Third Edition

Cataloging and Classification:
An Introduction

Lois Mai Chan

With the assistance of
Theodora L. Hodges

The Scarecrow Press, Inc.
Lanham, Maryland • Toronto • Plymouth, UK
2007

SCARECROW PRESS, INC.

Published in the United States of America
by Scarecrow Press, Inc.
A wholly owned subsidiary of
The Rowman & Littlefield Publishing Group, Inc.
4501 Forbes Boulevard, Suite 200, Lanham, Maryland 20706
www.scarecrowpress.com

Estover Road
Plymouth PL6 7PY
United Kingdom

British Library Cataloguing in Publication Information Available

Library of Congress Cataloging-in-Publication Data

Chan, Lois Mai.
    Cataloging and classification : an introduction / Lois Mai Chan ;
with the assistance of Theodora L. Hodges.—3rd ed.
        p.   cm.
    Includes bibliographical references and index.
    ISBN-13: 978–0-8108–5944–9 (alk. paper)
    ISBN-13: 978–0-8108–6000–1 (pbk. : alk. paper)
    ISBN-10: 0–8108–5944–0 (alk. paper)
    ISBN-10: 0–8108–6000–7 (pbk. : alk. paper)
    1. Cataloging—United States.   2. Classification—Books.
I. Hodges, Theodora, 1922–.   II. Title.
Z693.5.U6C48   2007
025.3—dc22   2007018729

∞ ™ The paper used in this publication meets the minimum requirements of
American National Standard for Information Sciences—Permanence of
Paper for Printed Library Materials, ANSI/NISO Z39.48-1992.
Manufactured in the United States of America.

CONTENTS

PREFACE

Since the publication of the second edition of *Cataloging and Classification: An Introduction*, the landscape, scope, and nature of bibliographic control in libraries have undergone enormous changes. Instead of depending primarily on their own holdings for providing information services, libraries now rely heavily on external or remote sources. These include those on the Internet and the Web, which have now become important milieus for knowledge discovery. Besides print and nonprint materials, libraries now also offer access to a range of digitized resources. Web resources, in particular, possess characteristics that are a far cry from those found among traditional library resources. To adjust to this new and highly varied environment, methods for describing and organizing library resources have also expanded and changed.

The adoption of the first two editions of this book by many library and information science programs as an introductory text for beginners in cataloging and classification, and by many cataloging departments as a training tool, has encouraged the preparation of the third edition. As in the case of the first two editions, the primary intended audience of the new edition consists of students in library and information science programs, beginning professionals working in the areas of resource description and organization, and public service librarians seeking a fuller understanding of the bibliographic control apparatus. It may also be useful to professionals in related fields who are concerned with knowledge organization, for example, indexers, abstractors, bibliographers, publishers, and information system designers. Individual chapters within the book may also be used separately in training or review classes dealing with information organization, storage, and retrieval.

The scope of this new edition is the analysis and representation of methods used in describing, organizing, and providing access to resources made available in or through libraries, including both the materials owned by the library (mostly physical items such as books, journals, and nonprint materials) and external resources such as those in electronic form that are accessible through the library's portal. In other words, the frame of reference for the book is today's library environment, and its emphasis is on the standards for bibliographic control that were developed over the years and have been widely adopted in the library field. It reports on recent developments in the retrieval arena, but technical details, particularly with regard to online systems, have been excluded because they vary from system to system and are subject to rapid changes. Two new chapters have been added to this edition of the book: chapter 4, containing a discussion of a number of widely used metadata schemas providing a brief overview of an important movement that is closely related to resource description and that began in the last decade of the twentieth century; and chapter 9, containing a discussion of FAST (Faceted Application of Subject Terminology), a newly developed subject controlled vocabulary.

This edition retains the overall outline of the second edition, presenting the essence of library cataloging and classification in terms of three basic functions: descriptive cataloging, subject access, and classification. It also covers authority work and the processing of cataloging records in both manual and electronic modes. Many chapters have been reorganized internally to provide a more logical progression of ideas and factual details. Within this framework, all chapters have been rewritten to incorporate the changes that have occurred during the interval between the second and third editions. In each part, the historical development and underlying principles of the retrieval mechanism at issue are treated first, because these are considered essential to an understanding of cataloging and classification. Discussion and examples of provisions in the standards and tools are then presented in order to illustrate the operations covered in each chapter. Throughout this edition, principles and practices in name and subject authority control are interspersed where appropriate.

Recent decades have witnessed the tremendous impact that changes in technology have had on cataloging and classification. Because of the great variety and idiosyncrasies of various online systems, no attempt has been made to focus on any particular online catalog system. Thus, it is in broad and general terms that online catalogs are discussed in this edition, with cataloging examples taken from a number of online systems. In reference to the computer processing of cataloging information, it is the MARC (machine-readable cataloging) system that is emphasized.

References to and discussion of MARC formats occur throughout the book. The MARC system and formats are introduced in chapter 1, and the development and architecture of MARC formats are discussed in considerable detail in chapter 16, with emphasis on their underlying structure and principles. In the chapters dealing with cataloging and classification operations, MARC tags and codes are given where appropriate. The chapter on the structure of the MARC formats is placed at the end of the book because it refers to concepts introduced throughout the earlier chapters and the details of the formats cannot be grasped until the complexities of what must be coded are mastered. Those who wish to study or teach the MARC formats along with cataloging operations may use chapter 16 and the earlier chapters simultaneously.

Each part of the book begins with a list of the standards and tools used in the preparation and processing of that part of the cataloging record covered, followed by suggested background readings selected to help the reader gain an overview of the subject to be presented. The list includes many works considered to be classics in the field. For those who wish to pursue the subject in greater depth, additional works are listed in the bibliography.

In this book, an attempt has been made to reflect current practice. Part One, which consists of chapter 1 only, provides a general overview of description, organization, and access relating to library resources within the context of the information environment in general, followed by a brief preview of the basic functions of cataloging and classification. Part Two, consisting of chapters 2, 3, and 4, covers resource description. Chapter 2, on the development of cataloging codes, places the current code in a historical context that brings out its organic nature and points out the inevitability of future changes. Chapter 3 addresses the foundations, principles, and standards of resource description, with the revised second edition of *Anglo-American Cataloguing Rules* as the main focus. At the time of preparing this edition, a new edition of cataloging rules, to be published under the title *Resources Description and Access* (RDA), is being developed. It was decided not to delay the publication of the third edition of this book until after the publication of RDA because various tools used in cataloging and classification are revised on different time schedules and at various intervals. Part Two concludes with chapter 4, a new chapter on metadata schemas.

Part Three, Access and Authority Control, consists of two chapters, 5 and 6, and covers the principles and concepts of authority control and names and titles as access points, plus the forms in which these access points appear in cataloging records.

Part Four, consisting of chapters 7–11 on subject representation and access, begins with a general chapter on subject access and controlled vocabularies followed by chapters discussing major subject access systems, including Library of Congress Subject Headings and Sears List of Subject Headings. A brief introduction of a specialized system, Medical Subject Headings, is also included. New to this edition is a chapter on the new subject access system called FAST (Faceted Application of Subject Terminology) currently under development at OCLC (Online Computer Library Center).

Part Five, Organization, covers the classification and categorization of library resources, with emphasis on the two major systems: the Dewey Decimal Classification and the Library of Congress Classification. The discussion and examples pertaining to the Dewey Decimal Classification in Part Five are based on Edition 22 of the DDC full version and Edition 14 of the DDC abridged version. The discussion of, and examples from, the Library of Congress Classification system are based on the most recent editions of classes in Library of Congress Classification. The examples make references to the print versions of these systems rather than the online version because the latter is subject to frequent changes and the fact that the former is more stable makes it easier for beginners and novices to navigate. Part Five also includes a discussion of the National Library of Medicine Classification as well as brief discussions of a number of other classification systems. Some of the systems that are seldom used or no longer in use but not necessarily inferior to those in use are included for the purpose of exposing students to ideas that challenge current practice and helping to illustrate the principles and theory embodied in different manifestations. The chapters on individual subject headings systems and classification schemes have been designed so that they may be used as a whole or selectively. For example, chapter 10, on Sears List of Subject Headings, may be used without first studying chapter 8, on Library of Congress Subject Headings; and in chapter 13, the sections on the abridged edition of the Dewey Decimal Classification can be used without first studying the section on the full edition. As a result, certain overlapping discussions or repetitions of similar points occur in these chapters. This method of presentation is used because certain library science programs are designed for specific types of libraries (for example, school libraries and media centers) and generally do not cover all systems of subject cataloging or classification.

Part Six consists of two chapters covering the encoding and processing of cataloging records.

It should be pointed out that this text is intended to be an aid in the study of these operations and their attendant tools and not as a substitute for the tools themselves. In other words, one cannot prepare a bibliographic description of a resource without resorting to *Anglo-American Cataloguing Rules* or classify an item without using a classification scheme. Therefore, the discussion concentrates on the essence of the rules and no attempt is made to replicate or reproduce the cataloging rules in the text.

Several of the chapters include exercises in order to reinforce the concepts covered; answers are given in appendix C. A glossary containing common terms in cataloging and classification, updated to reflect recent developments and current literature, is included, as is a bibliography of cataloging tools and selected writings in the field.

Examples illustrating various cataloging operations consist of extracts mostly from Library of Congress cataloging records. Complete MARC bibliographic and authority records are included in the appendixes to show how the parts fit together in the final cataloging product. Throughout this edition, one set of examples, the authority record for William A. Katz and the bibliographic record for the eighth edition of his book on reference services, is used to illustrate the structure of and relationship between authority and bibliographic records and the various manifestations of the same records in different cataloging systems. Appendix A also contains a set of records showing the cataloging of different manifestations and transformations of a particular work, Jane Austen's *Pride and Prejudice*.

I am indebted to many individuals for their contributions to the contents of this book and assistance in the preparation of this edition. Lynn El-Hoshy, Subject Specialist in the Cataloging Policy and Support Office of the Library of Congress, provided invaluable information regarding the Library of Congress Subject Headings (LCSH) system and LC policies for its application. Sally McCallum, Chief of Network Development and MARC Standards Office of the Library of Congress, reviewed the discussion on MARC formats. Professor Ian McIlwaine, Editor of the Universal Decimal Classification (UDC), revised and updated the section on UDC. Joseph Miller, Editor of Sears List of Subject Headings, helped interpret the list and headings. Professors Gerry Benoit (Simmons College) and Kwan Yi (University of Kentucky) patiently answered numerous questions regarding the encoding of cataloging and metadata records. In addition, I wish to acknowledge the generous help of the following: Dr. Theodora L. Hodges, formerly of the School of Library and Information Studies, University of California, Berkeley (now UC Berkeley School of Information), for editorial assistance in preparing the entire manuscript, especially in updating chapter 1, and in compiling the index; Megan Snyder, Sandy Rodriguez and Helen Morrison for providing bibliographic assistance and proofreading; Catherine Seago and Nancy Lewis for formatting many of the examples; Richard Douglas for preparing the graphics; and Dr. Martin Dillon for advice and guidance in the preparation of the manuscript. The Library of Congress and OCLC (Online Computer Library Center) provided cataloging examples used throughout the book. To all named above, I wish to express my deepest gratitude and appreciation.

PART ONE
INTRODUCTION

RECOMMENDED READING

Calhoun, Karen. "The Changing Nature of the Catalog and its Integration with Other Discovery Tools: Final Report, prepared for the Library of Congress, March 17, 2006," www.loc.gov/catdir/calhoun-report-final.pdf (19 Feb. 2007).

Cataloging and the Organization of Information: Philosophies, Practices, and Challenges at the Onset of the 21st Century. Binghamton, N.Y.: Haworth Press, 2000. Also published as Volume 30, Numbers 1–3 of *Cataloging & Classification Quarterly.*

Cochrane, Pauline A. "Universal Bibliographic Control: Its Role in the Availability of Information and Knowledge." *Library Resources & Technical Services* 34, no. 4 (October 1990): 423–31.

Hagler, Ronald. *The Bibliographic Record and Information Technology.* 3rd ed. Chicago: American Library Association, 1997. Chapter 1.

Markuson, Barbara Evans. "Bibliographic Systems, 1945–1976." *Library Trends* 25 (July 1976): 311–27.

Scott, Edith. "The Evolution of Bibliographic Systems in the United States, 1876–1945." *Library Trends* 25 (July 1976): 293–310.

Taylor, Arlene G. *The Organization of Information.* 2nd ed. Westport, Conn.: Libraries Unlimited, 2004.

Wilson, Patrick. *Two Kinds of Power: An Essay on Bibliographical Control.* Berkeley: University of California Press, 1978.

CHAPTER 1
INFORMATION RESOURCE MANAGEMENT: DESCRIPTION, ACCESS, ORGANIZATION

INTRODUCTION

The ways people look for information have changed enormously in the last fifty or sixty years. Up to the late 1940s, most people went to a library if they did not find what they wanted in the resources they had at home. There, besides finding a wealth of reference materials to consult, they could use the card catalog, whose brief item-by-item records organized by author, title, and subject showed what the library had and where it could be found on the shelves. In those days, printed books made up the most substantial part of most library collections, with journals and their attendant abstracting and indexing vehicles making up a lesser part, except in special-subject libraries. As the century wore on, however, more and more nonprint materials (sound recordings, visual materials, microforms, globes, dioramas, and so on) were gradually added. By late in the century, most library collections included a growing proportion of local-access electronic resources, and libraries began providing access to remote-access electronic resources as well.

Today, people have untold amounts of information available at their fingertips, whether at home, in school computer labs, in libraries, or in Internet cafes. What has made the difference, fundamentally, is the use of computers in processing information for storage and retrieval. Technology has made a major difference to library operations, as it has in so many other sectors of today's world. One example is that card catalogs have morphed to online catalogs called OPACs (online public access catalogs). OPACs not only offer access to local library holdings but also to a wide range of distant information sources; among examples are the full catalogs of major research libraries, the offerings of abstracting and indexing journals and other catalog-like services, and all the resources available through the Internet. Most modern OPACs allow quite sophisticated search options to users who are trying to hone in on material of interest.

There is no question that the Internet dominates today's information environment. With so many home computers, with computer labs in most schools, with Internet access offered by most libraries, and with "Internet cafes" in cities and towns almost worldwide, it is often the Internet that is first approached for information seeking. The Internet is a vast information store—so vast that a person submitting a query may well be told, on being given an initial response list of ten or twenty "hits," that there are thousands more. For many users, this may be sufficient, but for many others, this may not be a satisfactory response because there is no mechanism for them to efficiently select the best or most useful information that the Internet can offer. Thus, there is a downside in having easy access to what is apparently an unlimited supply of information.

The primary focus of this book is the mechanisms the library sector of the information community has developed for identifying and thereby providing a way for others to find the materials for which its sector is responsible.

In this context, it should be noted that traditional library catalogs, in whatever form, provided access to information at the level of a book or separately published document. Journals and other serials were listed under their titles, with information noting what volumes and issues their respective institutions held. However, users had to consult other tools to locate individual journal articles. Indexes to periodicals and journals as well as abstracting services were developed outside of the library community to fill this need. Early periodical indexes were manually prepared and published in print versions. Almost all are now online and referred to collectively as the online information industry. Most are proprietary but available to the public, free or for a fee.

In the library community, providing access to information consists of two prongs. The first is providing some sort of topical labeling to help those who are trying to zero in on a subject. The second is giving enough information about the item at hand that a searcher reading its description can tell whether the item to which it pertains is a fair match to what he or she had in mind when formulating the search. These are the prongs represented by the two sorts of information in traditional catalog records: (1) content information, such as subject headings, classification numbers, and, in some cases, content summaries; and (2) identification information (author and other responsible agents, title, publisher, place and date of publication, series membership, various control numbers, and so on).

When the power of the computer at search and retrieval first became apparent, there was some speculation in the library environment that, with the right programs, computers could greatly simplify, perhaps even take over, the somewhat tedious job of preparing items for search and retrieval. This was a heady prospect because constructing catalog records is a labor-intensive process requiring highly trained personnel and is thus very expensive. However, early expectations on how much could be done automatically proved overly optimistic. Searching by subject in full-text search systems delivered fairly satisfactory results when the amount of available information was relatively small but led to overwhelming retrieval sets as the amount of available information became enormous.

The information world of the first decade of the twenty-first century is complex, with many independent agencies and factors contributing to the overall picture. The situation is perhaps made more easily understandable through the realization that information resources and activities can be grouped into three different sectors. One is represented by the Internet and the designers of its components, another by libraries, and the third by the online information industry. Each of these sectors is constantly searching for improved and cost-effective means of making information available to those who seek it.

It is the library sector of the information community that has the longest history in respect to bibliographic access systems. The chapters of this book present an account of what has been done in that sector from early on to recent (2006) developments. Such an account has been considered essential preparation in the past for those entering the library-based profession and has also served as a helpful text for those in the profession who feel they would benefit from a systematic and analytic review. The account may even be of help to the information community at large.

Of particular interest, of course, are changes in all aspects of information retrieval that have come about since the beginning of the 1950s in what we may call the online age. Since then, most developments in the library and online information industry have rested on theoretical and practical developments in information technology—of which the most well-known and possibly the most significant are the Internet and the World Wide Web. It may therefore be instructive here to present parallel accounts of the milestones that each of the three sectors has passed on the road to their current positions. The Internet is featured here because it plays such an important role in current information-gathering activities. Developments in the online information industry are grouped with those in the library sector because their retrieval mechanisms are similar in many respects.[1]

TIMELINES IN INFORMATION ACCESS

Foundations, Both Environments

The first rumblings of the approaching tectonic shift in information processing and retrieval were heard in Vannevar Bush's 1945 "Atlantic Monthly" article,[2] in which he posited the future possibility of an online interactive information retrieval system he called Memex. Large computers, the necessary vehicles for such a system, were then in development. ENIAC, the country's first electronic computer, was operative the following year at the University of Pennsylvania, and in 1948, Bell Laboratories developed the transistor. In 1951, Remington-Rand built UNIVAC, the first commercial general-purpose electronic computer. The same year, Mortimer Taube presented a paper on coordinate indexing, and two years later, proposed an indexing system based on what he called "uniterms," a concept that underlay the future practice of keyword indexing. The Atlantic cable, a requirement for efficient communication between Europe and the United States, was laid in 1956. In the late 1950s, Hans Peter Luhn showed how the computer could be used to enable keyword searching, sorting, and content analysis of written texts,[3] and from that time on, computer technology was applied almost universally in the field. In September 1956, IBM began shipping RAMAC, the first hard drive: its capacity was 5 megabytes, it weighed a little over a ton, and it cost $50,000 (an estimated $350,000 today) to lease for a year.[4]

From then on, capacity increased as dramatically as its cost grew less. By 2006, a gigabyte of storage on a 3.5 inch hard drive may cost less than fifty cents.

1957–1970, the Internet Environment

In October of 1957, the USSR launched Sputnik, the world's first artificial satellite, a device the size of a basketball. The next month it launched Sputnik II, with a considerably bigger payload including a dog named Laika. These launches may be considered the beginning of the space age and also of the space race. The United States government reacted by funding programs aimed at regaining its former leading position in science and technology. An immediate step was setting up the Advanced Research Projects Agency (ARPA) in the Department of Defense. Another was establishing the National Aeronautics and Space Administration (NASA) in October 1958.[5] One of ARPA's projects was designing a computer "interface message" system. With its first IMP (Interface Message Processor) delivery, ARPANET,[6] the progenitor of the Internet, became operable in August 1969.

1957–1970, the Library and Online Information Industry Environment

In the early 1960s, the Library of Congress (LC) began working on developing a coding system to enable computer manipulation of library catalog records. The result was MARC, an encoding language whose name is based on the words *Machine Readable Cataloging*. LC began using it, and trial distribution of MARC tapes began in October 1966; by June 1968, approximately 50,000 coded records had been distributed to participating libraries. Libraries nationwide embarked on programs to convert their old catalog records in card form to ones that were machine-readable. Worldwide, many countries began developing their own MARC formats and cataloging-record conversion programs. In most libraries, early use of MARC was confined to printing catalog cards.

The early 1960s saw the emergence of various information databases run by corporations such as Lockheed Information Systems and the System Development Corporation (SDC) with support from government agencies such as NASA and the National Library of Medicine (NLM). Lockheed's RECON (later to become DIALOG) surfaced in 1965, and ERIC (Educational Resources Information Clearinghouse) in 1969. Throughout the sixties, batch-processing of data was the rule for most of these systems.

Another important trend in the 1960s was growth in international cooperation on bibliographical matters. In 1961, the International Conference on Cataloguing Principles, a conference that resolved many country-to-country cataloging differences, was held in Paris. *Anglo-American Cataloging Rules* (AACR) was published in 1967—a set of rules drafted according to the Paris Principles and governing how works were described and entered into a bibliographic database. In 1969, an international group began work on a standard order and content for describing monographic material, work which led to the family of International Standard Bibliographic Descriptions known as ISBDs.

Also, the sixties saw developments in indexing theory and practice. In 1961, Chemical Abstracts began regular publication of a KWIC (key word in context) index to its *Chemical Titles,* and; in 1964, the Institute for Scientific Information began producing a citation index for publications in science and technology.

1971–1980, the Internet Environment

1971 saw the first e-mail on ARPANET. University College of London connected with ARPANET in 1973, to make ARPANET's first international connection. In 1974, Vinton Cerf developed the basic architecture—TCP/IP (Transmission Control Protocol/Internet Protocol)—for a large complex network, and the same year saw the first published appearance of the term "Internet."

1971–1980, the Library and Online Information Industry Environment

One of the major developments in the seventies was the emergence of shared library cataloging systems. Prominent examples include RLIN (Research Libraries Information Network), OCLC (Ohio Colleges Library Center, later named Online Computer Library Center), and WLN (Washington Library Network, later named Western Library Network).

Another important development was the emergence of dial-up access to specialized informational databases. MEDLINE, for the medical community, was the first, in 1971. Not to be ignored in this context is the importance of the development and subsequent wide availability of personal computers. Radio Shack's TRS-80 personal computer was first marketed in 1976, and Apple II in 1977.

Interest in indexing languages continued during the decade, with

PRECIS (Preserved Context Index System) coming into use in England in 1974.

The MARC formats for encoding cataloging data were adopted as a national standard (ANSI Z39.2) in 1971, and as an international standard (ISO 2709) in 1973. On the international front, the 1973 IFLA (International Federation of Library Associations) Conference adopted the goal of Universal Bibliographic Control, under which a publication would be cataloged at the time and place of issue, with cataloging data available worldwide.

Finally, a second edition of the cataloging code AACR, noted above, was published in 1978; the new edition reflected the fact that library collections had by that time come to include many types of items—computer files being one example—for which earlier rules for description and access were inadequate.

1981–1990, the Internet Environment

MS-DOS surfaced in 1981, and 1982 saw the first use of the term "cyberspace." The first domain name was registered in 1985, and the entity that was to become America Online was founded that year also. In 1986, The National Science Foundation's NSFNET merged with, and then replaced, ARPANET. 1989 saw the rise of Compuserv and also AOL's debut. In 1990, a new system was being developed at CERN (originally the Center for European Nuclear Research). It combined hypertext and Internet technologies, and was called the World Wide Web.

1981–1990, the Library and Online Information Industry Environment

The 1980s saw the rounding-out of a trend that had begun somewhat earlier: the transformation of library catalogs from banks of catalog-card drawers to bibliographic databases accessed through personal computer screens. The new catalogs were known as OPACs, for online public-access catalogs. The first OPACs, now referred to as "first generation," allowed faster and easier searching, but were limited to on-site collections with search options not much beyond those of card or microfiche catalogs. Gradually, OPACs offered more and more sophisticated search options. By the late 1980s, OPACs had shown many improvements (including keyword searching with Boolean operations) which resulted in significantly improved access points. There were also provisions for truncation, index browsing, and more display options for search results. OPACs at this stage are generally referred to as "second generation" OPACs.

The online information industry also made great strides during this decade, with the creation of more databases and with search options becoming evermore sophisticated. There were also increasing efforts to provide additional end-user searching features.

1991–2000, the Internet Environment

In 1991, CERN released the World Wide Web (WWW, Web, or W3), which began as a networked information project at CERN under the direction of Tim Berners-Lee, now Director of the World Wide Web Consortium [W3C].[7] The Web became immediately popular, with the potential offered by hyperlinks capturing the imagination of the information community. In 1993, Mosaic, the first graphical Web browser, developed by the National Center for Supercomputing Applications (NCSA) at the University of Illinois, was released.

The United Nations went online in the same year. WebCrawler, the first full text search engine, became operational in 1994, enabling the harvesting of Web content and the creation of searchable indexes.[8] YAHOO!, Netscape Navigator, and Lycos also emerged in 1994, all offering full-text searching on the content of their databases. In the same year, Cambridge (MA) and Lexington (MA) became the nation's first wired communities. In 1995, Amazon.com, the programming language JAVA, and eBay appeared; in addition, AOL and Compuserv began offering Internet access. AOL bought Netscape in 1998, the same year that Google surfaced. For a year or two before the turn of the century, there was widespread anxiety that there would be a massive disruption of computer systems worldwide at midnight 31 December 1999 due to the century date change. Nothing happened. *Nupedia*, ancestor of *Wikipedia*, appeared in 2000.

1991–2000, the Library and Online Information Industry Environment

The nineties saw several major developments. Those responsible for MARC made gains in expansion and consolidation. USMARC merged with CANMARC to become MARC 21 in 1999 and 2000.

Library OPACs continued improving, with many commercial companies being set up to develop and maintain them. With the development of the Web browsers, OPACs moved to the World Wide Web and were sometimes called WebPACs. Web features such as hyperlinks and hypertext enabled many sophisticated features to be introduced into the Web-based OPACs, further enhancing search capabilities, access points, and display options.

On the theoretical front, an IFLA committee began work on developing a new base for determining the necessary factors for achieving optimum bibliographic retrieval: a study titled "Functional Requirements for Bibliographic Records" was published in 1998, its final report having been approved by the IFLA Section on Cataloguing in 1997.[9] Many new metadata schemas—special-purpose coding systems designed to cover different types of materials not well served by existing schemas—appeared during this decade. A prominent and fairly general one is the Dublin Core, developed at OCLC and aimed especially at Web materials. Work began on it in 1995.[10]

The Dublin Core schema calls for subject indicators, but traditional Library of Congress subject headings under their current rules for application are too cumbersome for that purpose. Accordingly, in 1998, OCLC began work on a subject heading system called FAST, the initials standing for Faceted Application of Subject Terminology.[11] FAST is based on the terminology of LCSH but uses simpler application rules. It is designed to be easier to apply, to offer more access points, to be flexible, and to be interoperable across disciplines and access environments. It is still under development at this writing.

2000–, the Internet Environment

In 2001, *Wikipedia* superseded *Nupedia*. The same year, the *New York Times* went on the Web, and Skype (an Internet phone service) was introduced. Google expanded over the next few years, offering GooglePrint, Gmail, GoogleEarth, and GoogleScholar. In 2004, Google not only announced an IPO (Initial Public Offering) of stock in its company, but also began scanning, and making searchable, the contents of five major research libraries. In 2005, Yahoo! counted three million visitors a month, and the one-billionth Internet user went online. In April 2006, a Google-Earthlink team and the city of San Francisco agreed to sign a contract for the team to install a WiFi (wireless fidelity) network for the whole city, to be free, or at very low cost, to users. At the same time, Earthlink was negotiating similar contracts with Philadelphia, PA, and Anaheim, CA.

2000–, the Library and Online Information Industry Environment

By 2002, AACR2 had undergone yet another revision. The consensus of the information community was that a new code was called for, a code that would include provisions for rapidly developing information items and packages and that would incorporate the conceptual framework set forth in the document, "Functional Requirements for Bibliographic Records."[12] The Joint Steering Committee for the Revision of AACR (JSC) began work on such a code, the tentative title for which is *RDA: Resource Description and Access*. JSC issued a prospectus for RDA in 2005 (revised June 2006) calling for comments from the information community.[13]

By 2007, OCLC's WorldCat contained over 85 million bibliographic records and one billion holding records.

As time progresses, online database providers continue to increase the contents of their databases and improve searching capabilities, with Web interfaces providing multiple options for users of differing degrees of skill and sophistication. Attempts are also being made to link search results to holdings of particular libraries.

Future Prospects

In 2006, OCLC made a bold move to provide free access to its vast World-Cat database (hitherto accessible to OCLC members only) through its Open WorldCat program.[14] This program enables Web users of popular Internet search, bibliographic, and bookselling sites such as Google, Yahoo! and Windows Live Academic to identify and locate library materials. For example, through the Google Book Search Beta,[15] a partner site in the OCLC Open WorldCat program, users can search for all sorts of library materials, retrieve bibliographic data based on the cataloging records, and locate copies in OCLC libraries by city, region, and country. Because most people start their information searches on the Web, the result of these initiatives is a convergence of access to both library and Web resources. Libraries are thus much more visible on the Web than they were before. These recent developments represent the first steps toward the vision of integrating library catalogs with open Web discovery tools.[16]

LIBRARY AND INTERNET ACCESS PROVISIONS

The trends revealed in the accounts above can be summarized as follows:

The Internet environment shows an accelerating increase in technological advances, coverage, and services, with no sign of slackening on any front. It has been international in scope and participation since the beginning. Services offered are mainly proprietary, a fact which means that little or no information is available about what methods the various search services use to produce their results.

The library environment, with a much longer history, took steps to enter the online age at its beginning, through its development of MARC and MARC-like coding systems. The online age continued the trends that had previously been in effect, working toward consistency on the one hand and expanded coverage on the other. The latter, in particular, focused on the types of materials that cataloging rules and coding systems are designed to handle. International cooperation on all fronts increased steadily over the fifty-year period at issue. Control mechanisms, for names, for surrogate design and content, and for topic designators, are still strong. OPACs, and more recently WebPACs, with increasingly sophisticated access provisions and search options, replaced card and book catalogs in almost all libraries,

It is appropriate here to consider information retrieval results from Internet and library or library-like search systems. At the end of a subject search on the Internet using full-text searching—the most common Internet search mode—the user is presented with a list of the leading documents in an enormously long list of links to information sources that contain his or her query term. There is no mechanism for telling that user of other documents on the same topic whose authors use a synonym for the submitted term. Furthermore, the number of hits in the list of retrieved documents is often at least in the thousands. Internet name searches may deliver many matches with little or nothing to differentiate them, with many in the list being the wrong fit for the wanted entity or individual.

Searches in online databases designed on similar patterns of library catalogs result in a smaller number of hits and a higher on-target rate. There are two main reasons for such precision. One is that such databases store brief representations of documents, representations drawn up by trained catalogers and indexers who have studied the documents to which the representations apply. The other is that modern systems such as OPACs are likely to have embedded synonym control, ensuring that a user wanting material about eyeglasses will get all the system has to offer even if his or her query term is "spectacles." If a given system lacks embedded controls, it at least presents users with *see* and *see-also* references. Modern systems do the same thing for names, so that users searching for an author's works will get all the material that author wrote, whether they search on the author's real name or a pseudonym. Synonym control also acts as a filter, using qualifiers for distinguishing ambiguous terms. Thus, users are not presented with material on both submitted terms and on their homographs, for example, on both waterfalls and eye-lens conditions in response to a search on "cataracts."

Why do the two systems deliver such different results? The key concept is "bibliographic control," a term in use for decades among librarians. Behind the phrase "bibliographic control" lie two other concepts, *recall* and *precision*. A system is said to have good recall if a search delivers almost everything in its collection or database that matches a submitted query. And it is said to have good precision if the search delivers almost nothing else. Although very few library systems rate a perfect score on these two measures, many come close.

BIBLIOGRAPHIC CONTROL

As a prelude to discussing the concept of bibliographic control with all its ramifications, it is useful to describe the role that adherence to standards has played in the library sector of the information community. Even late in the nineteenth century, librarians began to realize the advantages of standardizing practice and fostering cooperation among libraries. The need for codification of cataloging practice became particularly apparent as the use of cooperative or shared cataloging increased. Economically, shared cataloging is a boon for libraries, greatly reducing cataloging costs. However, libraries can benefit from shared cataloging only if the cataloging records in the catalogs of different libraries are compatible.

One reason for aiming for a high level of compatibility was the observation that user searches are more successful when document surrogates are consistent with others in the same system. Another is the fact that many practical aspects of library management are more efficient if records are consistent. Such consistency is especially important among records in a union catalog (i.e., a catalog of multiple collections) or in a union database with records coming from different sources. It is only if participating libraries follow the same cataloging rules and practices that optimum compatibility of records can be obtained.

Particularly since the late nineteenth century, numerous standards for bibliographic control have been developed. There are separate standards for bibliographic description, for subject and non-subject access, and for classification. For bibliographic description, the primary standard used in library catalogs in English-speaking countries is *Anglo-American Cataloguing Rules* (AACR), first published in 1967 and revised every few years ever since. For specific types of materials, such as archives and electronic resources, standards—called metadata schema—such as the *Encoded Archival Description* (EAD) and *Dublin Core* (DC) have emerged. For access, AACR includes rules for designating and formulating non-subject access points through names of persons, corporate bodies, titles, etc. Subject access points are determined by other standards such as *Library of Congress Subject Headings, Sears List of Subject Headings*, and *Medical Subject Headings*. For organization, the most commonly used schemes are the *Library of Congress Classification* and the *Dewey Decimal Classification*. These standards are discussed in detail in following chapters.

A library or other information system can keep its collection under bibliographic control when it follows these standards appropriately for the situation at hand. To understand why the provisions of various standards were designed as they are, one needs to consider the functions of bibliographic control mechanisms—in other words, what bibliographic control is supposed to achieve. Various thinkers over the years have written on this subject. A synopsis of the most influential statements follows.

FUNCTIONS OF BIBLIOGRAPHIC CONTROL

Among the earliest articulation of the functions of bibliographic control was Charles A. Cutter's statement of the "objects of the catalog" and the means for attaining them, found in Cutter's cataloging code, *Rules for a Dictionary Catalog*:[17]

Objects

1. To enable a person to find a book of which any of the following are known:

   a. the author
   b. the title
   c. the subject
2. To show what the library has:
   d. by a given author
   e. on a given subject
   f. in a given kind of literature
3. To assist in the choice of a book:
   g. as to its edition (bibliographically)
   h. as to its character (literary or topical)

Means

1. Author entry with the necessary references (for a and d)
2. Title entry or title reference (for b)
3. Subject entry, cross references, and classed subject table (for c and e)
4. Form entry and language entry (for f)
5. Giving edition and imprint, with notes when necessary (for g)
6. Notes (for h)

In the mid-twentieth century, the notable articulation of cataloging principles and theory came from Seymour Lubetzky. Lubetzky was a librarian at the Library of Congress and later a professor at the School of Library Services at the University of California, Los Angeles. His primary interest was descriptive cataloging, the functions of which he posited as:[18]

1. To describe the significant features of the book which will serve (a) to distinguish it from other books and other editions of the book, and (b) characterize its contents, scope, and bibliographical relations; and
2. To present the data in an entry which will (a) fit well with the entries of other books and other editions of this book in the catalog, and (b) respond best to the interests of the majority of readers.

Lubetzky was a prolific writer. His work underlay the deliberations of the International Conference on Cataloguing held in Paris in 1961. The Statement of Principles, also known as the Paris Principles, adopted by the Conference includes the following "Functions of the Catalogue":[19]

   The catalogue should be an efficient instrument for ascertaining
   2.1   whether the library contains a particular book specified by
         (a) its author and title, *or*
         (b) if the author is not named in the book, its title alone, *or*

  (c) if author and title are inappropriate or insufficient for identification, a suitable substitute for the title; and

2.2 (a) which works by a particular author and

  (b) which editions of a particular work are in the library.

This statement in turn laid the basis for the code that dominated the second half of the century: *Anglo-American Cataloguing Rules.*

More recently, in a document entitled *Functional Requirements for Bibliographic Records* (FRBR) and published in 1998, the requirements for bibliographic records have been redefined in relation to the following generic tasks that are performed by users when searching and making use of national bibliographies and library catalogs:[20]

- using the data to **find** materials that correspond to the user's stated search criteria (e.g., in the context of a search for all documents on a given subject, or a search for a recording issued under a particular title);
- using the data retrieved to **identify** an entity (e.g., to confirm that the document described in a record corresponds to the document sought by the user, or to distinguish between two texts or recordings that have the same title);
- using the data to **select** an entity that is appropriate to the user's needs (e.g., to select a text in a language the user understands, or to choose a version of a computer program that is compatible with the hardware and operating system available to the user);
- using the data in order to acquire or **obtain** access to the entity described (e.g., to place a purchase order for a publication, to submit a request for the loan of a copy of a book in a library's collection, or to access online an electronic document stored on a remote computer).

BIBLIOGRAPHIC CONTROL THROUGH SURROGATES

We now turn to a discussion of the various ways those in charge of different types of bibliographic systems operate their databases. Managers of large bibliographic systems, for the most part, turn to two different ways to set up items of database content for efficient storage and retrieval. One is to store the full text of whatever is posted or submitted and conduct searches on that. Most Internet and Web searches are on full text, and search engines such as Google apparently base their results on calculations involving term frequencies and links. (As noted above, the retrieval mechanisms most search engines use are trade secrets, so outsiders cannot know just how they work. Informal surveys, however, indicate that user satisfaction is high.) The other way to manage storage and retrieval for a collection of documents or other book-like materials is to construct and store *brief representations* of what is in the collection. This is what has been done for centuries, and is still being done, in the library environment. There, before the advent of computers, the only way to go directly to the full text of books or journals was to go to library or bookstore shelves, scan for a promising item, then pick it up and flip through its pages. Such a process was neither efficient nor ultimately satisfying for those who wanted to do systematic searches for information. Accordingly, throughout the history of bibliographic lists or catalogs, those in charge of a collection have created brief descriptions conveying the salient facts about the items they hold. Booksellers at the medieval Frankfurt book fairs drew up such descriptions, mostly in the form of brief-title listings. Librarians have done the same since the early days of the field, drawing up (and setting up for searching) descriptions that are referred to either as document surrogates or as bibliographic records—terms that are used interchangeably in the paragraphs that follow.

Surrogates present essential information about documents and other cataloged items: in brief, the responsible agent's name, title of work, publisher, date, content, and so on, to the extent those elements apply. Surrogates are constructed by human catalogers or indexers based on the actual content of the resource, and now follow a standard, internationally recognized pattern followed by libraries for at least part of their content. (Internationally, for description, the pattern followed by libraries is the *International Standard Bibliographic Description;*[21] in the Anglo-American cataloging environment, it is *Anglo-American Cataloguing Rules.*[22])

A more comprehensive account of surrogates is that they carry information on authors or other responsible agents, on co-authors if any, on other contributors such as illustrators or translators, on title (and subtitle if any), on edition, and on publisher, place of publication, and copyright. They also show series membership if any, and provide notes on anything unusual about the edition. Furthermore, they carry subject headings reflecting topical coverage, and classification numbers showing where the item can be located in a physical collection as well as how the item's topic fits into a hierarchical portrayal of human knowledge. In English-speaking countries, most subject headings are chosen from *Library of Congress Subject Headings*, a huge list of continuously updated headings that incorporates synonym control and suggests related, broader, and narrower terms as well. (In some situations, catalogers use headings from a smaller, somewhat simplified subject headings list known as the Sears List of Subject Headings.) Again in this country, most records carry classification numbers from both *Dewey Decimal Classification* and *Library of Congress Classification*. In individual library collections, class numbers are followed by *book numbers*, or *item numbers*, to sequence the item to which the record pertains among others in the same class position (and therefore in the same area of the shelves). Finally, records also carry other control numbers, such as the item's International Standard Book Number (ISBN) and its Library of Congress control number. (It should be noted here that surrogates carrying all the information detailed above are not appropriate to all storage and retrieval situations. A bookstore with a stock of a few thousand titles does not need surrogates to carry all the information that a library of millions or many hundreds of thousands requires in its surrogates.)

Another term for a document surrogate is a bibliographic record. Bibliographic records are the building blocks of a bibliographic file. Each bibliographic record pertains to an item in the collection represented in the file, and contains two primary kinds of information: first, enough data for the item to be identifiable in the context of the file, and, second, at least one assigned "access point." Names of authors are access points, as are titles and subject terms, as well as other entities, such as performers. In addition, there may be any number of computer-extracted words that also serve as access points. Broadly defined, a bibliographic record could be an entry in an index, in a bibliography, in a library catalog, or in any other text-based file. The amount and nature of information included in a record depend on the purposes for which the file is prepared. In some bibliographic files, such as scientific periodical indexes or catalogs of highly specialized libraries, it is appropriate that records provide extensive subject and/or descriptive information; in others, such as a short-title catalog of items published at a given place and time, very little information per item is often sufficient. Creating records of the kind just described requires highly trained personnel if the work is to be done well. One of the issues facing library-oriented information professionals at the present time is to determine whether current practice is cost-effective, and if not, how it might be made so.

An important factor in the cost of surrogate production stems from a long-held library-world tenet: name and synonym control. One of the principles behind the design of library-oriented retrieval mechanisms is that material on the same topic should be tagged with the same subject heading, not disbursed in an alphabetical array, as happens if some materials on timekeeping devices are labeled clocks, some watches, some timepieces, some chronographs, and so on. The same principle holds for names, whether personal, geographic, corporate, or named entities such as the Flatiron Building or a work such as the *Iliad*. To achieve a system reflecting the one-term-per-entity principle, catalogers had to work out a mechanism to show what terms or names should be preferred. The result for topical terms, built over more than a century, is *Library of Congress Subject Headings*, a list of preferred terms with directions on what references should be made to broader terms, narrower terms, and to related terms at the same hierarchical level, such as near-synonyms. The list also carries alternates to preferred terms called lead-in terms with references to the preferred term. (Lead-in terms are words searchers might use in looking for the topics denoted by the preferred term.) A similar mechanism exists for names, and a preferred-term list exists for them also. Constructing such lists, called authority lists because they are lists of authorized terms, is a highly labor-intensive undertaking because it takes extensive checking into both popular and professional or scientific literature to ascertain what is the most effective term to authorize or establish. The procedure involved is called authority work; it must be done whenever new terms or names are added to preferred lists and also whenever terms or names already in the list are changed. Authority work, needed in keeping subject and name lists up to date as well as dealing with new terms and names, is therefore the most costly aspect of the cataloging operation.

Another part of the cataloging operation, ubiquitous since computers first became an important factor in library work, is coding surrogates for computer manipulation; in other words, making them machine-readable. The Library of Congress began work on a workable coding system when it first became apparent that computers would be playing a significant role in library matters. The resulting system was MARC, which went into use in the late 1960s. Its current version, called the MARC 21 formats, is the standard encoding system for library materials, and is widely used around the world.

In recent years, a new concept and product has entered the information retrieval arena, the *metadata schema*. A rigorous definition of metadata is "structured data about data." Thus, a metadata schema provides a structure or standard format for recording data that bring out the essential characteristics of an information item or object. Although, in a broad sense, the term *metadata records* includes what are traditionally called catalogs and indexes, the term is used primarily for files designed to accommodate material that is not suited to standard cataloging rules and coding systems. Examples include archeological relics as well as various types of electronic resources.

Bibliographic files exist in many forms; within each form, one file may differ considerably from another in type of bibliographical material covered, the pattern followed in drawing up its records, amount of information provided per record, how records are organized, and how records may be retrieved. Bibliographic databases, which are bibliographic files in electronic form, show even more variation than manually prepared files because of the versatility and power of today's computers in handling bibliographic data and allowing different designs of online systems. It is through this power that bibliographic databases are able to offer users many more search and display options than were available in static systems.

Later chapters in this book discuss these various operations and tools in detail, with copious examples.

SURROGATE PRODUCTION

The bibliographic control methods used for centuries to help library users find information consist of three distinct but related operations: description, access-point provision, and organization. *Description* refers to the preparation of a surrogate or a brief representation containing essential elements of the original resources, thereby creating a bibliographic or metadata record. *Access-point provision* refers to designating selected elements in the representation which the user can use as means to gain "entry" to the representation. (In a card catalog or online or static browsing list, access points are the headings under which records appear.) Both of these operations are carried out in accordance with established standards, AACR in English-speaking countries. *Organization* refers to the method of arranging both surrogates and physical resources, also according to established orders, alphabetic (in most browsing lists or files), alpha-numeric (in Library of Congress classification order), or numeric (Dewey Decimal classification order).

Description

In a broad sense, *resource description* refers to the process and the product of presenting in a record, drawn up according to established standards, the essential facts concerning an information item. The resulting record in turn serves as the surrogate in the file or catalog for the full item itself. The purpose of resource description is to tell what the resource is, in enough detail to distinguish it from other items with similar descriptions, such as other editions or versions of the same work.

Different levels of description are appropriate to different situations. For some books, for instance, the title, the name of the author, and the location of the item are all that are needed in a description. On the other hand, descriptions in a rare-book dealer's sales list or catalog must be extensive and detailed. Furthermore, the sorts of information needed in descriptions vary according to what is being cataloged: the descriptions of museum items and other realia must include different elements than do descriptions of books. The same is true for descriptions of most non-book items (including films and sound recordings) and especially for electronic resources.

In the Anglo-American cataloging environment, the predominant standard for resource description of library materials is the most recent revision of AACR. As mentioned above, for material for which AACR is not suitable, various user communities have drawn up metadata schemas that provide a framework for resource description in which the details of the content elements are defined according to the needs of their communities. Therefore, metadata descriptions vary in content and in extent. When such factors apply, the most common elements of a metadata description include most of the elements specified in standard rules for description in addition to the community-specific elements for which the schemas were designed.

Conventions for bibliographic description have remained relatively steady, but not static, over the past several decades. To accommodate changes in the information environment, both AACR and the ISBDs have been revised on an ongoing basis. However, the unusually rapid proliferation of electronic resources, especially those available on the World Wide Web, has necessitated a re-examination of the way individual items are described for the discovery and retrieval of information. Standards for description can therefore be expected to change considerably in the coming years. The many new metadata schemas that have already emerged are part of this change.

Methods of displaying bibliographic records have also varied over the years, from early manuscript (handwritten) catalogs to OPACs. To enable the display of records electronically, the elements within the records are encoded according to one or another encoding scheme, such as the MARC (Machine-Readable Cataloging) formats, HTML (Hypertext Markup Language), XML (eXtensible Markup Language), and so on. MARC, the coding system widely used in the library environment—and in many others—is first presented at the end of this chapter and is discussed in detail in chapter 16 of this book. Many other encoding schemes, including those just mentioned, either are or can be made compatible with MARC.

Access

A catalog or a bibliographic database contains a collection of bibliographic records. Sizes of catalogs or databases vary greatly from hundreds to thousands to millions. To aid retrieval in *surrogate-based databases*, the record elements that are most frequently used by users to identify resources have traditionally been designated as access points. Typical access points include subject terms and non-subject elements such as the title, the name of the author(s), editors, translators, etc. To ensure consistency, standards concerning the designation or assignment of access points are followed.

Organization

The growing volumes of a library collection or a virtual collection of electronic resources require efficient methods of organization. Early on, for library collections, elaborate classification schemes were devised for shelf-arrangement, with the aim of enabling easy browsing and retrieval. Many such schemes are still in use, particularly, in the United States, the Dewey Decimal and the Library of Congress classifications. The same schemes are often also used for listing entries in a catalog or bibliography. A case can be made that electronic resources must also be organized in some logical and easy-to-navigate fashion if search and retrieval are to be made easier and more efficient. To date, for resources on the World Wide Web, relatively simple classification or categorical schemes are being used in some systems to guide users to desired subjects. In fact, the name of the search engine YAHOO! is said to reflect the phrase "Yet Another Hierarchically Organized Operating system." Hierarchical schemes have also been used in Web directories to display search results or to organize the links between and among retrieved items—typically uniform resource locaters (URLs).

Methods of displaying bibliographic records may or may not reflect how they are organized or sequenced *within* a bibliographic database. In manually maintained systems and in the early OPACs, what users saw reflected the internal organization of the system. In fully electronic systems, internal organization is hidden from users; however, in most modern systems, users are offered many options for how they want search results displayed.

LIBRARY CATALOGS

General Characteristics

A library catalog is a kind of bibliographic file. It differs from a bibliography or a periodical index in that all its records pertain to items in one or more libraries and carry information on where the items can be found. Most library catalogs represent a single institution's holdings (which may be distributed in many branches). Other catalogs show the holdings of several libraries or collections; these are called *union catalogs*.

A library catalog consists of a set of records that, like the records in other bibliographic files, provide data about the items in the collection or collections the catalog represents. The data in each record include, at least: (1) a bibliographic description giving the identification, publication, and physical characteristics of the resource; and, (2) for a physical item, a call number (consisting of the classification number based on the subject content and an item number based on the author, the title, or both) that indicates the physical location of the item in the collection. Most records also include subject terms which state succinctly the subject content of the resource.

Almost all library catalogs are *multiple access* files. This means that they offer many ways, or *access points*, to retrieve a particular record. In most card catalogs, there were often several cards for the same item, each filed under a heading that represented a different access point. This way of providing information about items in a collection—multiple access to records that provide sufficient details for identification plus characterization of content—helps users locate particular items or select items they judge relevant to the subject they are pursuing.

In library cataloging, it has long been the practice to designate one of the access points as the chief access point, or *main entry*. In most cases, the main entry is based on the author if such can be determined. Otherwise, the main entry is based on either the title or on the corporate body responsible for the content or the title. There are two reasons for main entry practice. First, it is the most efficient way to manage lists that are maintained manually. In the days of manually prepared cards, it was the convention to record all needed information on one card and to include only brief descriptions on other cards (called added entries) for the same item. In online situations, the original justification for designating a main entry no longer holds. But even for computer-stored lists, it remains helpful to have a standard convention for the way a bibliographic item should be cited. The main entry pattern (in other words, author/title) is the usual way of referring to a work, a fact that adds to its effectiveness as a consistent citation standard.

Forms of Catalogs

When catalog records were manually produced—handwritten, typed, or typeset—there were only a few options for physical form: book, card, and, to a limited extent, microform. Within these forms, considerations of cost and bulk placed a severe limit on the amount of information that could be included in a given record and on the number of access points that could be provided for it. As it did with access points, the advent of catalog automation made a major difference in the potential forms catalogs could take and in the variety of features an individual catalog could exhibit. In particular, automation removed the limits on record length that had prevailed in the manual environment.

The following brief account treats major catalog forms both historically and as they exist today.

Book Catalogs

The book catalog is a list in book form of the holdings of a particular library collection or group of collections, with the cataloging records displayed in page format. This is the oldest form of library catalog. Its items may be recorded by handwriting as in a manuscript catalog, by typing, or by a printing process. The oldest manuscript catalog goes back as far as the Pinakes compiled by Callimachus for the ancient Alexandrian library. The book-form catalog was the predominant form of library catalog until the late nineteenth century, when use of the card catalog began to spread. Even so, manually prepared book catalogs continued to be issued in small numbers for many years. Also, for a period around the middle of the last century, several major libraries published their whole catalogs in book form, the pages made up of photographs of their catalog cards, sequenced as they appeared in the catalog. Online catalogs, accessible from anywhere, eliminated the market for such publications.

Card Catalogs

In card catalogs, cataloging entries were recorded on 3 by 5 cards, one entry per card or set of cards. Each entry could then be revised, inserted, or deleted without affecting other entries. Before the card catalog, most library catalogs were in book form, either printed or looseleaf. When the card catalog was first introduced in the latter part of the nineteenth century, its advantage in ease of updating was immediately perceived, and libraries throughout the United States began adopting this form. The fact that, in 1901, the Library of Congress began distributing ready-made sets of catalog cards to subscribing libraries contributed to the card catalog's widespread use. For nearly a century, the card catalog was the predominant form of catalog in this country. It was catalog automation that eventually changed the picture, but not for well over a decade after its introduction: early catalog databases were used primarily to print sets of catalog cards.

Microform Catalogs

A microform catalog was a variant of the book catalog, and served in many situations as an interim device between card and online catalogs. It contained cataloging records in micro-image and required the use of a microform reader for viewing. The prevalent form of microform catalog was on microfiche, updated (that is, replaced by a new set of fiche showing additions and changes) on a regular basis, usually quarterly. The need for a microform reader, the handling of the fiche or film, and the display image all proved major psychological barriers for many users. For the early not-always-dependable online catalogs, however, the microform catalog provided a viable back-up.

Online Catalogs

When a library's users can retrieve catalog records directly from a computer database, the library is said to have an online catalog, usually called an OPAC—the letters standing for Online Public Access Catalog. The usual mode of display in an online catalog is through a computer terminal. In this mode, individual cataloging records or parts thereof are retrieved by means of access points or search keys and are displayed instantly on a monitor. Many OPAC terminals are accompanied by printers. Users gain numerous advantages from online catalogs, including instant feedback during the retrieval process and the availability of more access points than any manual catalog can offer. Furthermore, OPACs allow remote access so that the user does not have to be physically present in a library in order to search its catalog. Modern OPACs, sometimes called WebPACs, allow users to get to the Web and Internet and avail themselves of many of the features that search engines offer.

An online catalog can be integrated with other library operations such as cataloging, acquisitions, and circulation, resulting in an integrated online system. With an integrated system, the user is able not only to identify an item but also to ascertain whether the item is currently available for browsing or circulation. In some integrated systems, it is also possible to find out whether a particular item is on order.

Machine-readable cataloging records form the basic units of an online catalog. For a cataloging record to be machine-readable it must not only be input into a computer, but also its various elements must be tagged or labeled in such a way that they can be stored, manipulated, and eventually retrieved in all the ways that are appropriate for technical and reference services in libraries. In the early 1960s, in consultation with other major libraries, the Library of Congress began work on developing a protocol for coding bibliographic records. The emerging protocol was called the MARC format. Although there are other protocols for coding various kinds of records for computer storage and retrieval, MARC is the system that has prevailed for library records in this country and in many others. As noted earlier, the MARC format is briefly explained at the end of this chapter and is presented in greater detail in chapter 16.

CD-ROM Catalogs

A related catalog form is sometimes also referred to as an online catalog, although it is much less flexible. This is the *CD-ROM (Compact Disk-Read Only Memory) catalog*. For CD-ROM catalogs, a catalog database is periodically—usually quarterly—copied onto compact disks, which can be accessed through stand-alone microcomputers.

Displaying Cataloging Records

In a manually prepared book or card catalog, how the records or entries were arranged determined how they could be retrieved and displayed. There were two primary ways in which individual bibliographic entries could be assembled to form a coherent file: alphabetic, and systematic (or classified). In a classified catalog, the entries were arranged according to a chosen system of classification, resulting in subject collocation. This is a form of catalog arrangement that was popular in the nineteenth century but which, as a public tool, has become all but extinct in American libraries. In an alphabetical catalog or dictionary catalog, entries are organized in alphabetical sequence, with author, title, and subject headings interfiled. This form was introduced in the latter part of the nineteenth century and soon became predominant in this country.

How records in an online catalog are arranged internally is a matter of system design, and affects end-users only in the sense that one system may be easier to use and apparently deliver more satisfactory results than another. But how retrieved items appear on the screen also depends on system design, and here, end-users should be aware that many more options are open to them than were available in using a manual catalog. Results of a search are usually displayed in a default order, by date or by name, but in most systems the list may be re-sorted according to users' preferences.

CATALOGING OPERATIONS

One cannot discuss cataloging in today's library environment without acknowledging that catalogers in local libraries make heavy use of bibliographic records prepared elsewhere, a practice called *copy cataloging*. Sources of such records are the Library of Congress (LC) and, for those that are members of shared-cataloging networks or consortia, records prepared by other members. A *network* or *consortium* is an association of libraries with the main purpose of sharing resources including cataloging information. It maintains a cataloging database of contributed records that also includes records from the LC MARC database. Member libraries have direct online access to the database, and may use its records for verification of items to be purchased, for identification of items for interlibrary loan purposes, or for producing records for the local catalog. The largest network is OCLC (Online Computer Library Center), which has absorbed two other major networks, WLN (Western Library Network) and RLIN (Research Libraries Information Network). OCLC's WorldCat, containing over 85 million bibliographic records, is now the largest cataloging database in the world.

Despite the large role that copy cataloging plays in local libraries today, all professional catalogers have to be able to do full cataloging for an item—a process that is called *original cataloging*. During a cataloging department workday, many items may show up for which no cataloging copy exists. For these, after a reasonable wait, one must rely on original cataloging.

Cataloging Files

The catalog consists of two major files: the bibliographic file and the authority file. The bibliographic file contains cataloging records. This is the file that a library user interacts with. The authority file, on the other hand, is a cataloging tool that records the standardized forms of names and topical terms that have been authorized as headings, i.e., access points, along with their associated cross-references. The need for an authority file, and the work that goes into building one, are described briefly below, under "Authority Work" as well as in greater detail in chapters 5, 6, and 8. In manual systems, authority files were often maintained separately, one authority file for names and another for subject headings. In online catalog systems, they may either be one or two separate files; and either way, they may or may not be integrally linked to the bibliographic file.

Cataloging Procedures

Several distinct cataloging procedures are part of preparing an individual bibliographic record for a library: (1) resource description, the preparation of bibliographic descriptions and the determination of bibliographic access points; (2) subject analysis (often referred to as subject cataloging or the operation of assigning subject headings); (3) classification, the assignment of classification numbers and book numbers; and (4) authority work, the determination of the standardized forms of subject terms and names. For those doing online cataloging, an additional procedure is MARC tagging. Each of these activities is the focus of one or more later chapters in this book. Only a brief account of these activities is given in this introductory chapter.

The record resulting from the first three steps is called a *bibliographic record*. The result of authority work is referred to as the *authority record*.

Resource Description

Resource description, also called descriptive cataloging, consists of:

1. Drafting a set of information that includes the item's title, the agent responsible (most often the author), the edition, the place and date of publication, the publisher, a physical description, series membership if any, and any appropriate notes (such as "Includes index" or "Sequel to . . .");
2. Deciding what elements in the description should be the basis for access points; or, in other words, what the main and added entries should be;
3. Determining the proper form for the names and titles selected as main and added entries. (This last is called name authority work, which is described below.)

Descriptive cataloging in this country, and indeed in much of the world, is carried out according to accepted standards. The standards that have prevailed over the years are described in part two of this book. The one that is used in most English-speaking countries is *Anglo-American Cataloguing Rules*, second edition, revised (referred to as AACR2R) which was published in 1988 and updated annually. A new descriptive cataloging standard, named *RDA: Resource Description and Access*, is being drafted at the time of the writing of this book.

Subject Analysis

For each bibliographic record, appropriate subject headings are chosen from an authorized list. Most general libraries in this country use one of two authorized lists, *Library of Congress Subject Headings* (LCSH) for large libraries, and *Sears List of Subject Headings* for smaller ones. For specialized libraries, special subject headings lists, such as *Medical Subject Headings*, may be used. In some libraries, subject headings under which there are local listings are registered in a local subject authority file.

Traditionally, subject headings have been assigned from authorized lists only. In online catalogs, subject terms not derived from an authorized list are sometimes assigned to augment, or to take the place of, the authorized terms.

Classification

Classification requires fitting the primary topic of a work to the provisions of whatever classification scheme is being used. Most American libraries use either the *Library of Congress Classification* (LCC) or the *Dewey Decimal Classification* (DDC). Specialized libraries often use subject-oriented systems such as the *National Library of Medicine Classification*. After the appropriate class number has been chosen, an item number is added to form a call number. This too is done according to standard patterns, somewhat different for each system. The act of classifying also calls for adjusting the numbers indicated in the standards to fit the new item into the shelf array of existing items.

Authority Work

Authority work entails a procedure that spans both descriptive and subject cataloging. In order to fulfill the objective of the catalog as a tool for retrieving all works by a given author or all works on a given subject, the access points to bibliographic records are normalized and standardized. In other words, all works by a given author or on a given subject are listed under a uniform heading for that author or subject. To this end, each author's name and the name of each subject is "established" when used for the first time, and the decision is recorded in a record called the *authority record*. Furthermore, to allow access through variant names and different forms of a name or a subject, cross references to a given heading are provided in the catalog and also recorded in the authority record for that heading. The same is true for references between related headings. A fact worth noting is that while each bibliographic record represents a physical item or group of items in a collection, each authority record represents a person, corporate body, common title, or subject that may appear as an access point in any number of bibliographic records. The activities of authority control include both integrating standardized authority records into the local system and preparing authority records for those names and subjects not available from standard authority files.

When a new authority record must be made, considerable checking in reference and other sources, as well as considerable consultation, is often required to arrive at the decisions that are ultimately registered in it. Authority work, therefore, has long been regarded as the most time-consuming and costly aspect of cataloging.

MARC Tagging

In an automated cataloging environment, the cataloger also must supply the codes and other information needed for computer processing. In MARC records, for instance, there is considerably more information relating to the item than is called for in a standard bibliographic description. This added information includes various computer tags as well as codes for language, type of publication, and other attributes of the item being cataloged. Records are set up according to the various MARC formats, the most common being the MARC 21 formats, a set of related standards for handling different kinds of bibliographic and authority data records developed and maintained by the Library of Congress in cooperation with other libraries and organizations. For a more detailed discussion of the MARC 21 formats, see chapter 16 of this book.

A MARC record is made up of three parts. The first two, called *leader* and *directory*, contain information that aids in processing the record and are not the direct responsibility of catalogers; in modern installations, this information is "system supplied." It is the data in the main part of a MARC record that catalogers must learn how to create. This part of a MARC record is organized into fields and, for most fields, into component subfields. Each field is identified by a three-digit numerical code called a *field tag*, and each subfield is identified by an alphabetic or numeric *subfield code*. Certain fields contain two *indicators* containing values (in the form of a numeric character or a blank) that interpret or supplement the data in the field, for example, whether a personal name includes a surname or what kind of title is presented.

Examples of Cataloging Records

Introduction

The following examples of bibliographic and authority records present an overview of the cataloging procedures and their overall structures. The remaining chapters in the book provide details regarding individual components of the records.

The Bibliographic Record

The record shown below pertaining to a two-volume monographic work by William A. Katz illustrates the creation of bibliographic records.

(1) Classification data

Class number and item number:	**Z711 .K32 2002** *(based on Library of Congress Classification)*
Class number:	**025.552** *(based on Dewey Decimal Classification)*

(2) Descriptive data

   (a) Bibliographic description:

Title:	**Introduction to reference work**
Statement of responsibility:	**William A. Katz**
Edition statement:	**8th ed.**
Publication:	**Boston : McGraw-Hill, c2002.**
Physical description:	**2 v. ; 24 cm.**
Note:	**Contents: v. 1. Basic information services — v. 2. Reference services and reference processes.**
Note:	**Includes bibliographical references and index.**
Standard numbers:	**ISBN 0072441070 (v. 1 : alk. paper)** **ISBN 0072441437 (v. 2 : alk. paper)** **ISBN 0071120742 (international ed.)**

   (b) Bibliographic access points:

Author (main entry):	**Katz, William A., 1924-2004**

Title: **Introduction to reference
                                        work**

(3) Subject cataloging data
    Subject heading: **Reference services
                                        (Libraries)**
                                        (*based on Library of
                                        Congress Subject
                                        Headings*)
    Subject heading: **Reference
                                        books—Bibliography.**
                                        (*based on Library of
                                        Congress Subject
                                        Headings*)
(4) Electronic location and access

                                        **Publisher description
                                        http://www.loc.gov/
                                        catdir/description/
                                        mh021/00069536.html
                                        Table of Contents
                                        http://www.loc.gov/
                                        catdir/toc/mh021/
                                        00069536.html**

A Coded Bibliographic Record

To make the cataloging data machine-readable, each of the elements shown above must be coded. Figure 1-1 shows the bibliographic record for the Katz book from the OCLC WorldCat, with codes for the fields as defined in the MARC 21 bibliographic format. (Examples in this chapter carry the codes for the fields only; for a detailed discussion of other details relating to the MARC 21 formats, see chapter 16.)

To understand this MARC record, it is necessary to look at it in conjunction with Table 1-1 and the accompanying explanation. Table 1-1 shows the major MARC field tags for a bibliographic record. Individual fields are illustrated by a coded record (see Figure 1-1), which is also explained in turn.

Explanation of Table 1-1

In a MARC record, all the field tags are three digits long. The various kinds of fields are often referred to as the 00X fields, the 0XX fields, and the 1XX, 2XX, . . . fields.

The information ordinarily thought of as cataloging data is recorded in that part of the MARC structure called the variable fields. The variable fields, in turn, comprise two types: (1) control fields, and (2) data fields.

000 01061cam 2200289 a 4500
001   00069536
003 DLC
005 20040223170913.0
008 001222s2002   mau   b   001 0 eng
010    $a 00069536
020    $a0072441070 (v. 1 : alk. paper)
020    $a0072441437 (v. 2 : alk. paper)
020    $a0071120742 (international ed.)
040    $aDLC$cDLC$dDLC
050 00$aZ711$b.K32 2002
082 00$a025.5/52$221
100 1 $aKatz, William A.,$d1924-
245 10$aIntroduction to reference work /$cWilliam A. Katz.
250    $a8th ed.
260    $aBoston :$bMcGraw-Hill,$cc2002.
300    $a2 v. ;$c24 cm.
504    $aIncludes bibliographical references and index.
505 0 $av. 1. Basic information services -- v. 2. Reference services and reference processes.
650 0$aReference services (Libraries)
650 0$aReference books$vBibliography.
856 42$3Publisher description$uhttp://www.loc.gov/catdir/description/mh021/00069536.html
856 4 $3Table of Contents$uhttp://www.loc.gov/catdir/toc/mh021/00069536.html

FIGURE 1-1   Coded bibliographic record.

The control fields (00X) contain either a single data element or a series of fixed-length data elements. Such data plays an important role in computer processing of MARC records.

The data fields (01X-8XX) contain cataloging data. (These are shown line-by-line in Figure 1-1.) Fields 010-082 contain numbers and codes, such as standard book number, Library of Congress control number, and call numbers. Fields 100-8XX contain bibliographic and subject cataloging data: elements of a bibliographic description, main and added access points, and subject headings.

Some of the field tags can be seen to fall into groups. The 1XX fields are for different categories of main entry. The 4XX and 8XX fields pertain to series. The 5XX fields are for notes. The 6XX and 7XX fields are for subject added entries and name and title added entries, respectively. Field 856, a field added since the advent of electronic resources, holds information relating to electronic location and access.

Most fields are divided into subfields, identified by alphabetic or numeric codes preceded by a delimiter (represented by the symbol ‡ [a dagger], | [a vertical bar], or $ [a dollar sign, as used in this text], e.g., $b, $2, etc.). Generally, the first element in a field is subfield "$a," followed by other subfields. For instance, in the publication details field (260), "$a" is for place of publication, "$b" is for publisher, and "$c" is for date; and in

TABLE 1-1   MARC Tags for Frequently Occurring Data Fields in a
Bibliographic Record

Tag	Name
008	Coded control information
010	Library of Congress Control Number
020	International Standard Book Number
040	Cataloging Source
043	Geographic Area Code
050	Library of Congress Call Number
082	Dewey Decimal Classification Number
090	Local call numbers
100	Main Entry—Personal Name
110	Main Entry—Corporate Name
111	Main Entry—Meeting Name
130	Main Entry—Uniform Title
245	Title Statement
246	Variant title
250	Edition Statement
260	Publication, Distribution, etc. (Imprint)
300	Physical Description
440	Series Statement/Added Entry—Title
500	General Note
504	Bibliography, etc. Note
505	Formatted Contents Note
600	Subject Added Entry—Personal Name
610	Subject Added Entry—Corporate Name
611	Subject Added Entry—Meeting Name
650	Subject Added Entry—Topical Term
651	Subject Added Entry—Geographical Name
653	Index Term—Uncontrolled
700	Added Entry—Personal Name
710	Added Entry—Corporate Name
730	Added Entry—Uniform Title
740	Added Entry—Uncontrolled Related/Analytical Title
800	Series Added Entry—Personal Name
810	Series Added Entry—Corporate Name
811	Series Added Entry—Meeting Name

the Dewey Decimal classification number field (082), "$a" is for classification number, "$b" is for item number, and "$2" is for edition number (i.e., the number of the edition of DDC from which the classification number is taken). Some subfield codes have mnemonic value, for instance, "$d" in fields 100, 700, and 800 for personal name entry is for date of birth or birth/death dates, and "$l" in fields 1XX, 4XX, and 7XX for language of work. Table 1-1 does not show subfield codes, but some are shown in

Figure 1-1, the coded Katz record. (In some systems, the "$a" subfield code is often implicit and does not show in the record display.)

Explanation of Figure 1-1

Figure 1-1 shows the "full" MARC record for the Katz book. "Full" means here that virtually all elements and codes contained in the record are displayed. It is primarily library personnel who need to see coded records; in most cases, users of online catalogs are offered abbreviated or full but non-coded displays. Although some of what appears in the Katz MARC record has no obvious relation to what the user normally finds in the library catalog, most of what is shown in the MARC record is simply a different manner of displaying standard catalog information, with each element showing the codes that enable the data to be processed by the computer. The following explanation goes through the Katz MARC record element by element.

The first five lines (000 to 008) contain control data, such as the length, status, and type of the record, date of publication, illustrations, language, etc. Although most of the control data are of no direct interest to end-users and often not displayed in the public catalog, this coded information is essential to efficient record processing, especially in systems that allow searchers to specify such things as, "English language material only" or "only if there are illustrations" or "only if published since 2000."

The remaining lines of the record (data fields 010-856) present what many would call the heart of the MARC record. The three-digit number at the beginning of each line is its MARC field tag. Field by field, the Katz MARC record shows:

010   Library of Congress control number
040   Cataloging sources, e.g., DLC for the Library of Congress
020   International Standard Book Number (ISBN) for first volume
020   ISBN for second volume
020   ISBN for the international edition
050   LC call number (class number is first subfield; subfield b is for the item number)
082   Dewey class number
100   Personal name main entry heading for Katz (subfield d is for date of birth)
245   Title and statement of responsibility (the latter is subfield c; if there were a subtitle it would be subfield b)
250   Edition statement
260   Place of publication, publisher (subfield b), and date of publication (subfield c)

300   Number of volumes (it would be number of pages for a one-volume work) and size (subfield c)
504   Bibliography note
505   Contents note for the titles of each of the volumes
650   First topical subject heading
650   Second topical subject heading
856   Electronic location and access (publisher description)
856   Electronic location and access (table of contents)

The numerals 0 and 1 that appear between some field tags and the first subfield are *indicators*, the meanings of which are defined uniquely for each field. They are not shown in the analysis above; for details, consult chapter 16 of this book and *MARC 21 Concise Formats*.[23]

Once coded, the information contained in the MARC record can be manipulated by the computer to produce various cataloging products such as online catalog records, acquisitions lists, etc. While the layout of a catalog card was standardized, online display of records varies from system to system. Within a particular system, records may also be displayed in long or short formats.

Further examples of bibliographic records are shown in appendix A.

The Authority Record

An authority record contains essentially the following elements: the heading for a person, a corporate body, a place, a uniform title (i.e., the standardized title for a work that has appeared under different titles; for a fuller discussion see chapter 5 of this book), or a subject authorized for use as access points in bibliographic records; cross references from other names, titles, or terms not used for the heading, and to and from related headings; and, the sources used in establishing the heading.

For example, the name authority record for William A. Katz includes the following data:

Established heading:	**Katz, William A., 1924-2004**
Cross references:	Katz, Bill, 1924-2004
	Katz, Willis Armstrong, 1924-2004
	Katz, William, 1924-2004
Sources used:	Library Buildings Institute, Chicago, 1963. Problems in planning library facilities, 1964.
	His Your library, c1984: CIP t.p. (William Katz, SUNY at Albany)

Integrating print and digital
resources in library
collections, 2006: prelims.
(Dr. William (Bill) Katz; d.
Sept. 12, 2004)

A Coded Name Authority Record

In the MARC 21 formats, the codes used vary according to the type of headings and based on whether the heading appearing in the authority record is used as a name entry or a subject access point in the bibliographic record. Table 1-2 lists the tags for frequently occurring variable data fields in a name authority record in the MARC 21 format (for details regarding the structure of MARC 21 formats, see chapter 16).

Figure 1-2 shows the name authority record, coded with the field tags

TABLE 1-2   MARC Tags for Frequently Occurring Data Fields in an Authority Record

Tag	Name
008	Coded control information
010	Library of Congress Control Number
040	Cataloging Source
050	Library of Congress Call Number
100	Heading—Personal Name
110	Heading—Corporate Name
111	Heading—Meeting Name
130	Heading—Uniform Title
150	Heading—Topical Term
151	Heading—Geographic Name
400	See From Tracing—Personal Name
410	See From Tracing—Corporate Name
411	See From Tracing—Meeting Name
430	See From Tracing—Uniform Title
450	See From Tracing—Topical Term
451	See From Tracing—Geographic Name
500	See Also From Tracing—Personal Name
510	See Also From Tracing—Corporate Name
511	See Also From Tracing—Meeting Name
530	See Also From Tracing—Uniform Title
550	See Also From Tracing—Topical Term
551	See Also From Tracing—Geographic Name
663	Complex See Also Reference—Name
664	Complex See Reference—Name
670	Source Data Found
675	Source Data Not Found
680	Public General Note

```
000 00799cz  2200193n 4500
001 n  79092477
003 DLC
005 20060518052008.0
008 800507n| acannaabn        |a aaa
010   $an 79092477 $zn 93025121 $zn 97014023
035   $a(OCoLC)oca00324772
040   $aDLC$beng$cDLC$dDLC$dUkOxU$dSdMadT
100 1 $aKatz, William A.,$d1924-2004
400 1 $aKatz, Bill,$d1924-2004
400 1 $aKatz, Willis Armstrong,$d1924-2004
400 1 $aKatz, William,$d1924-2004
670   $aLibrary Buildings Institute, Chicago, 1963.$bProblems in planning library
facilities, 1964.
670   $aHis Your library, c1984:$bCIP t.p. (William Katz, SUNY at Albany)
670   $aIntegrating print and digital resources in library collections, 2006:$bprelims. (Dr.
William (Bill) Katz; d. Sept. 12, 2004)
```

FIGURE 1-2   Coded authority record.

based on the MARC 21 format, for the heading for William A. Katz. The
first five lines (numbered 000 to 008) show control data. (For details regarding control data, see chapter 16.) The remaining lines, containing
data fields, are analyzed below:

010	LC name authority control number
040	Record originated with LC and modified by other libraries
100	Authorized personal name heading for William A. Katz, with his birth and death dates
400	Form of name not used as the heading for Katz, from which a *see* reference would be made to the preferred heading
400	Another non-preferred form of name for Katz, from which a *see* reference would also be made
400	A third non-preferred form of name for Katz, from which a *see* reference would also be made
670	One of the sources in which the chosen form of Katz's name was found
670	A second source used in establishing Katz's name
670	A third source used in establishing Katz's name

The authority record shows the standardized heading to be used as an
access point in the catalog and also provides data for generating cross
references that link variant names and forms to the authorized heading.
The cross references may be displayed in different ways in the online
catalog. Further examples of name authority records are shown in appendix B.

As was the case with the coded Katz bibliographic record shown in
Figure 1-1 and the table of MARC 21 bibliographic tags (see Table 1-1
above), the coded Katz authority record can be best understood in con-

junction with Table 1-2, which shows the major fields and field tags in the MARC 21 Format for Authority Data. Some of the fields in the authority format parallel those in the format for bibliographic data: the control fields; and 1XX fields (with the authorized headings reflecting different types of names: 100 personal, 110 corporate, 111 meeting, and so on). Others are quite different; the 4XX fields show *see* references; the 5XX fields are for *see-also* references; and the 6XX fields are variously defined, including complex references, history notes, source for name choice, and notes identifying other sources used in establishing the heading.

In **authority** records (NR = not repeatable; R = repeatable):

100 Heading—Personal name (NR)
110 Heading—Corporate name (NR)
111 Heading—Meeting name (NR)
130 Heading—Uniform title (NR)
150 Heading—Topical term (NR)
151 Heading—Geographic name (NR)

400 *See from* tracing—Personal name (R)
410 *See from* tracing—Corporate name (R)
411 *See from* tracing—Meeting name (R)
430 *See from* tracing—Uniform title (R)
451 *See from* tracing—Geographic name (R)

500 *See also from* tracing—Personal name (R)
510 *See also from* tracing—Corporate name (R)
511 *See also from* tracing—Meeting name (R)
530 *See also from* tracing—Uniform title (R)
551 *See also from* tracing—Geographic name (R)

In **bibliographic** records:

100 Main entry—Personal name (NR)
110 Main entry—Corporate name (NR)
111 Main entry—Meeting name (NR)
130 Main entry—Uniform title (NR)

600 Subject added entry—Personal name (R)
610 Subject added entry—Corporate name (R)
611 Subject added entry—Meeting name (R)
630 Subject added entry—Uniform title (R)
650 Subject added entry—Topical term (R)
651 Subject added entry—Geographic name (NR)

700 Added entry—Personal name (R)
710 Added entry—Corporate name (R)

711   Added entry—Meeting name (R)
730   Added entry—Uniform title (R)

800   Series added entry—Personal name (R)
810   Series added entry—Corporate name (R)
811   Series added entry—Meeting name (R)
830   Series added entry—Uniform title (R)

Record Display

The same MARC record can be displayed in various formats and different degrees of fullness in the catalog for the users, depending on the type of library and user needs. The following examples show a full record display and a brief record display of the Katz book from the Library of Congress Online Catalog (http://catalog.loc.gov). In the public display, the MARC tags are replaced by labels that are easily recognized.

Full record display

LC Control No.:	**00069536**
Type of Material:	**Book (Print, Microform, Electronic, etc.)**
Personal Name:	**Katz, William A., 1924-2004.**
Main Title:	**Introduction to reference work / William A. Katz.**
Edition Information:	**8th ed.**
Published/Created:	**Boston : McGraw-Hill, c2002.**
Description:	**2 v. ; 24 cm.**
ISBN:	**0072441070 (v. 1 : alk. paper)**
	0072441437 (v. 2 : alk. paper)
	0071120742 (international ed.)
Contents:	**v. 1. Basic information services — v. 2. Reference services and reference processes**
Notes:	**Includes bibliographical references and index.**
Subjects:	**Reference services (Libraries)**
	Reference books — Bibliography.
LC Classification:	**Z711 .K32 2002**
Dewey Class No.:	**025.5/52 21**
Electronic File Information:	**Publisher description http://www.loc.gov/catdir/ description/mh021/ 00069536.html**

	Table of Contents
	http://www.loc.gov/catdir/toc/
	mh021/00069536.html
Links:	Publisher description
	Table of Contents

Brief record display

LC Control Number:	00069536
Type of Material:	Book (Print, Microform, Electronic, etc.)
Personal Name:	Katz, William A., 1924-2004.
Main Title:	Introduction to reference work / William A. Katz.
Edition Information:	8th ed.
Published/Created:	Boston : McGraw-Hill, c2002.
Description:	2 v. ; 24 cm.
ISBN:	0072441070 (v. 1 : alk. paper)
	0072441437 (v. 2 : alk. paper)
	0071120742 (international ed.)
Links:	Publisher description
	Table of Contents

CONCLUSION

This chapter has attempted to set the framework for a study of bibliographic control in the library environment, particularly in a general library. It began with an account of the difference between today's information world and that of two generations ago, briefly describing advances in the Internet along with parallel advances in the library environment and in the online information industry. It proceeded with discussions of the devices the library world has used to provide the best information services within its resources, taking into account how much impact technology has had on all phases of library and library-like operations. It attempts to show the general picture, defining bibliographic control and noting the various ways of achieving it in all environments where it is used—showing, at the same time, how its demands vary according to the nature of the material to be brought under control.

The discussion then turned to library catalogs. It proceeded to the major operations entailed in producing and maintaining a library catalog and its subsidiary files: description, access, and organization. All these topics are treated in extensive detail in subsequent chapters. Their order reflects the order of activities in producing a bibliographic record: drafting a description, deciding on name access points and forms of names, assigning subject headings, and classification. In conjunction, authority control, an operation essential for standardizing the access points to bibliographic records, is also considered. Emphasis is on standard Anglo-American cataloging practice, but along the way alternative means and tools are also discussed. Examples showing a bibliographic record and an authority record are included and briefly explained in order to present an integral picture of the cataloging process. The MARC structure is also introduced, but in-depth considerations of the MARC formats and other encoding schemes are left to the end of the book because their details cannot be fully understood until the complexities in what must be coded are mastered.

NOTES

1. Major sources used in drafting the following timelines were Charles P. Bourne and Trudi Bellardo Hahn, *A History of Online Information Services, 1963–1976* (Cambridge, Mass.: MIT Press, 2003); Trudi Bellardo Hahn, "Pioneers of the Online Age," in *Historical Studies in Information Science*, ed. Trudi Bellardo Hahn and Michael Buckland (Medford, N.J.: Published for the American Society for Information Science by Information Today, 1998), 116–31; Michael Kanellos, "The Hard Drive at 50: Half a Century of Hard Drives," *CNET News.com*, 11 September 2006, http://news.com.com/The+hard+drive+at+50/2009-1015_3-6112782 .html (19 Feb. 2007); Charles Meadow, "Online Database Industry Timeline," *Database*, 1988 October; Lucy Tedd, "OPACs Through the Ages," *Library Review* 43, no. 4 (1944): 27–37; Phyllis Richmond, *Introduction to PRECIS for North American Usage* (Littleton, Colo.: Libraries Unlimited, 1981); Joint Steering Committee for Revision of Anglo-American Cataloguing Rules, "RDA: Resource Description and Access," http://collectionscanada.ca/jsc/rda.html (19 Feb. 2007); and Quentin Hardy, "Can We Know Everything?" *California [UC Berkeley Alumni Magazine]*, 117, no. 2 (March/April 2006).

2. V. Bush, "As We May Think," *The Atlantic Monthly* 176, no. 1 (1945): 101–8, www.theatlantic.com/unbound/flashbks/computer/bushf.htm (19 Feb. 2007).

3. Heting Chu, *Information Representation and Retrieval in the Digital Age* (Medford, N.J.: Published for the American Society for Information Science and Technology by Information Today, 2003), 2–4.

4. Dan Fost, "Hard-driving valley began 50 years ago: And most other forms of data storage eventually became a distant memory," *San Francisco Chronicle*, Monday, September 11, 2006, www.sfgate.com/cgi-bin/article.cgi?=/c/a/ 2006/09/11/BUGH3L23T01.DTL (30 Mar. 2007).

5. "Sputnik and The Dawn of the Space Age," http://history.nasa.gov/ sputnik/ (updated February 21, 2003; accessed 19 Feb. 2007).

6. Michael Hauben, "History of ARPANET: Behind the Net—The Untold History of the ARPANET, Or—The 'Open' History of the ARPANET/Internet," www2.dei.isep.ipp.pt/docs/arpa.html (19 Feb. 2007).

7. George Laughead, Jr., "WWW-VL: History: Internet & W3 World-Wide Web," c2004–2005, http://vlib.iue.it/history/internet/ (19 Feb. 2007).

8. "WebCrawler: About WebCrawler," 2006, www.webcrawler.com/info .wbcrwl/search/help/about.htm (19 Feb. 2007).

9. IFLA Study Group on the Functional Requirements for Bibliographic Records, *Functional Requirements for Bibliographic Records, Final Report* (München: K. G. Saur, 1998). UBCIM Publications, New Series; v. 19. Also available at www .ifla.org/VII/s13/frbr/frbr.htm (19 Feb. 2007).

10. "History of the Dublin Core Metadata Initiative," http://dublincore.org/ about/history/ (19 Feb. 2007).

11. Edward T. O'Neill and Lois Mai Chan, "FAST (Faceted Application of Subject Terminology): A Simplified Vocabulary Based on The Library of Congress Subject Headings," *IFLA Journal* 29, no. 4 (December 2003): 336–42.

12. IFLA Study Group on the Functional Requirements for Bibliographic Records, *Functional Requirements for Bibliographic Records, Final Report.*

13. Joint Steering Committee for Revision of Anglo-American Cataloguing Rules, *RDA: Resource Description and Access: Prospectus,* www.collectionscanada .ca/jsc/rdaprospectus.html (19 Feb. 2007).

14. "Open WorldCat," www.oclc.org/worldcat/open/ (19 Feb. 2007).

15. "Google Book Search," http://books.google.com/ (19 Feb. 2007).

16. Karen Calhoun, "The Changing Nature of the Catalog and its Integration with Other Discovery Tools: Final Report, prepared for the Library of Congress, March 17, 2006," www.loc.gov/catdir/calhoun-report-final.pdf, (19 Feb. 2007).

17. Charles Ammi Cutter, *Rules for a Dictionary Catalog,* 4th ed. rewritten (Washington, D.C.: Government Printing Office, 1904; republished, London: The Library Association, 1953), 12.

18. Seymour Lubetzky, "Principles of Descriptive Cataloging," in *Studies of Descriptive Cataloging* (Washington, DC: Library of Congress, 1946), 25–33; also in *Foundations of Cataloging: A Sourcebook,* ed. Michael Carpenter and Elaine Svenonius (Littleton, Colo.: Libraries Unlimited, 1985), 104–12.

19. *Statement of Principles Adopted by The International Conference on Cataloguing Principles,* Paris, October 1961, www.ddb.de/standardisierung/pdf/paris_ principles_1961.pdf (19 Feb. 2007).

20. IFLA Study Group on the Functional Requirements for Bibliographic Records, *Functional Requirements for Bibliographic Records, Final Report.*

21. *ISBD (M): International Standard Bibliographic Description for Monographic Publications,* [prepared by] Working Group on the International Standard Bibliographic Description, 1st standard ed. (London: IFLA Committee on Cataloguing, 1974); and subsequent ISBDs.

22. *Anglo-American Cataloguing Rules,* 2nd ed., 2002 revision. Prepared under the direction of the Joint Steering Committee for Revision of AACR, a committee of: the American Library Association, the Australian Committee on Cataloguing, the British Library, the Canadian Committee on Cataloguing, Chartered Institute of Library and Information Professionals, the Library of Congress (Chicago: American Library Association, 2002).

23. *MARC 21 Concise Formats,* prepared by Network Development and MARC Standards Office (Washington, D.C.: Cataloging Distribution Service, Library of Congress, 2005); also available at: www.loc.gov/marc/bibliographic/.

PART TWO
DESCRIPTION

STANDARDS AND TOOLS

Anglo-American Cataloguing Rules. 2nd ed., 2002 revision. Prepared under
the direction of the Joint Steering Committee for Revision of AACR,
a committee of the American Library Association, the Australian
Committee on Cataloguing, the British Library, the Canadian Committee on Cataloguing, Chartered Institute of Library and Information Professionals, the Library of Congress. Chicago: American
Library Association, 2002-.

The Dublin Core Metadata Element Set: An American Standard. Developed
by the National Information Standards Organization, approved September 10, 2001, by the American National Standards Institute.
ANSI/NISO Z39.8s5-2001. Bethesda, Md.: National Information Standards Organization, 2001.

Gorman, Michael. *The Concise AACR2*. 4th ed., through the 2004 update.
Chicago: American Library Association, 2004.

Library of Congress Rule Interpretations. 2nd ed. Washington, D.C.: Cataloging Distribution Service, Library of Congress, 1989-. (Kept up to date
with quarterly updates and annual cumulations; also available
through Cataloger's Desktop by subscription, http://desktop.loc
.gov/).

RECOMMENDED READING

Caplan, Priscilla. "International Metadata Initiatives: Lessons in Bibliographic Control," in *Proceedings of the Bicentennial Conference on Bibliographic Control for the New Millennium: Confronting the Challenges of
Networked Resources and the Web: Washington, D.C., November 15–17,
2000*, sponsored by the Library of Congress Cataloging Directorate;

edited by Ann M. Sandberg-Fox. Washington DC: Library of Congress, Cataloging Distribution Service, 2001: 61–79. (Also available at: http://lcweb.loc.gov/catdir/bibcontrol/caplan_paper.html.)

Carpenter, Michael, and Elaine Svenonius. *Foundations of Cataloging: A Sourcebook*. Littleton, Colo.: Libraries Unlimited, 1985.

Cutter, Charles A. *Rules for a Dictionary Catalog*. 4th ed. rewritten. Washington, D.C.: Government Printing Office, 1904. Republished, London: The Library Association, 1953. First published under the title *Rules for a Printed Dictionary Catalogue* in 1876.

Dunkin, Paul S. Chapters 1–4 in *Cataloging U.S.A.* Chicago: American Library Association, 1969.

Gorman, Michael. "Descriptive Cataloguing: Its Past, Present, and Future." 79–94 in *Technical Services Today and Tomorrow*, Michael Gorman et al., 2nd ed. Edited by Michael Gorman. Englewood, Colo.: Libraries Unlimited, 1998.

Hsieh-Yee, Ingrid. *Organizing Audiovisual and Electronic Resources for Access: A Cataloging Guide*. Englewood, Colo.: Libraries Unlimited, 1999.

IFLA Study Group on the Functional Requirements for Bibliographic Records. *Functional Requirements for Bibliographic Records, Final Report*. UBCIM Publications, New Series, v. 19. München: K. G. Saur, 1998. Also available at: www.ifla.org/VII/s13/frbr/frbr.pdf (20 Feb. 2007).

International Conference on Cataloguing Principles, Paris, 1961. "Statement of Principles." In *Report of International Conference on Cataloguing Principles*, edited by A. H. Chaplin and Dorothy Anderson. London: Organizing Committee of the International Conference on Cataloguing Principles, 1963: 91–96.

Intner, Sheila S., Susan S. Laziner, and Jean Weihs. *Metadata and Its Impact on Libraries*. Westport, Conn.: Libraries Unlimited, 2006.

Jewett, Charles C. "Smithsonian Catalogue System." In *Smithsonian Report On the Construction of Catalogues of Libraries and of a General Catalogue and Their Publication by Means of Separate, Stereotyped Titles with Rules and Examples*, 3–19. 2nd ed. Washington, D.C.: Smithsonian Institution, 1853; also in *Foundations of Cataloging: A Sourcebook*, edited by Michael Carpenter and Elaine Svenonius, 51–61. Littleton, Colo.: Libraries Unlimited, 1985.

Joint Steering Committee for Revision of Anglo-American Cataloguing Rules. *A Brief History of AACR*. www.collectionscanada.ca/jsc/history.html (Last updated: 27 July 2005).

Lubetzky, Seymour. *Cataloging Rules and Principles: A Critique of the ALA Rules for Entry and a Proposed Design for Their Revision*. Washington, D.C.: Library of Congress, 1953.

Lubetzky, Seymour. "Principles of Descriptive Cataloging." In *Studies of Descriptive Cataloging*, 25–33. Washington, D.C.: Library of Congress, 1946; also in *Foundations of Cataloging: A Sourcebook*, edited by Michael

Carpenter and Elaine Svenonius, 104–12. Littleton, Colo.: Libraries Unlimited, 1985.

Osborn, Andrew D. "The Crisis in Cataloging." *Library Quarterly* 11 (October 1941): 393–411.

Taylor, Arlene G. *Introduction to Cataloging and Classification.* 10th ed. Westport, Conn.: Libraries Unlimited, 2006. Chapter 2.

Tillett, Barbara B. "FRBR (Functional Requirements for Bibliographic Records)." *Technicalities* 23, no. 5 (September/October 2003): 1, 11–13. Also available at: www.loc.gov/cds/FRBR.html.

CHAPTER 2
FOUNDATIONS, PRINCIPLES, AND STANDARDS OF RESOURCE DESCRIPTION

BIBLIOGRAPHIC DESCRIPTION AND SURROGATE RECORDS

In the print environment, keyword searching of texts was not an option; to help identify and choose relevant information items, users relied on brief descriptions of books and other library materials for indication of their characteristics and content. Each brief description contained what were considered to be essential attributes of a given item and served as its surrogate in the library's catalog.

In the early days of library service, cataloging was largely an individual activity for each library. Different libraries developed their own policies and practices in formulating surrogate records and in organizing them to form the catalogs they deemed most suitable for their purposes. Thus, cataloging records were presented in forms and styles that varied from library to library. Chapter 1 described how American librarians in the early part of the twentieth century came to value standardization of cataloging practice, and how various schemes and sets of rules merged to facilitate standardization. This chapter discusses the principles underlying the standards that emerged.

CONTRIBUTIONS TO CATALOGING THEORY

Over the past hundred or so years, many individuals and organizations have contributed to the development of standards and codes for bibliographic description, particularly through articulating basic tenets or principles and by setting standards. Early efforts at codifying cataloging practice were often the results of individual labors. As time went on, such efforts became more communal.

Some of the most influential cataloging concepts and principles, their proponents, and their impact are discussed briefly below.

Panizzi's Principles

Sir Anthony Panizzi (1797–1879), who worked as a cataloger and later became the Principal Librarian of the British Museum Department of

Printed Books, was responsible for formulating ninety-one rules to be used in compiling the catalog of the British Museum. These rules are hailed as "the ancestor of all modern library cataloging codes."[1] Some of the underlying principles of the rules were articulated in a letter, "Mr. Panizzi to the Right Hon. the Earl of Ellesmere.—British Museum, January 29, 1848."[2] Although some of the ideas and principles embodied in the rules and in his letter do not seem relevant to the current environment, many others, such as the objectives of a library catalog, the requirement for normalization of names (personal and corporate), the status of works modified or adapted from differing originals, and the requirement for uniformity in application of cataloging rules, still resonate in today's cataloging codes and practices.[3]

Jewett's Principles

Charles C. Jewett (1816–1868) was appointed Librarian and Assistant Secretary at the Smithsonian Institution soon after its establishment in Washington, D.C., in 1846. He embarked on an effort to establish a great national library, one that would incorporate within it a union catalog of the holdings of all public libraries in the United States. He envisioned the union catalog as the first step in a course that would lead eventually to a universal catalog.[4] To realize his vision of a "universal catalog," Jewett proposed two courses of action. The first was the use of entries embossed on separate stereotype plates in order to facilitate the production of such a catalog and, in addition, drastically reduce the cost of catalog production and maintenance, particularly in preparing new editions of the book catalog that was the predominant catalog form in his time. Jewett's second proposal was cooperative cataloging, a development he saw as necessary to building a universal catalog. Jewett's union catalog and cooperative cataloging ideas reverberated in later developments in library practice.

Cutter's Principles

Charles Ammi Cutter (1837–1903), a librarian at Harvard College who was later appointed the librarian of the Boston Athenaeum, was responsible for compiling *Rules for a Dictionary Catalog*, in which he claimed to "set forth rules in a systematic way or to investigate what might be called the first principles of cataloging."[5] These rules first appeared in 1876 as an adjunct to a government publication on the state of American libraries. Two statements that have been widely quoted in the literature and later cataloging codes are worthy of particular note. His statement, "The convenience of the public is always to be set before the ease of the cataloger,"[6] placed the focus of catalog design squarely on the user. The second often cited text from Cutter's *Rules* is the statement, cited in chapter 1 of this book, concerning the objectives of the catalog and the means for attaining them.[7]

Lubetzky's Principles

During the mid-twentieth century, Seymour Lubetzky (1898–2003), a librarian at the Library of Congress and later a faculty member of the School of Library Services at the University of California, Los Angeles, played an important role throughout his career in shaping the future direction of cataloging codes. He was a prolific writer and produced many publications about cataloging. Particularly influential are the following:

> *Studies of Descriptive Cataloging* (1946)[8]
> *Cataloging Rules and Principles* (1953)[9]
> *Code of Cataloging Rules* (1960)[10]
> *Principles of Cataloging* (1969)[11]

In his works, Lubetzky examined existing cataloging rules and called for a return to principles. In particular, he argued that rules for access points should be based on "condition of authorship" rather than on type of publication (which was called for in the then existing cataloging code). He advocated logical rather than situational rules. His insistence on a rationalized approach to cataloging standards based on objectives and principles laid the foundation for subsequent cataloging code development. He is credited for transforming cataloging codes "rich in rules" to those "rich in principle."[12]

Lubetzky's *Cataloging Rules and Principles*, recognized as his most important work, is divided into three parts. Part I presents a detailed analysis of specific rules in ALA (1949). Part II takes up the question of the "corporate complex" (again providing a perceptive analysis of the confusion regarding corporate authorship in existing codes), condemning ALA (1949) for many unnecessary rules such as those distinguishing between kinds of corporate bodies. In Part III, "Design for a Code," Lubetzky sets forth two objectives: "(1) to enable the user of the catalog to determine readily whether or not the library has the book he wants; (2) to reveal to the user of the catalog, under one form of the author's name, what works the library has by a given author and what editions or translations of a given work."

Paris Principles

In 1961, one of the most important events in the evolution of cataloging codes took place. The International Conference on Cataloguing Principles was held in Paris, October 9–18, 1961, under the auspices of the International Federation of Library Associations (IFLA). There were delegations from fifty-three countries and twelve international organizations. The discussion of cataloging principles was based on a draft statement circulated before the meeting. As a result of the conference, a statement of principles, which has become known as the "Paris Statement" or the "Paris Principles," was issued. It drew heavily upon Seymour Lubetzky's 1960 draft cataloging code, although its scope is limited to choice of entry and forms of headings. The work opens with a statement of the functions of the catalog, in essence a restatement of Lubetzky's and Cutter's objectives. The principles that follow rest logically on these objectives and are stated in specific terms and in considerable detail.

The Paris Statement represented a great step forward toward international agreement. One frequently cited feature of this document is its endorsement of corporate entry and natural, rather than grammatical, arrangement of title, which removes the major differences between the Anglo-American and the Germanic traditions of cataloging. (In German catalogs, titles were filed under their first substantive word.)

Since the appearance of the Paris Principles, many cataloging codes have been revised or developed according to their provisions, notably the *Anglo-American Cataloguing Rules*, the German Code (*Regeln für die alphabetische Katalogisierung* [RAK]), and the Swedish and Danish codes. The RAK represented a major revolution in Germanic cataloging in that the concept of corporate entry was introduced and use of the literal title (rather than the grammatical title) was accepted.

International Standard Bibliographic Description (ISBD)

After the Paris Conference, the next step toward greater international agreement was taken at the International Meeting of Cataloguing Experts, which was held in Copenhagen in 1969. At this meeting, an international working group was established for the purpose of developing a standard order and content for describing monographic material. The objectives of the new format for bibliographic description were defined as follows:

> . . . first, that records produced in one country or by the users of one language can be easily understood in other countries and by the users of other languages; second, that the records produced in each country can be integrated into files or lists of various kinds containing also records from other countries; and third, that records in written or printed form can be converted into machine-readable form with the minimum of editing.[13]

To fulfill these requirements, the order of bibliographic elements in a record was standardized and a special punctuation pattern distinguishing these elements was prescribed.

A document entitled *ISBD (M): International Standard Bibliographic De-*

scription (for Single Volume and Multi-Volume Monographic Publications) was issued in 1971. In the following years, this format was accepted and adopted by many national bibliographies. As often happens, the course of its application revealed many ambiguities and a need for more details in some areas. These deficiencies were discussed at the International Federation of Library Associations (IFLA) conference held in Grenoble, France, in 1973. After this conference, two documents were published: the first standard edition of *ISBD(M)* and a set of recommendations for *ISBD(S)* (for serial publications). The first standard edition of *ISBD(S)* was published in 1977.

In retrospect, after the development of *ISBD(M)* and *ISBD(S)*, it was considered desirable to develop a *general ISBD* that could serve as the framework for specific *ISBDs*. *ISBD(G): International Standard Bibliographic Description (General)* was published in 1977. Since then, other *ISBDs* have also been developed. The family of *ISBDs* now includes the following:

ISBD (A): International Standard Bibliographic Description for Older Monographic Publications (Antiquarian).

ISBD (CF): International Standard Bibliographic Description for Computer Files.

ISBD (CM): International Standard Bibliographic Description for Cartographic Materials.

ISBD (CR): International Standard Bibliographic Description for Serials and Other Continuing Resources.

ISBD (ER): International Standard Bibliographic Description for Electronic Resources.

ISBD (G): General International Standard Bibliographic Description.

ISBD (M): International Standard Bibliographic Description for Monographic Publications.

ISBD (NBM): International Standard Bibliographic Description for Non-Book Materials.

ISBD (PM): International Standard Bibliographic Description for Printed Music.

ISBD (S): International Standard Bibliographic Description for Serials.

Universal Bibliographic Control (UBC)

The theme of the thirty-ninth International Federation of Library Associations (IFLA) meeting in 1973 was the ideal of universal bibliographic control (UBC), and this concept was adopted as a goal for ultimate international cooperation. The ideal of UBC was first articulated at the International Meeting of Cataloguing Experts:

Efforts should be directed towards creating a system for the international exchange of information by which the standard bibliographic description of each publication would be established and distributed by a national agency in the country of origin . . .[14]

The basic idea of UBC is having each document cataloged only once, as near to the source of publication as possible, and making basic bibliographic data on all publications, issued in all countries, universally and promptly available in a form that is internationally acceptable.[15]

The fact that such a dream was even conceivable was due to the many encouraging developments toward international cooperation and standardization that had occurred in the field of cataloging in the preceding decades. The Paris Conference and the International Meeting of Cataloguing Experts in Copenhagen were two milestones on the road toward achieving the goal of UBC. The standards and agreements produced by these conferences played an important role in the revision of cataloging rules around the world.

Functional Requirements for Bibliographic Records (FRBR)

Another important occurrence was the development of Functional Requirements for Bibliographic Records (FRBR) by an IFLA study group in the mid-1990s. FRBR is a conceptual model for viewing the structure and relationships of bibliographic and authority records. Based on the four tasks performed by users when using catalogs or bibliographies—to find, to identify, to select, and to obtain a bibliographic entity—the study group formulated a model consisting of three groups of entities:[16]

- Group 1 entities consist of rigorous definitions and relationships among bibliographic entities called *work, expression, manifestation,* and *item.*
- Group 2 entities consist of *person* and *corporate body* that are related to Group 1 entities in terms of their roles with respect to *work, expression, manifestation,* and *item.*
- Group 3 entities concern the subjects of works, including concepts, objects, events, places, and any of the Group 1 or Group 2 entities.

Group 1 entities are defined as follows:

- *work* is a distinct intellectual or artistic creation;
- *expression* is the intellectual or artistic realization of a *work* in the form of alpha-numeric, musical, or choreographic notation, sound, image, object, movement, etc., or any combination of such forms;
- *manifestation* is the physical embodiment of an *expression* of a *work*; and,
- *item* is a single exemplar of a *manifestation*

Group 2 entities relate to bibliographic access points (discussed in part 3 of this book), and Group 3 entities relate to subject access points (discussed in part 4 of this book).

Barbara B. Tillett, Chief of the Cataloging Policy and Support Office at the Library of Congress, played a pivotal role in the development of FRBR.

Work on Group 1 entities has been completed and has resulted in the publication *Functional Requirements for Bibliographic Records, Final Report.*[17] Work on Groups 2 and 3 entities are in progress.

It is anticipated that the concepts brought forward in FRBR will provide an important approach to the development of future cataloging codes and to the future revision of current codes.

DEVELOPMENT OF STANDARDS

Since the middle of the nineteenth century, many cataloging codes, reflecting the principles discussed above, have been developed and published. Most of the earlier codes represented the efforts of individuals, but later ones result from corporate undertakings. The following is a brief discussion of the development of standards for resource description.

British Museum Cataloguing Rules (1839)

> British Museum. Department of Printed Books. *Rules for Compiling the Catalogues of Printed Books, Maps and Music in the British Museum.* Rev. ed. London: British Museum. Printed by order of the trustees, 1936.

The British Museum Cataloguing Rules (BM), also known as Panizzi's ninety-one rules, was drafted as a guide for the compilation of the British Museum catalogs. The rules, published in 1841 as part of the introductory matter for the British Museum's printed book catalog, with a revised edition published in 1936, reflect the functions of the catalog as an inventory list and finding list.

This set of rules is considered to be the first major cataloging code ever produced and is recognized as having had a substantial influence on later codes.

Jewett's Rules (1853)

> Jewett, Charles C. *Smithsonian Report on the Construction of Catalogues of Libraries, and Their Publication by Means of Separate, Stereotyped Titles, with Rules and Examples.* 2nd ed. Washington,

D.C.: Smithsonian Institution, 1853. Reprinted, Ann Arbor, Mich.: University Microfilms, 1961.

Charles C. Jewett was responsible for developing the code for the catalog of the Smithsonian Institution. The code contains thirty-three rules,[18] which were largely based on Panizzi's rules. Jewett advocated stringent and detailed rules that should leave little to the individual judgment of the cataloger.

A matter of particular interest is that Jewett's discussion of subject headings represents the earliest call for the codifying of subject heading practice.

Cutter's Rules (1876)

Cutter, Charles Ammi. *Rules for a Dictionary Catalog*. 4th ed. Rewritten. Washington, D.C.: Government Printing Office, 1904. Republished, London: The Library Association, 1953.

The first edition of this work appeared in 1876 with the title *Rules for a Printed Dictionary Catalogue*, which formed Part II of the U.S. Bureau of Education Publication, *Public Libraries in the United States*. It contains 369 rules covering descriptive cataloging, subject headings, and filing.

Cutter's purpose was to "investigate what might be called the first principles of cataloging." His code has had enormous influence on subsequent codes and cataloging practice in the United States. It became the basis for the dictionary catalog, which was to emerge as the predominant form of catalogs in general libraries in the United States.

AA (1908)

Catalog Rules: Author and Title Entries. American ed. Chicago: American Library Association, 1908.

AA (1908) represented the first joint effort between American and British librarians in developing a cataloging code. However, the two groups did not reach full agreements on all details and the code was published in two editions (English and American).

AA (1908) reflected the influence of previous codes—British Museum and Cutter—and, to a large extent, the then current practice of the Library of Congress, which had begun distributing printed cards in 1902. It owed a great deal to Cutter's rules; however, it did not include Cutter's statements of objects and means and also omitted any rules for subject headings. The major aim of the code was to meet the requirements of larger academic and research libraries. To a considerable extent, this focus has set the tone of subsequent codes, which have been drawn up primarily to respond to the needs of such libraries. In AA (1908), the particular needs of smaller libraries are only occasionally recognized through alternative rules.

Prussian Instructions

> *The Prussian Instructions: Rules for the Alphabetical Catalogs of the Prussian Libraries*. Translated from the 2nd ed., authorized August 10, 1908, with an introduction and notes by Andrew D. Osborn. Ann Arbor, Mich.: University of Michigan Press, 1938.

Originally developed as a standardized system of cataloging for Prussian libraries, the *Prussian Instructions* (PI) was adopted by many libraries in Germanic and Scandinavian countries.

The rules reflected two major differences in cataloging between the Germanic and the Anglo-American traditions. PI preferred entry under title instead of corporate entry. The second major difference was that grammatical arrangement of title is preferred over natural or mechanical arrangement.[19]

Vatican Code

> Vatican Library (Biblioteca Apostolica Vaticana). *Rules for the Catalog of Printed Books*. Translated from the 2nd Italian ed. by the Very Rev. Thomas J. Shanahan, Victor A. Schaefer, and Constantin T. Vesselowsky. Wyllis E. Wright, ed. Chicago: American Library Association, 1948. (3rd ed. in Italian appeared in 1949.)

The Vatican rules were developed for the purpose of compiling a general catalog of the printed books in the Vatican Library after its reorganization in the 1920s. The persons responsible were either Americans or American-trained local librarians. Therefore, American influence is evident, to the extent that it has been called an "international code with a definite American bias."[20] Its significance for American librarians lies in the fact that, for many years, the Vatican code was, as Wyllis Wright states in the foreword to the English translation, "the most complete statement of American cataloging practice."[21]

Probably the most comprehensive and best-structured code at the time, the Vatican code contained rules for entry, description, subject headings, and filing, with ample examples throughout.

ALA (1941 Draft)

> *ALA Catalog Rules: Author and Title Entries*. Preliminary American 2nd ed. Chicago: American Library Association, 1941.

During the early 1930s, there was a general feeling that the Anglo-American cataloging code needed revision. A Catalog Code Revision Committee under the American Library Association was established for this purpose. Although the plan was to cooperate with the Library Association of Great Britain and other national library associations, this intention was not fully realized because of the eruption of World War II.

The draft code was completed in 1941. The 88-page pamphlet AA (1908) had blossomed into a 408-page document. The reason for the elaboration, as stated in the preface, was the need for standardization required by centralized and cooperative cataloging. The committee felt that elaborate and precise detail was the means to accomplish this end. The code consists of two parts, one dealing with entry and headings and the other with description. Again, the rules for subject headings were omitted.

The 1941 draft code was dealt a heavy blow in June 1941 by Andrew D. Osborn's article entitled "The Crisis in Cataloging."[22] Osborn criticized the code for attempting to provide a rule for every situation or question that might come up, an approach he referred to as "legalistic." The consequence, Osborn maintained, was unnecessary multiplication of rules.

LC (1949)

> Library of Congress. *Rules for Descriptive Cataloging in the Library of Congress. Adopted by the American Library Association.* Washington, D.C.: Library of Congress, 1949.

Because of the extensive use of Library of Congress printed catalog cards by libraries in the United States, the Library of Congress decided to publish its descriptive cataloging rules, which were not totally compatible with the ALA rules.

In 1946, the Library of Congress published its *Studies of Descriptive Cataloging: A Report to the Librarian of Congress by the Director of the Processing Department*, which advocated simplification of cataloging details. As noted earlier, it was Lubetzky who was responsible for the studies. The Library of Congress responded favorably to the report and took its tenets into consideration as it proceeded to complete the work on the rules for description. A preliminary edition appeared in 1947, and the final edition in 1949 (LC 1949).

The rules cover bibliographic description only, excluding choice of entries (i.e., of access points), and forms of headings. Many types of materials are considered: monographs, serials, maps, relief models, globes and atlases, music, facsimiles, photocopies and microfilms, and incunabula.

ALA (1949)

> *ALA Cataloging Rules for Author and Title Entries.* 2nd ed. Clara Beetle, ed. Chicago: American Library Association, 1949.

Because the Library of Congress was revising its rules for description at the time, the American Library Association decided, in revising the 1908 ALA code, to omit the descriptive portion of the rules from the 1941 draft and include only the rules for entry and heading in the new ALA rules. This decision was made partly because individual libraries had been following LC practice (due to the availability of LC printed cards) and partly because that portion of ALA (1941) had not been very well received. As a result, the rules in ALA (1949) cover entry and headings only and had to be used in conjunction with LC (1949). Osborn's criticism of the 41 draft code did not seem to have much effect on ALA (1949). The rules in this code, in the opinion of many, are as pedantic, elaborate, and often arbitrary as those in the preliminary edition of 1941. Together, ALA (1949) and LC (1949) served as the standards for descriptive cataloging for American libraries until the appearance of the *Anglo-American Cataloging Rules* in 1967.

AACR (1967)

> *Anglo-American Cataloging Rules.* Prepared by the American
> Library Association, the Library of Congress, the Library
> Association, and the Canadian Library Association. North
> American text. Chicago: American Library Association, 1967.
> Reprinted in 1970 with supplement of additions and changes.

The strongest criticism of ALA (1949) was voiced in Lubetzky's *Cataloging Rules and Principles*,[23] which included a thorough and penetrating analysis of ALA (1949). Lubetzky criticized ALA (1949) for being unnecessarily long and confusing because it provided duplicate and overlapping rules to meet identical conditions. Related rules were scattered, he maintained, and there was a lack of logical arrangement and organization of the rules.

Lubetzky's report was received favorably; and another ALA Catalog Code Revision Committee, with Wyllis Wright as the chair, was established for the purpose of drafting a new code. In 1956, Lubetzky was appointed the editor of the new code.

In 1960, Lubetzky's *Code of Cataloging Rules, Author and Title Entry: An Unfinished Draft*[24] appeared. It begins with a statement of objectives, followed by specific rules developed on the basis of these objectives. Although not completed, the draft code gives indication of what can be accomplished by basing specific rules on basic principles. One major departure from previous codes is the determination of entry based on conditions of authorship rather than on types of work.

Lubetzky's work was exciting but also raised concerns among those involved in cataloging. It presaged a new era for cataloging, yet many were concerned about the cost such drastic changes would incur in implementation. This concern was to become a major factor in ensuing code revision work.

Lubetzky resigned as editor of the new code in 1962 and was succeeded by C. Sumner Spalding. Code revision proceeded on the basis of the work already done under Lubetzky and the Paris Principles. Cooperation between the American and British Library associations was also initiated. The new code *Anglo-American Cataloguing Rules* appeared in 1967. Because the British and the American communities failed to reach complete agreement on some of the details, two texts of the code were published: British Text and North American Text.

It was decided that the new code should include rules for both entry and description. Since the Paris Principles dealt with the problems of entry and headings only and there were yet no international guidelines for the development of the rules for description, LC (1949) was used as the basis for description of monographs and serials, as well as for the rules for cataloging nonprint materials in the North American text.

AACR (1967) was received with mixed feelings. Its logical arrangement and its emphasis on conditions of authorship rather than on types of work were considered to be a great improvement over the previous codes. However, some critics lamented the compromises made in the face of practical considerations and also the code's inadequate handling of nonprint materials.

AACR2 (1978)

> *Anglo-American Cataloguing Rules.* 2nd ed. Prepared by the American Library Association, the British Library, the Canadian Committee on Cataloguing, the Library Association, the Library of Congress. Edited by Michael Gorman and Paul W. Winkler. Chicago: American Library Association, 1978.

By 1973, it was felt that the appropriate time had come for an overhaul of the Anglo-American cataloging code. Certain significant developments since the publication of AACR in 1967 pointed to the desirability of a revision.[25] First, rapid progress toward the formulation of international standards for the description of monographs, serials, and other media indicated the need to redraft the AACR provisions for bibliographic description so that the code would facilitate the effort to promote international exchange of bibliographic data. Second, the rules for nonprint materials in AACR (1967) had been considered inadequate from the beginning, a situation which resulted in the proliferation of various cataloging codes for such materials. Only a complete revision of the rules for nonprint media could provide the standardization needed in this area. Third, the points of divergence between the separate North American and British texts of AACR had been gradually reconciled, leading to the prospect of a unified code. Furthermore, because there had been numerous piecemeal revisions and changes in the rules since 1967, the code had become rather inconvenient to use. Finally, the ideal of universal bibliographic control (UBC) and the development of the ISBDs were further important forces behind the revision of AACR (1967).

Michael Gorman and Paul W. Winkler were appointed editors of the second edition of AACR. In the revision, the Joint Steering Committee decided to conform to international agreements and standards, particularly the Paris Principles and the *ISBD*. As a result, in the second edition of AACR, the ISBDs formed the basis for Part I, which covers the rules for bibliographic description, and the Paris Principles underlie Part II, which contains the rules for access points. For the first time, rules for both description and access rested on international agreements. Furthermore, differences between the North American and the British texts of the first edition were reconciled, resulting in a single text.

AACR2R (1988)

> *Anglo-American Cataloguing Rules.* 2nd ed., 1988 revision. Prepared under the direction of the Joint Steering Committee for Revision of AACR, a committee of: the American Library Association, the Australian Committee on Cataloguing, the British Library, the Canadian Committee on Cataloguing, the Library Association, the Library of Congress. Michael Gorman and Paul W. Winkler, eds. Chicago: American Library Association, 1988.

In the early 1980s, three supplements containing revisions to AACR2 (1978) were issued. In addition, revisions that had yet to be published were also approved by the Joint Steering Committee for the Revision of AACR (JSC). Furthermore, a draft revision of the rules for computer files was prepared and published in 1986 in response to the ever-changing nature of computer files. With these changes, it was considered appropriate to issue a revised edition of AACR2. The JSC decided to call the new edition Second Edition 1988 Revision instead of the "third edition," perhaps because of the "anguished howls and monumental upheaval that greeted the advent of the original AACR2 in 1978,"[26] or the fact that "the rules have not been radically recast [nor was there] basic rethinking."[27]

Michael Gorman and Paul W. Winkler again served as the editors of the revised edition, which was published in 1988.

AACR2R (1998)

> *Anglo-American Cataloguing Rules,* 2nd ed., 1998 revision. Prepared under the direction of the Joint Steering Committee for Revision of AACR, a committee of: the American Library

Association, the Australian Committee on Cataloguing, the British Library, the Canadian Committee on Cataloguing, the Library Association, the Library of Congress; [editors, Michael Gorman and Paul W. Winkler]. Ottawa: Canadian Library Association; Chicago: American Library Association, 1998.

By the late 1990s, sufficient additions, deletions, and changes had been cumulated since 1988 to warrant a new issue of the second edition. A new revision of AACR2R containing the rules of the 1988 revision and the updates since then, was issued in 1998.

AACR2R (2002)

Anglo-American Cataloguing Rules. 2nd ed., 2002 revision. Prepared under the direction of the Joint Steering Committee for Revision of AACR, a committee of: the American Library Association, the Australian Committee on Cataloguing, the British Library, the Canadian Committee on Cataloguing, Chartered Institute of Library and Information Professionals, the Library of Congress. Chicago: American Library Association, 2002.

AACR2R (2002) contains changes and additions since 1998, particularly with regard to the treatment of electronic resources. Annual updates continue to be issued between editions.

The Concise AACR2

The concise AACR2. Prepared by Michael Gorman. 4th ed. Chicago: American Library Association; Ottawa: Canadian Library Association; London: Chartered Institute of Library and Information Professionals, 2004.

For libraries that do not need the details embodied in the full edition of AACR, a concise version, prepared by Michael Gorman, one of the editors of AACR, has been published at appropriate intervals since 1981. The current edition accompanies AACR2R (2002). The intent of the concise version, as stated in the general introduction to the latest edition, is "to convey the essence and basic principles of the second edition of the *Anglo-American Cataloguing Rules* (AACR2) without many of that comprehensive work's rules for out-of-the-way and complex materials."

RDA (Resource Description and Access)

In the early 2000s, discussion began on a new edition of AACR, which will include provisions for rapidly developing information items and packages (particularly electronic resources) and will incorporate the concepts set forth in the Functional Requirements for Bibliographic Records (FRBR). Furthermore, it will be made more hospitable to new and varying forms and types of information-bearing items than previous codes have been.

The JSC (Joint Steering Committee for Revision of *Anglo-American Cataloguing Rules*) is responsible for overseeing revision work. JSC is an international organization with representatives from American Library Association, Australian Committee on Cataloguing, The British Library, Canadian Committee on Cataloguing, CILIP: Chartered Institute of Library and Information Professionals, and the Library of Congress. In 2004, Tom Delsey was appointed editor.

Since December 2004, drafts of parts of AACR3 have been made available to the constituencies for review. Based on the responses to the draft, it was decided in 2005 to adopt a new working title: *RDA: Resource Description and Access*. The new code is scheduled to be released in 2009.[28]

Chapter 3 of this book discusses and gives examples of the rules for description contained in part one of AACR2R (2002). Descriptive—that is, non-subject—access points based on the rules in part two of AACR2R (2002) are discussed in chapters 5 and 6 of this book.

METADATA SCHEMAS

The rapid growth of the Internet and the proliferation of electronic resources have created a crushing need for better methods of describing and organizing them for efficient retrieval. Interest in such methods extends beyond the library community. Outside of the library community, cataloging standards are not well understood or widely applied. Even within the library profession, many feel that current cataloging rules are not only too complex for coping with electronic resources but may also be inadequate in other ways. In addition, current cataloging standards are not always suitable for describing and representing various types of resources such as archival, geospatial, or visual resources—nor are they tuned to the needs of different user communities such as those in the educational, publishing, government, and commercial sectors.

In the course of ten years, from the mid-1990s, numerous metadata schemas have been developed by various communities and groups concerned with managing electronic resources. Chapter 4 of this book contains a brief discussion of some of the more widely used metadata schemas.

NOTES

1. Anthony Panizzi, "Rules for the Compilation of the Catalogue," in British Museum, *The Catalogue of Printed Books in the British Museum* (London, 1841), vol.

1, p. v–ix; reprinted in Michael Carpenter and Elaine Svenonius, *Foundations of Cataloging: A Sourcebook* (Littleton, Colo.: Libraries Unlimited, 1985), 3–14.

2. Anthony Panizzi, "Mr. Panizzi to the Right Hon. the Earl of Ellesmere.—British Museum, January 29, 1848," in Great Britain, Commissioners Appointed to Inquire into the Constitution and Government of the British Museum, *Appendix to the Report of the Commissioner Appointed to Inquire into the Constitution and Management of the British Museum* (London: Her Majesty's Stationery Office, 1850), 378–95; reprinted in Carpenter and Svenonius, *Foundations of Cataloging: A Sourcebook*, 18–47.

3. Michael Carpenter, "Editor's Introduction: 'Mr. Panizzi to the Right Hon. the Earl of Ellesmere.—British Museum, January 29, 1848 [by] Sir Anthony Panizzi'," in *Foundations of Cataloging*, 15–17.

4. Elaine Svenonius, "Editor's Introduction: 'Smithsonian Catalogue System [by] Charles C. Jewett'," in *Foundations of Cataloging*, 49.

5. Charles Ammi Cutter, *Rules for a Dictionary Catalog*, 4th ed. rewritten (Washington, D.C.: Government Printing Office, 1904; republished, London: The Library Association, 1953), 3.

6. Cutter, *Rules for a Dictionary Catalog*, 6.

7. Cutter, *Rules for a Dictionary Catalog*, 12.

8. Seymour Lubetzky, "Analysis of Current Descriptive Cataloging Practice," in *Studies of Descriptive Cataloging* (Washington, D.C.: Library of Congress, Processing Department, 1946), 40–45; also in *Foundations of Cataloging*, 104–12.

9. Seymour Lubetzky, *Cataloging Rules and Principles: A Critique of the A.L.A. Cataloging Rules for Entry and a Proposed Design for Their Revision*, prepared for the Board on Cataloging and Classification (Washington, D.C.: Library of Congress, Processing Department, 1953); also in Seymour Lubetzky, *Writings on the Classical Art of Cataloging*, compiled and edited by Elaine Svenonius and Dorothy McGarry (Englewood, Colo.: Libraries Unlimited, 2001), 78–137.

10. Seymour Lubetzky, *Code of Cataloging Rules, Author and Title Entry: An Unfinished Draft for a New Edition of Cataloging Rules, Prepared for the Catalog Code Revision Committee*, with an explanatory commentary by Paul Dunkin (Chicago: American Library Association, 1960).

11. Seymour Lubetzky, *Principles of Cataloging: Final Report: Phase I: Descriptive Cataloging* (Los Angeles: Institute of Library Research, University of California, 1969).

12. Elaine Svenonius, "Development of Cataloging Rules: Editors' Introduction," in Lubetzky, *Writings on the Classical Art of Cataloging*, 152.

13. *ISBD (M): International Standard Bibliographic Description for Monographic Publications*, [prepared by] Working Group on the International Standard Bibliographic Description, 1st standard ed. (London: IFLA Committee on Cataloguing, 1974), vii.

14. *ISBD(M)*, vii.

15. Dorothy Anderson, *Universal Bibliographic Control: A Long Term Policy—A Plan for Action* (Munich: Verlag Dokumentation, Pullach, 1974), 11.

16. Barbara B. Tillett, "FRBR (Functional Requirements for Bibliographic Records)," *Technicalities* 23, no. 5 (September/October 2003): 1, 11–13. Also available at: www.loc.gov/cds/FRBR.html (7 Apr. 2007).

17. IFLA Study Group on the Functional Requirements for Bibliographic Records, *Functional Requirements for Bibliographic Records, Final Report* (München:

K. G. Saur, 1998). UBCIM Publications, New Series; v. 19. Also available at www.ifla.org/VII/s13/frbr/frbr.htm (20 Feb. 2007).

18. Charles C. Jewett, *Smithsonian Report on the Construction of Catalogues of Libraries, and Their Publication by Means of Separate, Stereotyped Titles, with Rules and Examples*, 2nd ed. (Washington, D.C.: Smithsonian Institution, 1853); Reprinted, Ann Arbor, Mich.: University Microfilms, 1961.

19. Paul S. Dunkin, *Cataloging U.S.A.* (Chicago: American Library Association, 1969), 11.

20. K. G. B. Bakewell, *A Manual of Cataloguing Practice* (Oxford: Pergamon Press, 1972), 32.

21. Vatican Library (Biblioteca Apostolica Vaticana), *Rules for the Catalog of Printed Books*, translated from the 2nd Italian ed. by the Very Rev. Thomas J. Shanahan, Victor A. Schaefer, and Constantin T. Vesselowsky; Wyllis E. Wright, ed. (Chicago: American Library Association, 1948), v.

22. Andrew D. Osborn, "The Crisis in Cataloging," *Library Quarterly* 11 (October 1941): 393–411.

23. Lubetzky, *Cataloging Rules and Principles*.

24. Lubetzky, *Code of Cataloging Rules, Author and Title Entry*.

25. "AACR 2: Background and Summary," *Library of Congress Information Bulletin* 37 (October 20, 1978): 640.

26. Margaret F. Maxwell, "AACR2R: Anglo-American Cataloguing Rules," *Library Resources & Technical Services* 33, no. 2 (April 1989): 179.

27. Michael Gorman, "AACR2R: Editor's Perspective," *Library Resources & Technical Services* 33, no. 2 (April 1989): 181.

28. Joint Steering Committee for Revision of *Anglo-American Cataloguing Rules*, "RDA: Resource Description and Access," www.collectionscanada.ca/jsc/rda.html (last updated 21 Mar. 2007).

CHAPTER 3
ANGLO-AMERICAN
CATALOGUING RULES:
DESCRIPTION

INTRODUCTION

Anglo-American Cataloguing Rules (AACR) is the most inclusive and detailed cataloging code used for descriptive cataloging in Australia, Canada, Great Britain, and the United States as well as in many other countries. The history of the development of this code was given in chapter 2. This chapter discusses the rules as laid out in the latest version of *Anglo-American Cataloguing Rules*, 2nd edition, 2002 revision (AACR2R).[1] Part I of AACR2R contains rules on bibliographic description; in other words, it gives instructions on how to represent the bibliographic and physical characteristics of the material being cataloged.

TYPES OF LIBRARY RESOURCES

For the purpose of bibliographic description, the following types of library resources have been identified by AACR2R (the term *resources* here is used to cover the range of types of materials in the library's own holdings as well as those available through the library's portal):

> Books, pamphlets, and printed sheets
> Cartographic materials
> Manuscripts (Including manuscript collections)
> Music
> Sound recordings
> Motion pictures and videorecordings
> Graphic materials
> Electronic resources
> Three-dimensional artefacts and realia
> Microforms
> Continuing resources

Appendix D of AACR2R and the glossary of this book give definitions of these terms.

The first chapter of AACR2R is devoted to bibliographic description of all types of materials and can be considered a general-guidance chapter. Each of the chapters numbered 2 through 12 in AACR2R provides rules for the description of a specific type of material. The rules in these later chapters often refer to chapter 1 for details applicable to all types of materials. Thus, neither chapter 1 nor any of the subsequent chapters for rules of description can be used alone. In cataloging a particular item, the cataloger begins with the chapter dealing with the specific type of material being cataloged, for example, chapter 2 for printed monographs, and then uses that chapter along with chapter 1. In some cases, three or more chapters dealing with specific types of materials may be required. For example, a digital map requires the use of chapters 1 (general rules), 3 (cartographic materials), and 9 (electronic resources). To facilitate use, the rules in these chapters have been numbered with a mnemonic device: for example, rule 1.5 deals with the physical description area, and so do rules 2.5 (for books), 3.5 (for cartographic materials), 4.5 (for manuscripts), and so on.

ISBD(G)

The *International Standard Bibliographic Description (General)*, developed by agreement between the International Federation of Library Associations (IFLA) and Joint Steering Committee for the Revision of AACR (JS-CAACR), first published in 1977, serves as a single framework for the description of all types of publications in all types of media, thereby ensuring a uniform approach in bibliographic description. Its major provisions are shown in Table 3-1.

The *ISBD(G)* was incorporated into chapter 1 of AACR2R as the general format for bibliographic description. Each of the chapters numbered 2 through 12 in AACR2R is based on a specialized *ISBD*. For example, the basis of the rules for the description of monographic materials in AACR2R is *ISBD(M): International Standard Bibliographic Description for Monographic Publications*, and the basis for the description of electronic resources is *ISBD(ER): International Standard Bibliographic Description for Electronic Resources*.

ORGANIZATION OF THE DESCRIPTION

The bibliographic description is divided into the following units, called *areas*, and presented in the order specified in AACR2R:

> Title and statement of responsibility
> Edition
> Material (or type of publication) specific details

TABLE 3-1 The ISBD(G)

Area	Prescribed preceding (or enclosing) punctuation for elements		Element
Title and statement		1.1	Title proper
responsibility area	[]	1.2	General material designation (*optional*)
	=	*1.3	Parallel title
	:	*1.4	Other title information
		1.5	Statements of responsibility
	/		First statement
	;		*Subsequent statement
2. Edition area		2.1	Edition statement
	=	*2.2	Parallel edition statement (*optional*)
		2.3	Statements of responsibility relating to the edition
	/		First statement
	;		*Subsequent statement
	,	*2.4	Additional edition statement
		2.5	Statements of responsibility following an additional edition statement
	/		First statement
	;		*Subsequent statement
3. Material (or type of resource) specific area			
4. Publication, distribution, etc. area		4.1	Place of publication, distribution, etc. First place
	;		*Subsequent place
	:	*4.2	Name of publisher, distributor, etc.
	[]	*4.3	Statement of function of distributor
	,	4.4	Date of publication, distribution, etc.
	(	*4.5	Place of manufacture
	:	*4.6	Name of manufacturer
	,)	*4.7	Date of manufacturer
5. Physical description area		5.1	Specific material designation and extent of resource
	:	5.2	Other physical details
	;	5.3	Dimensions
	+	*5.4	Accompanying material statement (*optional*)
6. Series area		6.1	Title proper of series or sub-series
	=	*6.2	Parallel title of series or sub-series
Note: A series statement is enclosed by parentheses. When there are two or more series statements, each is enclosed by parentheses.	:	*6.3	Other title information of series or sub-series
		6.4	Statements of responsibility relating to the series or sub-series
	/		First statement

			*Subsequent statement
;			
,	6.5		International Standard Serial Number of series or sub-series
;	6.6		Numbering within series or sub-series

7. Note area

8. Standard number (or alternative) and terms of availability area	=	*8.1	Standard number (or alternative)
	=	8.2	Key title
	:	*8.3	Terms of availability and/or price (*optional*)
	()	*8.4	Qualification (in varying positions) (*optional*)

* Can be repeated when necessary.

Source: International Federation of Library Association and Institutions. *(ISBD(G): General International Standard Bibliographic Description*: 2004 revision, www.ifla.org/VII/s13/pubs/isbdg2004.pdf (9 Oct. 2006).

Publication, distribution, etc.
Physical description
Series
Note(s)
Standard number and terms of availability

Each of these areas is further divided into a number of elements, which vary according to the type of material in hand. The following sections contain discussions of descriptive areas and elements pertinent to a wide range of materials.

OPTIONS

AACR2R contains a number of options, indicated by *Optional addition, Alternative rule,* or *Optionally.* These allow individual libraries or cataloging agencies to make decisions based on individual considerations in cases where two or more provisions are equally valid. Each library or cataloging agency must decide on whether or not to use each optional provision. Libraries using LC cataloging data will most likely conform to Library of Congress practice.

LIBRARY OF CONGRESS RULE INTERPRETATIONS

In its own use of AACR2R, the Library of Congress has made a number of modifications. Furthermore, some of the rules are open to different interpretations. To ensure consistency in application, the Library of Congress has been publishing its decisions regarding options, modifications, and interpretations in *Cataloging Service Bulletin*.[2] These decisions are cumulated in a publication entitled *Library of Congress Rule Interpretations* (LCRI),[3] which is updated quarterly and cumulated annually. Libraries and other information agencies that make use of LC cataloging data consult LCRI regularly in order to achieve consistency between their own cataloging and that of the Library of Congress and most other libraries.

LCRI is available in print version. It is also included in Cataloger's Desktop, an integrated, online system that also contains other cataloging tools, including AACR2R. Desktop is produced by the Library of Congress Cataloging Distribution Service and available as a subscription product on the Web.

SOURCES OF INFORMATION

AACR2R specifies sources of information to be used in describing a publication; in the case of a printed monograph, for example, such sources include the title page and the verso of the title page. Of these, the source of bibliographic data to be given first preference is called the *chief source of information*. The rules identify one or more chief sources of information for each type of material. Because bibliographic data such as the title and publication details are often repeated in slightly different forms in various locations in a publication—such as the cover and spine of a book, the verso of the title page, and the container or accompanying material—specifying the *chief source of information* helps to ensure consistency and uniformity in bibliographic description. Table 3-2 lists chief sources of information for different types of materials.

Chapters 2 through 12 (specific types of material) in AACR2R give prescribed sources of information for individual bibliographic areas in records for the type of material covered in each chapter. Information taken from sources other than those prescribed is enclosed in brackets.

Examples of chief sources of information with corresponding bibliographic descriptions are shown in Figures 3-1 to 3-6.

Following is the descriptive cataloging data for Figure 3-1:

> *Description:*
>   The organization of information / Arlene G. Taylor. — 2nd
> ed. — Westport, Conn. : Libraries Unlimited, 2004. — xxvii, 417
> p. : ill. ; 27 cm. — (Library and information science text series)
>   Includes bibliographical references (p. 385-405) and index.
>   Contents: Organization of recorded information — Retrieval
> tools — Development of the organization of recorded
> information in Western civilization — Encoding standards —
> Systems and system design — Metadata — Metadata :
> description — Metadata : access and authority control — Subject

TABLE 3-2   Chief sources of information

Type of Material	Source
Books, pamphlets, and printed sheets	Title page or its substitute
Cartographic materials (other than a printed atlas)	a. Cartographic item itself b. Container or case, the cradle and stand of a globe, etc.
Manuscripts	Manuscript itself Title page Colophon Caption, heading, etc. Content of the manuscript
Music	Title page or its substitute

Sound recordings:
  Disc
  Tape (open reel-to-reel)
  Tape cassette
  Tape cartridge
  Roll
  Sound recording on film
	
	Disc and label
	Reel and label
	Cassette and label
	Cartridge and label
	Label
	Container and label

Motion pictures and videorecordings	a. Item itself b. Its container (if integral part of item)
Graphic materials	Item itself including any labels, etc., permanently affixed to the item or a container
Electronic resources	The resource itself
Three-dimensional artefacts and realia	Object itself with any accompanying textual material and container
Microforms	Title frame or title card
Continuing resources: Printed	 Title page or its substitute of the earliest available issue

Nonprint resources:
    direct access electronic serials
    other nonprint resources
	
	The physical carrier or its labels
	What is specified in the rules

analysis — Systems for vocabulary control — Systems for categorization — Arrangement and display — Conclusion.
ISBN 1-56308-976-9

Main entry:
    Taylor, Arlene G., 1941-

THE ORGANIZATION OF INFORMATION

Second Edition

Arlene G. Taylor

Library and Information Science Text Series

U N L I M I T E D
A Member of the Greenwood Publishing Group
Westport, Connecticut • London

FIGURE 3-1   Title page of a book: Taylor, *The Organization of Information* (book)

Added entries:
   Title.
   Series.

Following is the descriptive cataloging data for Figure 3-2:

Description:
   Journal of Internet cataloging. — Binghamton, NY : Haworth Press, 1997- . — v. ; 25 cm.
   Quarterly
   Vol. 1, no. 1 (1997)-
   Title from cover; Vol. 1 published over three years, 1997-1999.
   Table of contents and abstracts from this journal can be found at the JIC home page.
   Also available via World Wide Web; OCLC FirstSearch Electronic Collections Online; Subscription required for access to abstracts and full text.
   ISSN: 1091-1367

Main entry:
   Title

FIGURE 3-2   Cover of a printed journal: *Journal of Internet Cataloging* (print journal)

> *Added entries:*
>   None

Following is the descriptive cataloging data for Figure 3-3:

> *Description:*
>   Lexington, Kentucky, street map : including Fayette County
>   vicinity map & portions of surrounding counties ; featuring horse

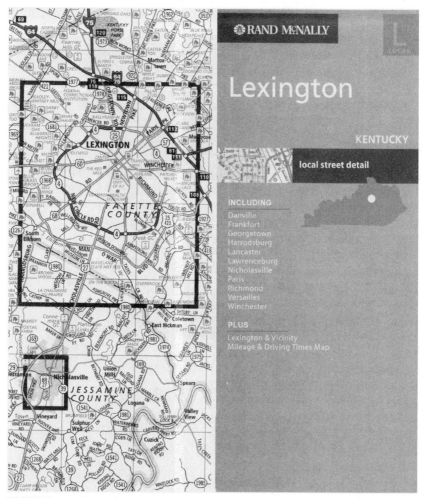

FIGURE 3-3 Part of a map, Universal Map (Firm): *Lexington, Kentucky, Street Map* (map)

farms, Lexington downtown map, . . . zip code boundaries / UniversalMAP. — UniversalMAP Lexington, Kentucky, street map. — Scale [ca. 1:31,000]. — Scale [ca. 1:150,000]. — Williamston, MI : UniversalMAP, [2004?]. — 2 maps : both sides, col. ; 60 x 57 cm. and 79 x 59 cm., folded to 24 x 11 cm.

Main entry:
    Universal Map (Firm)
Added entries:
    Title

FIGURE 3-4   A DVD and case: Verdi, *La Traviata* (videodisc)

FIGURE 3-4   Continued

Following is the descriptive cataloging data for Figure 3-4:

Description:
La traviata [videorecording] / Verdi. — London, England :
Decca, p1995. — 1 videodisc (135 min.) : sd., col. ; 4 3/4 in.
Opera.
Sung in Italian with subtitles in English, French, German, and
Chinese.
Angela Gheorghiu, soprano ; Frank Lopardo, tenor ; Leo
Nucci, baritone ; Orchestra and Chorus of the Royal Opera
House, Covent Garden ; Sir Georg Solti, conductor.
Director, Richard Eyre ; designer, Bob Crowley ; directed for
TV by Humphrey Burton and Peter Maniura.
Recorded at the Royal Opera House, Covent Garden, Dec.
1994.
DVD video; Dolby digital 5.1 surround sound; LPCM stereo.

Main entry:
Verdi, Giuseppe, 1813-1901
Added entries:
Gheorghiu, Angela

Lopardo, Frank
Nucci, Lee
Solti, Georg, 1912-1997
Title

Following is the descriptive cataloging data for Figure 3-5:

Description:
Online journal of space communication [electronic resource].
— Athens, OH : Institute for Telecommunications Studies, Ohio
University, 2002- . — Issue no. 1 (Apr. 2002)-
Four times a year
Title from caption (viewed Oct. 7, 2002).
Latest issue consulted: Issue no. 2 (July 2002).
Mode of access: World Wide Web.
A project of the Society of Satellite Professionals
International, hosted by: the Institute for Telecommunications
Studies, Ohio University.
Main entry:
Title
Added entries:
Society of Satellite Professionals International
Ohio University. Institute for Telecommunications Studies

Following is the descriptive cataloging data for Figure 3-6:

FIGURE 3-5   Home page for an online journal: *Online Journal of Space
Communication* (electronic journal)

FIGURE 3-6   Home page of a website: *American Variety Stage* (electronic resource)

Description:
American variety stage [electronic resource] : vaudeville and popular entertainment, 1870-1920 / American Memory, Library of Congress. — [Washington, D.C. : Library of Congress], 1996-
Computer data.
System requirements: World Wide Web (WWW) browser software.
Mode of access: Internet.
Title from title screen dated Oct. 31, 1996.
"Groups of theater posters and sound recordings will be added to this anthology in the future."
Multimedia collection containing digitized versions of

selected Library of Congress holdings. Represents diverse forms of popular entertainment, especially vaudeville, that thrived from 1870-1920. Includes 334 English and Yiddish language playscripts, 146 theater playbills and programs, sixty-one motion pictures, and 143 photographs and twenty-nine memorabilia items documenting the life and career of Harry Houdini.

Houdini — Theater playbills and programs — Sound recordings (coming soon) — Motion pictures — English playscripts — Yiddish playscripts.

Main entry:
    Title
Added entries:
    Library of Congress. National Digital Library Program
    Title: Vaudeville and popular entertainment, 1870-1920

PUNCTUATION

One of the unique features of the ISBDs is the prescribed punctuation marks. Their most prominent feature is using spaces before and after most of them—the exceptions are noted in the list below under "Space." A prescribed punctuation mark precedes each element in the description and signifies the nature of that element. The reason that ISBD prescribed punctuation marks differ considerably from standard prose punctuation is that they were selected to function as a signal or recognition device for the individual areas and elements in the bibliographic description. A person faced with a bibliographic record in an unknown language, for instance, can identify its statement of responsibility because it follows the space-slash-space after the title.

A summary of prescribed punctuation is given below.

Brackets

See *Parentheses; Square brackets.*

Colon

A colon precedes:

1. Each unit of other title information
2. The name of a publisher, distributor, printer, manufacturer, etc.
3. Other physical details (e.g., illustrations)
4. Terms of availability

A colon and a space separate introductory wording from the main content of a note.

Comma

A comma:

1. Separates units within a statement, e.g., phrases within a title, names of authors within a statement of responsibility
2. Precedes each subsequent edition statement
3. Precedes the date of publication, distribution, printing, manufacture, etc.
4. Precedes the ISSN of a series or subseries in the series area

Dash

A full stop, space, dash, space (. —) precedes each area in the description, unless the area begins a new paragraph.

Diagonal Slash

A diagonal slash precedes the first statement of responsibility.

Ellipses

See *Mark of omission*.

Equal Sign

An equal sign precedes:

1. A parallel title
2. An alternative numbering in the numeric or chronological designation area of a serial publication
3. A key-title in the standard number and terms of availability area

Full Stop (Period, in American English)

1. A full stop, space, dash, space (. —) precedes each area or repetition of an area. It is omitted if the area begins a new paragraph.
2. A full stop ends the last area in a paragraph.
3. A full stop is used as an abbreviation mark (e.g., 2nd ed.; 24 cm.). When the abbreviation mark occurs at the end of an area, the full stop which is apart of the prescribed punctuation is omitted (i.e., 2nd ed. —).

4. A full stop precedes the title of a supplement or section.
5. A full stop precedes the title of a subseries.

Hyphen

A hyphen follows the numeric or alphabetic designation, or both, and the date of the first issue of a serial publication.

Mark of Omission

A mark of omission (. . .) is used:

1. To indicate an abridged title proper or other title information
2. To indicate an omission from the statement of responsibility
3. To replace the date or numbering that varies from issue to issue in the title proper of a serial publication

Minus Sign

A minus sign is used to indicate the Southern Hemisphere when giving the declination of the center of a celestial chart.

Parentheses

Parentheses are used:

1. To enclose the details of printing or manufacture (place : name, date)
2. To enclose the full address of a publisher, distributor, etc. (if given) after the name of the place
3. To enclose physical details of accompanying material
4. To enclose each series statement
5. To enclose a qualification to the standard number or terms of availability
6. To enclose the continuous pagination of a multivolume monograph after the number of volumes
7. To enclose the statement of tactile data for material for the visually impaired
8. To enclose the statement of coordinates and equinox in the mathematical data area for cartographic materials
9. To enclose the number of records, statements, etc., after the designation for a computer file; the number of statements and/or bytes after the designation for a program file; the number of records and/or bytes in each file after the designation for a multipart file
10. To enclose the number of frames of a microfiche or a filmstrip and the playing time of a film or recording

11. To enclose a date following a designation that is numeric, alphabetic, or both, for a serial publication

Period

See *Full stop.*

Plus Sign

A plus sign:

1. Precedes a statement of accompanying material
2. Is used to indicate the Northern Hemisphere when giving the declination of the center of a celestial chart

Question Mark

A question mark is used to indicate a conjectural interpolation.

Semicolon

A semicolon precedes:

1. Each subsequent statement of responsibility
2. A second or subsequent named place of publication, distribution, etc.
3. Dimensions (e.g., size) in the physical description area
4. Subsequent statements of responsibility relating to a series or subseries
5. The numbering within a series or subseries
6. The projection statement for cartographic materials
7. A new sequence of numbering, etc., in the numeric, alphabetic, chronological, or other designation area for a serial publication

Slash

See *Diagonal slash.*

Space

A space precedes and follows each mark of prescribed punctuation, except the comma, full stop, hyphen, and opening and closing parentheses and square brackets. The comma, full stop, hyphen, closing parenthesis, and square bracket are not preceded by a space; the hyphen, opening parenthesis, and square bracket are not followed by a space.

Square Brackets

Square brackets are used:

1. To enclose information taken from outside the prescribed source or sources
2. To enclose the general material designation
3. To enclose a supplied statement of function of a publisher, distributor, etc.

When adjacent elements within one area are to be enclosed in square brackets, they are enclosed in one set of square brackets unless one of the elements is a general material designation, which is always enclosed in its own set of brackets. When adjacent elements are in different areas, each element is enclosed in a separate set of square brackets.

LEVELS OF DESCRIPTION

It was Charles A. Cutter, in his *Rules for a Dictionary Catalog*,[4] who first proposed the idea of three different levels of cataloging (short, medium, and full) to accommodate the different needs of libraries of different sizes and purposes. The first edition of AACR (1967) and the preceding ALA codes were each designed to respond to the needs of general research libraries and made only occasional alternative provisions for other types of libraries.

AACR2 (1978) remedied this situation by providing three levels of bibliographic description, reflecting Cutter's ideals of a flexible code. This provision continues in AACR2R.[5]

First Level (rule 1.0D1)

The first level contains at least the elements shown in the following schematic illustration:

> Title proper / first statement of responsibility, if different from main entry heading in form or number or if there is no main entry heading. — Edition statement. — Material (or type of publication) specific details. — First publisher, etc., date of publication, etc. — Extent of item. — Note(s). — Standard number

For example:

> *First level*
> Opportunities for education in urban and regional affairs at Canadian universities and community colleges / [by the] Policy

Planning Division, Central Mortgage and Housing Corporation. — 4th ed., 1973-74. — Central Mortgage and Housing Corporation, [1973?]. — xvii, 465 p. — English and/or French.

Second Level (rule 1.0D2)

The second level includes the following elements:

Title proper [general material designation] = parallel title : other title information / first statement of responsibility ; each subsequent statement of responsibility. — Edition statement / first statement of responsibility relating to the edition. — Material (or type of publication) specific details. — First place of publication, etc. : first publisher, etc., date of publication, etc. — Extent of item : other physical details ; dimensions. — (Title proper of series / statement of responsibility relating to series, ISSN of series ; numbering within the series. Title of subseries, ISSN of subseries ; numbering within subseries). — Note(s). — Standard number

For example:

Second level
Opportunities for education in urban and regional affairs at Canadian universities and community colleges [text] = Programmes de cours en affaires urbaines et régionales offerts par les universités et collèges communautaires canadiens / [by the] Policy Planning Division, Central Mortgage and Housing Corporation. — 4th ed., 1973-74 / edited by Ollie Crain. — Ottawa : Central Mortgage and Housing Corporation, [1973?]. — xvii, 465 p. ; 28 cm. — English and/or French.

Third Level (rule 1.0D3)

The third level represents full description and contains all elements set forth in the rules which are applicable to the item being described.

Policies on Descriptive Level

In respect to descriptive level, each library either chooses a level of description for all items cataloged for that library or establishes guidelines for the use of all three levels in the same catalog depending on the type of material being described. As a result, materials held by the same library or agency may be cataloged on different levels. Since the level of description is essentially a policy matter, each cataloging record carries an indication of the level at which the item has been described.

Some libraries define their own levels of cataloging based on their internal needs. For example, Library of Congress policies define the following levels: full level cataloging, copy cataloging, core level cataloging, minimal level cataloging, and collection level cataloging.[6] Its full level of description lies somewhere between the second and the third levels as defined by AACR2R. The Monographic Bibliographic Record Program (BIBCO), a part of the Program for Cooperative Cataloging (PCC), an international cooperative program coordinated jointly by the Library of Congress and PCC participants around the world,[7] has defined two levels of bibliographic records: *full record* and *core record*, which contain standard sets of bibliographic data elements that member libraries follow in creating cataloging records that can be shared and exchanged with minimal editing.

AREAS OF DESCRIPTION

AACR2R provides detailed rules with regard to each area of description, and numerous examples are included to illustrate those rules. The general rules are presented in the first chapter and rules for specific types of materials are given in chapters 2–12. The major areas and elements in the bibliographic description are discussed below, with examples. For each area and element, the AACR2R rule number and corresponding MARC tags and subfield codes are given. Neither the discussion nor the examples are intended to be exhaustive. It is essential to consult the texts of both AACR2R and the MARC 21 Formats for details and further examples.

In presenting data in a bibliographic description, information taken from the chief source of information is preferred. If the information required is unavailable or insufficient from the chief source, other sources are used. In chapters 2–12, which deal with specific types of materials, prescribed sources of information for each area are listed. Information taken from outside the prescribed source or sources is enclosed in brackets.

A mnemonic system of numbering rules and subrules is used in AACR2R. The first digit(s) in a rule number represents the chapter number followed by the digits for the rule and subrule number which is consistent throughout the other chapters in part I wherever feasible. For example, rule 1.1B Title proper in chapter 1 General rules is paralleled with rules 2.1B (title proper of books), 6.1B (title proper of sound recordings), 9.1B (title proper of electronic resources), etc.

Title and Statement of Responsibility Area (Mnemonic Rule: *.1) [MARC field 245]

This area contains the following elements: (1) title proper; (2) general material designation; (3) parallel titles; (4) other title information; and (5) statements of responsibility. Each of these is discussed in turn below.

1. Title proper (rule *.1B) [MARC field 245, subfield $a]

The title proper, which includes any alternative titles, is transcribed from the chief source of information exactly as to wording, order, and spelling, though not necessarily as to punctuation and capitalization. In print materials, the title proper is usually readily identifiable. It is often more difficult to determine the title proper of a website or Web page. Also, in manuscripts and nonprint materials, the title proper is often lacking and must be supplied. A supplied title is enclosed in brackets.

> 2004 Masters annual
> The American Bar Association legal guide for women
> Anglo-American cataloguing rules
> Bergin and Garfield's handbook of psychotherapy and behavior change
> The complete Dead Sea scrolls in English
> D-Lib magazine
> Grand Canyon geology
> Journal of American culture
> Online journal of space communication
> Principles of public international law
> Women, equality, and the French Revolution
> A study in scarlet ; The hound of the Baskervilles
> [Design of a dormitory]
> [Drift globe]
> [Harry Potter and the chamber of secrets—trailers]
> [Sea shells]

The rules for capitalization are presented in Appendix A in AACR2R. The first word of the title proper is always capitalized. Other words are capitalized according to the rules for the language involved. For English, the initial word and any proper names and proper adjectives in the title are capitalized, for example:

> A guide to the Library of Congress classification
> Metadata fundamentals for all librarians
> The organization of information

A long title proper may be abridged if this can be done without losing essential information. The first five words of the title proper are never omitted. The omissions are indicated by the mark of omission.

> Members of the Ancient and Honorable Artillery Company in the colonial period, 1638-1774 . . .

A title proper consisting of the title of a work and that of a part of the work not grammatically linked is recorded in two parts, separated by a period.

Bibliography on Holocaust literature. Supplement
Journal of the Chemical Society. Faraday transactions

2. General material designation (rule *.1C) [MARC field 245, subfield $h]

This is an *optional addition*. The general material designation [GMD], enclosed in square brackets, e.g., [electronic resource], indicates the broad
class of material to which the item being described belongs. For printed
or book-form material, the term *text* is used as the GMD. For certain forms
of materials, British and North American cataloging agencies use different terms as the general material designation. List 1 under rule 1.1C1 is
designed for British use, and list 2 for North American and Australian
use. For details of the lists, see chapter 1 of AACR2R.

Most libraries probably will choose to use the GMD for nonprint materials, but not otherwise. For example, the Library of Congress includes
the GMD only when cataloging the following types of material: electronic
resource, filmstrip, graphic, microform, motion picture, slide, sound recording, transparency, and videorecording.[8] Some examples:

> #10 [sound recording]
> MS-DOS/BASIC [electronic resource]
> Orienteering, what's that? [filmstrip]
> Platonis Res publica [microform]
> Respirators [motion picture]
> Sharing cultures with Ella Jenkins [sound recording]
> The adventures of a two-minute werewolf [videorecording]
> Dog days of Arthur Cane [videorecording]

3. Parallel titles (rule *.1D) [MARC field 245, subfield $b]

A parallel title is the title proper in another language and/or script. It
should not be confused with an alternative title or other title information,
which is not equivalent in meaning to the title proper.

> The one hundred new tales = Les cent nouvelles nouvelles
> International travel maps, Beijing, China, scale 1:20,000 (City),
>   1:100,000 (Region) = Guo ji lü you di tu, Beijing, bi li 1:20,000
>   (Beijing Cheng), 1:100,000 (Beijing Shi)
> Index universalis multilingualis : Deutsch-Französisch-Englisch-
>   Latein = Allemand-Francais-Anglais-Latin = German-
>   French-English-Latin = Germanicus-Francogallicus-
>   Anglosaxicus-Latinus.

4. Other title information (rule *.1E) [MARC field 245, subfield $b]

Other title information includes any title other than the title proper, the
parallel or series title(s), and any phrase appearing in conjunction with

the title proper. Subtitles, avant-titres, and phrases indicative of the character, contents, etc., of the item or the motives for, or occasion of, its production or publication, all fall into this category. Other title information is preceded by a space-colon-space (:) following the title proper or the general material designation.

> Skyscraper : the search for an American style, 1891-1941 : annotated extracts from the first 50 years of architectural record
>
> Living standards measurement study : abstracts of working papers 1-59
>
> Toxicology : a primer on toxicology principles and applications . . .
>
> Marbled paper : its history, techniques, and patterns : with special reference to the relationship of marbling to bookbinding in Europe and the Western world
>
> Nicholas of Cusa : in search of God and wisdom : papers from the American Cusanus Society
>
> The unfinished journey : American [sic] since World War II
>
> Chemistry [electronic resource]: balancing equations
>
> Growing up at the table [filmstrip] : teaching feeding skills to the mentally retarded child at home
>
> Konzert in A-Dur für Oboe d'amore (Oboe), Streicher und Basso continuo : Rekonstruktion nach BWV 1055 = Concerto in A major for oboe d'amore (oboe), strings, and basso continuo : reconstructed from BWV 1055
>
> Autism and creativity : is there a link between autism in men and exceptional ability?

5. Statements of responsibility (rule *.1F) [MARC field 245, subfield $c]

The statement of responsibility names the person or persons responsible for the intellectual or artistic content of the item being described, the corporate body or bodies from which the content emanates, or the persons or corporate bodies responsible for the performance of the content. The persons named may include writers, editors, compilers, adapters, translators, revisers, illustrators, reporters, composers, artists, photographers, cartographers, collectors, narrators, performers, producers, directors, and investigators. The statement or statements that appear prominently in the item are transcribed in the form in which they appear in the source of information. Words taken from sources other than those prescribed are enclosed in square brackets.

> Wake up, sir! : a novel / Jonathan Ames
>
> From biplane to Spitfire : the life of Air Chief Marshal Sir Geoffrey Salmond / by Anne Baker.

Sir Winston Churchill paintings / David Coombs, Minnie Churchill

Marketing / Michael J. Etzel, Bruce J. Walker, William J. Stanton

Command on the Western Front : the military career of Sir Henry Rawlinson 1914-18 / Robin Prior and Trevor Wilson

The library and reading of Jonathan Swift : a bio-bibliographical handbook. Part I, Swift's library in four volumes / Dirk F. Passmann, Heinz J. Vienken.

On Her Majesty's secret service [sound recording] : original motion picture soundtrack / [music composed, except where noted, by John Barry]

Standard handbook of machine design / [editors in chief,] Joseph E. Shigley, Charles R. Mischke, Thomas H. Brown, Jr.

Beyond the surface [sound recording] / 2nd Planet

Transformers / Bharat Heavy Electricals Limited

The Fish's tale / by the Fish, as told to Tish Rabe ; illustrated by Jan Gerardi

American Medical Association family medical guide / American Medical Association

Information retrieval (Z39.50) : application service definition and protocol specification : an American national standard / developed by the National Information Standards Organization

Social work practice with a difference : stories, essays, cases, and commentaries / [edited by] Alice A. Lieberman and Cheryl B. Lester

Sports leaders & success : 55 top sports leaders & how they achieve greatness / introduction by William J. O'Neil

Oak Grove Cemetery, Nacogdoches, Texas / [compiled by Mrs. Roy Dean Burk]

Clinical neuropsychology : a practical guide to assessment and management for clinicians / edited by Laura H. Goldstein and Jane E. McNeil

The 20th century / The Diagram Group, Victoria L. Chapman & David Lindroth

[Harry Potter and the chamber of secrets—trailers] / [production company unknown]

When a statement of responsibility in the source of information contains the names of four or more persons or corporate bodies, only the first named, followed by . . . [et al.], is included in the statement of responsibility in the cataloging record.

Streetwise Italian dictionary/thesaurus : the user friendly guide to Italian slang and idioms / Nicholas Albanese . . . [et al.].

Vector mechanics for engineers : statics and dynamics /
    Ferdinand P. Beer . . . [et al.]
Braunwald's heart disease : a textbook of cardiovascular
    medicine / edited by Douglas P. Zipes . . . [et al.].

When there are two or more statements of responsibility, each naming
one or more persons or corporate bodies performing different functions,
they are separated by a space-semicolon-space.

Sculpting & drama / project editors, Joanna Callihan, Lindsay
    Ann Mizer ; art director, Robert Sanford ; interior design and
    production, Christopher Fowler, Suzanne Reinhart
Life of an optimist / Sir David Gibbons, a.k.a. Grandpa ; with
    Allison Moir-Smith
Explorers of North America / [authors, Mike Graf, Kathleen
    McFarren ; illustrator, Lynn McClain]
Selected writings / Saint Thomas More. Together with, The life
    of Sir Thomas Moore / by William Roper ; edited by John F.
    Thornton and Susan B. Varenne ; preface by Joseph W.
    Koterski
Forgotten voices of World War II : a new history of World War II
    in the words of the men and women who were there /
    [compiled by] Max Arthur ; with an introduction by Sir
    Martin Gilbert
The illustrated encyclopedia of music : from rock, pop, jazz, blues
    and hip hop to classical, folk, world and more / general
    editor, Paul du Noyer ; consulting editors, Ian Anderson . . .
    [et al.] ; foreword by Sir George Martin
The new annotated Sherlock Holmes / by Sir Arthur Conan
    Doyle ; edited, with a foreword and notes by Leslie S.
    Klinger ; introduction by John le Carré ; with additional
    research by Patricia J. Chui

Titles and abbreviations of titles of nobility and British terms of honor
(Sir, Dame, Lord, and Lady) are included in the statement of responsibility. Other terms of address, honor, and distinction and initials of societies
are generally omitted, except when such a title is necessary either grammatically or for personal identification or when the name consists of a
given name or a surname only.

The art of living long / Louis Cornaro ; with essays by Joseph
    Addison, Lord Bacon, and Sir William Temple
Facts on file encyclopedia of art / edited by Sir Lawrence Gowing
Human races / by Stanley M. Garn [On title-page: by Stanley M.
    Garn, Ph.D.]
Stories of Charlemagne and the twelve peers of France from the

old romances / by the Rev. A.J. Church [*On title-page*: by the Rev. A. J. Church, M.A.]

Unity of the Brethren in Texas, 1855-1966 / written by the Christian Sisters Union Study Committee, Mrs. Jesse E. Skrivanek . . . [et al.]

Billy Bully bug : (learns a lesson in Hawaii) / word & music, "Mrs. B" ; illustrations, "Miss Jodi"

Hop on Pop / by Dr. Seuss

Edition Area (rule *.2) [MARC field 250]

This area contains four elements: (1) edition statement; (2) statements of responsibility relating to the edition; (3) statement relating to a named version of an edition; and (4) statements of responsibility relating to a named revision of an edition. Each is discussed below.

1. Edition statement (rule *.2B) [MARC field 250, subfield $a]

An edition statement found in an item, including one for the first edition, is transcribed. Standard abbreviations and numerals (in place of spelled-out words) are used (see Appendixes B and C of AACR2R).

2005 ed.
3rd ed.
1st U.S. ed.
39th ed.
4th ed., completely rev. and updated
Updated ed.
Rev. ed.
Tax release 3
Version 2
Preliminary ed.

2. Statements of responsibility relating to the edition (rule *.2C) [MARC field 250, subfield $b]

A statement of responsibility relating to one or more, but not all, editions is given after the edition statement instead of after the title.

Rev. ed. / Mrs. William Homer Watkins
3rd ed. / [edited by] William B. Pratt, Palmer Taylor
5th ed. / [edited] by Michael J. Lambert
Updated . . . June, 1981 / Ronning Cartography

3. Statement relating to a named revision of an edition (rule *.2D) [MARC field 250]

A statement, designating the item as a revision of an edition (a named reissue of a particular edition containing changes from that edition) is given after the edition statement and its statements of responsibility.

> 2nd ed., 2002 revision
> A new ed.
> Rev. 9th ed.

4. Statements of responsibility relating to a named revision of an edition (rule *.2E) [MARC field 250, subfield $b]

The statement relating to a named revision of an edition may be followed by its own statement(s) of responsibility, if any (rule *.2E).

Material (or Type of Publication) Specific Details Area (rule *.3) [MARC fields 254 (music), 255 (cartographic material), 256 (electronic resource), and 362 (continuing resources)]

This area is applicable only to the following types of material: cartographic materials, music, continuing resources, and, in some circumstances, microforms. For each type of material, this area is defined for specific details or unique characteristics as shown below.

1. Cartographic materials (rule 3.3) [MARC field 255]

Called *mathematical and other material specific data area*, this area contains the statement of scale, the statement of projection, and the statement of coordinates and equinox (optional).

> Historic Bath, Maine's city of ships / Maine Street Bath, Maine. — **Scale [1:18,000]. 1 in. = 1,500 ft.**
> DestinationMap Madrid / National Geographic ; manufactured by Laminating Services, Inc., Largo, FL. — **Scale 1:7,800**
> FastTrack Calgary. — **Scales differ**
> South East Asia, scale 1:4,000,000 : indexed / cartography by Pham Viet Hoa ; design and editorial, Naz Ali, Stephanie Henke. — **Scale 1:4,000,000 ; Lambert conformal conic proj. (E 92—E 158/N 28—S 16).**

2. Music (rule 5.3) [MARC field 254]

Called *musical presentation statement area*, this optional area records a statement appearing in the chief source of information indicating the physical presentation of the music, such as

Miniature score
Partitur

3. Cartographic materials, music and serials in microform (rule 11.3) [MARC fields 255, 254, 362]

In chapter 11 (Microforms) of AACR2R, this area is called *specific data for cartographic materials, music, and serials*. When cataloging a cartographic item, music, or serial in microform, the material (or type of publication) specific detail is given as in the case of such materials in printed form. In other words, rules 3.3, 5.3, and 12.3 are applied (see examples under sections 1 and 2 above and section 4 below).

4. Continuing resources (rule 12.3) [MARC field 362]

For serial publications, this area, called *numeric and/or alphabetic, chronological, or other designation area*, contains the numeric or alphabetic designation, or both, and/or the chronological designation relating to the first and last (if the serial is completed) issues.

> The AAPS Journal [electronic resource]. — Vol. 6, issue 03-
> The AIA Journal of Architecture : AIA J. — Spring 2003-
> American Journal of Applied Sciences. — Vol. 1, no. 1 (Jan./Mar. 2004)-
> Americana [electronic resource]: the Journal of American Popular Culture, 1900 to present. — Vol. 1, issue 1 (spring 2002)-
> Online Journal of Space Communication [electronic resource]. — Issue no. 1 (Apr. 2002)-
> Air Repair. — Vol. 1, no. 1 (July 1951)-v. 4, no. 4 (Feb. 1955)
> Journal of the Air Pollution Control Association. — Vol. 5, no. 1 (May 1955)-v. 36, no. 12 (Dec. 1986)

Publication, Distribution, etc., Area (rule *.4) [MARC field 260]

This area records information about the place, name, and date of all types of activities relating to the publishing, distributing, releasing, issuing, and manufacturing of the item being described.

If the item being described displays two or more places of publication, distribution, etc., or names of publishers, distributors, etc., the first-named place of publication, distribution, etc., and the corresponding publisher, distributor, etc., are recorded. However, if the first-named place is not in the home country of the cataloging agency and a place in the home country is named in a secondary position, with or without a corresponding publisher, etc., the latter is recorded also.

The elements in this area are recorded in the following order: (1) place of publication, distribution, etc.; (2) name of publisher, distributor, etc.; (3) statement of function of publisher, distributor, etc. (optional); (4) date of publication, distribution, etc.; and (5) place of manufacture, name of manufacturer, date of manufacture.

1. Place of publication, distribution, etc. (rule *.4C) [MARC field 260, subfield $a]

The place of publication, distribution, etc., is recorded in the form and the grammatical case in which it appears in the item. The name of the country, state, province, etc. (abbreviated according to Appendix B of AACR2R) is added to the name of a local place if it is considered necessary for identification, or for the purpose of distinguishing the place from others of the same name. The name of the country, state, province, etc. is enclosed in brackets if it does not appear in the prescribed sources of information.

> Philadelphia
> [Washington, D.C.]
> Albany, N.Y.
> Cambridge [England]
> Cambridge, Mass.
> Newbury Park, Calif.
> Oxonii
> Dordrecht, Netherlands
> Basel ; New York

If the place is not known, the abbreviation [S.l.] for *sine loco*, is given.

> [S.l.] : Lawson-Gould Music Publishers : Exclusively distributed by Alfred, c1990.

Optionally, the place of publication may be followed by the address of the publisher if it is not widely known.

> Portland, Me. (P.O. Box 658, Portland 04104-0658) : J. Weston Walch

This element is not applicable to the description of manuscripts or of naturally occurring objects.

2. Name of publisher, distributor, etc. (rule *.4D) [MARC field 260, subfield $b]

The name of the place is followed by the name of the publisher, distributor, etc., given in the shortest form in which it can be understood and identified internationally:

> New York : **McGraw-Hill**
> New York, NY : **Wiley**
> New York : **Random House Reference**
> [Chico, CA : **Department of Health and Community Services, California State University**]
> [Hollywood, Calif.] : **Americana, the Institute for the Study of American Popular Culture**
> Chichester, West Sussex, England; Hoboken, N.J. : **J. Wiley**
> Boston : Shambhala : **distributed in the U.S. by Random House**
> London : **Penguin**
> Washington, DC : **American Institute of Architects**

If the name of the publisher, distributor, etc., is not known, the abbreviation [s.n.], for *sine nomine*, is given.

> San Francisco : **[s.n.]**, 1972

3. Statement of function of publisher, distributor, etc. (optional) (rule *.4E) [MARC field 260, subfield $b]

A term that clarifies the function of the publisher, distributor, etc., may be added, if such function is not clear from the publisher statement.

> Belmont, Calif. : Brooks/Cole ; London : Thomson Learning **[distributor]**, c2006

4. Date of publication, distribution, etc. (rule *.4F) [MARC field 260, subfield $c]

The year of publication, distribution, etc., of the edition, revision, etc., named in the edition area is recorded in western-style Arabic numerals. If there is no edition statement, the year of the first publication of the edition to which the item belongs is recorded. If the date transcribed from the item is known to be incorrect, the correct date is added in square brackets.

> London : Penguin, 2004
> New York : Little, Brown and Co., 2005
> Chicago : [s.n.], **1964 [i.e. 1946]**
> Athens : University of Georgia Press, 2005

The date of distribution, if it is different from the date of publication, is added if considered significant.

It is optional to add the latest date of copyright following the date of publication, distribution, etc., if it is different.

If the dates of publication, etc., are not known, the copyright date or, lacking such, the date of manufacture is given in its place.

Boston : McGraw-Hill, **c2005**
Binghamton, NY : Haworth Information Press, **c2003**
Beverly Hills, CA : Maverick, **p2002**

If none of the dates discussed above can be assigned to the item being described, an approximate date of publication is given.

[Chicago] : Replogle Globes, Inc., **[1989?]** (*probable date*)
[Nacogdoches, Tex.] : Nacogdoches Historical Commission,
   [1963?]
New York: RCA, **[197-?]**
[ca. 1900] (*approximate date*)

If a multipart item contains more than one date, the earliest and the latest dates are recorded.

New York : Academic Press, **1969-1973**

If the multipart item is not yet complete, the earliest date followed by a hyphen (called an open entry) is given.

[United States] : MacNeil/Lehrer Productions, **c2003-**

For a manuscript, the date is given in this area unless it is already included in the title.

For an art original, unpublished photograph, or other unpublished graphic item (rule 8.4F2), the date of creation is recorded.

For a naturally occurring object (unless it has been mounted for viewing or packaged for presentation), no date is recorded. For artefacts not intended primarily for communication, the date of manufacture is recorded.

5. Place of manufacture, name of manufacturer, date of manufacture (rule *.4G) [MARC field 260, subfields $e, $f, $g]

If the name of the publisher is unknown, the place and name of the printer or manufacturer, if found in the item, are recorded in parentheses and following the place, name, and date of publication and/or distribution.

[S.l. : s.n.], c1987 **(Houston : Hart Graphics, Morin Division)**

The date of manufacture is included here if it has not been used in place of an unknown date of publication, distribution, etc.

Physical Description Area (rule *.5) [MARC field 300]

This area presents the physical characteristics of the item being cataloged. It contains the following basic elements: (1) extent of item (including specific material designation), (2) other physical details, (3) dimensions, and (4) accompanying material. The terms with which each type of material is described vary greatly. They are listed below.

1. Extent of item (including specific material designation) (rule *.5B) [MARC field 300, subfield $a]

The number of physical units and parts are recorded in Arabic numerals followed by the specific material designation (abbreviated according to Appendix B, AACR2R). The more common kinds of specific material designations used for different types of material are listed below. In the description, each of these terms is preceded by the number of units (e.g., 436 p., 3 film cassettes, etc.). For a multipart item that is not yet complete, the specific material designation alone, without the number, is given.

Books, pamphlets, and printed sheets

    v. (*for volume or volumes*)
    p. (*for page or pages*)
    leaf
    column
    broadside
    sheet
    portfolio

Cartographic materials

    atlas
    diagram
    globe
    map
    model
    profile
    remote-sensing image
    section
    view

Manuscripts

    leaf
    p.
    v.
    item (*for a collection of manuscripts*)
    ft. (*for a collection occupying more than 1 linear foot of shelf space*)

Music

>   score
>   condensed score
>   close score
>   miniature score
>   piano [violin, etc.] conductor part
>   vocal score
>   piano score
>   chorus score
>   part

Sound recordings

Each designation is followed by the playing time.

>   sound cartridge
>   sound cassette
>   sound disc
>   sound tape reel
>   sound track film

Motion pictures and videorecordings

Each designation is followed by the playing time.

>   film cartridge
>   film cassette
>   film loop
>   film reel
>   videocartridge
>   videocassette
>   videodisc
>   videoreel

Graphic materials

>   activity card
>   art original
>   art print
>   art reproduction
>   chart
>   filmslip
>   filmstrip
>   flash card
>   flip chart

photograph
picture
postcard
poster
radiograph
slide
stereograph
study print
technical drawing
transparency
wall chart

Electronic resources

computer chip cartridge
computer disk
computer optical disc
computer tape cartridge
computer tape cassette
computer tape reel

Three-dimensional artefacts and realia

art original
art reproduction
braille cassette
diorama
exhibit
game
microscope slide
mock-up
model

Microforms

aperture card
microfiche
microfilm
microopaque

Continuing resources

The specific material designation appropriate for the type of material to which the resource belongs, for example, filmstrips, computer disks, etc.

2. Other physical details (rule *.5C) [MARC field 300, subfield $b]

Other physical details are added for the following types of materials:

Books, pamphlets, and printed sheets (rule 2.5C)

> illustrative matter *(use for general illustrative matter and for specifying one or more of the following: coats of arms, computer drawings, facsimiles, forms, genealogical tables, music, plans, portraits, samples)*
> map

Cartographic materials (rule 3.5C)

> layout
> production method
> number of maps, etc., in an atlas
> col. *(for colour)*
> medium
> material
> mounting

Manuscripts (rule 4.5C)

> name of material (if not paper) on which a single manuscript is written (e.g., parchment, vellum), illustrative matter (same as graphic materials: rule 8.5C)

Music (rule 5.5C)

> illustrative matter (same as books: rule 2.5C)

Sound recordings (rule 6.5C)

> type of recording
> playing speed
> groove characteristic (analog discs)
> track configuration (sound track films)
> number of tracks (tapes)
> number of sound channels
> recording and reproduction characteristics

Motion pictures and videorecordings (rule 7.5C)

> aspect ratio and special projection characteristics (motion pictures)

sd. *(for sound characteristics)*
col. *(for colour)*
projection speed (motion pictures)

Graphic materials (rule 8.5C)

medium (chalk, oil, pastel, etc.) and the base (board, canvas, fabric, etc.) *(for art originals)*
process in general terms (engraving, lithograph, etc.) or specific terms (copper engraving, chromolithograph, etc.) *(for art prints)*
method of reproduction (photogravure, collotype, etc.) *(for art reproductions)*
double sided *(for charts and flip charts)*
sd. (for sound, if the sound is integral) *(for filmstrips, filmslips, flash cards, and slides)*
transparency or negative print *(for photographs)*
method of reproduction (blueprint, photocopy, etc.) *(for technical drawings)*
col., sepia, b&w, tinted, etc. *(for colour of all graphic media other than art originals, radiographs, and technical drawings)*

Electronic resources (rule 9.5C)

sd. *(for a resource specified to have sound or is known to produce sound)*
col. *(for a resource specified or known to display in two or more colours)*
file types (digital, PDF file; digital, mp3 file; etc.) *(for remote access resources)*

Three-dimensional artefacts and realia (rule 10.5C)

material (marble, glass, wood, plastic, etc.)
col. *(for colour)*

Microforms (rule 11.5C)

negative
ill. *(same as books, etc.)*
col. *(for colour)*

Continuing resources

Physical details appropriate to the type of material to which the resource belongs as outlined above.

3. Dimensions (rule *.5D) [MARC field 300, subfield $c]

The dimension of the item follows the extent of the item or other physical details (if present). The part of the item to be measured varies according to type of material.

Books, pamphlets, and printed sheets (rule 2.5D)

> in centimeters, to the next whole centimeter up, and in
>   millimeters if less than ten centimeters
> height of the volume or volumes
> height X width (if width is less than half the height or greater
>   than the height)

Cartographic materials (rule 3.5D)

> in centimeters, to the next whole centimeter up
> height X width (*for two-dimensional cartographic items, relief models,
>   and for atlases with the width less than half the height or greater
>   than the height*)
> height of the volume or volumes (*for atlases*)
> diameter (*for circular maps and globes*)

Manuscripts (rule 4.5D)

> in centimeters, to the next whole centimeter up
> height
> height X width (if width is less than half the height or greater
>   than the height)
> height X width X depth (*for collections of manuscripts in containers*)

Music (rule 5.5D)

> [*same as for books, pamphlets, etc.*]

Sound recordings (rule 6.5D)

> diameter of the disc in inches (*for sound discs*)
> gauge (width) in millimeters (*for sound track films*)
> dimensions of the cartridge and width of the tape (if other than
>   the standard measurement) in inches (*for sound cartridges and
>   sound cassettes*)
> diameter of the reel in inches and width of the tape (if other than
>   standard) in fractions of an inch (*for sound tape reels*)

Motion pictures and videorecordings (rule 7.5D)

> gauge (width) in millimeters and (if 8 mm) whether single,
> standard, super, or Maurer (*for motion pictures*)
> gauge (width) in inches or millimeters (*for videotapes*)
> diameter in inches (*for videodiscs*)

Graphic materials (rule 8.5D)

> height X width in centimeters (*for all graphic materials except films-*
> *strips, filmslips, and stereographs*)
> gauge (width) in millimeters (*for filmstrips and filmslips*)

Electronic resources (rule 9.5D)

> diameter in inches, to the next 1/4 inch up (*for discs/disks*)
> length of the side of the cartridge in inches to the next 1/4 inch
> up (*for computer cartridges*)
> length X height of the face of the cassette in inches, to the next 1/
> 8 inch up (*for computer cassettes*)
> appropriate dimensions in inches or in centimeters, rounding up
> as appropriate (*for other physical carriers*)

Three-dimensional artefacts and realia (rule 10.5D)

> dimensions of the object in centimeters to the next centimeter up,
> name and dimensions of container (if any)

Microforms (rule 11.5D)

> height X width in centimeters to the next centimeter up (*for*
> *aperture cards*)
> height X width in centimeters to the next centimeter up, if other
> than 10.5 X 14.8 cm. (*for microfiche*)
> width in millimeters (*for microfilms*)
> height X width in centimeters to the next centimeter up (*for*
> *microopaques*)

Continuing resources (rule 12.5D)

> dimensions appropriate to the type of material to which the
> resource belongs

4. Accompanying material (rule *.5E) [MARC field 300, subfield $e]

There are four ways of describing accompanying material:

1. Create a separate record.
2. Create a multilevel description (i.e., as an analytic as instructed in chapter 13 Analysis).
3. Record the details in a note.
4. Record the number of physical units in Arabic numerals and the name of the accompanying material at the end of the physical description.

Examples of physical description are given below:

Books, pamphlets, and printed sheets

v, 133 p. : ill. ; 22 cm.
2 v. ; 21 cm.
xv, 454, [26] p. : ill. ; 24 cm.
iv, 92 p. : col. ill. ; 31 cm.
xxi, 694 p. : maps ; 20 cm.
xiv, 1184 p. : ill. (some col.) ; 24 cm.
xxxii, 256 p., [16] p. of plates : col. ill. ; 24 cm.
xv, 220 p., [1] leaf of plates : ill. ; 24 cm.
4 v. : maps ; 28 cm.
1 v. (unpaged) ; 28 cm.
347 p. (large print) ; 23 cm.
14 p., 40 p. of plates : ill. ; 35 cm.

Cartographic materials

1 globe : col., plastic, on plastic and wood base ; 31 cm. in diam.
1 atlas (vi, 210 p.) : col. ill., col. maps ; 28 X 44 cm.
1 atlas (1 v. (various pagings)) : col. maps ; 28 cm.
1 map : col. ; 74 X 100 cm.
1 map : both sides, col. ; 170 X 56 cm., on sheet 95 X 59 cm., folded to 23 X 10 cm.
2 maps on 1 sheet : both sides, col. ; 69 X 99 cm. and 69 X 73 cm., sheet 69 X 99 cm., folded to 25 X 11 cm.

Manuscripts

[2], 35 leaves : parchment, ill. ; 30 X 60 cm.

Music

1 close score (vi, [2] p.) : 1 fascim. ; 30 cm.
1 score (7 p.) + 1 part (3 p.) ; 28 cm.

v. of music <2> : ill. ; 31 cm.
96 p. of music : col. ill. ; 28 cm.
1 score + 4 parts ; 29 cm.

Sound recordings

1 sound disc (1 hr., 20 min.) : digital ; 4 3/4 in.
2 sound files : digital preservation master, WAV file (96 kHz, 24 bit)
2 sound tape reels : analog, 7 1/2 ips, 2 track, stereo. ; 10 in. + 1 booklet (16 p.)
1 sound cassette : analog, stereo.
1 sound disc : digital, DTS ; 4 3/4 in. track

Motion pictures and videorecordings

2 film reels (ca. 20 min. each) : sd., col. ; 16 mm.
1 videodisc (50 min.) : sd., col. ; 8 in.
1 videocassette of 1 (Digital Betacam) (ca. 60 min.) : sd., col. ; 3/4 in. viewing copy
1 videocassette of 1 (D2) (ca. 60 min.) : sd., col. ; 19 mm. master
1 film cassette (40 min.) : sd., col. + 1 teacher's manual
12 film reels of 12 on 6 (ca. 99 min., 8,910 ft.) : sd., col. ; 35 mm. viewing print

Graphic materials

1 photograph : b&w ; 13 X 8 cm.
1 study print : col. ; 34 X 47 cm. + 1 teacher's guide
5 filmstrips (ca. 116 fr. each) : col. ; 35 mm. + 5 sound cassettes (98 min. : digital) + 5 teacher's guides

Electronic resources

5 computer disks ; 3 1/2 in. + 1 manual (loose-leaf) + 4 guides + 3 quick answer cards + templates
1 CD-ROM : ill., maps (some col.) ; 4 3/4 in.

Continuing resources

v. : ill. ; 28 cm.

In the description of different types of materials, the greatest variations occur in the physical description area. For more details and further examples, consult AACR2R.

Multimedia items (rule *.10)

If an item consisting of two or more components belonging to two or more distinct material types has been described in terms of the predominant component in the preceding areas, the physical description is also presented in terms of the predominant component with details of the subsidiary component given as accompanying material (cf. rule 1.10).

> 1 filmstrip (127 fr.) : col. ; 35 mm + 1 sound cassette

A multimedia item that has no predominant component is described as a kit if it has a collective title. The term [kit] or [multimedia] may be used as the general material designation and the physical description may be presented by one of the following methods:

1. Physical descriptions of all components are presented in the same statement.
   45 flash cards, 50 worksheets, 12 duplicating masters, teacher's guide ; in container 16 X 24 X 18 cm.
2. Physical description of each component is presented separately.
   1 filmstrip (74 fr.) : col ; 35 mm.
   1 sound disc (17 min.) : 33 1/3 rpm, mono. ; 12 in.
3. A general statement, if the item consists of a large number of heterogeneous components, is used.
   various pieces
   16 various pieces

Series Area (rule *.6) [MARC field 4XX]

Series area information is transcribed according to the corresponding rules in the title and statement of responsibility area. The series area contains the following elements:

1. Title proper of series (rule *.6B)
2. Parallel titles of series (rule *.6C)
3. Other title information of series (rule *.6D)
4. Statements of responsibility relating to series (rule *.6E)
5. ISSN (International Standard Serial Number) of series (rule *.6F)
6. Numbering within series (rule *.6G)
7. Subseries (rule *.6H)
8. More than one series statement (rule *.6J)

This area is not applicable to the description of manuscript texts. In describing a microform, the series to which the microform belongs is described in the series area, and the series to which the original belongs is recorded in a note. Examples of series statements are shown below:

(Mark Twain and his circle series)
(Harvard-Yenching Institute monograph series ; 58)
(McGraw-Hill series in marketing)
(Princeton theological monograph series ; 50)
(Shakespeare in performance)
(Schaum's easy outlines)
(Penguin classics)
(Glossarium artis ; Bd. 11)
(Publications in mediaeval studies ; 29)
(Series in machine perception and artificial intelligence ; v. 52)
(Studies in the history and interpretation of music ; v. 120)
(Broadway collector series)

If the item belongs to a subseries, which is named in the item along with the main series, both series are recorded within the same set of parentheses and separated by a full stop.

(American university studies. Series II, Romance languages and
    literature ; v. 227)
(Royal Historical Society studies in history. New series)

If the item belongs to two or more series, the series statements are enclosed in separate parentheses. (In MARC records, each series is recorded in a separate 4XX field.)

(LEA's organization and management series) (Series in applied
    psychology)
(Bulletin (American School of Prehistoric Research) ; no. 47)
    (Dolnovestonické studie ; sv. 10)
(Studies in the history of art (Washington, D.C.) ; 64) (Studies in
    the history of art (Washington, D.C.). Symposium papers ; 41)

Note Area (rule *.7) [MARC fields 5XX][9]

Useful descriptive information, which cannot be presented in the other areas, is given in notes. The notes may be based on information taken from any suitable source.

Some notes supplement or clarify information given in the preceding areas; others provide additional bibliographic information. In notes containing data relating to those in the preceding areas of description, similar prescribed punctuation is used, except that a full stop is used in place of a full stop-space-dash-space. When quotations from the item or from other sources are used as notes, they are enclosed in quotation marks.

The kinds of notes used are listed below, with examples.

1. Nature, scope, or artistic form (rule *.7B1)

(including frequency of continuing resources and system requirements and mode of access for electronic resources)

"Auction Catalogue 12"
Papers from a conference held in 2003
Four times a year
Semiannual
System requirements: Java-capable Web browser
Mode of access: World Wide Web

2. Language of the item and/or translation or adaptation (rule *.7B2)

English translation of Nicolas de Herberay's French translation
from the Spanish original
Greek text with English translation on facing pages ; introduction
and commentary in English
In English, with some Amharic
Russian text and English translation
Translation of: Atlas ba'sico de matematicas
Translation of a late Byzantine Greek poem

3. Source of title proper (rule *.7B3)

Title from cover
Title from disc label
Title from PDF file as viewed on 2/9/2006
Title from table of contents page (publisher's website, viewed Jan.
16, 2004)
Title from journal homepage (publisher's website, viewed Dec.
20, 2004)

4. Variations in title (rule *.7B4)

Alternate title: Anything else, la vie et tout le reste
Cover title: Biochemistry crash course
Title on disk: Sequoia and Kings Canyon national parks, middle
and south forks of the Kings River and north fork of the Kern
River, Tulare and Fresno counties, California
Spine title: The Volkmann Collection of the Zamorano 80

5. Parallel titles and other title information (rule *.7B5)

Parallel title on back of container insert: Tinagong paraiso
Subtitle on cover: Contemporary traditions, Highland roots &
island reels

6. Statements of responsibility (rule *.7B6)

Compiled by Pete Heywood

A project of the Society of Satellite Professionals International, hosted by: the Institute for Telecommunications Studies, Ohio University

Executive producers, Michael Ewing, Daniel Lupi, Jay Roach ; music by Teddy Castellucci ; cinematography by Jack N. Green ; editing by Jeff Gourson

Produced by the Music Division and the Recording Laboratory of the Library of Congress

7. Edition and history (rule *.7B7)

Based on the book by Nick Hornby

Articles reprinted from various issues of Sport magazine

Compilation from previously released albums

"Reprinted from Molecular and cellular biochemistry, Volume 242 (2003)."

Rev. ed. of: Fundamentals of human communication / Melvin L. DeFleur. 2nd. ed. c1998

Rev. ed. of: Heart disease / edited by Eugene Braunwald, Douglas P. Zipes, Peter Libby. 6th ed. 2001

Electronic version of: Journal of American studies

Previous ed. : London : Allen Lane, 1997

Previously published: Handbook of psychotherapy and behavior change. 4th ed. 1994

8. Material (or type of publication) specific details (rule *.7B8)

Type of Material	Note Regarding
Cartographic materials	Mathematical and other material specific details
Manuscripts	Place of writing
Music	Notation
Electronic resources	Type and extent of resource
Continuing resources	Bibliographic history and relationships with other resources

Examples of Material specific details notes:

Vol. 3, no. 4 omitted

Oriented with north toward the upper right

In staff notation and tablature, with chord symbols and guitar chord diagrams

9. Publication, distribution, etc. (rule *.7B9)

". . . co-published simultaneously as Science & technology libraries, volume 23, number 4, 2003"
Began in 2003
"First published in Great Britain by Little, Brown and Company, 2004"—T.p. verso
Originally published: Die Dalai Lamas. Stuttgart : Armodsche Art Publishers

10. Physical description (rule *.7B10)

Duration: 01:04:06
Duration: ca. 5:00
Digital sound on one compact disc stored in one film can (CGD 5946)
Maps on lining paper
Relief shown by gradient tints and spot heights
Folded map in pocket
One DVD in pocket attached to back cover lining paper

11. Accompanying material and supplements (rule *.7B11)

Accompanied by synopsis (16 p.)
Accompanied by forms on CD-ROM
Accompanied by: Preventing Child & Substance Abuse: a Parent's Guide
Accompanied by: "Chronologie der Dalai Lamas und Panchem Lamas im zeithistorischen Kontext" (2 p. : col. ill. ; 29 x 144 cm.), folded in pocket
Accompanied by: Drift Globe Guide. 15 p. : ill., maps ; 28 cm.
Kept up to date by 2004 supplement and 2005 cumulative supplement

12. Series (rule *.7B12)

Series statement from jacket
"A Continuing Legal Education series"—Cover
"Third in a series of four"—Pref.

13. Dissertations (rule *.7B13)

Thesis (Ph.D.)—Harvard University, 1999

14. Audience (rule *.7B14)

"Word problems don't have to freak you out—get wise! with cool lessons and activities for middle & high school students!"—Cover

Elementary grades through junior high school students
Senior high school students

15. Reference to published descriptions (rule *.7B15)

The Memoirs have been published in the Kentucky State
Historical Society register

16. Other formats (rule *.7B16)

Also available online
Issued also as video recording
Issued also in printed form

17. Summary (rule *.7B17)

Summary: A news website, which presents headline news,
  forums, essays, foreign news, and political wrap. Offers
  congressional news information and RealAudio segments of
  the latest news. The program features Jim Lehrer. A PBS
  website
Summary: Index to "Glossarium artis." Lists all German terms
  but only the most common French and English ones
Summary: Searchable, full-text versions of major Russian
  periodicals on social sciences and humanities. Features
  journals of the Russian Academy of Sciences, popular literary
  editions, and independent scholarly publications. Includes
  current issues as well as archives of back issues of journals
Summary: Henry plays a man who falls in love with Lucy, a
  woman with a short-term memory loss. Therefore, Lucy
  never remembers Henry and this proves to be a pain for him,
  as he has to gain her back every day

18. Contents (rule *.7B18)

Contents: v. 1. British Isles. The Salley gardens ; Little Sir
  William : The bonny Early o'Moray ; O can ye sew cushions? ;
  The trees they grow so high ; The ash grove ; Oliver Cromwell
  — v. 2. France. La Noël passée ; Voici le printemps ; Fileuse ;
  Le roi s'en va-t'en chasse ; La belle est au jardin d'amour ; Il
  est quelqu'un sur terre ; Eho! Eho! ; Quand j'étais chez mon
  père
Contents: Beijing (City) — Beijing (Region)
Incomplete contents: pt. 1. Mind and brain — pt. 2. Concepts —

pt. 3. Memory — pt. 4. Language — pt. 5. Intelligence — pt.
6. Reasoning and intuition
Includes: Historiography of the Californias, imprints of the
Colonial Period, 1522-1821 / W. Michael Mathes. First
published: California State Library Foundation Bulletin, no.
72, 2002, p. 16-25
Includes bibliographical references
Includes discography (p. 348-353) and index
Includes index
Includes bibliographical references (p. [135]-149) and index
Includes indexes, col. ill., inset of Forbidden City, and map of
Beijing transit

19. Numbers associated with the item (rule *.7B19)

(other than those presented in the Standard number and terms of availability area)

"NPS D-510, April 2004"
GBA3T4403 bnb

**20. Copy being described, library's holdings, and restrictions on use
(rule *.7B20) [MARC fields 506, 540]**

Library copy signed on t.p.: Fritzi Morrison
LC copy signed by compiler
Restricted: Copying allowed only for non-profit organizations

21. "With" notes (rule *.7B21)

With: The Bostonian Ebenezer. Boston : Printed by B. Green & J.
Allen, for Samuel Phillips,
1698—The cure of sorrow. Boston : Printed by B. Green, 1709.
Bound together subsequent to publication
Issued with: La traviata : highlights [sound recording] / Verdi.
[S.l.] : Decca, p1995

22. Combined notes relating to the original (rule *.7B22)

Previous ed.: Child psychology / E. Mavis Hetherington, Ross D.
Parke ; revised by Ross D. Parke and Virginia Otis Locke,
c2003
Rev. and expanded translation of: Taschenatlas der
Pharmakologie. 5th ed. c2004.

23. Item described (rule*.7B23)

Latest issue consulted: Vol. 1, no. 4 (Oct. 2004) (viewed Dec. 20, 2004)

Latest issue consulted: Vol. 3, issue 1 (spring 2004) (viewed from publisher's website Aug. 20, 2004)

Standard Number and Terms of Availability Area (rule *.8) [MARC fields 020 (ISBN), 022 (ISSN)]

This area contains the following elements: (1) standard number; (2) key-title; (3) terms of availability (optional); (4) qualification. This area does not apply to the description of manuscripts.

1. Standard number (rule *.8B) [MARC fields 020, 022, subfield code $a]

The number recorded is the International Standard Book Number (ISBN), International Standard Serial Number (ISSN), or any other internationally agreed upon standard number. *Examples:*

> ISBN 031610924X
> ISBN 3598116683 (set)
> ISBN 0071398759 (pbk. : alk. paper)
> ISBN 0375433651 (large print)
> ISBN 0808923056 (international ed.)
> ISBN 9780789736086
> ISSN 1544-5402

2. Key-title (rule *.8C) [MARC field 022]

Key-title, defined as "The unique name assigned to a bibliographic re-source by centres of the ISSN Network,"[10] applies to serial publications only. *Examples:*

> Key Title: E-journal of ethical leadership
> Key Title: Californian journal of health promotion (CD-ROM)

3. Terms of availability (rule *.8D) [MARC field 020, subfield $c]

This element is optional. *Examples:*

> Access limited to subscribers
> For sale ($295.00)
> For subscribers only; follow links to resource
> Free (members)

4. Qualification (rule *.8E) [MARC field 020, subfield $c]

A brief qualification is given if the item bears two or more standard numbers. *Examples:*

> ISBN 0-444-88812-8 (set). — ISBN 0-444-88242-1 (v. 1). —
> ISBN 0-226-67544-0 (cloth : alk. paper) : $19.95. — ISBN 0-226-
> 67545-9 (paper)
> ISBN 072160479X (single vol.) — ISBN 0721605095 (2 vol. set) —
> ISBN 0808923056 (international ed.) — ISBN 080892334X
> (Indian ed.) — ISBN 1416000380 (2 v. edition) — ISBN
> 1416000143 (single v. edition)

SUPPLEMENTARY ITEMS (RULE *.9)

A supplement, which is an item that complements or adds to an existing publication, can be treated in one of two ways: (1) as a separate item; (2) as a dependent item.

As a Separate Item

A separate cataloging record is created for the supplement. The supplement is linked to the main item by means of an added entry for the latter and a note explaining the relationship between the two.

As a Dependent Item

The supplement is recorded in the description of the main item as accompanying material, in a note, or in a multilevel description (as instructed in rule 13.6).

ANALYSIS

According to the rules in chapter 13 of AACR2R, Analysis refers to the "process of preparing a bibliographic record that describes a part or parts of a larger item, for which a comprehensive record might be made."[11] The bibliographic records for the parts are called *analytics* or *analytical entries.* The part or parts being described may be a monograph within a monographic series, a volume in a multi-volume set, or a part of a volume.

Analysis of Monographic Series and Multipart Monographs

An individual part or parts of a larger item or multipart monograph can be described in one of the following ways: (1) with analytical added entries; (2) in a separate record; (3) in a contents note; (4) using "in" analytics; or (5) using multilevel description.

Analytical Added Entries (rule 13.2)

An added entry (consisting of the part's main entry heading or of the title proper) is made in the comprehensive record for the larger work. In this case, the part should be named either in the title and statement of responsibility area or in the note area of the record for the main item.

In a Separate Record (rule 13.3)

In the case of a part of a monographic series or a multipart monograph, if the part being described has a distinctive title, a complete record describing the part may be created with details of the series or comprehensive item given in the series area.

In a Contents Note (rule 13.4)

The title or name and title of the part may be cited in a contents note in the comprehensive record for the larger work.

"In" Analytics (rule 13.5)

In this method, the part being analyzed is presented in the description, and the citation of the larger item is given in a note beginning with the word "In."

The record contains the following elements which are applicable to the item being described:

> Title and statement of responsibility area. — Edition area. — Numeric or other designation. — Publication, distribution, etc., area. — Extent and specific material designation of the part : other physical details ; dimensions. — Notes.
> *In* [Main entry. Uniform title of whole item]. Title proper / statement(s) of responsibility when necessary for identification. — Edition statement. — Numeric or other designation of a serial, or publication details of a monographic item.

Examples:

> Developing a national foreign newspaper microfilming program / John Y. Cole. — p. 5-17 ; 24 cm.
> *In* Library resources & technical services. — Vol. 18, no. 1 (Winter 1974)

C. A. Cutter's three-figure author table [electronic resource]. — Swanson-Swift revision. — Chicopee, Mass., Distributed by H. R. Huntting Co., 1969. — 29 p. ; 38 cm.
In Libraries Unlimited professional collection CD [electronic resource]. — Windows CD-ROM. — Englewood, CO ; Libraries Unlimited, 1995. — 1 computer laser optical disc : col. ; 4 3/4 in. + 1 guide.

Multilevel Description (rule 13.6)

AACR2R provides yet another method called "multilevel description" (rule 13.6) whereby the descriptive information is divided into two or more levels. The first level gives only information relating to the item as a whole, and subsequent levels give information relating to groups of parts or individual parts contained in the item.

NOTES

1. *Anglo-American Cataloguing Rules,* 2nd ed., 2002 revision. Prepared under the direction of the Joint Steering Committee for Revision of AACR, a committee of: the American Library Association, the Australian Committee on Cataloguing, the British Library, the Canadian Committee on Cataloguing, Chartered Institute of Library and Information Professionals, the Library of Congress (Chicago: American Library Association, 2002).
2. *Cataloging Service Bulletin.* No. 1– (Summer 1978–).
3. *Library of Congress Rule Interpretations* (Washington, D.C.: Cataloging Distribution Service, Library of Congress, 1989, 2002 Cumulation, with quarterly updates).
4. Charles Ammi Cutter, *Rules for a Dictionary Catalog,* 4th ed. rewritten. (Washington, D.C.: Government Printing Office, 1904), 11.
5. *Anglo-American Cataloguing Rules.* 2nd ed., 2002 revision, 14–15.
6. Library of Congress, Cataloging Policy and Support Office, "C1 Cataloging Priorities and Levels of Cataloging," www.loc.gov/catdir/cpso/c01.html (20 Feb. 2007).
7. Program for Cooperative Cataloging, "About the PCC." www.loc.gov/catdir/pcc/2001pcc.html. September 2, 2005 (20 Feb. 2007).
8. *Library of Congress Rule Interpretations,* 1.1C.
9. MARC 21 codes in the 500 series are used with notes, depending on their type; and unique subfield codes are defined for each 5xx field.
10. *Anglo-American Cataloguing Rules,* 2nd ed., 2002 revision, D-4.
11. *Anglo-American Cataloguing Rules,* 2nd ed., 2002 revision, 13-1.

CHAPTER 4
DUBLIN CORE AND OTHER
METADATA SCHEMAS

METADATA

The term "metadata" has been used by different communities to mean different things. Within the information community, it has been used since the early 1990s to mean data about other data. More elaborate definitions of metadata have been offered by various user communities. Some examples follow:

> Metadata is structured information that describes, explains, locates, or otherwise makes it easier to retrieve, use, or manage an information resource. Metadata is often called data about data or information about information.[1]

> Metadata are structured, encoded data that describe characteristics of information-bearing entities to aid in the identification, discovery, assessment, and management of the described entities.[2]

> [Metadata is] anything used to describe and or to organize *electronic, and primarily Web,* resources (born digital and digitized) for management and/or retrieval.[3]

> Metadata is . . . used to mean structured information about an information resource of any media type or format.[4]

> Metadata is structured information that describes the attributes of information packages for the purposes of identification, discovery, and sometimes management.[5]

Broadly defined, cataloging information, as data about data, can be considered a type of metadata. In most cases, however, the term metadata is used in reference to data created to describe or represent electronic resources. The term *metadata schema* refers to a set of elements designed with specific types of resources or user communities in mind.

During the past decade, numerous metadata standards or schemas have emerged. With regard to function, there are three main types of metadata:[6]

- *Descriptive metadata* describes a resource for purposes such as discovery and identification. It can include elements such as title, abstract, author, and keywords.
- *Structural metadata* indicates how compound objects are put together, for example, how pages are ordered to form chapters.
- *Administrative metadata* provides information to help manage a resource, such as when and how it was created, file type and other technical information, and who can access it.

This chapter focuses on descriptive metadata. Among existing metadata schemas, Dublin Core has emerged as the most widely used worldwide. The following sections of this chapter present brief discussions (with examples) of the Dublin Core and a number of other metadata schemas.

DUBLIN CORE

Introduction

On a cost-effectiveness basis, cataloging codes, with their extensive and detailed rules and their focus on material traditionally held by libraries, are not a satisfactory vehicle for characterizing the content of Internet and Web resources. Cataloging rules are costly to apply, in part because it takes professional training to use them well and in part because the per-item time required is relatively lengthy. They are also much more detailed than is needed for the bibliographical control of most Web resources.

Accordingly, a group of information professionals met in 1995 at OCLC (Online Computer Library Center) in Dublin, Ohio, to consider the matter. This meeting led to a new metadata schema aimed particularly at electronic resources such as those on the Web. This new schema came to be called the Dublin Core (DC). Another offshoot of the initial and subsequent Dublin meetings was the Dublin Core Metadata Initiative (DCMI), an open forum that oversees the continuing development of the Dublin Core and promotes other interoperable metadata standards. DCMI's activities include not only annual global conferences, workshops, and working groups organized around specific problem domains, but also both standards liaison and educational efforts to promote widespread acceptance of metadata standards and practices. Since the first DC meeting, which was sponsored by OCLC and the National Center for Supercomputing Applications (NCSA), was held in Ohio, there have been annual workshops held in different countries in the world, including Australia, Canada, China, Finland, Germany, Italy, Japan, Mexico, Spain, the United Kingdom, and the United States.

The original objective of the March 1995 Metadata Workshop held in

Dublin, Ohio, was to define a set of descriptive elements simple enough for non-catalogers, including authors themselves, to describe Web resources.[7] It began with thirteen elements and later, with the addition of the elements Description and Rights, was expanded to fifteen.

Since its inception, DC has been well received by many different information communities worldwide. In 2001, the Dublin Core Metadata Element Set was approved by the National Information Standards Organization as ANSI/NISO Standard Z39.85-2001 (updated May 2007).[8] In February 2003, it was approved as an international standard, ISO Standard 15836-2003.[9]

Dublin Core Element Set

The Dublin Core contains a set of fifteen elements.[10] These are listed below:

Element Name: title
Label: Title
Definition: A name given to the resource.

Element Name: creator
Label: Creator
Definition: An entity primarily responsible for making the resource.
Comment: Examples of a Creator include a person, an organization, or a service. Typically, the name of a Creator should be used to indicate the entity.

Element Name: subject
Label: Subject
Definition: A topic of the content of the resource.
Comment: Typically, Subject will be represented using keywords, key phrases or classification codes. Recommended best practice is to use a controlled vocabulary. To describe the spatial or temporal topic of the resource, use the Coverage element.

Element Name: description
Label: Description
Definition: An account of the resource.
Comment: Description may include but is not limited to an abstract, table of contents, graphical representation, or free-text account of the resource.

Element Name: publisher
Label: Publisher
Definition: An entity responsible for making the resource available.
Comment: Examples of a Publisher include a person, an organization, or a service. Typically, the name of a Publisher should be used to indicate the entity.

Element Name: contributor
Label: Contributor
Definition: An entity responsible for making contributions to the content of the resource.
Comment: Examples of a Contributor include a person, an organization, or a service. Typically, the name of a Contributor should be used to indicate the entity.

Element Name: date
Label: Date
Definition: A point or period in time associated with the life cycle of the resource.
Comment: Date may be used to express temporal information at any level of granularity. Recommended best practice is to use an encoding scheme, such as the W3CDTF profile of ISO 8601.

Element Name: type
Label: Resource Type
Definition: The nature or genre of the resource.
Comment: Recommended best practice is to use a controlled vocabulary (for example, the DCMI Type Vocabulary [DCMITYPE]). To describe the file format, use the Format element.

Element Name: format
Label: Format
Definition: The file format, physical medium, or dimensions of the resource.
Comment: Examples of dimensions include size and duration. Recommended best practice is to use a controlled vocabulary (for example, the list of Internet Media Types [MIME]).

Element Name: identifier
Label: Resource Identifier
Definition: An unambiguous reference to the resource within a given context.

Comment: Recommended best practice is to identify the resource by means of a string conforming to a formal identification system.

Element Name: source
Label: Source
Definition: A related resource from which the present resource is derived.
Comment: The described resource may be derived from the related resource in whole or in part. Recommended best practice is to reference the related resource by means of a string conforming to a formal identification system.

Element Name: language
Label: Language
Definition: A language of the resource.
Comment: Recommended best practice is to use a controlled vocabulary such as RFC 4646.

Element Name: relation
Label: Relation
Definition: A related resource.
Comment: Recommended best practice is to identify the resource by means of a string conforming to a formal identification system.

Element Name: coverage
Label: Coverage
Definition: The spatial or temporal topic of the resource, the spatial applicability of the resource, or the jurisdiction under which the resource is relevant.
Comment: Spatial topic and spatial applicability may be a named place or a location specified by its geographic coordinates. Temporal topic may be a named period, date, or date range. A jurisdiction may be a named administrative entity or a geographic place to which the resource applies. Recommended best practice is to use a controlled vocabulary such as the *Thesaurus of Geographic Names* (TGN). Where appropriate, named places or time periods can be used in preference to numeric identifiers such as sets of coordinates or date ranges.

Element Name: rights
Label: Rights
Definition: Information about rights held in and over the resource.
Comment: Typically, rights information includes a statement about various property rights associated with the resource, including intellectual property rights.

Although the original intention was to develop a simple and concise schema for describing Web resources, the Dublin Core has been used to describe other types of resources as well. In different applications, some users require more descriptive details than others. Thus, there are two different views with regard to the implementation of DC: the minimalist view supporting a minimum of elements and simple semantics and syntax and the structuralist view supporting greater extensibility through finer semantic distinctions. These different views have led to two approaches to the implementation of DC: the simple (unqualified) DC and the qualified DC with finer details allowed within each element. Simple Dublin Core consists of the original fifteen elements; qualified Dublin Core includes three additional elements (Audience, Provenance and RightsHolder), as well as a group of qualifiers that refine the semantics of the elements.[11] For example, the element SUBJECT may be qualified to indicate the nature (i.e., keyword, controlled vocabulary, or classification) and the encoding schema (MeSH, LCSH, DDC, LCC, etc.) of the value. The DCMI recognizes two broad classes of qualifiers:[12]

Element Refinement. These qualifiers make the meaning of an element narrower or more specific. A refined element shares the meaning of the unqualified element, but with a more restricted scope. A client that does not understand a specific element refinement term should be able to ignore the qualifier and treat the metadata value as if it were an unqualified (broader) element. The definitions of element refinement terms for qualifiers must be publicly available.

Encoding Scheme. These qualifiers identify schemes that aid in the interpretation of an element value. These schemes include controlled vocabularies and formal notations or parsing rules. A value expressed using an encoding scheme will thus be a token selected from a controlled vocabulary (e.g., a term from a classification system or set of subject headings) or a string formatted in accordance with a formal notation (e.g., "2000-01-01" as the standard expression of a date). If an encoding scheme is not understood by a client or agent, the value may still be useful to a human reader. The definitive description of an encoding scheme for qualifiers must be clearly identified and available for public use. The qualifiers for the 15 DC elements are shown in Table 4-1.

Users and implementers of the Dublin Core may define the qualifiers according to their needs. Following are examples of qualified Dublin Core Metadata records from OCLC's WorldCat:

(1) An online journal

> Title: **D-Lib magazine**
> Title.alternative: **Digital Library Magazine**
> Title.alternative: **D lib magazine**
> Identifier.LCCN: **sn 95004209**
> Identifier.NLCcn: **9709374**
> Identifier.NLCcn: **SR0084642**
> Identifier.ISSN: **1082-9873**
> Identifier.URI: **http://bibpurl.oclc.org/web/1110**
> Identifier.URI: **http://www.dlib.org/**
> Type.AACR2-gmd: **[electronic resource].**
> Contributor.nameCorporate: **Corporation for National Research Initiatives.**
> Contributor.nameCorporate: **D-Lib Forum.**
> Contributor.nameCorporate: **Federal High Performance Computing Program (U.S.). Information Infrastructure Technology and Applications Task Group.**
> Date.issued.MARC21-Date: **1995-9999**
> Date.issued.MARC21-362: **July 1995-**
> Description.note: **Title from journal home page (viewed Sept. 7, 1999).**
> Description.note: **Latest issue consulted: Vol. 11, no. 1 (Jan. 2005)(viewed Jan. 27, 2005).**
> Description: **Presents "D-Lib Magazine," a monthly electronic publication related to digital libraries. Includes commentaries and news articles. Offers an archive of back issues and a site search engine. Provides access to working groups, digital library research projects, events calendars, and related technical reports. Notes access terms and conditions and links to mirror sites. Links to the Corporation for National Research Initiatives, the coordinator of the magazine.**
> Language.ISO639-2: **eng**
> Publisher.place: **Reston, Va. :**
> Publisher: **Corp. for National Research Initiatives,**
> Relation.requires: **Mode of access: World Wide Web.**

TABLE 4-1 Dublin Core Summary Refinement and Scheme

DCMES Element	Element Refinement(s)	Element Encoding Scheme(s)
Title	Alternative	—
Creator	—	—
Subject	—	LCSH MeSH DDC LCC UDC
Description	Table of Contents Abstract	—
Publisher	—	—
Contributor	—	—
Date	Created Valid Available Issued Modified Date Accepted Date Copyrighted Date Submitted	DCMI Period W3C-DTF
Type	—	DCMI Type Vocabulary
Format	— Extent Medium	IMT — —
Identifier	— Bibliographic Citation	URI —
Source	—	URI
Language	—	ISO 639-2 RFC 1766
Relation	Is Version Of Has Version Is Replaced By Replaces Is Required By Requires Is Part Of Has Part Is Referenced By References Is Format Of Has Format Conforms to	URI

Coverage	Spatial	DCMI Point
		ISO 3166
		DCMI Box
		TGN
	Temporal	DCMI Period
		W3C-DTF
Rights	Access Rights	—
	License	URI

Source: Using Dublin Core–Dublin Core Qualifiers, http://dublincore.org/documents/usageguide/qualifiers.shtml (24 Oct. 2006).

Subject.class.LCC: **ZA4080**
Subject.class.NLM: **WWW**
Subject.class.NLM: **Z 669**
Subject.class.DDC: **025**
Subject.topical.LCSH: **Digital libraries • Periodicals.**
Subject.topical.LCSH: **Electronic publishing • Periodicals.**
Subject.topical.LCSH: **Libraries and electronic publishing • Periodicals.**
Subject.topical.LCSH: **Library information networks • Periodicals.**
Subject.topical.MeSH: **Information Storage and Retrieval.**
Subject.topical.MeSH: **Information Systems.**
Subject.topical: **Electronic journals.**
Subject.topical: **Digital libraries.**

(2) A sound recording

Title: **New York Philharmonic broadcast transcriptions • Carnegie Hall concert of July 9, 1944.**
Title.alternativeUniform: **Star-spangled banner (Song); • arr.**
Identifier.LCCN: **2003643451**
Type.AACR2-gmd: **[sound recording] :**
Type.radfg: **Western art music • Radio.**
Contributor.namePersonal: **Corigliano, John.**
Contributor.namePersonal: **Rosenker, Michael.**
Contributor.namePersonal: **Reiner, Fritz, • 1888-1963.**
Contributor.namePersonal: **Bach, Johann Sebastian, • 1685-1750. • Concertos, • violins (2), string orchestra, • BWV 1043, • D minor.**
Contributor.namePersonal: **Mozart, Wolfgang Amadeus, • 1756-1791. • Symphonies, • K. 551, C major.**
Contributor.namePersonal: **Strauss, Richard, • 1864-1949. Rosenkavalier (Opera). • Selections; • arr.**

Creator.nameCorporate.MEntry: **New York Philharmonic.**
Date.issued.MARC21-Date: **2003**
Description.note: **"Concert and broadcast recordings from the collection of Bruce Wellek."**
Description.note: **Compact disc.**
Description.tableOfContents: **The star-spangled banner / Smith ; Key — Concerto in D minor for two violins, BWV 1043 / J.S. Bach — Symphony no. 41 in C, K. 551, "Jupiter" / Mozart — Der Rosenkavalier : op. 59. Waltzes / Richard Strauss.**
Description.versionDetails.MARC21-533: **Digital master. • [Washington, D.C.] • : Peter Alyea, • 2002. 1 computer laser optical disc ; 4 3/4 in. • Contains 418 megabytes of • .WAV files. Duration: 57:06.**
Description.versionDetails.MARC21-533: **DAT original. • [Cleveland, Ohio] : • [Bruce Wellek], • [199-]. • 1 sound cassette : digital ; 2 1/2 x 3 in.**
Format.extent: **1 sound disc : • digital ; • 4 3/4 in.**
Publisher.place: **[Alexandria, Va.] :**
Publisher: **Al Schlachtmeyer,**
Relation.isPartOfSeries.MARC21-490: **The Reiner legacy ; • v. 12**
Relation.isPartOfSeries.MARC21-800: **Reiner, Fritz, • 1888-1963. • Reiner legacy ; v. 12.**
Subject.class.LCC: **ICD 26762 (Playback copy)**
Subject.class.LCC: **ICD 26811 (Digital master)**
Subject.class.LCC: **RGB 3006 (DAT original)**
Subject.topical.LCSH: **Concertos (Violins (2) with string orchestra)**
Subject.topical.LCSH: **Symphonies.**
Subject.topical.LCSH: **Operas • Excerpts.**
Subject.topical.LCSH: **Waltzes.**
Subject.topical.LCSH: **Live sound recordings.**

OTHER METADATA STANDARDS FOR RESOURCE DESCRIPTION

In addition to the Dublin Core, numerous other metadata schemas for resource description have also been developed and/or adopted by various information communities, such as libraries, museums, archives, art institutions, etc. Following is a brief description of some of the more widely used metadata schemas:

MODS (Metadata Object Description Schema)

MODS (Metadata Object Description Schema),[13] developed by the Library of Congress Network Development and MARC Standards Office in 2002, is a schema for a bibliographic element set that may be used for a variety of purposes, and particularly for library applications. It consists of a subset of MARC fields (see discussion in chapter 16) and uses language-based tags rather than numeric ones. The top level MODS elements include:

titleInfo	note
name	subject
typeOfResource	classification
genre	relatedItem
originInfo	identifier
language	location
physicalDescription	accessCondition
abstract	part
tableOfContents	extension
targetAudience	recordInfo

The following examples show the top elements in two MODS records:

(1) Carl Sandburg's *Arithmetic* (a book)

titleInfo	**Arithmetic**
name	**Sandburg, Carl, 1878-1967**
name	**Rand, Ted**
typeOfResource	**text**
originInfo	**San Diego, Harcourt Brace Jovanovich, c1993**
language	**eng**
physicalDescription	**1v. (unpaged) : ill. (some col.) ; 26 cm.**
abstract	**A poem about numbers and their characteristics. Features anamorphic, or distorted, drawings which can be restored to normal by viewing from a particular angle or by viewing the image's reflection in the provided Mylar cone.**
targetAudience	**juvenile**
note	**illustrated as an anamorphic adventure by Ted Rand.**
note	**One Mylar sheet included in pocket.**
subject	**Arithmetic**
subject	**Juvenile poetry**

subject	Children's poetry, American
classification	PS3537.A618 A88 1993
classification	811/.52
identifier	isbn: 0152038655
identifier	lccn: 92005291

(2) *Campbell County, Wyoming* (a map)

titleInfo	Campbell County, Wyoming
namePart	Campbell County Chamber of Commerce (Wyo.)
typeOfResource	cartographic
genre	map
originInfo	[Gillette, Wyo.] : Campbell County Chamber of Commerce
dateIssued	1982
issuance	monographic
language	eng
physicalDescription	1 map ; 33 x 15 cm.
note	this map reproduced by Campbell County Chamber of Commerce.
note	In lower right corner: Kintzels-Casper.
subject	Campbell County (Wyo.)—Maps
classification	G4263.C3 1982 .C3
recordInfo	DLC
	830222 [Record Creation Date]
	19830426000000.0 [Record Change Date]
recordIdentifier	5466714

For more details and encoding of MODS records, see chapter 16.

TEI (Text Encoding Initiative)

TEI (www.tei-c.org/) is an international standard providing guidelines for the preparation and interchange of electronic texts of literary and linguistic textual materials, such as fiction, drama, and poetry, for scholarly research in the humanities.

Originally sponsored by the Association of Computers in the Humanities (ACH), the Association for Computational Linguistics (ACL), and the Association of Literary and Linguistic Computing (ALLC), TEI is now maintained by the TEI Consortium.

The TEI's *Guidelines for Electronic Text Encoding and Interchange* (TEI P4), first published in April 1994 in print form, has undergone several

revisions. The latest version is available both in print and online (www
.tei-c.org/P4X/). A simplified version, called TEI Lite (www.tei-c.org/
Lite/), is a specific customization designed for the core TEI constituency.

TEI Header

Every TEI text has a header, which contains descriptive information, i.e.,
metadata, about the work. It is an "electronic title page," similar to the
title page of a printed work. The tags used to label individual parts of
the TEI header follow SGML (Standard Generalized Markup Language)
convention of using brackets to enclose element tags. (For more details
about SGML, see chapter 16.)

The header is introduced by the element <teiHeader> and has four
major parts:

1. File description <fileDesc> contains a full bibliographic description of an electronic file.
2. Encoding description <encodingDesc> documents the relationship
   between an electronic text and the source or sources from which it
   was derived.
3. Profile description <profileDesc> provides a detailed description
   of non-bibliographic aspects of a text, specifically the languages
   and sublanguages used, the situation in which it was produced,
   the participants, and their setting.
4. Revision description <revisionDesc> summarizes the revision history for a file.

The <fileDesc> element is mandatory. It contains a full bibliographic description of the file with the following elements:

<titleStmt>
    groups information about the title of a work and those
    responsible for its intellectual content.
<editionStmt>
    groups information relating to one edition of a text.
<extent>
    describes the approximate size of the electronic text as stored
    on some carrier medium, specified in any convenient units.
<publicationStmt>
    groups information concerning the publication or
    distribution of an electronic or other text.
<seriesStmt>
    groups information about the series, if any, to which a
    publication belongs.
<notesStmt>

collects together any notes providing information about a text additional to that recorded in other parts of the bibliographic description.

<sourceDesc>
supplies a bibliographic description of the copy text(s) from which an electronic text was derived or generated.

A minimal header has the following structure shown here with SGML coding:

```
<teiHeader>
  <fileDesc>
    <titleStmt> . . . </titleStmt>
    <publicationStmt> . . . </publicationStmt>
    <sourceDesc> . . . </sourceDesc>
  </fileDesc>
</teiHeader>
```

The <encodingDesc> element specifies the methods and editorial principles which governed the transcription of the text. Its use is highly recommended. It may be prose description or may contain elements from the following list:

<projectDesc>
describes in detail the aim or purpose for which an electronic file was encoded, together with any other relevant information concerning the process by which it was assembled or collected.

<samplingDecl>
contains a prose description of the rationale and methods used in sampling texts in the creation of a corpus or collection.

<editorialDecl>
provides details of editorial principles and practices applied during the encoding of a text.

<tagsDecl>
provides detailed information about the tagging applied to an SGML or XML document.

<refsDecl>
specifies how canonical references are constructed for this text.

<classDecl>
contains one or more taxonomies defining any classificatory codes used elsewhere in the text.

<fsdDecl>

identifies the feature system declaration which contains definitions for a particular type of feature structure.

<metDecl>
documents the notation employed to represent a metrical pattern when this is specified as the value of a met, real, or rhyme attribute on any structural element of a metrical text (e.g. lg, l, or seg).

<variantEncoding>
declares the method used to encode text-critical variants.

Examples of <projectDesc> and <samplingDesc>

<encodingDesc>
  <projectDesc>**Texts collected for use in the Claremont Shakespeare Clinic, June 1990.**
  </projectDesc>
</encodingDesc>
<encodingDesc>
  <samplingDecl>**Samples of 2000 words taken from the beginning of the text**
  </samplingDecl>
</encodingDesc>

The <profileDesc> element enables information characterizing various descriptive aspects of a text to be recorded within a single framework. It has three optional components:

<creation>
contains information about the creation of a text.
<langUsage>
describes the languages, sublanguages, registers, dialects, etc., represented within a text.
<textClass>
groups information which describes the nature or topic of a text in terms of a standard classification scheme, thesaurus, etc.

For example:

<creation>
  <date value = "1992-08">**August 1992**</date>
  <name type = "place">**Taos, New Mexico**</name>
</creation>

The <revisionDesc> element provides a change log in which each change made to a text may be recorded. The log may be recorded as a sequence of <change> elements each of which contains:

<date>
contains a date in any format.
<respStmt>
supplies a statement of responsibility for someone responsible for the intellectual content of a text, edition, recording, or series, where the specialized elements for authors, editors, etc., do not suffice or do not apply.
<item>
contains one component of a list.

For example:

<revisionDesc>
    <change><date>6/3/91:</date>
        <respStmt><name>EMB</name><resp>ed.</resp>
        </respStmt>
        <item>File format updated</item></change>
    <change><date>5/25/90:</date>
        <respSmt><name>EMB</name><resp>ed.</resp>
        <item>Stuart's corrections entered</item></change>
</revisionDesc>

The TEI header is usually placed at the beginning of the electronic resource that it describes. It can also function in detached form as a surrogate record in a separate list or catalog. Some libraries use TEI headers to derive MARC records for inclusion in their catalogs. Following is an example of a TEI header:[14]

<teiHeader>
    <fileDesc>
        <titleStmt>
            <title>Thomas Paine: Common sense, a machine-readable transcript</title>
            <respStmt><resp>compiled by</resp>
                <name>Jon K Adams</name>
            </respStmt>
        </titleStmt>
        <publicationStmt>
            <distributor>Oxford Text Archive</distributor>
        </publicationStmt>
        <sourceDesc>
            <bibl>The complete writings of Thomas Paine, collected and edited by Phillip S. Foner (New York, Citadel Press, 1945)
            </bibl>
        </sourceDesc>

```
</fileDesc>
</teiHeader>
```

EAD (Encoded Archival Description)

The Encoded Archival Description (EAD) is a standard for describing and encoding finding aids for archival materials. Finding aids are tools such as inventories, registers, indexes, and other documents created by archives, libraries, museums, and manuscript repositories for both managing and providing access to their collections.[15] Records for finding aids are different from cataloging records in that they are much longer and contain extensive narrative and explanatory information which is structured hierarchically.[16] EAD is used by many academic and research libraries, archives, historical societies, and museums to describe the finding aids for their special collections.

The EAD began in 1993 at the University of California, Berkeley. The goal was to create a standard for machine-readable finding aids used in archival work. At the same time, the original investigators wanted to include, in EAD records, information that went beyond what was found in traditional MARC records. As the EAD site states, the requirements for this project "included the following criteria: 1) ability to present extensive and interrelated descriptive information found in archival finding aids, 2) ability to preserve the hierarchical relationships existing between levels of description, 3) ability to represent descriptive information that is inherited by one hierarchical level from another, 4) ability to move within a hierarchical informational structure, and 5) support for element-specific indexing and retrieval."[17]

An EAD record typically contains a header similar to a TEI header. It describes the finding aid itself and contains a description of the archival collection as a whole as well as more detailed information about the records or series within the collection. In other words, the EAD header carries metadata about the finding aid itself.

The current version, maintained by the Library of Congress and the Society of American Archivists, is EAD DTD version 2002.[18] The EAD header contains the following elements:

```
<eadheader>
  <eadid>
  <filedesc>
    <titlestmt>
      <titleproper>
      <subtitle>
      <author>
      <sponsor>
    <editionstmt>
```

```
<publicationstmt>
    <addresses>
    <date>
    <num>
    <p>
    <publisher>
<seriesstmt>
<notestmt>
<profiledesc>
    <creation>
    <language>
<revisiondesc>
```

The following is based on an example of an EAD header from the EAD Application Guidelines, illustrating how to apply the "<titlepage>" tag:[19]

<eadheader>	
<eadid>	**loc.mss/eadmss.ms996001**
<filedesc>	
<titlestmt>	
<titleproper>	**Shirley Jackson**
<subtitle>	**A Register of Her Papers in the Library of Congress**
<author>	**Prepared by Grover Batts. Revised and expanded by Michael McElderry with the assistance of Scott McLemee**
<publicationstmt>	
<addresses>	**Washington, D.C. 20540-4860**
<date>	**1993**
<publisher>	**Manuscript Division, Library of Congress**
<notestmt>	**Edited full draft**
<profiledesc>	
<creation>	**Finding aid encoded by Library of Congress Manuscript Division**
<date>	**1996**
<language>	**English**
<revisiondesc>	
<change>	
<date>	**1997**
<item>	**Encoding revised**

VRA (Visual Resources Association) Core Categories

VRA is a documentation standard for image collections used by the visual resources community. It is designed for describing visual documents depicting works of art, architecture, and artifacts or structures from material, popular, and folk culture. Its purpose is to facilitate the sharing of information among visual resources collections about *works* and *images*. The standard is based on the Dublin Core with modifications. Some of the VRA elements are based on the Dublin Core elements such as title, creator, subject, and relation. Other elements such as measurements, material, and technique are added to enable a richer description of art works.

Core Element Set

The VRA Work Description (VRA Core Categories, Version 3.0, 2002) (www.vraweb.org/vracore3.htm) contains 19 elements,[20] each of which may contain one or more qualifiers to allow further specifications within the element:

Record Type

> Qualifiers: None
> Definition: Identifies the record as being either a WORK record, for the physical or created object, or an IMAGE record, for the visual surrogates of such objects.

Type

> Qualifiers: None
> Definition: Identifies the specific type of Work or Image being described in the record.

Title

> Qualifiers:
> Title.Variant
> Title.Translation
> Title.Series
> Title.Larger Entity
> Definition: The title or identifying phrase given to a Work or an Image. For complex works or series the title may refer to a discrete unit within the larger entity (a print from a series, a panel from a fresco cycle, a building within a temple complex) or may identify only the larger entity itself. A

record for a part of a larger unit should include both the title for the part and the title for the larger entity. For an Image record, this category describes the specific view of the depicted Work.

Measurements

Qualifiers:
Measurements.Dimensions
Measurements.Format
Measurements.Resolution
Description: The size, shape, scale, dimensions, format, or storage configuration of the Work or Image. Dimensions may include such measurements as volume, weight, area, or running time. The unit used in the measurement must be specified.

Material

Qualifiers:
Material.Medium
Material.Support
Description: The substance of which a work or an image is composed.

Technique

Qualifiers: None
Description: The production or manufacturing processes, techniques, and methods incorporated in the fabrication or alteration of the work or image.

Creator

Qualifiers:
Creator.Role
Creator.Attribution
Creator.Personal Name
Creator.Corporate Name
Description: The names, appellations, or other identifiers assigned to an individual, group, corporate body, or other entity that has contributed to the design, creation, production, manufacture, or alteration of the work or image.

Date

Qualifiers:
Date.Creation

Date.Design
Date.Beginning
Date.Completion
Date.Alteration
Date.Restoration
Description: Date or range of dates associated with the creation, design, production, presentation, performance, construction, or alteration, etc. of the work or image. Dates may be expressed as free text or numerical.

Location

Qualifiers:
Location.Current Site
Location.Former Site
Location.Creation Site
Location.Discovery Site
Location.Current Repository
Location.Former Repository
Description: The geographic location and/or name of the repository, building, or site-specific work or other entity whose boundaries include the Work or Image.

ID Number

Qualifiers:
ID Number.Current Repository
ID Number.Former Repository
ID Number.Current Accession
ID Number.Former Accession
Description: The unique identifiers assigned to a Work or an Image.

Style/Period

Qualifiers:
Style/Period.Style
Style/Period.Period
Style/Period.Group
Style/Period.School
Style/Period.Dynasty
Style/Period.Movement
Description: A defined style, historical period, group, school, dynasty, movement, etc. whose characteristics are represented in the Work or Image.

Culture

Qualifiers: None
Description: The name of the culture, people (ethnonym), or adjectival form of a country name from which a Work or Image originates or with which the Work or Image has been associated.

Subject

Qualifiers: None
Description: Terms or phrases that describe, identify, or interpret the Work or Image and what it depicts or expresses. These may include proper names (e.g., people or events), geographic designations (places), generic terms describing the material world, or topics (e.g., iconography, concepts, themes, or issues).

Relation

Qualifiers:
    Relation.Identity
    Relation.Type
Description: Terms or phrases describing the identity of the related work and the relationship between the Work being cataloged and the related work. Note: If the relationship is *essential* (i.e. when the described work includes the referenced works, either physically or logically within a larger or smaller context), use the Title.Larger Entity element.

Description

Qualifiers: None
Description: A free-text note about the Work or Image, including comments, description, or interpretation, that gives additional information not recorded in other categories.

Source

Qualifiers: None
Description: A reference to the source of the information recorded about the work or the image. For a work record, this may be a citation to the authority for the information provided. For an image, it can be used to provide information about the supplying Agency, Vendor, or Individual; or, in the

case of copy photography, a bibliographic citation or other description of the image source. In both cases, names, locations, and source identification numbers can be included.

Rights

Qualifiers: None
Description: Information about rights management; may include copyright and other intellectual property statements required for use.

Examples of VRA:[21]

(1) A record for a work of architecture

Record Type = **work**
Type = **architecture**
Type = **museums**
Title = **J. Paul Getty Museum**
Title.Variant = **Getty Museum**
Creator.Personal Name = **Meier, Richard**
Creator.Role = **architect**
Creator.Personal Name = **Olin, Laurie**
Creator.Role = **landscape architect**
Date.Creation = **1994-1997**
Location.Current Site = **Los Angeles, CA, US**
Culture = **American**
Subject = **art museums**
Subject = **research centers**
Relation.Part of = **Getty Center, Los Angeles, CA, US**

(2) A record for a slide

Record Type = **image**
Type = **slide**
Title = **entry level plan**
Creator.Personal Name = **John Cook**
Creator.Role = **photographer**
Date.Creation = **1998**
Location.Current Repository = **Cambridge, MA, US, Harvard Design School, Loeb Library, Visual Resources Department**
ID Number.Current Accession = **121401**
Subject = **entrances**
Subject = **floor plans**

Source = **Architecture, Dec., 1997, p.92**
Rights = **publisher**

ONIX (Online Information Exchange)

ONIX is an international metadata standard designed specifically to support electronic commerce applications. It was developed by publishers among the book industry trade groups in the United States and Europe and was designed to capture the images, cover blurbs, reviews, and other promotional information that can be used to enhance book sales. The main purpose of ONIX is to enable publishers to supply "rich" product information to Internet booksellers, and its major objective is to publicize and promote publishers' products by means of content-rich metadata.

Three bodies are involved in the development and maintenance of ONIX: Book Industry Communications (BIC) based in London, the Book Industry Study Group (BISG) based in New York, and EDItEUR (www.editeur.org/), an international steering group which is responsible for the maintenance of the ONIX standard. Version 2.1 of ONIX for Books was released in 2005.

An ONIX record contains bibliographic information as well as trade information. Libraries and information agencies have found the ONIX descriptions useful as starting points or as enhancements for resource descriptions for their own materials. Because much of this information is also included in library catalog records, ONIX records provide a source for ordinary cataloging information and for additional information, such as tables of contents, that is sometimes useful for enhancing cataloging records.

ONIX metadata can also be used as the beginning of a cataloging record to save money and effort in original cataloging. To facilitate this use, the Library of Congress initiated the Bibliographic Enrichment Advisory Team (BEAT) project to explore the feasibility of converting ONIX information for bibliographic use. The team created a crosswalk that maps elements between ONIX for Books and MARC 21;[22] it includes a mapping table in ONIX data element order and a record builder for creating MARC 21 records from ONIX data. Another approach to enriching cataloging records is to include hyperlinks in MARC records to ONIX information relating to the authors' or contributors' biographical information, and to the tables of contents and summaries contained in the ONIX records.

In the ONIX system, publishing data are organized in "ONIX messages" for transmission across networks and the Internet. The ONIX message contains data elements defined by XML tags, conforming to the ONIX DTD (Document Type Definition). A single ONIX message may contain data about multiple publications.

The ONIX DTD contains a set of over two hundred data elements in four groups:

1. The ONIX message header—containing information concerning the message being transmitted
2. Main Series Record (optional)—consisting of seven main elements with subelements, describing a series or "top level" of a series or subseries
3. Subseries Record—consisting of eight main elements with subelements, describing a subseries
4. Product Record—consisting of twenty-five main elements with subelements, describing an individual publication such as a book

The Product Record is the basic unit within an ONIX Product Information message. Table 4-2 lists the main elements in the Product Record.

Following is an example showing the part of an ONIX record that contains bibliographic and biographical information relating to a book:[23]

TABLE 4-2   ONIX Product Record Elements

PR.1.	Record Reference number, type, and source
PR.2.	Product Numbers
PR.3.	Product Form
PR.4.	Epublication Detail
PR.5.	Series
PR.6.	Set
PR.7.	Title
PR.8.	Authorship
PR.9.	Conference
PR.10.	Edition
PR.11.	Language
PR.12.	Extents and Other Content
PR.13.	Subject
PR.14.	Audience
PR.15.	Descriptions and Other Supporting Text
PR.16.	Links to Image/Audio/Video files
PR.17.	Prizes
PR.18.	Content Items
PR.19.	Publisher
PR.20.	Publishing Dates
PR.21.	Territorial Rights
PR.22.	Dimensions
PR.23.	Related Products
PR.24.	Supplier and Trade Data
PR.25.	Sales and Promotion Information

Source: Metadata Reference Guide: ONIX ONline Information eXchange, http://libraries
.mit.edu/guides/subjects/metadata/standards/onix.html (14 Nov. 2006).

Title	British English, A to Zed
Authorship	Schur, Norman W
BiographicalNote	A Harvard graduate in Latin and Italian literature, Norman Schur attended the University of Rome and the Sorbonne before returning to the United States to study law at Harvard and Columbia Law Schools. Now retired from legal practise, Mr Schur is a fluent speaker and writer of both British and American English
Edition	REV
EditionNumber	3
Language	eng
Extents and other content	493 [Pages]
Descriptions and other Text	BRITISH ENGLISH, A TO ZED is the thoroughly updated, revised, and expanded third edition of Norman Schur's highly acclaimed transatlantic dictionary for English speakers. First published as BRITISH SELF-TAUGHT and then as ENGLISH ENGLISH, this collection of Briticisms for Americans, and Americanisms for the British, is a scholarly yet witty lexicon, combining definitions with commentary on the most frequently used and some lesser known words and phrases. Highly readable, it's a snip of a book, and one that sorts out—through comments in American—the "Queen's English"—confounding as it may seem. Norman Schur is without doubt the outstanding authority on the similarities and differences between British and American English. BRITISH ENGLISH, A TO ZED attests not

only to his expertise, but also to his undiminished powers to inform, amuse and entertain.—Laurence Urdang, Editor, VERBATIM, The Language Quarterly, Spring 1988

Publisher	
Publisher Name	**Facts on File Inc**
PublicationDate	**1987**
Dimensions	
Measurement	**9.25 in**
Measurement	**6.25 in**
Measurement	**1.2 in**

NOTES

1. National Information Standards Organization (U.S.), *Understanding Metadata* (Bethesda, Md.: NISO Press, 2004), 1, www.niso.org/standards/resources/ UnderstandingMetadata.pdf (20 Feb. 2007).

2. Association for Library Collections & Technical Services, Committee on Cataloging, Description & Access, Task Force on Metadata, *Final Report* (CC:DA/ TF/Metadata/5), June 16, 2000, www.libraries.psu.edu/tas/jca/ccda/tf-meta6 .html (20 Feb. 2007).

3. Sheila S. Intner, Susan S. Lazinger, and Jean Weihs, *Metadata and Its Impact on Libraries* (Westport, Conn.: Libraries Unlimited, 2006), 6.

4. Priscilla Caplan, *Metadata Fundamentals for All Librarians* (Chicago: American Library Association, 2003), 3.

5. Arlene G. Taylor, *The Organization of Information*, 2nd ed. (Englewood, Colo.: Libraries Unlimited, 2004), 139.

6. National Information Standards Organization (U.S.), *Understanding Metadata*, 1.

7. National Information Standards Organization (U.S.), *Understanding Metadata*, 3.

8. *Dublin Core Metadata Element Set*, ANSI/NISO Z39.85-2007 (Bethesda, Md.: NISO Press, 2007). Available: www.niso.org/standards/resources/Z39-85 .pdf (6 June 2007).

9. *Information and Documentation—The Dublin Core Metadata Element Set*, ISO 15836: 2003 (E), www.niso.org/international/SC4/n515.pdf (20 Feb. 2007).

10. *Dublin Core Metadata Element Set.*

11. Diane Hillmann, "Using Dublin Core," 2005-11-07, http://dublincore .org/documents/2005/11/07/usageguide/ (20 Feb. 2007).

12. Dublin Core Metadata Initiative, "Using Dublin Core—Dublin Core Qualifiers," 07-11-2005, http://dublincore.org/documents/2005/11/07/usage guide/qualifiers.shtml (20 Feb. 2007)

13. MODS Metadata Object Description Schema, www.loc.gov/standards/ mods/ (20 Feb. 2007).

14. "TEI Headers," www.bibsys.no/elag97/foils/foil5.htm (20 Feb. 2007).

15. "Development of the Encoded Archival Description DTD," www.loc.gov/ead/eaddev.html (20 Feb. 2007).

16. National Information Standards Organization (U.S.), "Understanding Metadata," 6.

17. "Development of the Encoded Archival Description DTD," www.loc.gov/ead/eaddev.html (20 Feb. 2007).

18. Encoded Archival Description: Version 2002, www.loc.gov/ead/ (20 Feb. 2007).

19. "EAD Application Guidelines for Version 1.0: chapter 3. Creating Finding Aids in EAD: 3.6.1. EAD Header <eadheader>," www.loc.gov/ead/ag/agcre6.html#sec1ae (20 Feb. 2007).

20. Visual Resources Association Data Standards Committee, "VRA Core Categories, Version 3.0: a project of the Visual Resources Association Data Standards Committee," [last modified on 2/20/2002], www.vraweb.org/datastandards/vracore3.htm (2 Apr. 2007).

21. Visual Resources Association Data Standards Committee, "VRA Core Categories, Version 3.0."

22. Library of Congress, Network Development and MARC Standards Office, "ONIX to MARC 21 Mapping," 3 May 2005, www.loc.gov/marc/onix2marc.html (20 Feb. 2007).

23. Editeur, ONIX for Books: Product Information Message Product, Record Release 2.1, revision 02 15 July 2004, revised February 2005, p. 14–16, www.editeur.org (20 Feb. 2007).

PART THREE
ACCESS AND AUTHORITY CONTROL

STANDARDS AND TOOLS

Anglo-American Cataloguing Rules. 2nd ed., 2002 revision. Prepared under
the direction of the Joint Steering Committee for Revision of AACR,
a committee of the American Library Association, the Australian
Committee on Cataloguing, the British Library, the Canadian Committee on Cataloguing, Chartered Institute of Library and Information Professionals, the Library of Congress. Chicago: American
Library Association, 2002-.
Library of Congress Rule Interpretations. 2nd ed. Washington, D.C.: Cataloging Distribution Service, Library of Congress, 1989-. (Kept up to date
with quarterly updates and annual cumulations.)

RECOMMENDED READING

Auld, Larry. "Authority Control: An Eighty-Year Review." *Library Re-
sources & Technical Services* 26 (October/December 1982): 319–30.
Dunkin, Paul S. *Cataloging U.S.A.* Chicago: American Library Association,
1969, Chapters 3, 5–6.
Hagler, Ronald. *The Bibliographic Record and Information Technology.* 3rd ed.
Chicago: American Library Association, 1997. Chapter 3.
Maxwell, Robert L. *Maxwell's Guide to Authority Work.* Chicago: American
Library Association, 2002.
Perreault, Jean. "Authority Control, Old and New." *Libri* 32 (1982):
124–48.
Smiraglia, Richard. *The Nature of "A Work": Implications for Knowledge Or-
ganization.* Lanham, Md.: Scarecrow Press, 2001.
Talmacs, Kerrie. "Authority Control." 129–39 in *Technical Services Today
and Tomorrow.* 2nd ed. Englewood, Colo.: Libraries Unlimited.

Taylor, Arlene G. "Research and Theoretical Considerations in Authority Control." *Cataloging & Classification Quarterly* 9, no. 3 (1989): 29–57.

———. *Introduction to Cataloging and Classification.* 10th ed. Westport, Conn.: Libraries Unlimited, 2006. Chapters 6–8.

Tillett, Barbara B. "Authority Control: State of the Art and New Perspectives." *Cataloging & Classification Quarterly* 38, no. 3/4 (2004): 23–42.

———. "Considerations for Authority Control in the Online Environment." *Cataloging & Classification Quarterly* 9, no. 3 (1989): 1–13.

Wajenberg, Arnold S. "Authority Work, Authority Records, and Authority Files." 86–94 in *Technical Services Today and Tomorrow*, by Michael Gorman and Associates. Englewood, Colo.: Libraries Unlimited, 1990.

CHAPTER 5
ACCESS POINTS: NAME AND TITLE

INTRODUCTION

In information retrieval, the term *access point* refers to the mechanism that enables a user to discover a target document or other listed item. The access point can be a name, a term such as a keyword or combination of words, or an alphabetic, numeric, or alpha-numeric code. In other words, an access point is defined as a name, term, or code that can serve as a search key.

The access points discussed in this chapter are called descriptive access points and are based on information in bibliographic descriptions. Some access points are based on subjects, in which case they are called subject access points. These are discussed in later chapters.

Each metadata standard defines its own rules for determining both subject and descriptive access points. Although not all such rules follow the same pattern, most are founded on the same principles. The standard on which this chapter is based is Part II of *Anglo-American Cataloguing Rules, second edition, 2002 revision* (AACR2R)[1] because it contains the most elaborate and rigorous rules extant for determining bibliographic access points. It can therefore offer readers a thorough grounding in the principles and problems involved in bibliographic access.

There are four types of bibliographic access points in a catalog. They are often referred to as name and title access points.

1. Names of persons who perform certain functions:
   a. Authors
   b. Editors and compilers
   c. Translators
   d. Illustrators
   e. Other related persons (e.g., the addressee of a collection of letters; a person honored by a Festschrift)
2. Names of corporate bodies related to the item being described in a function other than solely as distributor or manufacturer
3. Titles
4. Names of series

Sometimes the access point or heading is in the form of a name-title combination, for example:

Johnson, Samuel, 1709-1784. Dictionary of the English language.

PRINCIPLES OF CHOICE OF ACCESS POINTS

Principles governing the choice of access points have evolved over the years. The milestones along this path are the writings of Charles Ammi Cutter (in 1876) and the Statement of Principles issued by the International Conference on Cataloguing Principles held in Paris in 1961.

Cutter's statements on the "objects" and "means"[2] of a catalog were cited in chapter 1. His first statement of "objects" embodies the principles relating to bibliographic access points. In order to "enable a person to find a book of which either a. the author [or] title is known," he wrote, the catalog must provide, for each work, an "Author entry with the necessary references" and a "Title entry or title reference." In other words, he prescribed access points under authors' names and under titles.

The Paris Statement of Principles, issued by the International Conference on Cataloguing Principles held in Paris in 1961, provides the foundation for AACR. It contains a statement relating to bibliographic access points:[3]

> 3. *Structure of the Catalogue*
> To discharge these functions [i.e., the location and collocation functions] the catalogue should contain
> 3.1   at least one entry for each book catalogued, and
> 3.2   more than one entry relating to any book, whenever this is necessary in the interests of the user or because of the characteristics of the book . . .
>
> 4. *Kinds of Entry*
> Entries may be of the following kinds: *main entries, added entries* and *references*.

CONCEPTS

Main Entry

It has long been the practice in library cataloging to designate one of the access points as the primary access point, or *main entry*. In most cases, the main entry is based on the author if such can be determined. Otherwise, the main entry is based on the title or on the corporate body responsible for the content.

There were two reasons for main entry practice. First, it has been and continues to be the most efficient way to manage lists that are maintained manually. In the days of handwritten or typed catalog cards, it was the convention to record all needed information on one card, called the *main entry* or *main entry card*, and to include only brief descriptions on other cards (called *added entries*) for the same item. For printed card sets, it was the record with the main entry heading that was duplicated; one card was filed as was, and added entry headings were typed on other cards as appropriate. Second, even for computer-stored lists where the main-entry/added-entry distinction would seem unnecessary, it remains helpful to have a standard convention for the way a bibliographic item should be cited. The main entry pattern (in other words, author/title) is the usual way of referring to a text, a fact that adds to its effectiveness as a citation standard.

The changing nature and format of information resources and the evolution of the library catalog from the card form to online have necessitated constant re-examination of the principles and rules, not only those relating to description but also regarding access points, particularly the notion of *main entry*.

With the introduction of the online catalog, the concept of main entry was challenged. It was questioned whether, in a multiple-entry file, particularly in an online catalog or database, the main entry had any real significance.[4] Some felt that since the user could retrieve the catalog record through any of the entries (or access points), they should have equal value.

Nonetheless, in AACR2R, the concept of main entry is still maintained as being valid at least under the following circumstances, when: a) making a single entry listing or b) making a single citation for a work (as required for entries for related works and for some subject entries). In addition, the concept of main entry is considered in assigning uniform titles and in promoting the standardization of bibliographic citations.[5]

Chapter 21 of AACR2R is devoted to the choice of access points and the designation of the main entry.

Authorship

As mentioned above, the rules for entry in AACR2R are largely based on the Paris Principles. The key statement regarding choice of main entry in the Paris statement is that the functions of the catalog "are most effectively discharged by an entry for each book under a heading derived from the author's name or from the title."[6] The author's name is, therefore, the primary choice as main entry. The author as main entry represents a long cataloging tradition. A brief examination of the concept of authorship may be helpful in understanding this tradition.

Definition of *Author*

Because the rules for the choice of entry are centered on the concept of authorship, it would seem that a clear, unambiguous definition of it would be needed for the effective application of the rules. Ironically, such a definition is difficult to achieve. The difficulty is attested by various attempts at defining the term *author* throughout the evolution of cataloging codes.[7]

Cutter: Author, in the narrower sense, is the person who writes a book; in a wider sense it may be applied to him who is the cause of the book's existence by putting together the writings of several authors (usually called the editor, more properly to be called the collector). Bodies of men (societies, cities, legislative bodies, countries) are to be considered the authors of their memoirs, transactions, journals, debates, reports, etc. (p. 14)

ALA (1908): 1. The writer of a book, as distinguished from translator, editor, etc. 2. In a broader sense, the maker of the book or the person or body immediately responsible for its existence. Thus, a person who collects and puts together the writings of several authors (compiler or editor) may be said to be the author of a collection. Corporate bodies may be considered the authors of publications issued in their name or by their authority. (p. xiii)

ALA Draft (1941): Same as ALA 1908 except that "corporate bodies" is replaced by "a corporate body."

ALA (1949): 1. The writer of a work, as distinguished from the translator, editor, etc. By extension, an artist, composer, photographer, cartographer, etc. 2. In the broader sense, the maker of the work or the person or body immediately responsible for its existence. Thus, a person who collects and puts together the writings of several authors (compiler or editor) may be said to be the author of a collection. A corporate body may be considered the author of publications issued in its name or by its authority. (p. 230)

AACR (1967): The person or corporate body chiefly responsible for the creation of the intellectual or artistic content of a work, e.g., the writer of a book, the compiler of a bibliography, the composer of a musical work, the artist who paints a picture, the photographer who takes a photograph. (p. 343)

AACR2 (1978, 1988, 1998, 2002): A personal author is the person chiefly responsible for the creation of the intellectual or artistic content of a work. (p. 21–26)

Personal Authorship

The concept of authorship in cataloging is rooted in the tradi
arly practice in the Western world. In the Orient, particularly in ancient
times, the title has been the main element of bibliographic identification;
the Western tradition, probably derived from the classical Greco-Roman
practice, has emphasized the author as the chief element of identification
of works.[8] Classical works, for instance, have generally been identified by
their authors—Homer, Plato, Herodotus, etc. On the other hand, the concept of authorship was not stressed in the Germanic tradition. Many of
the Germanic sagas, Anglo-Saxon poems, and early epics and tales are
anonymous and constitute the bulk of what is known as "anonymous
classics."

The concept of authorship remained somewhat vague and diffuse in
the Middle Ages. However, since the Renaissance, the practice of identifying works by their authors has prevailed in Western scholarship. This
concept of authorship was no doubt strengthened by the invention of
printing, which led to an author's rights in literary property. Now, even
in Asia, most modern works are identified by their authors, perhaps as a
result of the influence of Western practice.

The practice of assigning main entry under the author in library catalogs can be thought of as a reflection of Western scholarly tradition.

Corporate Authorship and Responsibility

Until the middle of the nineteenth century, the concept of authorship was
thought to apply mainly to personal authors. Corporate authorship as an
element of bibliographic identification (i.e., considering a corporate body
the author of a work), came later. Early bibliographies and catalogs did
not provide for entries under corporate bodies, nor did Germanic cataloging practice before the Germanic cataloging community began following
the Paris Principles. In the Anglo-American cataloging tradition, the recognition of corporate authorship began in the nineteenth century. The
rules for the British Museum Catalogue (1841) were the first major set of
rules to prescribe corporate author entries.[9]

As an entry element, corporate "authors" have always presented
problems. Lubetzky's attack on the "corporate complex"[10] resulted in a
thorough examination of the problem before the Paris Conference. Although the Paris Principles include specific guidelines relating to corporate authorship and corporate main entry, criticisms and discussions
following the publication of AACR (1967) and other cataloging codes
based on the Paris Principles demonstrated that the rules for works of
corporate authorship were open to diverse interpretations and were
therefore unsatisfactory. This state of confusion prompted Eva Verona's

study on corporate headings in the catalogs, national bibliographies, and cataloging codes of many countries. Her study revealed the chaotic state of corporate authorship at the time: "Among the great number of cataloguing codes recognizing corporate authorship, it is scarcely possible to find even two which interpret the concept in the same way."[11] One major problem was the lack of even a general agreement among different codes as to the definition of corporate authorship. As a result, efforts were made toward international consensus on the definition and treatment of corporate authorship.

Beginning with AACR2 (1978), a shift in the concept of corporate authorship took place. The role of corporate bodies as authors was redefined, and the code mandated that the term "corporate authorship" no longer be used. Instead, the rules in question are phrased in terms of works "emanating from" one or more corporate bodies, i.e., works issued by, caused to be issued by, or originating with, one or more corporate bodies.[12] Although AACR2R rules still provide for entering certain works under a corporate body, the number of instances in which corporate bodies are assigned as main entries has been greatly reduced. This shift in the concept of corporate authorship brought the Anglo-American cataloging rules closer than their predecessors to the Paris Principles—which also avoided the use of the term corporate authorship and replaced it with the concept of "corporate responsibility."

CHOICE OF MAIN ENTRY

For works written by one person, the choice of main entry presents little problem. However, when more than one person is responsible for the existence of the work, particularly if these persons perform different functions, the choice is less obvious. Throughout the evolution of the definition of the term author, an attempt has been made to exclude certain contributors to the work, such as translators, textual editors, illustrators, and publishers. On the other hand, corporate bodies are included, and until 1975, compilers and editorial directors of works were also given the status of author. In 1975, Rules 4 and 5 in AACR (1967) were revised to exclude compilers of collections and editorial directors in the choice of main entry. This principle is continued in AACR2 (1978, 1988, 1998, 2002).

Types of Main Entry

The main entry of a work is always either a personal name entry, a corporate name entry, or a title entry. Most book-form materials have main entry under personal authors, while many government publications are entered under corporate bodies. Serial publications and many nonprint and electronic resources usually have title main entries.

Conditions of Authorship

The choice of main entry is based on the condition of authorship of each work. The rules for the choice of entry in AACR2R are organized according to these conditions of authorship:

> Works for which a single person or corporate body is responsible
> Works of unknown or uncertain authorship or by unnamed groups
> Works of shared responsibility (works resulting from collaboration between two or more persons or corporate bodies performing the same kind of activity in the creation of the content of an item)
> Collections and works produced under editorial direction
> Works of mixed responsibility (i.e., previously existing works that have been modified; or, collaborations between two or more persons or corporate bodies performing different kinds of activities, for example, adapting or illustrating a work written by another person)

The following is a summary of the rules for the choice of descriptive access points. In the MARC 21 format, the 1XX fields are designated for main entry under personal authors, corporate bodies, and uniform titles. When the main entry is under the title proper, the indicator 0 in the first position in the 245 field is assigned.

Main Entry under Personal Author [MARC field 100]

1. Single personal authorship

For works of single personal authorship, main entry is under the author (rule 21.4A):

> Islands in the stream / Ernest Hemingway
> (main entry under the heading for Hemingway)

> A Benjamin Britten discography / compiled by Charles H. Parsons
> (main entry under the heading for Parsons)

> The complete silky terrier / Peggy Smith
> (main entry under the heading for Smith)

> Job evaluation [transparency] / Herbert H. Oestreich
> (main entry under the heading for Oestreich)

Carmen [sound recording] / George Bizet
(main entry under the heading for Bizet)

2. Shared responsibility

For works of shared responsibility, i.e., works produced by the collaboration of two or more persons who performed the same kind of activity
such as writing, adapting, or performing, main entry is under (a) principal author if indicated (rule 21.6B):

William S. Burroughs : a reference guide / Michael B. Goodman
    with Lemuel B. Coley
(main entry under heading for Goodman; added entry under the
    heading for Coley)

Beyond ambition : how driven managers can lead better and live
    better / Robert E. Kaplan with Wilfred H. Drath and Joan R.
    Kofodimos
(main entry under heading for Kaplan; added entries under the
    headings for Drath and Kofodimos)

Single market Europe : opportunities and challenges for
    business / Spyros G. Makridakis and associates
(main entry under the heading for Makridakis)

Or (b) author named first if responsibility is shared between two or three
persons and no principal author is indicated (rule 21.6C):

The making of an economist / Arjo Klamer and David Colander
(main entry under the heading for Klamer; added entry under
    the heading for Colander)

The intelligent design of computer-assisted instruction / Richard
    Venezky, Luis Osin
(main entry under the heading for Venezky; added entry under
    the heading for Osin)

Taliesin West [slide] / Julius Shulman & Jeffrey Cook
(main entry under the heading for Shulman; added entry under
    the heading for Cook)

Officially supported export credits : developments and
    prospects / G.G. Johnson, Matthew Fisher, and Elliot Harris
(main entry under the heading for Johnson; added entries under
    the headings for Fisher and Harris)

3. Mixed responsibility

For works of mixed responsibility, i.e., one to which different persons make intellectual or artistic contributions by performing different kinds of activity, including previously existing works that have been modified (e.g., adaptations, revisions, translations) and new works in which different persons or bodies performing different kinds of activity (e.g., collaborative work by a writer and an artist, reports of interviews), main entry is under:

(a) adapter for a paraphrase, rewriting, adaptation for children, or version in a different literary form (e.g., novelization, dramatization) (rule 21.10):

> Gone with the wind, the screenplay / Sidney Howard ; based on the novel by Margaret Mitchell
> (main entry under the heading for Howard; added entry (name-title) under the heading for Mitchell)

(b) writer of the text for a work that consists of a text for which an artist has provided illustrations (rule 21.11A):

> Bungalow fungalo / by Pegi Deitz Shea ; illustrated by Elizabeth Sayles
> (main entry under the heading for Shea; added entry under the heading for Sayles)

(c) artist for separately published illustrations (rule 21.11B):

> Blake's Grave : a prophetic book, being William Blake's illustrations for Robert Blair's The grave
> (main entry under the heading for Blake; added entry (name-title) under the heading for Blair)

(d) original author of an edition that has been revised, enlarged, updated, etc., by another person if the original author is still considered responsible for the work (rule 21.12A):

> Commonsense cataloging / Esther J. Piercy. — 2nd ed. / revised by Marian Sanner
> (main entry under the heading for Piercy; added entry under the heading for Sanner)

> Introduction to cataloging and classification. — Bohden S. Wynar. — 8th ed. by Arlene G. Taylor.
> (main entry under the heading for Wynar; added name-title entry under the heading for Taylor)

> Dewey decimal classification, 20th edition : a study manual / Jeanne Osborn ; revised and edited by John Phillip Comaromi

(main entry under the heading for Osborn; added entry under the heading for Comaromi and name-title added entry under the uniform title for Dewey decimal classification and relative index)

(e) reviser of an edition if the original author is no longer considered to be responsible for the work (rule 21.12B):

> Commonsense cataloging : a cataloger's manual / Rosalind E. Miller & Jane C. Terwillegar. — 4th ed.
> (main entry under the heading for Miller; added entry under the heading for Terwillegar)

> Wynar's introduction to cataloging and classification. — Rev. 9th ed. / by Arlene G. Taylor.
> (main entry under the heading for Taylor; added entry (name-title) under the uniform title heading for Wynar)

(f) commentator of a work consisting of a text and a commentary by a different person, if the latter is emphasized (rule 21.13B):

> Pylon / annotated by Susie Paul Johnson
> (contains also the text of Faulkner's Pylon)
> (main entry under the heading for Johnson; added entry (name-title) under the name-title heading for Pylon)

> The Theaetetus of Plato / Myles Burnyeat ; with a translation of Plato's Theaetetus by M.J. Levett, revised by Myles Burnyeat
> (main entry under the heading for Burnyeat; added entry (name-title) under the name-title heading for Theaetetus)

(g) author of the text of a work consisting of a text and a commentary by a different person, if the text is emphasized (rule 21.13C):

> A midsummer night's dream / William Shakespeare ; fully annotated, with an introduction, by Burton Raffel ; with an essay by Harold Bloom
> (main entry under the heading for Shakespeare; added entry under the heading for Raffel)

> The essential Wyndham Lewis : an introduction to his work / edited by Julian Symons
> (main entry under the heading for Lewis; added entry under the heading for Symons)

(h) original author of a translation (rule 21.14A):

> The distant friend / Claude Roy ; translated by Hugh Harter

(main entry under the heading for Roy)

(i) biographer-critic of a work by a writer accompanied by (or interwoven with) biographical or critical material, if the latter is emphasized (rule 21.15A):

> The life and letters of Frances Baroness Bunsen [microform] / by Augustus J.C. Hare
> (main entry under the heading for Hare; added entry under the heading for Bunsen)

(j) writer of a work accompanied by, or interwoven with, biographical or critical material by another person who is presented as editor, compiler, etc. (rule 21.15B):

> The China years : the life and letters of the Rev. & Mrs. Clifford V. Cook, China missionaries, 1925-52 / edited by Raymond Cook.
> (main entry under the heading for Clifford V. Cook; added entry under the heading for Raymond Cook)

Main Entry under Corporate Body [MARC fields 110 and 111

Main entry under a corporate body, defined as "an organization or group of persons that is identified by a particular name and that acts, or may act, as an entity,"[13] is restricted to those works that emanate from (i.e., are issued by or have been caused to be issued by or have originated with) a corporate body and fall into one or more of the following categories (rule 21.1B2):

1. Works of an administrative nature dealing with the corporate body itself or its internal policies, procedures, and/or operations, its finances, its officers and/or staff, or its resources (e.g., catalogues, inventories, membership directories):

    > Annual report / Maryland Environmental Service
    > (main entry under the heading for the Service)

    > Membership directory / Naval Reserve Association
    > (main entry under the heading for the Association)

2. Some legal, governmental, and religious works of the following types: laws (rule 21.31); decrees of the chief executive that have the force of law (rule 21.31); administrative regulations (rule 21.32); constitutions (rule 21.33); court rules (rule 21.34); treaties, etc. (rule

21.35); court decisions (rule 21.36); legislative hearings; religious laws (e.g., canon law); liturgical works (rule 21.39):

Massachusetts laws relating to municipal finance and taxation
(main entry under the heading for Massachusetts)

The Arizona Constitution : study guide
(main entry under the heading for Arizona)

3. Works that record the collective thought of the body (e.g., reports of commissions, committees, etc.; official statements of position on external policies):

Research strategies for the U.S. global change research program /
Committee on Global Change (U.S. National Committee for
the IGBP) of the Commission on Geosciences, Environment,
and Resources, National Research Council
(main entry under the heading for the Committee)

Report of the Committee on Fast Tracking East African
Federation, 26th November, 2004
(main entry under the heading for the Committee)

4. Works that report the collective activity of a conference (e.g., proceedings, collective papers), of an expedition (e.g., results of exploration, investigation), or of an event (e.g., an exhibition, fair, festival) falling within the definition of a corporate body (see 21.1B1), provided that the conference, expedition, or event is named in the item being cataloged:

Web technologies research and development [electronic
resource] : APWeb 2005 : 7th Asia-Pacific Web Conference,
Shanghai, China, March 29—April 1, 2005 : proceedings /
Yanchun Zhang . . . [et al.] (eds.)
(main entry under the heading for the conference; added entry
under the heading for Zhang)

5. Sound recordings, films, videorecordings, written records, etc. of performances resulting from the collective activity of a performing group as a whole where the responsibility of the group goes beyond that of mere performance, execution, etc. (for corporate bodies that function solely as performers on sound recordings, see rule 21.23):

Some kind of monster [sound recording] / Metallica
(main entry under the heading for the musical group Metallica)

Stand back [sound recording] : the anthology / the Allman
Brothers Band
(main entry under the heading for the musical group Allman
Brothers Band)

6. Cartographic materials emanating from a corporate body other
than a body merely responsible for their publication or distribution:

Atlas of the world / [prepared by National Geographic Maps for
the Book Division]
(main entry under the heading for National Geographic Maps)

7. Official communications from heads of state, heads of government, heads of international bodies, popes, patriarchs, bishops, etc.
(rule 21.4D1):

Encyclical letter, Ecclesia de Eucharistia, of his Holiness Pope
John Paul II : to the bishops, priests and deacons, men and
women in the consecrated life and all the lay faithful on the
Eucharist in its relationship to the Church / [John Paul II]
(main entry under the corporate heading for Pope John Paul II)

Iowa financial summary
(main entry under the corporate heading for the governor of
Iowa)

A report consistent with the Authorization for Use of Military
Force Against Iraq Resolution : communication from the
President of the United States transmitting a report including
matters relating to post-liberation Iraq as consistent with the
Authorization for Use of Military Force Against Iraq
Resolution of 2002 (Public Law 107-243)
(main entry under the corporate heading for President George W.
Bush; added entry under his personal heading)

Main Entry under Title [MARC field 245 with 0 as first indicator and field 130]

By way of elimination, works that do not fall into the categories of works
that require main entry under a person or a corporate body are entered
under the title (rule 21.1C). In other words, a work is entered under the
title when:

1. The personal authorship is unknown, uncertain, diffuse (i.e., authorship being shared among four or more persons without indi-

cation of principal responsibility), or cannot be determined, and the work does not emanate from a corporate body:

> Millionaire's shortbread / poems by Mary-Jane Duffy . . . [et al.] ;
> collages by Brendan O'Brien ; afterword by Gregory O'Brien
> (main entry under title; added entry under the heading for Duffy)

> American wits [sound recording]
> (main entry under title)

> Das Nibelungenlied = Song of the Nibelungs / translated from
> the Middle High German by Burton Raffel ; foreword by
> Michael Dirda ; introduction by Edward R. Haymes
> (main entry under the uniform title Nibelungenlied; added entry
> under the heading for Raffel)

2. It is a collection or a work produced under editorial direction that has a collective title:

> The Oxford anthology of English poetry / chosen and edited by
> John Wain
> (main entry under title; added entry under the heading for Wain)

> Critical essays on Canadian literature / editor, K. Balachandran
> (main entry under title; added entry under the heading for
> Balachandran)

> Encyclopedia Latina : history, culture, and society in the United
> States / Ilan Stavans, editor in chief ; Harold Augenbraum,
> associate editor
> (main entry under title; added entries under the headings for
> Stavans and Augenbraum)

3. It emanates from a corporate body but does not fall into any of the categories listed under rule 21.1B2 and is not of personal authorship:

> Community development : journal of the Community
> Development Society
> (main entry under title; added entry under the heading for the
> Society)

> Major savings and reforms in the President's 2006 budget /
> Executive Office of the President, Office of Management and
> Budget
> (main entry under title; added entries under the headings for the
> Executive Office of the President and the Office of
> Management and Budget)

Community polices and mountain areas : proceeding.
conference organised by the European Commission, Bru.
17 and 18 October 2002
(main entry under title; added entries under the headings for the
Commission)

4. It is accepted as sacred scripture by a religious group:

The Old Testament
(main entry under the uniform title for the Bible)

The principal Upanishads
(main entry under the uniform title for the Upanishads)

CHANGES IN TITLE PROPER (RULE 21.2)

Monographs in One Physical Part

If the title proper of a monograph in one physical part changes between
one edition and another, a separate main entry is made for each edition.

Monographs in More Than One Physical Part

If the title proper of a monograph in more than one physical part, e.g., a
multi-volume set, changes between parts, the title proper of the first part
is given as the title of the whole monograph. If another title proper appearing on later parts predominates, the later title proper is used as the
title proper for the whole monograph.

Serials

If the title proper of a serial changes between one volume or issue and
another, a separate main entry is made for each title in a separate record.

Air repair. — Vol. 1, no. 1 (July 1951)-v. 4, no. 4 (Feb. 1955)
(Continued by: Journal of the Air Pollution Control
Association)

Journal of the Air Pollution Control Association. — Vol. 5, no. 1
(May 1955)-v. 36, no. 12 (Dec. 1986)
(Continues: Air repair)
(Absorbed: APCA news Jan. 1960)
(Continued by: JAPCA)

JAPCA. — Vol. 37, no. 1 (Jan. 1987)-v. 39, no. 12 (Dec. 1989)

(Continues: Journal of the Air Pollution Control Association)
(Continued by: Journal of the Air & Waste Management
Association)

Journal of the Air & Waste Management Association. — Vol. 40,
no. 1 (Jan. 1990)-v. 42, no. 12 (Dec. 1992)
(Continues: JAPCA)
(Continued by: Air & Waste)

Air & waste : journal of the Air & Waste Management
Association. — Vol. 43, no. 1 (Jan. 1993)-v. 44, no. 12 (Dec.
1994)
(Continues: Journal of the Air & Waste Management
Association)
(Continued by: Journal of the Air & Waste Management
Association (1995))

Journal of the Air & Waste Management Association (1995). —
Vol. 45, no. 1 (Jan. 1995)-
(Continues: Air & waste)

Integrating Resources

If the title proper of an integrating resource changes, the record is revised
to replace the title proper with the new title and the description is revised
to reflect the new information. The earlier title is given in a note.

Heritage gateway to Colorado's digitization projects [electronic
resource]
(note: Former title: Colorado Digitization Project)

CHANGES OF PERSONS OR BODIES RESPONSIBLE FOR A WORK (RULE 21.3)

Monographs

In the case of a change in responsibility between the parts of a multipart
monograph, main entry is made under the person or corporate body that
has predominant responsibility. If none is predominant, main entry is
made under the heading appropriate to the first part. In the latter case,
if more than three persons or corporate bodies are responsible for the
completed work, main entry is made under the title.

Serials

A new record with a new main entry is created for a serial even if the title
proper remains the same and the numbering continues if (1) the heading

for a corporate body under which a serial is entered changes, (2) the main entry for a serial is under a personal or corporate heading and the person or corporate body is no longer responsible for the serial, or (3) the main entry for a serial is under the uniform title, which includes a corporate heading as a qualifier, and the corporate heading changes or the corporate body is no longer responsible for the serial.

Integrating Resources

When similar situations occur to an integrating resource, the existing record is revised to reflect the latest information. The earlier or former name is given in a note if considered important.

ADDED ENTRIES (RULES 21.29–21.30)

In addition to the main entry heading, added entries are assigned to cataloging records in order to provide additional access points through names and titles that are bibliographically significant. Added entries are generally made for potential access points not chosen as the main entry. They appear in the form of personal name headings, corporate name headings, titles, series, and name-title headings. A name-title heading consists of the name heading of a person or corporate body and the title of an item, e.g., **Faulkner, William, 1897-1962. Pylon.**

Added Entries under Personal Names [MARC field 700]

These are made for the following:

1. Collaborators (up to three) (If there are four or more collaborators, added entry is made for the first named only)
2. Writers
3. Editors and compilers (rarely made for a serial publication)
4. Translators (made in certain cases only)
5. Illustrators (made in certain cases only)
6. Other related persons. These are persons related to the work in a way other than being responsible for the creation of the content of the work (e.g., the addressee of a collection of letters, a person honored by a Festschrift)

Added Entries under Corporate Names [MARC fields 710 and 711]

An added entry is made under a corporate body that is prominently named in the work unless it functions solely as distributor or manufacturer. If four or more corporate bodies are involved in a particular work, an added entry is made under the first named only.

Added Entries under Titles [MARC field 245 with 1 as first indicator and MARC fields 730 and 740]

An added entry is made under the title proper if: (1) it has not been used as the main entry or (2) the title added entry is so similar as to duplicate the main entry heading or a reference to the main entry heading. An added entry is also made for any other title (cover title, caption title, running title, etc.) that differs significantly from the title proper.

Added Entries under Series [MARC fields 440 and 8XX]

An added entry is made under the heading for a series to which the item belongs except in the following cases:

1. if the items in the series are related to one another only by common physical characteristics
2. if the items in the series have been numbered primarily for stock control or to benefit from lower postage rates.

Analytical Added Entries

This is an added entry made for a work contained within the work being cataloged. The heading for the added entry is determined by the way the work contained would be entered, except that a name-title heading is used in cases requiring entry under a person or a corporate body.

Recording of Added Entries

In the MARC record, added entries are denoted by indicators in the 2XX fields and by field tags 440, 7XX, and 8XX.

NOTES

1. *Anglo-American Cataloguing Rules*, 2nd ed., 2002 revision, prepared under the direction of the Joint Steering Committee for Revision of AACR, a committee of the American Library Association, the Australian Committee on Cataloguing, the British Library, the Canadian Committee on Cataloguing, Chartered Institute of Library and Information Professionals, the Library of Congress (Chicago: American Library Association, 2002).

2. Charles Ammi Cutter, *Rules for a Dictionary Catalog*, 4th ed., rewritten

(Washington, D.C.: Government Printing Office, 1904; republished, London: The Library Association, 1953), 12.

3. International Conference on Cataloguing Principles, Paris, 1961, *Report of International Conference on Cataloguing Principles*, A. H. Chaplin and Dorothy Anderson, eds. (London: Organizing Committee of ICCP, 1963), 92.

4. For an examination of this issue, see M. Nabil Hamdy, *The Concept of Main Entry as Represented in the Anglo-American Cataloging Rules: A Critical Appraisal with Some Suggestions: Author Main Entry vs. Title Main Entry* (Littleton, Colo.: Libraries Unlimited, 1973).

5. *Anglo-American Cataloguing Rules*, 2nd ed., 2.

6. International Conference on Cataloguing Principles, Paris, 1961, *Report*, 92.

7. Paul S. Dunkin, *Cataloging USA* (Chicago: American Library Association, 1969), 24–26; cf. also Julia Pettee, "The Development of Authorship Entry and the Formulation of Authorship Rules as Found in the Anglo-American Code," *Library Quarterly* 6 (July 1936): 270–90; also in *Foundations of Cataloging: A Sourcebook*, ed. by Michael Carpenter and Elaine Svenonius (Littleton, Colo.: Libraries Unlimited, 1985), 75–89.

8. Dunkin, 23–24.

9. Ake I. Koel, "Can the Problems of Corporate Authorship Be Solved?" *Library Resources & Technical Services* 18 (Fall 1974): 349.

10. Seymour Lubetzky, *Cataloging Rules and Principles: A Critique of the A.L.A. Rules for Entry and a Proposed Design for Their Revision* (Washington, D.C.: Library of Congress, 1953), 16–35.

11. Eva Verona, *Corporate Headings: Their Use in Library Catalogues and National Bibliographies: A Comparative and Critical Study* (London: IFLA Committee on Cataloguing, 1975), 8–9.

12. *Anglo-American Cataloguing Rules*, 2nd ed., 288.

13. "Glossary," *Anglo-American Cataloguing Rules* (2002), appendix D-2.

CHAPTER 6
AUTHORITY CONTROL: FORMS
OF NAME HEADINGS AND
UNIFORM TITLES

FORMS OF ACCESS POINTS

Charles Ammi Cutter's "objects" and "means" of a catalog were cited in chapter 1. His second statement of "objects" embodies the principles, "To show what the library has . . . by a given author, on a given subject, [or] in a given kind of literature," and imposes the need to collocate all works by a given author or on a given subject under the same access point. The "means" to achieve that, according to Cutter, is to provide, for each author, title, and subject, a uniform entry with the necessary references.[1] When a particular author, title, or subject can be represented by different names or expressions, one is chosen as *the* entry, or authorized access point, under which all works by an author, all variant titles of a work, or all representations of a particular subject are gathered. The mechanism for achieving this gathering function is *authority control*.

PRINCIPLES OF AUTHORITY CONTROL

Underlying authority control is a set of principles, some of which apply to authority control in general, while others apply to name authority control or subject authority control specifically. Principles applying to name authority control are discussed below.

Principle of Uniform Headings

One of the functions of the catalog, as stated in both Cutter's rules and the Paris Principles,[2] is to ascertain which works by a particular author or on a specific subject are in the library. This is achieved by gathering all works by a particular author or on the same subject under a *uniform heading*, regardless of how many names or how many forms of a name an author has used or in how many ways a subject can be represented. This principle, when implemented in a catalog or other indexing medium, improves recall (i.e., the ratio of retrieved relevant items to all relevant items from a catalog) because no matter how many different names or different forms of a name have appeared in an author's works or in how many ways a subject can be described, all can be retrieved through the authorized heading established for the author or subject. The principle, however, has not always been rigidly applied. See the discussion below under "Choice of name."

In the case of personal name headings, the principle of uniform heading is observed in the *Anglo-American Cataloguing Rules* (AACR2R) with few exceptions. However, the principle is somewhat modified in the case of headings for corporate bodies, many of which undergo frequent name changes. How the names of corporate bodies are handled is discussed later in this chapter.

This principle also applies to title entries. When a work has appeared under various titles, one is chosen as the *uniform title*. Recent developments in revising cataloging rules have focused on the principles developed in the document *Functional Requirements for Bibliographic Records*[3] and discussed in chapter 2, specifically with regard to the use of the uniform title to relate the multiple facets of a "work" in terms of work, expression, manifestation, and item.

Uniform titles are discussed later in this chapter.

Principle of Unique Headings

The corollary of the principle of uniform heading (i.e., one heading for each person, corporate body, place, title, or subject) is that of *unique heading*. The principle of unique heading requires that each heading represent only one person, corporate body, place, title, or subject. For example, if two or more authors have the same name, the heading used for each is made unique by attaching additional elements: the most common modification is the addition of birth and death dates to author headings and of qualifiers to other entities. The reason for using unique headings is to improve precision (i.e., the ratio of retrieved relevant items to all retrieved items). When the unique heading is used as the access point, only works by the particular author represented by that heading will be retrieved, excluding works by other authors who happen to have the same name. Similarly, in subject representation, if a word or phrase has multiple meanings, each subject heading can represent one meaning only and the other meanings are expressed by different words or phrases.

The Authority Record

To ensure consistency, an authority record is created for each authorized heading for a proper name or a subject. An authority record is made when a heading is established, i.e., authorized for use as a main entry, an added entry, or subject entry, for the first time.

An authority record contains essentially the following elements:

1. The established heading for a person, a corporate body, a place, a uniform title (i.e., the standardized title for a work that has appeared under different titles; for a fuller explanation of uniform titles see the later discussion in this chapter), or a subject;
2. Cross references from other names, titles, or terms not used for the heading, and to and from related headings; and
3. The sources used in establishing the heading.

Until a change of the heading is necessitated by changes in the name or title, this established heading is used in cataloging records whenever the heading is required as an access point, whether as a main entry, an added entry, or a subject entry.

The following sections in this chapter focus on authority control for proper names, including those for persons, corporate bodies, and titles of works. Further discussion on subject authority control is found in chapter 7.

NAME AUTHORITY CONTROL

Previously, most libraries and bibliographic services maintained their own *name authority file* consisting of *name authority records* relating to the bibliographic records in the catalog. Currently the Library of Congress maintains a central authority file (http://authorities.loc.gov) for its own records plus those contributed by other libraries. The records are then shared by all libraries that need them.

Chapter 1 contains an example of a name authority record with MARC tags. Further examples of authority records are included in appendix B.

The process of creating name authority records and maintaining the name authority file is called *name authority control*. Name authority control has three main purposes: (a) to ensure that all works written by a particular author or related to the same corporate body are retrievable with the same access point (or under the same heading); (b) to ensure that a particular access point leads to works by a particular author or related to a particular corporate body only; and (c) to save the time and effort of having to establish the heading each time a work by the same author or related to the same corporate body is cataloged.

Frequently, persons and corporate bodies change their names or use different forms of their names. With a few exceptions, the rules require that in such cases, the new name or form of name be used as the authorized heading with *see* references from the old. As a result, the name authority record must be revised and the headings in all previously prepared bibliographic or metadata records affected by the change should be updated accordingly. This is an important—and costly—part of catalog and database maintenance.

In many online cataloging systems, the name authority file is linked to the bibliographic file so that when a heading has been updated in the authority record, the revised heading automatically replaces the obsolete heading or headings in all bibliographic records affected by the changed heading. Furthermore, appropriate cross references are automatically either generated or revised and obsolete references deleted.

HEADINGS FOR PERSONS

In the cataloging process, once a name has been chosen as an access point, the next step is to decide in what form this name is to appear in the bibliographic record. Chapters 22 through 25 of AACR2R are devoted to the forms of headings.

The determination of the form a personal name heading should take is normally based on information obtained from the chief sources of information in works by that person issued in his or her language. If the author has written other works, it is important to take into consideration the information they contain. If most of the author's works are not accessible, reference sources, particularly bibliographic and biographical sources, will have to be consulted. For persons who work in a nonverbal context (as do painters and performers) or who are not known primarily as authors, the headings are determined from reference sources issued in their languages. The headings for persons not primarily known as authors often need to be established for use as subject access points for works about them. Such headings are discussed under Biography in chapters 8 and 10.

There are three basic aspects in determining the uniform heading for a person: (1) choice of name; (2) choice of form; and, (3) choice of entry element. After these choices are made, further considerations include whether any other elements, such as titles of nobility and dates, should be added to the heading.

Choice of Name (rule 22.2)

A large number of people have used more than one name in their lifetimes. In many cases, an author writes under a name that is different from his or her real name or uses more than one name in his or her writings. In other cases, a person changes his or her name for one or another reason. If the catalog is to show what works by a particular author are in the library, all his or her works must be listed under the same name. Therefore, the first question that must be answered is: Which name should be used?

However, there is a further issue here. Is a person who writes necessarily only one author? If a person writes under two names for different purposes, could he or she not be considered two authors? A scientist who uses his or her real name in scientific works may choose to use a pseudonym in writing science fiction. It is not unreasonable to treat these works as if written by two different authors. In this case, this person's works may be listed under two different name headings in the catalog. The basic question is, then, can a person be more than one author? Over the years, the answer has sometimes been no and sometimes been yes, at least in practice if not officially sanctioned by cataloging rules.

In analyzing this problem in 1969, Paul S. Dunkin pointed out two basic approaches. He called the first the *rigid approach*. The person's real name is chosen as the heading, regardless of what other names or how many names the person has used. Dunkin called the second the *relaxed approach*. In this case, the heading is the author's name as it appears in the work being cataloged. If an author has used several names, his or her works would then be listed under several headings. In other words, "A uniform heading is not a uniform heading for an individual person. . . . Instead, it is the uniform heading for an author. But a person may be as many authors as he (or she or it) wishes."[4]

Before 1967, the ALA codes followed the first approach. As a result, all works by Lewis Carroll (pseudonym) were listed under the heading "Dodgson, Charles Lutwidge" (real name) and those by Novalis (pseudonym) appeared in the catalog under "Hardenberg, Friedrich, Freiherr von" (real name).

AACR (1967), based on the Paris Principles, adhered to neither approach strictly. It may be viewed as a modified rigid approach. Each person was allowed only one personal name heading, regardless of how many names the person may have used in his or her works. However, this name heading did not have to be the person's real name. The criterion for the choice of name rested on the principle of the most commonly known name, as evidenced in his or her works. The Paris Principles state that "the *uniform heading* should be the name by which the author is most frequently identified in editions of his works, in the fullest form commonly appearing there."[5]

AACR2 (1978) followed the same principle of choosing the predominant name as the heading. However, in the case of an author having used different pseudonyms without any one of them being predominant, the rules allowed as an option the use of the name appearing in each item as the heading for that item. As a result, when there is no predominant name, a person may have had more than one heading. This reflected the more "relaxed approach" mentioned by Dunkin and represented a softening of the principle of uniform heading.

In other words, in previous cataloging codes, the term author was more or less equated with the term "person." Each person was recognized as capable of being one author only. An author who deliberately established different identities in writing different kinds of works, such as fiction and scientific or political works, was represented by one uniform heading. AACR2 (1978) did, however, allow multiple headings for the same person in limited cases.

In 1988, as reflected in AACR2R, there was a major change: the AACR2R rules fully recognize that the same person may have "separate bibliographic identities" (rule 22.2B2) for different types of works. These separate bibliographic identities are then treated as different authors represented by different headings but connected with cross references. As a result, works for children written by Charles Lutwidge Dodgson are found under the heading for Lewis Carroll, and his scientific works are listed under Dodgson.

Furthermore, under AACR2R, multiple headings are established for contemporary authors who use one or more pseudonyms or use their real names and one or more pseudonyms but do not necessarily have separate bibliographic identities. For example, the twentieth century American novelist Stephen King wrote under his real name and pseudonyms Richard Bachman and Eleanor Druse. All three names are established as valid headings, and each is used as the main entry for works published under the particular name.

On the other hand, the principle of uniform headings is observed for all authors who are not contemporary and have not established separate bibliographic identities. For each author, the uniform heading is based on the name that is most commonly known.

For an author (other than one using a pseudonym or pseudonyms) who has changed his or her name, the heading is based on the latest name, unless an earlier name is better known.

Choice of Form of Name (rule 22.3)

Some names may appear in more than one form, varying in regard to fullness, language, or spelling. This is sometimes true even in an author's own works, and also in how the name appears in reference sources. Therefore, a decision must be made on what form to choose as the preferred heading.

1. Fullness

A person's name may vary in fullness, in terms of the number of elements involved or in terms of abbreviations or initials. Again, the basis for choice is the predominant or most commonly known form, e.g., **Friedrich Schiller** instead of *Johann Christoph Freidrich von Schiller* and **D.H. Lawrence** instead of *David Herbert Lawrence*.

2. Language

A person's name may appear in different languages, particularly in the case of famous authors and internationally known persons, e.g., **Domingo de Guzman** or **Saint Dominic; Quintus Horatius Flaccus** or **Horace; Karl V** and **Carlos I**, or **Charles V.** There is no one simple, clear-cut criterion for choice. The decision varies according to language, to type of name (given names or names containing surnames), and to chronological period. In general, there is a strong preference for well-established English forms and for Latin and Greek forms over vernacular forms.

3. Spelling

The same name may be spelled in more than one way, and a decision must be made regarding which spelling should be used in the heading. The basis for choice is official orthography or predominant spelling.

Choice of Entry Element (rules 22.4–22.11)

Most names contain more than one element, a simple example being given name and surname. Thus, for any name under consideration, after it has been determined which form to use, it must then be decided which element in the name is to be used as the entry word. The names of the majority of people living in modern times are entered under surname. Certain surnames, such as compound surnames and those with separately written prefixes, contain more than one word. In such cases, one of the words in the surname is chosen as the entry word. Some people, particularly royalty and people of earlier times, do not have surnames or do not use them. Headings for these people consist of their given names. Again, if the given name contains more than one word, the entry element must be determined.

The general principle for choice of entry element of a personal name is the person's preference (if known) or the way the name would normally be listed in authoritative alphabetic lists in his or her language or country.

1. Entry under surname (rule 22.5)

A name containing a surname is entered under that surname, e.g., **Shakespeare, William**. If the surname consists of several elements, one of them is chosen as the entry element, as follows.

Compound surnames. A surname consisting of two or more proper names is entered according to the preferred or established form (if known), e.g., **Day Lewis, C.** In other cases, entry is under the first element except for names of married women. The name of a married woman, except for those in Czech, French, Hungarian, Italian, or Spanish, that consists of a maiden name and husband's surname is entered under the husband's surname, for example, **Lindbergh, Anne Morrow**.

Surnames with separately written prefixes. Many surnames include an article or preposition or combination of the two. These names are entered according to the usage of the person's language or country of residence. Because usage varies among different languages and countries, separate rules are provided based on languages or language groups. For American and British names, the entry element is the prefix, e.g., **Van Den Hoven, Adrian**.

2. Entry under title of nobility (rule 22.6)

For persons who use their titles of nobility rather than their personal surnames in their works or are listed under their titles in reference sources, the entry element is the proper name in the title of nobility. The elements in the name are arranged in the following order: Proper name in the title, personal name in direct order, the term of rank in the vernacular, for example,

Shaftesbury, Anthony Ashley Cooper, Earl of

3. Entry under given name, etc. (rule 22.8)

A name that consists of a given name or given names only is entered under the part of name as listed in reference sources, e.g., **Thomas**, *of Sutton*; **Leonardo**, *da Vinci*.

4. Entry of Roman names (rule 22.9)

The name of a Roman active before A.D. 476 is entered according to the practice in reference sources, e.g., **Cicero, Marcus Tullius**.

5. Entry under initials, letters, or numerals (rule 22.10)

A name consisting of initials, or separate letters, or numerals, or consisting primarily of initials, is entered under the first initial, letter, or numeral, e.g., **H. D.; A. E.; 110908**.

6. Entry under phrase (rule 22.11)

A name consisting of a phrase or other appellation that does not include a forename, as well as a name consisting of a forename or forenames preceded by words other than a term of address or a title of position or phrase, is entered under the first element, e.g., **Dr. X; Poor Richard**, but **Seuss, Dr.**

Additions to Names (rules 22.12–22.16)

The following elements are added to the headings for persons.

1. Titles of nobility (rule 22.12)

The title of nobility is added after the name if the title appears commonly in association with the name in the person's works or reference sources.

> **Bismarck, Otto**, Fürst von

2. Saints (rule 22.13)

The word *Saint* is added after the name of a Christian saint (excluding popes, emperors, empresses, kings, or queens).

> **Francis,** *of Assisi, Saint*
> **Gregory I,** *Pope* (instead of Gregory, Saint, Pope)

3. Spirits (rule 22.14)

The word *(Spirit)* is added to a heading established for a spirit communication.

> **Twain, Mark** *(Spirit)*

4. Additions to names entered under surname only (rule 22.15)

The addition is in the form of a word or phrase associated with the name in works by the person or in reference sources.

> **Seuss,** *Dr.*

5. Additions to names entered under given name, etc. (rule 22.16)

Royalty. A phrase consisting of the title and the name of the state or people governed is added.

> **Louis XVI,** *King of France*
> **Akihito,** *Emperor of Japan*
> **Rainier III,** *Prince of Monaco*

Popes. The word *Pope* is added.

> **John Paul II,** *Pope*

Bishops, etc. The title or a phrase consisting of the title and the name of the latest see (if applicable) is added.

Anselm, *Saint, Archbishop of Canterbury*
Giles, *of Rome, Archbishop of Bourges*

Distinguishing Persons with the Same Name (rules 22.17–22.20)

As discussed earlier, the principle of unique headings requires that a particular heading should represent one person or author only. When two or more persons have the same name, additional elements normally are added to distinguish between them. The most common elements used for this purpose are the person's dates and/or fuller forms of the name. Optionally, these elements may be added to all personal names even when there is no need to distinguish between otherwise identical headings.

(a) Dates *(rule 22.17)*

> **Shakespeare, William,** 1564-1616
> **Eliot, T. S. (Thomas Stearns),** 1888-1965
> **Madonna,** 1958-
> **Pann, Anton,** *ca.* 1797-1854
> **Johnson, Benjamin,** fl. 1798
> **Goggans, Sadie,** b. 1888

(b) Fuller forms of the name *(rule 22.18)*

If a fuller form of a person's name is known and if the heading as prescribed does not include all of that fuller form, the fuller form of the name is added in parentheses. The fuller form may consist of spelled out forenames for initials included in the heading or forenames, surnames, or initials which are not part of the heading.

> **Cummings, E. E. (Edward Estlin),** 1894-1962
> **Jones, James C. (James Chamberlain),** 1809-1859
> **Johnson, Cathy (Cathy A.)**
> **Smith, G. E. Kidder (George Everard Kidder),** 1913-1997
> **Smith, John M. (John Martin),** 1942-
> **Smith, John M. (John Melvin),** 1940-

If the dates and fuller forms of the name are not available to distinguish between two or more identical headings, another element is used for this purpose. This element may be a suitable brief term, a term of address, title of position or office, initials of an academic degree, initials denoting membership in an organization, etc. (see rule 22.19B), e.g.,

Smith, J. Gregory, *Mrs.,* 1818-1905
Smith, John, *M.D.,* fl. 1710-1770

For headings in the form of given names only, see rule 22.19A. In rare cases when no suitable addition can be made, the heading in question is used without qualification.

GEOGRAPHIC NAMES IN HEADINGS

Geographic names are used in headings for various purposes: to distinguish between corporate bodies with the same name, as additions to other corporate names, and as headings for governments and non-governmental communities. Chapter 23 of AACR2R is devoted to the forms in which geographic names are to be presented in headings. Its major provisions are summarized below.

Language (rule 23.2)

The basic principle is to use the English form of the name of a place if there is one in general use. Otherwise, the vernacular form is used.

English form

> **Germany** (not Deutschland)
> **Naples** (not Napoli)
> **Munich** (not München)

Vernacular form

> **Sao Paulo**
> **Puerto Rico**
> **Rio de Janeiro**

Changes of Name (rule 23.3)

If the name of a place changes, both the former name and the current name may be used as appropriate (see rules 24.3E, 24.4C6).

Additions to Place Names (rule 23.4)

The name of a larger place (abbreviated according to appendix B in AACR2R) is added to the name of a place located within the larger place. Unless the place is located within one of the exceptional countries discussed below, this geographic qualifier normally consists of the name of the country, for example,

Naples (*Italy*)
Rio de Janeiro (*Brazil*)
Paris (*France*)

If the name of the country fails to distinguish between two places with the same name, the name of a smaller geographic entity is also added.

Friedberg (*Bavaria, Germany*)
Friedberg (*Hesse, Germany*)

In the case of a number of countries, the name of a jurisdiction immediately below the country level is used as the geographic qualifier. These exceptional countries include Australia, Canada, Malaysia, Great Britain, and the United States:

A place in a state, province, or territory in **Australia, Canada, Malaysia,** or **United States**	Add the name of the state, province, or territory
A place in the **British Isles**	Add *England, Ireland, Northern Ireland, Scotland, Wales, Isle of Man,* or *Channel Islands*

Examples:

Lexington (*Mass.*)
London (*England*)
London (*Ont.*)
Tyrone (*Northern Ireland*)

Geographic qualifiers are not added to the states, provinces, territories, etc., within the exceptional countries, for example,

England
Massachusetts
Northern Ireland
Ontario

HEADINGS FOR CORPORATE BODIES

Definition

A corporate body is defined as "an organization or group of persons that is identified by a particular name and that acts, or may act, as an entity."[6]

By this definition, corporate bodies include associations, institutions, business firms, radio and television stations, nonprofit enterprises, governments (including local jurisdictions), government agencies, religious bodies, local churches, conferences, expeditions, projects and programs, exhibitions, fairs, and festivals.

The three aspects involved in the determination of a personal name heading—choice of name, choice of form, and choice of entry element— also pertain to corporate headings. These are discussed below.

Choice of Name (rule 24.1)

Corporate bodies frequently undergo name changes. When a corporate body has been identified by more than one name, a decision must be made on which one will be represented in the authorized heading. For corporate name changes, the principle of uniform heading is suspended. While a personal author who has changed his or her name is normally represented by one heading only, a corporate body with a changed name is treated as a separate entity and represented by a different heading. In other words, each time a corporate body undergoes a name change, a new heading is established to be used in cataloging works issued by the body under that name. (However, when the heading is used as a subject access point, the latest heading is used.) As a result, the former names as well as the current one may all appear in the same catalog. This principle is called *successive entry*. A given corporate publication is entered under the name used at the time it appeared, with *see also* or explanatory references connecting the successive entries.

> **Society for Horticultural Science (U.S.)**
>   see also the later heading
> **American Society for Horticultural Science**
>
> **American Society for Horticultural Science**
>   see also the earlier heading
> **Society for Horticultural Science (U.S.)**

Choice of Form (rules 24.2–24.3)

As in the case of personal names, a corporate name may exist in different forms. Here, the principle of uniform heading generally applies, in that one of the variant forms is chosen to be used in the heading, with references from the other forms.

1. Fullness of Name (rule 24.2D)

If the name has appeared in various degrees of fullness, the criteria for choice (in the order of preference) are: the form found in the chief sources of information, the predominant form, or a distinctive brief form (including initials or an acronym).

> **American Library Association**
> {abbreviated form: ALA}
> **Henry E. Huntington Library and Art Gallery**
> {brief form: Huntington Library and Art Gallery}
> **Unesco**
> {full form: United Nations Educational, Scientific, and Cultural Organization}

Also, a conventional form of name in common use is preferred to the fuller, official name.

> **Westminster Abbey**
> {not Collegiate Church of St. Peter in Westminster, London, England}

2. Spelling (rule 24.2C)

If the form of the name varies in spelling, the following criteria (in the order of preference) are used: the form resulting from an official change in orthography, the predominant spelling, or the spelling found in the first item cataloged.

3. Language (rule 24.3)

While the basic principle is to choose the form in the official language of the body in question, the rules reflect a strong preference for the English form. This is particularly evident in the cases of ancient and international bodies, religious orders and societies, and governments.

> **United Nations**
> **International Federation of Library Associations and Institutions**

Modifications (rules 24.4–24.11)

In certain cases, modifications are made to the form chosen.

1. Additions (rule 24.4)

The following elements are sometimes added to the corporate name:

A. A general (or generic) qualifier is added if the name alone does not convey the idea of a corporate body, e.g.,

Queen Elizabeth (*Ship*)
Bon Jovi (*Musical group*)

B. The name of the place in which the corporate body is located is added in order to distinguish two or more bodies having the same name, e.g.,

National Research Foundation (*South Africa*)
National Research Foundation (*U.S.*)

Trinity University (*San Antonio, Tex.*)
Trinity University (*Waxahachie, Tex.*)

C. The name of the institution (with which the corporate body is commonly associated) instead of the local place name, is added to distinguish two or more bodies having the same name, e.g., **Institute of 1770 (Harvard University)**

D. The year of founding or the inclusive years of existence are added if the local place names fail to distinguish two or more bodies with the same name.

2. Omissions (rule 24.5)

Elements generally omitted from the heading are (1) initial articles, (2) citations of honors, and (3) terms indicating incorporation.

3. Other modifications (rules 24.6–24.11)

Names of certain types of corporate bodies require specific modifications: governments; conferences; exhibitions, fairs, festivals, etc.; chapters, branches, etc.; local churches; and radio and television stations.

Choice of Entry Element (rules 24.12–24.14)

When a corporate body is entered under its own name, the entry element is generally the initial word in the name with a few exceptions such as initial articles, ordinal numbers, and terms denoting royal privileges. Earlier cataloging codes often required the use of the name of the place in which the corporate body was located as the entry element, e.g.,

Pennsylvania. University.

This practice was discontinued in AACR. Most names are now entered directly, e.g.,

University of Pennsylvania.

The principle of entering a corporate body directly under its name applies to most corporate bodies except certain subordinate or related bodies and government bodies and officials.

1. Subordinate and Related Bodies (rules 24.12–24.13)

It is not easy to decide on the most satisfactory entry element for a subordinate or affiliated body because there are various factors that determine whether such a body should be entered under its own name or as a subheading under the higher body to which it belongs.

In the case of non-government bodies, a subordinate body or a related body is generally entered directly under its own name, with the exception of six types of subordinate and related bodies (see rule 24.13). These are subordinate bodies that are normally identified in close association with the names of their higher bodies or parent bodies, that have indistinctive names, or whose names contain a word implying subordination (e.g., division, department, committee, commission, etc.), e.g.,

> **Association of Graduates of American Universities.** *Nigeria Chapter*
> **Society of Gastroenterology Nurses and Associates.** *Core Curriculum Committee*
> **Society of Mining Engineers of AIME.** *Coal Division*
> **University of Illinois at Chicago.** *Library*

2. Direct or Indirect Subheading (rule 24.14)

Often, a corporate body is subordinate to another body which is subordinate to yet another higher body. In some cases, there may be several levels in the hierarchy. The general rule is to enter a subordinate body, after it has been decided that it should be treated as a subheading, under the lowest element in the hierarchy that is entered under its own name. In other words, all elements between the subheading and the higher element entered under its own name are omitted, unless the omission results, or is likely to result, in a conflict, i.e., two or more bodies with the same heading. Then, the name of the lowest element in the hierarchy that will distinguish between the bodies is interposed. A heading is *direct* when an intervening element has been omitted. An *indirect* heading includes intervening elements. For example,

Direct subheading

> **American Library Association.** *Acquisitions Committee*

Hierarchy:

> American Library Association

Resources Section
Acquisitions Committee

Indirect subheading

American Library Association. *Gay & Lesbian Task Force*.
Thesaurus Committee

Hierarchy:

American Library Association
Gay & Lesbian Task Force
Thesaurus Committee

Conferences, Congresses, Meetings, Etc. (rule 24.7)

By definition, conferences, congresses, meetings, etc., are a type of corporate body. Headings for these are established in the form: **Name of conference** (*number if any : date : place or institution*), for example,

Conference on Management of Water Resources in Ethiopia
(2004 : Addis Ababa, Ethiopia)
Symposium on "Facing Misuses of History" (1999 : Oslo,
Norway)
Symposium on Ferroelectric Thin Films (11th : 2002 : Boston,
Mass.)

Governments and Government Bodies (rules 24.3E, 24.6, 24.17–24.26)

Because of certain special characteristics of governments and government
bodies, separate rules concerning the entry element of their names are
provided.

The heading for a government is normally the conventional name,
i.e., the geographic name of the area over which the government exercises
jurisdiction, unless the official name is in common use. For example,

United States (*not* United States of America)
Kentucky (*not* Commonwealth of Kentucky)
Greater London Council

The rules in chapter 23 with regard to geographic names apply to headings of governments consisting of jurisdictional names. Some of these
rules, for instance, require the addition of the name of a larger place and/
or a type-of-jurisdiction qualifier. For example,

Chicago (Ill.)
Toronto (Ont.)
Edinburgh (Scotland)
Veracruz-Llave (Mexico : State)

A body created or controlled by a government is normally entered under its own name, with the exception of eleven types (rule 24.18) of government bodies that are entered as subheadings under the headings for the governments. The government agencies that are entered subordinately are those with indistinctive names, those whose names imply administrative subordination, and those which serve an executive, legislative, or judicial function. The subordinate body is entered as a direct or indirect subheading (rule 24.19) based on similar principles for other corporate bodies.

National Science Foundation (U.S.)
National Science Foundation (Colombo, Sri Lanka)
University of North Dakota
Library of Congress
United States. *Internal Revenue Service*
Texas. *Dept. of Agriculture. Rural & Urban Business Standards Division*
Florida. *Statewide Financial Reporting Section*
  Hierarchy:
    Florida
    Division of Accounting and Auditing
    Bureau of Accounting
    Statewide Financial Reporting Section

Government Officials (rule 24.20)

Certain government officials (heads of state, heads of governments or of international intergovernmental bodies, governors of dependent or occupied territories) have corporate headings in the form of: **Heading for government**. *Title of the office*, for example,

Chicago (Ill.). *Mayor*.

For heads of state, a separate heading is established for each incumbent in the form of **Heading for government**. *Title of the office (inclusive years of the reign or incumbency : name of person in brief form)*, e.g.,

United States. *President (1961-1963 : Kennedy)*
Arkansas. *Governor (1983-1992 : Clinton)*
France. *Sovereign (1814-1824 : Louis XVIII)*

As a result of this provision, each head of state has a corporate heading in addition to his or her personal heading. The corporate heading is used as the main entry for official communications with an added entry under the personal heading (see rule 21.4D1). The personal heading is used as the main entry for other works (see rule 21.4D2–D3). Works by popes, patriarchs, bishops, etc., are treated similarly.

> **Catholic Church.** *Pope (1978-2005 : John Paul II)*

UNIFORM TITLES

A uniform title is "the particular title by which a work is to be identified for cataloguing purposes."[7] The uniform title brings together under one heading the various manifestations (e.g., editions, translations) of a work regardless of how many different titles it has appeared under or how many titles the work is known by. This device is particularly important when the main entry of the work is under title. Without the use of a uniform title, the various manifestations of a work bearing different titles would be scattered throughout the catalog. It serves also to distinguish works with like titles. It is particularly useful for famous authors, such as Shakespeare, whose works have been published by many publishers in different countries under various titles. An example of a uniform title is: **Camus, Albert, 1913-1960. Carnets,** which was published in English under the title *Notebooks*.

The rules for uniform title do not apply to a manifestation of a work that is a revision or update in the same language as the original work. Revised and updated editions that have titles different from the original are treated as separate works with a note on the record for the later edition to make the connection between the revision or update and the original.

Chapter 25 of AACR2R provides rules for uniform titles. When a uniform title is chosen among variant titles of a work, cross references are made from titles not used as the uniform title (see rule 26.4).

Special rules are provided for the use of uniform titles in cataloging special types of materials such as manuscripts, legal materials, sacred scriptures, liturgical works, and music. However, to what extent these rules are applied in cataloging is a policy matter to be decided by individual cataloging agencies. The decision is normally based on the extent of the collection and on the nature and purpose of the collection (e.g., whether it is part of a research library).

Format

In a MARC record, the uniform title is coded with a special tag, such as 130 (if main entry is under the title) or 240 (if main entry is under the name of a person or corporate body) in the MARC 21 Format. In public display of the record, the uniform title is normally enclosed in brackets.

Anonymous Works Created before 1501

Almost all libraries apply the rules of uniform titles to the cataloging of anonymous works created before 1501. The rules pertaining to such works are summarized and discussed below.

Choice of Uniform Title (rule 25.4)

The criteria in the order of preference for choosing the title to be used as the uniform title are:

1. Title by which the work is identified in modern reference sources
2. Title most frequently found in modern editions
3. Title most frequently found in early editions
4. Title most frequently found in manuscript copies.

1. Language (rule 25.5C)

The title in the original language is used except for a work originally written in classical Greek or in another language not in the Roman script; for such works, an English title is preferred if there is one that is well-established. A list of uniform titles frequently found in library catalogs follows:

> **Arabian nights**
> **Aucassin et Nicolette**
> **Beowulf**
> **Chanson de Roland**
> **Everyman**
> **Gawain and the Grene Knight**
> **Havelok the Dane**
> **Mother Goose**
> **Nibelungenlied**

If the item being cataloged is in a language different from that of the original, the name of the language of the item is added to the uniform title.

> **Aucassin et Nicolette.** English

If two or more works bear the same title or if the uniform title is identical or similar to the heading for a person or corporate body, an appropriate qualifier is added.

Exodus (*Anglo-Saxon poem*)
Exodus (*Motion picture*)

Genesis (*Anglo-Saxon poem*)
Genesis (*Old Saxon poem*)

2. Special Rules for the Bible (rules 25.17–25.18A)

Sacred scriptures are entered under uniform titles. For the Bible, because of its numerous manifestations, certain elements are added in the form of subheadings to the uniform title. These are set forth in special rules. The general formula for the heading for a particular version of the Bible is given below. Elements that are not applicable in a particular case are omitted.

> **Bible.** [*O.T.* or *N.T.*]. [individual book or group of books].
> [language]. [version]. [year]
> e.g., **Bible.** *N.T. Mark. English. New King James. 1999*
>
> **Bible.** *English. Authorized. 2003*

For selections and miscellaneous extracts from the Bible, the elements are arranged in the following manner:

> **Bible.** [language]. [version]. *Selections.* [date]
> e.g., **Bible.** *English. Tyndale. Selections. 1996*
>
> **Bible.** [*O.T.* or *N.T.*]. [individual book or group of books].
> [language]. [version]. *Selections.* [date].
> e.g., **Bible.** *O.T. Pentateuch. English. Rosenberg. Selections. 1990.*

3. Other Sacred Scriptures (rules 25.18B–25.18M)

Rules pertaining to the uniform titles for other sacred scriptures, such as *Koran, Talmud,* and *Vedas,* are also provided. For example,

> **Koran.** *Surat al-Baqarah. English. 1993*
> **Talmud.** *Bezah. English*
> **Vedas.** *Rigveda. English. Selections*

REFERENCES

References, also called *cross references,* not only connect related headings in the catalog, but also give access to authorized headings from names, different forms of names, and uniform titles that are not used as headings.

Chapter 26 of AACR2R contains rules for making references. Because references are directly associated with both the choice of names and the forms used for them in headings, chapter 26 complements chapters 22 through 25; conversely, the rules for headings in these chapters often contain instructions for references in specific situations. In addition, the rules in chapter 26 provide general instructions covering all situations where references are appropriate. There are four kinds of references.

1. *See* reference. A *see* reference directs the user from a name or a form of the name or a title not used as a heading to the one chosen as a name heading or uniform title heading.
2. *See also* reference. A *see also* reference connects related authorized headings.
3. Name-title reference. This is a *see* or *see also* reference in the form of [*name. title*], e.g.,

   Shakespeare, William, 1564-1616. Hamlet
   United States. Treaties, etc.

   This form is used when the reference is made from a title entered under a personal or corporate heading.
4. Explanatory reference. This is a *see* or *see also* reference containing an explanatory note giving more explicit guidance to the user.

In making a reference, the name of a person, place, corporate body, or uniform title from which reference is made is structured according to the same rules for forms of headings in chapters 22 through 25 of AACR2R.

Before a reference is made, it is generally recommended that at least one bibliographic record appear under the heading referred to; otherwise, the reference would be "blind." It is general practice to record (or trace) on the name authority record for the established name heading the other names or forms of name *from* which references have been made. In the MARC authority format, simple *see* references are recorded in the 4XX fields, simple *see also* references in the 5XX fields, and explanatory references in the 66x fields. Complete MARC authority records are shown in appendix B of this book.

The most common kinds of references made to each type of heading are summarized below.

Personal Name Headings (rule 26.2)

See References [MARC authority field 400, 664]

See references are made *from* the following:

1. Names not used as the heading: real names, phrases used in lieu

of names, secular names, names in religion, earlier names, and later names

2. Forms of the name not used as the heading: full name, initials, different language form, different spelling, and different romanization

3. Different entry elements: elements of a compound name, part of surname following a prefix, prefix to surname used as entry element, part of surname following a prefix combined with surname, epithet or byname, etc.

See also References [MARC authority field 500, 663]

See also references are made between different headings for the same person when the person's works have been entered under more than one heading (cf. rule 26.2D1).

Examples of References for Personal Name Headings

Examples of personal name references are shown below:

Clinton, William J. (William Jefferson), 1946-
See
Clinton, Bill, 1946-

Doolittle, Hilda, 1886-1961
See
H. D. (Hilda Doolittle), 1886-1961

D., H. (Hilda Doolittle), 1886-1961
See
H. D. (Hilda Doolittle), 1886-1961

Eliot, Thomas Stearns, 1888-1965
See
Eliot, T. S. (Thomas Stearns), 1888-1965

George, David Lloyd, 1863-1945
See
Lloyd George, David, 1863-1945

Lloyd George, David Lloyd George, Earl, 1863-1945
See
Lloyd George, David, 1863-1945

Day-Lewis, Cecil 1904-1972
See
Day Lewis, C. (Cecil), 1904-1972

Lewis, C. Day (Cecil Day), 1904-1972
See
Day Lewis, C. (Cecil), 1904-1972

Day Lewis, C. (Cecil), 1904-1972
See also
Blake, Nicholas, 1904-1972

Blake, Nicholas, 1904-1972
See also
Day Lewis, C. (Cecil), 1904-1972

Plaidy, Jean, 1906-1993
For works of this author entered under other names, see also
Carr, Philippa, 1906-1993
Ford, Elbur, 1906-1993
Holt, Victoria, 1906-1993
Kellow, Kathleen, 1906-1993
Tate, Ellalice, 1906-1993

Note that some library online systems use "search under" instead of "see" and "search also under" instead of "see also."

Examples of personal name authority records, showing valid headings and references, are found in appendix B of this book.

Names of Corporate Bodies and Geographic Names (rule 26.3)

1. *See* references are made from variant names and different forms (language, spelling, romanization, initials, acronyms, full names, etc.) of a name. [MARC authority fields 410, 411, 451]
2. *See also* references are made between independently entered but related corporate headings. [MARC authority fields 510, 511, 551]
3. Typically, explanatory references are made between earlier heading(s) and later heading(s) of a corporate body. [**MARC authority fields 663, 664, 665, 666**]

Examples of corporate name references are shown below:

AMA
See
American Medical Association

IFLA
See
International Federation of Library Associations and Institutions

International Federation of Library Associations and
Institutions
See also the earlier heading
International Federation of Library Associations

International Federation of Library Associations
See also the later heading
**International Federation of Library Associations and
Institutions**

American National Red Cross
See also the later heading
American Red Cross

Boston Metropolitan Chapter of the American Red Cross
See
American Red Cross. Boston Metropolitan Chapter

American Red Cross. Boston Metropolitan Chapter
See also earlier heading
American National Red Cross. Boston Metropolitan Chapter

United States. State, Dept. of
See
United States. Dept. of State

United States. Public Health Service. National Institutes of Health
See
National Institutes of Health (U.S.)

Commonwealth of the Bahamas
See
Bahamas

Austria
See also the earlier headings
Austro-Hungarian Monarchy
Holy Roman Empire

Uniform Titles (rule 26.4)

1. *See* references are made from different titles and variants of the
   uniform title to the uniform title. **[MARC authority field 430]**
2. *See also* references are made to connect uniform titles of related
   works. **[MARC authority field 530]**

Examples of uniform titles are shown below.

Song of Roland

See
Chanson de Roland

Thousand and one nights
See
Arabian nights

Arabian nights. Sindbad the sailor
See
Sindbad the sailor

NOTES

1. Charles Ammi Cutter, *Rules for a Dictionary Catalog*, 4th ed., rewritten (Washington, D.C.: Government Printing Office, 1904; republished, London: The Library Association, 1953), 12.

2. International Conference on Cataloguing Principles, Paris, 1961, "Statement of Principles," in *Report of International Conference on Cataloguing Principles*, ed. A.H. Chaplin and Dorothy Anderson. (London: Organizing Committee of the International Conference on Cataloguing Principles, National Central Library, 1963), 91.

3. IFLA Study Group on the Functional Requirements for Bibliographic Records, *Functional Requirements for Bibliographic Records, Final Report* (München: K.G. Saur, 1998). UBCIM Publications, New Series; v. 19. Also available at www .ifla.org/VII/s13/frbr/frbr1.htm (22 Feb. 2007).

4. Paul S. Dunkin, *Cataloging U.S.A.* (Chicago: American Library Association, 1969), 29.

5. International Conference on Cataloguing Principles, 93.

6. *Anglo-American Cataloguing Rules*, 2nd ed., 2002 revision. Prepared under the direction of the Joint Steering Committee for Revision of AACR, a committee of the American Library Association, the Australian Committee on Cataloguing, the British Library, the Canadian Committee on Cataloguing, Chartered Institute of Library and Information Professionals, the Library of Congress (Chicago: American Library Association, 2002-), appendix D-2.

7. *Anglo-American Cataloguing Rules*, 2nd ed., 2002 revision, appendix D-9.

PART FOUR
SUBJECT ACCESS AND CONTROLLED VOCABULARIES

STANDARDS AND TOOLS

Library of Congress. Cataloging Policy and Support Office. *Subject Cataloging Manual: Subject Headings.* 5th ed. Washington, D.C.: Cataloging Distribution Service, Library of Congress, 1996- .

Library of Congress. Subject Cataloging Division. *Library of Congress Subject Headings.* 8th ed.-. Washington, D.C.: Cataloging Distribution Service, Library of Congress, 1975-. Published annually, with weekly updates: *Weekly Lists.* Also available as part of *Library of Congress Authorities.* http://authorities.loc.gov/.

Library of Congress, Subject Cataloging Division. *Subject Headings Used in the Dictionary Catalogs of the Library of Congress.* 1st ed.-7th ed. Washington, D.C.: Library of Congress, 1914–1966.

Medical Subject Headings 1st ed.- Bethesda, Md.: U.S. Dept. of Health and Human Services, Public Health Service, National Institutes of Health, National Library of Medicine, 1960–2003 (last printed version). Online version: www.nlm.nih.gov/mesh/ (22 Feb. 2007).

Sears List of Subject Headings. 18th ed. Edited by Joseph Miller, editor, and Joan Goodsell, associate editor. New York: H. W. Wilson Company, 2004.

RECOMMENDED READING

Bates, Marcia J. "Rethinking Subject Cataloging in the Online Environment." *Library Resources & Technical Services* 33, no. 4 (1989): 400–412.

Berman, Sanford, ed. *Subject Cataloging: Critiques and Innovations.* New York: Haworth, 1985.

Chan, Lois Mai. "Functions of a Subject Authority File." In *Subject Author-*

ities in the Online Environment: Papers from a Conference Program Held in San Francisco, June 29, 1987, sponsored by Resources and Technical Services Division, American Library Association, Library and Information Technology Association, Association of College and Research Libraries, Public Library Association. Edited by Karen Markey Drabenstott. ALCTS Papers on Library Technical Services and Collections, no. 1. Chicago and London: American Library Association, 1991.

————. Library of Congress Subject Headings: Principles and Application. 4th ed. Westport, Conn.: Libraries Unlimited, 2005.

Chan, Lois Mai, and Theodora Hodges, revised by Giles Martin. "Subject Cataloguing and Classification." In Technical Services Today and Tomorrow, by Michael Gorman and Associates, 2nd ed., 95–109. Englewood, Colo.: Libraries Unlimited, 1998.

Chan, Lois Mai, Phyllis Richmond, and Elaine Svenonius. Theory of Subject Analysis: A Sourcebook. Littleton, Colo.: Libraries Unlimited, 1985.

Coates, Eric. Subject Catalogues: Headings and Structure. London: Library Association, 1988.

Cutter, Charles A. Rules for a Dictionary Catalog. 4th ed. rewritten. Washington, D.C.: Government Printing Office, 1904. Republished, London: The Library Association, 1953. First published under the title Rules for a Printed Dictionary Catalogue in 1876 as Part II of the U.S. Bureau of Education Public Libraries in the United States.

Dunkin, Paul S. "What Is It About? Subject Entry." 65–95 in Cataloging U.S.A., Chicago: American Library Association, 1969.

Foskett, A. C. The Subject Approach to Information. 5th ed. London: Library Association Publishing, 1996.

Hagler, Ronald. The Bibliographic Record and Information Technology. 3rd ed. Chicago: American Library Association, 1997.

Haykin, David Judson. Subject Headings: A Practical Guide. Washington, D.C.: Government Printing Office, 1951.

Library of Congress Subject Headings: Principles of Structure and Policies for Application. Annotated version. Prepared by Lois Mai Chan for the Library of Congress. Washington, D.C.: Library of Congress, 1990.

Mann, Thomas. Library Research Models: A Guide to Classification, Cataloging, and Computers. New York: Oxford University Press, 1993.

Markey, Karen. Subject Searching in Library Catalogs Before and After the Introduction of Online Catalogs. OCLC Library, Information and Computer Science Series, no. 4. Dublin, Ohio: OCLC, 1984.

Miksa, Francis. The Subject in the Dictionary Catalog from Cutter to the Present. Chicago: American Library Association, 1983.

O'Neill, Edward T., and Lois Mai Chan. "FAST (Faceted Application of Subject Terminology): A Simplified Vocabulary Based on The Library of Congress Subject Headings," IFLA Journal 29, no. 4 (December

2003): 336–42. Also available: www.ifla.org/IV/ifla69/papers/010e
-ONeill_Mai-Chan.pdf (22 Feb. 2007).

"Principles of the Sears List of Subject Headings." xv–xxix in *Sears List of Subject Headings*. 18th ed., Joseph Miller, Editor; Joan Goodsell, Associate Editor (New York: H. W. Wilson Company, 2004).

Prevost, Marie Louise. "An Approach to Theory and Method in General Subject Heading." *Library Quarterly* 16 (April 1946): 140–51.

Studwell, William E. *Library of Congress Subject Headings: Philosophy, Practice, and Prospects*. New York: Haworth Press, 1990.

CHAPTER 7
PRINCIPLES OF CONTROLLED
VOCABULARIES AND SUBJECT
ANALYSIS

INTRODUCTION

In addition to author and title access points, library catalogs and other retrieval systems provide a subject approach to the records in their systems through access points based on the subject content of the documents or other resources on which their records are based. Subject access points, like access points based on author names and titles, serve the dual function of location and collocation.

There are two ways of searching by subject: (1) through words in parts of the records such as titles, notes (particularly contents notes), and/or the full text; and, (2) through words or phrases in the records that have been specifically assigned as index terms.

The first approach is called *keyword* or *free-text* searching. The available access points are words in the title or note areas of a bibliographic or metadata record or, increasingly, in the full text. In an online catalog that offers keyword searching, the user may use as an access point almost any of the words in a title or another searchable field, such as a note. The advantage of keyword searching is that information may be retrieved on the authors' own words, which often reflect the most current terminology in a particular subject field. The drawback is that when a user wishes to retrieve all information—or as much information as possible—on a given subject, he or she must search on all the synonyms for that subject.

The second approach is "controlled vocabulary" access. In this case, specific words or phrases designated as subject index terms are assigned to each bibliographic record, each term normally represents only one subject, and a given subject is normally represented by only one term. In other words, among possible synonyms one term is chosen as the subject index term. The searcher who uses a particular controlled term is then able to retrieve all records bearing that term. A controlled vocabulary also differentiates homographs by distinguishing between words with the same spelling but different meanings. As in the case of name authority control, the principles of uniform heading and unique heading also apply to controlled vocabularies.

A controlled vocabulary system depends on a master list of predetermined terms that can be assigned to documents. For most library catalogs, manual or online, these are called *subject headings*; for many abstracting and indexing systems they are called *descriptors* or perhaps simply *preferred* or *authorized* terms. Preferred terms are maintained in a *subject headings list* or *thesaurus*, which lists the subject access terms to be used in the cataloging or indexing operation at hand. When there are synonymous terms for a given subject, these terms are included in the list as *lead-in* or *entry* terms, and references under them direct the searcher to the authorized term for the subject. Authorized terms that are related in meaning are also linked by references: the links from lead-in terms are called *use* references, and the links to related terms are, depending on the types of relationship, called broader term (BT), narrower term (NT), and related term (RT).

Subject headings lists and thesauri require ongoing maintenance. This is accomplished through a control system, called *subject authority control*, which, for each term, documents the basis for decisions on the term, and on what links connect it with other terms. Reference and subject authority control are discussed in greater detail later in this chapter.

HISTORY OF SUBJECT ACCESS IN LIBRARY CATALOGS

Early library catalogs were primarily finding-lists providing author and catchword entries for each item along with a symbol indicating its location in the collection. The catchword entry played an important role in the evolution of subject headings. The catchword was usually the leading word in the title, but in cases where the leading word failed to express the subject content of a book, for example, *An Introduction to Physics*, another word from the title more indicative of the subject content, "Physics" in this example, was used as the entry word, i.e., an access point. This practice represented a step between the catchword entry and the true subject entry. Its use indicated that, by the middle of the nineteenth century, librarians had begun to be aware of the significance of the subject approach to library material.[1]

Depending on the type of catalog, subject access points may appear in different forms and configurations. When a heading contains terms from different levels of a hierarchy of subjects, it is called a *classed* or *classified entry*. When a heading contains the most specific word or phrase describing the subject, it is called a *specific and direct entry*.

The Classed or Classified Entry

The classed entry is probably the earliest form of subject access point. It begins with the term at the top of the hierarchy to which the subject being represented belongs, with each level in the hierarchy included in the subject heading so that a classed subject heading for "southern pines" would be:

Plants—Trees—Evergreens—Pines—Southern pines

When such access points are displayed systematically or hierarchically, they are collocated according to their subject relationships.

A subject catalog made up of classed entries is called a *classed catalog*. The order of progression of subjects is from the general to the specific. For most searches, using such a catalog effectively requires an accompanying alphabetical index listing individual terms to allow the subject to be approached from any level of the hierarchy. Probably, when classed catalogs were in general use, almost all had accessible indexes. Furthermore, if a classed catalog were offered today, keyword searching would ease the access problem. In American libraries, the classed catalog as a public tool was replaced in the late nineteenth century by the dictionary or alphabetical catalog. However, as a working tool, the classed catalog was retained in the form of "shelflists" until the advent of the online catalog. A shelflist was arranged according to whatever classification system a given library used. The main difference between a shelflist and a classed catalog was that a shelflist contained only one record for each item, filed by its classification number. The classed catalog, on the other hand, included multiple access points for documents that deal with more than one subject.

A variation on the classed catalog was the *alphabetico-classed catalog*, a hybrid of the classified approach and the alphabetical approach. In this form of catalog, the classed entries were arranged differently from those in the classified catalog. On each level of the hierarchy, the subject terms are arranged alphabetically rather than strictly by subject relationships. As a matter of fact, this is the arrangement adopted by most of the subject directories found on the Web today.

The Dictionary or Alphabetical Specific Catalog

An alphabetical specific entry is a controlled heading for a specific subject (without including terms for the higher levels of its subject hierarchy), e.g., *Southern pines*. It was introduced in the late nineteenth century by Charles Ammi Cutter. Entries are arranged in alphabetical order without regard to their subject relationships or hierarchical status; thus subject collocation is sacrificed for quick and direct access. A later development than classed or alphabetico-classed catalogs, it quickly and almost completely replaced other catalog forms in American libraries.

The Online Catalog

In online retrieval systems, including library catalogs, the internal arrangement of the records is of no concern to the end-users. What is important is the way retrieved records are displayed. Because the online catalog can display records based on words or text alphabetically or by class numbers, it provides the advantages of both the alphabetical and the classified catalogs. With the online catalog, the entry element of the subject heading is no longer a crucial issue in access and display. However, when libraries first put their catalogs online, their first step was to convert their existing records into machine-readable form. When new records were created, they were drawn up according to the same rules used in forming card catalog entries. As a result, the alphabetical specific headings that had been used in manual catalogs for a century were transferred to the online catalog with little structural change. Efforts to introduce changes that render subject headings more amenable to the online environment have been gradually implemented, and online capabilities now offer many possibilities for improved subject access.

SUBJECT VOCABULARIES

Before there was a standard list for subject headings, catalogers in individual libraries assigned subject headings as they saw fit. With the increase in interlibrary loan operations and the introduction of centralized cataloging through the distribution of Library of Congress (LC) printed cards, the advantages of having a standard list became apparent. Such a list would ensure consistency within the same library catalog as well as among catalogs of different libraries, thereby making retrieval easier for users who move from library to library as well as facilitating both interlibrary cooperation and the development of union catalogs.

In 1895, the first standard list for subject headings appeared. The *List of Subject Headings for Use in Dictionary Catalogs*, produced by an American Library Association (ALA) committee of which Cutter was a prominent member, was based on Cutter's principles. It went through three editions (1895, 1898, 1911). In 1910–1914, when LC began publishing its list under the title *Subject Headings Used in the Dictionary Catalogues of the Library of Congress*, later changed to *Library of Congress Subject Headings* (LCSH), it was found unnecessary to continue the ALA list.

Once LC began distributing printed cards at the beginning of the twentieth century, the Library's practice soon became the *de facto* standard for cataloging in the United States. After LC began publishing its subject headings list in 1914, it became a standard tool for subject cataloging in American libraries. Details on Library of Congress subject headings are given in chapter 8 of this book.

LCSH and its predecessors reflect the practice of a large research collection and neither were nor are always suited to medium-sized or small collections. Early on, the gap was filled by a list compiled by Minnie Earl Sears and first published in 1923 under the title *Subject Headings for Small*

Libraries. It was renamed *Sears List of Subject Headings* and has gone through eighteen editions so far, with the most recent appearing in 2004. Despite the relatively greater ease of using subject headings from LC cataloging copy, the *Sears* list is still favored for general collections in many small and medium-sized American libraries. Lists of subject headings have also been developed for special fields. The best known among these are *Medical Subject Headings* (MeSH) and FAST (Faceted Application of Subject Terminology). Chapters 8–11 of this book discuss these standard lists and systems in detail.

Both LCSH and the *Sears* list adopted the principles of the dictionary catalog first propounded by Cutter. However, LCSH and the *Sears* list differ in many respects. Details on each are given in chapters 8 and 10 respectively.

CUTTER'S PRINCIPLES OF SUBJECT CATALOGING

The rules for subject headings in a dictionary catalog were first set forth by Charles Ammi Cutter in his *Rules for a Dictionary Catalog*.[2] Writing on the subject approach, Cutter stated two objectives: (1) to enable a person to find a book of which the subject is known, and (2) to show what the library has on a given subject.[3] The first addresses the need to locate individual items, the second addresses the need to collocate materials on the same subject. It was on the basis of these needs that Cutter set forth his basic principles of subject entry. They are important because the impact of his principles on subject heading construction and maintenance is still discernible today. The basic principles of subject headings are described below.

The User and Usage

For Cutter, the most important consideration in the cataloging of library materials was "the best interest of the user." He called this principle "the convenience of the public."[4] He felt that catalogers should be concerned with "the public's habitual way of looking at things" and that these habits should not be ignored, even if they occasionally demand a sacrifice of logic and simplicity. On this principle, the public's usage becomes an important determining factor in selecting the terms and the forms of subject headings.

The principle, though unassailable in intent, is the hardest of Cutter's recommendations to implement effectively in a system designed for wide general use. One cannot define "user" and "usage" because there is no such thing as a "typical library user." Users come into the library with different backgrounds and different purposes, and there has never been an objective way to determine how they approach the catalog or what

their purposes are. As a result, in an attempt to follow Cutter's lead, catalogers have formed subject headings on the basis of what they assume to
be the needs and habits of users. Recent studies on user behavior, using
sophisticated methodology, have provided much more information regarding subject searching. However, because of the diversity of users and
their background and interests, it is still impossible to define a "typical
user."

Another approach to effective subject access is to attempt to develop
a system that adheres to strictly formed principles, on the assumption
that a logical and consistent system can be learned by its users. When one
looks beyond Cutter's insistence on reflecting general usage, one finds
that his early rules went a long way toward laying the groundwork for a
logical and consistent subject access apparatus.

In current subject heading systems, the most important factors,
evolved over the years, are (1) uniform and unique headings, (2) specific
and direct entry, (3) consistency and currency in terminology, and (4)
provision of cross references. All of these apply, just as forcefully, to non-
library surrogate systems as they do to library practice.

Uniform and Unique Headings

In order to show what a collection or a database has on a given subject, it
must adopt a principle of *uniform headings*, that is, it must bring under
one heading all the material dealing principally or exclusively with that
particular subject. This principle is similar to that requiring a uniform
heading for a given personal author. If a subject has more than one name
("ascorbic acid" and "Vitamin C," for instance), one must be chosen as the
valid or authorized heading. In general, its ideal is that the term chosen is
unambiguous and familiar to all users of the catalog. Similarly, if there
are variant spellings of the same term, e.g., "marihuana" and "mari-
juana," or different possible forms of the same heading, only one is used
as the heading. Examples of variant heading forms might be "Air quality"
versus "Air—Quality" or "Quality of air." One must be chosen, with the
others listed as lead-in terms. However, in a few cases, duplicate access
points are made for certain headings; for example, LC headings such as
United States—Foreign relations—Japan and **Japan—Foreign relations—United States** may both be valid, although they are two forms of
the same heading. The reason for duplicate access points is to provide
access under both United States and Japan in manual catalogs. In online
catalogs that provide searching on component parts of a heading, such
duplicate access points have less value.

The converse of the principle of uniform headings is *unique headings*;
that is, the same term should not be used to represent more than one
subject. If the same term must be used in more than one sense, as is often
the case when different disciplines or fields of knowledge are involved,

some qualification or clarification must be added so that it will be clear to the user which meaning is intended, e.g., "Cold" and "Cold (Disease)."

Specific and Direct Entry

The principle of *specific entry* governs both how subject headings are formed (thesaurus construction and maintenance) and how they are assigned to documents (indexing or subject cataloging). Regarding formulation, the principle requires that a heading be as specific as (i.e., no broader than) the topic it is intended to cover. In application, it requires that a work be assigned the most specific heading that represents its subject content. Ideally, the heading should be coextensive with (i.e., no broader or narrower than) the subject content of the work. The rule for specific entry was set forth by Cutter in his *Rules for a Dictionary Catalog*:

> Enter a work under its subject headings, not under the heading of a class which includes that subject. . . . Put Lady Cust's book on 'The Cat' under *Cat*, not under *Zoology* or *Mammals* or *Domestic animals*; and put Garnier's 'Le fer' under *Iron* not under *Metals* or *Metallurgy*.[5]

Cutter claimed that this rule is the main distinction between the dictionary catalog and the alphabetico-classed catalog. In an alphabetico-classed catalog, the subject "cats" would appear under a heading such as:

Zoology—Vertebrates—Mammals—Domestic animals—Cats

In this approach, the heading contains a series, or chain, of hierarchical terms beginning with, and therefore listed under, the broadest term and leading to the most specific. In other words, access is through the broadest term moving down the hierarchy to the term being sought. In the alphabetical approach, on the other hand, the subject is listed directly under its own name, in this case "Cats." In other words, the major characteristic of the alphabetical approach is that its entries are both *specific* and *direct*.

Consistent and Current Terminology

It follows from what has been said above, particularly regarding the justifications for uniform headings, that the terminology in headings should be both consistent and current. Two elements are particularly important here: synonymy and changing usage.

Choices among synonymous terms may require difficult decisions. By principle, common usage prevails when it can be determined. For example, a popular term is preferred to a scientific one in a general library and in standard lists of headings designed for general collections. Of course, the more specialized a library's collection and clientele, the more specialized its indexing terminology should be; special libraries, therefore, often develop their own thesauri or make extensive modifications of standard lists.

Changes in usage present many practical difficulties. A term may be chosen on the basis of common usage at the time it is established but become obsolete later on. For emerging subjects, it often takes time for terminology to crystallize. For example, when computers first appeared, the Library of Congress subject heading chosen for them was "Electronic calculating machines"; this was later changed to "Computers." Even when the revision of thesauri or subject heading lists keeps pace with needed changes, updating obsolete vocabulary in catalog records poses a workload problem. This is one reason changes to more current terms were sometimes slow in implementation in manual catalogs. In many online catalogs and databases where the bibliographic and authority files are linked, updating is easier: once a heading is changed, every record that was linked to the old heading can be automatically linked to the new.

Cross References

Three common types of *cross references* are used in the subject heading structure: (1) the *see (or use)* reference, (2) the *see also* [or *BT* (broader term), *NT* (narrower term), or *RT* (related term)] reference, and (3) the *general* reference.

See or USE References

To make sure that users who happen to consult the catalog under different names for (or different forms of the name of) a given subject will be able to locate material on it, *see* or *USE* references are provided to lead them from the terms they have looked under to the authorized heading for the subject in question. These references guide users *from* terms that are not used as headings *to* the authorized headings.

See Also (Including BT, NT, and RT) References

This type of reference connects headings that are related in some way, either hierarchically or otherwise. Unlike the *see* reference, a *see-also* reference relates headings that are all valid. The headings involved may overlap in meaning, but are not fully synonymous. If they were, they would not both be used in the catalog. By linking hierarchically related headings, *see also* (or BT for broader term and NT for narrower term) references guide the user to broader or more specific branches or aspects of a subject. By linking headings related non-hierarchically, *see-also* (or RT for related term) references provide users with additional access points to material related to their interests.

General Reference

While a *specific* reference directs the user from the term being consulted to another individual heading, a *general* reference directs the user to a group or category of headings instead of to individual members of the group or category. It is sometimes called a blanket reference; an example is "**Exhibitions—Awards** *see also* the subdivision Awards under names of individual exhibitions." An obvious advantage of using general references is economy of space: they obviate the need to make long lists of specific references.

SYNTAX AND APPLICATION

The subject content of an information resource or a document may consist of:

1. a single topic or concept, or multiple topics or concepts treated separately in a work, e.g., *Children; Children and young adults*
2. aspect(s) of a topic or concept, e.g., *Health care for children; Reading interests of children; Crimes against children*
3. two or more topics or concepts treated in relation to each other, e.g., *Children in popular culture; Effects of violence on children*

It is clear from this list that except for single topics or concepts, the subject content of a work cannot always or even often be represented by a single word or a simple adjectival phrase. When this is the case, specificity, i.e., how to represent the content as precisely as possible, must be achieved by other means. In this context, Mortimer Taube identified two types of specificity: "the specificity of a specific word or phrase and whatever degree of subdivision is allowed" and "the specificity achieved by the intersection, coordination, or logical product of terms of equal generality."[6] The first type of specificity is an aspect of vocabulary design and the second type relates to application.

In many cases, a phrase is used to combine two or more general terms, either of which is broader than the resulting heading, e.g., *Church and state; Intelligence testing for children; Fertilization of flowers; Effect of light on plants.* Another way to represent complexity is to use two or more separate terms without indicating the nature of their relationship; for example, a document might be assigned the two terms, *Flowers* and *Fertilization.* Such an approach leaves it to searchers to track down documents indexed with terms reflecting all the aspects of the topics that interest them.

At the heart of the *syntax* concept is the representation of complex subjects through combination, or coordination, of terms representing different topics or different aspects or facets (defined as families of concepts that share a common characteristic[7]) of a topic. In other words, the term "syntax" refers to how words are put together to form phrases. In subject representation, while a single topic may be expressed with a single word or a phrase, a complex topic is almost always expressed in the English language with multiple words. When and how to combine individual words to represent multiple or complex topics in a document is a central issue in both the design of a vocabulary and in its application.

There are two aspects of syntax: term construction and application syntax. Term construction, i.e., how words are chosen or put together to represent individual topics or concepts in the controlled vocabulary is a matter of principle; while application syntax, i.e., how terms are put together to reflect the contents of documents in the cataloging or metadata record, is a matter of policy, determined by practical factors such as user needs, available resources, and search engines and their capabilities.

For complex topics, term combination can occur at various stages in the process of information storage and retrieval:

1. during vocabulary construction;
2. at the stage of cataloging or indexing; or,
3. at the point of retrieval

The first two approaches result in the presence of pre-combined index terms in the bibliographic or index records, a process called *precoordination*. The third approach results in such records containing single-concept terms only, a process called *postcoordination*. The terms *precoordination* and *postcoordination* refer to "when" single-concept terms are combined to form complex subjects. These concepts are discussed below.

Precoordination

Whether the combination of words and phrases to represent complex topics occurs in the vocabulary or is created by the cataloger or indexer, the result of either practice is having complex subject terms stored in the records. This practice is called precoordination.

In a precoordinate system, the combination of multiple topics or facets may take place either before the heading enters the vocabulary (an approach called *enumeration*) or before it is assigned to a document (an approach called *synthesis*). A totally enumerative vocabulary is by definition precoordinated. On the other hand, a faceted controlled vocabulary—i.e., a system that provides individual terms in clearly defined categories, or facets—may be applied either precoordinately or postcoordinately. A faceted scheme hence offers greater possibility for combinations.

When words or phrases representing different topics or different facets of a topic are pre-combined at the point of vocabulary construction, we refer to the process as *enumeration*. In an enumerative vocabulary, both single-concept terms and multiple-concept terms are included. In an enumerative list, prepositions or other devices (punctuation or the structure of the string) are used to show how the terms are interrelated within a heading, for example,

Single-concept terms	Multiple-concept terms
Books	Books and reading
Children	Children—Books and reading
Discrimination	Children—Health and hygiene
Health	Children—Nutrition
Hygiene	Children and motion pictures
Internet	Discrimination against people
Reference services (Libraries)	with disabilities
Motion pictures	Internet in library reference
Nutrition	services
People with disabilities	Oil pollution of groundwater
Plucked instruments	Recorders (2) with plucked
Popular culture	instrument
Reading	Ensemble
Recorders	Teenagers—Alcohol use
Teenagers	Teenagers—Books and reading
Violence	Violence in popular culture

Because it is not possible to list all combinations, there is no completely enumerative controlled vocabulary. Controlled vocabularies devised in early times tend to be partially enumerative. Many began as largely enumerative lists, but became less so as the volume of material to be covered increased and the subject matter treated became more complicated. Two examples of partially enumerative schemes are *Library of Congress Subject Headings* (LCSH) and *Sears List of Subject Headings*. In applying such lists, precoordinated headings, when available, are assigned to works on complex subjects, and new precoordinate headings are constantly being established. In this approach, cataloging consists basically of finding the best match between the work being cataloged and the available pre-combined headings. With the use of prepositions and other connecting words, precoordinated headings are often more expressive than what can be achieved by postcoordination. For example, the heading, **Effect of poison on plants** is more precise in meaning than combining the separate terms **Plants**, **Poison** with the Boolean operator *AND*.

The other approach, called *synthesis*, is to list the concepts and topics individually as single-concept subject headings or descriptors, which then can be combined by the indexer or cataloger during the process of indexing or cataloging or by the user when searching for complex subjects. When individual terms in the controlled vocabulary are divided into distinctive categories or facets, such as thing/object, place, time, form, the list is called *faceted*.

Postcoordination

Because no system can be totally precoordinate, often complex topics are represented by assigning single concepts headings to bibliographic records, allowing the combination to take place at the point of retrieval. This concept is referred to as *postcoordination*. Postcoordination allows the user to combine the terms as appropriate at the point of searching. It can be easily seen that postcoordination is more flexible, allowing for infinite combinations of concepts. However, because it was not easy for the user to combine concepts in the book or card catalog, early cataloging practice tended to take the precoordinate approach. Postcoordination is favored in the online environment, because computer searching enables Boolean and other sophisticated operations. Other advantages of postcoordination include the ease in maintaining a vocabulary consisting of simple terms while allowing infinite combinations among the terms at retrieval.

Subject heading lists typically contain both single-concept headings and enumerated complex headings, while thesauri contain single-concept terms, called *descriptors*, only. Subject vocabularies used in MARC records are typically precoordinated subject heading strings, while controlled vocabularies used in online databases are mostly single-concept descriptors to be combined by the searcher as required.

SUBJECT AUTHORITY CONTROL

Any retrieval system offering both controlled terminology and a cross-reference apparatus must have a means of maintaining control over the vocabulary and the references. Librarians and other retrieval systems personnel have devised such a means, referred to as *authority control*. The principles of authority control in general and name authority control devices were discussed in chapter 6; subject authority control systems follow much the same pattern.

Subject authority systems have two main purposes: to ensure uniformity and consistency in subject heading terminology and cross references. To these ends, headings are *established*, i.e., authorized when they are used for the first time, and *subject authority records* are set up for them.

Name and subject records in a library system may be kept in separate files or databases or in a combined name/subject authority file. Currently, LC's name and subject authority records can be searched through the same authorities interface at the Library's website (http://authori ties.loc.gov).

Subject Authority Record

A subject authority record contains the following information: the established heading; scope notes, if any; cross references made from synonyms and those made to and from other headings; and the sources or authorities on which the decision on the heading form was based. For example, the authority record for the Library of Congress subject heading **International librarianship** contains the following data:

Established heading: **International librarianship**

Scope note:	Here are entered works on the activities, cooperation, exchange, etc., in librarianship at the international level. Works on the study and analysis of the libraries and library systems of different countries are entered under Comparative librarianship.
Used-for (see) reference from:	Librarianship, International
Broader term reference:	International cooperation
	Library science
Related term reference:	Comparative librarianship
	Library cooperation
Narrower term reference:	Bibliography, International

Levels of Subject Authority Control

There are at least two levels of subject authority control: central and local. On the first level, a central agency, such as—in the case of the United States—the Library of Congress, the National Library of Medicine, or the H. W. Wilson Company—maintains the subject authority file, making changes to existing headings and cross references as well as adding new ones.

On the local level, a library devises a subject authority apparatus that ensures conformity and currency of the subject headings and cross references appearing in its own catalog. Most American libraries rely on one of the standard subject headings lists, such as LCSH or the *Sears* list, and create local subject authority records only for headings not yet appearing in the standard list. In some libraries, newly established headings are simply recorded in a *subject headings list*, along with needed maintenance information. Local subject authority work then includes correcting erroneous headings and cross references, updating obsolete headings, and adding or revising cross references necessitated by new headings. The design and capabilities of a given online catalog system determine what methods of local subject authority control are best suited to that system.

Functions of a Subject Authority File

In the library setting, a subject authority file[8] serves a number of functions:

Cataloging. In subject cataloging, the subject authority file serves as the source of indexing vocabulary and as the means of verifying or validating headings assigned to individual cataloging records. With the subject authority file, a cataloger can ensure that the same heading is assigned to all works on a particular subject, and that each heading represents only one particular subject. Furthermore, by consulting the subject authority file, the cataloger can ensure that all headings assigned to cataloging records conform to the established forms.

Catalog maintenance. Even after cataloging records have been created, adjustments must be made from time to time as a result of heading changes. When existing headings are revised or new headings are added, cross references are often affected and should be adjusted. The subject authority file, reflecting the most current status of headings and cross references, serves as the source for verification and validation.

Retrieval. Enhanced retrieval must be considered the ultimate function of subject authority control, because the purpose of normalizing subject access points is to enable the user to retrieve relevant information. There are two ways in which the subject authority file can aid the user in retrieval. First, the subject headings displayed in the subject authority file show the user the terminology and form of subject access points in the catalog. Second, the cross references guide the user to related headings when the user's input terms fail to retrieve useful records. For either function, of course, the subject authority file must be available to the user.

GENERAL METHODS OF SUBJECT ANALYSIS

No matter what the subject access system within which a subject cataloger or indexer is working, subject analysis of a particular work or document involves basically three steps: (1) determining the overall subject content of the item being cataloged, (2) identifying multiple subjects and/or subject aspects and interrelationships, and (3) representing both in the language of the controlled vocabulary at hand.

(1) The most reliable and certain way to determine the subject content is to read or examine the work in detail. Since this is not always practical

for reasons of cost, catalogers usually have to use other means. Titles are sometimes but not always a fair indication of content. *An Introduction to Chemistry* is undoubtedly what its title implies, but *Tourist Attraction* is a novel rather than a travel book. Therefore, it is always advisable to look beyond the title for the subject content of the work. Other features of the work often provide information relating to content. These include abstracts if any, tables of contents, chapter headings, prefaces, introductions, indexes, book jackets, slipcases, and any other accompanying descriptive material—the latter two being particularly helpful in the case of nonprint materials and for electronic resources. When these elements fail to provide a clear picture of what the work is about, external sources, such as bibliographies, catalogs, review media, and other reference sources, may prove helpful. Occasionally, subject specialists may have to be consulted, particularly when the subject matter is unfamiliar to the cataloger or indexer.

(2) The next step is to identify the main and subsidiary subjects, including different aspects of the subject such as author's point of view, time, and place. A work may deal with several subjects separately, or deal with two or more subjects in relation to each other. The interrelationships of subjects in a work are called *phase relations*. Some examples of phase relations follow:

Influence phase. The influence of one thing, one concept, or one person on another is a very common approach in scholarly works.

Bias phase. Some works on a particular subject have a bias toward, or aim at, a specific group of readers or audience; for example, *Fundamentals of Physical Chemistry for Premedical Students*.

Tool or application phase. This relationship is particularly common among scientific or technical works; for example, *Chemical Calculations: An Introduction to the Use of Mathematics in Chemistry*.

Comparison phase. This relationship is common in literary and social science studies.

(3) The final step is to represent the content according to a particular system or scheme. The first two steps are the same in all subject analysis operations. The third step varies according to whether representation is through subject headings, indexing terms, or classification numbers. In many cases, the cataloger or indexer starts with a tentative wording or phrasing, and tries to match it in the tool being used.

ASSIGNING SUBJECT HEADINGS: GENERAL GUIDELINES

Although policies regarding subject heading assignment may vary from library to library and agency to agency, certain general practices are followed by most libraries and information agencies in the United States.

These are discussed below. For specific guidelines for assigning headings from a particular subject headings list, catalogers and indexers should consult the following chapters in this book, the introduction to the subject list, and the cataloging manual of the system.

Levels of Subject Cataloging

The levels of indexing, i.e., whether subject representation is provided for both parts and comprehensive whole, depend on the policy of the indexing agency. In some, indexing is primarily at the work-as-a-whole (such as a monograph or a journal) level; in others, it is at the level of chapter or article content. In catalogs in American libraries prepared according to the *Library of Congress, Sears,* or the *National Library of Medicine Library,* subject headings are assigned to each item to bring out the overall content of the work being cataloged. Occasionally, subject headings for parts of a work are also assigned. These are called *analytical* entries (for a component part such as a short story, play, or chapter) or *partial contents* entries (for a substantial portion of a work).

Headings for individual persons, families, corporate bodies, places, etc. are assigned if they are considered significant to the work as a whole.

Specific (Co-Extensive) Entry

The heading that represents precisely the subject content of the work is assigned as the primary subject heading, unless such a heading does not exist and cannot be established. In the absence of a coextensive heading, a broader or more general heading may be used. In such cases, the broader heading is the most *specific* authorized heading in the hierarchy that covers the content of the work. In many cases, several headings may be assigned in order to cover different aspects of a subject.

With a few exceptions, a general heading which comprehends the specific primary heading is not assigned as an additional heading to a work dealing with only the specific subject. For example, the subject heading **Science** is not assigned to a work on chemistry, which receives the heading **Chemistry**.

Number of Headings

The number of headings assigned to each work depends on the nature of its content, the structure of available headings, and the policies established by the cataloging agency. It is the policy of the Library of Congress, for example, to allow the assignment of up to ten subject headings for an individual item. The ideal situation is one in which one heading will suffice to express the subject of the work being cataloged. However, in many cases more than one heading may be required because the subject content of a particular work cannot be totally expressed in a single heading. Furthermore, headings are sometimes assigned to bring out secondary topics or concepts treated in the work.

Certain categories of works, such as general periodicals and individual works of fiction, are not usually given subject headings.

Multitopical and Multi-Element Works

For a multitopical or multi-element work, more than one heading may be required; what is done in a given library or cataloging agency depends on the policy of the agency in question. The following guidelines reflect Library of Congress practice, and may be followed by libraries using LCSH or the *Sears* list.

A multitopical work (one that deals with two or three distinctive subjects or concepts separately) is assigned two or three separate headings, unless the two or three subjects constitute approximately the totality of a general subject; in the latter case, the heading for the general subject is used. For example, a book about Chinese and Japanese literature is assigned two headings, one for each literature, but a book about Greek and Latin literature is assigned the heading for classical literature. When a work deals with four or more subjects, all of which form parts of a larger subject, it is given the heading for the larger subject, for instance, "**South America—Description and travel**" for a work about traveling in Argentina, Brazil, Chile, and Ecuador. When individual subjects in a work do not belong to a particular broad subject, they are given separate headings if there are no more than four; for more than four topics, the general practice is to use either several very general headings or a form heading only, e.g., "**French essays.**"

For a multi-element work (one that features a single central topic considered from different aspects or containing various elements such as form, place, and time) the most desirable heading is one that brings out all these aspects or elements. If such a heading is not available, a new heading may be established or several headings may be used as appropriate. Whether all the concepts, aspects, and elements identified in the subject of a work should be represented in the catalog depends on the types of users for whom the catalog is intended. The main criterion is the potential value or usefulness of the headings for the users.

The methods and procedures outlined above represent general approaches to subject cataloging. Individual systems often have special policies or guidelines. These are discussed in the following chapters.

NOTES

1. Julia Pettee, *Subject Headings: The History and Theory of the Alphabetical Subject Approach to Books* (New York: H. W. Wilson Company, 1947), 151.

2. Charles Ammi Cutter, *Rules for a Dictionary Catalog*, 4th ed. rewritten (Washington, D.C.: Government Printing Office, 1904); first published in 1876.

3. Cutter, 12.

4. Cutter, 6.

5. Cutter, 66.

6. Mortimer Taube, "Specificity in Subject Headings and Coordinate Indexing," *Library Trends* 1 (October 1952): 222.

7. David Batty, "WWW—Wealth, Weariness or Waste: Controlled Vocabulary and Thesauri in Support of Online Information Access," *D-Lib Magazine*, November 1998, www.dlib.org/dlib/november98/11batty.html (22 Feb. 2007).

8. Lois Mai Chan, "Functions of a Subject Authority File," in *Subject Authorities in the Online Environment: Papers from a Conference Program Held in San Francisco, June 29, 1987,* sponsored by Resources and Technical Services Division, American Library Association, Library and Information Technology Association, Association of College and Research Libraries, Public Library Association, edited by Karen Markey Drabenstott. ALCTS Papers on Library Technical Services and Collections, no. 1 (Chicago and London: American Library Association, 1991).

CHAPTER 8
LIBRARY OF CONGRESS
SUBJECT HEADINGS

INTRODUCTION

Library of Congress Subject Headings (LCSH) is a list of subject headings originally developed by the Library of Congress for use in its cataloging records. The list was begun in 1898 and first published in 1914 under the title *Subject Headings Used in the Dictionary Catalogues of the Library of Congress.*[1] Since then, it has become the standard list used by most large general libraries in the United States as well as by many special libraries and some smaller libraries; it is also used in many libraries in other countries. The list has gone through many editions. Beginning with the eighth, the title was changed to *Library of Congress Subject Headings* (LCSH).

LCSH is essentially a subject authority list; in other words, it is a list of terms authorized by the Library of Congress for use in its own subject cataloging. Libraries using LCSH for subject authority control have relied on the list and follow Library of Congress policies and practices as *de facto* standards. Yet for subject cataloging there is no formal code of rules comparable to *Anglo-American Cataloguing Rules* for descriptive cataloging. In 1984, in response to the expressed need of the library community for a guide to subject cataloging, the Library of Congress began publishing its internal instructions for subject cataloging in *Subject Cataloging Manual: Subject Headings.*[2] This manual, now in its 5th edition (1996, with semi-annual updates), contains detailed instructions for establishing and assigning subject headings but is not cast in the form of a subject cataloging code. In 1990, a document entitled *Library of Congress Subject Headings: Principles of Structure and Policies for Application,*[3] was published. This document serves as a succinct statement of the principles and policies governing LCSH, with respect to both construction of subject headings and their application. The following discussion is based on the *Subject Cataloging Manual* and its statement of principles and policies.

To use LCSH effectively, it is important to realize its scope: what it contains and what it does not contain. Its most prominent feature is the set of headings authorized for use as subject access points in bibliographic records. It also contains many terms that are not authorized as headings but are included as *lead-in* (also called *non-preferred* or *entry*) terms to help users as well as catalogers find the applicable authorized term for a topic at issue. Cross references under the lead-in terms give directions to the associated authorized headings. However, not all authorized subject headings appear in LCSH: catalogers may derive headings from the Name Authority File or, acting under established policies, construct suitable headings on their own. In other words, many subject headings appearing in LC's bibliographic records are not listed in LCSH. A list of the principal categories of headings omitted appears in the introduction to the printed version of the list. These omissions include: (1) headings residing in the Name Authority File, (2) headings containing free-floating phrases such as . . . **Metropolitan Area,** . . . **Region,** etc., (3) certain music headings, and (4) headings with free-floating subdivisions.

FORMAT OF LIBRARY OF CONGRESS SUBJECT HEADINGS AND MARC CODING

Since 1986, the list has been available in electronic form, which can be used as such, and from which other versions are published. Since 1988, the print version of LCSH has been published annually. The electronic version is available on the World Wide Web (as part of *Classification Web*). The *Subject Authorities* database containing LCSH is also available via Internet FTP. In this book, the following terms are used to refer to the various versions:

LCSH. The Library of Congress Subject Headings system in general and the list in whatever form

Subject Authorities. The electronic version (the online version of the *Authorities* file available at the LC website, http://authorities.loc.gov, includes subject authority records as well as name authority records)

Library of Congress Subject Headings. The print version

Classification Web. The web version that contains both LCSH and the Library of Congress Classification schedules

Subject Authority Records

In the print version of LCSH, authorized headings appear in boldface type, e.g., **Art; Berries; Business and education; Digital music players; Rural-urban relations;** etc. Each valid heading is followed by scope notes, cross references, and subdivisions, if any.

Entries printed in lightface Roman are not to be used as subject headings: they are the lead-in terms (i.e., synonyms or variants of regular headings) followed by cross references to the authorized headings. Examples of entries are shown below:

Adventures and adventurers—Computer games
USE Computer adventure games

Berries *(May Subd Geog)*
  [SB381-SB386 (Culture)]
  BT   Fruit
       Fruit-culture
  RT   Cookery (Berries)
  SA   *names of berries, e.g.* Strawberries
  NT   Amelanchier
       Blueberries
       Canned berries
       Frozen berries
       Huckleberries
       Ornamental berries
       Rubus
  —Harvesting *(May Subd Geog)*
  —Varieties *(May Subd Geog)*

Computer adventure games *(May Subd Geog)*
  [GV1469.22-GV1469.25]
  UF   Adventures and adventurers—Computer games
       Adventure games, Computer
       Games, Computer adventure
  BT   Adventure games
       Computer games
  SA   *subdivision* Computer games *under subjects*
  NT   Island of Kesmai (Game)
       Queen: The Eye (Game)

Fine arts
  USE Art
       Arts

Foreign relations
  USE *subdivision* Foreign relations *under names of countries*
       International relations

Games, Computer adventure
  USE Computer adventure games

In the electronic *Subject Authorities* file encoded according to MARC 21 authority formats, each **main heading** or **main heading—subdivision** combination is represented by a separate authority record. The valid heading and the references are identified by specific tags. Each subdivision within a heading is identified by a subfield code. The field tags and subfield codes used in subject authority records are shown below.

Heading fields:
  150   Heading—Topical term
  151   Heading—Geographic name
  155   Heading—Form/genre
Common subfields:
  $v Form subdivision
  $x General subdivision
  $y Chronological subdivision
  $z Geographic subdivision
Tracing fields:
  260   Complex see reference—subject
  360   Complex see also reference—subject
  450   See from tracing—Topical term
  451   See from tracing—Geographic name
  455   See from tracing—Genre/Form term
  550   See also from tracing—Topical term
  551   See also from tracing—Geographic name
  555   See also from tracing—Genre/Form term
Common subfields:
  $i Explanatory text
Note fields:
  667   Nonpublic general note
  670   Source data found
  675   Source data not found
  680   Public general note
  681   Subject example tracing note
Common subfields:
  $a Defined variously in each field
  $b Information found
  $i Explanatory text

Field 150 includes form headings as well as topical headings. The MARC 21 authority record related to the heading **Computer adventure games** from the Library of Congress *Authorities* is shown below:

LC Control Number:	sh 85029475
HEADING:	Computer adventure games
000	00626cz 2200217n 450
001	4681749
005	19970626103922.5
008	860211i| anannbabn |a ana
035	## $a (DLC)sh 85029475
010	## $a sh 85029475
040	## $a DLC $c DLC $d DLC
053	#0 $a GV1469.22 $b GV1469.25

150	## $a Computer adventure games
360	## $i subdivision $a Computer games $i under subjects
450	## $a Adventure and adventurers $v Computer games
450	## $a Adventure games, Computer
450	## $a Games, Computer adventure
550	## $w g $a Adventure games
550	## $w g $a Computer games

(| = no attempt to code; # = blank; $ = subfield delimiter)

Subject Headings in Bibliographic Records

In the MARC bibliographic record, subject headings are identified by field tags, which include the following:

600   Personal name heading
610   Corporate name heading
630   Uniform title
650   Topical heading
651   Geographic name heading
655   Index term—Genre/Form

Subfield codes for fields 600, 610, and 630 are similar to those in fields 100, 110, and 130 in a name authority record. Subfield codes for fields 650, 651, and 655 are similar to those in fields 150, 151, and 155 in a subject authority record.

The Library of Congress has also made use of field 653 *Index term— Uncontrolled* for additional subject entries that are not taken from LCSH nor constructed from established subject/thesaurus-building rules.

For examples of coded subject headings in bibliographic records, see Figure 1-1 in chapter 1 and appendix A of this book.

MAIN HEADINGS: FUNCTIONS, TYPES, SYNTAX, AND SEMANTICS

Subject headings may be categorized into various types according to their functions. A *topical heading* represents a concept or object treated in a work. It reflects what the work is *about*. When headings are used to represent the physical or bibliographic form of the item being cataloged, they are called *form/genre headings*. A *form/genre heading* reflects what the work *is* rather than what it is *about*. Proper names may also be used as subject headings for works focusing on individual persons, corporate bodies, places, and other named entities. These are called *headings for named enti-ties.*

Topical and Form Headings [MARC authority field 150; bibliographic field 650]

A topical or form heading may contain one or more words. A one-word heading represents a single object or concept while a multiple-word heading may represent either a single concept or object or multiple concepts or objects. A heading may also carry a subdivision or subdivisions that bring out one or more aspects of the main subject. A heading containing more than one concept may appear either in the form of a phrase heading or a heading with subdivisions; this is called an *enumerated heading*, i.e., a pre-combined complex heading in the list.

Syntax

On the basis of their syntactical structure, topical and form headings may be divided into two main categories: single-noun headings and phrase headings.

Single-Noun Headings

The simplest form of main heading consists of a noun or substantive, e.g., **Cabbage; Cats; Economics; Poetry; Locomotion; Cataloging; Poor.** Some single-noun headings are followed by a qualifier, which is discussed in the section on Semantics below.

Phrase Headings

When a subject or concept cannot be properly expressed by a single noun, a phrase is used. There are several patterns of phrase headings: adjectival, conjunctive, prepositional, inverted, and free-floating. These are dis-cussed individually below:

Adjectival Phrase Headings. These are the most common type of phrase headings; they consist of a noun or noun phrase with an adjectival modifier. The adjectival modifier can be in one of several forms: a com-mon adjective, a proper adjective, a geographic name, a noun modifier, or a noun in the possessive case, e.g., **Alien films; Educational websites; Gospel singers; English literature; California sea lion; Library science; Cowper's glands; Carpenters' squares;** etc.

Conjunctive phrase headings. These headings consist of two or more nouns, noun phrases, or both, with or without modifiers, connected by the word *and*. This form serves two purposes: (1) to express a reciprocal relationship between two general topics discussed at a broad level from the perspectives of both topics, e.g., **Literature and science; Church and social problems**; etc.; (2) to connect subjects that are often treated together in works because they are similar, opposite, or closely associated, for example, **Emigration and immigration; Open and closed shelves; Debtor and creditor; Children's encyclopedias and dictionaries; Bolts and nuts**; etc. (This pattern of heading is no longer used by LC in establishing new headings; current policy requires separate headings be established.)

Prepositional Phrase Headings. These headings consist of nouns, noun phrases, or both, with or without modifiers, connected by a preposition, e.g., **Breach of contract**. Such phrase headings usually serve one of two purposes: (1) to express complex relationships between topics which cannot be represented by a single noun or a conjunctive phrase, e.g., **Electric discharges through gases; Federal aid to youth services; Internet in children's libraries**; etc., or (2) to represent a concept or object that cannot be stated in English in any other way than by using a prepositional phrase, e.g., **Boards of trade; Figures of speech; Fathers of the church**; etc.

Inverted phrase headings. In many cases, a phrase heading is inverted in order to bring a significant word into a prominent position as the entry element, e.g., **Chemistry, Organic; Maps, Statistical; Bridges, Steel plate deck; Knowledge, Sociology of**; etc. In a manual catalog or a single-entry listing or display, the inverted form brought together headings containing the same initial word for the purpose of subject collocation. The inverted form is no longer used in newly established headings, except where a pattern of inverted headings in the same category already exists.

Free-floating phrase headings. A number of terms or phrases are designated as free-floating components which may be combined with any heading within designated categories to form new phrase headings, for example,

> [Name of city] Metropolitan Area
> [Name of city] Suburban Area
> [Name of geographic feature] Region

The resulting combinations are usually not listed in LCSH.

> Washington <u>Metropolitan Area</u>
> Mississippi River <u>Region</u>

Semantics

Respecting semantics or terminology, LCSH is a controlled-vocabulary list, a list that is designed to offer uniform and unique subject terminology. A main heading represents a topic: a thing, a concept, a process, an activity, a person, an organization, a geographic or jurisdictional entity, an event, a fictional construct, etc. Controlled vocabulary builders, working on the principle of uniform headings discussed in chapter 7 and following accepted design principles, try to avoid using multiple terms that have the same meaning as valid headings; in LCSH, this is done by authorizing only one term from a set of synonyms as the valid heading.

A second design consideration, in accordance with the principle of unique headings, is to avoid headings that have more than one meaning. Many English words or phrases have more than one meaning. In constructing a controlled vocabulary, one method for solving the problem of multiple meanings is to choose an acceptable synonym that is unambiguous. Often, however, the most appropriate term for a topic may have multiple meanings. LCSH solves the problem of multiple meaning in part by adding a *qualifier* (a second term enclosed in parentheses) to resolve the ambiguity. Examples are **Chairs (Cathedra)**; **Cold (Disease)**; and **Pool (Game)**.

A qualifier may also be used to provide context for obscure or technical terms, in which case it usually takes the form of the name of a discipline or of a category or type of things, e.g., **Charge transfer devices (Electronics)**; **Chlorosis (Plants)**; and **Semantic integration (Computer systems)**.

Semantic confusion also arises with authorized terms that are close or overlapping in meaning to other authorized terms. This problem is resolved through the use of scope notes. Many headings in LCSH are provided with scope notes that (a) define the heading's scope, (b) specify the range of subject matter to which it is applied in LC cataloging records, (c) distinguish between related headings, or (d) state which of several meanings of a term is the one to which its use in LC catalogs is limited. The following examples are illustrative.

College graduates

Here are entered works on college graduates as a socio-economic group. Works on college graduates in relation to their alma maters are entered under Universities and colleges—Alumni and alumnae.

Drafts

Here are entered works dealing in general with orders for the payment of money drawn by one party on another, and including non-negotiable instruments such as postal money-orders, cashier's checks, "Anweisungen," etc. Works on bills of exchange both foreign and domestic are entered under the heading Bills of exchange.

Growth factors

Here are entered works on a group of polypeptides that control cellular responses such as cell multiplication by mechanisms analogous to classical endocrine hormones.

Headings for Named Entities [MARC authority fields 100, 110, 111, 130; bibliographic fields 600, 610, 611, 630]

Proper names are often needed as subject headings, and very few are listed in LCSH. The Name Authority File gives the established form for a large number of proper names, including names for persons, corporate bodies, and jurisdictions. Qualifiers are added as prescribed by *Anglo-American Cataloguing Rules*, second edition 2002 revision (AACR2R). Names used as subjects but not covered by AACR2R (for example, names of geographic features and fictitious characters) are established by the Library of Congress according to principles and policies compatible to those in AACR2R. These headings are listed in LCSH.

The following sections discuss three categories of name headings: personal names, corporate names, and geographic names.

Personal Names [MARC authority field 100; bibliographic field 600]

To facilitate retrieval, the same personal name heading is used for works *by* and *about* a person, for example, **Shakespeare, William, 1564-1616; Austen, Jane, 1775-1817**. Personal name headings are established according to AACR2R and stored in the Name Authority File.

Certain types of personal name headings, including family name headings, headings for gods and goddesses, and headings for legendary and fictitious characters, are used only as subject headings. These are established and included in LCSH and the Subject Authority File. Examples are given below:

> **Bakewell family**
> **Lincoln family**
> **Aphrodite (Greek deity)**
> **Baal (Deity)**
> **Venus (Roman deity)**
> **Robin Hood (Legendary character)**
> **Snoopy (Fictitious character)**

Corporate Names [MARC authority field 110; bibliographic field 610]

Names of corporate bodies are used as subject headings for works that describe their origin and development and analyze and discuss their organization, function, and activities. Corporate name headings, established and stored in the Name Authority File, are used for this purpose. Thus, a corporate subject heading conforms to the main or added entry heading for the same entity. The most common types of corporate bodies are associations and firms, governments and their agencies, institutions, committees, and commissions, for example,

> **American Library Association**
> **United States. Food and Drug Administration**
> **Johns Hopkins University**
> **University of Kentucky. Dept. of English**

Geographic Names[4] [MARC authority field 151; bibliographic field 651]

Names of places and geographic features may appear as main headings or as subdivisions under topical or form headings. For a given place, the form of the geographic name should be the same when used in either position. There are two types of geographic names: jurisdictional and non-jurisdictional.

Jurisdictional Names. Geographic names, also called *jurisdictional headings*, that serve as subject as well as bibliographic access points are established according to AACR2R and stored in the Name Authority File. For example,

> **Madrid (Spain)**
> **New Jersey**
> **Seattle (Wash.)**

Non-Jurisdictional Names. Non-jurisdictional geographic names, including names of natural geographic features, can be used as subject headings even though they are not used as bibliographic access points. Such names, established according to the policies discussed below, are listed in LCSH. If the name exists in more than one language form, English is generally preferred. Furthermore, in many cases, qualifiers are added in order to make the headings unique or compatible with jurisdictional headings.

Two types of qualifiers are used with geographic names: geographic and generic.

Geographic Qualifiers. The term *geographic qualifier* refers to the addition of the name of a larger geographic entity (normally the name of the country) to a place name. The descriptive cataloging rules governing jurisdictional names are followed for non-jurisdictional names as far as applicable. For places in certain countries, including Australia, Canada, Great Britain, Malaysia, and the United States, the name of the appropriate first-order political subdivision (i.e., state, province, constituent country, etc.) is used as the geographic qualifier, e.g., **Sheep River (Alta.)**, **Ben Nevis (Scotland)**, **Albany (N.Y.)**, etc.

The name of a natural feature generally does not require a geographic qualifier unless it is contained wholly within one or two jurisdictions or when there are two or more entities bearing the same name, e.g.,

> **Amazon River**
> **Himalaya Mountains**
> **Ohio River Valley**
> **Berkel River (Germany and Netherlands)**
> **Table Rock Lake (Mo. and Ark.)**
> **Ventana Wilderness (Calif.)**
> **San Juan River (Colo.-Utah)**
> **San Juan River (Colombia)**
> **San Juan River (Nicaragua and Costa Rica)**
> **Golden Triangle (Pittsburgh, Pa.)**
> **Golden Triangle (Southeast Asia)**

Generic Qualifiers. The names of many natural features contain a generic term, e.g., **Ohio River**; **Baltic Sea**. If it is necessary to distinguish between headings and/or cross references that have the same name and geographic qualifier, a generic qualifier is added to the non-jurisdictional name:

> **Big Bear Lake (Calif.)** [heading for the city]
> **Big Bear Lake (San Bernardino County, Calif. : Lake)**
> [heading for the lake in San Bernardino County. There are four other Big Bear Lakes.]
>
> Marco Island (Fla.) USE **Marco (Fla.)**
> [heading and reference for the city]
> **Marco Island (Fla. : Island)**

Entry Element.[5] When a geographic name consists of more than one element, the elements are rearranged so that the distinctive portion of the name occurs in the initial position. Two situations account for the majority of inverted geographic names.

In the first situation, the inverted form is used when the name of a natural geographic feature consists of a generic term, such as "lake" or "valley," followed by the specific name, e.g.,

> **Fuji, Mount (Japan)**
> **Superior, Lake**
> **Mexico, Valley of (Mexico)**

but

> Rocky Mountains
> Beaver Creek (McCreary County, Ky.)
> Indian Lake (Ohio)

In the second situation, the inverted form is often used when the geographic heading consists of a geographic name preceded by a directional adjective which is not an integral part of the proper name, e.g.,

> Africa, Southern
> California, Northern
> Texas, East

but

> South Africa
> North Dakota
> East China Sea

SUBDIVISIONS [MARC SUBFIELDS $V, $X, $Y, $Z]

A main heading may be subdivided by one or more of four kinds of subdivisions: form, topical, period, and geographic. In many cases, there may be several subdivisions following a main heading. The result is a string of elements, e.g., **United States—History—Civil War, 1861-1865—Naval operations—Submarine**.

Most **heading—subdivision** combinations are specifically authorized by the Library of Congress as allowable subject strings. However, some commonly used form and topical subdivisions have been given a different status: they are of general application (under stated conditions) and are known as *free-floating subdivisions*. These are discussed later in this chapter.

In the print version of LCSH, under a main heading, period subdivisions (arranged chronologically) appear first, followed by form and topical subdivisions (arranged alphabetically), and then by geographic subdivisions (in a separate alphabetical sequence).

Form Subdivisions [MARC subfield $v]

Form subdivision has been defined as an extension of a subject heading based on the bibliographic or physical form, or literary or artistic genre, in which the material in a work is organized and/or presented.[6] While a main heading normally expresses what the work is *about*, a form subdivision represents what it *is*, i.e., what form the treatment of the subject takes.[7] Different works may deal with the same subject but not be the same kind of work; in other words, they are in different bibliographical forms, e.g.,

> **Engineering—Examinations, questions, etc.**
> **—Indexes**
> **—Periodicals**
> **Gardens—Pictorial works**
> **—Poetry**

Topical Subdivisions [MARC subfield $x]

In general, LCSH does not authorize any **topical heading—subdivision** combination where the subdivision represents a species or part or kind of the subject represented by the main heading; in other words, by policy, there should be no authorized headings of the type, "Biology—Botany". Such a heading is characteristic of a classified catalog and is against the principle of specific entry, which excludes genus-species or class-inclusion relationships. Typically, a topical subdivision limits the concept expressed by a main heading to a special subtopic; very often, a subdivision represents an activity or operation applied to or associated with the subject denoted by the main heading. For example, the heading **Agriculture—Accounting** means accounting as applied to the field of agriculture and does not mean accounting as a kind or division of the subject agriculture. This type of topical subdivision is used extensively in LCSH.

Free-Floating Form and Topical Subdivisions

In order to ensure consistency and better control of subject strings, subdivisions and main headings may not be combined randomly. As a rule, each new combination of a subdivision with a main heading must be approved by an editorial committee at the Library before its use becomes authorized.

An exception to the rule stated above is a group of widely used subdivisions called *free-floating subdivisions*. The term refers to those form or topical subdivisions which may be used without prior authorization under a particular subject or name heading, where applicable and appropriate. Consequently, these **main heading—subdivision** combinations may appear on LC bibliographic records without being listed in LCSH.

Free-floating subdivisions are listed either separately (apart from main headings) or under representative main headings called *pattern headings*, with the intention that these subdivisions may be combined with appropriate main headings in the same subject category at the time of application. There are four categories of free-floating subdivisions: those of general application, those to be used only under specific categories of headings, those controlled by pattern headings, and those indicated by "multiples."

A combined list of all free-floating subdivisions appears in *Free-Floating Subdivisions: An Alphabetical Index*,[8] which serves as an index to *Subject Cataloging Manual: Subject Headings*,[9] in which more detailed explanations and instructions are found.

Free-Floating Subdivisions of General Application

Form and topical subdivisions that are applicable to a large number of headings are designated as free-floating subdivisions of general application. Following are some examples of general free-floating subdivisions.

—Abstracts
—Examinations
—Lighting
—Literary collections
—Periodicals—Indexes
—Software
—Study and teaching

Under each subdivision in the free-floating subdivisions lists in *Subject Cataloging Manual: Subject Headings*, instruction is given as to the kinds of headings to which the particular subdivision is applicable. For example, the subdivision —Lighting is applicable only under main headings representing vehicles, structures, buildings, rooms, installations, etc.

Free-Floating Subdivisions under Specific Types of Headings

Many subdivisions are authorized for use as free-floating subdivisions under specific categories of main headings only. Separate lists of free-floating subdivisions have been established and published in *Subject Cataloging Manual: Subject Headings*[10] for use with the following categories of main headings: classes of persons; ethnic groups; names of corporate bodies; names of persons; names of places; and names of bodies of water, streams, etc. The following headings, although not listed in LCSH, are valid headings that were constructed using these free-floating subdivisions.

Actors—Political activity
Asian-Americans—Race identity
American Library Association—Employees
Hong Kong (China)—Description and travel
Milton, John, 1608-1674—Political and social views
Bush, George W. (George Walker), 1946—Inauguration, 2001
Colorado River (Colo.—Mexico)—Navigation

Free-Floating Subdivisions Controlled by Pattern Headings

Certain form or topical subdivisions are common in a particular subject field. Instead of authorizing them heading by heading and repeating them under each heading within the same category, they are listed under a chosen heading in the category. This chosen heading then serves as a *pattern heading* of subdivisions for headings in that category. The applicable subdivisions are displayed under the pattern heading in LCSH and in the Subject Authority File. Topical and form subdivisions listed under a pattern heading may be transferred and used with another heading in the same category even though the combination does not appear in LCSH. For example, under **English language**, the pattern heading for languages, the subdivision —**Pronoun** is listed. Therefore, the combination **Japanese language—Pronoun** may be used, even though the combination does not appear in the list as such.

Table 8-1 shows the pattern headings designated for each subject category. For example, headings for individual corporate bodies may be subdivided according to the patterns listed in the table.

Catholic Church (as model for Christian denominations)
United States. Congress (for legislative bodies)
United States. Army (for armies of other countries)
United States. Navy (for navies of other countries)
Harvard University (for individual educational institutions)

As are other elements of LCSH, the provisions under pattern headings are under continual review. Therefore, the latest edition of LCSH plus its weekly updates, the subject authority file, or the latest edition and update of *Subject Cataloging Manual: Subject Headings* should be consulted for complete and current lists of subdivisions under pattern headings.

Free-Floating Subdivisions Indicated by "Multiples"

Certain subject headings carry "multiple subdivisions," a device naming a few examples as suggestions for analogous subdivisions, for example,

Birth control—Religious aspects—Buddhism, [Christianity, etc.]
Vietnam War, 1961-1975—Foreign public opinion—Austrian, [British, etc.]

In both these examples, the subdivision and the terms given in square brackets serve as examples of similar subdivisions that may be used without prior authorization, e.g.,

Vietnam War, 1961-1975—Foreign public opinion—French

TABLE 8-1   Pattern Headings in LCSH

Subject Field	Category	Pattern Heading(s)	
RELIGION	Religious and monastic orders	Jesuits	H 1186
	Religions	Buddhism	H 1185
	Christian denominations	Catholic Church	H 1187
	Sacred works (including parts)	Bible	H 1188
HISTORY AND GEOGRAPHY	Colonies of individual countries	Great Britain— Colonies	H 1149.5
	Legislative bodies (including Individual chambers)	United States. Congress	H 1155
	Military services (including armies, navies, marines, etc.)	United States—Armed Forces	H 1159
		United States. Air Force	
		United States. Army	
		United States. Marine Corps	
		United States. Navy	
	Wars	World War, 1939–1945	H 1200
		United States—History— Civil War, 1861–1865	
SOCIAL SCIENCES	Industries	Construction industry	H 1153
		Retail trade	
	Types of educational institutions	Universities and colleges	H 1151.5
	Individual educational institutions	Harvard University	H 1151
	Legal topics	Labor laws and legislation	H 1154.5
THE ARTS	Art	Art, Italian	H 1148
		Art, Chinese	
		Art, Japanese	
		Art, Korean	
	Groups of literary authors (including authors, poets, dramatists, etc.)	Authors, English	H 1155.2
	Literary works entered under author	Shakespeare, William, 1564–1616. Hamlet	H 1155.6
	Literary works entered under title	Beowulf	H 1155.8
	Languages and groups of languages	English language	H 1154
		French language	
		Romance languages	
	Literatures (including individual genres)	English literature	H 1156
	Musical compositions	Operas	H 1160
	Musical instruments	Piano	H 1161
		Clarinet	

SCIENCE AND TECHNOLOGY	Land vehicles	Automobiles	H 1195
	Materials	Concrete	H 1158
		Metals	
	Chemicals	Copper	H 1149
		Insulin	
	Organs and regions of the body	Heart	H 1164
		Foot	
	Diseases	Cancer	H 1150
		Tuberculosis	
	Plants and crops	Corn	H 1180
	Animals	Fishes	H 1147
		Cattle	

Source: Library of Congress, Subject Cataloging Division, *Subject Cataloging Manual: Subject Headings*, 5th ed. Washington, D.C.: Library of Congress, 1996. H1146, p.3–5.

Chronological Subdivisions [MARC subfield $y]

Chronological (also called period or time) subdivisions are used with headings for the history of a place or subject. Certain subject areas—such as history, politics and government of individual countries, music, art, and national literatures—lend themselves particularly to historical or chronological treatment.

Many chronological subdivisions are listed individually under the appropriate headings in LCSH. Those unique to specific places or topics are generally not free-floating. On the other hand, chronological subdivisions by century and a few specific dates have been established as free-floating subdivisions under certain categories of main headings, for example:

Under headings for art:

—10th century
—11th century
—12th century
—13th century
etc.

Under topical headings:

—History—To 1500
—History—16th century
—History—17th century
—History—18th century
—History—19th century
—History—20th century
—History—21st century

Under headings for Christian denominations:

—History—Modern period, 1500-
—History—1965-

These subdivisions may be used under individual corporate name headings or topical headings to which the free-floating subdivision —History can be assigned appropriately, for example, **Friendship—History—18th century**. However, if the resulting heading conflicts with an enumerated heading containing an established chronological subdivision in LCSH, the latter takes precedence. In other words, the free-floating chronological subdivisions may be used when they do not contradict enumerated headings. Chronological subdivisions in LCSH appear in various forms. Examples are given below.

(1) The name of a monarch, a historical period, or an event followed by dates:

American literature—Revolutionary period, 1775-1783
France—History—Louis XIV, 1643-1715
United States—History—Civil War, 1861-1865

(2) The preposition "to" followed by a date:

French literature—To 1500

(3) Dates alone:

China—Civilization—1976-2002
Greece—History—1453-1821

(4) The name of the century:

Japanese fiction—19th century
United States—History—20th century

(5) An inverted "noun, adjective" heading:

Architecture, Ancient
Architecture, Baroque
Architecture, Medieval
Architecture, Renaissance
Architecture, Rococo
Architecture, Romanesque

The modifiers in these noun/adjective headings in fact denote both period and subject characteristics. They are generally not considered to be true chronological subdivisions and therefore are interfiled alphabetically with other subdivisions that have no period connotation.

Frequently, both a broad period subdivision and period subdivisions covering lesser epochs or specific events falling within the broad period are listed under the same main heading. However, they are not usually used together for the same work; the heading closest to the period treated in the work being cataloged is the one chosen.

> **Great Britain—History—Norman period, 1066-1154**
> **—History—Medieval period, 1066-1485**
> **—History—1066-1687**
> **—History—Angevin period, 1154-1216**
> **—History—Plantagenets, 1154-1399**
> **—History—13th century**
> **—History—14th century**
> **—History—Wars of the Roses, 1455-1485**

For example, the heading **Great Britain—History—Norman period, 1066-1154** is assigned to a work such as *The Reign of William Rufus and the Accession of Henry the First*, while the heading **Great Britain—History—1066-1687** is used with a work covering the history of England from 1200 to 1640.

Exercise 8-1

Assign Library of Congress subject headings to the following topics: main headings and headings with topical and/or form subdivisions.

1. Journal of geographical information science
2. Geometric function theory in several complex variables
3. The communicative ethics controversy
4. Dictionary of concepts in recreation and leisure studies
5. Geography in the curriculum
6. Proceedings of a conference on condensed matter, particle physics and cosmology
7. A handbook for counseling the troubled and defiant child
8. Construction materials: types, uses, and applications
9. Control theory of distributed parameter and applications: proceeding of a conference
10. An introduction to urban geographic information systems
11. Paleontology of vertebrates
12. The adolescent in the family
13. The rhythm and intonation of spoken English
14. The biblical doctrine of salvation
15. An English-Swedish, Swedish-English dictionary
16. A historical study of the doctrine of the Trinity
17. ABC: A child's first book

18. Twenty-three days with the Viet Cong: an American soldier's experience
19. The principal voyages and discoveries of the English nation to 1600
20. Public attitudes toward life insurance

Geographic Subdivisions [MARC subfield $z]

A geographic subdivision[11] indicates the origin or the locality of the main topic and may be used after subjects that lend themselves to geographical treatment (i.e., that show variations when treated in or with regard to different places). Headings that may be subdivided by place carry the designation (*May Subd Geog*) immediately after their listing in LCSH. This information also appears in the name and subject authority records.

Geographic subdivision is essentially accomplished by inserting the name of a place, e.g., a city, a province, a country or other political entity, a region, or a geographic feature into a subject heading string; there are, however, established conventions governing form of geographic name, and citation order within the string.

A main heading or a main heading—subdivision combination may be subdivided by place either *directly* or *indirectly*, depending on the place in question.

Direct Geographic Subdivision

With *direct* geographic subdivision, the name of the place follows the heading or another subdivision immediately without the interposition of the name of a larger geographic entity, e.g.,

> **Music—Africa**
> **Education—Curricula—Japan**
> **Art—Great Britain**
> **Education, Elementary—United States**

Indirect Geographic Subdivision

With *indirect* geographic subdivision, the name of a larger geographic entity, normally the name of a country, is interposed between the main heading and the place in question (e.g., **Music—Austria—Vienna**). Indirect subdivision has the effect of gathering material on a particular subject under the name of the larger geographic entity. With a few exceptions, geographic names are entered indirectly after a heading when the place in question falls wholly within a country, for example,

> **Charities—Italy—Florence**
> **Cities and towns—France—Brittany**

Municipal government—Spain—Castilla y León
Rural development projects—Kenya—Coast Province
Wool industry—Government policy—Italy—Naples (Kingdom)

Exceptions are made when the larger divisions of certain countries are entered directly without the name of the country as an intervening element. These exceptional countries are:

Country	Divisions
Canada	Provinces
Great Britain	Constituent countries
United States	States

For example,

Agriculture—Florida
Music—British Columbia
Geology—Scotland

In addition, the names of the following cities are assigned directly: Jerusalem, Vatican City, and Washington, D.C., for example,

Rabbis—Jerusalem

When the place in question falls within a division (called a first-order political division) in one of the exceptional countries, the name of the first order political division, instead of the name of the country, is used as the intervening element in an indirect geographic subdivision, for example,

Music—British Columbia—Vancouver
Geology—Scotland—Highlands
Minorities—Missouri—Saint Louis

No more than two levels of geographic subdivision are used within a given heading, for example,

Horse breeders—Kentucky—Lexington
[*not* Horse breeders—Kentucky—Fayette County—Lexington]

In local subdivision, the latest name of any entity whose name has changed during the course of its existence is always used, regardless of the form of the name appearing in the work cataloged. For example, the heading **Banks and banking—Congo (Democratic Republic)—Kinshasa** is assigned to a work about banks in Leopoldville.

Similarly, local subdivision reflects the present territorial sovereignties of existing nations, regardless of whatever past territorial division is described in the work being cataloged. For a region or jurisdiction that existed in the past under various sovereignties, it is the name of the country currently in possession (as long as the region or jurisdiction is located wholly within that country) that is used. For instance, the heading **Education—France—Alsace** is assigned to a work about the status of education in Alsace in 1910 when it belonged to Germany.

When subdividing indirectly, if the geographic qualifier of the subordinate entity is identical to the name of the country or the name of the first-order political subdivision of an exceptional country, the geographical qualifier is omitted to avoid redundancy, e.g.:

> **Yangtze River** (*China*) [as a main heading]
> [*but*] **Stream measurements—China—Yangtze River**
>
> **Guadalajara** (*Spain : Province*) [as a main heading]
> [*but*] **Transportation—Spain—Guadalajara** (*Province*)

When the qualifier and the country subdivision are not identical, the qualifier is retained, e.g.:

> **Great Lake** (*Tas.*) [as a main heading]
> **Boats and boating—Australia—Great Lake** (*Tas.*)

In summary, the following places are entered *directly*:

1. Countries or larger geographic entities
2. The first order political divisions of Canada, Great Britain, and the United States
3. Any jurisdiction or region which does not lie wholly within a single existing country or within a first-order political subdivision of Canada, Great Britain, and the United States, including: (A) historic kingdoms, empires, etc., e.g., **Diplomatics—Holy Roman Empire**; and (B) geographic features and regions, such as continents and other major regions, bodies of water, mountain ranges, and so on, for instance, **Europe; Sahara; Great Lakes; Mexico, Gulf of; Rocky Mountains; Nile River Valley**.
4. Islands or groups of islands situated some distance from land masses, even if they do not represent autonomous political rules, for instance, **Geology—Falkland Islands**
5. The cities of Jerusalem and Washington, D.C., for example, **Museums—Washington (D.C.)**
6. Vatican City

The following places are entered *indirectly*:

1. Places below the level of the first order political divisions of Canada, Great Britain, and the United States

2. Places of the following types when they fall wholly within one of the other countries:
   - subordinate political jurisdictions, such as provinces, districts, counties, cities, etc., with the exceptions noted above
   - historic kingdoms, principalities, etc., e.g., **Jesuits—Italy—Naples (Kingdom)**
   - geographic features and regions, such as mountain ranges, bodies of water, lake regions, watersheds, metropolitan areas, etc.
   - islands situated within the territorial limits of the country in question

Order of Subdivisions

The citation order (i.e., the order in which elements are strung together in a heading) normally follows the patterns below:

(1) When the string begins with a geographic heading, the elements are generally arranged in the following citation order:

[Place]—[Topic]—[Time]—[Form]

For example,

> **England—Civilization—17th century—Sources**
> **Great Britain—Court and courtiers—History—16th**
>   **century—Sources**
> **United States—History—Civil War, 1861-**
>   **1865—Sources—Juvenile literature**

(2) When the string begins with a topical heading, one of the following citation orders is used:

(a) **[Topic]—[Place]—[Topic]—[Time]—[Form]**
[When (*May Subd Geog*) follows the main heading but not the topical, period, or form subdivision]

For example,

> **Farm buildings—Kentucky—Fayette County—Heating and**
>   **ventilation**
> **Nobility—Great Britain—History—16th century—Sources**

(b) **[Topic]—[Topic]—[Place]—[Time]—[Form]**
[When (*May Subd Geog*) follows the topical, period, or form subdivision]

For example,

Farm buildings—Specifications—Kentucky—Fayette County

Art—Collectors and collecting—United States—History—20th century—Exhibitions

Exercise 8-2

Assign Library of Congress subject headings to the following topics: geographic headings and headings with geographic and/or chronological subdivisions.

1. A. Assign subject headings on the social conditions of the following places.
   Athens, Georgia
   Athens, Greece
   Brittany, France
   Cambridge, Great Britain
   Munich, Germany
   New York (the city)
   Ottawa, Canada
   Tennessee
   Rio de Janeiro (the state), Brazil
   Mississippi Valley
1. B. Assign subject headings on art originated in places listed under A.
2. Assign subject headings to the following topics.
   A. Events leading to the American Civil War, 1837-1861
   B. A history of slavery and slave trades in Sub-Saharan Africa
   C. Profile of Ontario's provincial electoral districts based on statistics collected in the 1986 census
   D. Popular culture in the United States during the Cold War
   E. Lobbying for social changes in the United States
   F. Christian life and the church in the Holy Roman Empire during the tenth century
   G. Essays on the Hungarian Protestant Reformation in the 16th century
   H. Violence in American families
   I. Managing social services in the United States: designing, measuring, and financing
   J. U.S-Japan economic relations since World War II
   K. Social relations in Elizabethan London
   L. Public school choice in American education
   M. The gypsies of Eastern Europe
   N. The Taiwan uprising of February 28, 1947
   O. Working women look at their home lives

P. Norman illumination of manuscripts at Mont St. Michel, 966-1100
Q. Life in a Japanese Zen Buddhist monastery
R. The German community in Cincinnati
S. A pictorial guide to San Francisco
T. A catalog of Great Britain railway letter stamps

CROSS REFERENCES

As discussed in chapter 6, cross references are provided in the catalog for two purposes: (1) to guide the users from their search terms to valid headings, and (2) to link related headings. In LCSH, the main types of relationships among subject headings expressed by cross references are equivalence, hierarchy, and association.

Equivalence Relationships [MARC authority field 45X]

USE references direct searchers from the unauthorized or non-preferred terms they may have chosen to the authorized or valid headings for the subject in question. *USE* terms include synonyms, alternative spellings (including singular and plural forms), alternative endings, changed or cancelled headings, abbreviations and acronyms, phrases in different word order, and occasionally opposite terms that are often treated together in works. Examples of *USE* references are shown below.

Archeology
USE **Archaeology**

Electronic calculating-machines
USE **Computers**

German hymns
USE **Hymns, German**

Hothouses
USE **Greenhouses**

Illiteracy
USE **Literacy**

Nonlinear logic
USE **Fuzzy logic**

UFOs
USE **Unidentified flying objects**

In LCSH, reciprocal entries appear under the valid headings with the symbol "UF" (used for) preceding the non-preferred terms, for example,

Archaeology
UF Archeology

Computers
UF Electronic calculating-machines
[former heading]

Fuzzy logic
UF Nonlinear logic

Greenhouses
UF Hothouses

Hymns, German
UF German hymns

Literacy
UF Illiteracy

Unidentified flying objects
UF UFOs

Hierarchical Relationships [MARC authority field 55X]

Hierarchical references indicate topics that are either broader or narrower in scope than the one in question. Two symbols are used for these purposes: *BT* (broader topic) and *NT* (narrower topic), for example:

Poetry
BT Literature
NT Children's poetry
Classical poetry
Lyric poetry
Odes

Lyric poetry
BT Poetry
NT Ballads
Dithyramb
Odes
Sonnets

Odes
BT Lyric poetry
Poetry

Sonnets
   BT Lyric poetry

Headings connected by the *BT* or *NT* references are all valid headings. Each heading is connected to the heading or headings on the level immediately above or below it in the appropriate hierarchy or hierarchies. Therefore, there is no direct link between the heading **Poetry** and the heading **Sonnets** or **Dithyramb**. However, this policy may be relaxed where the hierarchies are not well or clearly defined. For instance, the heading **Odes** is linked to both **Poetry** and **Lyric poetry**. In MARC authority records, the broader topics are traced in field 55X in the record for the narrower topic.

Associative Relationships [MARC authority field 55X]

The symbol *RT* (related topic) is used to link headings that are related in concept but not in a hierarchical sense. Such references are usually made for the following types of relationships: headings with meanings that overlap to some extent, headings representing a discipline and the object studied, and headings representing persons and their fields of endeavor. Examples are shown below.

Aliens
   RT Immigrants

Entomology
   RT Insects

Law
   RT Jurisprudence
      Legislation

Physicians
   RT Medicine

In the print version of LCSH as well as in MARC authority records, instructions for *RT* references are provided under both terms involved, e.g.,

Aliens
   RT Immigrants

Immigrants
   RT Aliens

Medicine
   RT Physicians

Physicians
RT Medicine

General References

In addition to the references discussed above, there is a type of general or blanket reference, represented by the symbol *SA* (see also), which refers from one heading to a group of headings or to subdivisions used under other headings, e.g.,

Courts of last resort
SA *names of individual supreme courts*

Cranberries
—Diseases and pests
SA *names of pests, e.g.*, Cranberry root-worm

Atlases
SA *subdivision* Maps *under names of countries, cities, etc., and under topics*

The following entry, taken from LCSH, illustrates the different types of cross references associated with the heading **Library education**.

Library education
UF Education for librarianship
Librarians—Training of
Librarians, Education of
Librarians, Training of
Library school education
Library science—Study and teaching
BT Education, Higher
Professional education
RT Library schools
SA *subdivision* Study and teaching *under special subjects, e.g.*
Book selection—Study and teaching
NT Interns (Library science)
Library education (Continuing education)
Library institutes and workshops

In explanation, the cross references mean that: (1) "Education for librarianship," "Librarians—Training of," "Librarians, Education of," "Librarians, Training of," "Library school education," and "Library science—Study and teaching" are synonymous terms not used as valid headings for the concept represented by the subject heading **Library education**; (2) **Education, Higher** and **Professional education**—both valid headings—represent broader concepts; (3) **Library schools** represents a concept related to the heading **Library education,** but not in a hierarchical sense; (4) as a subdivision, **—Study and teaching** is used under specific subjects relating to library education; and, (5) **Interns (Library science), Library education (Continuing education),** and "**Library institutes and workshops**" represent narrower topics. Figure 8-1 shows the MARC authority record for the heading **Computers.**

ASSIGNING LC SUBJECT HEADINGS: PRECOORDINATION VS. POSTCOORDINATION

When a precoordinate heading that would suit a particular work is not enumerated in LCSH, a heading may be constructed by combining elements according to appropriate procedures. Especially since the mid-1970s, the Library of Congress has relied more on synthesis than enumeration for precoordinate complex headings. This development is consistent with the progress taking place in the field of indexing. As

000 01143cz 2200325n 4500
001 sh 85029552
003 DLC
005 20020611123401.0
008 860211i| anannbabn |b ana
010   $ash 85029552
040   $aDLC$cDLC$dDLC
053 0$aQA75.5$bQA76.95$cMathematics
053 0$aTK7885$bTK7895$cElectrical engineering
150   $aComputers
360   $iheadings beginning with the word$aComputer
450   $aAutomatic computers
450   $aAutomatic data processors
450   $aComputer hardware
450   $aComputing machines (Computers)
450   $aElectronic brains
450   $wnne$aElectronic calculating-machines
450   $aElectronic computers
450   $aHardware, Computer
550   wgaComputer systems
550   wgaCybernetics
550   wgaMachine theory
550   $aCalculators
550   $aCyberspace
680   $iHere are entered works on modern electronic computers first developed after 1945. Works on present-day calculators, as well as on calculators and mechanical computers of pre-1945 vintage, are entered under$aCalculators.
681   $iNote under$aCalculators

FIGURE 8–1   MARC subject authority record

Svenonius states, "Probably the most significant development in index language construction in the twentieth century is the move from largely enumerative index languages to largely synthetic ones."[12]

Synthesis, or constructing subject heading strings, in LCSH is achieved mainly through the use of free-floating subdivisions, a device that allows the combination of a main term with terms representing common aspects of subjects without requiring that each combination be authorized. Typically, such synthesized headings do not appear in the list. Thus, many highly complex headings appear in bibliographic records but not in *Library of Congress Subject Headings*, for example,

> **France—History—Revolution, 1789-1799—Literature and the revolution**
> **Lawyers—United States—Discipline—Cases**
> **Social sciences—Study and teaching (Graduate)—United States**
> **Teenagers—Books and reading—United States**

Synthesis renders a precoordinate subject indexing system much more flexible because it allows many more possible combinations than an enumerative system can accommodate.

When cataloging a work on a complex subject for which there is no coextensive heading and for which one cannot be synthesized, subject catalogers at the Library of Congress and those at cooperating libraries have two options. They may either propose a new heading as required for the work being cataloged (a procedure currently preferred) or choose to use several existing headings (i.e., take the postcoordinate approach) if the topic in question appears to be new but is judged to be not yet discrete and identifiable.

ASSIGNING LC SUBJECT HEADINGS: SPECIAL MATERIALS

General guidelines for assigning subject headings are discussed in chapter 7. The Library of Congress has also established policies regarding subject heading assignment for specific types of works. Some of the most common types are discussed below. The examples shown follow the format of the print version of LCSH, where the subdivisions are preceded by the symbol dash (—) rather than by the MARC codes.

Electronic Resources

There are no specific overall guidelines or policies regarding subject headings assigned to electronic resources. There are, however, subdivisions used specifically with electronic resources of various types. A number of subdivisions are used to indicate the electronic form, for example,

—**Computer games**
—**Databases**
—**Juvenile software**
—**Software**

Examples of subject headings containing these subdivisions are shown below:

Adobe GoLive [electronic resource] : *Web workgroup server CD*
1. **websites—Authoring programs—Software.**

Nickel takes on teasing [electronic resource]: *a clickable social skill story*
1. **Social skills—Study and teaching (Elementary)—Juvenile software.**
2. **Teasing—Prevention—Juvenile software.**

FreeBooks4Doctors [electronic resource] : *promoting free access to medical books*
1. **Medical literature—Databases.**
2. **Medicine—Databases.**

Stanley. Wild for sharks! [electronic resource]
1. **Sharks—Juvenile software.**
2. **Computer games—Juvenile software.**
3. **Sharks—Interactive multimedia.**

The following subdivisions, on the other hand, are used for works *about* specific types of electronic resources; in other words, they are topical subdivisions, not form subdivisions:

—**Computer network resources**
—**Computer programs**
—**Computer simulation**

For example,

European history highway : a guide to Internet resources / Dennis A. Trinkle and Scott A. Merriman, editors
1. **Europe—History—Research.**
2. **History—Computer network resources.**
3. **Internet.**

There are no special subdivisions designating Internet resources or Web resources. The subdivision —**Databases** is not used under subjects for electronic resources that are essentially textual in nature and that do not fit the definition of a database (i.e., a collection of logically interrelated data stored together in one or more computerized files, usually created and managed by a database management system[13]). Such materials include articles, conference proceedings, literary works, reference-type works, etc. Many Web resources are of such nature and, as a result, are assigned subject headings similar to those assigned to print materials. Examples of subject headings assigned to Internet and Web resources are shown below:

> *Reclaiming the Everglades* [electronic resource] : *South Florida's natural history, 1884-1934* / University of Miami Library, Florida International University Libraries, and Historical Museum of Southern Florida
> 1. **Nature conservation—Florida—Everglades.**
> 2. **Everglades (Fla.)—History.**

> *The Angry Kid series* [electronic resource]
> 1. **Animated films—Catalogs.**

Examples of subject headings assigned to works *about* electronic resources are shown below:

> *Database and data communication network systems : techniques and applications* / edited by Cornelius T. Leondes
> 1. **Distributed databases.**
> 2. **Computer networks.**

> *Microsoft Office XP step by step courseware* / Microsoft Corporation
> 1. **Business—Computer programs.**

> *Online ecological and environmental data* / Virginia Baldwin, editor
> 1. **Environmental sciences—Computer network resources.**
> 2. **Environmental sciences—Databases.**

> *Rules of play : game design fundamentals* / Katie Salen and Eric Zimmerman
> 1. **Computer games—Design.**
> 2. **Computer games—Programming.**

Literature

There are two main types of works in the field of literature:[14] (1) literary works and (2) works *about* literature. A literary work may consist of a collection of works by two or more authors, or an individual work or a collection of works by one author. A work about literature may focus on literature in general, in a particular language or from a particular nationality, on a particular period and/or genre of literature, on a particular author, or on a particular work. Subject headings are assigned to bring out various aspects including language, nationality, genre or form, theme, character, authorship, etc.

Anthologies and Collections of Literary Works by Two or More Authors

For an anthology or collection of works by two or more authors, one or more literary form headings with appropriate subdivisions are assigned:

Literature—Collections
[for an anthology of world literature not limited to any language or genre]

Drama, Medieval
[for an anthology or collection of Medieval drama not limited to a particular language or nationality; note that the subdivision —Collections, is not used]

American drama—20th century
[for a collection of 20th century American plays]

In each of these cases, the literature heading represents the form or genre rather than the subject content of the work. The subdivision —Collections is not free-floating and may be used with a given heading only when so listed in LCSH. The distinction between a collection of and a discussion of literature is indicated by adding to the latter the subdivision —History and criticism, e.g., French literature—20th century—History and criticism.

If a collection is organized around a particular theme, additional topical headings with appropriate literary form subdivisions are also assigned. Examples of literary anthologies and collections:

The Norton anthology of modern and contemporary poetry / edited by Jahan Ramazani, Richard Ellmann, Robert O'Clair
1. American poetry—20th century.
2. English poetry—20th century.
3. American poetry—19th century.
4. English poetry—19th century.

Anthology of African American literature / Keith Gilyard, Anissa Wardi
1. American literature—African American authors.
2. African Americans—Literary collections.

Works Written by Individual Authors

Headings representing major literary genres, e.g., **American drama** or **German fiction**, are *not* assigned to individual literary works except in the case of literary works for children, which do receive form headings. In other words, the heading **American fiction—19th century** is not assigned to Mark Twain's *The adventures of Tom Sawyer* nor the heading **English poetry—19th century** to Tennyson's *In memoriam*. In the case of collected works by one author, a literary form heading is assigned only when the form is highly specific, e.g., **Allegories; Fables; Fairy tales; Radio stories; Amateur theater; Carnival plays; Children's plays; College and school drama; Didactic drama; Radio plays; Sonnets, American;** and **Concrete poetry**. The literary form heading is also assigned when it combines a theme with the literary form, for example, **War poetry** or when it combines in one heading a nationality or language and a highly specific genre, e.g., **Sonnets, American; Love stories, French**.

For a drama or poem featuring a specific theme or based on the life of a real person, a topical heading in the form of the topic or the personal name with the subdivision **—Drama** or **—Poetry** is used.

If a collection of works in various forms by an individual author centers around a particular theme, a topical heading with the subdivision **—Literary collections** is used, for example,

> *In a house by the sea* / Sandy Gingras
> 1. **Seaside resorts—Literary collections.**
> 2. **Vacation homes—Literary collections.**
> 3. **Beaches—Literary collections.**

For a collection of novels or stories by an individual author, the form subdivision **—Fiction** is assigned only under an identifiable topic, e.g.,

> **Automobile racing—Fiction**

For an individual novel or story, one or more topical headings with the subdivision **—Fiction** may be assigned. In addition, many libraries, including the Library of Congress, assign genre/form headings to selected works. These headings come from a separate controlled vocabulary entitled *Guidelines on Subject Access to Individual Works of Fiction, Drama, Etc.,*[15] for example,

> *The virtues of war : a novel of Alexander the Great* / Steven Pressfield
> 1. **Alexander, the Great, 356-323 B.C.—Fiction.**
> 2. **Greece—History—Macedonian Expansion, 359-323 B.C.—Fiction.**
> [Genre/form heading:
> Biographical fiction.
> War stories.]

Henry V / edited by John Crowther
1. Henry V, King of England, 1387-1422—Drama.
2. Great Britain—History—Henry V, 1413-1422—Drama.
[Genre/form heading:
Historical drama.]

Sequoyah / Robert J. Conley
1. Sequoyah, 1770?-1843—Fiction.
2. Cherokee Indians—Fiction.
3. Kings and rulers—Fiction.
[Genre/form heading:
Biographical fiction.]

Works about Literature in General

Works about literature in general are assigned appropriate headings regarding the approach, type, or form of literature treated in the work, e.g.,

> **Literature—History and criticism**
> [for histories of literature in general and works evaluating the character and qualities of works of literature]
> **Criticism**
> [for works on the principles of literary criticism, not used with a work of criticism]
> **Poetics**
> **American fiction—20th century—History and criticism**
> **Drama—20th century—Congresses**
> **Poetry, Modern—19th century—Bibliography**

Works discussing the relationship between literature and other subjects are given headings such as **Literature and technology; Literature and science; Music and literature;** and **Religion and literature.**

Discussions about particular themes in literature are assigned **[Subject** or **theme] in literature** in addition to other appropriate literature headings, for instance,

> **Politics in literature**
> [for a study of political themes in twentieth-century American fiction, assign this heading in addition to **American fiction—20th century—History and criticism**]
> **Soldiers in literature**
> **War in literature**

A discussion about a particular place or person as a theme or character in literature, fiction, drama, poetry, etc., is given the heading **[name of person** or **place** in AACR2R form]—**In literature** (a free-floating subdivision), for instance,

Shakespeare, William, 1564-1616—In literature
New York (N.Y.)—In literature

It is easy to confuse the situations in which the heading [Name of person or place]—Drama or [Name of person or place]—Poetry is used with those in which the heading [Name of person or place]—In literature is appropriate. The former is used for a drama or poem featuring the person or place named as a character, while the latter is used for a discussion of (i.e., a work *about*) the person as a character or the place as a subject in literature. Following are examples of works about literature:

Humanism and machinery in Renaissance literature / Jessica Wolfe
1. **English literature—Early modern, 1500-1700—History and criticism.**
2. **Humanism in literature.**
3. **Machinery in literature.**
4. **Mechanics in literature.**
5. **Renaissance—England.**
6. **Humanists—England.**

Nation & novel : the English novel from its origins to the present day / Patrick Parrinder
1. **English fiction—History and criticism.**
2. **National characteristics, English, in literature.**
3. **Nationalism and literature—Great Britain.**
4. **Nationalism in literature.**

Plotting early modern London : new essays on Jacobean City comedy / edited by Dieter Mehl, Angela Stock, Anne-Julia Zwierlein
1. **English drama—17th century—History and criticism.**
2. **English drama (Comedy)—History and criticism.**
3. **City and town life in literature.**
4. **London (England)—In literature.**

Works about Individual Authors: Biography and Criticism

A work about an individual author is assigned a personal name heading in AACR2R form with or without a subdivision. For subdivisions, consult the list for free-floating subdivisions under names of persons.

Kafka, Franz, 1883-1924
Thoreau, Henry David, 1817-1862—Political and social views
Goethe, Johann Wolfgang von, 1749-1832—Dramatic works
[Note that this heading, assigned to works *about* Goethe's plays, is different from the heading Goethe, Johann Wolfgang von, 1749-1832—Drama, which is assigned to plays featuring Goethe as a character.]

The subdivision —**Biography** is not used under the name of a person, including literary authors. However, a subdivision denoting a biographical approach such as —**Correspondence** or —**Interviews** may be assigned. In addition, a second heading representing the class of persons to which the author belongs is also assigned, e.g.,

> *Edgar Allan Poe* / by Aaron Frisch
> 1. **Poe, Edgar Allan, 1809-1849—Juvenile literature.**
> 2. **Authors, American—19th century—Biography—Juvenile literature.**

> *Conversations with Jack Kerouac* / edited by Kevin J. Hayes
> 1. **Kerouac, Jack, 1922-1969—Interviews.**
> 2. **Authors, American—20th century—Interviews.**
> 3. **Beat generation—Interviews.**

Critical works without biographical information are assigned the personal name heading with the subdivision —**Criticism and interpretation** and/or another more specific subdivision designating criticism, e.g.,

> *Shakespeare* / by Mark Van Doren ; introduction by David Lehman
> 1. **Shakespeare, William, 1564-1616—Criticism and interpretation.**

> *Mark Twain : the fate of humor* / James M. Cox
> 1. **Twain, Mark, 1835-1910—Criticism and interpretation.**
> 2. **Twain, Mark, 1835-1910—Humor.**
> 3. **Humorous stories, American—History and criticism.**

Works about Individual Works

For a work that contains criticisms or commentaries on another work, including literary works, the uniform title for the work commented on is assigned in addition to other appropriate headings. If the work commented on is of known authorship, a [**Name. Title**] subject heading is used, as shown in the asterisked headings in the following examples:

> *Temporal circumstances : form and history in the Canterbury tales* / Lee Patterson
> 1. **Chaucer, Geoffrey, d. 1400—Criticism and interpretation—History.**
> *2. **Chaucer, Geoffrey, d. 1400. Canterbury tales.**
> 3. **Tales, Medieval—History and criticism.**
> 4. **Christian pilgrims and pilgrimages in literature.**

Charlotte Brontë's Jane Eyre / Harold Bloom, editor
*1. Brontë, Charlotte, 1816-1855. Jane Eyre.
2. Governesses in literature.

For a work about a foreign title, the uniform title consists of the author's name and the title in the original language regardless of the language in which the criticism is written, e.g.,

Thomas Mann's Death in Venice : a reference guide / Ellis Shookman
*1. Mann, Thomas, 1875-1955. Tod in Venedig.
2. Mann, Thomas, 1875-1955—Criticism and interpretation.

For a work about another work of unknown authorship, the subject heading consists of the title alone, e.g.,

Atlantic monthly

For a work about an anonymous classic or a sacred work, the subject heading is in the AACR2R form of the uniform title, e.g.,

Arabian nights
Beowulf
Bible. N.T. John
Chanson de Roland
Nibelungenlied
Pearl (Middle English poem)

Biography

Collective Biography

When a work consists of four or more life histories, it is generally considered a collective biography.[16] The heading **Biography** is assigned to a collective biography not limited to a place or a specific class of persons. When the persons treated in a collective biography belong to a specific period, a period subdivision is added, e.g., **Biography—20th century**. When the persons are from a particular place, the subject heading consists of the name of the place with the subdivision **—Biography**, e.g., **Illinois—Biography**. In addition, topical headings are assigned as appropriate. Examples of general collective biography are shown below:

Oxford dictionary of national biography : in association with the British Academy : from the earliest times to the year 2000 / edited by H.C.G. Matthew and Brian Harrison

1. Great Britain—Biography—Dictionaries.

The presidents, first ladies, and vice presidents : White House biographies, 1789-2005 / Daniel C. Diller and Stephen L. Robertson
1. White House (Washington, D.C.)—History.
2. Presidents—United States—Biography.
3 Presidents' spouses—United States—Biography.
4. Vice-Presidents—United States—Biography.

When the persons belong to a particular ethnic group or a particular profession or subject field, the appropriate term for the members of that group with the subdivision —**Biography** is used as the subject heading, e.g.,

> Arabs—Biography
> Chinese Americans—Biography
> Artists—Biography
> Authors, English—19th century—Biography
> Dentists—Biography
> Physicists—Biography

The subdivision —**Biography** is also used under names of corporate bodies and historical events, periods, etc., for example,

> United States. Army—Biography
> United States—History—Revolution, 1775-1783—Biography

When the required term referring to a special class of persons is not available in LCSH, an established subject heading consisting of the name of the relevant subject or discipline with the subdivision —**Biography** (not free-floating in this case), as listed in LCSH, is used, e.g.,

> Art—Biography
> [for all kinds of people associated with art, including artists, dealers, collectors, museum personnel, etc.]

If the work contains lists of works of authors active in particular fields as well as biographical information about those authors, the subdivision —**Bio-bibliography** is used under names of countries, cities, etc. and under subjects, for example,

> California—Bio-bibliography
> English literature—Early modern, 1500-1700—Bio-bibliography

American literature—Asian American authors—Bio-
bibliography—Dictionaries

This subdivision is not used with names of individual persons.

Individual Biography

For the biography (including autobiographical writings such as diaries
and correspondence) of an individual, three types of headings may be
assigned: (1) the name of the biographee, (2) a class-of-persons heading,
and (3) other appropriate headings.

(1) The name of the biographee in AACR2R form is assigned. If the biography focuses on a specific aspect of the person's life, an appropriate
subdivision taken from the list, "Free Floating Subdivisions Used under
Names of Persons"[17] is added. Note that the subdivision —**Biography** is
not used under names of individual persons.

> **Freud, Sigmund, 1856-1939—Correspondence**
> **Gandhi, Mahatma, 1869-1948—Political and social views**
> **Twain, Mark, 1835-1910**

(2) In addition to the personal name heading, a *class-of-persons* heading in
the form of **[Class of persons]—[Place]—[Subdivision indicating type
of biographical work]** is assigned. This practice in effect violates the general principle of *not* assigning a general heading and a specific heading
encompassed in the general heading to the same work. The doubling (i.e.,
assigning both a specific heading and a general heading to the same
work) is done for the purpose of collocating biographies of persons in the
same field or with similar characteristics. For example, a biography of the
basketball player Michael Jordan is assigned the following headings:

> *Michael Jordan : basketball player* / Mike McGovern
> 1. **Jordan, Michael, 1963-**
> 2. **Basketball players—United States—Biography.**

A biography of Barbara Bush is assigned the following headings:

> *Reflections : life after the White House* / Barbara Bush
> 1. **Bush, Barbara, 1925-**
> 2. **Bush, George, 1924-**
> 3. **Presidents' spouses—United States—Biography.**

(3) For a partial biography or a biography which includes material about
the field in which the biographee was involved, an additional topical
heading or headings may be assigned to bring out the subject, e.g.,

Tony Blair : the making of a world leader / Philip Stephens
1. **Blair, Tony, 1953-**
2. **Labour Party (Great Britain)—Biography.**
3. **Prime ministers—Great Britain—Biography.**
4. **Great Britain—Politics and government—1997-**

To a work about a statesman, ruler, or head of state which contains information about his or her personal life, three types of headings are assigned: (1) the personal name heading with applicable subdivision(s), (2) the class-of-persons heading with appropriate subdivision(s), and (3) a heading for the event or period of the country's history in which the person was involved, e.g.,

Elizabeth I : always her own free woman / edited by Carole Levin, Jo Eldridge Carney, and Debra Barrett-Graves
1. **Elizabeth I, Queen of England, 1533-1603.**
2. **Queens—Great Britain—Biography.**
3. **Great Britain—History—Elizabeth, 1558-1603.**

If the work contains mainly biographical material, the first two types of headings are assigned:

True myths : the life and times of Arnold Schwarzenegger : from pumping iron to governor of California / Nigel Andrews
1. **Schwarzenegger, Arnold.**
2. **Motion picture actors and actresses—United States—Biography.**
3. **Governors—California—Biography.**

If the work presents the history of the jurisdiction for the period or events in which a statesman or ruler participated but contains less than 20% biographical material, the class-of-persons heading is omitted, e.g.,

Blair's wars / John Kampfner
1. **Blair, Tony, 1953- —Influence.**
2. **Great Britain—Foreign relations—1997-**
3. **Great Britain—Military policy.**
4. **Great Britain—Foreign relations—United States.**
5. **United States—Foreign relations—Great Britain.**

Corporate headings, such as **Great Britain. Sovereign (1660-1685 : Charles II)**, which are used in descriptive cataloging as main or added entries, are not used as subject entries. Instead, the personal name heading and the appropriate heading for the history of the period are used.

Exercise 8-3

Assign Library of Congress subject headings to the following topics. (Literature and biography)

1. A history of modern German literature
2. Essays on American and British fiction
3. A study of the themes of order and restraint in the poetry of Philip Larkin, a British author
4. Women and literature in France
5. Irony in Rabelais
6. Memoirs of Richard Nixon
7. Columbus and the age of discovery
8. Bibliographies of studies in Victorian literature for the years 1975-1984
9. A critical study of characterization in Jacobean tragedies
10. A commentary on the epistles of Peter and Jude
11. A study of the theme of friendship in fifteenth-century Chinese literature
12. Mary Stuart in sixteenth and seventeenth century literature: a critical study
13. A reader's guide to Walt Whitman
14. A journal of twentieth-century Spanish literature

Subject Headings for Children's Literature

Library of Congress List of Juvenile Headings

The Library of Congress also developed a special list of subject headings for children's literature. In 1965, the library initiated the Annotated Card (AC) Program for children's materials, with the purpose of providing more appropriate and extensive subject cataloging for juvenile titles through more liberal application of subject headings and through the use of headings more appropriate to juvenile users. In some cases, existing Library of Congress subject headings were reinterpreted or modified in order to achieve these purposes; in other cases, new headings were created. The result is a separate list of subject headings that represent exceptions to the master list of LC headings. It was first published in 1969 as *Subject Headings for Children's Literature*. Beginning with the eighth edition of LCSH, the list, now entitled *AC Subject Headings*, has been included in the print version of LCSH, where it precedes the master list. Subject authority records for AC headings are included in the authority file and may be searched and viewed in LC's Web Authorities service (authorities .loc.gov).

In application, this list must be used in conjunction with the master list.

Subject Cataloging of Children's Materials

In LC cataloging records for materials intended for children up through age fifteen or the ninth grade, two sets of subject headings are assigned:

(1) regular headings implying juvenile nature or with juvenile subdivisions, and (2) alternative headings (called AC headings) for children's materials. These are discussed below:

Regular Headings Implying Juvenile Nature or with Juvenile Subdivisions

Topical or non-fictional juvenile materials are assigned appropriate topical headings with juvenile subdivisions such as —Dictionaries, Juvenile; —Juvenile films; —Juvenile humor; —Juvenile literature (used only for nonliterary works); —Juvenile sound recordings (not used with musical sound recordings); and —Juvenile software.

Juvenile belles lettres are assigned juvenile literary form headings such as **Children's plays** and **Children's poetry**. In addition, topical headings with juvenile literary form subdivisions (—**Juvenile drama; —Juvenile fiction; —Juvenile poetry**) are assigned to bring out themes, places, etc.

This method is usually used when children's materials are integrated into the general collection of the library.

Alternative Headings for Children's Materials

For libraries that maintain separate collections and/or catalogs for children, alternative headings consisting of regular LC subject headings without juvenile subdivisions are provided on LC cataloging records. These headings are supplemented by headings from *AC Subject Headings*, which contain additional headings designed for use with children's materials and are not in LCSH or are different in form from those found in LCSH.

For juvenile belles lettres, topical headings with literary form subdivisions are assigned more liberally than in the case of adult materials in order to provide topical access to such materials. Many topical headings, which are not generally used with adult literature, are assigned to juvenile fiction and drama.

In CIP (cataloging-in-publication) information found on the verso of the title page in most trade books, including children's materials, prepared by the Library of Congress, the AC subject headings, which may or may not differ from the regular headings, are enclosed in brackets. In MARC records, AC headings are identified by the second indicator 1 in 6XX fields.

Examples of subject headings assigned to children's materials are shown below. AC subject headings are enclosed in brackets.

A *season of hope* / by Lauren Brooke
1. **Horses—Juvenile fiction.**
2. **Fathers and daughters—Juvenile fiction.**
3. **Heartland (Imaginary place)—Juvenile fiction.**

[Horses—Fiction.
Fathers and daughters—Fiction.
Heartland (Imaginary place)—Fiction.]

A apple pie / Gennady Spirin
1. Nursery rhymes.
2. Alphabet rhymes.
3. Children's poetry.
[Nursery rhymes.
Alphabet.]

Horsing around : jokes to make ewe smile / by Diane L. Burns . . . [et al.] ; pictures by Brian Gable
1. Animals—Juvenile humor.
2. Wit and humor, Juvenile.
[Animals—Humor.
Jokes.
Riddles.]

The American heritage children's science dictionary
1. Science—Dictionaries, Juvenile.
[Science—Dictionaries.]

Bunny day / photographs by Michael Scott
1. Easter—Juvenile fiction.
2. Infants—Juvenile fiction.
[Easter—Fiction.
Babies—Fiction.]

1001 facts about insects / written by Laurence Mound . . . [et al.]
1. Insects—Miscellanea—Juvenile literature.
[Insects—Miscellanea.]

NOTES

1. Library of Congress, Catalog Division, *Subject Headings Used in the Dictionary Catalogues of the Library of Congress* (Washington, D.C.: Government Printing Office, Library Branch, 1910–1914).

2. Library of Congress, Subject Cataloging Division, *Subject Cataloging Manual: Subject Headings*, prelim. ed. (Washington, DC: Library of Congress, 1984).

3. Lois Mai Chan, *Library of Congress Subject Headings: Principles of Structure and Policies for Application* (Washington, D.C.: Library of Congress, 1990).

4. Library of Congress, Cataloging Policy and Support Office, *Subject Cataloging Manual: Subject Headings*, 5th ed. (Washington, D.C.: Library of Congress, 1996), H690.

5. Library of Congress, Cataloging Policy and Support Office, *Subject Cataloging Manual: Subject Headings*, 5th ed., H690, 6.

6. Chan, *Library of Congress Subject Headings*, 17.

7. Chan, *Library of Congress Subject Headings*, 27.

8. Library of Congress, Cataloging Policy and Support Office, *Free-Floating Subdivisions: An Alphabetical Index* (Washington, D.C.: Library of Congress, Cataloging Distribution Service, 1989–).

9. Library of Congress, Cataloging Policy and Support Office, *Subject Cataloging Manual: Subject Headings*, 5th ed., H1095.

10. Library of Congress, Cataloging Policy and Support Office, *Subject Cataloging Manual: Subject Headings*, 5th ed., H1100, H1103, H1105, H1110, H1140, H1145.5.

11. Library of Congress, Cataloging Policy and Support Office, *Subject Cataloging Manual: Subject Headings*, 5th ed., H807, H830.

12. Elaine Svenonius, "Design of Controlled Vocabularies." In *Encyclopedia of Library and Information Science*, Allen Kent, ed. (New York: Marcel Dekker, 1990), Vol. 45, Supp. 10, 88.

13. Library of Congress, *Subject Cataloging Manual: Subject Headings*, H1520.

14. Library of Congress, Cataloging Policy and Support Office, *Subject Cataloging Manual: Subject Headings*, 5th ed., H1155.2, H1155.4, H1155.6, H1155.8.

15. Association for Library Collections & Technical Services, Cataloging and Classification Section, Subject Analysis Committee, Subcommittee on the Revision of the Guidelines on Subject Access to Individual Works of Fiction, *Guidelines on Subject Access to Individual Works of Fiction, Drama, Etc.*, 2nd ed. (Chicago: American Library Association, 2000).

16. Library of Congress, Cataloging Policy and Support Office, *Subject Cataloging Manual: Subject Headings*, 5th ed., H1330.

17. Library of Congress, Cataloging Policy and Support Office, *Subject Cataloging Manual: Subject Headings*, 5th ed., H1110.

CHAPTER 9
FAST (FACETED APPLICATION
OF SUBJECT TERMINOLOGY)

INTRODUCTION

The phenomenal growth of electronic resources and the emergence of numerous metadata schemes for their description have spurred a re-examination of the way subject data might be efficiently and effectively provided for Web resources. There is a need, particularly, for subject access methods that can handle a large volume of materials without incurring as much effort and cost as is needed for providing access to traditional library materials.

In 1998, OCLC (Online Computer Library Center) began exploring a new approach to subject vocabulary while in the process of searching for a subject access system that would optimize the use of technology for Dublin Core metadata records. In keeping with the premises of the Dublin Core, it was determined that a subject vocabulary suitable for the Web environment has the following functional requirements:[1]

- It should be simple in structure (i.e., easy to assign and use) and easy to maintain;
- It should provide optimal access points; and,
- It should be flexible and interoperable across disciplines and in various knowledge discovery and access environments, not the least among which is the online public access catalog (OPAC).

In creating a new subject schema, two key decisions are required: (1) defining the semantics (the choice of vocabulary); and, (2) formulating the syntax (precoordination vs. postcoordination). Regarding the semantics, OCLC decided to retain the vocabulary of *Library of Congress Subject Headings* (LCSH). By adapting its vocabulary, compatibility with LCSH is ensured. As a subject vocabulary, LCSH offers several advantages:[2]

- It is a rich vocabulary covering all subject areas, easily the largest general indexing vocabulary in the English language;
- There is synonym and homograph control;
- It contains rich links (cross references) among terms;
- LCSH is a de facto universal controlled vocabulary and has been

translated or adapted as a model for developing subject heading systems by many countries around the world;
- It is compatible with subject data in MARC records;
- With a common vocabulary, automated conversion of LCSH to the new schema is possible; and,
- The cost of maintaining the new schema is minimized since many of the changes to LCSH can be incorporated into the new schema.

While the rich vocabulary and semantic relationships in LCSH provide subject access beyond the capabilities of keywords, its complex syntax has often proven a stumbling block to wider use. Such complexity also runs counter to the basic premises of simplicity and semantic operability of the Dublin Core. For these reasons, OCLC decided to devise a simplified syntax using the LCSH vocabulary. The resulting scheme would be a controlled vocabulary built on the terminology and relationships already established in LCSH. In application, syntax would be separated from semantics, with the result that the application process would be simplified, but the richness of vocabulary in LCSH would be retained. The resulting schema would be much easier to use and maintain. Furthermore, with the change, computer technology could be used to greater advantage in both the assignment and the maintenance of subject data as well as in subject authority control.

DEVELOPMENT

This new method, called FAST (Faceted Application of Subject Terminology), is based on the existing LCSH vocabulary, but applied with a simpler syntax than that currently used by libraries following Library of Congress application policies.

Based on the structure of the Dublin Core Metadata scheme, subject-related data, i.e., topic, place, time, and form, that have been traditionally assembled in the subject string assigned to MARC records are scattered in the following elements:[3]

Subject

A topic of the content of the resource. Typically, Subject will be expressed as keywords, key phrases, or classification codes that describe a topic of the resource. Recommended best practice is to select a value from a controlled vocabulary or formal classification scheme.

Coverage

The extent or scope of the content of the resource. Typically, Coverage will include spatial location (a place name or geographic coordinates), temporal period (a period label, date, or date range) or jurisdiction (such as a named administrative entity). Recommended best practice is to select a value from a controlled vocabulary (for example, the Thesaurus of Geographic Names [TGN]) and to use, where appropriate, named places or time periods in preference to numeric identifiers such as sets of coordinates or date ranges.

Type

The nature or genre of the content of the resource. Type includes terms describing general categories, functions, genres, or aggregation levels for content. Recommended best practice is to select a value from a controlled vocabulary (for example, the DCMI Type Vocabulary [DCT]).

While an LC subject heading may contain elements representing different facets (i.e., topical, geographic, chronological, form, and name), or aspects, of the main heading, in FAST, for the sake of simplicity and semantic interoperability, headings belonging to different facets are assigned as separate headings. In this sense, FAST is a postcoordinate scheme based on distinctive facets. By separating the facets, FAST is more in line with the basic premises and characteristics of the Dublin Core.

Since many FAST users are not expected to be trained subject catalogers, automated authority control must play a significant role in ensuring the quality of the subjects assigned. The application rules could be greatly simplified by fully establishing all headings in the new schema, thus eliminating most of the rules for heading construction and greatly simplifying authority control. In summary, the FAST schema is:

- Based on the LCSH vocabulary;
- Designed for the electronic environment;
- A postcoordinated faceted vocabulary;
- Usable by people with minimal training and experience; and,
- Amenable to automated authority control.

FACETING OF SUBJECT-RELATED ELEMENTS

FAST consists of seven subject facets and a form/genre facet. Headings in the subject facets reflect what the work being cataloged or indexed is *about*. Subject facets include the following:

- Topic
- Place (geographic)
- Time (chronological)
- Person

- Corporate body
- Event
- Title of works

On the other hand, form/genre headings represent what a work *is*. Examples of the differences in heading formulation and assignment between LCSH and FAST are shown below:

Title: *Bank consolidation and small business lending : it's not just bank size that matters*
    LC subject headings:
        Small business—United States—Finance.
        Bank loans—United States.
        Bank mergers—United States.
    FAST headings:
        Topical: **Small business—Finance**
        Bank loans
        Bank mergers
        Geographic: **United States**
Title: *Alcohol and aging*
    LC subject headings:
        Alcoholism—United States—Psychological aspects.
        Older people—Alcohol use—United States.
        Aging—United States.
    FAST headings:
        Topical: **Alcoholism—Psychological aspects**
        Older people—Alcohol use
        Aging
        Geographic: **United States**
Title: *Churches of Florence*
    LC subject headings:
        Church architecture—Italy—Florence.
        Florence (Italy)—Buildings, structures, etc.
        Florence (Italy)—Church history.
    FAST headings:
        Topical: **Church architecture**
        Buildings and structures
        Geographic: **Italy—Florence**
        Form: **Church history**
Title: *Economic & financial review*
    LC subject headings:
        Finance—United States—Periodicals.
        Banks and banking—United States—Periodicals.
        United States—Economic policy—1993-2001—Periodicals.

United States—Economic policy—2001—Periodicals.
FAST headings:
Topical: **Finance**
Banks and banking
Geographic: **United States**
Period: **Since 1993**
Form: **Periodicals**

Topic

Topical headings consist of topical main headings, which may be subdivided by topical subdivisions. Except for the fact that each heading contains elements belonging to the same facet only, the FAST topical headings look very similar to the established form of LCSH topical headings, for example,

Banks and banking
Electronic contracts
Hospitals—Administration—Data processing
Music and tourism
Nuclear reactors—Shutdown
Older people—Abuse of—Investigation
Space vehicles—Orbital assembly
Teenagers—Sleep
Web archives

A difference between LC and FAST practice is that all free-floating topical subdivisions in LCSH are part of the established form of the FAST heading and all "multiple" subdivisions are expanded. However, rather than establishing all possible combinations, only those that have actually been used will be established. For example, headings based on the following heading with multiple subdivisions are fully established in the Subject Authority File.

In LCSH:
Love—Religious aspects—Buddhism, [Christianity, etc.]
In FAST:
Love—Religious aspects—Buddhism
Love—Religious aspects—Christianity
Love—Religious aspects—Islam
Love—Religious aspects—Hinduism
Etc.

Geographic

Unlike LCSH, in which place names used as main headings appear in direct order (e.g., **Paris (France)**) but take the indirect form (**—France—**

Paris) when used as subdivisions, all FAST geographic names are established and used in indirect order, except for top level headings such as names of continents and most countries. Furthermore, first-level geographic names are limited to those from the *MARC Code List for Geographic Areas*.[4] This approach results in a hierarchical structure, from larger areas to those within them, for all geographic names. The following examples illustrate the differences between geographic headings in LCSH and in FAST:

LCSH	FAST
Los Angeles (Calif.)	California—Los Angeles
Tokyo (Japan)	Japan—Tokyo
Morgan line	Europe—Morgan line
Worcester County (Md.)	Maryland—Worcester County
Cochabamba (Bolivia : Dept.)	Bolivia—Cochabamba (Dept.)
Coventry (England)	England—Coventry
Great Lakes (North America)	Great Lakes
Italy	Italy
Chinatown (San Francisco, Calif.)	California—San Francisco—Chinatown

The last example above shows that FAST allows a three-level construction in formulating geographic headings. Three-level headings are limited to the following types of places:

• City sections
• Neighborhoods
• Interchanges
• Sites within a city
• Geographic features within a city
• Bays and similar bodies of water that are not associated with top-level bodies of water
• Bridges and tunnels within a city or closely associated with a city

Examples:

Ohio—Columbus—German Village
British Columbia—Victoria—Point Ellice Bridge
Minnesota—Minneapolis—Loring Park
Ontario—Lake Rosseau—Portage Bay

An advantage of the hierarchical structure is scalability. For applications where detailed geographic representation for local places is not required, first-level geographic headings may be sufficient and second- and third-level headings could be eliminated.

Time

FAST chronological headings reflect the actual time periods of coverage for the resources. All chronological headings are expressed as either a single numeric date or as a date range. For example, the default time period associated with the period, **Wars of the Huguenots, 1562-1598,** would be 1562 to 1598. However, in reducing this subdivision to simply a date range, the name of the war is lost. To prevent this loss of information and access point, period subdivisions with topical terms are established as topical headings as well. For instance, the subdivision **Wars of the Huguenots (1562-1598)** is represented as both a topical heading **Wars of the Huguenots, 1562-1598** and a chronological heading **1562-1598,** ensuring that both the period and topical aspects are retained in the appropriate facets. Further, since a chronological heading should reflect the actual time period covered, for a work covering only a single battle, e.g. one that occurred in 1565, the chronological heading would be limited to that single year. In addition, LC chronological headings with established periods are also retained. Examples of chronological headings:

> **To 1500**
> **1914-1918**
> **1945**
> **1942-1945**
> **Since 1987**
> **221 B.C.-220 A.D.**
> **From 500 to 570 million years ago**
>   [Corresponding to the Cambrian period]

Names of Persons, Corporate Bodies, Events, and Uniform Titles

Other than headings for places, headings for other types of proper names (including persons, corporate bodies, events, and uniform titles) that have been used as subject headings are extracted from MARC records prepared by the Library of Congress and OCLC member libraries. These headings are derived from LC subject headings containing such names, which in turn are based on the headings found in the Name Authority File,[5] a file maintained by the Library of Congress. For information about the types and forms of proper name headings, see discussions in chapters 5 and 6 of this book.

Examples of proper name headings and uniform titles used as FAST subjects include:

> **Charles II, King of France, 823-877**
> **Einstein, Albert, 1879-1955**

Teresa, Mother, 1910-1997
American Library Association
United Nations
Paris Peace Conference
Birds (Motion picture)
Beowulf
Dead Sea scrolls
American Civil War (1861-1865)
Rose Bowl (Football game)

Form/Genre

Form data are treated as a distinct facet. All free-floating subdivisions taken from Library of Congress subject headings are established as separate form/genre headings. Other FAST form/genre headings are identified by extracting form subdivisions from enumerated and assigned topical and geographic headings in MARC records. For example,

Bibliography—Catalogs
Biography—Dictionaries
Catalogs
Controversial literature
Directories
Records and correspondence
Rules
Slides
Statistics
Textbooks
Translations

FAST AUTHORITY FILES

The FAST authority files are derived from unique Library of Congress topical and geographic subject headings assigned to records in OCLC's WorldCat as well as those appearing in the name authority file. The FAST authority files are built from LCSH headings extracted from MARC records in OCLC's WorldCat and then broken into FAST facets. For example the LCSH heading France—History—Wars of the Huguenots, 1562-1598—Pamphlets results in the following FAST headings:

Topical:	**Wars of the Huguenots**
	History
Geographic:	**France**
Period:	**1562-1598**
Form:	**Pamphlets**

Because of its wide acceptance, the MARC 21 format for authority data[6] was adopted for the creation of FAST authority records. Following is an example of a FAST authority record with MARC 21 field tags:

LDR nz n
001   fast 611370
003   OCoLC
005   20041024193304.0
008   041024zneanz‖babn n ana d
040   OCoLC $b eng $c OCoLC $f fast
050   RC684.D5
150   Heart $x Diseases $x Diet therapy
550   Heart $x Diseases $x Nutritional aspects
550   Heart $x Diseases $x Treatment
688   LC usage: 84 (2006)
688   OCLC usage: 651 (2006)
750   0 Heart $x Diseases $x Diet therapy $0 (DLC)sh 85059656

At this writing, work on the FAST authority files is near completion. The FAST authority records will be extensively tested and evaluated. The evaluation will determine if the FAST team has achieved its goal of creating a new subject schema for metadata that retains the rich vocabulary of LCSH while being easy to maintain, apply, and use.

MODULAR APPROACH

FAST adopts a modular approach toward maintaining its term lists. This means that each facet forms a distinct and discrete group of headings in a separate file. These lists may be used together or separately. In a particular application, some facets may not be required. For example, in indexing a collection of naturally occurring objects, the chronological and personal name headings may not be applicable.

Furthermore, one or more of the facets may be used with other standard lists, for instance, topical headings from FAST may be used with geographic headings from the *Getty Thesaurus of Geographic Names* (TGN).[7]

NOTES

1. Lois Mai Chan, Eric Childress, Rebecca Dean, Edward T. O'Neill, and Diane Vizine-Goetz, "A Faceted Approach to Subject Data in The Dublin Core Metadata Record," *Journal Of Internet Cataloging* 4 (1/2) (2001): 35–47.

2. ALCTS/CCS/SAC/Subcommittee on Metadata and Subject Analysis, *Subject Data in the Metadata Record: Recommendations and Rationale: A Report*, 1999,

www.ala.org/ala/alctscontent/catalogingsection/catcommittees/subjectanalysis/ metadataandsubje/subjectdata.htm (25 Feb. 2007).

3. *Dublin Core Metadata Element Set*, ANSI/NISO Z39.85-2001 (Bethesda, Md.: NISO Press, 2001). Available: www.niso.org/standards/resources/Z39-85.pdf (25 Feb. 2007).

4. Library of Congress, Network Development and MARC Standards Office, *MARC Code List for Geographic Areas*, Web version, www.loc.gov/marc/geoareas/gacshome.html (25 Feb. 2007).

5. *Library of Congress Authorities*, http://authorities.loc.gov (25 Feb. 2007).

6. Library of Congress, Network Development and MARC Standards Office, *MARC 21 Format for Authority Data: Including Guidelines for Content Designation* (Washington, D.C.: Cataloging Distribution Service, Library of Congress, 1999).

7. *Getty Thesaurus of Geographic Names* ([Los Angeles, Calif.]: J. Paul Getty Trust, c1999–), also available at: www.getty.edu/research/conducting-research/vocabularies/tgn/ (25 Feb. 2007).

CHAPTER 10
SEARS LIST OF SUBJECT
HEADINGS

INTRODUCTION

In the early 1920s, because neither Library of Congress Subject Headings (LCSH) nor the earlier American Library Association (ALA) list (described in chapter 8) was judged suitable for the access needs of small and medium-sized general libraries, Minnie Earl Sears developed a new list with smaller libraries in mind. Recognizing the advantages of compatibility in creating her list, she decided to follow the general principles that underlie Library of Congress subject headings, with certain exceptions to meet the particular needs of small libraries. Therefore, although the Sears list is not an abridgment of LCSH, it is similar in principle, format, and structure.

The first edition of *List of Subject Headings for Small Libraries* appeared in 1923. Since then, the list has gone through many editions, the most recent being the eighteenth.[1] Sears was responsible for the first three (1923, 1926, and 1933). With the sixth edition (1950), the title was changed to *Sears List of Subject Headings*. Joseph Miller is the editor of the current edition, which appeared in 2004.

Today, the Sears list is used widely by school libraries and small public libraries in the United States. Thus, the Sears and the Library of Congress lists together serve as the two standard lists for subject headings for general libraries in the United States.

Throughout the history of the Sears list, its editors have followed the general principles set forth by Minnie Earl Sears, i.e., close parallels with Library of Congress Subject Headings (LCSH) with variations and modifications as appropriate for smaller libraries. Recent editions of the Sears list also have incorporated headings from the Library of Congress's Subject Headings for Children's Literature, with a few exceptions where Sears headings are in a slightly different form. The variations, however, do not affect basic structure and principles. These are the principles of alphabetical specific headings first enunciated by Charles A. Cutter: specific and direct entry, common usage and literary warrant, uniformity (i.e., uniform headings), and syndetic devices.[2] Such variations as there are usually occur in the following areas: terminology (e.g., **Social work** instead of *Social service*), spelling (e.g., **Archeology** instead of *Archaeol-*

ogy), word order (e.g., **Colleges and universities** instead of *Universities and colleges*), and a lower degree of specificity (e.g., combining closely related headings such as *Art, Greek* and *Art—Greece* into **Greek Art** only). In format, the Sears list resembles the print version of LCSH. Headings and their subdivisions used as subject access points in a catalog are printed in boldface type. Those printed in lightface roman are non-preferred terms; they are synonymous terms or variant forms of authorized headings and are followed by "USE" references to the terms that are used as headings. Sample entries are shown below.

Biological rhythms: 571.7
    UF   Biological clocks
            Biology—Periodicity
            Biorhythms
    BT   **Cycles**
    NT   **Jet lag**

Computer music: 786.7
    BT   **Music**
    RT   **Computer sound processing**
            Electronic music

Conundrums
    USE   **Riddles**

Cookery, American
    USE   **American cooking**

Digital libraries: 025.00285
    UF   Electronic libraries
            Virtual libraries
    BT   **Information systems**
            Libraries

Electronic libraries
    USE   **Digital libraries**

Except for very general subject headings, each valid heading in Sears is followed by one or more classification numbers taken from the Abridged Dewey Decimal Classification. Since the Sears list is designed for use in small libraries, the corresponding DDC numbers are seldom carried out more than four places beyond the decimal point. Following common practices in controlled vocabularies, related terms are included under each heading and the relationships among headings are indicated by commonly used symbols.

The following sections of this chapter discuss and explain the basic technical features of the Sears list. The topics covered are main headings, cross references, subdivisions, classes of headings omitted from the list, and subject headings for biography and literature. Readers should note that, because the Sears list is a close parallel to LCSH, much of what is said about it repeats or overlaps what was said in chapter 8 about LCSH. This repetition is unavoidable; many readers will need all pertinent information on the Sears list gathered into one chapter.

Sears headings consist of single nouns, compounds, adjective-noun phrases, and prepositional phrases. The list contains cross references, and provides for subdivisions of headings. Many terms that can be used in subject cataloging according to the Sears list do not appear explicitly in the list, but must be supplied by catalogers. All these topics are discussed and explained below.

MAIN HEADINGS

Topical Headings

Topical headings consist of words or phrases representing concepts or objects that depict the content of the works being cataloged. They can be in the form of single noun headings, phrase headings, or compound headings.

Single Noun Headings

Most of the broad fields of knowledge, concepts, and concrete objects are represented by headings consisting of a single noun, e.g., **Chemistry**; **Education**; **Law**; **Democracy**; **Books**; **Rocks**; **Water**; etc. When a noun has more than one meaning, a qualifier is added in parentheses to limit the heading to one concept or object e.g., **Bridge (Game)** or **Masks (Sculpture)**. The choice of the singular or the plural form depends on the term involved. In general, abstract concepts are represented by the singular noun, e.g., **Credit**, while concrete objects are represented by the plural, e.g., **Books**. Sometimes both the singular and the plural forms of a noun are used as headings. In such cases, they carry different meanings, e.g., **Essay** (the technique) and **Essays** (the works); or **Art** (for visual arts) and **Arts** (for arts in general).

Phrase Headings

Phrase headings are used when a subject or concept cannot be properly or precisely expressed by a single noun. Types of phrase headings include compound headings, adjectival headings, and prepositional phrase headings.

Compound Headings

Compound headings consist of two nouns or noun phrases connected by the word *and*. They are used mainly for the following purposes: (1) to connect topics or concepts which are usually treated together in works, e.g., **Scouts and scouting; Clothing and dress; Cliff dwellers and cliff dwellings**; (2) to connect opposite subjects that are usually treated together in works, e.g., **Debtor and creditor; Open and closed shop**; and (3) to express a relationship between two concepts or things, e.g., **Church and education; Philosophy and religion.**

Adjectival Headings

The most common type of adjectival headings consists of a noun or noun phrase with one or more adjectival modifiers, e.g., **English language; Space flight; Air-cushion vehicles; College students; Children's songs;** etc.

Prepositional Phrase Headings

Some concepts are expressed by nouns or noun phrases connected by prepositions that express their relationships, e.g., **Cooking for the sick; Electricity in agriculture; Religion in the public schools;** or **Devotional literature for children;** etc.

Form Headings

A form heading describes the form or genre of the work rather than its subject content. In other words, a form heading represents what the work *is* rather than what it is *about*. In the Sears list, form refers to the intellectual form, such as literary and artistic genres and forms of presentation, rather than the physical form, such as sound recordings or motion pictures. Examples of form headings include:

> **Book reviews**
> **Children's poetry**
> **Children's songs**
> **Indexes**
> **Short stories**

Headings such as **Sound recordings** and **Motion pictures** are used for works *about* sound recordings or motion pictures, etc. The scope note found under the particular heading indicates the usage, for example,

> **Sound recordings** (May subdiv. geog.) **621.389; 780.26**

is used for general materials and for materials on sound recordings that emphasize the content of the recording rather than the format. Materials about the format are entered under the format, e.g. **Compact discs.** Materials about the equipment or the process by which sound is recorded are entered under **Sound—Recording and reproducing.**

> SA   types of sound recordings, e.g. **Compact discs** and types of music with the subdivision *Sound recordings*, e.g. **Opera—Sound recordings** [to be added as needed]

Geographic Headings

Geographic names, both jurisdictional names and names representing geographic features, may appear as main headings or as subdivisions. Only a few geographic headings, e.g., **North America, United States, Ohio, Chicago (Ill.), Rocky Mountains**, appear in the Sears list as examples or to show cross references and subdivisions. Others are to be added by the cataloger as needed. They are formulated according to *Anglo-American Cataloguing Rules* (AACR2R),[3] for example, **Thailand, Tokyo (Japan)**, and **Mississippi River.**

Name Headings

Names of persons, families, corporate bodies, literary and artistic works, etc. may also be used as subject headings for works about them. Only a few name headings are included in the list, for example, **Napoleon I, Emperor of the French, 1769-1821; Shakespeare, William, 1564-1616; Lincoln family**, etc. Other names are to be added as needed.

The form of a personal heading and its cross references are established according to AACR2R in order that works written by and about the same person can be collocated in the catalog. The name authority record (explained in chapter 6) established for a person as an author serves to determine the form of both author and subject headings for that person. If a person whose name is required as a subject heading has not appeared as an author in the catalog, a name authority record should be established according to the same procedure as in descriptive cataloging. Examples of names of persons as subject headings are:

> **Boone, Daniel, 1734-1820**
> **Bush, George, 1924-**
> **Madonna, 1958-**

By way of exception, a few personal headings are included in the list. For example, **Jesus Christ** is included because of unique subdivisions; **Shakespeare, William, 1564-1616** is included as a "key" to show subdivisions that may be used under names of other voluminous authors—in other words, it serves as a "pattern" heading; and **Napoleon I, Emperor of the French, 1769-1821—Drama** is included because it is used as an example under the heading **Drama.**

CROSS REFERENCES

Cross references are used for two reasons: first, to guide users who consult the catalog under terms that are not used as subject headings to those terms that are and, second, to call users' attention to materials related to the topics being consulted. Cross references also help catalogers select the most appropriate headings for the work being cataloged. While a heading may appear many times in the catalog, each reference is made only once regardless of how many times the heading involved has been assigned to bibliographic records. Cross references appear in three forms: specific *see* references, specific *see also* references, and general references. When any heading in the Sears list has cross references associated with it, coded instructions appear under the heading to indicate what should be done. These instructions are described and explained in the following sections.

Specific *See* References

Specific *see* references appear under unauthorized terms, and indicate that another term should be used. In the Sears list, instruction for making *see* references, indicated by a preceding UF, is given after the authorized heading. The symbol UF (used for) means that references are to be made **from** the terms that follow **to** the heading immediately above it, e.g.,

> **Physicians**
> > UF   Doctors
> **Modern history**
> > UF   History, Modern

This means that in the printed Sears list, the lead-in terms "Doctors" and "History, Modern" are followed by references, indicated by the symbol *USE*, to the authorized headings **Physicians** and **Modern history** respectively, e.g.,

> Doctors
> > USE   **Physicians**
> History, Modern
> > USE   **Modern history**

It also means that if a cataloger is adding a record to the catalog using the subject heading **Physicians** for the first time, he or she should check to ensure that the catalog includes a USE reference to **Physicians** from the lead-in term "Doctors."

In general, USE references are made from synonymous or near-synonymous terms, and from inverted forms that are not used as subject headings. Occasionally, a USE reference is made from a more specific term that is not used as a heading to the more general term that is used, for example,

> Cooking utensils
> USE   **Kitchen utensils**

Specific *See Also* References

A *see also* reference connects a heading to a related heading or headings; such a reference is made only when the library has material listed under both headings. A *see also* reference is made for one of two purposes: to refer from a general subject to more specific parts of it (a downward hierarchical reference) and vice versa. A *see also* reference may also connect two related headings of more or less equal specificity (a same-level reference).

See also references, indicated by the symbols NT (narrower term), BT (broader term), and RT (related term) are listed directly under appropriate headings. In addition, reverse instructions are given under the headings referred to. For instance, for the headings **Bees,** Sears shows the following:

> **Bees**
> BT   **Insects**
> RT   **Beekeeping**
>   **Honey**
>
> **Beekeeping**
> BT   **Agriculture**
> RT   **Beehives**
>   **Bees**
>
> **Honey**
> BT   **Food**
> RT   **Bees**
>
> **Insects**
> BT   **Animals**
> NT   **Ants**
>   **Bees**
>   Etc.

General References

A general reference, in the form of SA (for *see also*), covers an entire category or class of headings rather than an individual heading. This device is used to save space in both the subject headings list and in the library catalog. A general explanation or direction is given instead of a long list of individual headings, e.g.,

Dogs
  SA types of dogs, e.g. **Guide dogs**; and names of specific breeds of dogs [to be added as needed]

Electronic musical instruments
  SA types of instruments, e.g. **Synthesizer (Musical instrument)** [to be added as needed]

Rivers
  SA names of rivers [to be added as needed]

Army
  USE **Armies**
       Military art and science
       and names of countries with the subhead *Army*, e.g.,
       United States. Army [to be added as needed]

Examples of Cross References

Following is an example of the different types of cross references required for a particular heading.

Carving (Decorative arts) (May subdiv. geog.) **731.4; 736**
  UF Carving (Arts)
  SA types of carving, e.g. **Wood carving** [to be added as needed]
  BT **Decorative arts**
  NT **Wood carving**
  RT **Sculpture**

Under the terms and headings referred to and from the authorized heading **Carving (Decorative arts)**, there are reciprocal references pointing back to the heading:

Carving (Arts)
  USE **Carving (Decorative arts)**

Decorative arts
  NT **Carving (Decorative arts)**

Wood carving
    BT   Carving (Decorative arts)

Sculpture
    RT   Carving (Decorative arts)

SUBDIVISIONS

In the Sears list, many general subjects are subdivided to indicate their specific aspects or to provide a subarrangement for a large number of works on the same subject. There are several types of subdivisions: subject or topical; form; period or chronological; and place, local, or geographic.

Subject or Topical Subdivisions

A subject or topical subdivision added to a main heading brings out a specific aspect or characteristic of the general subject, e.g.,

English language—Business English
English language—Dialects
English language—Etymology
Education—Curricula
Education—Finance

Form Subdivisions

A form subdivision expresses the intellectual or literary form of the work being cataloged, e.g.,

Animals—Poetry
Chemistry—Dictionaries
Chicago (Ill.)—Maps
Motion pictures—Catalogs
Sports—Fiction

Because many form subdivisions and some topical subdivisions are so common that they are applicable to many subjects, they are not enumerated under each heading with which they may be used but instead are listed together in the introduction to the Sears list (pages xlv–l, 18th edition). These subdivisions are equivalent to the free-floating subdivisions in LCSH. Because these common subdivisions may be used under subject headings where applicable, the following combinations may be assigned by the cataloger even though they are not actually so listed:

Librarians—Biography
Libraries—Directories
Piano music—Discography
Railroads—Maps
Space sciences—Periodicals

In addition to the list of common subdivisions mentioned above, instructions for the use of these subdivisions are also provided in the list itself under the appropriate terms, e.g.,

Bibliography
SA   subjects and names of persons and places with the subdivision *Bibliography*, e.g.
      Agriculture—Bibliography; Shakespeare, William, 1564-1616—Bibliography; United States— Bibliography; etc. [to be added as needed]
Maps
SA   types of maps, e.g. **Road maps**; subjects with the subdivision *Maps*, e.g. **Geology—Maps**; and names of countries, cities, etc., and names of wars with the subdivision *Maps* [to be added as needed]

It should be noted that some of the subdivisions represent the physical form or medium of the work, for example, **—Computer software; —Data- bases**; and **—Sound recordings**. However, they are used as topical subdivisions for works *about*, not as form subdivisions for works *in*, these forms. Thus, the heading **Opera—Sound recordings** is assigned to a work *about* operatic sound recordings, not the recordings themselves.

Exercise 10-1

Assign subject headings from the Sears list to the following topics.

1. Reading habits of adolescents
2. Advertising and selling by mail
3. Encyclopedia of science and technology
4. *Library Journal*
5. Handbook of chemistry and physics
6. History of the First World War
7. *Journal of Plant Pathology*
8. A list of scientific journals
9. *Time* (magazine)
10. A Russian-English dictionary of medical terms
11. A bibliography of library and information science
12. Opportunities in textile careers

13. An amateur photographer's handbook
14. *Sears List of Subject Headings*

Geographic Subdivisions

Many works deal with a subject with regard to a specific locality. For a subject that lends itself to such treatment, the Sears list authorizes geographic subdivisions; such authorization is indicated by a parenthetical statement, (May subdiv. geog.), following the main heading. For example, a heading such as **Flowers** (May subdiv. geog.) indicates that the following headings, though not listed, are valid as subject entries:

> **Flowers—United States**
> **Flowers—Hawaii**
> **Flowers—Honolulu (Hawaii)**

Period or Chronological Subdivisions

National history lends itself to chronological treatment. In the Sears list, chronological or period subdivisions are provided under the history of the United States and other countries about which American libraries are likely to have sizeable collections. Period subdivisions appear as further subdivisions under the subdivision —**History**.

> **United States—History—1600-1775, Colonial period**
> **United States—History—1689-1697, King William's War**
> **United States—History—1755-1763, French and Indian War**
> **United States—History—1775-1783, Revolution**
> **United States—History—1861-1865, Civil War**
>
> **Japan—History—0-1868**
> **Japan—History—1868-1945**
> **Japan—History—1945-1952, Allied occupation**
> **Japan—History—1952-**

Even though **United States** is a key heading, the period subdivisions listed under it may not be used under headings of other countries, because each country has a unique history and the period subdivisions appropriate to one country may not apply to other countries.

Exercise 10-2

Assign subject headings from the Sears list to the following.

1. Museums in New York City
2. Popular songs in the U.S.A.

3. Alternative work hours
4. Canadian foreign policy, 1945-1954
5. *The Eisenhower Years: A Historical Assessment*
6. Party politics in Australia
7. Directory of hospitals in Athens, Georgia
8. The reign of Elizabeth, 1558-1603
9. A pictorial guide to San Francisco
10. *Famous American Military Leaders*
11. *Norwegian Folk Tales: A Collection*
12. *Getting to Know Iran and Iraq*
13. *The Land and People of Switzerland*

Key Headings for Subdivisions

Many subdivisions are applicable to headings in a particular category. Instead of enumerating these subdivisions under each heading in the category, one heading is chosen as the "key" heading under which typical subdivisions are listed; in other words, they are analogous to pattern headings in LCSH. The following headings serve as the key patterns for subdivisions in Sears:

Category	Key heading
Authors	**Shakespeare, William, 1564-1616**
Ethnic groups	**Native Americans**
Languages	**English language**
Literature	**English literature**
Places	**United States**
	Ohio
	Chicago (Ill.)
Public figures	**Presidents—United States**
Wars	**World War, 1939-1945**

The subdivisions listed under them may be used whenever appropriate with other headings in the same categories. For example, the subdivisions listed under **World War, 1939-1945** may be used with the heading for another war, e.g., **Persian Gulf War, 1991—Causes.**

Order of Subdivisions

When a subject heading contains multiple subdivisions, the order of the subdivisions within the string follows the practice of LCSH:

[Topical]—[Geographic]—[Chronological]—[Form]
[Geographic]—[Topical]—[Chronological]—[Form]

For example,

American literature—Southern States—Bibliography
United States—Civilization—1960-1970—Periodicals

HEADINGS TO BE ADDED BY THE CATALOGER

Sears contains the headings that are most commonly used in small libraries and is not intended to be an exhaustive list of subject headings. Personal names, corporate names, and other proper names are potential
subject headings because many works are written about individual persons, institutions, places, events, and so on. However, it is not practical or
even possible to include in the subject headings list all possible names
that may become subjects of works. Headings needed in cataloging but
not listed may be added, according to specific instructions.[4] The "SA"
references in the list provide instructions on creating headings in areas
most frequently needed, for example,

Tools (May subdiv. geog.)
   SA   types of tools [to be added as needed]
Trees (May subdiv. geog.)
   SA   types of trees, e.g., **Oak** [to be added as needed], in the
         singular form

As a result, any catalog using the Sears list will likely show many assigned subject headings that do not appear in the list. Furthermore, when
new names are needed as subject headings, the cataloger must derive the
appropriate form. Most names that do not appear in the subject list are
proper names for persons, families, places, or corporate bodies. In addition, certain types of common names may also be added as needed. Such
headings are created by the cataloger according to descriptive cataloging
rules or following established headings in the same subject category or as
shown in examples.
     The arrays given below list the categories of headings that are not in
Sears but are likely to be needed in addition to headings in the list:

Topical Subjects

1. Types of common things—foods, tools, sports, musical instruments, etc. (e.g., **Carrots; Spinach; Pork; Hammers; Badminton;
   Harpsichord;** etc.)
2. Types of plants and animals—fruits, flowers, birds, fishes, etc.
   (e.g., **Grapefruit; Carnations; Swallows; Trout; Kangaroos;** etc.)
3. Types of chemicals and minerals (e.g., **Chlorite; Glycine; Potas-
   sium; Topaz;** etc.)

4. Types of enterprises and industries (e.g., **Horse industry**, etc.)
5. Types of diseases (e.g., **Measles**)
6. Names of organs and regions of the body (e.g., **Kidney; Legs;** etc.)
7. Names of languages, language groups, and national literatures (e.g., **Turkish language; Austrian literature;** etc.). **English language** and **English literature** serve as key headings for subdivisions.
8. Names of ethnic groups and nationalities (e.g., **Oneida Indians; Belgians; Germans;** etc.). **Native Americans** serves as the key for subdivisions under ethnic group or native people.
9. Names of wars, battles, treaties, etc. (e.g., **Waterloo, Battle of, 1815; Portsmouth, Treaty of, 1905**). The heading **World War, 1939-1945** serves as the key for subdivisions under any war, and in some cases under individual battles.

Geographic Headings

1. Names of political jurisdictions—countries, states, cities, provinces, etc.
   Very few geographical or place names are listed as such in Sears. Those which are included serve as key headings for treatment of analogous headings. Geographical or place names fall into several different categories, as described below.
   A. Countries (e.g., **India; Belgium**, etc.). A number of countries are included to show their unique period subdivisions. The heading **United States** serves as a key heading for topical and form subdivisions. The subdivisions (except period subdivisions which are not transferable) under **United States** may be used with names of other countries, e.g., (**India—Geography; Belgium—Population**).
   B. States (e.g., **Colorado; Wyoming**, etc.). **Ohio**, as a key state, is listed with subdivisions which can be used under names of other states.
   C. Provinces, etc. (e.g., **Scotland; Ontario; British Columbia;** etc.).
   D. Cities (e.g., **San Francisco (Calif.); Athens (Ga.); Dijon (France); etc.). The name of the country or the state (if in the United States) is added to the name of a local place in accordance with AACR2R for geographic names. For subdivisions, Chicago (Ill.)** serves as the key city.
2. Groups of states, groups of countries, alliances, etc. (e.g., **Baltic States**).
3. Names of geographic features—regions, mountain ranges, island groups, individual mountains, individual islands, rivers, river valleys, oceans, lakes, etc.

A. Mountain ranges and individual mountains (e.g., **Smokey Mountains; Mont Blanc;** etc.)
B. Island groups and individual islands (e.g., **Virgin Islands; Jamaica;** etc.)
C. River valleys and individual rivers (e.g., **Ohio Valley; Mississippi River;** etc.)
D. Regions, oceans, lakes, etc. (**Indian Ocean; Kentucky Lake;** etc.)

Names

Works about individual persons, corporate bodies, and other works are assigned as subject headings in the form of name or uniform title headings established according to descriptive cataloging rules so that they are compatible with headings used as main and added entries.

1. Personal names—individual persons and families. (The heading for the name of a family consists of the family name followed by the word **family,** e.g., **Kennedy family; Brontë family;** etc.)
   A. **Shakespeare, William, 1564-1616,** serves as the key for subdivisions under voluminous authors and under other individual persons as appropriate.
   B. **Presidents—United States** serves as the key heading for subdivisions under the presidents, prime ministers, governors, etc., and in some cases under the names of individual presidents, prime ministers, etc.
2. Corporate names—names of associations, societies, government bodies, religious denominations, business firms, performing groups, colleges, libraries, hospitals, hotels, ships, etc.
   A. Names of associations, societies, clubs, etc. (e.g., **American Chemical Society; American Library Association;** etc.)
   B. Names of government bodies (**United States. Navy; California. Legislature;** etc.)
   C. Names of religious denominations (e.g., **Methodist Church;** etc.)
   D. Names of institutions: colleges, libraries, hospitals, etc. (e.g., **Smith College; Florida State University; New York Public Library; Massachusetts General Hospital;** etc.)
   E. Names of hotels, retail stores, ships, etc. (e.g., **Christina (Ship);** etc.)
3. Uniform titles—anonymous literary works, newspapers, periodicals, sacred scriptures, motion pictures, etc.

Exercise 10-3

Assign subject headings from the Sears list to the following.

1. Swedish word origins
2. *Poems for Thanksgiving* (by various American authors)
3. Russian grammar
4. *The Peace Corps in Action*
5. *Chemicals of Life: Enzymes, Vitamins, Hormones*
6. A history of the American Medical Association
7. NATO and Europe
8. The German community in Cincinnati
9. *Wonders of the Himalayas*
10. A travel guide to Estonia, Latvia, and Lithuania
11. *The Department of Defense: A History*
12. Sparrows of Asia

SUBJECT HEADINGS FOR SPECIAL TYPES OF MATERIALS

Certain types of library materials require special treatment; of these, the most common are biography and literature.

Subject Headings for Biography

Collective Biography

A work containing biographies of more than three persons is treated as a *collective biography*. A subject heading covering the entire group is assigned, instead of individual personal headings. Various kinds of collective biographies are discussed below:

General Biography

If a collective biography is not limited to any geographic area, time period, or subject field or a particular class of people, for example, Van Loon's *Lives*, the general form heading **Biography** is assigned. For a work *about* biography, the heading **Biography as a literary form** is used. For biographical reference works that are arranged in dictionary form, e.g., *Webster's Biographical Dictionary* or *International Who's Who*, the heading **Biography—Dictionaries** is used.

Local Biography

When a collective biography contains lives of people from a particular geographic area or a specific ethnic group, e.g., *Who's Who in Australia*, *Canadian Who's Who*, and *Who's Who among African Americans*, the subject heading is in the form of the geographic or ethnic name with the subdivision —**Biography** or —**Biography—Dictionaries:**

> Australia—Biography—Dictionaries
> Canada—Biography—Dictionaries
> African Americans—Biography

Classes of Persons

When a collective biography contains lives of persons of a particular subject field or a class, a subject heading is assigned in the form of the term representing the members of the field or the class, e.g., **Chemists; Explorers; Philosophers; Sailors;** etc. In some cases, the heading may be divided geographically, e.g., **Actors—United States; Composers—Germany; Statesmen—Great Britain;** etc. In other cases, the adjective form is used, e.g., **American poets; English dramatists.**

When there is no appropriate term to represent the members of a field or when the name of the class or group refers to the subject in general rather than to individuals, the heading assigned is in the form of the name of the field or group with the subdivision —**Biography:**

> Baseball—Biography
> France—History—1789-1799, Revolution—Biography
> Women—Biography

Individual Biography

For a biography of one, two, or three individuals, the name of each individual is assigned as a subject heading; the form of the heading should agree with the established heading of the same person used as the main or added entry in descriptive cataloging. A biography of Robert F. Kennedy, for example, is assigned the heading,

> **Kennedy, Robert F., 1925-1968—Biography.**

A biography of two or three of the Kennedy brothers would be assigned headings under the name of each.

Frequently, when the biography of a person also contains material about the field in which the person is concerned, a second subject heading representing the subject field is added. For example, if the biography of President John F. Kennedy contains a substantial amount of material on his administration, a second heading **United States—History—1961-1974** is assigned in addition to the personal heading.

For persons about whom there is a large amount of material, subdivisions are used for subarrangement. The heading **Shakespeare, William, 1564-1616** serves as the "key" for subdivisions to be used under other voluminous authors when there is a large amount of material. The subdivisions listed under the heading **Presidents—United States** may be used under headings for individual presidents, prime ministers, and other rulers. In small libraries, for most individual biographies, the personal name alone without any subdivision is sufficient as the heading.

For autobiographical writings, including journals, memoirs, and letters in addition to autobiographies, a subject heading identical to the author entry is often assigned. This is important in searching, because it allows the separate retrieval of works *by* and *about* the person.

The headings used with collective biographies are not assigned to individual biographies. For example, the heading **Musicians** or **Musicians—United States** is not used with a biography of Billy Joel. However, a reference is made from the collective heading to the individual headings, e.g.,

> **Musicians** (May subdiv. geog.)
> SA   types of musicians and names of individual musicians [to be added as needed]

Subject Headings for Literature

There are two distinctive categories of works in the field of literature: (1) works *about* literature, and (2) literary works or specimens. These receive different treatment in subject cataloging.

Works about Literature

These works, in which literature *is* the subject, are treated like other works with subject headings representing the content and the scope of the works, e.g.,

> **Literature**
> [with or without subdivisions depending on the scope]
> **American literature**
> [use **English literature** as the key for subdivisions]
> **Drama**
> **German drama—History and criticism**
> **Essay**
> **English essays—History and criticism**

Many of the more general literature headings are subdivided for special aspects. These may be used when appropriate. In addition, the general subdivisions listed in the Sears introduction (pages xlv–l) may also be used when appropriate. Note that the subdivision —**History and criticism**, instead of —**History**, is used with literature headings.

The headings discussed above do not apply to works about individual authors or about works written by them. A work about an individual author or about his or her works is assigned a heading in the form of the author's name, e.g., **Dickens, Charles, 1812-1870**. The heading for Shakespeare serves as a key for subdivisions used with voluminous authors.

In addition to headings representing literary forms or genres, topical headings are also assigned to bring out the themes of the works. Headings for topics in literature are assigned according to the pattern shown under the following heading:

> **Literature—Themes: 809**
> SA   subjects, racial and ethnic groups, and classes of persons in literature, e.g. **Dogs in literature; Women in literature**; etc. and names of persons, families, and corporate bodies with the subdivision *In literature*, e.g. **Napoleon I, Emperor of the French, 1769-1821—In literature** [to be added as needed]

Literary Works

In these works, literature is the *form* rather than the *subject*. There are two categories of literary works: collections of works of more than one author, and single or collected works by individual authors.

Collections of Works of More Than One Author

A literary form heading, e.g., **Essays; American drama—Collections**; etc., is assigned to a collection of works of more then one author. To differentiate a topical heading from a form heading containing the same term, the singular form is used as the topical heading (for a work *about* the literary form) and the plural form, when there is one, is used as the form heading (for literary collections). When there is no acceptable plural form of a noun, the subdivision —**Collections** is added, for example:

Subject heading	*Form heading for collections*
Essay	**Essays**
Short story	**Short stories**
Literature	**Literature—Collections**
Spanish literature	**Spanish literature—Collections**
Poetry	**Poetry—Collections**
English poetry	**English poetry—Collections**

Topical and geographic headings are often assigned to collections of novels, poems, and plays to bring out predominant topics, places, persons, or historical events. To distinguish between factual accounts of these topics and aspects from literary or imaginative works, the subdivisions —Fiction, —Poetry, or —Drama are added to the latter, e.g.,

> **Basketball—Fiction**
> **United States—History—1861-1865, Civil War—Fiction**
> [for a work such as *Gone with the Wind* by Margaret Mitchell]
> **Lincoln, Abraham, 1809-1865—Drama**
> [for a work such as *Abe Lincoln in Illinois* by Robert E. Sherwood]
> **Napoleon I, Emperor of the French, 1769-1821—Poetry**

Works by Individual Authors

For collected or individual works by individual authors, no literary form heading is assigned if the works are in one of the major forms such as drama, fiction, and poetry. However, for collected works in a minor form such as parodies, satire, and short stories by an individual author, headings similar to those used with collections by more than one author are assigned as instructed. The scope note under a particular heading gives instruction regarding its applicability to collected and/or individual works, for example,

Drama: 808.2; 808.82

Use for general materials on drama, not for individual works. . . . Collections of plays are entered under **Drama—Collections; American drama—Collections; English drama—Collections**; etc.

English drama: 822

Use for general materials about English drama, not for individual works.

Short stories: 808.83

Use for collections of short stories by one author or by several authors . . .

Science fiction: 808.3; 808.83

May be used for individual works, collections, or materials about fiction based on imagined developments in science and technology.

For example, **English drama** is not assigned to a play written by Shakespeare, nor **American fiction** to Hemingway's novel *The Old Man* *and the Sea.* On the other hand, E. A. Poe's *Selected Tales,* a collection of short stories, is assigned the heading **Short stories.** Minor literary forms are not listed under the national adjectives.

In the eighteenth edition of Sears, many form or genre headings, based on the *Guidelines on Subject Access to Individual Works of Fiction, Drama, Etc.,*[5] issued by the American Library Association, were added to enhance access to individual works of fiction, poetry, drama, and other imaginative works. The assignment of minor literary form and genre headings, such as **Ballads; Horror fiction;** and **Science fiction,** to individual works of literature is in keeping with the ALA *Guidelines.*

Exercise 10-4

Assign subject headings from the Sears list to the following:

1. Lives of famous French dramatists
2. *American Men and Women of Science*
3. Short stories: a collection
4. Stories of Maupassant
5. Commentaries on the New Testament
6. Life of Pablo Picasso
7. Modern American secret agents
8. Famous New Yorkers
9. Life of Daniel Boone
10. *The Agony and the Ecstasy* (an American novel based on the life of Michelangelo)
11. *Best Sports Stories*
12. *A Day in the Life of President Johnson* (Lyndon B.)
13. *The Combat Nurses of World War II*
14. *Book of Poetry for Children*
15. *A Man for All Seasons* (an English drama based on the life of Sir Thomas More)
16. *A Study of Mark Twain's Novels*

Subject Headings for Nonprint Resources

For nonprint materials, including electronic resources, users of the Sears list are advised to follow the same principles they would use for print materials. Form subdivisions are not used under topical headings to bring out physical format such as motion pictures, slides, sound recordings, computer files, etc., because "AACR2 provides the option of using general material designations (GMD) at the end of the title proper to alert users to the general class of material to which an item belongs."[6]

NOTES

1. *Sears List of Subject Headings*, 18th ed., Joseph Miller, Editor; Joan Goodsell, Associate Editor (New York: H. W. Wilson Company, 2004).

2. For a discussion of these principles, see "Principles of the Sears List of Subject Headings," in *Sears List of Subject Headings*, 18th ed., xv–xxix.

3. *Anglo-American Cataloguing Rules*. 2nd ed., 2002 revision. Prepared under the direction of the Joint Steering Committee for Revision of AACR, a committee of: the American Library Association, the Australian Committee on Cataloguing, the British Library, the Canadian Committee on Cataloguing, Chartered Institute of Library and Information Professionals, the Library of Congress. (Chicago: American Library Association, 2002–.)

4. *Sears List of Subject Headings*, xl.

5. Association for Library Collections & Technical Services, Cataloging and Classification Section, Subject Analysis Committee, Subcommittee on the Revision of the Guidelines on Subject Access to Individual Works of Fiction, *Guidelines on Subject Access to Individual Works of Fiction, Drama, Etc.*, 2nd ed. (Chicago: American Library Association, 2000).

6. "Principles of the Sears List of Subject Headings," xxxii.

CHAPTER 11
MEDICAL SUBJECT HEADINGS

INTRODUCTION

Library of Congress Subject Headings (LCSH) and *Sears List of Subject Headings* are not the only systems of subject cataloging used in American libraries and information agencies. Most, but not all, of the others are designed for special subject fields. This chapter discusses *Medical Subject Headings* (MeSH) as an example of a specialized subject vocabulary.

MeSH is the system designed and used by the National Library of Medicine (NLM) for assigning medical subject headings or indexing terms to books and journal articles in the biomedical sciences. It has gained considerable acceptance outside of NLM and is now widely used by both health sciences libraries and the abstracting and indexing services that serve the field.

BRIEF HISTORY

In the 1940s, a subject authority file on cards was established at NLM for use in its bibliographies and catalogs.[1] Its headings followed the patterns set by LCSH but were not quite the same. Early on, NLM had had two access systems—one for citations to medical books and one for indexing journal articles. In the early 1950s, NLM decided to integrate the two by constructing a thesaurus of medical subject headings (MeSH) to be used by both NLM catalogers and by indexers of journal literature for both *Index Medicus* and its online version MEDLINE. MEDLINE is now a part of PubMed, a service of the U.S. National Library of Medicine that includes over 16 million citations from MEDLINE and other life science journals for biomedical articles back to the 1950s. It also includes links to full-text articles and other related resources.

MeSH was originally based on *Library of Congress Subject Headings* (LCSH) but has departed considerably from it. Over the years, MeSH has become an increasingly faceted system so that most searching is done using postcoordination. This is true particularly when MeSH functions as an indexing tool for the 4,800 or so of the world's leading biomedical journals for the MEDLINE/PubMED® database. NLM also uses MeSH for the NLM database that includes cataloging records for the books, documents, and audiovisual materials acquired by the Library.[2]

The first official publication of the medical subject headings list appeared in 1954 under the title *Subject Heading Authority List Used by the Current List Division, Armed Forces Medical Library*.[3] Beginning in 1960, the list has been published under the title *Medical Subject Headings*.[4]

MeSH now exists in two versions:

1. An online version accessible on the NLM website (www.nlm.nih .gov/mesh) and available for downloading in several data formats, including XML, ASCII MeSH, and MeSH/MARC.
2. A print version published in January of each year. Until 2003, it came out in three volumes: the *Annotated Alphabetic List*, *MeSH Tree Structures*, and *Permuted MeSH*. Since then, an alphabetic list and the tree structures have been published annually. Currently, *Medical Subject Headings* (familiarly known as the black and white MeSH and formerly known as the *Supplement to Index Medicus*) combines the alphabetic list and the tree structures in a single publication.

STRUCTURE OF MeSH

MeSH descriptors, also called MeSH headings, are organized into categorized lists called "tree structures" that show hierarchical relationships among terms. *Tree Structures*[5] consists of a categorical arrangement placing each heading in relationship to other headings that represent similar areas and concepts. A system of "tree numbers" (each consisting of a capital letter followed by one or more digits) is used to reflect the hierarchies.

The tree structures first appeared in 1963 (in the second edition of MeSH) with thirteen main categories. There are currently sixteen main categories:

A. Anatomy
B. Organisms
C. Diseases
D. Chemicals and Drugs
E. Analytical, Diagnostic, and Therapeutic Techniques and Equipment
F. Psychiatry and Psychology
G. Biological Sciences
H. Physical Sciences
I. Anthropology, Education, Sociology and Social Phenomena
J. Technology, Industry, Agriculture
K. Humanities
L. Information Science
M. Named Groups

N. Health Care
V. Publication Characteristics
Z. Geographic Locations

Each category is subdivided into one or more subcategories, with headings arranged hierarchically in each. Each heading is accompanied by the full tree number giving the location of the heading in the "tree." If a topic represented by a given heading belongs in more than one subcategory, that heading may appear in several places in the *tree structures*. When a concept appears in more than one hierarchy, it is assigned multiple tree numbers. For example, the descriptor **Asthma** appears in the following "trees":

> Respiratory Tract Diseases [C08]
>   Bronchial Diseases [C08.127]
>   **Asthma** [C08.127.108]
>   Asthma, Exercise-Induced [C08.127.108.110]
>   Status Asthmaticus [C08.127.108.880]
>
> Respiratory Tract Diseases [C08]
>   Respiratory Hypersensitivity [C08.674]
>   **Asthma** [C08.674.095]
>   Asthma, Exercise-Induced [C08.674.095.110]
>   Status Asthmaticus [C08.674.095.880]
>
> Immune System Diseases [C20]
>   Hypersensitivity [C20.543]
>   Hypersensitivity, Immediate [C20.543.480]
>   Respiratory Hypersensitivity [C20.543.480.680]
>   **Asthma** [C20.543.480.680.095]
>   Asthma, Exercise-Induced [C20.543.480.680.095.110]
>   Status Asthmaticus [C20.543.480.680.095.880]

The tree structures provide a classificatory approach to medical subjects,[6] manifesting hierarchical principles and providing a logical basis for the cross references. In online retrieval, the tree numbers, also called descriptor codes, can be used to search for related subjects.

TYPES OF MeSH TERMS

MeSH contains the following types of terms:[7] **Descriptors** (main headings), **Qualifiers**, **Publication Types**, **Geographics**, and **References**.

Descriptors

Descriptors, also called *main headings*, represent main topics. Most descriptors are topical, in the form of single words or phrases. Examples are:

Acrylic Resins
Asthma
Blood Pressure
Nurses
Nurses' Aides
Nursing Administration Research
Pediatrics
Pulmonary Circulation
Respiratory System
Therapeutics
Thermal Conductivity
Vinyl Compounds

Some phrase headings are inverted in order to collocate significant terms, for example,

Nurses, Male
Respiration, Artificial
Respiratory Therapy Department, Hospital
Therapy, Computer-Assisted

The following examples show the authority records for the descriptors **Asthma** and **Blood Pressure**:

MeSH Heading	Asthma
Tree Number	C08.127.108
Tree Number	C08.381.495.108
Tree Number	C08.674.095
Tree Number	C20.543.480.680.095
Annotation	do not coord with BRONCHIAL DIS for X ref ASTHMA, BRONCHIAL; / drug ther: consider also ANTI-ASTHMATIC AGENTS; ASTHMA, CARDIAC see DYSPNEA, PAROXYSMAL is available
Scope Note	A form of bronchial disorder associated with airway obstruction, marked by recurrent attacks of paroxysmal dyspnea, with wheezing due to spasmodic contraction of the bronchi.
Entry Term	Asthma, Bronchial
Entry Term	Bronchial Asthma
See Also	Anti-Asthmatic Agents
Allowable Qualifiers	BL CF CI CL CN CO DH DI DT EC EH

EM EN EP ET GE HI IM ME MI
MO NU PA PC PP PS PX RA RH RI
RT SU TH UR US VE VI

Unique ID   D001249

MeSH Heading   Blood Pressure
Tree Number   G09.330.553.400.114
Annotation   GEN; note specifics; "arterial" pressure
                       = BLOOD PRESSURE and not also
                       ARTERIES unless a specific artery;
                       pressure within a specific vessel:
                       coord vessel / physiol (IM) +
                       BLOOD PRESSURE (NIM); do not
                       add SYSTOLE, DIASTOLE or
                       PULSE unless particularly
                       discussed; with diseases coord IM
                       with disease / physiopathol (IM),
                       not / blood (IM): Manual 23.28;
                       blood pressure vs
                       HYPERTENSION &
                       HYPOTENSION: Manual 23.27 +
Scope Note   PRESSURE of the BLOOD on the
                       ARTERIES and other BLOOD
                       VESSELS.
Entry Term   Systolic Pressure
Entry Term   Diastolic Pressure
Entry Term   Pulse Pressure
See Also   Hypertension
See Also   Hypotension
Allowable Qualifiers DE ES GE IM PH RE
Unique ID   D001794

Qualifiers

A *qualifier*, formally called a *subheading*, is used to qualify a main heading by specifying one of its aspects. Qualifiers are used with descriptors to collocate those documents concerned with a particular aspect of a subject. Not every qualifier is suitable for use with every main heading. The list of Qualifiers by Allowable Category[8] contains 62 subject categories and the qualifiers assigned to those categories. The following example shows allowable categories under headings relating to general drugs and chemicals

> **D LIST—General Drugs and Chemicals**
> AA /analogs
> AD /admin

AE /adv eff
AG /agon
AI /antag
AN /anal
BL /blood
CF /csf
CH /chem
CL /class
CS /chem syn
CT /contra
DU /diag use

There are two types of qualifier: topical and publication type. Examples of qualifiers are shown below:

Topical Qualifiers

administration & dosage
analysis
diagnosis
embryology
standards
therapeutic use

Example of authority record for a qualifier:

Subheading	administration & dosage
Record Type	Q
Entry Version	ADMIN
Abbreviation	AD
Scope Note	Used with drugs for dosage forms, routes of administration, frequency and duration of administration, quantity of medication, and the effects of these factors.
Annotation	subhead only; for routes of administration, timing, amounts of doses; not for "dosage" in Romance languages (= / analysis) ; see MeSH scope note in Introduction; indexing policy: Manual 19.8.2; DF: /admin or /AD
Online Note	search policy: Online Manual; use: main heading/AD or AD (SH) or SUBS APPLY AD
History Note	66; used with Category D 1966-90 forward
Date of Entry	19731227

Revision Date	20030722
Date Established	19660101
Unique ID	Q000008

Publication Characteristics

Qualifiers for type of publication[9] indicate what the item *is*, i.e., its genre, rather than what it is *about*. Examples include:

Abbreviations [Publication Type]
Abstracts [Publication Type]
Atlases [Publication Type]
Congresses [Publication Type]
Directory [Publication Type]
Handbooks [Publication Type]
Indexes [Publication Type]
Periodicals [Publication Type]
Popular Works [Publication Type]

Geographics

Geographics include continents, regions, countries, states, and other geographic subdivisions. They are listed in category Z of the tree structures but do not appear in the alphabetical list. Examples include:

Afghanistan
Africa
Africa, Eastern
Africa, Central

Hawaii
Hebrides
Honduras
Hong Kong

New South Wales
New York
New York City
New Zealand

Pacific Islands
Pacific Ocean

Rhode Island
Romania
Rome

Entry Vocabulary

There are three categories of entry vocabulary: *see* references, *see also* (or *see related*) references, and *consider also* references.[10]

1. Entry terms, or *see references*, include cross references from synonyms or closely related terms to descriptors. In searching, they may be used interchangeably with preferred descriptors. *See* references indicate that information related to the term in question is found under its *descriptor*, i.e., the authorized term for the subject. Not all such terms are synonyms of the descriptors to which they refer. They are, however, designed to lead from a user's entry term to valid headings, and are made from synonyms, near-synonyms, abbreviations, alternate spellings, and other alternate forms. Because of their narrow focus, some terms are not useful as subject headings and are listed instead as cross references. Examples include:

AORTA/radiography see **AORTOGRAPHY**
HYPERTENSION see **BLOOD PRESSURE, HIGH**
NURSERY SCHOOLS see **SCHOOLS, NURSERY**
RESPIRATORS see **VENTILATORS, MECHANICAL**
VIDINE see **CHOLINE**
BAREFOOT DOCTORS see **COMMUNITY HEALTH AIDES**

2. *See also* or *see related* references indicate the presence of other headings that relate to the topic conceptually but do not occur in the same subcategory of the MeSH Tree Structures. *See also* references are made regularly between an organ and a procedure (e.g., **Aorta** See Also **Aortography**); between an organ and a physiological Process (**Bone and Bones** See Also **Osteogenesis**); between a physiological process and a related disease (**Blood Pressure** See Also **Hypertension**); and between an organ and a drug acting on it (**Bronchi** See Also **Bronchoconstrictor Agents**).

3. *Consider also* references are used primarily with anatomical descriptors. They refer to other descriptors that relate to the topic linguistically, i.e., to groups of descriptors beginning with a common stem rather than to a single descriptor, for example,

Brain
    consider also terms at **CEREBR-** and **ENCEPHAL-**
Heart
    consider also terms at **CARDI-** and **MYOCARDI-**
Kidney
    consider also terms at **GLOMERUL-, NEPHR-, PYEL-,** and **RENAL**

CATALOGING INSTRUCTIONS

In 1998, the National Library of Medicine installed the Voyager Integrated Library System. One of the components of Voyager is LocatorPlus, NLM's online public access catalog (OPAC). LocatorPlus is available at http://locatorplus.gov. Since then, NLM has harmonized its cataloging and indexing practices in order to facilitate cross-file searching through the NLM Gateway. The Library also made a decision to stop using the traditional subject heading strings on its internal bibliographic records. However, on request from many users, NLM now reconstructs heading strings on those records which are distributed to bibliographic utilities and other licensees.

In addition to LocatorPlus, NLM has an alternative search interface: the NLM Catalog (available at www.ncbi.nlm.nih.gov/entrez/query.fcgi ?DB = nlmcatalog). It provides access to NLM bibliographic records for journals, books, audiovisuals, computer software, electronic resources, and other materials using the NCBI (National Center for Biotechnology Information) Entrez system. The NLM Catalog links to LocatorPlus for access to NLM holdings information.

NLM's website "Use of Medical Subject Headings for Cataloging"[11] sets out specific instructions regarding its cataloging practices, including how to construct traditional subject heading strings. These are summarized below.

Assigning Main Headings

As is true for other controlled vocabularies, catalogers and indexers are instructed to find and use the most specific MeSH descriptor or heading that is available to represent the main focus of the work. Additional descriptors or headings may then be assigned to bring out secondary topics and to enhance access. An example given on the MeSH website illustrates this practice:[12]

> For example, articles concerning Streptococcus pneumoniae will be found under the descriptor Streptococcus Pneumoniae rather than the broader term Streptococcus, while an article referring to a new streptococcal bacterium which is not yet in the vocabulary will be listed directly under Streptococcus. Accordingly, the user may consult the trees to find additional subject headings which are more specific than a given heading, and broader headings as well. For example, under Abnormalities, there are specific abnormalities:
> Abnormalities C16.131
> Abnormalities, Drug Induced C16.131.042
> Abnormalities, Multiple C16.131.077

Alagille Syndrome C16.131.077.065
Angelman Syndrome C16.131.077.095

Because MeSH descriptors are used in both indexing and cataloging, instructions in MeSH include those specifically noted for cataloging. Such annotations are prefaced by the word "CATALOG" under each heading, for example, "CATALOG: do not use" or "CATALOG: use NAF [name authority file] only."

Assigning Two or More Main Headings

If the topic in question contains more than one concept or facet, catalogers may employ one or more of the three following methods:

1. using two or more main headings
2. using a precoordinated main heading
3. using a main heading and a subheading, including topical, geographic, form, or language subheadings

If a publication deals with two or more subjects that are subordinate to a broad heading, up to three separate, specific headings are assigned. If more than three subjects are involved, the broad heading encompassing the individual specific topics in the tree structure is assigned. If the specific subjects are not within a tree, as many specific headings as necessary are assigned.

Representation of Complex Subjects

In applying MeSH, complex subjects can be represented in three ways:[13]

1. Postcoordination: Using two or more separate descriptors, leaving it to the searcher to infer the connection. For example, jejunal enteritis may be expressed by assigning separately the terms **Jejunum** and **Enteritis**.
2. Precoordination at the point of indexing: using qualifiers in conjunction with appropriate descriptors. For example, a deficiency of monoamine oxidase may be indexed as **Monoamine Oxidase/ deficiency**. The direct linkage of the qualifier to the descriptor to which it relates avoids the possibility of false coordination that may occur if two descriptors are used to represent a single concept.
3. Precoordination in the vocabulary: MeSH includes many precoordinated descriptors for frequently encountered subjects. When a descriptor-qualifier combination is available, it is assigned in preference to using two separate descriptors. For example, if MeSH has a precoordinated descriptor such as Heart Surgery, the indexer or cataloger uses it rather than a descriptor-qualifier combination.

Assigning Precoordinated Headings

As noted earlier, if a precoordinated main heading is available, it is used instead of two or more separate headings; for example, the phrase heading **NURSING RESEARCH** takes precedence over the two separate headings **NURSING** and **RESEARCH**. However, two headings are assigned for public health research, **PUBLIC HEALTH** and **RESEARCH**, because there is no phrase heading for the topic research in public health.

The citation order of precoordinated heading strings is not the same for records in LocatorPlus and for those in distributed records. In the MARC View of LocatorPlus, subject headings appear in the following format:[14]

> 650 _2$a   Main Heading $x topical subheading
> 651 _2$a   Geographic location $x topical subheading
> 655 _7$a   Publication type (formerly form division) $2 mesh
> 659 _7$a   Genre/publication type $2 mesh

The order of the main headings and subheadings on distributed records is:

> 650 _2$a   Main Heading $x topical subheading $z geographic
>   location $v publication type/genre [former form
>   subheading] $x language
> 650 _2$a   Main Heading $x topical subheading $x age group $z
>   geographic location $v Publication type/genre
>   [former form subheading] $x language

Assigning Topical Subheadings

Under a particular main heading, the cataloger or indexer may assign only those topical subheadings included in the allowable qualifier list for that heading. These can be found in the MeSH heading record in the MeSH Browser.

In cataloging a particular work, if no more than three topical subheadings are applicable to a given main heading, multiple headings containing the main heading and appropriate topical subheadings are assigned. When more then three topical subheadings are applicable, the main heading is assigned without topical subheadings.

Geographic Locations

In NLM's Web-based catalogs (including the Web-based OPAC, Locator-Plus, and an Entrez-base search interface), main headings, or main heading and topical subheading combinations, are not qualified by geographic, form, or language terms. This is because geographic descriptors and publication types (PTs), previously known as form divisions, are carried in separate fields. Retrieval is accomplished postcoordinately by using either main headings or main heading/topical subheading combinations.

On the other hand, in distributed records, geographic locations are included in the subject headings, for example,

> 650_2 $a Hepatitis, Viral, Human $x prevention & control $z Minnesota.
> 650_2 $a Needs Assessment $z Minnesota.

Language

MeSH headings in the LocatorPlus record do not contain language subfields in the subject string since this information is encoded in the MARC 21 language field (041). They are however included in distributed records, for example,

> 65012 $a Medicine $v Dictionary $x English.
> 65012 $a Medicine $v Dictionary $x French.

Publication Types

Publication types, formerly known as "form subheadings," are used to indicate the form of the overall publication. Not all available publication types are used in cataloging. Those that are used fall into two categories:[15]

Publication Types Used as Form Divisions

These may be added as form subdivisions in a subject heading string (MARC 21 650 subfield $v in distributed records or MARC 21 field 655 (Genre/Form) in LocatorPlus). Examples include:

> **Bibliography**
> **Biography**
> **Case Report**
> **Collected Works**
> **Congresses**
> **Dictionary**
> **Laboratory Manuals**
> Etc.

For example:

> In LocatorPlus:
> 650 12 $a   Kidney Diseases
> 655 _7 $a   **Congresses** $2 mesh

On distributed records:
650 12 $a   Kidney Diseases $v **Congresses**

Publication Types Used as Genres

These are not added to subject heading strings but are assigned separately in MARC 21 field 655 on distributed records and in field 659 (a locally defined field) in LocatorPlus. Examples include:

Academic Dissertations
Almanacs
Book Reviews
Festschrift
Newspaper article
Posters
Practical Guideline
Etc.

For example:

In LocatorPlus:
650 12 $a   Renal Dialysis
659 _7 $a   **Practice Guideline** $2 mesh
In distributed records:
650 12 $a   Renal Dialysis
655 _7 $a   **Practice Guideline** $2 mesh

Because the descriptive and coded portions of a bibliographic record contain the physical format information pertinent to each item, such information is not part of the MeSH subject string.

MARC Coding

In bibliographic records, MARC 21 codes used with MeSH headings are similar to those used with Library of Congress subject headings:

600   Personal name heading
610   Corporate name heading
630   Uniform title
650   Topical heading
651   Geographic name heading

The first indicator in the 650 field indicates the "Level of subject:"

#—No information provided
0—No level specified
    The level of the term could be determined but is not specified.

1—Primary
The term describes the main focus or subject content of the material.
2—Secondary
The subject term describes a less important aspect of the content of the material.

The second indicator in each 6XX field indicates the source vocabulary; for example, 0 indicates LC headings, and 2 indicates MeSH headings.

CATALOGING EXAMPLES

The following examples illustrate the cataloging of medical publications using MeSH headings. Library of Congress subject headings are shown for the purpose of comparison.

Tutorials in paediatric differential diagnosis / edited by David Field, David Isaacs, John Stroobant. 2005
1. **Diagnosis, Differential—Child.**
2. **Diagnosis, Differential.**
[LC subject headings:
1. **Children—Diseases—Diagnosis**
2. **Diagnosis, Differential.**]

The respiratory system / David Petechuk. 2004
1. **Respiratory System.**
2. **Respiratory Tract Diseases.**
[LC subject headings:
1. **Respiratory organs—Diseases.**
2. **Respiratory organs.**
3. **Respiration.**]

Children, ethics, and modern medicine / Richard B. Miller. 2003
1. **Ethics, Clinical.**
2. **Pediatrics.**
3. **Ethics, Medical.**
[LC subject headings:
1. **Pediatrics—Moral and ethical aspects.**
2. **Medical ethics.**
3. **Children—Diseases—Treatment—Moral and ethical aspects.**]

Introduction to human anatomy and physiology / Eldra Pearl Solomon. 2003
1. **Anatomy.**
2. **Physiology.**

[LC subject headings:
1. **Human physiology.**
2. **Human anatomy.**]

Say it in Spanish : a guide for health care professionals / Esperanza Villanueva Joyce, Maria Elena Villanueva. 2004
 1. **Medicine—Phrases—English.**
 2. **Medicine—Phrases—Spanish.**
[LC subject headings:
 1. **Medicine—Dictionaries.**
 2. **Spanish language—Conversation and phrase books (for medical personnel).**
 3. **Spanish language—Dictionaries—English.**]

Running in place : how the Medicaid model falls short, and what to do about it / Eliot Fishman. 2002
 1. **Medicaid—organization & administration.**
 2. **Medicaid—economics.**
 3. **Models, Economic—United States.**
 4. **State Government—United States.**
[LC subject headings:
 1. **Medicaid.**
 2. **Medical policy—United States.**]

The psychodynamics of addiction / edited by Martin Weegmann and Robert Cohen. 2002
 1. **Behavior, Addictive—psychology.**
[LC subject headings:
 1. **Compulsive behavior.**
 2. **Compulsive behavior—Treatment.**]

The clinical interview of the child / Stanley I. Greenspan, with Nancy Thorndike Greenspan. 2003
 1. **Interview, Psychological—child.**
 2. **Interview, Psychological—infant.**
[LC subject headings:
 1. **Mental illness—Diagnosis.**
 2. **Interviewing in child psychiatry.**
 3. **Child psychology.**]

NOTES

1. "The National Library of Medicine," in *Encyclopedia of Library and Information Science*, ed. Allen Kent (New York: Marcel Dekker, 1986), v. 41 (Supp. 6): 231–56.

2. National Library of Medicine (U.S.), "Fact Sheet: Medical Subject Headings (MeSH®)," www.nlm.nih.gov/pubs/factsheets/mesh.html (25 Feb. 2007).

3. National Library of Medicine (U.S.), *Subject Heading Authority List Used by the Current List Division, Armed Forces Medical Library* (Washington, D.C.: 1954).

4. *Medical Subject Headings* (Bethesda, Md.: National Library of Medicine, 1960-2003 [last printed version]; online version: www.nlm.nih.gov/mesh/ (25 Feb. 2007).

5. National Library of Medicine (U.S.), "Medical Subject Headings: MeSH Tree Structures," www.nlm.nih.gov/mesh/intro_trees2007.html (25 Feb. 2007).

6. Susan L. Gullion, "Cataloging and Classification: Classification and Subject Cataloging," in *Handbook of Medical Library Practice*, ed. Louise Darling, David Bishop, Lois Ann Colaianni, 4th ed. (Chicago: Medical Library Association, 1983), 269.

7. National Library of Medicine (U.S.), "Medical Subject Headings: Features of the MeSH Vocabulary," www.nlm.nih.gov/mesh/intro_features2006.html (25 Feb. 2007).

8. National Library of Medicine (U.S.), "Medical Subject Headings: Qualifiers by Allowable Category—2007," www.nlm.nih.gov/mesh/topcat2007.html (25 Feb. 2007).

9. National Library of Medicine (U.S.), "Medical Subject Headings: Publication Characteristics—Scope Notes," 2007, www.nlm.nih.gov/mesh/pubtypes 2007.html (25 Feb. 2007).

10. National Library of Medicine (U.S.), "Medical Subject Headings: Entry Terms and Other Cross-References," www.nlm.nih.gov/mesh/intro_entry2007 .html (25 Feb. 2007).

11. National Library of Medicine (U.S.), "Medical Subject Headings: Use of Medical Subject Headings for Cataloging—2007," www.nlm.nih.gov/mesh/cat practices2007.html (25 Feb. 2007).

12. National Library of Medicine (U.S.), "Medical Subject Headings: Use of Medical Subject Headings for Cataloging—2007," www.nlm.nih.gov/mesh/cat practices2007.html (25 Feb. 2007).

13. National Library of Medicine (U.S.), "Medical Subject Headings: Use of Medical Subject Headings for Cataloging—2007."

14. National Library of Medicine (U.S.), "Medical Subject Headings: Use of Medical Subject Headings for Cataloging—2007."

15. National Library of Medicine (U.S.), "Medical Subject Headings: Use of Medical Subject Headings for Cataloging—2007."

PART FIVE
ORGANIZATION OF LIBRARY RESOURCES

STANDARDS AND TOOLS

Cutter, C. A. C. A. Cutter's Three-Figure Author Table. Swanson-Swift revision. Chicopee, Mass.: H.R. Huntting Company, 1969.

Cutter, C. A. C. A. Cutter's Two-Figure Author Table. Swanson-Swift revision. Chicopee, Mass.: H. R. Huntting Company, 1969.

Cutter, C. A. Cutter-Sanborn Three-Figure Author Table. Swanson-Swift revision. Chicopee, Mass.: H. R. Huntting Company, 1969.

Dewey, Melvil. Abridged Dewey Decimal Classification and Relative Index. Ed. 14. Edited by Joan S. Mitchell, Editor in Chief; Julianne Beall, Giles Martin, Winton E. Matthews, Jr., Gregory R. New, Assistant Editors. Dublin, Ohio: OCLC, Online Computer Library Center, Inc., 2004.

Dewey, Melvil. Dewey Decimal Classification and Relative Index: Devised by Melvil Dewey. Ed. 24. Edited by Joan S. Mitchell, Editor in Chief; Julianne Beall, Giles Martin, Winton E. Matthews, Jr., Gregory R. New, Assistant Editors. Dublin, Ohio: OCLC, Online Computer Library Center, Inc., 2003.

Library of Congress. Library of Congress Classification Weekly Lists. No. 1, January 2002. www.loc.gov/catdir/cpso/cpso.html#class.

Library of Congress. Cataloging Policy and Support Office. Classification. Washington, D.C.: Library of Congress, 1901–.

Library of Congress. Cataloging Policy and Support Office. Subject Cataloging Manual: Classification. Washington, D.C.: Library of Congress, 1992–.

Library of Congress. Cataloging Policy and Support Office. Subject Cataloging Manual: Shelflisting. 2nd ed. Washington, D.C.: Library of Congress, 1995–.

Library of Congress. Classification Web: World Wide Web Access to Library of

Congress Classification and Library of Congress Subject Headings.
www.loc.gov/cds/classweb (24 Oct. 2006).
National Library of Medicine (U.S.). *NLM Classification.* 2002–. www.nlm
.nih.gov/class/.

RECOMMENDED READING

Chan, Lois Mai. *A Guide to the Library of Congress Classification.* 5th ed.
Englewood, Colo.: Libraries Unlimited, 1999.
Chan, Lois Mai, and Joan S. Mitchell. *Dewey Decimal Classification: Princi-
ples and Application.* 3rd ed. Dublin, Ohio: OCLC Online Computer
Library Center, 2003.
Comaromi, John P. *Book Numbers: A Historical Study and Practical Guide to
Their Use.* Littleton, Colo.: Libraries Unlimited, 1981.
——. "Conception and Development of the Dewey Decimal Classifica-
tion." *International Classification* 3 (1976): 11–15.
——. *The Eighteen Editions of the Dewey Decimal Classification.* Albany,
N.Y.: Forest Press Division, Lake Placid Education Foundation, 1976.
Dunkin, Paul S. "Where Does It Go? Call Numbers." 96–137 in *Cataloging
U.S.A.* Chicago: American Library Association, 1969.
Foskett, A. C. *The Subject Approach to Information.* 5th ed. London: Library
Association Pub, 1996.
"Introduction to the Dewey Decimal Classification." In *Dewey Decimal
Classification and Relative Index.* Ed. 22. Vol. 1, xxvii–lxiii.
"Introduction to the Dewey Decimal Classification." In *Abridged Dewey
Decimal Classification and Relative Index.* Ed. 14. xxiii–xlvi.
Koch, Traugott, and Michael Day. *The Role of Classification Schemes in In-
ternet Resource Description and Discovery.* Last updated: 28-Jan-1999.
www.ukoln.ac.uk/metadata/desire/classification/ (25 Feb. 2007).
LaMontagne, Leo E. *American Library Classification with Special Reference to
the Library of Congress.* Hamden, Conn.: Shoe String Press, 1961.
Lehnus, Donald J. *Book Numbers: History, Principles, and Application.* Chi-
cago: American Library Association, 1980.
Marcella, Rita, and Arthur Maltby. *The Future of Classification.* Aldershot,
Eng.; Brookfield, Vt.: Gower, 2000.
Palmer, Bernard I. *Itself an Education: Six Lectures on Classification.* 2nd ed.
London: Library Association, 1971.
Ranganathan, S. R. *Elements of Classification; Based on Lectures Delivered at
the University of Bombay in December 1944 and in the School of Librarian-
ship in Great Britain in December 1956.* 2nd ed., revised and rewritten.
Edited by B. I. Palmer. London: Association of Assistant Librarians,
Section of the Library Association, 1959.

CHAPTER 12
CLASSIFICATION AND CATEGORIZATION

DEFINITION

Classification, broadly defined, is the process of organizing knowledge into some systematic order. It has been considered the most fundamental activity of the human mind. The essential act of classification is the multi-stage process of deciding on a property or characteristic of interest, distinguishing things or objects that possess that property from those which lack it, and grouping things or objects that share a common property or characteristic into a class. Other essential aspects of classification are establishing relationships among classes and making distinctions within classes to arrive at broader and finer divisions. Those who devise and use library classification schemes do much the same thing. The classification of library materials can thus be seen as a special application of a much more general human intellectual activity.

Library classification in particular has been defined as "the systematic arrangement by subject of books and other material on shelves or of catalogue and index entries in the manner that is most useful to those who read or who seek a definite piece of information."[1] Although this definition covers what may be done in-house to serve the needs of a specialized audience, traditionally, library classification has involved labeling materials in a collection according to the provisions of an inclusive, usually hierarchically arranged, scheme. The labels, called notation, usually in the form of numerals or letters or a combination of both, served a dual function: to arrange items in a logical order on library shelves, and to provide a systematic display of bibliographic entries in printed catalogs, bibliographies, and indexes. It should be noted here that "logical order" is not the same for every circumstance. In any collection, the most appropriate basis for determining groups varies according to the needs of the collection. For example, library materials may be grouped by author, physical form, size, date of publication, or subject. In modern library classification systems, subject is the predominant characteristic for grouping.

In addition to shelving and display, classification is used as a tool for collection management, e.g., facilitating the creation of specialized branch libraries and the generation of discipline-specific holdings lists. In online public access catalogs (OPACs), classification also serves a direct retrieval function because class numbers can be used as access points to MARC records.

In today's teeming information world, classification may have a wider role to play, a fact that has been recognized by many in the library community. In 1999, the ALCTS (Association of Library Collections and Technical Services) Subcommittee on Metadata and Subject Analysis recommended that subject access through classification be extended to other metadata records by including class numbers, but not necessarily item numbers, from existing classification schemes in metadata records for Web resources.[2] In the same year, its related committee, the ALCTS Subcommittee on Metadata and Classification, identified seven functions of classification: location, browsing, hierarchical movement, retrieval, identification, limiting/partitioning, and profiling.[3]

With the rapid growth of networked resources over the last two decades, the enormous amount of information available on the Web has cried out for systematic organization. In some cases, classification systems have been called into play. Many library portals that in the beginning offered only alphabetical listing and/or keyword searching have adopted a directory approach based on broad subject categorization schemes when their collections of electronic resources became voluminous and unwieldy.[4] In parallel, many Web designers have turned to classification as a supplementary navigational tool, so that during the last decade or so, subject categorization devices that are similar to broad classification schemes have become fairly popular among Web information providers. However, not many such devices provide the rigorous hierarchical structure and careful conceptual organization found in traditional classification schemes. In both milieus, some of the adopted schemes are based on existing classification systems, such as the Dewey Decimal Classification (DDC) and the Library of Congress Classification (LCC); others are the fruit of in-house labor.

The reason for the turn toward more systematic subject control lies in the fact that subject categorization defines narrower domains within which term searching can be carried out more efficiently and thus enables the retrieval of more relevant results. In fact, combining subject categorization with term searching has proven to be an effective and efficient approach in resource discovery and data mining. In this regard, classification or subject categorizing schemes function as information filters, used "to quickly eliminate large segments of a database from consideration of a query."[5] Furthermore, classification schemes can also serve as switching mechanisms across different languages and different controlled vocabularies.[6]

In the library context, *classification* as a term refers both to the development of schemes for the systematic display of all aspects of the various fields of knowledge and to the art of arranging books or other objects in conformity with such schemes. In other words, it is used both for the creation of a classification scheme and for its application. For clarity in discourse, the people who are involved in these two processes are given different names. The inventor or creator of a classification scheme or a person who is engaged in the theory of classification is called a *classificationist*, while the person who applies such a scheme is referred to as a *classifier*.

BASIC CONCEPTS

The traditional ideas of library classification were borrowed from the logical or philosophical principles of classification. Classification begins with the universe of knowledge as a whole and divides it into successive stages of classes and subclasses, with a chosen characteristic, also called *facet*, as the basis for each stage. For a broad subject area, called a main class, the progression is from general to specific, forming a hierarchical or "tree" structure in which each class is a *species* of the class on the preceding level and a *genus* to the one below it. The array of classes on each level, usually mutually exclusive and totally exhaustive categories, form a coordinate relationship to one another and are collocated according to the affinity of their relationships. Classification according to hierarchical principles, with biological taxonomy the prevailing model, was in a particularly active stage of development during the latter part of the nineteenth century. The Dewey Decimal Classification (DDC) and the Library of Congress Classification (LCC), the most widely used library classification systems today, both originated at that time and reflect the general intellectual climate of the era. Each would be seriously out of date by now were it not for the fact that each organization, OCLC's Dewey Services and LC's Cataloging Policy and Support Office, are conscientious about undertaking revisions and issuing updates.

With a particular hierarchy, the basis for division within a class into subclasses and sub-subclasses may vary considerably from subject to subject. For example, architecture can be classified according to schools and styles, periods, or types of buildings. Literature can be divided by language, genre/form, or period. Each characteristic is called a *facet*. Figure 12-1 illustrates the division of literature in DDC based on the three facets named above.

The coordinate elements on each level or stage of division form an *array*, e.g., **American literature, English literature, German literature**, etc. The term *chain* refers to a string of subjects, each of which represents a different level in the hierarchy, e.g., **Literature—English literature— English poetry—Elizabethan poetry**. There is not always a built-in or natural order of the characteristics or facets in each class. For example, although language is a natural first-order division for literature, the next divisions could be first by form and then by period, or equally reasonably

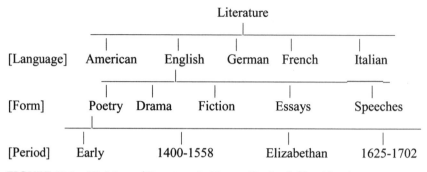

FIGURE 12-1   Division of literature in Dewey Decimal Classification

the other way around; just as many readers, presumably, would like to see Victorian novels, drama, poetry and so on in close array as would like to see English poetry arranged chronologically. The original designers of classification systems made what they considered appropriate decisions on principles of division, class by class; and then they and their successors tried to maintain consistency within each class on how facets were determined and developed. Order of facets is called *citation order*.

Traditional library classification schemes tend to list all subjects and their subdivisions and provide ready-made symbols for them. Such a scheme is referred to as *enumerative* classification. Among existing library classification schemes, LCC is considered the most fully enumerative.

Modern classification theory, on the other hand, places emphasis on *facet analysis* and *synthesis*—the *analysis* (or breaking up) of a subject into its component parts and the *synthesis* (or reassembling) of those parts as required by the document to be represented. Instead of enumerating all subjects in a hierarchical structure, modern theory argues that a classification scheme should identify the basic components of subjects and list under each discipline, or main class, the elements or aspects that are topically important within that class. Each class has its own class-specific *facets*. For instance, the class Education might have a facet for Persons Taught, a facet for Subjects Taught, a facet for Educators, a facet for Methods of Instruction, a facet for Educational Institutions, and so on. In addition, recurring or common facets, such as form divisions, geographical divisions, and chronological divisions, are listed separately for application to all classes. In applying such a scheme, the act of classification essentially consists of identifying appropriate component facets and synthesizing (i.e., combining) them according to a predetermined *citation formula*. A system based on these principles is called a *faceted* or *analyticosynthetic classification*. An example is the Colon Classification.[7]

Some classification systems provide minute details under each class or subject, while others provide broad subject divisions only. The former are referred to as *close classification*, and the latter as *broad classification*.

NOTATION

Each classification scheme adopts a system of symbols to represent its classes and divisions. The purpose of such a device, called *notation*, is to furnish a brief designation of subjects (and sometimes their relationships as well) and to provide a sequential order for arrangement of library materials, particularly for shelf location.

In some classification systems, the notation consists of all letters; in others, all numbers; and in still others, a combination of both. A *pure notation* is one in which only one type of symbol is used: an example is the notation of DDC which consists of Arabic numerals. A system that employs more than one type of symbol is called a *mixed notation*: an example is the combined letters and Arabic numerals in the notation of LCC.

A *hierarchical notation* is one that reflects the structural order or hierarchy of the classification, while an *expressive notation* is one that expresses relationships among coordinate subjects. The notation used with DDC is hierarchical, and that of the Universal Decimal Classification is both hierarchical and expressive. The notation of LCC is neither.

Another feature of some notation schemes is internal *mnemonics*, or aids to memory. In this context, the term means that when a given topic recurs in the scheme, it is represented consistently by the same symbol. For example, in DDC, poetry is represented by the number 1, hence, 811 (American poetry), 831 (German poetry), 841 (French poetry), and so on. Correspondingly, 3 often pertains to Germany, and 4 to France.

COMPONENTS OF A CLASSIFICATION SCHEME

A classification scheme consists typically of the following components:

Schedule: the entire sequence of class numbers and captions arranged in class number order

Tables: consisting of additional numbers used in conjunction with numbers from the schedule

Index: a list of index terms with corresponding class numbers

Additional documentation: introduction, manual or instructions on use, glossary, etc.

HOW TO CLASSIFY

Classifying and assigning subject headings both begin with the same intellectual process: determining the subject content and identifying the principal concepts in the work under consideration. This process was described in the chapter on subject cataloging. Much of what was said in that chapter applies here, but the two processes are not fully parallel. One difference, of course, is that while in subject cataloging the content of a work is represented by verbal terms, in classification it is notation (based of course on verbal terms in classification schedules) that carries the meaning. A more important difference is that, because in American libraries classification was traditionally used mainly as a shelving or location device, only one class number is chosen for each work; in subject cataloging, on the other hand, any number of subject headings may be assigned to a work. (Of course, where classification is considered a major retrieval device, as in libraries with a classed catalog or bibliographies arranged by classification numbers, two or more different classification numbers may also be assigned to a given work, with one of them being used as an indication of shelf location.)

Choosing a Number: General Guidelines

If the subject, or overall content, of the work in hand focuses on a clearly defined topic, classifying it is a relatively simple operation. One needs simply to choose the appropriate number from the scheme being used. However, a work may deal with more than one topic, or more than one aspect of a topic: different topics may be treated together as parts of a broader topic; they may be brought together by the author because they are affinitive topics considered separately; they may be treated in terms of their relationship to each other; or, finally, a given topic may be treated from an interdisciplinary point of view. Faceted classification schemes such as the Universal Decimal Classification or Colon Classification provide for combining class numbers to bring out every topic or aspect treated in a multitopical work. However, such combinations are not always possible with traditional schemes such as DDC or LCC; classifiers working in traditional situations often have to choose one number from two or more numbers that represent the different topics or aspects treated in the work.

The use of each classification system involves certain unique procedures, and, for DDC, LCC, and the National Library of Medicine (NLM) Classification, these procedures are discussed in detail in later chapters. The following discussion focuses on some of the general principles and guidelines that apply to the classification of library resources in general.

1. Consider Usefulness

When a work can be classed in more than one number in a scheme, consider where it will be most useful to the users.

2. Make Topic the Primary Consideration

When the classification scheme allows alternatives, in general, class by topic, then by place, time, and form, except in literature, where language and literary form are what matter most.

3. Use the Most Specific Number Available

Class a work in the most specific number that will contain it. There may not be an exact number for every topic encountered, however. When there is no specific number for the work, place it in the next most specific category above it, depending on which scheme is used. For example, classify a history of Chicago in the number for Chicago, if available; if not, place it in the number for the next larger geographic unit, i.e., the county, state, or country, for which the scheme makes provision.

4. Do not Classify from the Index Alone

The index or indexes that accompany each classification scheme provide help in locating specific class numbers. However, the chosen number should always be checked in the schedules to ensure that the topic of the work being classified has been placed properly in the overall structure of the scheme and that the instructions in the schedules restricting or elaborating the use of the number have been observed.

Choosing a Number: Multitopical Works

There is no hard and fast rule for the choice of a number for a multitopical work. The following guidelines[8] are generally applicable.

1. Determine the Dominant Topic or the Phase Relations

Dominant Topic

Classify under the dominant topic, if one can be determined. If the topics are treated separately, a ready indication of preponderance may be the amount of space devoted to each. Another gauge is the author's apparent intention or purpose.

Phase Relations

The situation with a work in which the different topics are viewed in relationship to each other is more complicated. In such a case, an analysis of the relationship may help to determine the emphasis of the work. *Phase relations*, in other words, the interrelationships among topics treated in a work, were discussed earlier in the chapter on subject cataloging. In classification, the following considerations apply.

Influence Phase. Classify a work about the influence of one thing or person on another under the topic or person being influenced.

Bias Phase. Classify a work on a particular subject written with a "bias" toward, or aiming at, a specific group of readers (for example, *Fundamentals of Physical Chemistry for Premedical Students*), under the topic (physical chemistry), not the element to which it is "biased" (premedical or medical sciences).

Tool or Application Phase. Classify a work such as *Chemical Calculations: an Introduction to the Use of Mathematics in Chemistry* under the topic (chemistry) instead of the tool (mathematics).

Comparison Phase. Class under the topic emphasized or under the first topic.

Note: It should be stressed that the preceding are only *general* guidelines. If a work on the influence of one topic or one person on another clearly places emphasis on the topic or person exerting the influence, it should be classed with that topic or person. Similarly, if a work on a topic written for a specific group of readers is of little value to other readers, it should be classed under the number reflecting the intended readers.

2. Class under First Topic

If the dominant topic cannot be ascertained—for instance, when works treating two or three topics separately or in comparison do not give any indication of preponderance—class under the first topic treated, unless instructed otherwise in the scheme. In DDC, *first* means the one coming first in the schedules. For example, a work dealing equally with Judaism (296) and Islam (297) would be placed in 296. Without such specific instructions, *first* may mean the topic treated first in the work.

3. Class under Broader Topic

Class under the broader topic a work dealing with two or three topics that are subdivisions of a broader topic and that together constitute the major portion of that topic, for instance, choosing the number for classical languages for a work about Greek and Latin. Likewise, for a work dealing with four or more topics, all of which are divisions of a broader topic, class under the number that covers them all; for example, use the number for chemistry (540) for a work about physical (541), analytical (543), inorganic (546), and organic (547) chemistry.

CALL NUMBERS

To distinguish individual bibliographic items on the same subject, an *item number* (also called *book number*) is added to the class number to form a "call number" as a location symbol for the item in the library's collection. The term "call number" probably originated from the fact that in the earlier days most libraries had closed stacks, and a library user would have to "call" for a book from the collection by means of its unique number.

Many libraries adopt the principle of unique call numbers. Each item in the library is assigned a number different from any other call number in the collection. In this sense, the call number serves as the true address of the item. The call number consists of the class number followed by one or more elements based on the bibliographic characteristics of the item, such as the author's name, the title, the edition, the date of publication, the volume number, etc.

There are various ways of composing a call number, depending on the size of the collection and the classification system used. The procedures for assigning call numbers are discussed in the following chapters on individual classification schemes.

MARC CODING FOR CLASSIFICATION AND ITEM NUMBERS

In *MARC 21 Format for Bibliographic Data*, the following fields contain data relating to call numbers based on classification systems discussed in this book:

050   Library of Congress call number
        Indicators:
           First—Existence in LC collection
           # (blank) = No information provided
               A call number assigned by an organization other than LC.
           0 = Item is in LC
           1 = Item is not in LC
           Second—Source of call number
           0 = Assigned by the Library of Congress (LC)
           4 = Assigned by agency other than LC
        Subfield codes:
           $a = Classification number (R)
           $b = Item number (NR)
           $3 = Materials specified (NR)
               The part of the described materials to which the field applies
           $6 = Linkage (NR)
           $8 = Field link and sequence number (R)
060   National Library of Medicine (NLM) call number
        Indicators:
           First—Existence in NLM collection
           # (blank) = No information provided
               A call number assigned by an organization other than LC.

0 = Item is in NLM
1 = Item is not in NLM
Second—Source of call number
0 = Assigned by NLM
4 = Assigned by agency other than NLM
Subfield codes:
$a = Classification number (R)
$b = Item number (NR)
$8 = Field link and sequence number (R)

080   Universal Decimal Classification number
082   Dewey Decimal call number
Indicators:
First—Type of edition
0 = Full edition
1 = Abridged edition
Second—Source of call number
# (blank) = No information provided
0 = Assigned by LC
4 = Assigned by agency other than LC
Subfield codes:
$a = Classification number (R)
$b = Item number (NR)
$2 = Edition number (NR)
$6 = Linkage (NR)
$8 = Field link and sequence number (R)

090-099   Local call numbers

MODERN LIBRARY CLASSIFICATION SYSTEMS

Many library classification systems have been developed in modern times, some for general collections and others for specialized subject collections. The following chapters discuss in detail the major systems used by American libraries and make a brief presentation of the salient characteristics of a number of other classification systems along with information on their conception and development.

NOTES

1. Arthur Maltby, *Sayers' Manual of Classification for Librarians*, 5th ed. (London: Andre Deutsch, 1975), 15.

2. ALCTS/CCS/SAC/Subcommittee on Metadata and Subject Analysis, *Subject Data in the Metadata Record: Recommendations and Rationale: A Report*, 1999, www.ala.org/ala/alctscontent/catalogingsection/catcommittees/subjectanalysis/metadataandsubje/subjectdata.htm (25 Feb. 2007).

3. ALCTS/CCS/SAC/Subcommittee on Metadata and Classification, *Final Report* (1999), www.ala.org/ala/alctscontent/catalogingsection/catcommittees/subjectanalysis/metadataandclass/metadataclassification.htm (25 Feb. 2007).

4. Thomas J. Waldhart, Joseph B. Miller, and Lois Mai Chan, "Provision of Local Assisted Access to Selected Internet Information Resources by ARL Academic Libraries," *Journal of Academic Librarianship* 26, no. 2 (March 2000): 100–109.

5. Robert R. Korfhage, "The Matching Process," In *Information Storage and Retrieval* (New York: Wiley, 1997), 79–104.

6. Lois Mai Chan, "Exploiting LCSH, LCC, and DDC to Retrieve Networked Resources," in *Proceedings of the Bicentennial Conference on Bibliographic Control for the New Millennium: Confronting the Challenges of Networked Resources and the Web,* Washington, D.C. November 15–17, 2000, sponsored by the Library of Congress Cataloging Directorate, ed. Ann M. Sandberg-Fox (Washington, D.C., Library of Congress, November 2001), 164.

7. S. R. Ranganathan, *Colon Classification,* 6th ed., reprinted with amendments (Bombay: Asia Publishing House, 1963).

8. "Introduction to the Dewey Decimal Classification," in *Dewey Decimal Classification and Relative Index,* ed. 22, ed. Joan S. Mitchell, Editor in Chief; Julianne Beall, Giles Martin, Winton E. Matthews, Jr., Gregory R. New, Assistant Editors (Dublin, Ohio: OCLC, Online Computer Library Center, Inc., 2003), vol. 1, xli–xlv; Paul S. Dunkin, *Cataloging U.S.A.* (Chicago: American Library Association, 1969), 116–22; William Stetson Merrill, *Code for Classifiers,* 2nd ed. (Chicago: American Library Association, 1939), 3–7.

CHAPTER 13
DEWEY DECIMAL
CLASSIFICATION

HISTORY

The Beginning

The publication in 1876 of a pamphlet entitled *A Classification and Subject Index for Cataloguing and Arranging the Books and Pamphlets of a Library* marked the beginning of the Dewey Decimal Classification (DDC), which was soon adopted by many libraries in the United States and later by libraries around the world. Today, in its twenty-second edition (2003), the Dewey Decimal Classification is the most widely used library classification system in the world.[1] The scheme has been translated into more than thirty languages, including Arabic, Chinese, French, German, Greek, Hebrew, Icelandic, Italian, Korean, Norwegian, Russian, Spanish, Swedish, and Vietnamese. It is used in more than 20,000 libraries in 135 + countries around the world. In the United States, DDC users include academic, public, special, and school libraries.

DDC was conceived as a classification of knowledge for the purpose of organizing a library. Melvil Dewey (1851–1931), the founder of the system named after him, was assistant librarian at Amherst College when he developed the scheme. In the preface to the first edition (1876), Dewey states that the system was developed early in 1873 as a result of several months' study of some hundreds of books and pamphlets and of over fifty personal visits to various American libraries.

The 1876 edition, consisting of merely forty-four pages and published anonymously, contains a brief preface outlining Dewey's principles, the schedules for ten main classes subdivided decimally to form a total of 1,000 categories numbered 000–999, and an alphabetical subject index. The division of main classes was based on an earlier classification system (1870) devised by W. T. Harris, who, in turn, based his scheme on an inverted order of Francis Bacon's classification of knowledge.[2] Bacon divides knowledge into three basic categories (history, poesy, and philosophy), corresponding to the three basic faculties of the human mind (memory, imagination, and reason). The classifications of Bacon, Harris, and Dewey are compared in Table 13-1.

TABLE 13-1   Classification Systems of Bacon, Harris, and Dewey

Bacon		Harris	Dewey
[Original]	*[Inverted]*		
		Science	
History	Philosophy	Philosophy	General works
(Memory)		Religion	Philosophy
		Social and	Religion
		political science	Sociology
		Natural sciences	Philology
		and useful arts	Science
			Useful arts
		Art	
Poesy	Poesy	Fine arts	Fine arts
(Imagination)		Poetry	Literature
		Pure fiction	
		Literary miscellany	
		History	
Philosophy	History	Geography and	History
(Reason)		travel	Biography
		Civil history	Geography and
		Biography	travel
		Appendix	
		Miscellany	

In his new classification scheme, Dewey introduced two new features: relative location and relative index. Prior to Dewey, books in libraries were numbered according to the chronological order in which they were acquired, and that order determined their locations on the shelves. Such a practice meant that each book had a fixed location. The Dewey system, on the other hand, numbers books in terms of their relationship to one another without regard to the shelves or rooms where they are placed. Relative location allows infinite interposition; new and reclassified books are placed with others on the same subject. In the relative index, Dewey brings together under one term the locations in the scheme of a subject which, in many cases, falls in several fields of study and is scattered under different numbers.

Early Editions

The second edition (1885) of DDC, a considerable expansion from the 1876 edition, contained a number of relocations—i.e., shifts of subjects from certain numbers to other numbers. This edition set the notational pattern for all subsequent editions. It was also in this edition that Dewey laid down his famous injunction of the "integrity of numbers." Being a pragmatist and a realist, Dewey was fully aware that a system that changed substantially from edition to edition would not be acceptable to librarians, because changes, particularly relocations, necessitate reclassification—a labor-intensive operation. Therefore, in the preface to the second edition, Dewey declared that the numbers may be considered "settled," and henceforth there would be expansions when necessary but as few relocations as possible. This policy had a stabilizing effect on subsequent revisions of DDC, particularly in the early editions. Nonetheless, in order to cope with new developments in knowledge, certain major changes could not be avoided.

Dewey himself supervised DDC revision through its thirteenth edition, working until his death in 1931. His interest in simplified spelling was reflected in the early schedules, e.g., Filosofy and Geografy.

The fourteenth edition followed the editorial policies that had governed work on earlier editions: expansion in detail as required, but little change in basic structure. The expansion, however, had not always been balanced, and there were many underdeveloped areas.

Fifteenth Edition

With the fifteenth edition, it was decided that a new approach was necessary in order to give the scheme a more even structure and to keep up with new developments in knowledge, particularly in science and technology. Several innovations were introduced: details were cut back until all subjects reflected more or less equal degrees of subdivision; a large number of subjects were relocated; the index was pruned drastically; and the simplified spelling used in earlier editions was discontinued. The magnitude of the changes was considerable, for instance, some 31,000 entries in the fourteenth edition were reduced to 4,700 in the fifteenth edition.

After the publication of the fifteenth edition in 1951, it soon became clear that the changes were too much for practicing librarians, most of whom refused to accept the new edition and continued to use the fourteenth. Criticism of the fifteenth edition was fierce and vehement. Many critics even pronounced the system "dead."

Sixteenth Edition and Later Editions

The sixteenth edition, under the editorship of Benjamin A. Custer, appeared in 1958. This edition reflected a return to the former policy of detailed enumeration but incorporated some of the innovative features of the fifteenth edition, such as standard spelling, current terminology, and a pleasing typographical presentation.

The seventeenth through nineteenth editions, also under the editorship of Custer, continued to develop along similar lines. Attempts were made to keep pace with knowledge while maintaining "integrity of numbers" to the greatest reasonable extent.

Edition 20, under the editorship of John P. Comaromi, assisted by Julianne Beall, Winton E. Matthews, Jr., and Gregory R. New, appeared in 1989. The classification, by then, had grown into a four-volume set. A classifiers' manual, which was first issued as a separate publication after the appearance of Edition 19, was incorporated into Edition 20, following the index. Edition 21, begun under the leadership of Comaromi and continued under the editorship of Joan S. Mitchell, appeared in 1996. Edition 22 was published in 2003.

Under the direction of Mitchell, DDC has gone through considerable internationalization, resulting in the adoption and translation of the scheme into many languages around the world. In recent editions, to render the system more useful and useable to users outside of the United States, American biases in the treatment of certain subjects such as religion and law have been gradually removed.

PUBLICATION OF THE CLASSIFICATION

Versions of DDC

The Dewey Decimal Classification is issued in two versions: full and abridged.[3] After the publication of the second edition (1885) of DDC, it became obvious that a short form of the classification would be better suited to the needs of small and slowly growing libraries. Accordingly, an abridged edition of the scheme, about two-fifths the size of the full edition, was issued in 1894. In the beginning, the abridged edition was revised when the need arose; later, it was considered desirable to follow each full edition with an abridged edition. The present abridged edition 14 (2004) accompanies the full edition 22 (2003).

From its first appearance, the abridged edition has been designed specifically for small collections: the elementary and secondary school libraries, small public libraries with collections not expected to grow beyond 20,000 titles, and other relatively small collections of a general nature. It is used by most of the school libraries and many small libraries in the United States, and is also widely used in other countries, particularly in Great Britain, Canada, and Australia.

The numbers in the abridged version are based on those in the full edition. They are shorter and do not represent the complexities of topics to the extent expressed by the full numbers.

Formats of DDC Schedules

Until 1993, DDC was published in a print format only. Since then, it has been issued in electronic forms as well. WebDewey, the current electronic format, was based on two earlier versions of machine-readable DDC: Electronic Dewey (a DOS version) and Dewey for Windows. The current Web-based version, a parallel of the full edition 22 but updated continuously, was first released by OCLC in 2000 and is currently available through "OCLC Connexion," the interface for online cataloging at OCLC. The Abridged WebDewey contains the content of abridged edition 14.

REVISION

Current Procedures for Revision

An editorial team, consisting of the Editor-in-Chief and assistant editors, oversees, and is responsible for, DDC revision. The editorial office is a part of the Bibliographic Access Divisions at the Library of Congress. OCLC (Online Computer Library Center), the publisher of DDC, has a contractual arrangement with the Library of Congress for the editorial work. Between these two organizations is a group called the Decimal Classification Editorial Policy Committee, composed of practicing librarians and library educators, which advises both the editors and OCLC concerning matters relating to the revision of DDC; the Committee examines proposed revisions and makes appropriate recommendations. The DDC editorial office is located in the Decimal Classification Division at the Library of Congress, which is responsible for assigning DDC numbers to LC cataloging records. The close proximity of the editorial staff and DDC classifiers ensures consistency and a great degree of coordination between the revision and the application of the system.

Presently, the print version of DDC is being issued at approximately seven to ten year intervals. Between the publications of the print editions, the schedules and tables are regularly reexamined. Revisions of existing numbers and index entries, and provisions for new subjects, are made as required. This policy, called "continuous revision," was adopted after the publication of Edition 19 in order to ensure currency of the scheme. Results of continuing editorial work are incorporated into WebDewey immediately, and each new print edition now represents a snapshot of the classification at the time of printing.

Forms of Revision

Revisions usually take the following forms:

Expansion

This method is used to introduce new subjects as well as to provide more minute and specific subdivisions under existing subjects. The numerical notational system of DDC is such that new subjects can only be introduced as subdivisions under existing subjects. This is a reasonable approach since new subjects seldom emerge totally independent of existing knowledge but usually appear as an offspring or outgrowth of an existing field. For existing knowledge, as library material proliferates, more minute subdivisions of existing topics are also required.

Reduction and Discontinuation

Occasionally, existing subdivisions that are rarely used are discontinued and the subtopics are classed with the more general topic. In rare cases, a table or an entire section in the schedule may be eliminated. In Edition 22, for instance, the entire Table 7 Persons was removed in favor of direct use of notation already available in the schedules and in notation -08 from Table 1.

Relocation

In each edition, a number of existing topics are moved to different locations (i.e., numbers) in the scheme. Relocation is usually an attempt to meet one of the following goals:

1. To eliminate dual provisions when two or more numbers have the same meaning or overlap to a large extent. For example, before Edition 22, the topic Motion pictures, radio, television was represented by both 306.485 and 302.234. In Edition 22, 306.485 was eliminated so that all material on the subject is now classed in 302.234.
2. To make room for new subjects when there is no available number. For example, in Edition 18 of DDC, Antarctica was moved from the area notation -99 to -989 in order that -99 could be used for Extraterrestrial worlds. In general, a number vacated as a result of relocation is not reused until a later edition. However, in this case, the urgency to accommodate the Extraterrestrial worlds outweighed this policy of "starvation."
3. To provide uniformity of development for parallel subjects.
4. To reflect realignment of fields of knowledge. A new subject, which had been introduced as a subdivision under an existing subject, may turn out to belong more properly in a different field of knowledge. For example, Astronautics, which was originally placed in 629.1388 (as a subdivision under Aeronautics) was moved to 629.4 (as one of the "other branches" of engineering).
5. To rectify an improper placement by moving the topic to where it really belongs. For example, in Edition 18, Yiddish language and literature, formerly in 492.49 and 892.49 (as subdivisions of He-

braic languages and literature) were relocated to 437.947 and 839.09 (as branches of Germanic languages and literatures).

Extensive Revisions

In each edition, selected classes, divisions, or sections undergo extensive revision. The main outline remains basically the same, but selected portions are reworked and expansions are provided for new topics. Examples include 370 Education, 580 (Plants (Botany)), and 590 (Animals (Zoology)) in Edition 21. Class 200 Religion was revised extensively during a two-edition span (editions 21 and 22) in order to reduce Christian biases.

Completely Revised Schedules

A completely revised schedule, previously called a "phoenix schedule," represents the most drastic form of revision. With this method, an entire schedule, such as 780 (Music) in Edition 20 and 340 (Law) in Edition 18, is reconstructed without regard to previous divisions. The policy of integrity of numbers is suspended and the editors are not hampered by notational constriction in rearranging existing subjects and inserting new subjects. As a result, massive relocations occur within that schedule. In recent editions, the following schedules have been revised completely:

301-307	(Sociology), 324 (The political process), and -41 and -42 (area notation for Great Britain in Table 2) in Edition 19
780	(Music) and -711 (Area notation for British Columbia in Table 2) in Edition 20
570	(Biology and life sciences) in Edition 21

There is no completely revised schedule in Edition 22.

New Schedules

Occasionally, the schedule for a particular subject is completely reworked and moved to a new location so that there is no conflict with the old schedule. An example of a new schedule is the 004-006 (Data processing and Computer science) revision that was developed and published separately between Editions 19 and 20. The new schedule was eventually incorporated into Edition 20.

BASIC PRINCIPLES

Classification by Discipline

To say that classification groups together materials on the same subject is an oversimplification. In fact, both the Dewey Decimal Classification and the Library of Congress Classification, the two major systems in use in this country, are classifications by discipline. The division of main classes and subclasses is based on academic disciplines, or fields of study, rather than on subject. Such division means that the same subject may be classed in more than one place in the scheme. For example, the subject "family," depending on the author's approach and perspective, may be classed in ethics, religion, sociology, social customs, family planning, home economics, or genealogy.

In the Dewey Decimal Classification, knowledge was initially divided into ten main classes that mirrored the recognized academic divisions of Dewey's time: General works, Philosophy, Theology, Sociology (later Social sciences), Philology, Natural science, Useful arts, Fine arts, Literature, and History (see Table 13-1). Some of these are not considered disciplines today, but rather areas of study, each of which includes several academic disciplines. Based on the curriculum of a modern university, one would group such fields as Philosophy, Languages, Fine arts, and Literature as disciplines under the area of Humanities, in parallel with other areas of study such as Social sciences and Physical sciences, each of which also contains various disciplines. In DDC, however, Philosophy, Languages, Literature, etc., remain as coordinate subjects with Social sciences, Pure sciences, and Technology/Applied sciences. This fact alone makes the scheme somewhat uneven in the extent to which its basic organization of knowledge matches what prevails in the world today. Furthermore, over the last hundred years, the advancement of knowledge in different fields has varied considerably in both quantity and velocity, so that some classes, such as 100 Philosophy and 400 Language, have remained fairly stable throughout successive editions while others, such as 500 Science and 600 Technology, have undergone tremendous development and expansion. Thus, disparity in treatment from class to class has been compounded. Table 13-2 shows the current distribution of topics over the system.

Structural Hierarchy

Each of the ten *main classes* is divided into ten *divisions*, and each division is divided into ten *sections*, with further subdivisions made as required. Each level, divided on a base of ten because of the notational system, is subordinate to the level above it, thus forming a hierarchical structure that progresses from the general to the specific (see Figure 13-1).

In general, arrangement is first by discipline, then by subject with various levels of subject subdivisions, then by geographic and/or period specification, and then by form of presentation. Exceptions to this pattern are found in Literature (800) and in History (900). In the 800 class, arrangement of belles-lettres is first by the discipline (literature), then by original language, then by literary form, and then by period of composi-

TABLE 13-2 Outline of DDC.

Second Summary
The Hundred Divisions

000	Computer science, knowledge & systems	500	Science
010	Bibliographies	510	Mathematics
020	Library & information sciences	520	Astronomy
030	Encyclopedia & books of facts	530	Physics
040	[Unassigned]	540	Chemistry
050	Magazines, journals & serials	550	Earth sciences & geology
060	Associations, organizations & museums	560	Fossils & prehistoric life
070	News media, journalism & publishing	570	Life sciences; biology
080	Quotations	580	Plants (Botany)
090	Manuscripts & rare books	590	Animals (Zoology)
100	Philosophy	600	Technology
110	Metaphysics	610	Medicine & health
120	Epistemology	620	Engineering
130	Parapsychology & occultism	630	Agriculture
140	Philosophical schools of thought	640	Home & family management
150	Psychology	650	Management & public relations
160	Logic	660	Chemical engineering
170	Ethics	670	Manufacturing
180	Ancient, medieval & eastern philosophy	680	Manufacture for specific uses
190	Modern western philosophy	690	Building & construction
200	Religion	700	Arts
210	Philosophy & theory of religion	710	Landscaping & area planning
220	The Bible	720	Architecture
230	Christianity & Christian theology	730	Sculpture, ceramics & metalwork
240	Christian practice & observance	740	Drawing & decorative arts
250	Christian pastoral practice & religious orders	750	Painting
260	Christian organization, social work & worship	760	Graphic arts
270	History of Christianity	770	Photography & computer art
280	Christian denominations	780	Music
290	Other religions	790	Sports, games & entertainment
300	Social sciences, sociology & anthropology	800	Literature, rhetoric & criticism
310	Statistics	810	American literature in English
320	Political science	820	English & Old English literatures
330	Economics	830	German & related literatures
340	Law	840	French & related literatures
350	Public administration & military science	850	Italian, Romanian & related literatures
360	Social problems & social services	860	Spanish & Portuguese literatures
370	Education	870	Latin & Italic literatures
380	Commerce, communications & transportation	880	Classical & modern Greek literatures
390	Customs, etiquette & folklore	890	Other literatures
400	Language	900	History
410	Linguistics	910	Geography & travel
420	English & Old English languages	920	Biography & genealogy
430	German & related languages	930	History of ancient world (to ca. 499)
440	French & related languages	940	History of Europe
450	Italian, Romanian & related languages	950	History of Asia
460	Spanish & Portuguese languages	960	History of Africa
470	Latin & Italic languages	970	History of North America
480	Classical & modern Greek languages	980	History of South America
490	Other languages	990	History of other areas

Consult schedules for complete and exact headings

Source: *Summaries DDC: Dewey Decimal Classification* (Dublin, Ohio: OCLC, 2003), 8. Reproduced with permission from OCLC.

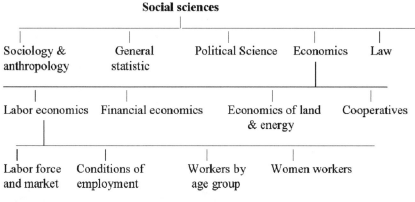

FIGURE 13-1   Hierarchical structure from general to specific

tion. In the 900 class, geography and history of individual continents are arranged first by place, then by period, topic, and form.

NOTATION

Symbols

Dewey adopted a pure notation based on Arabic numerals: each topic in the scheme is represented by a number expressed in Arabic numerals only, with decimal expansion as needed, e.g., 030, 150, 346.73046956, etc. Such a notation has the advantages of being widely recognized and transcending most language barriers.

Main classes and divisions in DDC are organized around a base of ten, a characteristic of the Arabic numeral system. Main classes are numbered 0 through 9, as shown in Table 13-2. Further divisions and subdivisions follow the decimal principle, for example,

> 5 Science
> 51 Mathematics
> 52 Astronomy and allied sciences
> 53 Physics
> 54 Chemistry and allied sciences
> etc.

For such numbers to be considered sequential, there must be a leading decimal. However, to make its notation easier to grasp, DDC uses three-digit numbers for its main classes, for the divisions of main classes, and for major sections of those divisions; zeros are put in as fillers in the numbers for main classes, so each contains at least three digits. Thus, we have

500 for the main class Science, and 510 for one of its major branches, Mathematics. When more than three digits are needed to specify a topic, a decimal point is placed after the third digit, giving numbers such as 512.56 and 512.546. In sequential arrangement and shelving, as decimal numbers, 512.546 precedes 512.56.

Notational Hierarchy

The DDC notation reflects the hierarchical order of the classification, showing the relationship between each level of knowledge and its superordinate and subordinate elements. Each of the ten main classes is divided into ten divisions represented by the second position in the notation. Thus, in 500 (Sciences & mathematics), 510 through 590 are used for the major branches of science, e.g., 510 (Mathematics), 520 (Astronomy & allied sciences), 530 (Physics), 540 (Chemistry & allied sciences), etc. Each division, in turn, is divided into ten sections, represented by the number in the third position of the notation, e.g.,

> 510   Mathematics
> > 511   General principles of mathematics
> > 512   Algebra
> > 513   Arithmetic
> > 514   Topology
>
> 540   Chemistry and allied sciences
> > 541   Physical chemistry
> > 542   Techniques, procedures, apparatus, equipment and materials
> > 543   Analytical chemistry

The system allows further subdivision into various degrees of specificity by means of a continued decimal notation. The decimal point is always placed after the third digit, followed by as many digits as required by the subject matter. The notation never *ends* with a zero after the decimal point, since a terminal zero after a decimal point has no value.

As the classification progresses from the general to the specific, each level of division is indicated by the addition of one new digit. The following example illustrates the hierarchical structure present in both the notation and the classificatory categories, carried to three digits beyond the decimal point:

> 500   Natural sciences and mathematics
> > 510   Mathematics
> > > 516   Geometry
> > > > 516.3   Analytic geometries
> > > > > 516.37   Metric differential geometries
> > > > > > 516.375   Finsler geometry

There are, however, a few exceptions to the hierarchical structure, as is the case for Life Science, Biology (570), Plants (Botany) (580), and Animals (Zoology) (590); most scientists would consider it more reasonable to make botany and zoology subtopics under biology rather than coordinate topics. Nevertheless, the intention, in general, is that the classificatory structure be hierarchical and, as such, be reflected in the notation.

Mnemonics

In assigning numbers to subjects, Dewey frequently used consistent numbers for recurring subjects. For example, Italy is regularly represented by the notation 5, which recurs in numbers related to that country: 945 (history of Italy); 914.5 (Description of Italy); 450 (Italian language); 554.5 (Geology of Italy); 195 (Italian philosophy); and 035 (General encyclopedic works in the Italian language). In literature, the number 1 represents poetry, thus, 821 (English poetry); 851 (Italian poetry); 895.11 (Chinese poetry); etc. This device helps readers memorize or recognize class numbers more easily. Furthermore, it has enabled the system to develop from an enumerative system to a more nearly analytico-synthetic scheme in which many elements in a class number can be readily isolated and identified.

In the earlier editions, the mnemonic device was used most prominently in the following areas: form divisions, geographical divisions, languages, and literature. As the analytico-synthetic nature of the system increased, the mnemonic device has become standard practice for some aspects of the system.

Enumeration versus Synthesis

DDC began as a basically enumerative system, in that the numbers for individual subjects, including compound and complex subjects, are listed as such in the scheme. In the second edition, however, the table for form divisions was introduced; also, there was the provision that certain numbers in the scheme were to be divided like certain other numbers, particularly those pertaining to geographic subdivision. Thus, a limited amount of synthesis, or number building, existed from the early editions.

In Edition 17, an areas table for geographic subdivisions was introduced. Then, in Edition 18, more tables were added. The tables provide numbers for frequently occurring subtopics or aspects that may be used with base numbers representing main topics throughout the schedules.

EVALUATION

A great deal has been written about the merits and the weaknesses of the Dewey Decimal Classification. Following is a brief summary of some of the opinions.

Merits

1. It is a practical system. The fact that it has survived many storms in more than one hundred and thirty years and is still the most widely used classification scheme in the world today attests to its practical value.
2. Relative location was an innovation introduced by Dewey, even though it is now taken for granted.
3. The relative index brings together different aspects of the same subject scattered in different disciplines.
4. The pure notation of Arabic numerals is universally recognizable. People from any cultural or language background can adapt to the system easily.
5. The self-evident numerical sequence facilitates display and shelving.
6. The hierarchical nature of the notation expresses the relationships between and among the class numbers. This characteristic particularly facilitates online searching and browsing. The searcher can broaden or narrow a search by reducing or adding a digit to the class number.
7. The classification structure and notation progresses from the general to the specific and renders the scheme particularly suitable for organizing electronic resources for browsing and navigating.
8. The use of the decimal numbering system enables infinite expansion and subdivision.
9. The mnemonic nature of the notation helps users navigate within the system.
10. The continuous revision and publication of the schedules at regular intervals ensure the currency of the scheme.

Weaknesses

1. An Anglo-American bias is particularly obvious in 900 (Geography and history), and 800 (Literature). Furthermore, 200 (Religion) shows a heavy bias toward American Protestantism. However, such biases have been gradually removed from recent editions.
2. Related disciplines are often separated, e.g., 300 (Social sciences) from 900 (Geography and history); and 400 (Languages) from 800 (Literature).
3. The proper placements of certain subjects have also been questioned; for example, Library science in general works (000s), Psychology as a subdivision under Philosophy (100s), and Sports and Amusements in The arts (700s).
4. In 800, literary works by the same author are scattered according

to literary form when most scholars would prefer to have them grouped together.

5. The base of ten limits the hospitality of the notational system by restricting the capacity for accommodating subjects on the same level of the hierarchy to nine divisions.

6. The different rate of growth in various disciplines has resulted in an uneven structure. Some classes, such as 300 (Social sciences), 500 (Natural sciences), and 600 (Technology), have become overcrowded.

7. Even though an existing subject can be expanded indefinitely by virtue of the decimal system, no new numbers can be inserted between coordinate numbers (e.g., between 610 and 620) even when required for the accommodation of new subjects. The present method of introducing a new subject is to include it as a subdivision under an existing subject.

8. While the capacity for expansion is infinite, it also results in lengthy numbers for specific and minute subjects. The long numbers have been found inconvenient, particularly when the system is used as a shelving device.

ASSIGNING CALL NUMBERS

A call number based on the Dewey Decimal Classification consists of two parts: the *class number* and the *book* or *item number*. The class number reflects the main subject content of the item. The book or item number consists of one or more elements based on the bibliographic characteristics, such as the name of the author and/or the title of the item. The construction of the DDC call number is discussed below.

CLASS NUMBERS [MARC 21 FIELDS 082, 09X, SUBFIELD $a]

The class number may be derived from the full edition or the abridged edition.

As a result of the influence of modern classification theory, DDC has become less enumerative and increasingly analytico-synthetic or faceted in recent editions. Many numbers that can be assigned to resources are not listed as such in the schedules. Instead, they must be built from base numbers found in the schedules and numbers in the tables. The discussion below illustrates how class numbers enumerated in the schedules are expanded as needed through notational synthesis—in other words, by what is called *number building*—in the full and abridged editions of DDC.

NUMBER BUILDING: FULL EDITION

The discussion and examples in this section are based on the full edition. A similar discussion based on the abridged edition is found later in this chapter. The *main* or *base* number is always taken from the schedules. The additional elements may come from either the schedules or the tables, or both, and are added to the base number. (In this context, "added" means "tacked onto" not added in the arithmetical sense.) The order of the elements in each case is determined by instruction in the schedules or tables. In building a number, the decimal point is first removed. After the process of synthesis is completed, a decimal point is inserted after the third digit.

Combining Schedule Numbers

Adding an Entire Number to a Base Number

A bibliography of physics	016.53
1. The main number for bibliographies and catalogs of works on specific subjects or in specific disciplines with a note to "add to base number 016 notation 001-999" the number for the specific subject	016
2. The number for Physics	530
3. The subject number added to the base number	016.530
4. The resulting number with a decimal point after the third digit and the removal of the terminal 0 after the decimal point	016.53

Paper industry	338.47 676.2
1. Base number for Secondary industry of services and specific products, with instruction to add 001-999	338.47
2. Number for Paper production	676 2
3. (2) added to (1)	338 47 676 2
4. With decimal point inserted	338.47 676 2

Adding a Fraction of a Number or Fractions of Numbers to a Base Number

A general Russian periodical	057.1
1. Number for all serial publications as indicated in the index	050

2. Number in schedule for serial
   publications in Slavic languages, with
   instruction: "Add to base number 057
   the numbers following 037 in 037.1-
   037.9"   0<u>57</u>
3. The number in the sequence for
   Russian   037.<u>1</u>
4. The number following 037 added to (2)   0<u>57</u> 1
5. With decimal point inserted   0<u>57</u>.1

A Presbyterian guide to Christian life   <u>248.485</u>
1. Base number for Guides to Christian
   life with instruction: "Add to base
   number 248.48 the numbers following
   28 in 280.2-289"   <u>248.48</u>
2. The number for the Presbyterian
   Church in the sequence   28<u>5</u>
3. The number following 28 added to (1)   <u>248</u> <u>485</u>
4. With decimal point inserted   <u>248</u>.<u>485</u>

Photographs of scientific subjects   <u>779.95</u>
1. Base number for photographs with
   instruction: "Add to base number 779
   the numbers following 704.94 in
   704.942-704.949"   <u>779</u>
2. The most appropriate number in the
   sequence Iconography of other specific
   subjects, with instructions: "Add to
   base number 704.949 notation 001-999"   704.94<u>9</u>
3. The number for Science   <u>500</u>
4. (3) added to (2)   704 949<u>500</u>
5. The number following 704.94 added to
   (1)   <u>779</u> <u>9500</u>
6. With decimal point inserted and
   terminal 0s removed   <u>779</u>.<u>95</u>

Exercise 13-1

Assign Decimal Classification numbers to the following topics:

1. India under the British rule
2. Discipline of students through punishments in the public schools
3. Television commercials
4. A thesaurus of water resources terms
5. Planning public library buildings
6. A bibliography on diagnostic x-ray techniques

7. *American Libraries* (official journal of the American Library Association)
8. Commentaries on the Gospel of John
9. Colligative properties of electrolytic solutions
10. Unemployment in library services
11. Embryology of vertebrates
12. Curriculum design in schools
13. The Bolshevik Revolution and the Civil War in Russia
14. *Journal of Physical Oceanography*

Adding Notation(s) from the Tables to a Base Number

In Edition 22 of DDC, there are six tables:

Table 1. Standard Subdivisions
Table 2. Geographic Areas, Historical Periods, Persons
Table 3. Subdivisions for the Arts, for Individual Literatures, for Specific Literary Forms
Table 3A. Subdivisions for Works by or about Individual Authors
Table 3B. Subdivisions for Works by or about More than One Author
Table 3C. Notation to be Added Where Instructed in Table 3B, 700.4, 791.4, 808-809
Table 4. Subdivisions of Individual Languages and Language Families
Table 5. Ethnic and National Groups
Table 6. Languages

Notations from all tables, except 3 and 4, may be used throughout the entire schedules. Notations from Table 1 may be used wherever applicable. Notations from Tables 2, 5, and 6 are used only when instructed. However, notations from Tables 2 and 5 may also be added, according to instructions, to -09 and 089 respectively, in Table 1, and the results are then used as standard subdivisions, i.e., may be used whenever appropriate.

Tables 3 and 4 apply only to certain schedules: Table 3 to the 800s and parts of 700s and Table 4 to 420-490. These, too, are used only when specifically instructed.

All notations from the tables are preceded by a dash, indicating that these are not complete class numbers but must be used in conjunction with main numbers from the schedules. In some cases, a notation from one table may be added to one found in another table, and the combination is then attached to the appropriate main number from the schedules to form a complete class number.

Table 1: Standard Subdivisions

After a specific class number has been chosen for a work, the classifier should then consider whether further specification concerning the bibliographic form or the author's approach is desirable, i.e., whether any of the standard subdivisions is applicable. Table 1 lists nine categories of standard subdivisions which are further subdivided into more detailed specifications. All notations for standard subdivisions begin with a 0, e.g., -01, -07154.

Notations from tables are never used alone, or as main numbers. With the exception of -04, the classifier does not need any specific instruction in the schedules in order to add the notations for standard subdivisions, unless there is a specific instruction to the contrary. Appropriateness and applicability are the general guides. For example, for a journal of inorganic chemistry, the standard subdivision -05 (for serial publications) is added to the base number 546 to form the number 546.05.

Standard subdivision notations and their meanings are given in Table 1. However, under certain numbers in the schedules, a few standard subdivisions may be listed when these subdivisions have special meanings or when extended notation is provided for the subject in question. For example under 610 (Medicine and Health), the standard subdivisions -06 (i.e., 610.6) and -07 (i.e., 610.7) have extended meanings, such as 610.696 (Medical relationships) and 610.73 (Nursing and services of allied health personnel).

The standard subdivision -04 is reserved for special topics which have general application throughout the regular subdivisions of certain specific subjects. Therefore, it varies from subject to subject and is to be used only when the special topics are spelled out in the schedules, for example, the subdivisions .04-.049 found under 331 (Labor economics).

Before adding a standard subdivision to a base number, the classifier should remove all the terminal zeros which are used as fillers in the base number. Therefore, standard subdivision -03 added to the base number 100 results in 103, not 100.03. A journal of library science is classed in 020.5, not 020.05.

However, there are exceptions to this rule. In many cases, notations beginning with -0, -00, or even -000 have been assigned meanings other than those for standard subdivisions. In these cases, the classifier is instructed to use more than one zero for standard subdivisions, e.g.,

320   Political science (Politics and government)
      .01-.09 Standard subdivisions
      [Hence, 320.03 for an encyclopedia of political science]
338   Production
      .001-.008 Standard subdivisions
      [Hence, 338.005 for a journal of Production]
620   Engineering and allied operations

.001-.009 Standard subdivisions
[Hence, 620.009 for a history of engineering]

When a standard subdivision (e.g., 507) or a span of standard subdivisions (e.g., 516.001-.009) is specifically named in the schedules, it is understood that the sub-subdivisions to these standard subdivisions may be used (e.g., 507.4 for science museums, or 516.0076 for review and exercises in geometry) unless there are contrary instructions in the schedules.

Certain standard subdivision concepts, particularly for geographical treatment, are displaced to nonzero numbers. For example, insurance in France is represented by the number 368.944 (Insurance in France) instead of 368.00944. When zeros are to be removed, there are clear indications and/or directions in the schedules.

Although standard subdivisions may be applied wherever they are appropriate, there are certain restrictions on their use. In addition to specific restrictions appearing in the schedules relating to individual numbers (e.g., 362.[09] *Do not use; class in* 362.9), certain general restrictions are set forth in the "Introduction" to DDC:[4]

1. The classifier should not add standard subdivisions when they are redundant. In other words, for a history of the United States, do not add -09 to 973, which already means history of the U.S. Likewise, it is redundant to add -03 to 423, which already means a dictionary of the English language.
2. Standard subdivisions should be added to the number chosen for a work only when the content of the work is equivalent to the whole, or "approximately the whole" meaning of the number. In other words, standard subdivisions are not used when the work in hand deals with a subject more specific than the content of the number, i.e., when the subject represented in the work does not have its own specific number. For example, a history of classification systems is classed in 025.4309, but a history of the Russian Library-Bibliographical Classification, which does not have its own number, is classed in 025.43, instead of 025.4309. In other words, the standard subdivision is not added unless the content of the work being classified covers the whole, or approximately the whole, of the subject represented by the main number. This is called the "approximate-the-whole" rule. In the case of multiterm headings of class numbers, instructions are provided with regard to the addition of standard subdivisions, for example, under the number 514.32 Systems and spaces [in Topology], there is a note: Standard subdivisions are added for either or both topics in heading. In this example, both "systems" and "spaces" are considered to "approximate-the-whole."
3. With a few exceptions noted below, the classifier should not add

one standard subdivision to another standard subdivision unless there are specific instructions to do so. When two or more standard subdivisions are applicable to a work, choose one. In choosing a standard subdivision, observe the table of preference found at the beginning of Table 1 (vol. 1, p. 186), e.g., 020.7 for Journal of Education for Librarianship rather than 020.5 or 020.705. On the other hand, the use of more than one standard subdivision is allowed in the following cases:

a. With standard subdivision -04 (Special topics) because of its unusual nature as a *standard* subdivision

b. With standard subdivisions which have extended meanings, e.g., 610.7305 for a journal of nursing, although both -073 and -05 appear to be standard subdivisions. The subdivision -073 under the number 610 has been given an extended meaning and there is a specific instruction in the schedule to add further standard subdivisions.

c. With standard subdivision concepts which have been displaced to non-zero numbers, e.g., 368.944068 (Management of insurance in France).

Furthermore, standard subdivisions may be extended by adding notation from other tables when so instructed; when this is the case, the resulting number is treated as an extended standard subdivision. For example, notation 3-9 from Table 2 may be added to standard subdivision -09 to specify treatment of the main topic by specific continents, countries, etc. Thus, the notation -769 may be added to the standard subdivision -09 to form -09769 for treatment of a topic in Kentucky. The following examples show the application of standard subdivisions:

The use of computers in education worldwide	370.285
1. Education	370
2. Standard subdivision for computer applications from Table 1	-0 285
3. (2) added to (1) (without terminal zero) with decimal point inserted	370.285

Management of welfare services	361.0068
1. Social problems and social welfare with indication of an extra zero for standard subdivisions	361.0
2. Standard subdivision for management from Table 1	-068
3. (2) added to (1) with decimal point inserted	361.0068

Table 2: Geographic Areas, Historical Periods, Persons

Notation from Table 2, providing representation of geographic areas, historical periods, and persons relating to the main subject, may be used with numbers throughout the schedules as instructed. It is used in the following ways.

1. Used directly when so noted with numbers from the schedules

Geology of Iceland	554.912
1. Geology, with instruction to add area notation 4-9 to base number 55	55
2. Area notation for Iceland from Table 2	-4 912
3. (2) added to (1) with decimal point inserted	554.912

A journal of higher education in Japan	378.5205
1. Higher education, with instruction: "Add to base number 378 notation 4-9 from Table 2"	378
2. Area notation for Japan	-52
3. (2) added to (1) as instructed	378 52
4. Standard subdivision for serial publications	-05
5. (4) added to (3)	378.5205

Emigration from Italy to New York City	325.245097471
1. Base number for emigration from specific continents, countries, localities	325 2
2. Area notation for Italy	-45
3. (2) added to (1) as instructed	325 245
4. Standard subdivision for New York City	-097471
5. (4) added to (3)	325.245097471

North Dakota education law	344.7840702632
1. Labor, social service, education, cultural law in specific jurisdictions and areas	344 .3-.9
2. Area notation -784 for North Dakota added to base number 344	344 784
3. Education law	344.07
4. (2) and (3) combined as instructed under 344.3-.9	344 78407
5. Special form division for collected laws as listed under 342-347	-02632
6. (5) added to (4)	344.7840702632

2. Used through interposition of notation -09 from Table 1. Under -093-099 in Table 1, there is an instruction to add area notation 3-9 from Table 2 to base number -09, e.g., -0973, for historical, geographical, and persons-treatment of a subject with regard to the United States. Once an area number is added to -09, the entire combination (e.g., -0973) becomes a standard subdivision. Since -09 is a standard subdivision and can be added to any number from the schedules as desired, virtually every number in the DDC system can be subdivided geographically. However, when direct geographic subdivision is provided as illustrated above, it takes precedence over the use of -09 and its subdivisions.

Shopping centers in the United States	381.110973
1. Number for Shopping centers, with no direct provision for geographic subdivision	381 11
2. Standard subdivision for United States	-0973
3. (2) added to (1)	381.110973
Paper industry in England	338.4767620942
1. Number for Paper industry as constructed under Paper industry on p. 334	338 476762
2. Standard subdivision for England	-0942
3. (2) added to (1)	338.4767620942

3. Used when so noted with numbers from other tables

American Chemical Society	540.6073
1. Number for Chemistry	540
2. Standard subdivision from Table 1 for national organizations	-0 60
3. Area notation -73 for the United States from Table 2 added to (2) as instructed	-0 6073
4. (3) added to (1)	540.6073
American Physical Society (Similar to the example above, except that the number 530 requires two 0s for standard subdivisions)	530.06073
A history of descriptive research in Library Science in Great Britain	020.723
1. Number for library and information science	020
2. Standard subdivision for descriptive research	-0 723
3. Standard subdivision for historical and geographical treatment of Great Britain	-0941

4. (2) added to (1) (Since the classifier has
been advised not to add one standard
subdivision to another one, (2) is
chosen over (3) according to the order
of precedence for standard
subdivisions.)   020.723

4. Used with another number from Table 2

Foreign relations between Japan and Great
Britain   327.41052
  1. Base number for foreign relations
    between specific nations as listed under
    327.3-327.9   327
  2. Area notation for Japan   -52
  3. Area notation for Great Britain   -41
  4. As instructed, add area notation for
    one nation to the base number, add 0
    and to the result add area notation for
    the other nation. The order of the area
    notations is determined by the
    emphasis of the work. If Japan is
    emphasized.   327 52041
  5. If Great Britain is emphasized.   327 41052
  6. "If emphasis is equal, give priority to
    the nation or region coming first in
    Table 2."   327.41052

Exercise 13-2

1. Assign Decimal Classification numbers to the subjects listed in
   Table 13-3.
2. Assign Decimal Classification numbers to the following topics.
   A. Financial management of special education in Ohio
   B. Brooklyn Public Library
   C. History of classical languages
   D. A dictionary of modern music and musicians
   E. Popular music in the United States
   F. European immigrants in the United States during the 1930s
   G. The government of American cities
   H. Statistical methods used in social sciences
   I. Foreign relations between Russia and Japan
   J. The Nazi spy network in Switzerland during World War II
   K. Social conditions in Japan after World War II
   L. Masterpieces of painting in the Metropolitan Museum of Art:
   an exhibition catalog

TABLE 13-3   DDC Area Notation, Exercise 13-B(1)

	United States	Tennessee	Scotland	Egypt
Area table notation				
History of				
Tourist guide to				
Newspapers from				
Folk songs from				
Political condition in				
Geology of				

M. Life and health insurance laws (United States)
N. Illinois rules and regulations for fire prevention and safety, as amended 1968
O. Arizona library laws (a compilation)
P. Tourist trade in Russia after World War II

Table 3: Subdivisions for the Arts, for Individual Literatures, for Specific Literary Forms

Notation from Table 3 is used, when applicable, with the base numbers for individual literatures identified by an asterisk (*) under 810-890, and also with specific instructions under 808-809 and certain numbers in the 700s in the schedules. Number building for literature and music calls for the most complex procedures in the DDC system. The application of Table 3 is discussed later in this chapter, under "Classification of Literature."

Table 4: Subdivisions of Individual Languages and Language Families

Notations from Table 4 are used with base numbers for individual languages identified by an asterisk (*) under 420-490 in the schedules. The classifier's first task is to identify the language in hand.

Verbs in the German language	435.6
1. Base number for German language	43
2. Subdivision for verbs from Table 4	-56
3. (2) added to (1) with decimal point inserted	435.6

Bilingual dictionaries are a special case. Since a bilingual dictionary involves two languages, the classifier must first determine which language is to be used as the base number. Instructions for choosing the base number are given under -32—39 in Table 4. If the entry words are given in only one language with equivalent words in the second language, the number for the first language is used as the base number, for example,

A German-French dictionary	433.41
1. Base number for the German language	43
2. Subdivisions for bilingual dictionaries	-32-39
3. Language notation for the French language from Table 6	-41
4. (3) added to (2) and (1)	433.41

A bilingual dictionary containing entry words in both languages is classed as instructed, usually with the number for the language lesser known to the users as the base number.

An English-Spanish, Spanish-English dictionary	463.21
1. Base number for Spanish as the "more useful" for English-speaking users	46
2. Subdivision for bilingual dictionaries	-32-39
3. Languages notation (-21) for English from Table 6 added to the subdivision for dictionaries (-3) in Table 4	-3 21
4. (3) added to (1) with decimal point	463.21

As instructed under -32—39 in Table 4 (vol.1, p. 655), "If classification with either language is equally useful, give priority to the language coming later in 420-490."

A German-French, French-German dictionary	443.31
1. Base number for French, since it is greater than the number for German, i.e., 43	44
2. Subdivision for bilingual dictionaries	-32-39
3. Language notation (-31) for German from Table 6 added to the subdivision for dictionaries (-3) in Table 4	-3 31
4. (3) added to (1) with decimal point	443.31

Table 5: Ethnic and National Groups

Notations from Table 5 are used with those numbers from the schedules and other tables to which the classifier is instructed to add ethnic and national groups notation.

Social groups among the Hindis   305.89143
  1. Base number for ethnic and national
     groups with instruction to add
     notation 05-9 from Table 5   305 8
  2. Notation for Hindis from Table 5   -9143

Decorative arts of the Chinese   745.089951
  1. Base number for Decorative arts   745
  2. Standard subdivision for treatment
     among specific ethnic and national
     groups with instruction to add
     notation 05-9 from Table 5   -089
  3. Notation for Chinese from Table 5   -951

Table 6: Languages

Notations from Table 6 represent the language aspect, or facet, of a main subject and are used with base numbers from the schedules. They are added as instructed, a procedure similar to that employed with Tables 2 and 5.

A French Bible   220.541
A Swahili Bible   220.596392
The Old Testament in French   221.541
The Old Testament in Swahili   221.596392
The Book of Job in French   223.10541
The Book of Job in Swahili   223.10596392
A general Japanese periodical   059.9 56

Exercise 13-3

Assign Decimal Classification numbers to the following subjects or titles.

 1. Swahili grammar
 2. A bibliography of anonymous works in German
 3. A Chinese-English, English-Chinese dictionary
 4. Islamic painting
 5. Jewish population in the Netherlands
 6. *La Raza: the Mexican-Americans*
 7. An exhibition of twentieth century American art from a Long Island collection
 8. Jewish families in New York City
 9. A German version of the New Testament
10. World War II letters of Barbara Wooddall Taylor and Charles E. Taylor

11. Italian-American women in Nassau County, New York, 1925-1981
12. Teaching English reading in the secondary school
13. The Spanish-speaking people from Mexico in the United States
14. Native Americans in the United States, 1820-1890

Classification of Literature

In classifying literature, the subject or topical aspect is secondary to language, literary form, and period, which are the main facets of literature. Other facets include style, mood, themes, and subjects. In general, the DDC numbers for works by or about individual authors reflect primary facets only, while those for collection and criticism of more than one author bring out other facets as well.

Citation Order

With a few exceptions, the citation order for the different facets in a class number for literature is:

1. The main class, *Literature*, is represented by the base number.
2. Language is the second element in the number, e.g., 82- for English literature, 891- for Chinese literature, and so on. When the work is not limited to any language, a zero is used to fill the second digit, e.g. 80- for world literature.
3. Literary form is the third element. Mnemonics are employed, e.g, -1 for poetry, -2 for drama, etc. Hence, 821 for English poetry, 891.2 for Chinese drama, and 820 for English literature not limited to a particular form.
4. Period, if applicable, follows literary form, e.g., 811.1 (colonial American poetry).
5. For literature written by more than one author and works about such literature, standard subdivisions with rather elaborate subsubdivisions for feature and theme are represented as further subdivisions under -08 (collections) and -09 (history and criticism).

The citation order varies when a collection by more than one author is not limited to a particular language/nationality or a literary form.

Examples

In DDC, number-building for literature, particularly literature of specific languages, is more complex than in other situations involving number building. Table 3 is devised for use with numbers in the 700 and 800 classes as instructed. It contains three parts:

Table 3A.   Subdivisions for Works by or about Individual
            Authors
Table 3B.   Subdivisions for Works by or about More than One
            Author
Table 3C.   Notation to be Added Where Instructed in Table 3B,
            700.4, 791.4, 808-809

Fortunately, very detailed instructions for carrying out the process are
provided in the DDC manual (vol. 1, pages 162–67), with brief step-by-
step instructions printed at the beginning of Table 3 (vol. 1, pages 616–17).
These should be studied carefully. The following examples illustrate the
many possible combinations of facets in classifying literature. The examples are divided by various types of literary works and works about literature: (1) collections of literature by more than one author, (2) works about
literature, (3) works written by individual authors, (4) works about individual authors, and (5) works about individual works.

1. Collections of literature by more than one author

An anthology of world literature	<u>808.8</u>
A collection of nineteenth-century literature	
(Facet: Period)	<u>808.80034</u>
1. Base number for a collection of	
literature from specific periods	<u>808.800</u>
2. Standard subdivision for early	
nineteenth century from Table 1	-090<u>34</u>
A collection of Christmas literature (Facet:	
Feature/theme)	<u>808.80334</u>
1. Base number for a collection of	
literature displaying specific features	<u>808.80</u>
2. Notation from Table 3C for themes	
relating to holidays	-<u>334</u>
A collection of nineteenth-century poetry	
(Facets: Form plus Period)	<u>808.81034</u>
1. Base number for a collection of poetry	
from a specific period	<u>808.810</u>
2. Period notation from Table 1	-090<u>34</u>
A collection of Christmas poetry (Facets: Form	
plus Feature/theme)	<u>808.819334</u>
1. Base number for a collection of poetry	
displaying specific features	<u>808.819</u>
2. Notation from Table 3C for holidays	-<u>334</u>

An anthology of Spanish literature (Facet:
Language)   860.8
  1. Base number for Spanish literature   86
  2. Subdivision for collections from Table
    3B   -0 8

A collection of eighteenth-century Spanish
literature (Facets: Language plus period)   860.8004
  1. Base number for Spanish literature   86
  2. Notation from Table 3B for collections
    of literary texts in more than one form,
    with instruction to add from Table 3C   -0 800
  3. Notation from Table 3C for specific
    periods   -01-09
  4. Notation for the eighteenth century
    from the period table for Spanish
    literature in the schedule (vol. 3, p. 795)   4

A collection of Spanish poetry (Facets:
Language plus Form)   861.008
  1. Base number for Spanish literature   86
  2. Notation from Table 3B for a collection
    of poetry   -1 008

A collection of eighteenth-century Spanish
drama (Facets: Language plus Form plus
Period)   862.408
  1. Base number for Spanish literature   86
  2. Notation from Table 3B for drama of
    specific periods   -21-29
  3. Notation for the eighteenth century
    from period table for Spanish literature   4
  4. Notation for collections of literary texts   08

A collection of American Christmas poetry
(Facets: Language plus Form plus Feature/
theme)   811.0080334
  1. Base number for American literature   81
  2. Collections of poetry featuring
    holidays (Tables 3B and 3C)   1 0080334

A collection of nineteenth-century American
Christmas poetry (Facets: Language plus
Form plus Period plus Feature/theme)   811.3080334
  1. Base number for American literature   81
  2. Poetry (Table 3B)   11-19

3. Nineteenth century (period table for
   American literature)   <u>3</u>
4. Collections featuring holidays (Tables
   3B and 3C)   -<u>080334</u>

2. Works about literature

Using examples similar to those listed above, one may build the following
numbers for works about literature:

A history of world literature	<u>809</u>
A study of nineteenth-century literature	<u>809</u>.<u>034</u>
A study of Christmas literature	<u>809</u>.<u>93334</u>
A study of nineteenth-century poetry	<u>809</u>.<u>1034</u>
A study of Christmas poetry	<u>809</u>.<u>19334</u>
A history of Spanish literature	<u>860</u>.<u>9</u>
A study of eighteenth-century Spanish literature	<u>860</u>.<u>9004</u>
A study of Spanish poetry	<u>861</u>.<u>009</u>
A study of eighteenth-century Spanish drama	<u>862</u>.<u>409</u>
A study of American Christmas poetry	<u>811</u>.<u>009334</u>
A study of nineteenth-century American Christmas poetry	<u>811</u>.<u>309334</u>

3. Works written by individual authors

Because DDC classes literature by form, the works of an individual author may be classed in different numbers if the author wrote in different
literary forms.

The notation for works written by individual authors contains the
following facets: Literature (<u>8</u>), language, form, and period, e.g.,

The Adventures of Huckleberry Finn by Mark Twain (Novel)	<u>813</u>.<u>4</u>
The Celebrated Jumping Frog of Calaveras County, and Other Stories by Mark Twain	<u>813</u>.<u>4</u>
Essays by G. K. Chesterton	<u>824</u>.<u>912</u>
The Heart of Midlothian by Sir Walter Scott (Novel)	<u>823</u>.<u>7</u>
The Lady of the Lake by Sir Walter Scott (Poems)	<u>821</u>.<u>7</u>

Selected and collected works by individual authors are classed according
to literary forms in the same numbers as individual works without the
use of -<u>08</u>, the subdivision notation for collections by more than one author, e.g.,

| *Short Stories* by Sir Walter Scott | 823.7 |
| *Selected Tales* by Edgar Allen Poe | 813 .3 |

When the collected works are in different forms, the problem is then which number to use. In general, the number for the predominant form is chosen, e.g.,

The Annotated Waste Land, with T. S. Eliot's	
Contemporary Prose	821.912
Emerson's Prose and Poetry : Authoritative Texts,	
Contexts, Criticism	814.3

When no predominant form can be determined, or when the collection includes works in a variety of forms, the number -8 for Miscellaneous writings (from Table T3A) further subdivided by period and ending in -09 is used, e.g.,

The Wit and Wisdom of Mark Twain	818.409
Stories, Poems, and Other Writings, by Willa	
Cather (American Novelist, 1874-1947)	818.309
The Sayings of Sir Walter Scott	828 .709
The Best of Oscar Wilde: Selected Plays and	
Literary Criticism	828.809

In DDC, literary authors do not receive individual unique class numbers as in the Library of Congress Classification. Authors writing in the same form and the same period share the same number. For example, all late nineteenth century American novelists are assigned the number 813.4. The only exception to this rule is Shakespeare *as a dramatist*, to whom the unique number 822.33 has been assigned.

In many libraries, fiction in English is not classified. Instead, it is assigned the letter *F* and subarranged alphabetically by author.

4. Works about individual authors

Works *about* an individual author are classed in the same number as assigned to the author's works, as instructed in Table 3A (vol. 1, p. 617), e.g.,

Ezra Pound: A Collection of Critical Essays	811.52
A Study of the Sonnets of Shakespeare	821.3
Aldous Huxley: A Study	823.912
An Essay on the Genius and Writings of Pope	821.5

In literature, it is often difficult to separate biography and criticism of an author. Therefore, they are usually both classed in the 800s, e.g.,

Henry James: a Study of the Short Fiction   813.4
The Selected Letters of Ralph Waldo Emerson   814.3
In the Footsteps of Hans Christian Andersen   839.8136

Note that the standard subdivision -0924 for individual biography is not used.

5. Works about individual works

Individual works and works about them are classed in the same numbers, as instructed in Table 3A. The subdivision -09 is not used, e.g.,

A critical study of Thackeray's *Vanity Fair*   823.8
A study of Marlowe's *Doctor Faustus*   822.3

Exercise 13-4

Assign Decimal Classification numbers:

1. A collection of German literature for and by Jews
2. Characterization in Jacobean (English 1606–1625) tragedies: a critical study
3. A collection of devotional poetry from colonial America
4. A collection of seventeenth-century French drama
5. A history of science fiction in the United States
6. A study of the theme of friendship in fifteenth-century Chinese literature
7. Abraham Lincoln in American literature: a critical study
8. A study of the theme of alienation in twentieth-century American fiction
9. The diaries of Mark Twain
10. A history of Irish Gaelic poetry in the early period
11. A study of the theme of love in twentieth-century American poetry
12. A study of the characters in seventeenth-century French drama
13. A study of Shakespeare's tragedies by Clifford Leech
14. Collected poems of Byron
15. The art of writing short stories
16. An anthology of American short stories
17. Literary history of the United States: twentieth century
18. A study of French Renaissance tragedy
19. A study of feminine fiction in England, 1713-1799
20. Study of literary criticism in Finnish universities

21. Essays on Russian and Polish literature
22. Interpret the following Decimal classification numbers:

338.4769009421
338.926091724
551.2109989
782.4215520941
917.92003

Segmentation Mark

Dewey numbers assigned from the full edition by the Library of Congress and many other libraries carry a segmentation mark (a slash (/) or a prime mark (')). It is used to indicate the end of an abridged number (as provided in the abridged edition), for example, 025.2/1, 823/.7, and 338.4/76661097409041. This practice facilitates the assignment of abridged DDC numbers when full numbers for the same works are available.

NUMBER BUILDING: ABRIDGED EDITION

It is a characteristic of the abridged edition to provide a broad classification without minute details. Thus, in many cases, the classifier will find that the abridged edition does not supply a number for a subject as specific as the content of the work being classified. When this is the case, the classifier should choose the most specific base number that the edition provides.

The abridged edition does, however, provide for a certain degree of notational synthesis, or number building; as it, like the unabridged DDC, is a partially analytico-synthetic scheme. For number building in the abridged edition (as in the full), the main or base number is always taken from the schedules. To begin with, all decimal points are removed. Additional elements may come from either the schedules or the tables, or both. The order of the elements in each case is determined by instructions in the schedules or tables. After the process of number building is completed, a decimal point is inserted after the third digit.

It is assumed that those readers who use the abridged DDC edition and have little interest in the full edition may turn directly to this section without studying what was said above about notational synthesis in the previous section on the full edition. This section has therefore been written to stand more or less alone, and so, necessarily, much of what was said above is repeated here.

Combining Schedule Numbers

Adding an Entire Number to a Base Number

Bibliography of adult education	<u>016</u>.<u>374</u>
1. The number for a subject bibliography with the instruction: "Add to base number 016 notation 001-999," meaning any class number can be added to 016 to obtain the number for a bibliography of that subject	<u>016</u>
2. Adult education	<u>374</u>
3. (2) added to (1) with decimal point inserted	<u>016</u>.<u>374</u>

Adding a Fraction of a Number to a Base Number

An Interpretation of the Old Testament	<u>221</u>.<u>6</u>
1. Number for the Old Testament with a note under 221.1-221.9: "Add to base number 221 the numbers following 220 in 220.1-220.9"	<u>221</u>
2. The number in that range meaning an interpretation	220.<u>6</u>
3. The number following 220 added to (1)	<u>221</u>.<u>6</u>

Exercise 13-5

Assign Dewey Classification numbers (abridged edition) to the following topics or titles:

1. Magnetism of the earth
2. Guidance and counseling in schools
3. Cataloging and classification of books in libraries
4. *Séance: A Book of Spiritual Communications*
5. A bibliography of bacteriology
6. Landscaping for homes
7. Acquisition of audiovisual materials in libraries
8. The causes of the Civil War
9. A bibliography of local transportation
10. The kinesiology of weight lifting
11. Designing dormitories
12. *Kentuckiana: A Bibliography of Books about Kentucky*
13. A concordance to modern versions of the New Testament
14. A critique of Marx's *Das Kapital*

15. Smallpox vaccination
16. Newspapers in Russia
17. Position of women in the Old Testament
18. Paintings from the United States
19. An atlas of the moon
20. Public library administration
21. Greek mythology
22. How to prepare for college entrance examinations

Adding Notation(s) from the Tables to a Base Number

In the abridged edition, there are four tables:

Table 1: Standard Subdivisions
Table 2: Geographic Areas and Persons
Table 3: Subdivisions for Individual Literatures, for Specific
       Literary Forms
Table 4: Subdivisions of Individual Languages

Notations from Table 1 are applicable throughout the schedules wherever appropriate. Those from Table 2 also apply to all classes but can be used only when instructed. Table 3 applies only to the numbers -810–890 and is used only when specifically instructed. Likewise, Table 4 applies to the numbers 420–490 and is also used only when specifically instructed.

All notations from the tables are preceded by a dash, indicating that these are not complete class numbers but must be used in conjunction with numbers from the schedules. In some cases, a notation from one table may be added to one from another table, and the combination is then used with the appropriate base number from the schedules.

Table 1: Standard Subdivisions

After a specific number has been chosen for a work, the classifier should then consider whether further specification concerning the bibliographic form or the author's approach is desirable, i.e., whether any of the standard subdivisions is applicable. Table 1 lists nine categories of standard subdivisions, which are further subdivided into more detailed specifications. All notations for standard subdivisions begin with a 0, e.g., -01 and -075.

Notations from tables are never used alone or as main numbers. With the exception of -04, the classifier does not need any specific instruction in the schedules in order to add the notations for standard subdivisions. Appropriateness and applicability are the general guide. For example, for a journal of inorganic chemistry, the standard subdivision -05 (for serial publications) is added to the base number 546 to form the number 546.05.

The standard subdivision -04 is reserved for special topics which have general application throughout the regular subdivisions of certain specific subjects, e.g., 604, and its subdivisions. Therefore, it varies from subject to subject and is to be used only when the special topics are spelled out in the schedules.

In adding a standard subdivision to a base number, the classifier should first remove all the zeros which are used as fillers. When this is done, for instance, standard subdivision -03 added to the base number 100 results in 103, not 100.03. A journal of library science is classed in 020.5, not 020.05.

However, there are exceptions to the single-zero rule. In many cases, notations beginning with 0 have been assigned meanings other than those for standard subdivisions. In these cases, the classifier is instructed to use more than one zero for standard subdivisions, e.g.,

> 300   Social sciences
> Use 300.1-300.9 for standard subdivisions
> [Hence, 300.3 for an encyclopedia of social sciences]
> 551.7   Historical geology
> .7001-.7009 Standard subdivisions
> [Hence, 551.7007 for education and research in historical geology]
> 620   Engineering and allied operations
> 620.001-.009 Standard subdivisions
> [Hence, 620.005 for a journal of engineering]

When a standard subdivision (e.g., 507) or a span of standard subdivisions (e.g., 516.001-.009) is specifically named in the schedules, it is understood that the sub-subdivisions to these standard subdivisions may be used when applicable (e.g., 507.4 for science museums, or 516.0076 for review and exercises in geometry) unless there are contrary instructions in the schedules.

Although standard subdivisions may be applied wherever they are appropriate, there are certain restrictions on their use. In addition to restrictions appearing in the schedules relating to specific numbers (e.g., do not use 362.09; class in 362.9), certain general restrictions are set forth in the "Introduction" to the abridged edition:[5]

1. The classifier should not add a standard subdivision when it is redundant, i.e., when the subdivision means the same as the base number. Therefore, for a history of the United States, do not add -09 to 973, which already means history of the U.S.
2. The classifier should not add one standard subdivision to another standard subdivision unless there are specific instructions to do so. When two or more standard subdivisions are applicable to a work, choose one according to the table of preference, which is

found at the head of Table 1, e.g., choosing -068 over -09 and choose -09 over -05.

3. Unless there are instructions in the schedules permitting their use, the classifier should be cautious about adding a standard subdivision to the number chosen for a work that deals with a subject more specific than the content of the number, i.e., when the subject represented in the work does not have its own specific number. For example, a history of special libraries is classed in 026.0009, but a history of medical libraries, which does not have its own number, is classed in 026, instead of 026.0009. In other words, the standard subdivision is not added unless the content of the work being classified covers the whole, or approximately the whole, of the subject represented by the main number. This is called the "approximate-the-whole" rule.

When the caption of a number contains two topics, instruction is provided as to whether standard subdivisions may be added to both topics, to either topic, or to one of the topics only, e.g.,

> 327.1   Foreign policy and specific topics in international relations
> Standard subdivisions are added for foreign policy

Certain standard subdivision concepts, particularly for geographical treatment, are displaced to non-zero numbers. For example, political campaigns in the United States are classed in 324.973 instead of 324.0973. In such cases, the full range of standard subdivisions may be added further, for example, maps of American political campaigns, 324.973022.

Table 2: Geographic Areas and Persons

Area notation specifies the historical or geographical treatment of a subject and may be used with numbers throughout the schedules as instructed. It is used in the following ways:

1. Used directly when so noted with numbers from the schedules

Geology of Latvia	554.796
1. Base number for regional geology	55
2. Area notation for Latvia from Table 2	-4 796
3. (2) added to (1) with decimal point inserted	554.796
Postage stamps from Japan	769.56952
1. Base number for postage stamps: historical geographic, persons treatment	769 569

2. Area notation from Table 2 for Japan   -52
3. (2) added to (1) with decimal point
   inserted   769.56952

A history of Thailand   959.3
1. Base number for general history of
   specific countries. Cf. note under 930-
   990   9
2. Area notation for Thailand from Table
   2   -59 3
3. (2) added to (1) with decimal point
   inserted   959.3

2. Used through the interposition of notation -09 from Table 1. In Table 1, under -093-099, there is an instruction to add area notation 3-9 from Table 2 to base number -09, e.g., -0973 for historical and geographical treatment of a subject with regard to the United States. The combination is then treated as one standard subdivision. Since -09 is a standard subdivision and therefore can be added to any number from the schedules when appropriate, virtually every number in the DDC system can be subdivided geographically, unless there is specific instruction in the schedules not to use the standard subdivision under the particular number.

Economic geology of Germany   553.0943
1. Base number for economic geology   553
2. Standard subdivision for geographic
   treatment for Germany   -0943
3. (2) added to (1) with decimal point
   inserted   553.0943

When direct geographic subdivision as explained earlier is provided, it takes precedence over the use of -09 and its subdivisions.

Exercise 13-6

Assign Decimal Classification numbers (abridged edition) to the following topics or titles:

1. How to teach cooking
2. A scientist's view with regard to life on Mars
3. Labor union discrimination against black American textile workers
4. Rocks from the moon
5. Flora and fauna of Alaska
6. Nursing education

7. A history of Kentucky during the Civil War
8. Monetary policy of France
9. History of political parties in Australia
10. An encyclopedia of engineering
11. A travel guide to Florida
12. A bibliography of Ohio imprints
13. A history of Christian churches in Iowa
14. Journal of political science
15. Farming in Iowa
16. A history of New Orleans
17. Interior decoration in Sweden
18. Social conditions in China
19. A history of Singapore
20. A collection of fairy tales
21. A gardener's handbook on diseases of flowers
22. Political conditions in the United States
23. Geology of Iran
24. *American Restaurants Then and Now*
25. United States policy toward Latin America
26. Kentucky folklore
27. Macroeconomic policy in Britain, 1974-1987
28. *Early Education in the Public Schools in Massachusetts*

Table 3: Subdivisions for Individual Literatures, for Specific Literary Forms

Notation from Table 3 is used with the base numbers for individual literatures according to add-notes found under subdivisions of individual literatures in 810-890 in the schedules. It is not used for individual literatures that lack instructions to add from Table 3. A number for literature usually contains the following elements:

1. The main class, *Literature*, is represented by the base number 8.
2. *Language* is the second element, e.g., 82- for English literature, 891.7 for Russian literature, etc. When the work is not limited to any language, the -0- is used to fill the second digit, e.g., 80- for world literature.
3. *Literary form* is the third element. Mnemonics are employed, e.g., -1 for poetry, -2 for drama, etc., hence, 821 (English poetry), 891.72 (Russian drama), etc. When the work covers more than one form, the -0 is used, e.g., 820, English literature not limited to any particular form.
4. A standard subdivision when applicable, e.g., 830.5 (a journal of German literature) is the fourth element.

Different types of literary works are classified in the following ways:

Collections of literature by more than one author

An Anthology of World Literature	<u>808</u>.<u>8</u>

An Anthology of World Drama <u>808</u>.<u>82</u>
  1. Base number for a collection of literary
     texts in specific forms from more than
     one literature <u>808</u>.<u>8</u>
  2. The number following 808 meaning
     drama -<u>2</u>
  3. (2) added to (1) <u>808</u>.<u>82</u>

An Anthology of English Literature <u>820</u>.<u>8</u>
  1. Base number for English literature <u>82</u>
  2. Notation for collections of literary texts
     from Table 3 -<u>0</u> <u>8</u>

An Anthology of French Poetry <u>841</u>.<u>008</u>
  1. Base number for French literature <u>84</u>
  2. Notation from Table 3 for a collection
     of poetry by more than one author -<u>1</u> <u>008</u>

Works about literature

A History of World Literature <u>809</u>

A Study of World Drama <u>809</u>.<u>2</u>
  1. Base number for a critical appraisal of
     literature in specific forms <u>809</u>
  2. Number following 808 in 808.1-808.7
     meaning drama, i.e., 808.<u>2</u> -<u>2</u>

A History of English Literature <u>820</u>.<u>9</u>
  1. Base number for English literature <u>82</u>
  2. Notation from Table 3 for a history of
     more than one form by more than one
     author -<u>0</u> <u>9</u>

An Outline of French Literary History <u>840</u>.<u>90002</u>
  1. Base number for French literature <u>84</u>
  2. Notation from Table 3 for history,
     description, appraisal of literature in
     more than one form by more than one
     author -<u>0</u> <u>9</u>

3. Standard subdivision from Table 1 for
an outline, with two extra zeros as
instructed under -09 in Table 3   <u>0002</u>

Works written by individual authors. In DDC, literature is classified by form; works by a given author who writes in different literary forms are classed in different numbers according to their forms. Standard subdivisions are not used with works by individual authors.

Poems by Henry Wadsworth Longfellow	<u>811</u>
Ivanhoe by Sir Walter Scott	<u>823</u>
Charles Lamb's *Essays*	<u>824</u>

In many libraries, all fiction is grouped together without regard to language and assigned a simple notation *F* with the author's name or a *Cutter number* (see discussion on pages 363–65).

Selected and collected works by individual authors are classed in the same numbers as individual works, e.g.,

Selected Poems by Edgar Allen Poe	<u>811</u>
Plays by Christopher Marlowe	<u>822</u>

When the collection contains works in various forms, the number for the predominant form or the form by which the author is best known is chosen, e.g.,

The Writings of Mark Twain	<u>813</u>
Selected Prose and Poetry by Ralph Waldo Emerson	<u>814</u>

By way of exception, William Shakespeare as a dramatist receives a unique number, 822.3; dramatic works written by him and works about him are classed in this number.

Works about individual authors. Works about individual authors are classed in the same numbers as the works written by them, as instructed in Table 3. The standard subdivision -<u>09</u> is not used.

A Study of Longfellow's Poems	<u>811</u>
Commentary on Homer's Iliad	<u>883</u>
A Critical Appraisal of Sir Walter Scott's Novels	<u>823</u>

Table 4: Subdivisions of Individual Languages

Notation from Table 4 is used with base numbers for individual languages that are identified by an asterisk (*) under 420-490 in the schedules.

A Dictionary of the Russian Language	491.73
1. Base number for Russian	491.7
2. Notation for dictionaries from Table 4	-3
English Word Origins	422
1. Base number for English	42
2. Notation for etymology from Table 4	-2

Classification of Biography

Under 920 in the schedules, several methods of classing biographies of specific classes of persons are presented. The preferred treatment is to class both individual and collected biographies of persons associated with a specific subject with the subject, using standard subdivisions notation -092 from Table 1, e.g.,

A Biography of Melvil Dewey	020.92
Biographical Directory of Librarians in the United States and Canada	020.92
A Biography of Abraham Lincoln	973.7092
Presidents of the United States	973.092

Note that biographies of heads of states are classed in the numbers for the history of their periods instead of in the number for political science. Some libraries may find it desirable to use one of the optional methods:

1. Class both individual and collected biographies of persons associated with a specific subject in 920.1-928, e.g.,

A Biography of Melvil Dewey	920.2
Biographical Directory of Librarians in the United States and Canada	920.2
A Biography of Abraham Lincoln	923
Presidents of the United States	923

2. Class all individual biographies regardless of subject orientation in 92 or B and all collected biographies regardless of subject orientation in 92 or 920 without subdivision, e.g.,

A Biography of Melvil Dewey	92 or B
Biographical Directory of Librarians in the United States and Canada	92 or 920
A Biography of Abraham Lincoln	92 or B
Presidents of the United States	92 or 920

3. Class individual biographies of men in 920.71 and of women in 920.72.

Exercise 13-7

Assign Decimal Classification numbers (abridged edition) to the following topics:

1. A history of American literature
2. An encyclopedia of Norwegian literature
3. A biography of President Lyndon Baines Johnson
4. A biography of Walter Cronkite, news broadcaster
5. A teacher's handbook of Latin literature
6. A critical study of twentieth-century drama
7. An English-Japanese, Japanese-English dictionary
8. A critical study of Russian novels
9. A history of Chinese poetry
10. The collected works of Henry Fielding
11. A handbook for sign language teachers
12. A critical study of the Afro-American as a character in American fiction
13. Remedial reading for French
14. A collection of Portuguese essays (by various authors)
15. A study of political themes in twentieth-century British literature

ITEM OR BOOK NUMBERS [MARC FIELDS 082, 09X, SUBFIELD $b]

One of the functions of a class number is to provide a shelf-location mark for a physical item in a library. In this capacity, the shelf mark for each item must be unique. Because many books are on the same subject and share the same class number, additional elements are added to the class number to create a unique shelf mark, generally referred to as a "call number." A call number contains the class number plus one or more of the following: an item number (based on the main entry), a work mark (usually based on the title of the work), a date, and a volume or issue number.

In cataloging records prepared by the Library of Congress, the DDC number does not include the item number. Also, when DDC is used for the purpose of organizing Web resources, the item number is generally omitted.

Several kinds of item or book numbers, also referred to as author notation (or number), may be employed with DDC class numbers. The simplest form, used by many small school, public, and church libraries, is the initial based on the main entry, in most cases the author's last name, for example:

512   822.3
D   M

For slightly larger collections, more letters from the main entry or author's last name may be used, hence:

512   822.3
Dic   Mar

An extreme of this method is to use the author's complete surname, e.g.,

512   822.3
Dickenson   Marlowe

However, this device is clumsy and used by very few libraries, in spite of its ability to distinguish between authors' names that begin with the same letters.

Cutter Numbers

Most libraries use a device called Cutter numbers, named after its designer, Charles Ammi Cutter. Developed originally for use with the Cutter Expansive Classification, it is now widely used with the Dewey Decimal Classification. A simplified form is used with the Library of Congress Classification and is described in chapter 14.

In the Cutter number system, the author number is derived by combining the initial letter or letters of the author's last name with numbers from a numerical table that was designed to ensure an alphabetical arrangement of names, for example, D556 (Dickens), D557 (Dickenson), and D558 (Dickerson). This device provides a shorter author number which is also easier to arrange and to read on the shelves.

There are three Cutter tables: *Two-Figure Author Table,*[6] *Three-Figure Author Table,*[7] and the *Cutter-Sanborn Table,*[8] listed in the order of increasing details. The following instruction is based on the *Three-Figure Author Table.* The Cutter number is constructed according to the following procedures:

1. Locate in the Cutter table the first few letters of the author's surname or corporate name which is the *main entry* of the work. Use only the bold face letters shown in the combination and the Arabic numbers next to it, e.g.,

Dewes   514
Dewey   515
Dewil   516

Based on the above figures, the Cutter number for Melvil Dewey is *D515.*
Certain letters in the alphabet appear more frequently as initial letters

of names. In order to keep the Cutter numbers short, two letters are used in a combination for names beginning with a vowel or the letter *S*, and three letters are used for names beginning with the letters *Sc*, e.g.,

813.54	813.54	813.54	813.54
Ed98	Sch56	Sm64	V896

2. Where there is no Cutter number in the table that fits a name exactly, use the first of the two numbers closest to the name, e.g., *T325* for Thackeray, based on:

Thacher	325
Thad	326

3. Cutter numbers are treated decimally. Therefore, when required, any number can be extended by adding extra digits at its end. For example, if *Sm52* has been assigned to Benjamin Smith and *Sm53* has been assigned to Charles Smith, and a Cutter number must be provided for Brian Smith, the number Sm525 can then be used. The filing order is Sm52, Sm525, Sm53. The number 5 or 6 is often chosen as the extra digit in order to leave room on both sides for future interpolation.

For the same reason, although the tables provide many numbers ending in the numeral 1, it is advisable to add a digit and not to use a Cutter number ending in 1, because it places a limit on expansion. For example, use L5115 instead of L511 for David Lee. Furthermore, avoid using zero, because it is easily confused with the letter *o*, and, if possible, use some means to distinguish the number 1 from the letter *l*, such as substituting the lower-case script form (*l*) for the latter.

4. When two authors classified in the same number share the same Cutter number in the table, assign a different number for the second author by adding a digit, e.g., M315 for Heinrich Mann and M3155 for Thomas Mann. If Thomas Mann has been assigned the number M315 before a number for Heinrich Mann is required, the number M3145 then can be used for the latter.

5. Names beginning with Mc, M', and Mac are treated as though they were all spelled Mac. The apostrophe is ignored, i.e., O'Hara being treated as Ohara.

6. When the main entry is under title, the Cutter number is based on the first word (disregarding initial articles) of the title. *Encyclopaedia Britannica* is assigned En19. Therefore, it is more accurate to state that the Cutter number is derived from the main entry of the work which may or may not be a personal author.

7. An exception is made for biographies. In order to group all biographies of a person together, the Cutter number is based on the name of the biographee instead of the main entry. For example, all biographies of Napoleon are grouped in the Cutter number N162. In many libraries,

this practice is extended to include works about corporate bodies, particularly firms and institutions.

Unique Call Numbers

As mentioned above, when two or more authors with the same last name write on the same subject, they are assigned different author or Cutter numbers, e.g., D557 for David Dickenson and D558 or D5575 for Robert Dickenson. When the same author has written more than one work on a particular subject, further devices—work marks, edition marks or date of publication, and copy and volume numbers—are added to create unique call numbers. These are discussed below.

Work Mark

A *work mark* (sometimes called a *work letter*) is added to the Cutter number to distinguish different titles on the same subject by the same author. Work marks usually follow the Cutter number directly, and consist of the first letter or letters (in lower case) from the first word (disregarding initial articles) in the title. The following examples show the pattern.

512
D557i   *Introduction to Algebra* by D. Dickenson

512
D557p   *Principles of Algebra* by D. Dickenson

512
D557pr   *Progress in Algebra* by D. Dickenson

813.4
J233a   *The Ambassadors* by Henry James

813.4
J233am   *The American* by Henry James

813.4
J233p   *The Portrait of a Lady* by Henry James

In some cases, when books in a series by the same author on the same subject all begin with the same word, it is customary to use the first letter from each key word in the titles, e.g.,

738.2
H324ce   Hayden's *Chats on English China*

738.2
H324co   Hayden's *Chats on Old China*

738.2
H324cr   Hayden's *Chats on Royal Copenhagen Porcelain*

Practices in assigning work marks vary slightly from library to library, as there are no definitive rules concerning this aspect of cataloging. The approach shown in the examples here represents one of various alternatives and should not be taken as the *only* method.[9] Nonetheless, they illustrate the basic function of the call number, which is to provide a unique symbol for each item of library material and to ensure a logical arrangement of works that share the same class number.

Exercise 13-8

Assign Cutter numbers and work marks to the following titles:

1. 973 Adams, Henry. *History of the United States of America.* 1962
2. 973 Adams, Henry. *The Formative Years: a History of the United States during the Administration of Jefferson and Madison.* 1948
3. 973 Adams, James Truslow. *The March of Democracy.* 1932–33
4. 973 Adams, Randolph G. *The Gateway to American History.* 1927
5. 973 Adams, Randolph G. *Pilgrims, Indians and Patriots: The Pictorial History of America from the Colonial Age to the Revolution.* 1928
6. 973 Baldwin, Leland Dewitt. *The Stream of American History.* 1965
7. 973 Bancroft, George. *History of the United States of America, from the Discovery of the Continent to 1789.* 1883–85
8. 973 Beals, Carleton. *American Earth: the Biography of a Nation.* 1939
9. 973 Schlesinger, Arthur Meier. *New Viewpoints in American History.* 1922
10. 973 Schlesinger, Arthur Meier. *Political and Social History of the United States, 1829–1925.* 1925
11. 973 Schouler, James. *History of the United States of America under the Constitution.* 1880–1913
12. 973 Sellers, Charles G. *A Synopsis of American History.* 1963
13. 973 Shaler, Nathaniel S. *The United States of America.* 1894
14. 973 Sheehan, Donald H. *The Making of American History.* 1950
15. 973 Sherwood, James. *The Comic History of the United States.* 1870
16. 973 *Six Presidents from the Empire State.* 1974
17. 973 Smith, Dale O. *U.S. Military Doctrine: A Study and Appraisal.* 1955
18. 973 Smith, Goldwin. *The United States: An Outline of Political History, 1492–1871.* 1893

Work marks are particularly important in cases where many items are classed under the same number, for example, B (Biography) and F (Fiction). Work marks for biographies and literary works therefore merit special consideration.

Cutter Numbers for Biography

In order to group all biographies of the same person together on the shelf, the Cutter number is taken from the name of the biographee instead of the author. All biographies of George Washington are cuttered under W277, and the work mark is then taken from the first letter of the main entry—which is usually the author's surname. The work mark *a* is used for all autobiographical writings in order to place such works before biographies written by other people. A biography written by an author whose surname begins with the letter *a* is then assigned two letters as the work mark, e.g., W277ad (for Adams, etc.). When there is more than one autobiographical work, an arbitrary Arabic number may be added to the work mark. For example,

W277a	Washington, George. *Autograph Letters and Documents of George Washington Now in Rhode Island Collections*
W277a1	Washington, George. *Affectionately Yours, George Washington: A Self-Portrait in Letters of Friendship,* edited by T. J. Fleming
W277a2	Washington, George. *Last Will and Testament of George Washington of Mount Vernon*
W277ad	Adams, R. G. *Five Radio Addresses on George Washington*
W277b	Bellamy, F. R. *The Private Life of George Washington*
W277d	Delaware. Public Archives Commission. *George Washington and Delaware*
W277h	*Honor to George Washington and Reading about George Washington*

Cutter Numbers for Literary Works

In the Dewey Decimal Classification, critical appraisals and biographies of individual authors are classed in the same numbers as those assigned to their works; thus, they share the same class number and Cutter number. It is then the function of the work mark to distinguish the works written *by* and those written *about* an author. In this area particularly, libraries vary in their practices. For example, some libraries use an additional Cutter number for works about individual authors. There are as yet no standards or rules in this regard. The following is presented as an example of a workable mechanism. In many libraries, the practice outlined in this section also applies to philosophers and artists when works written by and about them are classed in the same numbers.

Works by Individual Authors

These are assigned work marks taken from the titles, e.g.,

821.5	Pope, Alexander
P8115d	*The Dunciad*
P8115ep	*An Epistle from Mr. Pope to Dr. Arbuthnot*
P8115es	*An Essay on Criticism*
P8115ess or P8115esm	*An Essay on Man*
P8115r	*The Rape of the Lock*

Biography and Criticism of Individual Authors

Since critical appraisals and biographies of an individual author share the same class number and Cutter number with the author's works, they require special work marks if the library does not wish to interfile these two categories of works. The most common device is to insert the letter z between the Cutter number and the work mark, e.g.,

P8115zc   Clark, D. B. *Alexander Pope*

P8115zr   Russell, J. P. *Alexander Pope: Tradition and Identity*

With the use of the letter z, works *about* Pope will be filed after works written *by* him. The letter z in this case is followed by the regular work mark based on the main entry. In this way, the letter z alone is reserved for any title by the author with the first word beginning with the letter z, e.g.,

833.912
M317z   Mann, Thomas. *Der Zauberberg*

M317zl   Lehnert, Herbert. *Thomas-Mann-Forschung*

In some libraries, serial publications devoted to the study of an individual author are assigned the work mark zz so that these publications will be filed after other critical works about the author, e.g., M317zz for *Blätter der Thomas Mann Gesellschaft*.

As an alternative of using the letter z as a work mark for works about an author, a second Cutter number based on the main entry of the work may be used, e.g.,

821.5

P8115   Clark, D. B.
C547   *Alexander Pope*

821.5
P8115   Russell, J. P.
R914   *Alexander Pope: Tradition and Identity*

Works about Individual Works

If the library wishes to have individual works and the critical works about them stand together on the shelf, work marks may be used as a device for such an arrangement. The capital letter Z is inserted between the work mark for the work criticized, and the work mark is based on the critic's surname, e.g.,

821.5
P8115dZs   Sitter, J. E. *The Poetry of Pope's Dunciad*

P8115dZw   Williams, A. L. *Pope's Dunciad: A Study of Its
           Meaning*

This practice may be extended to include translations of literary works if one wishes to have the original work and the translations stand together, e.g.,

833.912   Mann, Thomas
M317b   *Bekenntnisse des Hochstaplers Felix Krull*

M317bE   *Confessions of Felix Krull, Confidence Man*

The letter E stands for an English translation. In some libraries, the letter x is used as a work mark for an author's collected works, and the letter y for works such as bibliographies and concordances of individual authors, e.g.,

821.5   Pope, Alexander
P8115xb   *Complete Poetical Works*, edited by H. W.
           Boynton

P8115xd   *Poetical Works*, edited by H. Davis

P8115ya   Abbott, E., comp. *A Concordance to the Works of
           Alexander Pope*

The only problem in this practice is that an individual work with a title beginning with the letter z would then be separated from other individual works. An alternative is to use the letter a as a work mark for collected works, similar to the treatment of autobiographies. In this case, collected

works of an author would precede individual works, an arrangement preferred by many libraries. Bibliographies and concordances would then be
treated like other works about the author.

The works written *by* and *about* an individual author are therefore
arranged in the following order:

> Collected works (arranged by date or by editor)
> Individual works (arranged alphabetically by title)
>> Original text
>> Translations (subarranged alphabetically by language and
>> then by translators' names)
>> Critical appraisals (subarranged alphabetically by the critics'
>> names)
> General critical appraisals not limited to a single work
> (subarranged by the critics' names)
> Serial publications devoted to the study of the author

For example,

833.912 M317a	Mann, Thomas *Gesammelte Werke*
M317t	*Der Tod in Venedig*
M317tE	*Death in Venice*
M317z	*Der Zauberberg*
M317zE	*The Magic Mountain*
M317zZm	Miller, R. D. *The Two Faces of Hermes: A Study of Thomas Mann's Novel, "The Magic Mountain"*
M317ze	Eichner, H. *Thomas Mann*
M317zs	Schroter, K. *Thomas Mann*
M317zz	*Blätter der Thomas Mann Gesellschaft*

It should be noted that in filing, capital letters precede lowercase letters.

Shakespeare constitutes a special case because of the large number of
editions and translations of his works and of works about him. In DDC,
he has been given a special class number, 822.33. Since no other author
shares that class number, it would be redundant to base the Cutter number on his name. Therefore, a special scheme of Cutter numbers based on
titles has been developed. It appears in the DDC schedules following the
class number 822.33.

In the case of anonymous classics, the Cutter number is based on the uniform title, and the work mark may be taken either from the title of the version being cataloged, or from the editor, translator, or the person most closely associated with the edition, e.g.,

821.1	Pearl (Middle English poem)
P316c	*The Pearl*; with an introductory essay by S. P. Chase
P316g	*Pearl*; edited by E. V. Gordon
P316zk	Kean, P. M. *The Pearl: An Interpretation*

For various versions of the Bible, since the class number already represents the Bible, its parts (i.e., the Old and New Testaments), or individual books, it would be redundant to cutter under title. The Cutter number is then based on the name of the version, the name of the editor, or, lacking such, on the name of the publisher.

For libraries with large collections of other sacred scriptures, a similar arrangement may be used.

Edition Mark

Many works appear in different editions, which share the same class and Cutter numbers. In order to create a unique call number for each edition, an edition mark in the form of a number is usually added after the work mark or a date under the Cutter number, e.g.,

| 025.431 | 025.431 | 025.431 | 025.431 |
| D515d17 | D515d18 | D515d19 | D515d20 |

or

025.431	025.431	025.431	025.431
D515d	D515d	D515d	D515d
1965	1979	1989	2003

Some libraries use dates as edition marks for all works; others use both methods in the same catalog. The choice of method in each case depends on appropriateness; for instance, dates are usually used when editions are not numbered. When there is more than one edition of a work within a year—as is often the case with literary works—a letter is added arbitrarily to the date, e.g., 1976a, 1976b, 1976c, etc.

Copy and Volume Number

When a work is published in more than one volume or when the library has more than one copy of a work, a volume or copy number, or in some cases both, is added to the call number on the physical volume in order to provide a unique address for each item in the collection, e.g.,

025.431	025.431
D515d19	D515d20
v.2	v.1
	copy 2

The copy designation does not appear in the bibliographic record, since the record represents the entire work rather than an individual copy. The volume number may or may not appear there depending on whether the record has been created for that particular volume or for the entire work.

Prefixes to Call Numbers

When a particular item is to be shelved in a special location or out of its ordinary place, a prefix may be added to the call number. The most commonly used prefix is the letter *R* for books in the reference collection, e.g.,

R
031
En19

Prefixes are also used for large-size books, books in special collections, and nonprint materials.

Exercise 13-9

Complete the call numbers for the following titles:

1. 92 Arthur, Sir G. *Concerning Winston Spencer Churchill* [1874–1965]
2. 92 Ashley, M. P. *Churchill as Historian* [W. S. Churchill, 1874–1965]
3. 92 Bullock, A. L. C. *Hitler: A Study in Tyranny*
4. 92 Churchill, Jennie Jerome, 1854–1921. *The Reminiscences of Lady Randolph Churchill*
5. 92 Churchill, Randolph S., 1911–1968. *Winston S. Churchill* [1874–1965]
6. 92 Churchill, Winston, Sir. 1874–1965. *A Roving Commission: My Early Life*
7. 92 Churchill, Winston, Sir, 1874–1965. *Lord Randolph Churchill* [1849–1895]
8. 92 Fishman, J. *My Darling Clementine* [wife of W. S. Churchill]
9. 92 Gardner, B. *Churchill in Power* [W. S. Churchill, 1874–1965]

10. 92 Graebner, W. *My Dear Mr. Churchill* [W. S. Churchill, 1874–1965]
11. 92 Hackett, Francis. *What Mein Kampf Means to America*
12. 92 Hitler, Adolph. *Mein Kampf*
13. 92 Hitler, Adolph. *My Battle*
14. 92 James, R. R. *Lord Randolph Churchill* [1849–1895]
15. 92 Kraus, R. *Young Lady Randolph* [Churchill, 1854–1921]
16. 92 Leslie, Anita. *Jennie: The Life of Lady Randolph Churchill* [1854–1921]
17. 92 Leslie, Anita. *Lady Randolph Churchill: The Story of Jennie Jerome* [1854–1921]
18. 92 Martin, R. G. *Jennie: The Life of Lady Randolph Churchill* [1854–1921]
19. 92 Smith, B. F. *Adolph Hitler: His Family, Childhood and Youth*

Now complete the call numbers for the following titles:

1. 823.8 Brook, G. L. *The Language of Dickens*
2. 823.8 Churchill, R. C. *A Bibliography of Dickensian Criticism*
3. 823.8 Dickens, Charles. *Eine Geschichte von zwei Städten* [a German translation of *A Tale of Two Cities*]
4. 823.8 Dickens, Charles. *Hard Times*
5. 823.8 Dickens, Charles. *Historia de dos Ciudades* [a Spanish translation of *A Tale of Two Cities*]
6. 823.8 Dickens, Charles. *Paris et Londres en 1793* [a French translation of *A Tale of Two Cities*]
7. 823.8 Dickens, Charles. *Les temps difficiles* [a French translation of *Hard Times*]
8. 823.8 Dickens, Charles. *Schwere Zeiten* [a German translation of *Hard Times*]
9. 823.8 Dickens, Charles. *A Tale of Two Cities.* 1934
10. 823.8 Dickens, Charles. *A Tale of Two Cities.* 1970
11. 823.8 Dickens, Charles. *Zwei Städte, Roman aus der französischen Revolution von Charles Dickens* [a German translation of *A Tale of Two Cities* by B. Dedek, 1924]
12. 823.8 *Dickens Studies Newsletter*
13. 823.8 *The Dickensian: A Magazine for Dickens Lovers*
14. 823.8 Hayward, A. L. *The Dickens Encyclopedia*
15. 823.8 *Twentieth Century Interpretations of A Tale of Two Cities: A Collection of Critical Essays*

NOTES

1. Melvil Dewey, *Dewey Decimal Classification and Relative Index.* Ed. 22, ed. Joan S. Mitchell, Editor in Chief, Julianne Beall, Giles Martin, Winton E. Matthews,

Jr., Gregory R. New, Assistant Editors (Dublin, Ohio: OCLC Online Computer Library Center, Inc., 2003), v.1, xxxix.

2. Arthur Maltby, *Sayers' Manual of Classification for Libraries*, 5th ed. (London: Andre Deutsch, 1975), 121. John Phillip Comaromi, on the other hand, argued that Hegel provided the philosophic underpinnings of Harris's and Dewey's classification systems (cf. his *The Eighteen Editions of the Dewey Decimal Classification* [Albany, N.Y.: Forest Press Division, Lake Placid Education Foundation, 1976], 29).

3. Melvil Dewey, *Abridged Dewey Decimal Classification and Relative Index*. Ed. 14, ed. Joan S. Mitchell, Editor in Chief, Julianne Beall, Giles Martin, Winton E. Matthews, Jr., Gregory R. New, Assistant Editors (Dublin, Ohio: OCLC Online Computer Library Center, Inc., 2004).

4. "Introduction," in Melvil Dewey, *Dewey Decimal Classification and Relative Index*. Ed. 22, v. 1, lii–liv.

5. "Introduction" in Melvil Dewey, *Abridged Dewey Decimal Classification and Relative Index*. Ed. 14, xxxviii.

6. Cutter, C. A. *C. A. Cutter's Two-Figure Author Table*. (Swanson-Swift revision. 1969) Chicopee, Mass.: H. R. Huntting Company, 1969.

7. Cutter, C. A. *C. A. Cutter's Three-Figure Author Table*. (Swanson-Swift revision. 1969) Chicopee, Mass.: H. R. Huntting Company, 1969.

8. Cutter, C. A. *Cutter-Sanborn Three-Figure Author Table*. (Swanson-Swift revision. 1969.) Chicopee, Mass.: H. R. Huntting Company, 1969.

9. See also John P. Comaromi, *Book Numbers: A Historical Study and Practical Guide to Their Use* (Littleton, Colo.: Libraries Unlimited, 1981); and, Donald J. Lehnus, *Book Numbers: History, Principles, and Application* (Chicago: American Library Association, 1980).

CHAPTER 14
LIBRARY OF CONGRESS
CLASSIFICATION

INTRODUCTION

During most of the nineteenth century, the Library of Congress collection was organized according to a system devised by Thomas Jefferson. When the Library moved into its new building in 1897, however, the Jeffersonian system was found to be inadequate for a collection that had grown to over one and a half million pieces. Two other classification systems, the Dewey Decimal Classification (DDC) and Charles A. Cutter's Expansive Classification (EC) (see discussion in chapters 13 and 15), had emerged during the last few decades of the nineteenth century and were in use in many other libraries in the nation, but neither was considered suitable for the Library of Congress. It was decided to construct a new system, to be called the *Library of Congress Classification* (LCC), and work began on its development.

From the beginning, individual classes were developed by different groups of specialists working under the direction of J. C. M. Hanson and Charles Martel; the schedules, each of which contained an entire class, a subclass, or a group of subclasses, were published separately. Thus, unlike most other classification systems, LCC was not the product of one mastermind. Indeed, it has been called "a coordinated series of special classes."[1]

Today, the Library of Congress Classification consists of twenty-one classes displayed in over forty separately published print schedules and a large database. Its provisions are continually updated, and information on additions and changes is made widely available to the library community. Although LCC was originally designed expressly for the Library of Congress collection, it has been adopted by most large academic and research libraries, as well as by some large public libraries. During the 1960s, in particular, there was a trend among academic libraries previously using DDC or other systems to switch to LCC. There were several reasons for the trend: (1) the basic orientation of LCC toward research libraries; (2) the economic advantage offered by LC cataloging services—libraries can simply adopt whole call numbers as they appear on LC cataloging records; and (3) the increasing ease with which many libraries can bring up full LC MARC records online and add them to their own catalog databases. The fact that LCC is used in so many libraries has had some impact on its development; Library of Congress catalogers no longer focus solely on the Library's own needs as they revise and expand the schedules.

In the Web environment, the potential of using LCC as a tool for organizing Internet resources has also been considered and experimented on.[2] An example of using LCC in a portal is the CyberStacks(sm) system on the Iowa State University website.[3]

HISTORY

From its earliest days, the two persons primarily responsible for the design and working out of the new Library of Congress Classification were J. C. M. Hanson and Charles Martel. They chose Cutter's Expansive Classification (EC) as their chief guide, with considerable modification of the EC notation. Some of the early parallels, particularly for Class Z (Book Arts in Cutter; Bibliography and Library Science in LCC) were very close. Table 14-1, a comparison of Cutter's outline and Hanson's first outline, shows how much the two schemes resembled each other in broad divisions.

For notation, it was decided at the outset to adopt a three-element pattern: first, single capital letters for main classes (H for Social sciences, P for Language and literature, Q for Science, and so on) with one or two capital letters for their subclasses (H for General works on social sciences, HA for Statistics, QD for Chemistry, and so on); second, Arabic integers from 1 to 9999 for subdivisions; and third, Cutter numbers (letter/number strings read decimally) for individual books.[4] Gaps were left for future expansion. Before many decades, parts of the schedules became crowded as knowledge developed. To accommodate new topics, decimal expansion of the original integers was allowed in some cases, and so was the use of Cutter numbers for some topical subdivisions. More recently, three capital letters have been used for some subclasses.

Class Z was chosen as the first schedule to be developed because its subject matter included the bibliographical works necessary for work on all the other schedules. The Class Z draft was adopted by the Library of Congress in 1898, although the schedule was not published until 1902. From the beginning, the LC Classification schedules have been developed and published separately, each on its own timetable. The first schedule to be published was Class E-F, *America, History and Geography* (1901). A full system outline appeared in 1904, by which time the classification of Classes D, E-F, M, Q, R, S, T, U, and Z had been completed and work was under way on Classes A, C, G, H, and V. By 1948, all but one schedule had been completed and published; the exception was Class K (Law). The first schedule of this class, KF (United States law), was published in 1969, and schedules for other subclasses of law have appeared since.

TABLE 14-1 Cutter's Outline and Hanson's First Outline

Cutter's Outline	*Hanson's First Outline*
General works	Polygraphy; Encyclopedia; General Periodicals; Societies
Philosophy	Philosophy
Religion	Religion; Theology; Church history
Christianity	
Historical sciences	Biography; and studies auxiliary to history
Biography	General history; periods; and local
History	America; history and geography
Geography and travel	Geography and allied studies
Social sciences	Political science
Demotics, Sociology	Law
Civics	Sociology
Legislation	Women; Societies; clubs, etc.
	Sports and amusements
	Music
	Fine arts
Sciences and Arts	Philology; Literature
Natural history	
Botany	Science; Mathematics; Astronomy; Physics; Chemistry
Zoology	Natural history, general; Geology Zoology; Botany
Medicine	Medicine
Useful arts. Technology	Useful arts; Agriculture
Constructive arts	Manufactures
Fabricative arts	Engineering
Art of War	Military and Naval science; light houses; lifesaving; fire extinction
Recreative arts. Music	Special collections
Fine arts	
Language	
Literature	
Book arts	Bibliography (Book arts)

Source: John Phillip Immroth, *A Guide to the Library of Congress Classification*, 2nd ed. (Littleton, Colo.: Libraries Unlimited, 1971), 20–21.

BASIC PRINCIPLES AND STRUCTURE

Overall Characteristics

Like the other classification systems originating in the nineteenth century, the Library of Congress Classification is basically a classification by disci-

pline. Main classes, established to accommodate all subject areas represented in the LC collection, correspond to major academic areas or
disciplines. Main classes are divided into subclasses, which in turn reflect
individual disciplines or their branches. Classes or subclasses are then
further subdivided by topic and/or by form, place, or time. The structure
of LCC, therefore, is hierarchical, progressing from the general to the specific. One striking difference between LCC and most other modern classification systems is that it is essentially an enumerative scheme in that
most subject subdivisions are listed in highly specific detail and compound or multi-faceted subjects are specifically listed as such in the
schedules. Even many common divisions, including those for form, are
also individually listed under their applicable subjects. Such detailed
enumeration means that relatively little notational synthesis, or number
building, is required. There are many tables, but these are included
mainly as a device for saving space in the schedules; they are usually
used for pinpointing specific numbers within a range of numbers given
after a caption in a schedule. Thus, tables in LCC have quite a different
purpose from those in the Dewey Decimal Classification and other systems, where numbers can be quite literally "built." LCC's degree of enumeration is only one way in which it differs dramatically from DDC.
Another is that, because of the use of letters as notation for representing
main classes and subclasses, there is room for a substantially larger number of them.

It should be borne in mind that in its details LCC was not designed
as a universal system (i.e., a system that details all existing subjects), but
rather as one specifically tailored to Library of Congress needs. In other
words, it was based on the "literary warrant" of the materials already in,
and being added to, the Library of Congress itself. To a considerable extent, this fact partly explains the seemingly uneven distribution of LCC
notation, especially its preponderance in history and other social sciences.
Table 14-2 shows the current state of LCC classes and subclasses in terms
of what the schedules are and how many volumes are devoted to each.
The table provides an overview of how LCC's coverage is distributed over
areas of knowledge. A list of separately published schedules of LCC appears on the inside cover of each printed schedule.

Main Classes

The rationale for the arrangement of LCC's main classes was explained
by Charles Martel,[5] one of the persons responsible for the original planning and supervision of the development of the system. The class of general works (A), not limited to any particular subject, leads the scheme. It
is followed by the class containing philosophy and religion (B), which
sets forth theories about human beings in relation to the universe. The
next classes in the sequence, history and geography (C-G), cover such

TABLE 14-2   LCC Main Classes and Schedules

A	General works (1 volume)
B	Philosophy. Psychology. Religion (3 volumes)
	B–BJ; BL–BQ; BR–BX
C	Auxiliary Sciences of History (1 volume)
D	History: General and History of Europe, Asia, etc. (2 volumes)
	D–DR; DS–DX
E–F	History: America (1 volume)
G	Geography. Maps. Anthropology. Recreation (1 volume)
H	Social Sciences (1 volume)
J	Political Science (1 volume)
K	Law (12 volumes)
	K Tables; K; KB; KD; KDZ, KG–KH; KE; KF; KJ–KKZ; KJV–KJW;
	KK–KKC; KL–KWX; KZ
L	Education (1 volume)
M	Music and Books on Music (1 volume)
N	Fine Arts (1 volume)
P	Language and Literature (9 volumes)
	P–PZ Tables; P–PA; PB–PH; PJ–PK; PL–PM; PN; PQ; PR, PS, PZ; PT
Q	Science (1 volume)
R	Medicine (1 volume)
S	Agriculture (1 volume)
T	Technology (1 volume)
U–V	Military Science. Naval Science (1 volume)
Z	Bibliography. Library Science. Information Resources (General) (1 volume)

concepts as the human abode and the source of humanity's means of subsistence, humans as affected by and affecting their physical milieu, and the mind and soul of humanity in transition from primitive to advanced culture. The next group, classes H-L, deals with the economic and social evolution of human beings. Classes M-P (music, fine arts, and language and literature) concern human aesthetic and intellectual development and state. Classes B-P form the group of the philosophico-historical and philological sciences. The second large group, Classes Q-V, embraces the mathematico-physical, natural, and applied sciences. Bibliography, which in many libraries may be distributed throughout different subject classes, shares the same class (Z) with Librarianship.

Because different persons were responsible for the development of the individual classes, a given class may display unique features. The use of tables and the degree and method for notational synthesis often vary from schedule to schedule. However, certain features are shared by all schedules: the overall organization, the notation, the method and arrangement of form and geographic divisions, and many tables. (These will all be discussed in detail later in the chapter.) The organization of divisions within a class, subclass, or subject originally followed a general pattern, often called Martel's seven points. Briefly, these are (1) general form divisions; (2) theory/philosophy; (3) history; (4) treatises or general works; (5) law/regulation/state-relations; (6) study and teaching; and (7) special subjects and subdivisions of subjects. Subsequent additions and changes have clouded this pattern to some extent, but it is generally still discernible. Since the development of the K (Law) schedules, legal topics relating to specific subjects have been moved to Class K.

Subclasses

Each of the main classes, with the exception of E and F, is divided into subclasses that represent disciplines or major branches of the main class. Class Q, for example, is divided into the following subclasses:

Q	Science (general)
QA	Mathematics
QB	Astronomy
QC	Physics
QD	Chemistry
QE	Geology
QH	Natural History (General)—Biology (General)
QK	Botany
QL	Zoology
QM	Human anatomy
QP	Physiology
QR	Microbiology

Divisions

Each subclass is further divided into divisions that represent components of the subclass. For example, the subclass chemistry has the following divisions:

QD	*Chemistry*
1-65	General
	Including Alchemy
71-142	Analytical chemistry
146-197	Inorganic chemistry
241-441	Organic chemistry
415-436	Biochemistry
450-801	Physical and theoretical chemistry
625-655	Radiation chemistry
701-731	Photochemistry
901-999	Crystallography

Each of the divisions, in turn, has subdivisions specifying different aspects of the subject, such as form, time, place, and more detailed subject subdivisions. Table 14-3 shows a portion of the subdivisions under Inorganic chemistry.

NOTATION

Symbols

As mentioned earlier, the Library of Congress Classification uses a mixed notation of letters and Arabic numerals to construct call numbers. Main classes are represented by a single letter, e.g., K (Law), N (Fine arts), and Q (Science). Most subclasses are represented by double or triple letters, e.g., QD (Chemistry), DJK (History of Eastern Europe), and KFF (Law of Florida). Classes E and F, the earliest classes to be developed, have not been divided into subclasses.

An interesting feature of the LCC notation is that, in most schedules, the single letter stands for the class as a whole as well as for its first subclass, usually general works relating to the subject as a whole, but sometimes, its most prominent subclass, which is narrower in scope. For example,

      Class H: Social Sciences
         Subclass H: Social Sciences (General)
      Class N: Fine arts
         Subclass N: Visual arts
      Class P: Language and literature
         Subclass P: Philology. Linguistics

Divisions within subclasses are represented by Arabic numbers from 1 to 9999 (as integers) with possible decimal extension, and/or with further subdivision indicated by Cutter numbers (a combination of a capital letter and one or more numerals). An item number (also in the form of a Cutter number) and in most cases the year of publication completes the call number. Typical forms of LC call numbers are:

		Class number
DJK	SD	One, two, or three capital letters
7	207	Integer 1 to 9999
.5		Possible decimal extension
.H36	.P57	*Item number*
2004	2004	*Year of publication*
		Class number
HD	N	One, two, or three capital letters

TABLE 14-3 Portion of Subdivisions under Inorganic Chemistry

QD	Chemistry
	Inorganic chemistry
	Cf. QD475, Physical inorganic chemistry
	Cf. QE351 + Mineralogy
146	Periodicals, societies, congresses, serial publications
147	Collected works (nonserial)
148	Dictionaries and encyclopedias
	Nomenclature, terminology, notation, abbreviations
149	History
149.5	General works
149.7.A-Z	By region or country, A-Z
	Early works through 1800
150	General works, treatises, and advanced textbooks
151	1801–1969
151.2	1970–2000
151.3	2001-
151.5	Elementary textbooks
152	Addresses, essays, lectures
152.3	Special aspects of the subject as a whole
152.5.A-Z	Special topics, A-Z
	Mathematics
	Reaction mechanisms see QD502.5
152.5.M38	Study and teaching. Research
153	General works
153.5	Outlines, syllabi, etc.
154	Problems, exercises, examinations
155	Laboratory manuals
155.5	Handbooks, tables, formulas, etc.
156	Inorganic synthesis
	Electric furnace operations
	Cf. QD277, Electric furnace operations (Organic)
157	Nonmetals
161	General works
162	Gases
163	Chemistry of the air
	Cf. TD881 +, Air pollution
165	Halogens: Bromine, chlorine, fluorine, iodine
167	Inorganic acids
	Cf. QD477, General theory of acids and bases
169.A-Z	Other, A-Z
169.C5	Chalcogenides
	Heavy water, *see* .W3
	Water
	Cf. GB855 + Natural water chemistry
	Metals
169.W3	Cf. TN600 +, Metallurgy

171	General works, treatises, and textbooks
172	By group, A-Z
172.A3	Actinide elements
172.A4	Alkali metals
172.A42	Alkaline earth metals
172.I7	Iron group
172.M4	Magnesium group
172.P8	Platinum group
172.P88	Precious metals
172.R2	Rare earth metals
172.S6	Spinel group
172.S93	Superheavy elements
	Cf. QC796.2 Nuclear physics
172.T52	Titanium group
172.T6	Transition metals
172.T65	Transplutonium elements
172.T7	Transuranium elements

9651	6530	Integer 1 to 9999
.9		Possible decimal extension
.D6	.N6	Cutter number for further subdivision of subject
D69	H64	*Item number*
2004	2003	*Year of publication*

No LC call number contains more than two Cutter numbers. Call numbers for certain types of maps and atlases, however, may contain three letter-number combinations that appear to be triple Cutter numbers.

An important characteristic of LCC notation is that it is not hierarchical beyond the class/subclass level. In other words, the notation does not necessarily reflect whatever general/specific relationships are inherent in the scheme itself. There has been some criticism of LCC's non-hierarchical notation.[6] On the other hand, the absence of notational hierarchy can be viewed as an advantage for LCC. For one thing, most of its class numbers are thereby relatively brief and are thus easily manageable for shelving purposes. For another, in part because relationships are largely ignored, LCC notation is remarkably hospitable.

Hospitality

A classification system with its attendant notation is said to be *hospitable* if it can readily accommodate expansion. Compared with the Dewey system, especially, the LCC notation stands out for its hospitality. One reason is that, from the beginning, generous notational provision was made for future expansion. At the class level, the alphabet provides a broad base for division by major subject area or discipline, broad enough that not all letters are used; I, O, X, and Y have not been assigned to any subjects and so are available for later or specialized use. At the subclass level, generous gaps have been left between two-letter combinations, and these too are available for future expansion or specialized use. An example of specialized use is found in the LCC-based National Library of Medicine Classification; it has adopted the vacant letter W for Medicine and the unused span QS-QZ for Pre-clinical sciences. Finally, there is the option of interpolating three-letter combinations to denote new subclasses.

Within subclasses, expansion is usually achieved by using vacant numbers, but when this is not feasible, two other methods can be used: decimal extension and Cutter numbers. Regarding decimal extensions, the absence of hierarchy allows their use for coordinate subjects or even for subjects broader than those represented by shorter numbers. For Cutter numbers, their alphabetical base and broad decimal extensibility make them especially suitable for alphabetical arrangement of subtopics or for geographic subdivision.

Mnemonics

LCC lacks the mnemonic aids found in some other systems. There is some use of mnemonics in Class A, where the second letter for the subclass is taken from the name of the subject covered, e.g., AC for Collections, AE for Encyclopedias, AS for Societies, etc.

EVALUATION OF THE LIBRARY OF CONGRESS CLASSIFICATION

The Library of Congress Classification[7] has both strong and weak points, both supporters and detractors. Ideally, someone making decisions on a classification system for a *new* collection would look for one with provisions most suitable for the nature and size of that collection. A medical library, for instance, is best organized by a classification system with deeply detailed provisions for medical topics. Other considerations include the availability of cataloging copy (i.e., of ready-to-use records) and frequency of update of provisions. For existing collections already classed by one system or another, one thing can be said with some force: there must be strong reasons for change, because accomplishing a change is very demanding in terms of personnel and other resources. In this context, the following lists of LCC's merits and weaknesses may be helpful.

Merits

1. It is a practical system that has proven to be satisfactory. "It is a triumph for pragmatism."[8]

2. It is based on the literary warrant of the resources in the Library of Congress collection, and of those in academic and research libraries that are members of SACO, a subject authority cooperative.
3. It is largely an enumerative system that requires minimal notational synthesis, or number building.
4. Each schedule was developed by subject specialists rather than by "generalists."
5. Its notation is compact and hospitable.
6. There are frequent additions and changes, stemming for the most part from what is needed in the day-to-day cataloging work at LC and cooperating libraries, and these are made readily available to the cataloging community.
7. The need for reclassification of large blocks of material is kept to a minimum because, to ensure stability of class numbers, few structural changes have been made over the years. (This advantage is also a disadvantage: see point 6 under "Weaknesses," below.)

Weaknesses

1. Its scope notes are inferior to those of the Dewey Decimal Classification.
2. There is much national bias in emphasis and terminology.
3. Too few subjects are seen as compounds. Multitopical or multi-element works for which specific provisions have not yet been made cannot be classified with precision.
4. Alphabetical arrangements are often used in place of logical hierarchies.
5. There is little clear and predictable theoretical basis for subject analysis.
6. As a result of maintaining stability, parts of the classification are obsolete in the sense that structure and collocation sometimes do not reflect current conditions.

THE SCHEDULES: REVISION AND PUBLICATION PATTERNS

Revision

Revision and expansion of LCC take place continuously. Changes are the responsibility of the Cataloging Policy and Support Office at the Library of Congress, with assistance from catalogers at the Library of Congress as well as those at cooperating libraries. Additions and changes often originate with catalogers who become aware of subjects not previously provided for or who discover anomalies as they attempt to find classification placements for new materials. Proposals are reviewed at weekly meetings of an editorial committee composed of representatives of the Office and other catalogers; if approved, a new or changed number is put into effect immediately and entered into the *Library of Congress Classification Weekly List,* posted on the Office's website (www.loc.gov/catdir/cpso/cpso.html#class). These changes and additions are incorporated into the LCC database and subsequent revisions of individual schedules.

Another publication that is helpful in keeping LCC current is *Super LCCS: Gale's Library of Congress Classification Schedules Combined with Additions and Changes through [previous year].*[9] Updated annually, this publication offers the advantage of consulting all currently valid numbers in one source. Each volume combines in one sequence the latest edition of every Library of Congress Classification schedule together with all additions, changes, and deletions. *Super LCCS* is also available on microfiche.

Publication Patterns for Revised Schedules

There is no regular timetable for issuing revised editions for individual LCC schedules; new issues are prepared as needed, independently of one another. Schedules in science and technology have been revised more frequently than those in humanities or some of the schedules in social sciences. Since the conversion of the schedules into electronic format in the 1990s, the Library has been able to update schedules much more frequently than previously.

Format of Schedules

LCC schedules are now available in two formats:

Print schedules. This is the standard format that has existed from the inception of the scheme. Since the conversion of the schedules into MARC format, print schedules have been issued at much greater frequencies than before.

Electronic version. The electronic version of LCC is available on the Web as *Classification Web* (www.loc.gov/cds/classweb). The website includes both the *Library of Congress Classification* and *Library of Congress Subject Headings,* with links between many of the class numbers and their LCSH equivalents. In addition, it displays correlations among LCC, LCSH, and OCLC's WebDewey, as they are found in LC bibliographic records.

Indexes

In the print version, each schedule contains its own index. A combined index for the entire scheme exists only in the electronic version. It represents a merger of indexes from individual volumes and is browsable in *Classification Web*.

APPLYING THE LIBRARY OF CONGRESS CLASSIFICATION: INSTRUCTIONS AND EXAMPLES

The Library of Congress Classification is highly enumerative with little need for synthesis. There are, however, many places in the schedules where the classifier needs to use tables, and the application rules for these must be learned. Furthermore, in some cases use of Cutter numbers with LCC is quite complex.

The following instructions and examples are based on LCC schedules H, P, Q, and S. They cover such matters as characteristics of arrays of numbers within classes or subclasses, types of LCC tables, the special Cutter number table used with LCC, Cutter numbers as part of class numbers, double and successive Cutter numbers, and Cutter number variations such as "A" and "Z" Cutter numbers. The focus is on understanding how LCC works in order to use it according to Library of Congress policies and practices. In most collections classified by LCC, a large number of new records originate from LC itself; it is generally considered important that records prepared locally should be consistent and compatible with LC practice. Only if this is the case can the full advantage of using LC cataloging copy be realized.

Library of Congress Classification Schedules

To use LCC efficiently, one must be familiar with the format and physical characteristics of the schedules. As noted earlier, the print version comprises over forty separately published schedules, and the electronic version consists of a large database of class number entries and an index. The print schedules are similar in format, with the following elements found in most of them: (1) a preface; (2) a synopsis of the subclasses; (3) an outline of the major divisions within subclasses; (4) the main array of provisions giving all details except those which need to be extrapolated through the use of tables; (5) any applicable tables; (6) an index.

Class Numbers [MARC field 050, subfield $a]

The primary task in classifying according to any system is the same as it is in subject cataloging: identifying the subject content of, and the principal concepts in, the work in hand. The next task is to express that content (even when multiple concepts are involved) as accurately as possible within the provisions of the classification system with which one is working. Given the structure and nature of LCC, most subjects can be found enumerated in the schedules, with whatever form, period, geographic, and topical subdivisions as provided; thus no notational synthesis is required. In other cases, there are tables to be used as directed, usually within a range of numbers listed in the main schedule or subdivisions by means of Cutter numbers. Finding the optimal classification placement often requires judicial use of whatever indexes are available, careful attention to any scope notes or other placement directions pertaining to the subject at issue, and persistent study of the list of captions preceding and following what one has selected as a starting point. It may involve using a table or constructing complicated Cutter numbers.

Table 14-4, taken from the schedule for Class Q, Science, shows typical divisions of a scientific subject, and also illustrates the possible helpfulness of "cf." and "see" references.

As can be seen from Table 14-4, the numbers QC120-129.5 contain form, period, and geographic divisions of the subject, Descriptive and experimental mechanics. A journal on this subject is classed in QC120 and a current treatise on the subject is classed in QC125.2. Numbers beginning with QC133 provide topical divisions of the subject, such as Dynamics, Motion, etc. Each of the topical divisions may have its own subdivisions, depending on literary warrant. More elaborate subdivisions appear under Fluids and Fluid mechanics than under Dynamics; thus, a handbook on Fluid mechanics is classed in QC145.3. When no form divisions are provided under a particular subject, the number designated for General works is used for all forms; a handbook on Dynamics is therefore classed in QC133.

Cutter Numbers [MARC field 050, subfield $b]

As mentioned earlier, the Cutter number is used in LCC for two purposes: as a further extension of the class number (as part of subfield $a, e.g., $a HD9651.9.D6 $b D69 2004) and as an item or book number. A Cutter number consists of a capital letter followed by an Arabic number; the number is read decimally and the decimal point precedes the letter, e.g., .T7, .T7324, .T745, .T8, etc. The decimal feature of Cutter numbers is important, because it allows for infinite interpolation on the decimal principle.

Because, in most cases, subject provisions in LCC are developed in greater detail than those in the Dewey system, not as many items are likely to be assigned the same class number. Therefore, the elaborate Cutter tables used with DDC are not needed for constructing LCC item numbers. Instead, a relatively simple Cutter table, shown in Table 14-5,[10] is used.

Since the table provides only a general framework for the assignment of numbers, the symbol for a particular name or work is constant only

TABLE 14-4   Divisions of a Subject: Class Q, Science: QC, Physics

QC Physics
Descriptive and Experimental Mechanics

For theoretical and analytical mechanics see *QA801–939*
Cf. *QC71.82–73.8* Force and energy (General)
Cf. *QC176–176.9* Solid state physics
Cf. *TA349–359* Applied mechanics

QC120	Periodicals, societies, congresses, serial publications
QC121	Collected works (nonserial)
QC121.6	Dictionaries and encyclopedias
QC121.8	Nomenclature, terminology, notation, abbreviations
	History
	For general history of mechanics see *QA802*
QC122	General works
QC122.2.A-Z	By region or country, A-Z
QC123	Early works through 1800
	General works, treatises, and advanced textbooks
QC125	1801–1969
QC125.2	1970–
QC127	Elementary textbooks
QC127.3	Popular works
QC127.4	Juvenile works
QC127.6	Addresses, essays, lectures
	Study and teaching. Research
QC128	General works
QC129	Problems, exercises, examinations
QC129.5	Laboratory manuals
QC131	Special aspects of the subject as a whole
	Dynamics. Motion
	Cf. *QA843–871* Analytic mechanics
QC133	General works, treatises, and textbooks
QC133.5	Juvenile works
QC135	Kinematics
QC136	Vibrations
	Cf. *QA865–867.5* Analytic mechanics (Dynamics)
	Cf. *QA935–939* Vibrations of elastic bodies
	Cf. *QC231* Sound
	Cf. *TA355* Engineering
QC137	Inertia
	Including Mach's principle
	Velocity. Speed
	Cf. *QC233* Velocity of sound
	Cf. *QC407* Velocity of light
QC137.5	General works, treatises, and textbooks

(continues)

TABLE 14-4   Continued

QC137.52	Juvenile works
	Fluids. Fluid mechanics
	Including liquids
	Cf. *QA901–930* Analytic mechanics
	Cf. *TA357–359* Applied fluid mechanics
QC138	Periodicals, societies, congresses, serial publications
QC139	Dictionaries and encyclopedias
QC140	Nomenclature, terminology, notation, abbreviations
QC141	History
QC142	Early works through 1500
	General works, treatises, and textbooks
QC143	1501–1700
QC144	1701–1800
QC145	1801–1969
QC145.2	1970–
QC145.24	Juvenile works
QC145.26	Addresses, essays, lectures
QC145.28	Study and teaching
QC145.3	Handbooks, tables, formulas, etc.
QC145.4.A-Z	Special properties of liquids, A-Z
QC145.4.A25	Acoustic properties
QC145.4.C6	Compressibility
QC145.4.D5	Diffusion
QC145.4.E45	Electric properties
QC145.4.E9	Expansion
QC145.4.M27	Magnetic properties
QC145.4.O6	Optical properties

under a particular class number. Each entry must be added to the existing entries in the shelflist in such a way as to preserve alphabetical order in accordance with filing rules.

Cutter Number as Part of Class Number

In Table 14-3, under QD149.7, the caption "By region or country, A-Z" indicates that Cutter numbers are to be used for geographic division of the subject, History of inorganic chemistry. In Table 14-4, QC145.4 carries the caption "Special properties of liquids, A-Z." This means that individual properties are represented by Cutter numbers after the main class number. For example, the class number for the subject of expansion of fluids contains the following elements:

QC	Double letters for the subclass, Physics
145.4	Arabic number meaning special properties of liquids
.E9	Cutter number for expansion

TABLE 14-5 Cutter

1. *After initial vowels*								
for the second letter:	b	d	l-m	n	p	r	s-t	u-y
use number:	2	3	4	5	6	7	8	9

2. After the initial letter *S*								
for the second letter:	a	ch	e	h-i	m-p	t	u	w-z
use number:	2	3	4	5	6	7	8	9

3. After the initial letters *Qu*							
for the second letter:	a	e	i	o	r	t	y
use number:	3	4	5	6	7	8	9
for initial letters *Qa-Qt*							
use numbers:	2–29						

4. After other initial *consonants*							
for the second letter:	a	e	i	o	r	u	y
use number:	3	4	5	6	7	8	9

5. For *expansion*							
for the letter:	a-d	e-h	i-l	m-o	p-s	t-v	w-z
use number:	3	4	5	6	7	8	9

Letters not included in the table are assigned the next higher or lower number as required by previous assignments in the particular class.

The arrangements in the following examples illustrate possible applications of this table:

Vowels		S		Q		Consonants	
IBM	.I26	Sadron	.S23	*Qadduri	.Q23	Campbell	.C36
Idaho	.I33	*Scanlon	.S29	*Qiao	.Q27	Ceccaldi	.C43
*Ilardo	.I4	Schreiber	.S37	Quade	.Q33	*Chertok	.C48
*Import	.I48	*Shillingburg	.S53	Queiroz	.Q45	*Clark	.C58
Inman	.I56	*Singer	.S57	Quinn	.Q56	Cobblestone	.C63
Ipswich	.I67	Stinson	.S75	Quorum	.Q67	Cryer	.C79
*Ito	.I87	Suryani	.S87	Qutub	.Q88	Cuellar	.C84
*Ivy	.I94	*Symposium	S96	*Qvortrup	.Q97	Cymbal	.C96

[The Cutter numbers marked by the asterisk (*) reflect the adjustments made to allow for a range of letters on the table, e.g., l-m, or for letters not explicitly stated, e.g., h after an initial consonant.]

Cutter Number as Item Number

Each call number contains an item number generally based on the main entry of the work. Its main purpose is to distinguish different works on the same subject that have been given the same class number. If the Cutter number taken from the table has already been assigned to another work, it is adjusted for the work being classified. The following example illustrates the assignment of Cutter number for authors writing on the same topic:

	Barro, Robert J.
HB172.5.B37	*Money, expectations, and business cycles : essays in macroeconomics*
	Barron, John M.
HB172.5.B375	*Macroeconomics*
	Baumol, William J.
HB172.5.B38	*Macroeconomics: principles and policy*

According to the Cutter table, names beginning with Bar- are assigned the Cutter number .B37. In this case, because .B37 has already been assigned to Barro, the Cutter number assigned to Barron was adjusted as .B375.

If the same author has written more than one work on a subject, the Cutter numbers are adjusted in a similar manner. Because .B37 has been assigned to Barro's *Money, expectations, and business cycles*, his other book, *Macroeconomics*, arriving in the library after the first book, was then assigned the number .B36, to maintain the alphabetical sequence by title:

	Barro, Robert J.
HB172.5.B36	*Macroeconomics*
HB172.5.B37	*Money, expectations, and business cycles: essays in macroeconomics*

In order to place a translation of a work with the original text, the call number of the original work with an extension of the item number is assigned to the translation, for example,

	Remmert, Reinhold
QA331.R46	*Funktionentheorie* [original work in German]
QA331.R4613	*Theory of complex functions* [an English translation of the above title]

The Table for Translations[11] (see Table 14-6) is used unless there are specific instructions for subarranging translations in the schedules.

In Table 14-6, the letter x represents the Cutter number assigned to the original work. The Arabic numerals representing languages may be adjusted to accommodate translations in languages other than the ones shown in the table. For instance, for a Bulgarian translation, one may use .x13 if the original work is in English or .x125 if the original is in a language other than English.

Double Cutter Numbers

When a class number includes a Cutter number as a subdivision, a second Cutter number is added as the item or book number, resulting in a double

TABLE 14-6 Translations

.x	Cutter number for original work
.x12	Polyglot
.x13	English translation
.x14	French translation
.x15	German translation
.x16	Italian translation
.x17	Russian translation
.x18	Spanish translation

Cutter number. For example, a work about computer security is assigned the following call number:

> *Techniques and applications of digital watermarking and content protection* / Michael Arnold, Martin Schmucker, Stephen D. Wolthusen. 2003
>
> | | |
> |---|---|
> | QA | Double letters meaning Mathematics |
> | 76.9 | Arabic number meaning topics about Computers |
> | .A25 | First Cutter number for the topic Access control; computer security |
> | A76 | Item number for the main entry under Arnold |
> | 2003 | Date of publication |

Note that only one decimal point, preceding the first Cutter number, is required for double Cutter numbers. (The first decimal in the call number above results from numerical expansion of the schedule notation, and thus is not part of the Cutter sequence.)

Call numbers for biography often contain double Cutter numbers, one for the biographee and one for the biographer, e.g., a biography of LeBron James, by David Lee Morgan, Jr.:

> *LeBron James : the rise of a star* / David Lee Morgan, Jr. 2003
>
> | | |
> |---|---|
> | GV | Double letters for Recreation and leisure |
> | 884 | Arabic number meaning a biography associated with basketball |
> | .J36 | First Cutter number for James |
> | M67 | Second Cutter number for Morgan |
> | 2003 | Date of publication |

In rare instances, both Cutter numbers may be extensions of the class number and the call number will then not include an item number.

Successive Cutter Numbers

Successive Cutter numbers are a series of consecutive Cutter numbers (e.g., .F3, .F4, .F5) or decimal extensions of a Cutter number (e.g., .F32,

.F33, .F34, .F35) in an established sequence. They are used when certain works are to be grouped on the shelves in an established order. An example is the additional digits for a translation (e.g., 14, French) attached to an item number. Frequently in the schedules and in tables, there are instructions to use successive Cutter numbers. They are used most frequently in tables for internal subarrangement (see examples in the section: Tables for Internal Subarrangement).

A and Z Cutter Numbers

In some cases, under a class number, a span of Cutter numbers at the beginning or at the end of the alphabetical sequence is assigned special meanings. These spans are called "A" Cutter numbers or "Z" Cutter numbers, respectively. The "A" Cutter numbers are used most frequently for form divisions such as periodicals or official publications, for example,

QC	PHYSICS
174.4	Quantum statistics
174.4.A1	Periodicals, societies, congresses, serial publications
174.4.A2	Collected works (nonserial)
174.4.A6-Z	General works, treatises, and textbooks

The Cutter numbers .A1 and .A2 are used for serial publications and nonserial collected works. A3-.A5 are not used at present. A treatise on quantum statistics by an author named Adams, which is normally assigned the Cutter number .A3 according to the Cutter table, will receive a Cutter number greater than .A6.

The "Z" Cutter numbers are often assigned to special divisions of the subject such as biography and criticism of a literary author, or corporate bodies associated with the subject.

UA	ARMIES: ORGANIZATION, DISTRIBUTION, ETC.
	By region or country
	Europe
	France
	Army
	Artillery
705.A1-.A5	Documents
.A6-.Z4	General works
.Z5	Bataillons d'artillerie à pied
.Z6	Regiments. By number and author

Dates in Call Numbers

Dates in LC call numbers serve two functions. A date may be part of the class number; at various points in the schedules there are dates listed explicitly, or there are instructions about using them. A date may also be part of an item number; the date of imprint or copyright is now added to the Cutter numbers for all monographs and to later editions of serials.

Date as Part of Class Number

The following example shows a case in which a date is called for as part of a class number.

HB	Economic theory
3717	History of crises
1929	Date of the crisis

In such cases, the item number and date of publication follow the first date to complete the call number, i.e., HB3717 1929 .G68 2003.

Date of Publication in Item Numbers

The date of publication is added to an item number for all monographic publications (including most types of nonprint materials) and to later editions of serials. An example is shown below.

Economic growth / Robert J. Barro, Xavier Sala-i-Martin. 2nd ed. c2004

HD	Industries. Land use. Labor
75.5	Mathematical models
.B37	Item number based on the main entry, Barro
2004	Date of publication

Since different editions of the same work receive the same class and item numbers, they are distinguished by dates of publication.

	Reagan, Nancy
E878.R43A3 1989	*My turn : the memoirs of Nancy Reagan* (Random House, c1989)
E878.R43A3 1990	*My turn : the memoirs of Nancy Reagan* (Thorndike Press large print edition, 1990)

	Heyne, Paul T.
HB171.5.H46 1990	*The economic way of thinking.* 6th ed. 1990
HB171.5.H46 2003	*The economic way of thinking.* 10th ed. 2003

If different dates are shown in the work, the date to be used in the call number is based on the imprint or copyright date given in the "publication, distribution, etc." area in the bibliographic record.

If there is more than one edition of the same work published in the same year, a lowercase letter (called a *work letter*) is added to the date. The work letters are assigned in the following manner:

[date]   Original work
[date]a   A facsimile or photocopy edition, the date being that of the original
[date]b   A variant edition published in the same year
[date]c   Another variant edition
etc.

For supplements and indexes, *Suppl., Suppl. 2*, etc. and *Index, Index 2*, etc. are added after the date.

Exercise 14-1

Assign LC call numbers (**i.e., class number + item number and date**) to the following works:

1. *Gardens for the new country place : contemporary country gardens and inspiring landscape elements* / by Paul Bennett ; [principal photography by Betsy Pinover Schiff]. 2003
2. *Ramanujan's lost notebook* / George E. Andrews, Bruce C. Berndt. 2005- [Ramanujan was a mathematician from India]
3. *World guide to scientific associations and learned societies* / [editor, Helmut Opitz]. 8th ed. 2002
4. *The philosophy of science and technology studies* / Steve Fuller. 2006
5. *Sedimentary geology : sedimentary basins, depositional environments, petroleum formation* / Bernard Biju-Duval ; translated from the French by J. Edwin Swezey and Traduclair Translation Company. 2002
6. Conference on Recent Advances in Operator-Related Function Theory (2004 : Dublin, Ireland). *Recent advances in operator-related function theory.* 2006
7. *Evolution of herbivory in terrestrial vertebrates : perspectives from the fossil record* / edited by Hans-Dieter Sues. 2000
8. *U.S. development aid—an historic first : achievements and failures in the twentieth century* / Samuel Hale Butterfield ; foreword by Maurice Williams. 2004
9. *Magnetic leadership : are you a good enough leader to be hired by the best employees?* / Victor Downing. 2005
10. *Back to the drawing board : designing corporate boards for a complex world* / Colin B. Carter and Jay W. Lorsch. 2004
11. *Methods of discovery : heuristics for the social sciences* / Andrew Abbott. 2004
12. *Boss talk : top CEOs share the ideas that drive the world's most success-*

ful companies / the editors of the Wall Street Journal ; introduction by Tom Peters. 2002

13. *Pension plans : IRS programs for resolving deviations from tax-exemption requirements : report to the Chairman, Subcommittee on Oversight, Committee on Ways and Means, House of Representatives* / United States General Accounting Office. 2000. [main entry under: United States. General Accounting Office.]

14. *Women workers in brick factory : sordid saga from a district of West Bengal* / Amal Mandal. 2005

15. *The economic dynamics of environmental law* / David M. Driesen. 2003

TABLES

Tables represent recurring patterns of subdivision. Those familiar with other classification systems will find a basic difference between LCC tables and those used in other systems. The tables in the Dewey system, for instance, provide additional segments to be *attached* to a main class number, extending it lengthwise to render it more specific. In LCC, with the exception of those for subdivisions that are represented by Cutter numbers, the tables are a device for locating the desired number within a range of numbers given in the schedule. Usually, the number given in the table is *added* (in the arithmetic sense) instead of attached to the base number from the schedule. The base number is normally given in the schedule under the class number or numbers for which the table is to be used.

There are two types of tables in LCC: tables of general application and tables of limited application. Tables of general application include (1) the biography table, (2) the translation table mentioned earlier, and (3) geographic tables based on Cutter numbers. These tables were initially used with only a few schedules but are now applicable throughout the schedules whenever called for. In turn, there are two kinds of LCC tables that are limited in their application: one applies to a whole class or subclass, and the other (referred to as "tables for internal subarrangement") is used with specific spans of numbers. These tables are applied only according to specific directions in the schedules.

In the print version of LCC, tables appear either in the schedules or in *Subject Cataloging Manual: Shelflisting*.[12]

Tables of General Application

Several tables for general application are discussed with illustrations below.

Tables for Geographic Division by Means of Cutter Numbers

Two methods for geographic subdivision are used in LCC. One is through regular class numbers within the schedules; the other is through the use of tables containing Cutter numbers.

Regions and Countries Table. The Regions and Countries Table provides alphabetical arrangement of countries by means of Cutter numbers. It is used whenever the schedule gives the instruction "By region or country, A-Z." This table is found in *Subject Cataloging Manual: Shelflisting.*[13] Table 14-7 shows portions of the table.

The following examples illustrate its application.

Canada's federal marine protected areas strategy. c2005

QH	Natural history (general)
91.75	Marine parks and reserves: By region or country, A-Z
.C2	Canada (according to "Regions and Countries Table")
C36	Cutter number for the main entry under the title, *Canada's federal . . .*
2005	Date of publication

Micro enterprise development in Ghana / by Richard Jinks Bani. 2003

HD	Industries. Land use. Labor
2346	Small business. Medium-sized business: By region or country, A-Z
.G4	Ghana (according to "Regions and Countries Table")

TABLE 14-7   Regions and Countries (Portions)

Abyssinia, *see* Ethiopia		Cambodia	.C16
Afghanistan	.A3	Cameroon	.C17
Africa	.A35	Canada	.C2
Africa, Central	.A352	Canary Islands	.C23
Africa, East	.A353		
Africa, Eastern	.A354		
Africa, French-		France	.F8
Speaking West	.A3545	French Guiana	.F9
Africa, North	.A355	Ghana	.G4
Spain	.S7	United States	.U6
Sri Lanka	.S72	Upper Volta, *see* Burkina Faso	
Sudan	.S73	Uruguay	.U8
Sudan (region)	.S74	Uzbekistan	.U9
Surinam	.S75	Vanuatu	.V26
		Vatican City	.V3

B36   Cutter number for the main entry, Bani
2003   Date of publication

Although the table is applied universally, the Cutter number assigned to a particular country may sometimes vary under different class numbers, depending on what already *exists* in the shelflist. For example, although, in the table, *.U6* is the Cutter number listed for the United States, in the following example, .U5 is assigned instead.

Abortion—murder or mercy? : analyses and bibliography / Francois B. Gerard (compiler). 2001
HQ   The family. Marriage. Woman
767   Abortion
.5   By region or country, A-Z
.U5   United States
A2655   Cutter number for the main entry under title, *Abortion . . .*
2001   Date of publication

Table of American States and Canadian Provinces. This table, containing an alphabetical list of the states and regions of the United States and provinces in Canada, is used when the instruction "By state, A-W" or "By province, A-Z" appears under numbers assigned to the United States or Canada in the schedule. The table is found in *Subject Cataloging Manual: Shelflisting.*[14] The following examples illustrate its use.

The state of North Dakota : economic, demographic, public service, and fiscal conditions : a presentation of selected indicators / by Randal C. Coon, F. Larry Leistritz. 2003
HC   Economic history and conditions
107   United States, by region or state
.N9   North Dakota (according to the table "American States and Canadian Provinces")
C66   Item number based on the main entry, Coon
2003   Date of publication

Industry and society in Nova Scotia : an illustrated history / Jim Candow, editor. 2001
HC   Economic history and conditions
117   Canada (the seventh number in the range HC111-120 assigned to Canada in the main schedule, chosen according to Table H15 in the schedule), by state, etc., A-Z
.N8   Nova Scotia (according to the table "American States and Canadian Provinces")

I53   Item number based on the main entry under title:
         Industry and . . .
2001   Date of publication

Biography Table

When works about a person, including autobiography, letters, speeches, and biography, are classed in a number designated for individual biography, they are subarranged according to the Biography table. This table (reproduced in Table 14-8) contains extensions (in the form of successive Cutter numbers) of the Cutter number (represented by .x in the table) assigned to the individual or biographee.

Application of the Biography table results in double Cutter numbers: the first Cutter number (shown as .x in the table) is for the biographee and the second is taken from the table. The use of "A" Cutter numbers for autobiographical writings in this table results in works written by the biographee to be filed before works written by other people about him or her. The following example illustrates the use of the Biography table.

> *The autobiography of William Sanders Scarborough : an American journey from slavery to scholarship* / edited and with an introduction by Michele Valerie Ronnick ; foreword by Henry Louis Gates, Jr. c2005
>
> E   History: United States
> 185.97   Elements in the population—African Americans—Individual biography
> .S28   First Cutter number for Scarborough
> <u>A3</u>   Second Cutter number (for autobiography) from the Biography Table
> 2005   Date of publication

TABLE 14-8   Biography

.x	Cutter number for the biographee
.xA2	Collected works. By date
.xA25	Selected works. Selections. By date
	Including quotations
.xA3	Autobiography, diaries, etc. By date
.xA4	Letters. By date
.xA5	Speeches, essays, and lectures. By date
	Including interviews
.xA68-Z	Individual biography, interviews, and criticism
	By main entry
	Including criticism of selected works, autobiography, quotations letters, speeches, interviews, etc.

Tables of Limited Application

Tables Applicable to an Individual Class or Subclass

Many LCC schedules contain tables that apply to an entire class or subclass. Examples are the author tables used throughout the schedules for Class P, Language and literature; the form tables used in the schedules of Class K, Law; and the geographic tables in Class H, Social sciences, and in Class S, Agriculture. These may be Cutter tables, numerical tables, or a combination of both. In the print version, they usually appear at the end of the schedule to which they apply, immediately before the index.

In the print version, Subclasses in Class K, Law, are issued in separate volumes, but they share the same tables. Instead of repeating the tables in each volume, a separate volume containing tables only is issued. This arrangement is also true of Class P, Language and literature.

In using a table that contains Cutter numbers, the appropriate Cutter number, adjusted if necessary, is simply attached to the main number from the schedule.

In applying a numerical table, the following steps should be followed:

1. Find the range of numbers in the schedule within which the subject being represented falls, and note its base number.
2. Determine the appropriate table to be applied to the specific range of numbers.
3. Select the number in the table that represents the specific subject or aspect appropriate to the item being classified, and fit the number (usually by simple substitution or addition) into the range of numbers from the schedule.

Geography tables in Class S. An example of numerical tables is the "Geographical Distribution Tables" in Class S, Agriculture. A portion of Table S2 is reproduced in Table 14-9.

The following example illustrates the application of Table S2.

Development of forest resources in the European part of the Russian Federation / by A.I. Pisarenko . . . [et al.]. 2001

SD	Forestry
207	Number meaning a history of forestry in Russia
.D48	Cutter number for the main entry under the title, *Development of* . . .
2001	Date of publication

The number SD207 is determined by following the steps outlined below:

1. In schedule S, the numbers SD145-245 have been assigned to the history of forestry subdivided geographically.

TABLE 14-9   Geography (Portions of S2) from Class S

S2

	America
	North America
1–2	Canada
3–4	Mexico
5–6	Central America
7–8	West Indies
33	Europe
35–36	Great Britain. England
37–38	Wales
59–60	Norway
61–62	Portugal
63–64	Russia. Soviet Union. Russia (Federation)

2. These class numbers are to be used with Table S2 for specific countries.
3. The number 63, meaning Russia (General Works), from Table S2 is added to the base number 144 as given in the schedule.

Geography tables in Class H. The "Tables of Geographical Divisions" in Class H consist of a group of ten tables (Tables H1–H10) providing detailed geographic divisions. They are used with spans of numbers given in the main schedules with specific instructions indicating which table is to be used in a particular case.

For example, to classify a work about the standard of living in Asia and Europe, the first step is to find the appropriate class number or numbers in the schedule:

HD	INDUSTRIES. LAND USE. LABOR
	Labor. Work. Working Class
	Cost and standard of living
6981-7080	By region or country. (Table H1 modified)

The instruction indicates that numbers from "Table H1 modified" are to be added to HD6980. A portion of Table H1 is reproduced as Table 14-10. (The term "Modified" refers to variations from the table, noted in the schedule.) The number designated for Asia in Table H1 is 68. This number is added to the base number HD6980 (instead of 6981, which is the first number in the range, not the base number) to obtain the desired number, HD7048. Attaching the item number for the main entry and the date of publication yields the desired call number, HD7048.L58 2005. This number is analyzed below:

> *Living standards in the past : new perspectives on well-being in Asia and Europe* / edited by Robert C. Allen, Tommy Bengtsson, and Martin Dribe. 2005

TABLE 14-10   Geographical Divisions (Portions of H1) in Class H

H1	*Tables of Geographical Divisions*
1	America. Western Hemisphere
	North America
2	General works
	United States
3	General works
4	Northeastern States. New England
5	Middle Atlantic States. Middle States
15	Canada
15.25	Saint Pierre and Miquelon Islands
	Asia
68	General works
	Middle East. Near East
68.2	General works
	Caucasus
68.215	General works
68.22	Armenia

HD	Industries. Land use. Labor
7048	Cost and standard of living in Asia
.L58	Cutter number for the main entry under the title, *Living . . .*
2005	Date of publication

Since the schedule does not provide for period subdivision, the chronological aspect of the book is not represented in the class number.

The following example illustrates the use of Table H19 (Table for Industries and Trades) in Class H. In the schedule for Class H, chemical industries are given the span of numbers HD9650-9660 with the instruction to use Table H19 (Table for Industries and Trades [10 nos.]). A work about the Dow Chemical Company in the United States, written by Jack Doyle, is classed in HD9651.9 .D6D69 2004.

Trespass against us : Dow Chemical & the toxic century / Jack Doyle. 2004	
HD	Industries. Land use. Labor
9651	Second number (according to Table H19) in the range HD 9650-9660 assigned to chemical industries—United States in the schedule
.9	By firm, A-Z (1.9.A-Z in Table H19)
.D6	Cutter number for Dow Chemical
D69	Cutter number for the main entry, Doyle
2004	Date of publication

Author tables in Class P. The author tables in Class P present special features because provision has to be made for a large number of related works. Their use is illustrated below. Works written by and those about an individual literary author are classed together in LCC. Each author is assigned a range of numbers, a number, or a Cutter number. The literature tables used with authors, originally published in the appropriate schedules of Class P, have been revised, renumbered, and published together in a separate volume entitled *Library of Congress Classification: P-PZ: Language and Literature Tables.* These tables provide patterns for subarrangement of works by and about literary authors. The following examples illustrate the use of author tables in Class P.

> *The best short stories of Mark Twain* / edited, with a preface and notes, by Lawrence I. Berkove ; introduction by Pete Hamill. 2004
>
> | PS | American literature |
> |---|---|
> | 1302 | Third number ("2" in Table P-PZ31 modified) in the range of 1300–1348 assigned to Clemens, Samuel Langhorne (Mark Twain) for selected works |
> | .B47 | Item number based on the name of the editor, Berkove, as instructed in Table P-PZ31 |
> | 2004 | Date of publication |

> *The adventures of Huckleberry Finn* / Mark Twain ; with an introduction by John Seelye ; notes by Guy Cardwell. 2003
>
> | PS | American literature |
> |---|---|
> | 1305 | Number (within the range of 5–22 designated for separate works by an author with 49 numbers in Table P-PZ31) assigned specifically to *The adventures of Huckleberry Finn* |
> | .A1 | Cutter number (according to Table P-PZ41, "Table for Separate works (1 no.)"), meaning the text of the work arranged by date (if no editor is given) |
> | 2003 | Date of publication |

> *Great tales and poems of Edgar Allan Poe.* [2003]
>
> | PS | American literature |
> |---|---|
> | 2602 | Third number (2) in the range 0–49 in Table P-PZ31 for selections fitted into the range of numbers PS2600–2648 assigned to Poe in the schedule |
> | 2003b | Date of publication, with the letter b to indicate a variant edition published in the same year |

No Cutter number is assigned to this work because the author's name, Poe, is already implied in the class number, and no editor is given.

The following examples illustrate the application of Table P-PZ32 for Alexander Pope, an author assigned nineteen numbers.

The Dunciad : in four books / edited by Valerie Rumbold. 1999
PR   English literature
3625   Number assigned to *Dunciad* in the schedule (within
            the range of numbers (25-30) for separate works
            according to Table P-PZ32, i.e., PR3625-3630 for Pope)
.A2   Text arranged by editor (according to Table P-PZ41,
            Table for Separate Works (1 no.))
R86   Item number based on the name of the editor,
            Rumbold
1999   Date of publication

More solid learning : new perspectives on Alexander Pope's Dunciad /
edited by Catherine Ingrassia, Claudia N. Thomas. c2000
PR   English literature
3625   Number for *Dunciad*
.M67   Cutter number (within the range of .A7-Z for criticism
            according to Table P-PZ41) based on the main entry
            under the title: *More* . . .
2000   Date of publication

Tables for Internal Subarrangement

Tables designed for use with specific spans of numbers are scattered
throughout the schedules. Such tables are used for subarrangement
within a span of numbers and may contain form, period, geographic,
and/or subject elements. They range from a few lines of instructions to
several pages.

Table 14-11 contains an example of tables for internal subarrangement from Class H, found under HE215–300.

For example, a work about transportation and communications in
Canada is classed in HE215. In Table H1 (partially reproduced in Table
14-7), Canada is assigned the number of 15, which is to be added to the
base number HE200 shown in Table 14-11 to form the number HE215.
Adding the item number results in HE215.A15T7a, which is analyzed
below:

Annual report to Parliament / Transportation Safety Board of
Canada. 199?-
HE   Transportation and communications
215   Number for Canada, resulting from adding the
            number 15 from Table H1 to the base number 200
.A15   First Cutter number meaning serial publications from
            internal table HE215/1 for 1-number countries (i.e.,
            countries that have been assigned one Cutter number
            each)

TABLE 14-11 Internal (HE)

HE	Transportation and Communications
	By region or country
215–300	Other regions or countries (Table H1)
	Add country number in table to HE200
	Under each:
	Apply Table HE215/1 for 1 number countries
	Table for transportation and communication, by country (1 number)
.A15	*Periodicals. Societies. Serials*
.A2	*General works*
.A3	*Ancient*
.A5	*Medieval*
.A7-.Z5	*Modern*
.Z7A-.Z7Z	*Local, A-Z*
	Apply Table HE215/2 for 1 number regions
	Table for transportation and communication, by region (1 number)
.A15	*Periodicals. Societies. Serials*
.A2	*General works*
.A3	*Ancient*
.A5	*Medieval*
.A7-.Z5	*Modern*

T7	Second Cutter number for the main entry, Transportation Safety . . .
a	Work letter for a serial publication

A general work on the same subject is classed in HE215.A2:

Weather and transportation in Canada / edited by Jean Andrey and Christopher Knapper. c2003

HE	Transportation and communications
215	Number for Canada, resulting from adding the number 15 from Table H1 to the base number 200
.A2	Cutter number meaning general works from internal table HE215/1 for 1-number countries
W43	Second Cutter number for the main entry under the title, *Weather* . . .
2003	Date of publication

   Some internal tables are simple, containing only two or three numbers. An example is the table under HD3616.A-Z shown in Table 14-2. Table 14-12 contains a small table (using successive Cutter numbers, .x, .x2, .x3, .x4). Note that the first Cutter number in the small table is .x (e.g.,

TABLE 14-12   Internal (HD)

HD	Industries. Land Use. Labor
	Industry
	Industrial policy. The state and industrial organization
3616.A-Z	By region or country, A-Z
	Under each country (except the United States):
	.x *Periodicals. Societies. Serials*
	.x2 *History*
	.x3 *Public policy*
	.x4A-.x4Z *Local, A-Z*

.C2 for a periodical on industrial policy in Canada) instead of .x1 (.C21) because the use of a Cutter number ending in the digit "1" limits the possibility of interpolation and is therefore generally avoided. Furthermore, the digit 1 is used to introduce a successive Cutter number for a translation, for example, .C214 for a French translation and .C215 for a German translation of a work assigned the Cutter number .C2.

An example of applying the small internal table is shown below:

> *Between public and private : readings and cases on Canada's mixed economy* / edited by Diane Jurkowski, George Eaton. c2003
> | HD | Industries. Land use. Labor |
> |---|---|
> | 3616 | Industrial policy by region or country |
> | .C23 | Cutter number (.C2 for Canada according to the Regions and Countries Table) with the successive number (3) for public policy based on the internal table under 3616.A-Z |
> | B48 | Item number based on the main entry under the title, *Between . . .* |
> | 2003 | Date of publication |

In many cases, call numbers are constructed by using a combination of different types of tables. An example is given below.

> *Working across boundaries : collaboration in public services* / Helen Sullivan and Chris Skelcher. 2002
> | HD | Industries. Land use. Labor |
> |---|---|
> | 4148 | Public policy regarding state industries and public works |
> | .S85 | Cutter number for the main entry, Sullivan |
> | 2002 | Date of publication |

In this example, the main number HD4148 is constructed as follows:

1. Locate the appropriate range of numbers in the schedule:
   HD4001-4420.7 Industry

                  Industrial policy. The state and industrial organization

                      State industries. Public works. Government ownership

                          By region or country

                              Other regions or countries (Table H9)

                                Add country number in table to HD4000
2. Consult Table H9 for the numbers assigned to Great Britain: 141-150
3. Consult the internal table HD4001/1 for 10 number countries, under HD4001-4420.7:

       8   Public policy
4. Choose the eighth number in the range 141-150: 148
5. Add 148 to 4000: 4148

Exercise 14-2

Assign LC call numbers to the following works:

1. *Monetary and financial management in Asia in the 21st century* / editor, Augustine H. H. Tan. 2002. [main entry under the title]
2. *Communism in history and theory : the European experience* / Donald F. Busky. 2002
3. *A tough act to follow? : the Telecommunications Act of 1996 and the separation of powers* / Harold W. Furchtgott-Roth. 2006
4. *Ben Jonson in the Romantic Age* / Tom Lockwood. 2005
5. *Staging anatomies : dissection and spectacle in early Stuart tragedy* / Hillary M. Nunn. 2005
6. *Love's sacrifice* / John Ford ; edited by A. T. Moore. 2002
7. *The Brontës* / Patricia Ingham. 2006
8. *Medieval images, icons, and illustrated English literary texts : from Ruthwell Cross to the Ellesmere Chaucer* / Maidie Hilmo. 2004
9. *Kelly's people* / Walter Wager. 2002 [late 20th century American author]
10. *Miss Lulu Bett and stories* / Zona Gale ; edited by Barbara H. Solomon and Eileen Panetta. 2005
11. *All's well that ends well* / [William Shakespeare] ; edited by Russell Fraser ; with an introduction by Alexander Leggatt. 2003. [Table PR4: A2 = by editor]
12. *Reinventing King Arthur : the Arthurian legends in Victorian culture* / Inga Bryden. 2005

13. *Jane Austen and religion : salvation and society in Georgian England /* Michael Giffin. 2002

14. *Mark Twain himself : a pictorial biography /* produced by Milton Meltzer. 2002

NOTES

1. Arthur Maltby, *Sayers' Manual of Classification for Librarians*, 5th ed. (London: Andre Deutsch, 1975), 175.

2. Diane Vizine-Goetz, "Using Library Classification Schemes for Internet Resources," OCLC Internet Cataloging Project Colloquium Position Paper, last edited 11/23/99, http://staff.oclc.org/~vizine/Intercat/vizine-goetz.htm (25 Feb. 2007); "The Role of Classification Schemes in Internet Resource Description and Discovery: Work Package 3 of Telematics for Research Project DESIRE (RE 1004): Current Use of Classification Schemes in Existing Search Services," www .ukoln.ac.uk/metadata/desire/classification/class_4.htm (25 Feb. 2007).

3. CyberStacks(sm), August 24, 1998, www.public.iastate.edu/~CYBER STACKS/homepage.html (25 Feb. 2007).

4. J. C. M. Hanson, "The Library of Congress and Its New Catalogue: Some Unwritten History," in *Essays Offered to Herbert Putnam by His Colleagues and Friends on His Thirtieth Anniversary as Librarian of Congress: 5 April 1929.* (New Haven: Yale University Press, 1929), 186–87.

5. Leo E. LaMontagne, *American Library Classification with Special Reference to the Library of Congress* (Hamden, Conn.: Shoe String Press, 1961), 254.

6. Maltby, *Sayers' Manual of Classification for Librarians*, 180.

7. Cf. Maltby, *Sayers' Manual of Classification for Librarians*, 187, 174–89; see also J. Mills, *A Modern Outline of Library Classification* (London: Chapman & Hall, Ltd., 1967), 89–102; and A. C. Foskett, *The Subject Approach to Information*, 4th ed. (Hamden, Conn.: Linnet Books; London: Clive Bingley, 1982), 409–17.

8. Maltby, 187.

9. *Super LCCS: Gale's Library of Congress Classification Schedules combined with additions and changes through . . .* (Detroit: Gale Research, Inc., c1994-).

10. "Call Number," in Library of Congress, Cataloging Policy and Support Office, *Subject Cataloging Manual: Shelflisting*, 2nd ed. (Washington, D.C.: Library of Congress, 1995), G060.

11. "Translations," in Library of Congress, *Subject Cataloging Manual: Shelflisting*, G150, p. 1.

12. Library of Congress, Cataloging Policy and Support Office, *Subject Cataloging Manual: Shelflisting*.

13. "Regions and Countries Table," in Library of Congress, *Subject Cataloging Manual: Shelflisting*, G300.

14. "American States and Canadian Provinces," in Library of Congress, *Subject Cataloging Manual: Shelflisting*, G302, pp. 1–2.

CHAPTER 15
NATIONAL LIBRARY OF MEDICINE CLASSIFICATION AND OTHER MODERN CLASSIFICATION SCHEMES

INTRODUCTION

The preceding two chapters presented the two classification systems used by most of the general libraries in the United States as well as by many other libraries around the world. This chapter discusses in some detail a system that was designed for a special library. It also describes, briefly, some of the other library classification systems that have arisen since the last quarter of the nineteenth century. These latter systems show how much classification schemes may differ from one another, and also illustrate many aspects of classification theory.

NATIONAL LIBRARY OF MEDICINE CLASSIFICATION

Introduction

The National Library of Medicine (NLM) has developed its own classification system as well as its own indexing thesaurus—*Medical Subject Headings* (MeSH), described in chapter 10. The NLM Classification is an example of a special-subject classification system that was expressly designed to be fully compatible with an extensive, existing general classification system. In this case the general system is the Library of Congress Classification (LCC) which, as noted in chapter 14, was designed with many "empty spaces" in its notational array of main classes and major subclasses. What the original designers of the NLM Classification proposed was a classification scheme that would: (1) follow LCC in both style of classification and general pattern of notation; (2) develop its own classification scheme for medicine and related subjects, fitting it into LCC's vacant class W; and (3) develop its own scheme for the pre-clinical sciences, using LCC's vacant subclasses QS through QZ (in LCC main class

Q for science). In response, the Library of Congress agreed with NLM that the main class W and subclasses QS to QZ would be permanently excluded from LCC.

For any material in its collection that does not fall within either medicine or the pre-clinical sciences, NLM uses LCC as it stands except for Class R (Medicine), Subclasses QM (Anatomy), QP (Physiology), and QR (Microbiology), and Class Z provisions for medicine-related bibliographies.

The resulting National Library of Medicine Classification system has many advantages for a specialized medical library such as NLM. The classificational development of the subject matter that is its primary concern is fully under its control, while provisions for peripheral subjects are developed and kept up to date by outside specialists, in this case the Library of Congress staff. Yet the two parts of the system are fully compatible. More specifically, its advantages are: (1) currency in arrangement of medical material and in terminology; (2) compatibility in terminology with *Medical Subject Headings*;[1] (3) compatibility in notation with LCC; (4) the presence of NLM call numbers in both the NLM Web catalog and LOCATORplus, its online catalog database; and (5) the presence of both NLM class numbers and LCC class numbers on most, if not all, LC MARC records for materials in health sciences. This dual provision, which results from NLM's involvement in the Library of Congress cooperative cataloging program, is especially helpful to libraries with collections classified by both LC and NLM systems.

Brief History and Current Status

In the early 1940s, a survey at the U.S. Army Medical Library (now the National Library of Medicine) indicated the need for a specialized classification scheme for the books in the Library. In 1948, a preliminary edition of such a scheme was prepared by Mary Louise Marshall. This edition was modified and revised by Dr. Frank B. Rogers in 1950 and published in 1951 as the first edition of the *Army Medical Library Classification*.[2] The second edition was published in 1958 under the title *National Library of Medicine Classification*. The third edition appeared in 1964, the fourth in 1978, and a revision of the fourth in 1981. The most recent print edition, the fifth edition, revised, was published in 1999.[3] Beginning with the 2002 edition, the *National Library of Medicine Classification* is published only in electronic form[4] and is updated annually.

Although originally designed for the Army Medical Library, now the National Library of Medicine (NLM), the NLM scheme is also used by most of the other major medical libraries in the United States and in many countries around the world.

Basic Principles and Structure

The NLM Classification comprises two major subject groups. The first group, divided into eight subclasses, QS through QZ, contains the preclinical sciences. The second group, Class W, contains twenty-seven subclasses within medicine and related subjects: beginning with the health professions in general, followed by public health and medical practice, then by diseases, physiological systems, medical specialties, hospitals, nursing, and the history of medicine. An outline of the first-order divisions of the NLM Classification is shown in Table 15-1.

Within a particular schedule for a subclass and, in some cases, under a main subject, the numbers 1–33 (e.g., WI 1-33.1 and WO 201-233.1) are used for form divisions such as society publications, collected works, history, dictionaries and encyclopedias, tables and statistics, and atlases and pictorial works. In the schedules for physiological systems, form divisions are followed by general divisions and then by division by organ. For example, a brief outline of subclass WI is given below:

DIGESTIVE SYSTEM
WI 1-150   Reference Works. General
    WI 101-113   Anatomy. Physiology. Hygiene
    WI 140-150   Diseases. Diagnosis. Signs and Symptoms
WI 200-250   Stomatognathic System. Esophagus
WI 300-387   Stomach
WI 400-575   Intestines
    WI 400-480   Intestines (General)
    WI 500-512   Small Intestine
    WI 520-560   Large Intestine
    WI 575   Peritoneum
WI 600-650   Anus. Rectum
WI 700-770   Liver. Biliary Tract
WI 800-830   Pancreas
WI 900-970   Abdomen. Abdominal Surgery

Divisions by organ have priority over diseases, which are subsumed under the organ or region chiefly affected, regardless of special emphasis on diet, drug, or other special form of therapy.

Materials treating several subjects that fall into different areas of the classification are classed by emphasis. If no emphasis is apparent, they are classed with the first subject treated.

Notation

As mentioned earlier, it was planned from the beginning that the notation for the NLM Classification would be compatible with that for LCC; and that, for material that did not fall within the areas covered by its own system, NLM would use provisions from LCC proper. One necessary con-

TABLE 15-1   Outline of the National Library of Medicine Classification

PRE-CLINICAL SCIENCES
QS   Human Anatomy
QT   Physiology
QU   Biochemistry
QV   Pharmacology
QW   Microbiology and Immunology
QX   Parasitology
QY   Clinical Pathology
QZ   Pathology

MEDICINE AND RELATED SUBJECTS
W   Health Professions
WA   Public Health
WB   Practice of Medicine
WC   Communicable Diseases
WD   Disorders of Systemic, Metabolic or Environmental Origin, etc.
WE   Musculoskeletal System
WF   Respiratory System
WG   Cardiovascular System
WH   Hemic and Lymphatic Systems
WI   Digestive System
WJ   Urogenital System
WK   Endocrine System
WL   Nervous System
WM   Psychiatry
WN   Radiology. Diagnostic Imaging
WO   Surgery
WP   Gynecology
WQ   Obstetrics
WR   Dermatology
WS   Pediatrics
WT   Geriatrics. Chronic Disease
WU   Dentistry. Oral Surgery
WV   Otolaryngology
WW   Ophthalmology
WX   Hospitals and Other Health Facilities
WY   Nursing
WZ   History of Medicine
19th   Century Schedule

Source: U.S. National Library of Medicine, *Outline of the NLM Classification* (Bethesda, Md.: National Library of Medicine, 2002–), www.nlm.nih.gov/class/OutlineofNLMClassifica tionSchedule.html (1 Mar. 2007).

dition for the implementation of these plans was that NLM would not use the LC schedules for Class R (Medicine) and Subclasses QM through QR (Anatomy, Physiology, and Microbiology); another was that LC would not seek to develop Class W or Subclasses QR through QZ, which were, in a sense, "ceded" to NLM. Within these limitations, the NLM notational system is fully compatible with that for LCC.

Class Numbers [MARC field 060, subfield $a]

A typical NLM class number consists of one or two capital letters followed by an Arabic number of up to three digits with possible decimal extensions, for example, **W 1, QS 22.1, QY 350, W 40.1**, and **WK 700**. Triple capital letter combinations are used in classifying some nineteenth-century publications. Also, in some cases, Cutter numbers are used for subject subdivision. With respect to notational capacity, the NLM Classification allows a range of 1–999 integers under each main class or subclass, in contrast to the range of 1–9999 in LCC. The NLM Classification is a relatively broad classification system, leaving specificity in subject analysis to the Medical Subject Headings system and its tree structures.

Cutter Numbers [MARC field 060, subfield $b]

NLM Cutter numbers, used primarily as item numbers and occasionally for subject subdivisions, differ from those used in LCC. The difference springs from the fact that there may be a large number of works written on any one of the topics enumerated in the NLM scheme for which the relatively simple Cutter number table used for item numbers in LCC does not suffice. Instead, NLM uses the more detailed *Cutter-Sanborn Three-Figure Author Table*[5] for item numbers. Even then, numbers from this table may need to be adjusted to accommodate the many books that are crowded into NLM's broad class numbers. Work letters, taken from the first word in the title disregarding initial articles, are added to distinguish works on the same subject by the same author, and publication dates are routinely added to records for monographs, as they are in LCC. Illustrations of NLM item numbers appear in the cataloging examples on pages 418–21. Note that NLM does not use a period before the item number, even though the numbers are read decimally.

Examples of Cutter numbers used for subject subdivisions, where a simpler Cutter number scheme suffices, are given below.

QW	MICROBIOLOGY. IMMUNOLOGY	
	138	Enterobacteriaceae
	138.5	Specific organisms, A-Z
	.E5	Enterobacter
	.E8	Escherichia
	.K5	Klebsiella
	.P7	Proteus

.S2   Salmonella
.S3   Serratia
.S4   Shigella
.Y3   Yersinia

Cutter numbers are not used as item numbers for nonprint materials. Instead, the system uses a media code consisting of a serial number following a brief alphabetic notation representing type-of-material (e.g., AV for sound recordings, VC for videorecordings, etc.). For examples, see pages 420–21.

Geographic Table

There is only one table in the NLM Classification system: Table G for geographic subdivisions, which is based on a modified Cutter pattern. The world is divided into ten regions, each of which is assigned a capital letter as follows:

> A—United States (Federal Government)
>   AA1—United States (as geographical area)
> D—Americas
> F—Great Britain
> G—Europe
> H—Africa
> J—Middle East and Asia
> K—Australasia
> L—Islands of the Pacific and Indian Oceans
> M—International Agencies
> P—Polar Regions

Within each region, subdivisions are provided for subordinate units, for example,

> AA1—United States
> AA4—Alabama
> AA5—Alaska
> AA6—Appalachian Region
>
> FA1—Great Britain
> FE5—England
> FG9—Guernsey
> FI7—Northern Ireland
> FM2—Isle of Man
> FS2—Scotland
> FW3—Wales
>
> M—International agencies (General or not listed below)
> MA4—Allied Forces

MF6—Food and Agricultural Organization of the United Nations
MI3—International Labour Office
MU5—United Nations

Table G is used mainly with serial government publications and with hospital publications. However, there are some numbers in the schedules that expressly call for the use of Table G, for example,

> **QV   PHARMACOLOGY**
> 11   History (Table G)
> 11.1   General coverage (Not Table G)
>
> 32   Laws (Table G)
>   (*Used for both monographs and serials*)
> 32.1   General coverage (Not Table G)
>   (*Used for both monographs and serials*)

In these cases, the decimal extension .1 is used for material covering areas broader than any of the areas represented in Table G. A history of pharmacology in a particular geographic area is classed in QV 11 plus a number from Table G, while a general history of pharmacology is classed in QV 11.1.

Index

There is a detailed index to the NLM schedules, with major terms chosen to conform to those in MeSH. In the index, major terms are arranged alphabetically with sub-terms indented under them. Each major term or sub-term is followed by a class number or range of numbers, including numbers from LCC. The example below shows these features.

> Lasers
>   Applied optics TA 1671-1707
>   Biomedical application (General) WB 117
>   Diagnostic use WB 288
>   In dentistry (General) WU 26
>   In surgery see Laser Surgery WO 511
>   Physics QC 685-689.5
>   Therapeutic use WB 480
>   Used for other purposes, by subject
>   See also special topics under Radiation, Non-ionizing
>   See also Holography

Classification of Special Types of Materials

Certain types of materials receive special treatment in the NLM Classification. These include bibliographies, serial publications, and early publications.

Bibliography

The call number for a bibliography in a topic listed in the NLM schedules begins with the letter Z, followed by the class number for the particular subject of the bibliography. A bibliography outside of the scope of the NLM Classification is assigned a number from Class Z of the Library of Congress Classification. Examples of class numbers for bibliographies are shown below:

Z 675.D3	A list of general holdings of a dental library
Z 7144.I8	A bibliography of isotopes
ZQT 35	A bibliography of biomedical mathematics
ZW 1	A bibliography of general medical serials
ZWB 100	A bibliography of works on medicine practice
ZWD 700	A bibliography of aviation medicine

Serial Publications

Serials are classified in the form number W 1 with the exceptions noted below:[6]

1. Government Administrative Reports or Statistics. Serial government publications that are administrative or statistical in nature are classed in W 2. Integrated reports of administrative and/or statistical information on several hospitals under government administration are also classed in W 2. Serials classified in W 2 are sub-arranged by jurisdiction according to Table G.
2. Hospital Administrative Reports or Statistics. Serial hospital publications that are administrative or statistical in nature, including reports of single government hospitals, are classed in WX 2. Serials classified in WX 2 are sub-arranged geographically according to Table G.
3. Directory, Handbooks, etc. Certain publication types, such as directories, handbooks, etc., issued serially are classed in form numbers used also for monographs. For example, directories, whether monographic or serial in nature, are classed for the publication type Directory in form number 22 [for example, W 22; WX 22]. Numbers used for both types of publications are identified in the schedules with the parenthetical note "(Used for both monographs and serials)". The appropriate LC schedule is used for the above defined publication types when their subjects fall outside the scope of the NLM Classification.
4. Bibliographies and Indexes. Serial publications of bibliographies or indexes are classed according to the instructions in the section on Bibliographies above. Unless otherwise noted, the classification

numbers for bibliographies may be used for both monographs and serials.

5. Schedule numbers for special forms. Some publication forms are individually listed in the schedules, with the numbers marked with an asterisk (*). They are used for both monographs and serial publications, for example,

WB   PRACTICE OF MEDICINE
*22   Directories (of health resorts and/or special systems of therapeutics) (Table G)
*22.1   General coverage (Not Table G)

Early Publications

1. Nineteenth-century titles

A "19th Century Schedule," which is a simplified version of the NLM Classification, is provided for the classification of works published 1801–1913, except nineteenth-century bibliographies. This special schedule appears at the end of the NLM schedules. An excerpt from this special schedule is shown below:

QS   Anatomy
QS 22   Directories (Table G)
QSA   Histology
QSB   Embryology

WB   Practice of medicine
WB 22   Directories (Table G)
WBA   Popular medicine
WBB   Diagnosis

2. Early printed books

Books published before 1801 and Americana (early imprints from North, South, and Central America and the Caribbean islands) are classed in WZ 230–270, a section of the classification specially designed for such works.[7] These books are arranged alphabetically by author under the classification number for the period during which they were printed. Reprints and translations of pre-1801 works are classified in WZ 290–292, and modern criticism of early works in WZ 294.

Cataloging Examples

Application of the NLM Classification system is illustrated in the following examples. Notice that all MARC records of medical literature prepared by NLM for the Library of Congress through its shared cataloging program contain both Class R (LCC) and Class W (NLM) numbers, as shown in some of the following examples.

Cardiovascular health and disease in women / [edited by] Pamela S. Douglas. 2nd ed. c2002

WG	Cardiovascular system
120	Cardiovascular diseases
C267485	Cutter number for the main entry under the title, *Cardiovascular . . .*
2002	Date of publication

[LC call number: RC682 .C4 2002]

Microbiology / Vikas Bhushan . . . [et al.]. 4th ed. c2005

QW	Microbiology and Immunology
18.2	Educational materials
M6216	Cutter number for the main entry under the title, *Microbiology . . .*
2005	Date of publication

[LC call number: QR46 .B465 2005]

Evidence-based acute medicine / edited by Sharon E. Straus . . . [et al.]. 2002

WB	Practice of Medicine
102	Clinical medicine
E925	Cutter number for the main entry under the title, *Evidence-based . . .*
2002	Date of publication

[LC call number: RC64 .E95 2002]

Medical publishing in 19th century America . . . / Francesco Cordasco. 1990

WZ	History of medicine
345	Medical writing and publishing
C794m	Cutter number for the main entry, Cordasco, and work letter (m) for the title
1990	Date of publication

[LC call number: Z473 .C764 1990]

Medical physiology : a cellular and molecular approach / Walter F. Boron, Emile L. Boulpaep. Updated ed. c2005

QT	Physiology
104	General works
B7356m	Cutter number for the main entry, Boron, and work letter (m) for the title
2005	Date of publication

[LC call number: QP34.5 .B65 2005]

Paediatrics and child health / Mary Rudolf, Malcolm Levene. 2nd ed. 2006

WS	Pediatrics
200	General works
L657p	Cutter number for the main entry, Levene, and work letter (p) for the title
2006	Date of publication

[LC call number: RJ45 .R86 2006]

Women in medicine : career and life management / Marjorie A. Bowman, Erica Frank, Deborah I. Allen. 3rd ed. c2002

W	Health Professions
21	Medicine as a profession
B787w	Cutter number for the main entry, Bowman, and work letter (w) for the title
2002	Date of publication

[LC call number: R692 .B69 2002]

Acid related diseases : biology and treatment / Irvin M. Modlin, George Sachs. 2nd ed. c2004

WI	Digestive System
350	Peptic ulcer
M692a	Cutter number for the main entry, Modlin, and work letter (a) for the title
2004	Date of publication

[LC call number: RC821 .M63 2004]

Cutter numbers are not assigned to audiovisual and locally accessed electronic resources.

My mom's my hero [sound recording] : *secondhand smoke campaign* / Environmental Protection Agency, Consumer Federation of America Foundation, American Medical Association. [2003?]

WA	Public Health
754	Air pollution and pollutants
2004 AV-0193	AV number assigned to sound recordings

Three times the fun with kids [videorecording] / CDS ; Visualeyes Corporation. 2003

WU	Dentistry. Oral Surgery
480	Pediatric dentistry. Dental care for children
VC no.20 2003	VC number assigned to videorecordings

The basics of sleep [electronic resource]. [2005?] [A CD-ROM]

2005 AV-0228	AV number assigned to locally accessed electronic resources

Internet resources are generally assigned class numbers without item numbers:

> *Acta crystallographica. Section F, Structural biology and crystallization communications* [electronic resource]. Vol. 61, pt. 1 (Jan. 2005)-
> W   Health Professions
> 1   Serials

> *Moving medical innovations forward* [electronic resource] : *new initiatives from HHS* / U.S. Department of Health and Human Services. [2005]
> QY   Clinical Pathology
> 4   General works

OTHER MODERN LIBRARY CLASSIFICATION SYSTEMS

In addition to the library classification systems discussed previously, a number of other systems have been developed in modern times. The following account presents the salient characteristics of the most notable, along with information on their conception and development. They are listed in chronological order by date of publication of their first editions.

Although some of the systems are no longer in use, they are included here not only because they are part of the history of librarianship but also because they illustrate different ways of classifying bibliographical materials. In designing new retrieval schemes, an appropriate classification framework is one of the keys to effective design. A comparison of the different principles and structures that characterize the many classification systems can be a fruitful exercise.

Expansive Classification (Charles Ammi Cutter, 1837–1903)

Brief History

Cutter first designed the Expansive Classification (EC) for the Boston Athenaeum, where he was librarian. He later recognized its value as a general library classification system and, with certain modifications and refinements, made it available to other libraries by publishing it over the years 1891–1893.[8]

Cutter continued work on his seven-stage scheme, the first of which was intended for small libraries, and the seventh for a collection of 10 million volumes. Unfortunately, he died before its completion. EC was adopted by a number of American libraries. However, perhaps particularly because there has never been a mechanism or organizational support for updating the scheme, libraries have long ceased to adopt it. The latest survey, conducted in the 1970s, revealed that it was used then by only a dozen American and Canadian libraries, most of which were special or small public libraries.[9]

Basic Principles and Characteristics

The Expansive Classification is perhaps best known today because it served as a model for the early development of the Library of Congress Classification (LCC). However, it presents several interesting features in its own right. The most striking is that the same basic organizational approach to recorded knowledge was developed at several levels of fullness. Cutter was very much aware of the fact that a village library and a national library have vastly different needs, so he decided to work out a system that could meet the needs of all sizes of libraries. EC was therefore prepared in seven versions, called classifications, in increasing fullness of detail. The first has eight main classes with rather broad subdivisions. The second has fifteen main classes and the third through sixth have twenty-seven; these are shown in Table 15-2. The idea of providing varying degrees of fullness to suit the needs of individual libraries is in keeping with Cutter's proposal of the full, medium, and short catalogs for libraries of different sizes.[10] A similar principle, followed to a lesser degree, was adopted by both the Dewey Decimal Classification (DDC) (two versions, full and abridged) and the Universal Decimal Classification (three versions, full, medium, and abridged).

In arranging the subdivisions of each main class, Cutter claims to have followed an evolutionary order; that is, placing the subdivisions of each subject in the order that evolutionary theory assigns to their appearance in creation. For example, Science in general proceeds from the molecular to the molar (a term used in physics, to denote the whole as distinguished from its constituent elements), from number and space, through matter and force, to matter and life. In Book arts, the subdivisions follow the history of the book from its production through its distribution, to its storage and use in libraries, and ends with its description, i.e., bibliography.

For notation, Cutter used capital letters for main classes and subdivisions, e.g.

X	Language
XDG	Grammar
XDHZ	Parts of speech
XDI	Noun
XDIW	Adjective

TABLE 15-2   Outline of the Expansive Classification

A	General works
B	Philosophy
BR	Religion (except the Christian and Jewish)
C	Christian and Jewish religions
D	Ecclesiastical history
E	Biography
F	History
G	Geography and travels
H	Social Sciences
I	Sociology
J	Government; Politics
K	Legislation; Law; Woman; Societies
L	Science in general; Physical sciences
M	Natural history
N	Botany
O	Zoology
Q	Medicine
R	Useful Arts (technology)
S	Engineering; Building
T	Manufactures; Handicrafts
U	Defensive and preservative arts
V	Recreative Arts: Sports; Theatre
VV	Music
W	Fine Arts
X	Language
Y	Literature
Z	Book Arts

The notation is thus kept shorter than that in a system using only Arabic numerals. However, it is not expressive.

For forms and geographic areas, Cutter devised two tables of common subdivisions, designated by Arabic numerals, that were applicable throughout the system. The following lists, the first in its entirety, the second an excerpt, illustrate these tables.

Forms:	.1	Theory; Philosophy
	.2	Bibliography
	.3	Biography
	.4	History
	.5	Dictionaries; Encyclopedias
	.6	Yearbooks; Directories
	.7	Periodicals
	.8	Societies
	.9	Collections

For example, XDG.4 designates History of grammar.

Areas:	30	Europe
	32	Greece
	35	Italy
	45	England, Great Britain
	47	Germany
	80	America
	83	United States

For example, with IU denoting Schools, IU45 is for English schools and IU83 is for schools in the United States.

For subarrangement of books on the same subject, Cutter devised an extensive system of author or item numbers to be used with his classification. Ironically, this part of Cutter's achievement, which has become known as the Cutter number system, has survived the classification itself; it is now widely used with the Dewey and the NLM systems, and a version of it, considerably simplified, is used with the Library of Congress Classification.

Universal Decimal Classification

Brief History

The Universal Decimal Classification (UDC) is an adaptation and expansion of the Dewey Decimal Classification. It was originally developed for the purpose of compiling a classified index to a universal bibliography that would list all publications, including books and articles in periodicals (*Répertoire bibliographique universel*). This project was initiated in 1895 by the Institut International de Bibliographie (IIB) located in Brussels, which moved from Belgium to the Netherlands in 1931 and became the Fédération Internationale de Documentation (FID). Paul Otlet and Henri La Fontaine, two Belgian lawyers who were responsible for the initial development of UDC, decided to base the new system on DDC, which by the end of the nineteenth century had become a highly successful and widely known library classification system. Because much more detail and minute specifications are needed for indexing journal articles than were available in DDC, the Institute obtained Melvil Dewey's permission to expand and modify DDC to suit the purpose of a universal bibliography.

The first edition was in French; it was published between 1904 and 1907[11] under the title *Manual du Répertoire bibliographique universel*. A second French edition appeared in the 1920s and a third in German in the 1930s. Belgium remains responsible for the French edition to the present day. The first English edition began appearing in the 1940s and other language editions were produced in a range of levels of detail. Apart from the first three, no other complete edition has appeared in the form originally envisaged, but smaller editions in varying sizes have been produced over the years and at the present time, there are editions of varying sizes in some thirty-eight languages.[12]

By the 1930s, the project of the universal bibliography was abandoned, but the development of UDC as a general scheme for classification and indexing continued. It has been adopted widely in Europe (especially Eastern Europe), in South America, and in North Africa.

In the recent past, many changes have taken place both in the management of UDC and in the way in which UDC is maintained and published. In 1989, the FID found that the elaborate revision system that had long been in place had become too unwieldy and that revision was proceeding too slowly. The cost of maintaining the classification was also a concern. Therefore, an international Task Force was established to consider the future potential of the scheme and to make recommendations including, if that were the finding, the possible cessation of the classification.[13]

The Task Force reported in 1990 and recommended that the scheme should continue, having found considerable enthusiasm from the results of its international survey. It recommended that a machine-readable database should be created and that this should become a Master File from which all future versions should be created. It also proposed that this file should be limited to some 60,000 records in order to make revision manageable and that the unevenness of some of the classes should be rectified.

Soon afterward, in 1992, the Universal Decimal Classification Consortium, consisting of UDC publishers, was formed. The Consortium collectively took over responsibility for the classification. At the same time, the FID relinquished its sole responsibility for UDC and became a partner in the new consortium. (FID itself ceased to exist in 2000.) The Consortium members are all publishers of the classification, in many cases standards organizations. Anyone who wishes to translate the scheme into a major world language must first become a member. Other language editions are produced under license.[14]

In order to create a machine-readable file as quickly as possible, the Consortium used as a basis the 1985 Medium English Edition published by the British Standards Institution (BSI) together with subsequent extensions and corrections. The Master Reference File was completed in 1992, the same year the Consortium came into being. This file, known as MRF, is the authoritative version of the classification. It is in English and is updated annually on January 1st, subsequent to the publication of the annual *Extensions and Corrections to the UDC* which are issued in the previous November. It now has some 66,000 records and is available under license in ASCII text or as a CDS/ISIS database export (ISO 2709). Published versions are the responsibility of the individual publisher either by virtue of being a member of the Consortium or under license. All published versions in English are the property of the British Standards Institution which maintains an online service.[15] An abridged edition in English was published in 2002. A printed standard edition is in preparation.

Responsibility for UDC rests with the Executive Committee of the Consortium which meets three or four times per year in The Hague, the Netherlands. The actual work on the scheme is divided between the day to day running of the business—which is undertaken by the UDC Administrator at the headquarters in the Royal Library in The Hague—and revision work which is the responsibility of the Editor in Chief and a small group of assistants who meet on a monthly basis. Revision is also undertaken by other interested persons around the world, who communicate their proposals by e-mail.

Revision of the classification not only has to contend with developments in knowledge and in classification theory, but also has to correct errors of previous revisers. For example, Table 1k-05, the Table of Persons, originally devised for use in Class 3—Social sciences, was later extended for use with Class 61—Medicine and eventually became a table of general application. However, there were numerous places in the classification where persons were enumerated with an entirely different notation: revision was therefore needed to accommodate the new use of Table 1K = 05. As with all other classification schemes, there is a constant struggle to establish a helpful order while maintaining a stable, predictable arrangement, because changes in a classification are very unpopular with the user community. For the most part, these problems are handled in three different ways: (1) an increased use of facet analysis, (2) the elimination of cross-classification, and (3) the use of the colon to handle interdisciplinary topics.

Revision is of two kinds. There is the creation of a totally new class, as has happened with such disciplines as Theology, Management, Biotechnology, Environmental science, and Tourism. However, there is also a constant "patching up," as has been undertaken with Education, Domestic science and Architecture. In addition, the Area Table is continuously updated with the current policy being to remove all alphabetical extensions and to spell out areas with their own notation (e.g. in South America, the Middle East, the Indian Subcontinent, and Africa) and provide equal detail for all parts of the world. Details from non-English versions of the scheme are incorporated into the Master Reference File; examples are the locally produced expansions for France, Estonia, and Macedonia.

There are some deviations from the original DDC base. For example, Language and Linguistics and Literature, which are separated in classes 400 and 800 in DDC, are collocated in UDC in Class 8. Management, seen as a generally applicable discipline, has a totally new and coherent class, located at 005. In the same manner, a new class Computer science was created at 004. The emptying of Class 4, formerly Language and Linguistics, has freed up space for a totally new class and there is a proposal to use it for Psychology and Medicine. The latter class is in the process of a total reconstruction and revision. It is a deliberate policy, when a total revision is undertaken, not to reuse the same numbers, so libraries which do not wish to alter their practices can continue to use the "old" notations.

Basic Principles and Characteristics

UDC follows the basic outline of the Dewey system in the majority of its main classes and major subdivisions: these are delineated in Table 15-3. It is thus a general classification scheme covering all fields of knowledge. The DDC provisions, however, required extensive expansion in order to meet the needs of a system intended to serve as an indexing tool for a universal bibliography. In the subsequent proliferation of subject subdivisions, the progression is from general to specific, and division is based as far as possible on mutually exclusive classes. Efforts are also made to collocate related topics. This task is made more manageable than it would be in most other schemes because the synthetic nature of UDC permits notations from different parts of the scheme to be linked using a colon as the connecting symbol. Table 15-3 shows the outline of the Universal Decimal Classification.

Features of the UDC include:

1. it is a general classification covering the universe of information;
2. it is a classification designed for all bibliographic purposes, from shelf arrangement to the organization of resources on the Internet;
3. it is continuously being developed into a faceted classification from an enumerative one;
4. it was designed for bibliographic use but has proved eminently suitable for library use;

TABLE 15-3   Outline of the Universal Decimal Classification

0	Generalities (Including Computer science. Management)
1	Philosophy. Psychology
2	Religion. Theology
3	Social sciences
4	(Vacant at present)
5	Mathematics and Natural sciences
6	Applied sciences. Medicine. Technology
7	The arts. Recreation. Entertainment. Sport
8	Language. Linguistics. Literature
9	Geography. Biography. History

5. it is an aspect classification in which a phenomenon is classed according to the concept or discipline in which it is considered; and,
6. it is an analytico-synthetic classification permitting the expression of a compound concept by linking two separate concepts notationally.

Because of their differences in initial purpose and later development, there are several aspects in which UDC has moved a long way from DDC. Especially noticeable is that an attempt has been made to remove all national biases. However, a western, or occidental, viewpoint is still detectable, especially in Class 3 (Social sciences). The bias is more likely to be European rather than American. Especially commendable in this regard is the revision of Class 2 (Religion) which now treats each major religion equally and provides sets of auxiliary tables that permit detailed specification. By arranging the various world religions in a historical order, a logical and unbiased arrangement is achieved.

For notation, UDC followed DDC in adopting a base notation of Arabic numerals, including a decimal after the third digit; such notation is particularly advantageous for an international bibliographical system because it is universally recognizable with virtually infinite possibilities for expansion. UDC notation departs from DDC notation in not requiring three-digit integers as base numbers; in other words, UDC does not use zeros as fillers. Every digit is considered a decimal, and the decimal point is inserted to break up the notation—normally after every third digit—rather than signifying the break between ordinal and decimal numbers. For example, Religion is represented by 2 instead of 200, as it is in DDC. Divisions and subdivisions of main classes are represented by additional digits, e.g., 63 Agriculture, 633 Field crops, 633.1 Cereal, corn, grain. All revisions adhere to a strictly hierarchical notation, so it is immediately obvious that one concept is subordinate to another.

As noted above, because it serves as an indexing tool, UDC is required to have many more detailed subdivisions than a scheme designed mainly for shelving purposes. Perhaps for this reason, over the years, UDC has adopted modern classification theory more readily than DDC and has incorporated many of the features of a faceted scheme. It provides for a considerable degree of synthesis through combining subjects and concepts by means of auxiliary devices. There are common auxiliaries—such as form, period, and place—that apply to all classes, and special auxiliaries that apply to certain parts of the schedules. The distinguishing aspect of UDC's provisions for synthesis, however, is that topics and subtopics in disparate parts of the schedules can be combined as required by means of connecting symbols (called *facet indicators*) that not only provide links but show the nature of the relationship. Table 15-4 lists these facet indicators and their meanings. The examples which follow demonstrate that UDC notation is both hierarchical (i.e., capable of

TABLE 15-4   Facet Indicators in the Universal Decimal Classification

Symbol	Meaning
+	Combining two closely related topics, separated by the classification
/	Combining two or more consecutive numbers
:	Simple relationships between two subjects
::	Connecting symbol indicating the order of the component numbers in a compound number
=	Language
(0 . . .)	Form
(1/9)	Place
(=0/9)	Race and nationality
" . . ."	Time
A/Z	Alphabetical subarrangement
-02	Properties
-03	Materials
-04	Processes, operations
-05	Persons
[. . .]	Denoting subordinate concepts
*	Connecting non-UDC concepts to a UDC number

Following are examples of UDC numbers:

94(735.5 + 736.9)	History of Virginia and Kentucky
94(735.5)	History of Virginia
94(736.9)	History of Kentucky

026:61 (058.7)	Directory of medical libraries
026	Libraries
61	Medicine
(058.7)	Directory

61 (038) = 111 = 131.1	Italian-English dictionary of medicine
61	Medicine
038	Dictionary
= 111	English
= 131.1	Italian

821.311'19'	Twentieth-century Italian literature
821.311	Italian literature
"19"	Twentieth century

Example of a hierarchy:

(73)	United States of America (USA)
(734)	States of the northeastern USA
(734.7/.8 + 737.1/.6)	States bordering the Great Lakes
(734.7/.9)	Middle Atlantic states
(734.7)	New York (state)

(continues)

TABLE 15-4   Continued

Symbol	Meaning
(734.711 + 734.912)	Boroughs and counties of New York metropolitan area
(734.711)	New York metropolitan area within New York state
(734.711.1)	Borough of Manhattan (= New York County = Manhattan Island)
(734.711.2/.5)	Boroughs and counties of Long Island
(734.711.2)	Borough of Brooklyn (= Kings County)

representing hierarchical relationships) and expressive (i.e., capable of representing associative relationships).

UDC is a powerful system, one that is particularly suited to the machine environment: retrieval algorithms can be written that can either refine or expand subject searches just through operations on the class numbers. It has the advantage of being able to capitalize on its hierarchical structure and its synthetic devices and has made increasing use of facet analysis. Recent revisions such as Class 2—Religion are totally faceted. All revisions have their hierarchies clearly distinguished by the notation. Unlike DDC, it is able to adapt to different levels of need, from the highly complex technical environment to the children's library. In the English-speaking world it is most often found in specialized situations but, in other parts of the world, the reverse is the case; and, in countries such as Spain, Croatia, or Romania, it is universally used in public libraries. Because of its flexible structure, it is less able to impose a rigid order in the component parts of a class number. This is not a problem online, but can create difficulties for shelf arrangement or for the ordering of bibliographical or other listings. In this respect, it is less attractive than DDC. The standard citation order, however, is the recommended one and the recent addition of Common Auxiliary Tables for commonly recurring properties and activities goes a long way toward meeting this problem.

Subject Classification (James Duff Brown, 1862–1914)

Brief History

The Subject Classification, developed by James Duff Brown, (1862–1914) has now faded into obscurity, but is worth consideration for its interesting features. The classification originated as a protest. Toward the end of the nineteenth century, the Dewey system, already widely used in the United States, was gradually gaining ground in Britain also. Brown, who was dissatisfied with the Dewey system because of its obvious American bias and other weaknesses, set out to devise a British system. The Subject Classification (SC) first appeared in 1906, with a second edition in 1917, three years after Brown's death. The third (1939) edition was edited by J. D. Stewart. Prior to his work on SC, Brown was responsible for two other schemes. The *Quinn-Brown Classification* (in collaboration with John Henry Quinn) was developed in 1849. It was modified by Brown and published in 1898 as the *Adjustable Classification*.[16]

Although SC had enough viability in its early years to merit the 1939 edition, in the end it failed to win over British libraries and only a small number adopted it. Failure to keep the system up to date may have been the crucial factor in its obsolescence.

Basic Principles and Characteristics

In its arrangement of the main classes, SC follows an order of "scientific progression." Brown's theory was that, in the order of things, matter and force came first; they gave rise to life and then to mind. Finally, mind was followed by the making of its record. Table 15-5 shows the SC outline.

Brown is most famous for his "one-place theory," which assumes that materials on a concrete subject are more useful grouped together in one place than scattered according to the author's standpoint or discipline. This is the major difference between his system and other schemes such as DDC and LCC. Although the subject Iron may be treated from such standpoints as Metallurgy, Mineralogy, Inorganic chemistry, Geology, Economics, or Industry, in SC, all materials on the subject Iron are grouped together with locations determined on the principle of placing each subject as near as possible to the science on which it is based. Hence, Iron is classed under Mineralogy, Apple under Botany, and Music under Acoustics, which is, in turn, a subdivision of Physics. Applications follow

TABLE 15-5   Outline of the Subject Classification

A	Generalia
	Matter and Force
B-D	Physical Science
	Life
E-F	Biological Science
G-H	Ethnology. Medicine
I	Economic biology. Domestic Arts
	Mind
J-K	Philosophy and Religion
L	Social and Political science
	Record
M	Language and Literature
N	Literary Forms. Fiction. Poetry
O-W	History and Geography
X	Biography

their theoretical base: Chemical technology under Chemistry, and Mining under Geology.

Brown adopted a simple mixed notation: main classes are represented by single capital letters and subdivisions by Arabic numerals, e.g.,

N	Literary forms and texts
N000	Fiction
N100	Poetry
N110	Forms of poetry
N114	Lyric poetry—English

Brown also provided a Categorical Table for commonly used subdivisions; its provisions can be used throughout the scheme. Thus, limited notational synthesis is provided by combining the main number with a number from the Categorical Table (for the subdivision of subjects) representing form or other divisions, as shown below:

.0	Generalia
.00	Catalogues. Lists
.01	Monarchs. Rulers
.02	Subdivisions for rearrangement
.1	Bibliography
.2	Encyclopedias. Dictionaries
.10	History (for general use in all classes)

For example,

I229.10 History of gardening in England.

Colon Classification (Shiyali Ramamrita Ranganathan, 1892–1972)

Brief History

The Colon Classification (CC) was developed by S. R. Ranganathan, a prominent librarian from India who is considered by many to be the foremost theorist in the field of classification because of his contributions to the theory of facet analysis and synthesis. His writings on classification, the best known of which is *Prolegomena to Library Classification*,[17] form the basis of modern classification theory. The Colon Classification is a manifestation of Ranganathan's theory, which has had a major influence on all currently used classification and indexing systems. CC itself, however, has not been widely used even in India.

The first edition of *Colon Classification* was published in 1933. The sixth edition[18] appeared in 1963. Over the years, as Ranganathan refined and redefined his thinking about classification, each edition reflected the progress of his theory. Drastic changes took place between editions, and stability was sacrificed for the sake of keeping up with knowledge as well as with classification theory.

Ranganathan died before completing the seventh edition, which had been in preparation for many years. M. A. Gopinath continued what was begun by Ranganathan. So far, only the first volume (containing the schedules) of three projected volumes of the seventh edition had been published.[19]

Basic Principles and Characteristics

In the Colon Classification, knowledge is divided into more or less traditional main classes; these are shown in Table 15-6. However, the similarity between CC and other classification systems ends here.

CC is a faceted scheme. Each class is broken down into its basic concepts or elements according to certain characteristics, called *facets*. In isolating these component elements, Ranganathan identified five fundamental categories, often referred to as PMEST: Personality (entity in question), Matter (materials, substances, properties, etc.), Energy (operations, processes, activities, etc.), Space (geographical areas and features), and Time (periods, dates, seasons, etc.). When classifying a document, the classifier identifies the component parts that reflect every aspect and element of the subject content and puts them together according to a structural procedure, called a *facet formula*, which has been individually designed for each main class. Thus, unlike enumerative classification schemes, CC does not list complete, ready-made numbers in its schedules. A combination, or *synthesis*, of notation is tailored for each work in hand.

In addition to subject subdivisions in each main class, there are certain common subdivisions (called *isolates* in the CC system), which can be applied throughout the entire scheme. These include form and language isolates.

The basic ideas of facet analysis and synthesis had been present in earlier classification schemes, notably in the form divisions in Dewey's system, the common subdivisions and the local list in Cutter's classification, and the Categorical Table in Brown's classification, but it was left to Ranganathan to systematize and formalize the theory. Its influence is particularly apparent in the revision of UDC and the Bibliographic Classification. In addition, revision of DDC, particularly in recent editions, shows increasing use of facet analysis and synthesis, most noticeably in the auxiliary tables added since Edition 18.

Notation for the Colon Classification is extremely mixed and complex. It combines Arabic numerals, capital and lowercase letters, some Greek letters, brackets, and certain punctuation marks. The Generalia

TABLE 15-6   Outline of the Colon Classification, Main Classes

Main Classes	
01	Generalia
1	Universe of subjects
2	Library
3	Book science
4	Mass communication
8	Management
B	Mathematics
C	Physics
D	Engineering
E	Chemistry
F	Technology
G	Biology
H	Geology
I	Botany
J	Agriculture
K	Zoology
L	Medicine
M	Useful arts
Δ	Mysticism
N	Fine arts
O	Literature
P	Linguistics
Q	Religion
R	Philosophy
S	Psychology
T	Education
U	Geography
V	History
W	Political science
X	Economics
Y	Sociology
Z	Law

classes are represented by Arabic numerals. Main classes are shown by capital letters of the Roman alphabet and certain Greek letters. Basic concepts and elements under each main class are represented mainly by Arabic numerals, e.g.,

L	Medicine		
2		Digestive system	
27			Large intestine
2721			Caecum

Common subdivisions, called common isolates, are shown in lowercase letters, capital letters, or Arabic numerals, e.g.,

4	Asia
5	Europe
52	Italy
5215	Sicily

r	Dry
u	Rainy
v	Monsoonish

L	1700-1799 A.D.
N	1900-1999 A.D.
Z	Future

In formulating a class number, certain punctuation marks are used as facet indicators to show the nature of the element being presented. The following meanings have been assigned to them:

(,)	connecting symbol for Personality
(;)	connecting symbol for Matter
(:)	connecting symbol for Energy
(.)	connecting symbol for Space
(')	connecting symbol for Time

In Edition 7 of CC, additional connecting symbols were introduced, for example, = (equal to) as in the space isolate 1 = (Q,7) for the Muslim area of the world, where 1 means the world and Q,7 means Islam. Following are examples of CC class numbers:

Research in the cure of the tuberculosis of lungs by X-Ray, conducted in India in 1950s
L,45;421:6;253:f.44'N5

L	Medicine
45	Lungs
421	Tuberculosis
6	Treatment
253	X-Ray
f	Research
44	India
N5	1950

Discharge of partnership in Indian Law
Z,44,315,7

Z	Law
44	India
315	Partnership
7	Discharge

Eradication of virus in rice plants in Japan (1971)
J,381;421:5.42′N7

J	Agriculture
381	Rice
421	Virus disease
5	Prevention
42	Japan
	et
N7	1970s

Bibliographic Classification (Henry Evelyn Bliss, 1870–1955)

Brief History

Henry Evelyn Bliss, a librarian in the College of the City of New York for nearly half a century, devoted more than thirty years of his life to the study of classification and the development of the Bibliographic Classification (BC). The publication of the scheme took thirteen years, from 1940 to 1953. In the course of its development, Bliss also produced numerous articles and books on classification. Among his best-known works are *Organization of Knowledge and the System of the Sciences* (1929) and *Organization of Knowledge in Libraries and the Subject Approach to Books* (1933; 2nd ed., 1939). The latter embodies the theory on which his classification scheme was based and includes an outline of the scheme.

Before the full schedules were published, an expansion of the outline appeared in a one-volume work entitled *A System of Bibliographic Classification* (1935).

Although BC was not widely adopted in the United States, it received much attention in Britain. In 1967, an abridged *Bliss Classification* was published there by the School Library Association. A Bliss Classification Association was formed in Britain, which has assumed responsibility for maintaining and updating the scheme. A second edition, entitled *Bliss Bibliographic Classification*,[20] under the editorship of J. Mills and V. Broughton, began publication in 1977 in separate volumes. Currently, not all schedules in the second edition have been published.

Basic Principles and Characteristics

From the beginning, several principles guided Bliss's work. These are consensus, collocation of related subjects, subordination of special to general, gradation in speciality, and the opportunity for alternative locations and treatments.

Respecting **consensus**, Bliss asserted that "knowledge should be *organized in consistency with the scientific and educational consensus, which is* *relatively stable* and tends to become more so as theory and system become more definitely and permanently established in general and increasingly in detail."[21] He believed that such an order would be the most helpful to library users, and he tried to reflect scientific and educational consensus in arranging his main and subordinate classes.

The original Bliss Classification was essentially an "aspect" classification—in other words, classification by discipline—in which information on individual "phenomena" is scattered over many disciplines and subdisciplines. For instance, Iron is subordinated variously to Chemistry, Chemical technology, Mineralogy, Mining, Industrial economics, and so on.

Bliss acted on his ideas of **collocation of related subjects** by bringing them into close proximity in his schedules. For example, certain pure sciences are collocated with the appropriate technology. This idea is similar to Brown's. However, Bliss did not carry it to the extremes Brown used in the Subject Classification. Bliss brought together only those pure sciences and technology which are most likely to be used together.

In developing subclasses and subdivisions, Bliss followed the principle of **subordination of special to general** in bringing special subjects under comprehensive general subjects. In arranging coordinate topics under them, the principle of **gradation in speciality** was followed. The premise of this principle is that certain derivative subjects draw on the findings of other subjects. In a classification scheme, the subject that borrows from another is considered to be more specialized than the latter and should follow it. For example, mathematics is a science that many other sciences draw on, and therefore, it is placed at the very beginning of the classification.

Bliss recognized that, frequently, a subject may be placed with equal usefulness in two or more possible locations in the scheme. In order to render the system useful to the largest number of users, **alternative locations** are provided in the scheme for these subjects. For example, Economic history can be subordinated to General history or classed in Economics. There are a large number of alternative provisions in BC, and this feature is enhanced even further in the new edition. Alternative locations might be to place Religion between History and the Occult or to put it at the end of the scheme, or to concentrate all Technology together in class U instead of subordinating the more science-oriented ones with the appropriate science (e.g., Chemical technology with Chemistry).

Bliss also realized that in some cases a body of material may be organized in different but equally useful ways. He made many provisions for **alternative treatment** in the schedules. A notable example is his four modes of classifying literature:

1. Separating literary history from texts;
2. Putting literary history and texts together;

3. Using (1) for modern literature and (2) for earlier literature;
4. Same as (3) except that modern texts are classed by form rather than by author.

In the new edition, referred to below as BC2,[22] the editors have taken into consideration advances in classification theory since Bliss died, particularly explicit citation orders and explicit filing order, and the principles of facet analysis based on Ranganathan's work. The second edition of BC adopts the facet analytical theory[23] developed by the members of the United Kingdom Classification Research Group. S. R. Ranganathan's original five categories (Personality, Matter, Energy, Space, and Time) were expanded into a set of thirteen categories:

Thing—kind—part—property—material—process— operation—patient—product—by-product—agent— space—time

In addition, a standard citation order, enabling combination between categories, has also been developed, based on the principles of progression from general to special, increasing concreteness of terms, and pragmatic order derived from literary warrant and preferred arrangements of documents.[24]

While the main outline of the first edition was largely retained, many of the internal details have undergone radical revision. Each class has been given a fully faceted structure. Furthermore, the vocabulary has been thoroughly revised and greatly enlarged, as well as organized into explicitly named facets and arrays.

At the beginning of the scheme, the new edition provides classes for comprehensive works (called Generalia attributes, Generalia processes, and Generalia entities), but with the option of placing these works with the most suitable "aspect" or discipline. Many new subjects have been added, such as Media science, Recording and reproduction techniques, Data processing, etc.

Bliss's notation was simple, with Generalia classes represented by Arabic numerals, subject classes by single capital letters, and subclasses and subdivisions by a combination of capital letters, e.g.,

U	Technology, useful arts
UE	Engineering
UHC	Construction techniques
UHV	Architecture, planning and building
UJ	Architectural practice and design

Bliss constantly emphasized the desirability of brief notation. The wide base provided by the use of the letters in the alphabet makes brevity more easily achievable, but, inevitably, entails a sacrifice of expressivity. (Many designers of classification schemes have made the same choice). The new BC edition has retained most of the notational features of the original. In the earlier edition, lowercase letters and arbitrary symbols were also used, but these have been abandoned in the new edition.

Outline of Bliss Bibliographic Classification

Table 15-7 shows an outline of the current BC2 main schedules. Table 15-8 contains excerpts from auxiliary schedules in BC2.

The main features of BC2 are summarized as follows:[25]

- The main class order is based on closely argued theoretical principles; these are the principle of gradation, supplemented by that of integrative levels, developed by Feibleman and others.
- Each main class, and every subclass demanding it (whatever its hierarchical level) is fully faceted; i.e., the vocabulary is organized rigorously into clearly defined and easily grasped categories. For example, Human biology and medicine is organized into Types of persons, Parts and systems of the person, Processes in the person, Actions on the person, Agents of actions.
- A comprehensive and consistent citation order is observed throughout, making the position of any compound class highly predictable. For example, the citation order in medicine is the order of the facets listed above; so a work on nursing child victims of cancer would go under (Type of person) Paediatrics—(Processes)—Pathological—Cancer—(Actions on) Nursing. This reflects the Standard Citation Order in which, for any subject, the primary (first cited) facet is that reflecting the purpose of the subject (its defining system, end-product, etc.) followed by its Types, Parts, Processes, Actions, Agents—always in that order. Medicine is definable as the study and treatment of biological processes in humans—hence the citation order in the above example.
- The filing order consistently maintains general-before-special. [Thus,] HMY Nursing in general files before HQE Cancer in general, which files before HXO Paediatrics in general. The subject *Children—Cancer—Nursing* files after all of them at HXO QEM Y, being more specific. Note that the initial letter for this class (H) is dropped when combining subclasses.
- The notation is fully faceted and synthetic. Any class may be qualified by all the classes following it in citation order (and therefore filing before it). The notational base is very wide—35 characters (1/9, A/Z). It is also purely ordinal, i.e., it does not attempt the impossible task of always reflecting hierarchy. These two features produce classmarks which are exceptionally brief in relation to their speci-

TABLE 15-7   Outline of the Bliss Bibliographic Classification (Second Edition)

Class	Subject
Introduction and Auxiliary schedules	
2/9	Generalia, Phenomena, Knowledge, Information science & technology
A/AL	Philosophy & Logic
AM/AX	Mathematics, Probability, Statistics
AY-B	General science, Physics
C	Chemistry, Chemical Engineering
D	Space & Earth sciences
	Astronomy
	Geology
	Geography
E/GQ	Biological sciences
E	Biology
	Biochemistry
	Genetics
	Virology
F	Botany
G	Zoology
GR	Agriculture
GU	Veterinary science
GY	Applied Ecology, Human environment
H	Physical Anthropology, Human biology, Health sciences
I	Psychology & Psychiatry
J	Education. Rev. ed.
K	Society (includes Social sciences, sociology & social anthropology)
L/O	History (includes Archaeology, biography and travel)
P	Religion, Occult, Morals and ethics
Q	Social welfare & Criminology. Rev. ed.
R	Politics & Public administration
S	Law
T	Economics & Management of economic enterprises
U/V	Technology, Engineering
W	Recreation, Arts, Music
X/Y	Language, Literature

ficity (number of compounded concepts defining the class). For example, the class of a work on the nurse as a caregiver for terminal patients and their families is exactly represented by the classmark HPK PEY FBG K. No other general scheme can approach this degree of specificity without significantly longer classmarks. No symbols other than numbers and letters are needed in BC2.

• Fully detailed alphabetical indexes to all classes are provided, using the economies of chain procedure.

TABLE 15-8 Excerpts from Auxiliary Schedules in BC

Schedule	Divisions	
1. Common subdivisions	2EN	Nonbook materials
	2WHU	Government publications
	5V	Bibliographies
	6C	Research in the subject
	7	History (*see* Schedule 4)
	8	Places, localities in the subject (*see* Schedule 2)
	9	Biography
1A. Persons	A	Persons in the subject
	CP	Relations to community, society
	JD	Minority groups
	NS	Families
	RC	Refugees
	AS	Regions by climate
2. Place	BAJ	Regions by land and resource use
	BC	Urban
	D	Europe
	O	Asia
	RB	China
	X	America
	Y	U.S.A.
3. Language	G	American aboriginal languages
	PB	Indo-European languages
	WB	Germanic
	X	German, Dutch, English
3A. Ethnic Groups	BS	Europiforms
	G	American aborigines
	KY	Northeast Asian groups
	L	Japanese
4. Periods of Time	DF	4000 B.C.
	EV	000 A.D.
	FX	1300
	GZ	1500
	Q	1900
	S	2000

Examples of Application

The following examples illustrate the application of BC2:[26]

> Questionnaires on changes in marriage patterns among Muslims in France: KVF QSP BKC E7N
> K   Society

K7N   Questionnaires
KCE   Social change
KPB K   Muslims
KQS   Marriage
KVF   France
Unemployment in rural communities in India: KVQ EOM MUR
KMU R   Rural communities
KOM   Unemployed persons
KVQ E   Indian society
Field studies of kinship in hunter-gatherer societies: KSX JPG 9V
K9V   Field studies
KPG   Kinship
KSX J   Hunter-gatherer societies
Community care policy: QEN AGP
Q   Social welfare
QAG P   Policy
QEN   Community care

The Common Auxiliary Schedules (from the BC2 volume Introduction and Auxiliary Schedules) are used to specify place, date, language, or form:

European child protection services : training pack for careers: QLJ JE8 D2F P
QLJ JE Child protection services
8D   Europe
2FP   Multimedia

NOTES

1. *Medical Subject Headings* (Bethesda, Md.: National Library of Medicine, Library Operations, Medical Subject Headings Section, 1960–2003, last printed version); online version: www.nlm.nih.gov/mesh/ (25 Feb. 2007).

2. United States Army Medical Library, *Army Medical Library Classification: Medicine. Pre-clinical Sciences: QS-QZ, Medicine and Related Subjects: W,* 1st ed. (Washington, DC: Government Printing Office, 1951).

3. *National Library of Medicine Classification: A Scheme for the Shelf Arrangement of Library Materials in the Field of Medicine and Its Related Sciences,* 5th ed. revised, NIH Publication no. 00-1535 (Bethesda, Md.: National Library of Medicine, 1999).

4. United States, National Library of Medicine, *NLM Classification* (Bethesda, Md.: National Library of Medicine, 2002–), www.nlm.nih.gov/class/ (25 Feb. 2007).

5. Charles Ammi Cutter, *Cutter-Sanborn Three-Figure Author Table,* Swanson-Swift revision (Chicopee, Mass.: H. R. Huntting Company, 1969).

6. *NLM Classification Practices: Serial Publications,* www.nlm.nih.gov/class/nlmclassprac.html#Serial (25 Feb. 2007).

7. "Early Printed Books," *National Library of Medicine Classification,* www.nlm.nih.gov/class/nlmclassprac.html#Early (25 Feb. 2007).

8. C. A. Cutter. *Expansive Classification: Part 1: The First Six Classifications.* Boston: C. A. Cutter, 1891–1893.

9. Robert L. Mowery. "The Cutter Classification: Still at Work." *Library Resources and Technical Services,* 20 (Spring 1976): 154–56.

10. Charles A. Cutter, *Rules for a Dictionary Catalog,* 4th ed. rewritten. U. S. Bureau of Education, Special Report on Public Libraries, Part II (Washington, D.C.: Government Printing Office, 1904), 13.

11. I. C. McIlwaine, *The Universal Decimal Classification: A Guide to Its Use* (The Hague: UDC Consortium, 2000), Chap. 1.

12. Aida Slavic, "UDC Translations: A 2004 Survey Report and Bibliography," *Extensions and Corrections to the UDC* 26 (2004): 58–80.

13. I. C. McIlwaine, "The Work of the System Development Task Force," in *The UDC: Essays for a New Decade;* ed. Alan Gilchrist and David Strachan (London: Aslib, 1990), 19–27.

14. UDC Consortium, www.udcc.org (25 Feb. 2007).

15. UDC Online, 2005, www.udconline.net (25 Feb. 2007).

16. James Duff Brown. *Adjustable Classification for Libraries, with Index* (London: Library Supply Company, 1898).

17. S. R. Ranganathan, *Prolegomena to Library Classification,* 3rd ed., assisted by M. A. Gopinath (London: Asia Publishing House, 1967).

18. S. R. Ranganathan, *Colon Classification,* 6th ed., reprinted with amendments (Bombay: Asia Publishing House, 1963).

19. S. R. Ranganathan, *Colon Classification,* Edition 7, revised and edited by M. A. Gopinath (Bangalore: Sarada Ranganathan Endowment for Library Science, 1987); cf. P. Dhyani, "Colon Classification Edition 7—An Appraisal," *International Classification* 15, no. 1 (1988): 13.

20. Henry Evelyn Bliss. *Bliss Bibliographic Classification,* 2nd ed., ed. J. Mills and Vanda Broughton, with the assistance of Valerie Lang (London; Boston: Butterworths, 1977-).

21. Henry Evelyn Bliss, *The Organization of Knowledge in Libraries,* 2nd ed. (New York: The H. W. Wilson Company, 1939), 42–43.

22. J. Mills. "The New Bliss Classification," *Catalogue and Index,* 40 (Spring 1976): 1, 3–6.

23. *The Bliss Bibliographic Classification,* last modified 21 September 2004, www.sid.cam.ac.uk/bca/bcclass.htm (25 Feb. 2007).

24. *The Bliss Bibliographic Classification.*

25. *The Bliss Bibliographic Classification: History and Description,* www.sid.cam.ac.uk/bca/bchist.htm (25 Feb. 2007).

26. *The Bliss Bibliographic Classification.*

PART SIX
ENCODING FORMATS AND
PRODUCTION OF CATALOGING
AND METADATA RECORDS

STANDARD AND TOOLS

MARC 21 Concise Formats, prepared by Network Development and
  MARC Standards Office, Library of Congress, 2000 ed. Washington,
  D.C.: Library of Congress, Cataloging Distribution Service, 2000–.
*MARC 21 Format for Authority Data: Including Guidelines for Content Desig-
  nation,* prepared by Network Development and MARC Standards Of-
  fice, Library of Congress, in cooperation with Standards and Support,
  National Library of Canada. Washington, D.C.: Library of Congress,
  Cataloging Distribution Service; Ottawa: National Library of Canada,
  1999–.
*MARC 21 Format for Bibliographic Data: Including Guidelines for Content Des-
  ignation,* prepared by Network Development and MARC Standards
  Office, Library of Congress, in cooperation with Standards and Sup-
  port, National Library of Canada. Washington, D.C.: Library of Con-
  gress, Cataloging Distribution Service, 1999–.
*MARC 21 Format for Classification Data: Including Guidelines for Content
  Designation,* prepared by Network Development and MARC Standards Office, Library of Congress in cooperation with Standards and
  Support, National Library of Canada. Washington, D.C.: Cataloging
  Distribution Service, Library of Congress, 2000–.
*MARC 21 Format for Holdings Data: Including Guidelines for Content Desig-
  nation,* prepared by Network Development and MARC Standards Of-
  fice, Library of Congress, in cooperation with Standards and Support,
  National Library of Canada. Washington, D.C.: Cataloging Distribution Service, Library of Congress, 2000–.

RECOMMENDED READING

Avram, Henriette D. *MARC: Its History and Implications.* Washington, DC: Library of Congress, 1975.

Byrne, Deborah J. *MARC Manual: Understanding and Using MARC Records.* 2nd ed. Englewood, Colo.: Libraries Unlimited, 1998.

Fritz, Deborah A., and Richard J. Fritz. *MARC21 for Everyone: A Practical Guide.* Chicago: American Library Association, 2003.

Furrie, Betty. *Understanding MARC Bibliographic: Machine-Readable Cataloging.* 7th ed. Washington, D.C.: Cataloging Distribution Service, Library of Congress, 2003. Also available: www.loc.gov/marc/umb (25 Feb. 2007).

Library of Congress, MARC Development Office. *Information on the MARC System.* 4th ed. Washington, DC: Library of Congress, 1974.

The MARC21 Formats: Background and Principles. Prepared by MARBI in conjunction with Network Development and MARC Standards Office, Library of Congress. Revised November 1996. Washington, D.C.: Cataloging Distribution Service, Library of Congress, 1996. Also available at: www.loc.gov/marc/96principl.html/ (25 Feb. 2007).

OCLC. *OCLC Online Computer Library Center.* www.oclc.org/ (25 Feb. 2007).

Taylor, Arlene G. *Introduction to Cataloging and Classification.* 10th ed. Westport, Conn.: Libraries Unlimited, 2006. Chapters 3, 19–20.

Understanding MARC Authority Records: Machine-Readable Cataloging. Prepared by Network Development and MARC Standards Office, Library of Congress. 2nd ed. Washington, D.C.: Cataloging Distribution Service, Library of Congress, 2004. Also available at: www.loc.gov/marc/uma/ (25 Feb. 2007).

CHAPTER 16
MARC FORMATS AND
ENCODING SCHEMAS

INTRODUCTION

Previous chapters have discussed in detail the standards for creating bibliographic and authority records. To set up such records for computer manipulation, for printing or browsing or any of the myriad of other things a computer can do with its data, elements in or pertaining to the records must be coded according to a standard format or markup language. The one used in the library community is MARC, an acronym based on MAchine-Readable Cataloging. In the Web environment, other encoding schemas, based on SGML (Standard Generalized Markup Language) and XML (eXtensible Markup Language), also come into play.

A MARC format contains codes for labeling individual areas, elements, sub-elements, and other pertinent data in a given cataloging record. MARC formats began to emerge in the 1960s. Initially, individual countries developed their own; examples include USMARC for American libraries, UKMARC for British libraries, and CANMARC for Canadian libraries. Not much later, the International Federation of Library Associations (IFLA) developed an international schema called UNIMARC. In the interest of exchanging and sharing cataloging data internationally, and also because of the cost of maintaining such formats, many countries have since decided to adopt or convert to UNIMARC or USMARC. In 1999, USMARC and CANMARC were harmonized to become MARC 21, the name chosen in honor of the approaching new century.

Minimal information on MARC was presented in the first chapter of this book. Here the formats are discussed in considerable detail, in terms of both their historical background and their basic structure.

MARC 21: HISTORY

The MARC 21 formats are a set of standards developed for the purpose of representing and communicating machine-readable descriptive metadata about information items—particularly, but not solely, bibliographic items.[1] Work on the formats started in the mid- to late 1950s, when the

Library of Congress (LC) began investigating the possibility of automating its internal operations. In the early 1960s, the Council on Library Resources provided financial support for two exploratory studies. One examined the feasibility of applying automated techniques to the Library of Congress's internal operations. The other considered possible methods of converting the data on LC catalog cards to machine-readable form in order to print bibliographic products by computer. These studies generated a great deal of interest and enthusiasm. As a result, a pilot project, called *MARC*, was initiated in January 1966 to test the feasibility and utility of having LC distribute machine-readable cataloging data on tape to user libraries. For the pilot project, sixteen libraries of different types and geographic locations were chosen to receive MARC tapes. Trial distribution began in October 1966. By June 1968, approximately 50,000 cataloging records for English-language book materials had been converted to machine-readable form and distributed to the participating libraries. (By comparison, in 2007, the number of records in OCLC's WorldCat came to more than 85 million.) The results of the MARC pilot project were sufficiently encouraging for LC to proceed on a full-scale basis. The original MARC book format was refined and became the MARC II format for monographs.

It is the Network Development and MARC Standards Office of the Library of Congress that is responsible for the development and maintenance of the MARC 21 formats. The MARC Distribution Services, a part of LC's Cataloging Distribution Service, was established in March 1969 to disseminate MARC records to subscribing libraries and institutions. It has been doing so, in increasing volume, ever since. Initially, the cataloging data being distributed was limited to records for currently cataloged English-language monographic material,[2] but over the years coverage has been broadened to include a range of types of material, in many languages.

The MARC structure was adopted as a national standard (ANSI standard Z39.2)[3] in 1971 and as an international standard (ISO Standard 2709)[4] in 1973.

Also in 1973, the American Library Association committee working on machine-readable forms of bibliographic information became a MARC advisory committee working with LC on changes and refinements in MARC formats. (The committee is known by its acronym, MARBI.) Other representatives from the American library and bibliographic community and national libraries also participate in the continuing development of MARC. In 1982, a set of principles was prepared and published.[5] The Library of Congress continues to hold principal responsibility for the maintenance and publication of the MARC 21 formats, but all proposed changes are discussed at MARBI meetings and published after MARBI approval.

Initially, the MARC formats were intended as communications formats for the purpose of transmitting machine-readable data from the Library of Congress to users in the library community. But with wide adoption and use, LC MARC became known as USMARC and later, beginning in 1999, as MARC 21.

The MARC 21 formats have been translated in various degrees of fullness into many different languages. Many libraries worldwide use the English versions and their equivalents in other languages.

TYPES OF MARC 21 FORMATS

There are currently five types of MARC 21 formats: (1) for bibliographic data, (2) for authority data, (3) for classification data, (4) for holdings data, and (5) for community information. The first four types are used for bibliographic information, while the fifth is for structuring information relating to individuals, organizations, programs or services, events, and other such entities. These formats have been published in separate volumes. It is the first four types of MARC 21 formats that are used in creating and maintaining bibliographic and authority records.

(1) *MARC 21 Format for Bibliographic Data*[6] is designed to cover bibliographic information for various types of materials, including books, maps, music, sound recordings, visual materials, continuing resources, electronic resources, and mixed materials. Initially, separate formats were prepared for different media—books, serials, etc.—and there were differences in the provisions for each medium, differences that were soon seen to cause problems in application.[7] For example, bibliographic items that fall into more than one category, such as nonprint materials in serial form, could not fit adequately into one format. Although bibliographic items in many media may be issued in serial form, provisions for serial publications or products were inconsistent among the various formats. Furthermore, comparable elements in different formats were not always handled consistently. In practice, the multiplicity of formats made maintenance and systems support difficult and cumbersome. As a result, in the early 1990s, the various medium-specific formats were rationalized and integrated into a single format.

(2) *MARC 21 Format for Authority Data*[8] is intended for use by persons who create and maintain authority records. It contains specifications for encoding and identifying data elements in authority records, including those for name headings, name/title headings, uniform title headings, topical term headings, extended headings (i.e., headings with subdivisions), and references to headings.

(3) *MARC 21 Format for Classification Data*[9] is designed for identifying data elements in classification records. In effect, a classification record is an "authority record" for a class number. It is intended for use by persons who (a) create and maintain classification records, (b) arrange the publi-

cation of classification schemes from machine-readable data, and (c) design and maintain systems for processing classification records and entering them into the appropriate database. The format contains features particularly amenable to the two major classification schemes in use in the United States: *Dewey Decimal Classification* (DDC) and *Library of Congress Classification* (LCC).

(4) *MARC 21 Format for Holdings Data*[10] is designed for identifying the data elements in MARC holdings reports (i.e., reports indicating the holdings of individual libraries) for both serial and nonserial items. As such, it contains provisions for recording copy-specific information of any particular item, plus information that is peculiar to the holding library. It is designed to allow the potential use of the format to interface with automated control systems such as union catalogs, automatic serials claiming, and interlibrary loan systems. It is intended for use by those who create and maintain MARC 21 holdings information.

LEVELS OF MARC 21 FORMATS

To accommodate the needs of different types and sizes of libraries and different levels of use, MARC 21 is issued in three levels according to fullness of detail: full, concise, and "LITE."

The full and concise versions contain all format types, while MARC 21 LITE is limited to the bibliographic format only. MARC 21 Concise has all data elements contained in the full version but with less explanatory detail. MARC 21 LITE, on the other hand, contains fewer data elements and even fewer explanatory details. The LITE format is extensible; if more details are needed than defined in each format, details from the full format may be added selectively.

MARC 21 Full

The full versions are the most inclusive in respect to details.

MARC 21 Concise

For those who do not need the elaborate explanatory details in the individual formats, a concise version including all formats, entitled *MARC 21 Concise Formats*, has also been published.[11] The nature and purpose of this version are stated as:

> The *MARC 21 Concise Formats* provide in a single publication a quick reference guide to the content designators defined in each MARC format. It provides a concise description of each field, [of] each character position of the fixed-length data element fields, and of the defined

indicators in the variable data fields. Descriptions of subfield codes and coded values are given only when their names may not be sufficiently descriptive. Examples are included for each field. (www.loc .gov/marc/concise/concise.html#general_intro)

MARC 21 LITE

In 2001, an even simpler version for bibliographic data, called *MARC LITE*, was developed for use in simple cataloging and metadata records. The nature and purpose of this version are stated as:

> The *MARC 21 LITE Bibliographic Format* is a subset of the markup defined in the full MARC 21 Bibliographic Format. It includes all essential data elements that are needed to create bibliographic descriptions of information items. It is a true subset of the data elements in the complete *MARC 21 Format for Bibliographic Data* and does not collapse or change any data tagging found in the full format. Records using only the elements in this document are valid MARC records and may be integrated with fuller records without alteration. If elements from the full format are needed for special reasons in an implementation, they can always be added to LITE records by the implementer or user. (www.loc.gov/marc/bibliographic/lite/gen intro.html)

AVAILABILITY OF MARC 21 FORMATS

The MARC 21 formats are available in various publication types and are also found in many cataloging tool packages. The full version and the concise version are published in print form. The full version consists of five volumes, one for each type. The concise version contains in one volume all five types of format. The formats are also available on the Library of Congress website (www.loc.gov/marc/), along with other MARC-related documents and tools. MARC LITE is available only in electronic form from the LC website.

The full version of MARC 21 is also included in Cataloger's Desktop, which is available by subscription from the Cataloging Distribution Service of the Library of Congress.

ARCHITECTURE OF MARC 21 FORMATS

The general architecture of the various formats is much the same for all formats. The separately published formats, which include instructions on application as well as the format definitions and provisions themselves, are enormously complex and detailed. For beginners and those interested in an overview of the formats, the concise version offers essential details sufficient for an understanding of MARC architecture.

It is helpful to consider the basic structure of the MARC 21 formats in three perspectives: what is the overall structure, what is included, and how is all the content organized? It should be borne in mind that a MARC record in the communications format consists of a sequential string of characters, with a blank space counting as a character. For example, the sequence "MARC format" equals eleven characters. A typical coded bibliographic record consists of hundreds of such sequences. (The MARC records taken from the Library of Congress online catalog and from OCLC's Worldcat shown throughout this book have been re-formatted for easy reading.)

Certain control characters used in the MARC record are given arbitrary graphic representation in various displays of MARC records. For example, in different contexts or systems, the subfield limiting character may be represented by the dollar sign ($), the vertical bar (|), or by the dagger (‡). The field and record terminators are often omitted from record displays, but never from the actual record.

In this text, the following graphics are used:

> \# = blank (indicating a positive or fixed value, for example, in the indicator)
> $ = subfield limiting character
> @ = field terminator
> % = record terminator

Figure 16-1 shows a cataloging record in the MARC communications format (along with a field-by-field analysis) as it stands before individual elements are formatted for display.

Structural Components of the MARC 21 Format

Three elements form the basis of the MARC 21 format: record structure, content designators, and data content:

> (1) The record structure is the overall framework for the MARC record.
> (2) The content designators are a set of symbols by which data in the record are identified and manipulated; these include field tags, indicators, and subfield codes (see explanation below).
> (3) The data content is field-by-field record-specific information (bibliographic data, authority data, classification data, etc.). Data content is what is usually thought of as "catalog information," and is usually defined by standards outside the

(a)

```
01066cam  2200289 a 450000100130000000030004000130050017000170080041000
340100017000750200035000920200003500127020003500162040001800197050000200
021508200170023510000340025224500550028625000120034126000350035330000001
900388504005100407505009000458650003500548650003500583586000850061885600
07300703@   00069536 @DLC@20040223170913.0@001222s2002    mau        b
  001 0 eng  @  $a   00069536 @ $a0072441070 (v. 1 : alk. paper)@  $a
0072441437 (v. 2 : alk. paper)@  $a0071120742 (international ed.)@  $a
DLC$cDLC$dDLC@00$aZ711$b.K32 2002@00$a025.5/52221@1 $aKatz, William A.
,$d1924-2004.@10$aIntroduction to reference work /$cWilliam A. Katz.@
  $a8th ed.@  $aBoston :$bMcGraw-Hill,$cc2002.@  $a2 v. ;$c24 cm.@  $aI
ncludes bibliographical references and index.@0 $av. 1. Basic informat
ion services -- v. 2. Reference services and reference processes.@ 0$a
Reference services (Libraries)@ 0$aReference books$vBibliography.@423P
ublisher description$uhttp://www.loc.gov/catdir/description/mh021/0006
9536.html@4 $3Table of Contents$uhttp://www.loc.gov/catdir/toc/mh021/0
0069536.html@%
```

(b)

Leader	01066cam##2200289#a#4500
Directory entries	001001300000
	003000400013
	005001700017
	008004100034
	010001700075
	020003500092
	020003500127
	020003500162
	040001800197
	050002000215
	082001700235
	100003400252
	245005500286
	250001200341
	260003500353
	300001900388
	504005100407
	505009000458
	650003500548
	650003500583
	856008500618
	856007300703

FIGURE 16-1 MARC record in the communications format for Katz, William A., *Introduction to reference work*. 8th ed. 2002: a bibliographic record (a) and a field-by-field analysis (b), with $ = delimiter, @ = field terminator, % = record terminator, and # = blank

@

Data fields
###00069536#@DLC@20040223170913.0@
001222s2002####mau######b####001#0#eng##@
##$a###00069536#@
##$a0072441070#(v.#1#:#alk.#paper)@
##$a0072441437#(v.#2#:#alk.#paper)@
##$a0071120742#(international#ed.)@
##$aDLC$cDLC$dDLC@
00$aZ711$b.K32#2002@
00$a025.5/52221@1#$aKatz,#William#A.,$d1924-2004.@
10$aIntroduction#to#reference#work#/$cWilliam#A.#Katz.@##$a8th#ed.@
##$aBoston#:$bMcGraw-ill,$cc2002.@
##$a2#v.#;$c24#cm.@
##$aIncludes#bibliographical#references#and#index.@
0#$av.#1.#Basic#information#services#--
#v.#2.#Reference#services#and#reference#processes.@
#0$aReference#services#(Libraries)@
#0$aReference#books$vBibliography.@
423Publisher#description$uhttp://www.loc.gov/catdir/description/mh021/00069536.html@
4#$3Table#of#Contents$uhttp://www.loc.gov/catdir/toc/mh021/00069536.html@%

FIGURE 16-1   (Continued)

> formats, such as cataloging rules, classification schemes,
> subject vocabularies, code lists, etc.

Units in a MARC 21 Record

Another way to look at what constitutes a MARC record is in terms of
units. The term "unit" here refers to an item of MARC-tagged information. Any MARC record consists of the following units:

(1) *Data element*: This is the lowest unit of information. It may be only
one character long, for example, the code for record status. It may be a
numeric string, such as an International Standard Book Number, a copyright date, or an LC control number, or it may be a character string, such
as an author's full name. Also, it may be of fixed or variable length:

(a) *Fixed-length element*: This is an element that is always expressed by
the same number of characters, e.g., the coding of a language is always
three characters long.

(b) *Variable-length element*: This is an element (such as an author's
name, a series title, an edition statement, etc.) the length of which cannot
be predetermined.

(2) *Field*: A field is a collection of data elements, such as a main entry
which consists of the data elements for the person's name and possibly a
title of nobility or the dates of his or her birth and death. Some fields
consist of only one data element, such as the LC Control Number. All of

the fields in a MARC record end with a field terminator which, however, is often not shown in a record display. Each field terminator indicates that the next character in the MARC string begins a new field.

(3) *Record*: A record is a collection of fields treated as a unit, e.g., a bibliographic record, an authority record, or a classification record. In a string of records, each one ends with a record terminator (not always shown in record displays), indicating that the next character in the MARC string begins a new record.

Organization of a MARC 21 Record

A final way to look at what makes up a MARC record is to consider how its distinct parts are organized. There are three main sections: the leader, the directory, and the fields. Figure 16-2 shows the three-part structure.

(1) The *leader*, fixed at twenty-four characters (positions 0–23), is the first field in a MARC record. It provides particular information for processing the ensuing record, data such as total length, status (e.g., new, deleted, or corrected), type (e.g., books, maps, sound recordings, or name authority or subject authority), base address of data, and encoding level (full, minimal, complete, incomplete, etc.). Each specific bit of leader information is entered at a prescribed position in the leader. The leader does not need a field terminator because its length is fixed: the system is set up to "realize" that position 24 is where the directory begins.

(2) The *directory* is a computer-generated index to the locations of the control and data fields within a record. It is similar to the table of contents in a book. It begins at record position 24 and lists the various data fields in the record, giving their respective locations by starting character position. Directory data are system-computed after a record is entered—the cataloger does not have to supply them. The directory consists of a series of fixed-length (twelve characters each) entries, one for each of the fields that contain data presented later in the record. The elements in each directory entry are: the field tag (such as 100 for a personal name main entry); the field length (how many characters—letters, numbers, punctuation marks, subfield codes, and blanks—are in that field); and its starting character position in the record. A record's directory has as many of these twelve-character entries as there are fields in the record. It ends with a field terminator. Figure 16-3 shows the outline of a directory entry.

Leader	Directory	Data fields

FIGURE 16-2 MARC 21 record structure

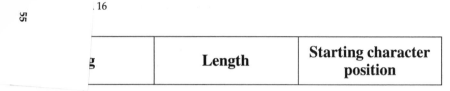

5	Length	Starting character position

FIGURE 16-3   Outline of directory entries

(3) The *fields* contain the essence of the record, i.e., cataloging, authority, classification, or holdings data. Each field is identified by a three-character numeric tag stored in the directory. The field tag identifies the nature of each field in the record: personal name main entry, corporate name main entry, title, subject, and so on. At the end of each field is a field terminator. There are two types of fields: *control fields* and *data fields*.

Control fields are numbered 00X (e.g., 001, 005, 008); they contain either a single data element or a series of fixed-length data elements identified by relative character position.

Data fields are numbered 01X–8XX; most of the fields in the range of 010–09X are for various numbers or codes (e.g., 020 for ISBN, 050 for LC call number, 082 for DDC number) while the ones in the range of 100–8XX are for bibliographic, subject, and linking information, in other words, what is usually considered cataloging information. The 9XX fields contain local data.

Two kinds of content designators are used within data fields: *indicators* and *subfield codes*. The indicators are two one-character positions containing values that interpret or supplement the data found in the field. Not every field uses indicators; those which have not been defined are kept as blanks in the string. The subfield codes identify the data elements within the field that require separate manipulation. Each subfield code is an alphabetic or numeric character which is preceded by a character ($ in this text) called a *delimiter*; for example, $d and $2. Each subfield delimiter and code is followed by the appropriate data, defined independently for each field.

Figure 16-4 shows an example of a data field and its corresponding directory entry in a bibliographic record.

Some fields, such as the 100 (main entry) or 250 (edition) fields, occur only once in each record. Others, such as those for subject headings or index terms, may be repeated. Similarly, some subfields are also repeatable. The repeatability (R) or nonrepeatability (NR) of each field and subfield is indicated in the MARC 21 formats.

What a given content designator means varies considerably from one MARC 21 format to another. This is shown in the contrast between the two tables included in the first chapter for bibliographic and authority data respectively. Nevertheless, there are similar patterns. The schemas below, for bibliographic data, illustrate the sort of things that may be

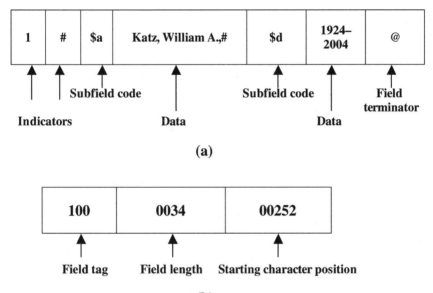

FIGURE 16-4   A variable data field in a bibliographic record (a) and the corresponding directory entry (b)

found in other formats. Fields in the *bibliographic* record are grouped into blocks identified by the first character of the tag, which normally indicates the function of the data within the record.

0XX	Control information, identification and classification numbers, etc.
1XX	Main entry fields
2XX	Titles and title-related fields (title, edition, imprint)
3XX	Physical description, etc. fields
4XX	Series statement fields
5XX	Note fields
6XX	Subject access fields
7XX	Added entry fields other than subject or series; linking fields
8XX	Series added entry fields, holdings, location, etc. fields
9XX	Reserved for local implementation

Within the 100, 400, 600, 700, and 800 blocks, the type of information (e.g., personal name, corporate name, uniform title, and geographic name) is often identified by the second and third characters of the tag.

X00	Personal names
X10	Corporate names

X11	Meeting names
X30	Uniform titles
X40	Bibliographic titles
X50	Topical terms
X51	Geographic names

Indicators and subfield codes are defined individually for each field. For example, the main entry personal name field (tag 100) in a bibliographic record uses the first indicator position to specify the type of personal name according to the following codes:

0—Forename
1—Surname
3—Family name

The second indicator, left as a blank, is undefined. If the main entry is in the form of a personal name, the most commonly used subfield codes are the following:

Code	Subfield
$a	Personal name
$b	Numeration
$c	Titles and other words associated with a name
$d	Dates associated with a name

For example see Figure 16-4(a). Wherever feasible, parallel content designation is used in the various formats. For example, the same subfield codes shown above are used in fields containing personal names in both the bibliographic and authority formats.

It is the coding in a MARC record that allows it to be processed by the computer for various uses and various types of display. There are many circumstances when library personnel need to see and work with fully coded records. Catalog maintenance is one, but other sectors of the library often need them too. OPAC records can be displayed in various formats and levels of detail. They do not show MARC coding, but it is the codes that make such variety possible. It is also the codes that enable many of the sophisticated search options available in today's OPACs. Thus, it can be seen that the same cataloging information, once coded, can be tailored for use in different environments and for different purposes—online catalogs, acquisitions lists, circulation records, etc. The flexibility is great: the design of each online catalog system determines what can be done with the coded catalog data.

MARC-RELATED FORMATS

In addition to the three levels of MARC 21 formats, a number of other formats have been developed by the Library of Congress to facilitate the use of MARC records in different environments. All of these standards have been developed and are maintained by the Network Development and MARC Standards Office of the Library of Congress with input from MARBI and from users.

Three of these standards—MARCXML, MODS, and MADS—are discussed below. Because these standards are encoded in XML (eXtensible Markup Language), a brief introduction to the markup languages used to process electronic data is in order.

SGML (Standard Generalized Markup Language)

A markup language is used to indicate how a document or text is to be structured and presented. The term has its origin in the publishing field. Before a book or journal is published, a copyeditor or "markup" person goes through the manuscript and writes instructions on the margins regarding the font, type, size, etc. for the typesetter. SGML (Standard Generalized Markup Language) was developed to process digital data. SGML is derived from IBM's Generalized Markup Language (GML), developed in the 1960s by Charles Goldfarb, Edward Mosher, and Raymond Lorie. By 1986, GML had been adopted by the International Standards Organization (ISO) and was promulgated as "ISO 8879:1986 Information Processing—Text and office systems—Standard Generalized Markup Language (SGML)." The standard, which is rather complex, was adopted by agencies that require tremendous amounts of data to be processed from text files, notably the U. S. Department of Defense and the Association of American Publishers.

SGML is not a markup language itself but it is a meta-language that is used to define markup languages. By 1992, experiences in using markup had led researchers at the Centre européen pour la recherche nucléaire (or European Organization for Nuclear Research, now commonly referred to as the European Laboratory for Particle Physics, or just "CERN"), to create the HTML (Hypertext Markup Language), an application of SGML. HTML is a markup language designed for displaying documents on Web browsers.

SGML also serves as a meta-meta-language, which means that meta-languages can be created based on SGML. XML (eXtensible Markup Language) is an example of such an implementation of SGML.

XML (eXtensible Markup Language)

XML, an instantiation or implementation of part of SGML, was developed and maintained by the World Wide Web Consortium (W3C).[12] An important feature of XML is that it allows documents to contain data about themselves *within* the document, the same way that MARC records contain the directory. This means the data carry with them specifications that guide their processing, independent of any specific software application. XML was initiated mainly to serve as a simpler and easier-to-implement meta-markup language than SGML with all of the needed concepts embodied within it. The first version of XML specification was published in 1996. The current version of XML specification is the fourth edition of the 1.0 version, as of September 29, 2006. The XML Recommendation (www .w3.org/2001/XMLSchema.html) contains a set of specifications that guide the creation of XML-tagged records of information resources.

Today XML has grown into an all-purpose and all-pervasive way to insert structure into full-text documents and to create flexible surrogates, or metadata, for other objects. The use of XML has become so pervasive that it led Catherine Ebenezer to declare: "Every serious Web technology is now expected to define its relationship to XML."[13] The characteristics of XML can be summarized briefly as follows:

- XML is a simplified implementation of SGML;
- XML consists of a subset of SGML specifications;
- Like SGML, XML is a meta-markup language for text documents;
- Unlike HTML, XML is not a markup language for indicating display options.

In other words, XML tags assign meaning to the data (e.g., <title>**Paradise Lost** </title>), while HTML tags indicate how the data are to be displayed (e.g., <b>**Paradise Lost**</b>). Elliotte Rusty Harold and W. Scott Means summarize the purposes and benefits of XML as follows:[14]

Flexibility: XML allows users to invent the elements based on their needs.

Syntax: The XML Recommendation defines a grammar for XML documents that indicates where tags may be placed, what they must look like, which element names are legal, how attributes are attached to elements, etc.

Semantics: The markup in an XML document describes the structure of the document, i.e., the document's semantics. That is, XML supports a structural and semantic markup language.

Extensibility: XML can be extended and adapted to meet many different needs.

Interoperability: Individuals or organizations may agree to use only certain tags, forming tag sets called XML applications. As a result, XML documents based on the same XML application are interoperable.

Portability: XML is a simple, well-documented, straightforward data format, offering the possibility of cross-platform, long-term data formats. XML documents are text-based and can be read with any tool that can read a text file.

Similar to HTML tags, XML tags are indicated by angled brackets "<"and ">." Tags are case sensitive (e.g., <B> is not the same as <b>), and each starting tag (e.g.,) must have a corresponding ending tag (e.g.,).

DTD (Document Type Definition) and XML Schema

As mentioned earlier, XML is a meta-language. The application of XML in a particular domain, such as in libraries, is called an XML application; and an XML document is a realization of an XML application. An XML application is a formal definition for a document type that conforms to the XML specification. In each XML application, the elements (tags), attributes, and structural rules that are permitted in an XML document must be specified.

There are several ways of creating an XML application. The languages for creating such applications are Document Type Definitions (DTDs) and the XML Schema. The terms DTD or XML Schema are often used to refer to XML applications as well as to the schemas themselves. In general, the XML Schema language provides a more precise grammar than does the DTD format. Thus, using the XML Schema is preferred in situations that require quite sophisticated rules or controls governing the elements and attributes of what is being coded. In an XML application, a formal grammar specifies which elements can be used, how those elements can be used, and what contents and attributes are valid.

Details regarding XML applications are beyond the scope of this book. Rather, the primary focus here is on XML *documents*, in other words, on instances of XML applications. By definition, an XML document is a document combining content data and an XML grammar specified in a particular XML application.

Two simple examples of XML documents are shown below. These documents contain the same content, but the first illustrates the use of a DTD, while the second shows the use of an XML Schema.

Example of an XML document using a DTD:

```
1    <?xml verson="1.0" encoding="ISO-8859-1"?>
2    <!DOCTYPE record SYSTEM "simpleRecord.dtd">
3    <record>
4        <title> cataloging and classification </title>
5        <author>
6            <first_name> lois </first_name>
7            <middle_name> mai </middle_name>
8            <last_name> chan </last_name>
9        <edition> third edition </edition>
10       <subject> cataloging </subject>
11       <subject> classification </subject>
12   </record>
```

An XML document is divided into two parts: XML *declaration* and XML *content*. In the declaration, a variety of external information, such as XML version, encoding scheme, and validation, is stated. In the example above, the first two lines constitute the declaration. The first line indicates the currently used version of XML (1.0) and the encoding schema (ISO-8859-1 character set). The second line indicates that this document is written in conformance with the syntax of the DTD described in a file called *simple Record.dtd* and that the DTD file is located within the same directory as the XML document.

Lines 3–12 contain a mix of document content and a set of valid elements and attributes written according to the grammar described in the *simpleRecord.dtd* file in the example. Every XML document must have a single root element that contains all document content. In this example, the content begins with the third line where the root element <record> of the XML document is declared. Under the root element, four nested elements (*title, author, edition,* and *subject*) are declared. Under the *author* element, there is another nested hierarchical structure showing the sub-elements *first_name, middle_name,* and *last_name.* There are two instances of the *subject* element. Each element must be enclosed within a pair of opening and closing tags, for instance, the pair of <title> as an opening tag and </title> as a closing tag, with the element content given between the tags. An element name indicates what the element content is. For example, the *title* element contains the title "cataloging and classification."

The following shows the same XML document using an XML Schema:

```
1    <?xml version = "1.0" encoding = "ISO-8859-1"?>
2    <record
3        xmlns:xsi = "http://www.w3.org/2001/XMLSchema-
         instance"
4        xsi:noNamespaceSchemaLocation = "book.xsd">
5        <title> cataloging and classification </title>
6        <author>
7            <first_name> lois </first_name>
8            <middle_name> mai </middle_name>
9            <last_name> chan </last_name>
10       <edition> third edition </edition>
11       <subject> cataloging </subject>
12       <subject> classification </subject>
13   </record>
```

In this example, the first line indicates that this is an XML document conforming to XML version 1.0 and that the encoding schema is the ISO-8859-1. According to the XML Schema Recommendation ("http://www

.w3.org/2001/XMLSchema"), all possible sets of elements and attributes for an XML application should be pre-defined and pre-declared in *namespaces*, and the links between these elements and attributes and their corresponding namespaces must be explicitly or implicitly stated in the XML document. Such links, with the prefix *xsi*, indicate which namespace is to be used for which element and/or attribute. The XML Schema Language specifies two special namespaces: in the first one ("http://www.w3.org/2001/XMLSchema"), all standard schema elements are defined; and in the other ("http://www.w3.org/2001/XMLSchema-instance"), four attributes are defined. For example, the "noNamespaceSchemaLocation" attribute in line 4 is one of the four attributes.

In the example above, two attributes are specified in the top element *record*, as shown in lines 3 and 4. Line 3 begins with the term *xmlns*. "xmlns" stands for "XML Namespace." (A namespace is the equivalent of the name of a table in relational databases. The namespace, among other things, guides computer programs parsing the record to know the correct XML Schema for a given element. This is useful because once an XML Schema has been created, it is then easy to share it.)

The combination of "xmlns:xsi =" is a reserved word in the XML Schema Language for referencing a namespace specified in the ensuing URI (Uniform Resource Identifier), in this case "http://www.w3.org/2001/XMLSchema-instance." This reference means that all four attributes specified in the particular namespace can be used within the record element or any attributes prefixed *xsi*.

In line 4, the "noNamespaceSchemaLocation" attribute is declared, which gives the location of the XML Schema to be used in this document. More specifically, it means that the designated XML Schema (*book.xsd*) is to be used for elements that are not included in any namespace. In this example, since no other XML Schema is declared anywhere else for the five different elements (record, title, author, edition, subject), the file *book.xsd* will be used for the attributes of the elements.

To summarize, SGML is a set of abstract specifications for creating markup languages, such as XML for marking up the *structure* of the data and HTML for marking up the *presentation* of data. Since it does not contain fixed sets of terms (elements and attributes) or their relationships, the creators of SGML applications can build selected sets of elements and attributes for their particular domains. This has led to numerous SGML/XML applications for different domains. The flexibility of SGML-based applications enables documents to be encoded in unlimited ways. There is no reason why, for instance, an XML schema for literature could not have both a tag called "<protagonist>" for adult readers and a tag called "<main_character>" for young adult readers.

XML provides a flexible and adaptive means of storing, structuring, and identifying information, without prescribing how the information is displayed or used. Additional tools, such as XSL (eXtensible Stylesheet

Language) and CSS (Cascading Style Sheets), are used for processing and manipulating XML data and for handling the proper display of XML-tagged data.

The main features of XML include:

- XML is hierarchical, with a root element and parent and child elements.
- An XML schema is usually stored in a separate file and then is associated with XML documents by references to namespaces.
- There is no fixed or standard set of valid elements and attributes for an XML application; the developer can create them.
- XML is an open standard (non-proprietary), sharable by all.
- Data to be encoded in an XML document can be of any type.
- Data encoded in XML are valid and well-formed.
- The syntax of XML is easily processed by software and machines, because many programming languages, especially Java, include resources (called "libraries") for computer programs to parse XML records.
- Natural language tags make XML understandable to humans.
- Record content data are completely separate from presentation or display instructions.
- Creating and using shared DTDs or XML schemas increases interoperability (sharing) of the data.

XML in Library Applications

XML makes it possible to update legacy XML-based cataloging and metadata records and to create new XML-based text records that can be searched across various database systems. Furthermore, the well-structured text in XML-coded records makes catalog and metadata records amenable to full-text parsing and other techniques found in information retrieval systems.

There is a trend in Integrated Library Systems (ILS) to integrate access to all sorts of materials and resource types. Since the record structure of an XML-coded record is open and available (that is, the Schema itself is available along with any records that have been tagged following its provisions), it is possible to create meta-search systems and to incorporate data based on multiple metadata schemes within a single record. For instance, OCLC's WorldCat accepts both MARC and DC (Dublin Core) tags.

In the end, the power of XML enables librarians to convert MARC data to be used in an XML environment and to adjust document content to adapt to new devices and new user needs. Use of XML also facilitates the easy transfer of data between systems.

The following sections discuss the application of SGML and XML to standards for structuring and processing catalog and metadata records.

MARCXML

XML, originally designed to meet the challenges of large-scale electronic publishing, is now also playing an important role in the exchange of a wide variety of cataloging data and metadata on the Web. To enable MARC users to work with MARC data in the Web environment and in ways specific to their needs, the Network Development and MARC Standards Office of the Library of Congress has developed a framework called MARCXML, by casting MARC data in an XML framework. Based on XML, MARCXML enables the representation of MARC 21 data in an XML environment. It allows users to work with MARC data in ways specific to their needs. The framework itself includes many components such as schemas, stylesheets, and software tools. Along with the MARCXML schema, LC also provides a variety of XML tools, including stylesheets for transforming and displaying the data.[15] The tools LC provides also permit libraries to convert their old MARC records to MARCXML, to MODS (Metadata Object Description Schema), or to Dublin Core or other metadata records.

The MARCXML schema retains the semantics of MARC 21. However, some structural elements in MARC 21, such as the length of field and starting position of field data in directory entries, are not needed in an XML record. MARC's leader and the control fields are treated as data strings, and its fields are treated as subelements. Nevertheless, all of the essential data in a MARC record can be converted and expressed in XML.

Figure 16-5(a) and (b) show the same work encoded in the MARC 21 bibliographic format and in MARCXML. Figure 16-5(a) is the complete MARC 21 record for Carl Sandburg's *Arithmetic*. Figure 16-5(b) is the MARCXML record for the same work. (As all XML records are required to do, the first line of the XML record, <?xml version = "1.0" encoding = "UTF-8" ?>, declares the XML version and the encoding schema. Line 2 indicates that the root of this record is "record." The second part of this line gives information about the XML Namespace: http://www .loc.gov/MARC21/slim.)

MODS (Metadata Object Description Schema)

As mentioned in chapter 4, the MODS (Metadata Object Description Schema)[16] is a metadata schema for creating original resource description records that consist of selected data from the MARC 21 Bibliographic format. For encoding, it uses XML.

MODS consists of a subset of twenty bibliographic elements based on the MARC 21 Format for Bibliographic Data, selected specifically for

(a)

```
000 01142cam  2200301 a 4500
001   92005291
003 DLC
005 19930521155141.9
008 920219s1993    caua  j      000 0 eng
010   $a   92005291
020   $a0152038655 :$c$15.95
040   $aDLC$cDLC$dDLC
042   $alcac
050 00$aPS3537.A618$bA88 1993
082 00$a811/.52$220
100 1 $aSandburg, Carl,$d1878-1967.
245 10$aArithmetic /$cCarl Sandburg ; illustrated as an anamorphic adventure by Ted Rand.
250   $a1st ed.
260   $aSan Diego :$bHarcourt Brace Jovanovich,$cc1993.
300   $a1 v. (unpaged) :$bill. (some col.) ;$c26 cm.
500   $aOne Mylar sheet included in pocket.
520   $aA poem about numbers and their characteristics. Features anamorphic, or distorted,
drawings which can be restored to normal by viewing from a particular angle or by viewing the
image's reflection in the provided Mylar cone.
650  0$aArithmetic$xJuvenile poetry.
650  0$aChildren's poetry, American.
650  1$aArithmetic$xPoetry.
650  1$aAmerican poetry.
650  1$aVisual perception.
700 1 $aRand, Ted,$eill.
```

(b)

```xml
<?xml version="1.0" encoding="UTF-8" ?>
<record xmlns="http://www.loc.gov/MARC21/slim"
xmlns:xsi="http://www.w3.org/2001/XMLSchema-instance"
xsi:schemaLocation="http://www.loc.gov/MARC21/slim
http://www.loc.gov/standards/marcxml/schema/MARC21slim.xsd">
  <leader>01142cam a2200301 a 4500</leader>
  <controlfield tag="001">  92005291 </controlfield>
  <controlfield tag="003">DLC</controlfield>
  <controlfield tag="005">19930521155141.9</controlfield>
  <controlfield tag="008">920219s1993    caua  j      000 0 eng </controlfield>
  <datafield tag="010" ind1=" " ind2=" ">
   <subfield code="a">  92005291 </subfield>
  </datafield>
  <datafield tag="020" ind1=" " ind2=" ">
   <subfield code="a">0152038655 :</subfield>
   <subfield code="c">$15.95</subfield>
  </datafield>
  <datafield tag="040" ind1=" " ind2=" ">
   <subfield code="a">DLC</subfield>
   <subfield code="c">DLC</subfield>
   <subfield code="d">DLC</subfield>
  </datafield>
  <datafield tag="042" ind1=" " ind2=" ">
   <subfield code="a">lcac</subfield>
  </datafield>
  <datafield tag="050" ind1="0" ind2="0">
```

FIGURE 16-5 Carl Sandburg's *Arithmetic*: a MARC 21 record (a) and MARCXML record (b)

```xml
      <subfield code="a">PS3537.A618</subfield>
      <subfield code="b">A88 1993</subfield>
   </datafield>
   <datafield tag="082" ind1="0" ind2="0">
      <subfield code="a">811/.52</subfield>
      <subfield code="2">20</subfield>
   </datafield>
   <datafield tag="100" ind1="1" ind2=" ">
      <subfield code="a">Sandburg, Carl,</subfield>
      <subfield code="d">1878-1967.</subfield>
   </datafield>
   <datafield tag="245" ind1="1" ind2="0">
      <subfield code="a">Arithmetic /</subfield>
      <subfield code="c">Carl Sandburg ; illustrated as an anamorphic adventure by Ted
Rand.</subfield>
   </datafield>
   <datafield tag="250" ind1=" " ind2=" ">
      <subfield code="a">1st ed.</subfield>
   </datafield>
   <datafield tag="260" ind1=" " ind2=" ">
      <subfield code="a">San Diego :</subfield>
      <subfield code="b">Harcourt Brace Jovanovich,</subfield>
      <subfield code="c">c1993.</subfield>
   </datafield>
   <datafield tag="300" ind1=" " ind2=" ">
      <subfield code="a">1 v. (unpaged) :</subfield>
      <subfield code="b">ill. (some col.) ;</subfield>
      <subfield code="c">26 cm.</subfield>
   </datafield>
   <datafield tag="500" ind1=" " ind2=" ">
      <subfield code="a">One Mylar sheet included in pocket.</subfield>
   </datafield>
   <datafield tag="520" ind1=" " ind2=" ">
      <subfield code="a">A poem about numbers and their characteristics. Features
anamorphic, or distorted, drawings which can be restored to normal by viewing from a
particular angle or by viewing the image&apos;s reflection in the provided Mylar
cone.</subfield>
   </datafield>
   <datafield tag="650" ind1=" " ind2="0">
      <subfield code="a">Arithmetic</subfield>
      <subfield code="x">Juvenile poetry.</subfield>
   </datafield>
   <datafield tag="650" ind1=" " ind2="0">
      <subfield code="a">Children&apos;s poetry, American.</subfield>
   </datafield>
   <datafield tag="650" ind1=" " ind2="1">
      <subfield code="a">Arithmetic</subfield>
      <subfield code="x">Poetry.</subfield>
   </datafield>
   <datafield tag="650" ind1=" " ind2="1">
      <subfield code="a">American poetry.</subfield>
   </datafield>
   <datafield tag="650" ind1=" " ind2="1">
      <subfield code="a">Visual perception.</subfield>
```

FIGURE 16-5 Continued

```
  </datafield>
  <datafield tag="700" ind1="1" ind2=" ">
   <subfield code="a">Rand, Ted,</subfield>
   <subfield code="e">ill.</subfield>
  </datafield>
 </record>
```

FIGURE 16-5   Continued

supporting the description of electronic resources and objects. As such, it is a rich, library-oriented XML metadata schema. Yet, although it is a simpler schema than the MARC 21 Bibliographic Format, it retains compatibility with MARC 21. It also provides multiple linking functions.

For encoding, MODS uses language-based tags rather than numeric ones. The top level MODS elements include:

> **titleInfo**
> **name**
> **typeOfResource**
> **genre**
> **originInfo**
> **language**
> **physicalDescription**
> **abstract**
> **tableOfContents**
> **targetAudience**
> **note**
> **subject**
> **classification**
> **relatedItem**
> **identifier**
> **location**
> **accessCondition**
> **part**
> **extension**
> **recordInfo**

There are a great number of subelements and attributes for MODS listed on the Library of Congress' website (www.loc.gov/standards/mods/). Figure 16-6 contains the MODS record for *Lexington, Kentucky, Street Map*.

The following example, based on the title field (MARC tag 245) only, shows the parallel and coordination among MARC, MARCXML, and MODS:

> **MARC**
> [245] 14$a**The heart of Midlothian** / $c **Sir Walter Scott**

(a)

```xml
<?xml version="1.0" encoding="UTF-8"?>
<mods xmlns="http://www.loc.gov/mods/v3"
xmlns:xsi="http://www.w3.org/2001/XMLSchema-instance" version="3.1"
xsi:schemaLocation="http://www.loc.gov/mods/v3
http://www.loc.gov/standards/mods/v3/mods-3-1.xsd">
  <titleInfo>
    <title>Lexington, Kentucky, street map</title>
    <subTitle>including Berea, Burgin, Curdsville, Cynthiana, ... & Winchester ;
featuring airports, cemeteries, Fayette County vicinity map, ... zip code
boundaries</subTitle>
  </titleInfo>
  <titleInfo type="alternative">
    <title>UniversalMAP Lexington, Kentucky, street map</title>
  </titleInfo>
  <name type="corporate">
    <namePart>Universal Map (Firm)</namePart>
    <role>
      <roleTerm authority="marcrelator" type="text">creator</roleTerm>
    </role>
  </name>
  <typeOfResource>cartographic</typeOfResource>
  <genre authority="marc">map</genre>
  <originInfo>
    <place>
      <placeTerm type="code" authority="marccountry">miu</placeTerm>
    </place>
    <place>
      <placeTerm type="text">Williamston, MI</placeTerm>
    </place>
    <publisher>UniversalMAP</publisher>
    <dateIssued>[2006?]</dateIssued>
    <dateIssued encoding="marc">2006</dateIssued>
    <issuance>monographic</issuance>
  </originInfo>
  <language>
    <languageTerm authority="iso639-2b" type="code">eng</languageTerm>
  </language>
  <physicalDescription>
    <extent>2 maps : both sides, col. ; 60 x 57 cm. and 79 x 59 cm., folded to 24 x 11
cm.</extent>
  </physicalDescription>
  <tableOfContents>Lexington, Kentucky [Lexington metropolitan area] --
Lexington, Kentucky [Lexington region road map].</tableOfContents>
  <note type="statement of responsibility">UniversalMAP.</note>
  <note>Title from panel.</note>
  <note>At head of title: UniversalMAP.</note>
```

FIGURE 16-6 MODS record for Carl Sandburg's *Arithmetic* (a) and *Lexington, Kentucky, Street Map* (b).

(b)

```
<note>Includes indexes, ancillary map of Central Lexington, and inset of "Major
highway systems of Kentucky."</note>
<subject>
  <cartographics>
    <scale>Scale [ca. 1:31,000].</scale>
  </cartographics>
</subject>
<subject>
  <cartographics>
    <scale>Scale [ca. 1:150,000].</scale>
  </cartographics>
</subject>
<subject authority="lcsh">
  <geographic>Lexington (Ky.)</geographic>
  <topic>Maps</topic>
</subject>
<subject authority="lcsh">
  <geographic>Lexington Metropolitan Area (Ky.)</geographic>
  <topic>Maps</topic>
</subject>
<subject authority="lcsh">
  <topic>Roads</topic>
  <geographic>Kentucky</geographic>
  <geographic>Lexington region</geographic>
  <topic>Maps</topic>
</subject>
<classification authority="lcc">G3954.L4 2006 .U51</classification>
<identifier type="isbn">0762546727</identifier>
<identifier type="lccn">2006458616</identifier>
<recordInfo>
  <recordContentSource authority="marcorg">DLC</recordContentSource>
  <recordCreationDate encoding="marc">060905</recordCreationDate>
  <recordChangeDate encoding="iso8601">20060905161002.0</recordChangeDate>
  <recordIdentifier source="DLC">  2006458616</recordIdentifier>
</recordInfo>
</mods>
```

FIGURE 16-6   Continued

MARCXML
```
<datafield tag="245" ind1="1" ind2="4">
    <subfield code="a">The heart of Midlothian</
        subfield>
    <subfield code="c">Sir Walter Scott</subfield>
    </datafield>
```
MODS
```
<titleInfo><nonSort>The</nonSort><title>heart of
    Midlothian</title></titleInfo>
<note type="statementOfResponsibility">Sir Walter
    Scott</note>
```

MADS (Metadata Authority Description Schema)

MADS (Metadata Authority Description Schema)[17] is an XML schema for an authority element set that may be used to provide metadata about agents (people, organizations), events, and terms (topics, geographics, genres, etc.). MADS records may also include elements such as topical, temporal, genre, geographic, or occupation.

MADS is compatible with the MARC 21 Authorities format. It was intended to be a companion to MODS and so was designed to be as consistent and compatible with MODS as possible. The relationship between MADS and MARC 21 Authorities parallels that between MODS and MARC 21 Bibliographic.

MADS also uses language-based tags. A MADS record contains the same basic components as found in a MARC authority record:

> Authorized heading
> Related heading(s) (see also reference(s))—attributes:
> > earlier
> > later
> > parentOrg
> > broader
> > narrower
> > etc.
> Variant heading(s) (see reference(s))—attributes:
> > equivalent
> > acronym
> > abbreviation
> > translation
> > etc.
> Other elements (e.g., notes, affiliation, url, identifier, etc.)

Examples of MADS records are shown in Figures 16-7 and 16-8.

METADATA RECORDS ENCODED IN SGML AND XML

SGML and XML are also used to encode metadata records. The content definitions of some of the widely used metadata schemas are given in chapter 4. The following examples show metadata records encoded in SGML or XML.

Dublin Core

The example in Figure 16-9, extracted from OCLC's Connexion, shows the XML version of an unqualified Dublin Core record for a map. In this

(1) Personal heading: **Katz, William A.**

```xml
<?xml version="1.0" encoding="UTF-8"?>
<mads:mads xmlns:mads="http://www.loc.gov/mads/"
xmlns:xsi="http://www.w3.org/2001/XMLSchema-instance"
xmlns:mods="http://www.loc.gov/mods/v3" xmlns:xlink="http://www.w3.org/1999/xlink"
version="1.0" xsi:schemaLocation="http://www.loc.gov/mads/
http://www.loc.gov/standards/mads/mads.xsd http://www.loc.gov/mods/v3
http://www.loc.gov/standards/mods/v3/mods-3-2.xsd">
  <mads:authority>
    <mads:name type="personal" authority="naf">
      <mads:namePart>Katz, William A</mads:namePart>
      <mads:namePart type="date">1924-2004</mads:namePart>
    </mads:name>
  </mads:authority>
  <mads:variant type="other">
    <mads:name type="personal">
      <mads:namePart>Katz, Bill</mads:namePart>
      <mads:namePart type="date">1924-2004</mads:namePart>
    </mads:name>
  </mads:variant>
  <mads:variant type="other">
    <mads:name type="personal">
      <mads:namePart>Katz, Willis Armstrong</mads:namePart>
      <mads:namePart type="date">1924-2004</mads:namePart>
    </mads:name>
  </mads:variant>
  <mads:variant type="other">
    <mads:name type="personal">
      <mads:namePart>Katz, William</mads:namePart>
      <mads:namePart type="date">1924-2004</mads:namePart>
    </mads:name>
  </mads:variant>
  <mads:note type="source">Library Buildings Institute, Chicago, 1963. Problems in
planning library facilities, 1964</mads:note>
  <mads:note type="source">His Your library, c1984: CIP t.p. (William Katz, SUNY at
Albany)</mads:note>
  <mads:note type="source">Integrating print and digital resources in library collections,
2006: prelims. (Dr. William (Bill) Katz; d. Sept. 12, 2004)</mads:note>
  <mads:identifier type="lccn">n 79092477 </mads:identifier>
  <mads:identifier type="lccn" invalid="yes">n 93025121 </mads:identifier>
  <mads:identifier type="lccn" invalid="yes">n 97014023 </mads:identifier>
  <mads:recordInfo>
    <mods:recordContentSource authority="marcorg">DLC</mods:recordContentSource>
    <mods:recordCreationDate encoding="marc">800507</mods:recordCreationDate>
    <mods:recordChangeDate
encoding="iso8601">20060518052008.0</mods:recordChangeDate>
    <mods:recordIdentifier source="DLC">n 79092477 </mods:recordIdentifier>
    <mods:languageOfCataloging>
      <mods:languageTerm authority="iso639-2b" type="code">eng</mods:languageTerm>
    </mods:languageOfCataloging>
  </mads:recordInfo>
</mads:mads>
```

FIGURE 16-7   MADS record for a personal name heading

(2) Subject heading: **Reference services (Libraries)**

```
<?xml version="1.0" encoding="UTF-8"?>
<mads:mads xmlns:mads="http://www.loc.gov/mads/"
xmlns:xsi="http://www.w3.org/2001/XMLSchema-instance"
xmlns:mods="http://www.loc.gov/mods/v3" xmlns:xlink="http://www.w3.org/1999/xlink"
version="1.0" xsi:schemaLocation="http://www.loc.gov/mads/
http://www.loc.gov/standards/mads/mads.xsd http://www.loc.gov/mods/v3
http://www.loc.gov/standards/mods/v3/mods-3-2.xsd">
  <mads:authority>
    <mads:topic authority="lcsh">Reference services (Libraries)</mads:topic>
  </mads:authority>
  <mads:related type="broader">
    <mads:topic>Information services</mads:topic>
  </mads:related>
  <mads:related type="broader">
    <mads:topic>Public services (Libraries)</mads:topic>
  </mads:related>
  <mads:variant type="other">
    <mads:topic>Libraries</mads:topic>
    <mads:topic>Reference department</mads:topic>
  </mads:variant>
  <mads:variant type="other">
    <mads:topic>Library reference services</mads:topic>
  </mads:variant>
  <mads:variant type="other">
    <mads:topic>Reference work (Libraries)</mads:topic>
  </mads:variant>
  <mads:identifier type="lccn">sh 85112201 </mads:identifier>
  <mads:recordInfo>
    <mods:recordContentSource authority="marcorg">DLC</mods:recordContentSource>
    <mods:recordCreationDate encoding="marc">030513</mods:recordCreationDate>
    <mods:recordChangeDate
encoding="iso8601">20030617130318.0</mods:recordChangeDate>
    <mods:recordIdentifier source="DLC">sh 85112201 </mods:recordIdentifier>
  </mads:recordInfo>
</mads:mads>
```

FIGURE 16-8   MADS record for a subject heading

application, the prefix "rdf: RDF xmlns:rdf = " is used as the reference to the URI of the namespace.

EAD (Encoded Archival Description)

Figure 16-10 contains an example of a fully encoded <eadheader> element.[18]

ONIX (Online Information Exchange)

Figure 16-11 shows a portion of an ONIX record containing bibliographic information about a book.[19]

```xml
<?xml version="1.0"?>
<rdf:RDF xmlns:rdf=http://www.w3.org/1999/02/22-rdf-syntax-ns#
xmlns:dc=http://purl.org/dc/elements/1.0/
xmlns:dcq="http://purl.org/dc/qualifiers/1.0/">
<rdf:Description about=" 2006458616">
<dc:title>Lexington, Kentucky, street map : including Berea, Burgin, Curdsville,
Cynthiana, ... & Winchester ; featuring airports, cemeteries, Fayette County vicinity map,
... zip code boundaries /</dc:title>
<dc:title>UniversalMAP Lexington, Kentucky, street map</dc:title>
<dc:coverage>a 31000</dc:coverage>
<dc:coverage>a 150000</dc:coverage>
<dc:coverage>Scale [ca. 1:31,000].</dc:coverage>
<dc:coverage>Scale [ca. 1:150,000].</dc:coverage>
<dc:creator>Universal Map (Firm)</dc:creator>
<dc:format>2 maps : both sides, col. ; 60 x 57 cm. and 79 x 59 cm., folded to 24 x 11
cm.</dc:format>
<dc:publisher>Williamston, MI :</dc:publisher>
<dc:publisher>UniversalMAP,</dc:publisher>
<dc:date>2006</dc:date>
<dc:description>Title from panel.</dc:description>
<dc:description>At head of title: UniversalMAP</dc:description>
<dc:description>Includes indexes, ancillary map of Central Lexington, and inset of "Major
highway systems of Kentucky."</dc:description>
<dc:description>Lexington, Kentucky [Lexington metropolitan area] -- Lexington,
Kentucky [Lexington region road map].</dc:description>
<dc:identifier> 2006458616</dc:identifier>
<dc:identifier>0762546727</dc:identifier>
<dc:language>eng</dc:language>
<dc:subject> <rdf:Description> <dcq:subjectQualifier>class</dcq:subjectQualifier>
<rdf:value>G3954.L4 2006 .U51</rdf:value> </rdf:Description> </dc:subject>
<dc:subject> <rdf:Description> <dcq:subjectQualifier>geographic</dcq:subjectQualifier>
<rdf:value>Lexington (Ky.)--Maps.</rdf:value> </rdf:Description> </dc:subject>
<dc:subject> <rdf:Description> <dcq:subjectQualifier>geographic</dcq:subjectQualifier>
<rdf:value>Lexington Metropolitan Area (Ky.)--Maps.</rdf:value> </rdf:Description>
</dc:subject>
<dc:subject> <rdf:Description> <dcq:subjectQualifier>topical</dcq:subjectQualifier>
<rdf:value>Roads--Kentucky--Lexington region--Maps.</rdf:value> </rdf:Description>
</dc:subject>
<dc:type>Map data</dc:type>
</rdf:Description>
</rdf:RDF>
```

FIGURE 16-9 Encoded Dublin Core record

```
<eadheader audience="internal" langencoding="ISO 639-2"
findaidstatus="edited-full-draft">
        <eadid systemid="dlc" encodinganalog="856">loc. mss/eadmss.ms996001
        </eadid>
        <filedesc>
                <titlestmt>
                        <titleproper>Shirley Jackson</titleproper>
                        <subtitle>A Register of Her Papers in the Library of
                        Congress</subtitle>
                        <author>Prepared by Grover Batts. Revised and
                        expanded by Michael McElderry with the assistance of
                        Scott McLemee
                        </author>
                </titlestmt>
                <publicationstmt>
                        <date>1993</date>
                        <publisher>Manuscript Division, Library of Congress
                        </publisher>
                        <address>
                                <addressline>Washington, D.C. 20540-
                                4860</addressline>
                        </address>
                </publicationstmt>
                <notestmt>
                        <note>
                                <p>Edited full draft</p>
                        </note>
                </notestmt>
        </filedesc>
        <profiledesc>
                <creation>Finding aid encoded by Library of Congress
                Manuscript Division,
                        <date>1996.</date>
                </creation>
                <langusage>Finding aid written in
                        <language>English.</language>
                </langusage>
        </profiledesc>
        <revisiondesc>
                <change>
                        <date>1997</date>
                        <item>Encoding revised</item>
                </change>
        </revisiondesc>
</eadheader>
```

FIGURE 16-10   Encoded EAD header

```
<Product>
  <RecordReference>1234567890</RecordReference>
  <NotificationType>03</NotificationType>
  <ProductIdentifier>
    <ProductIDType>02</ProductIDType>
    <IDValue>0816016356</IDValue>
  </ProductIdentifier>
  <ProductForm>BB</ProductForm>
  <Title>
    <TitleType>01</TitleType>
    <TitleText textcase = "02">British English, A to Zed</TitleText>
  </Title>
  <Contributor>
    <SequenceNumber>1</SequenceNumber>
    <ContributorRole>A01</ContributorRole>
    <PersonNameInverted>Schur, Norman W</PersonNameInverted>
    <BiographicalNote>A Harvard graduate in Latin and Italian literature, Norman
Schur attended the University of Rome and the Sorbonne before returning to the
United States to study law at Harvard and Columbia Law Schools. Now retired
from legal practise, Mr Schur is a fluent speaker and writer of both British and
American English</BiographicalNote>
  </Contributor>
  <EditionTypeCode>REV</EditionTypeCode>
  <EditionNumber>3</EditionNumber>
  <Language>
    <LanguageRole>01</LanguageRole>
    <LanguageCode>eng</LanguageCode>
  </Language>
  <NumberOfPages>493</NumberOfPages>
  <BASICMainSubject>REF008000</BASICMainSubject>
  <AudienceCode>01</AudienceCode>
  <OtherText>
    <TextTypeCode>01</TextTypeCode>
    <Text>BRITISH ENGLISH, A TO ZED is the thoroughly updated, revised, and
expanded third edition of Norman Schur's highly acclaimed transatlantic
dictionary for English speakers. First published as BRITISH SELF-TAUGHT
and then as ENGLISH ENGLISH, this collection of Briticisms for Americans,
and Americanisms for the British, is a scholarly yet witty lexicon, combining
definitions with commentary on the most frequently used and some lesser known
words and phrases. Highly readable, it's a snip of a book, and one that sorts out
– through comments in American – the "Queen's English" – confounding as it
may seem.</Text>
  </OtherText>
  <OtherText>
    <TextTypeCode>08</TextTypeCode>
```

FIGURE 16-11   Encoded ONIX record

```
        <Text>Norman Schur is without doubt the outstanding authority on the
        similarities and differences between British and American English. BRITISH
        ENGLISH, A TO ZED attests not only to his expertise, but also to his
        undiminished powers to inform, amuse and entertain. – Laurence Urdang,
        Editor, VERBATIM, The Language Quarterly, Spring 1988 </Text>
    </OtherText>
    <Imprint>
        <ImprintName>Facts on File Publications</ImprintName>
    </Imprint>
    <Publisher>
        <PublishingRole>01</PublishingRole>
        <PublisherName>Facts on File Inc</PublisherName>
    </Publisher>
    <PublicationDate>1987</PublicationDate>
    <Measure>
        <MeasureTypeCode>01</MeasureTypeCode>
        <Measurement>9.25</Measurement>
        <MeasureUnitCode>in</MeasureUnitCode>
    </Measure>
    <Measure>
        <MeasureTypeCode>02</MeasureTypeCode>
        <Measurement>6.25</Measurement>
        <MeasureUnitCode>in</MeasureUnitCode>
    </Measure>
    <Measure>
        <MeasureTypeCode>03</MeasureTypeCode>
        <Measurement>1.2</Measurement>
        <MeasureUnitCode>in</MeasureUnitCode>
    </Measure>
    <SupplyDetail>
        <SupplierSAN>1234567</SupplierSAN>
        <AvailabilityCode>IP</AvailabilityCode>
        <Price>
            <PriceTypeCode>01</PriceTypeCode>
            <PriceAmount>35.00</PriceAmount>
        </Price>
    </SupplyDetail>
</Product>
```

FIGURE 16-11   Continued

NOTES

1. Henriette D. Avram, *MARC: Its History and Implications* (Washington, D.C.: Library of Congress, 1975); Walt Crawford, *MARC for Library Use: Understanding Integrated USMARC* (Boston: G. K. Hall & Co., 1989), 203–41.

2. Library of Congress, MARC Development Office, *Information on the MARC System*, 4th ed. (Washington, D.C.: Library of Congress, 1974), 1.

3. American National Standards Institute, *American National Standard Format for Bibliographic Information Interchange on Magnetic Tape*, ANSI Z39.2-1971 (New York: ANSI, 1971); current ed.: *Information Interchange Format*, ANSI/NISO Z39.2-1994 (R2001) (Bethesda, Md.: NISO, 1994); also available: www.niso.org/standards/resources/Z39-2.pdf (25 Feb. 2007).

4. International Organization for Standardization, *Documentation: Format for Bibliographic Information Interchange on Magnetic Tape* ISO 2709 (Geneva: The Organization, 1973); 2nd ed. ([Geneva]: ISO, 1981).

5. John Attig, "The USMARC Formats—Underlying Principles," *Information Technology and Libraries* 1, no. 2 (June 1982): 169–74.

6. *MARC 21 Format for Bibliographic Data: Including Guidelines for Content Designation*, prepared by Network Development and MARC Standards Office, Library of Congress, in cooperation with Standards and Support, National Library of Canada (Washington, D.C.: Library of Congress, Cataloging Distribution Service, 1999–).

7. Walt Crawford, *MARC for Library Use: Understanding Integrated USMARC* (Boston: G. K. Hall & Co., 1989), 221–22.

8. *MARC 21 Format for Authority Data: Including Guidelines for Content Designation*, prepared by Network Development and MARC Standards Office, Library of Congress, in cooperation with Standards and Support, National Library of Canada (Washington, D.C.: Library of Congress, Cataloging Distribution Service; Ottawa: National Library of Canada, 1999–).

9. *MARC 21 Format for Classification Data: Including Guidelines for Content Designation*, prepared by Network Development and MARC Standards Office, Library of Congress in cooperation with Standards and Support, National Library of Canada (Washington, D.C.: Cataloging Distribution Service, Library of Congress, 2000–).

10. *MARC 21 Format for Holdings Data: Including Guidelines for Content Designation*, prepared by Network Development and MARC Standards Office, Library of Congress, in cooperation with Standards and Support, National Library of Canada (Washington, D.C.: Cataloging Distribution Service, Library of Congress, 2000).

11. *MARC 21 Concise Formats*, prepared by Network Development and MARC Standards Office, Library of Congress (Washington, D.C.: Library of Congress, Cataloging Distribution Service, 2000– ; updated annually).

12. Extensible Markup Language (XML), www.w3.org/XML/ (25 Feb. 2007).

13. Catherine Ebenezer, "Trends in Integrated Library Systems," *VINE* 32, no. 4 (2003): 19.

14. Elliotte Rusty Harold and W. Scott Means, *XML in a Nutshell*, 3rd ed. (Sebastopol, Calif.: O'Reilly, 2004), 4, 6.

15. MARCXML: MARC 21 XML Schema, www.loc.gov/standards/marc xml/ (25 Feb. 2007).

16. MODS Metadata Object Description Schema, www.loc.gov/standards/mods/ (25 Feb. 2007).

17. MADS Metadata Authority Description Schema, www.loc.gov/standards/mads/ (25 Feb. 2007).

18. "EAD Application Guidelines for Version 1.0: chapter 3. Creating Finding Aids in EAD: 3.6.1. EAD Header <eadheader>," www.loc.gov/ead/ag/agcre6.html#sec1ae (25 Feb. 2007).

19. Editeur, *ONIX for Books: Product Information Message Product*, Record Release 2.1, revision 02 15 July 2004, revised February 2005, 14–16, www.editeur.org (25 Feb. 2007).

CHAPTER 17
PRODUCING AND
PROCESSING CATALOGING
RECORDS

INTRODUCTION

The preceding chapters have focused primarily on the intellectual operations of preparing cataloging records: drafting a description, determining access points (both those based on names and titles and those based on subject content), ensuring uniform and unique headings, assigning classification numbers, and coding cataloging information for computer manipulation. This chapter treats a more practical question: how and by whom cataloging is done.

In cataloging any given item, there are two ways to proceed. The first, called *copy cataloging,* is to make the fullest possible use of records prepared elsewhere—records that are called *cataloging copy.* The second, called *original cataloging,* is to do the cataloging in house, from scratch. In any given library with a general collection, it is typical to find a mix of both, with fully original cataloging restricted to items for which no outside record is available. The more specialized the library or indexing agency, of course, the fewer outside records are likely to be suitable if any can be found at all.

In strict copy cataloging, a local cataloging record is based on an outside record with minimum modification to fit the item being cataloged. Nonetheless, in many cases of copy cataloging, a high level of professional judgment may be needed once a candidate outside record is found: first, to be sure that the record in question matches the item in hand; second (if it does match), to determine whether the item was adequately cataloged by the originating agency; and third, to alter, add, or delete cataloging elements to suit local needs. Thus, there are elements of original cataloging even in what is usually considered copy cataloging. In general libraries, nevertheless, most local cataloging departments stay as close as possible to strict copy cataloging because doing so has been found to bring about a large increase in the productivity of cataloging staff.

Where do outside records come from? Where can they be found? Two facets of the cataloging process come into play here: centralized cataloging and shared cataloging. *Centralized cataloging* describes the situation in which cataloging records are prepared by one agency and made available to subscribers; *shared cataloging* describes the situation in which cataloging records are contributed by two or more libraries or agencies to a central database and made generally available.

In the history of cataloging in the United States, the Library of Congress (LC) has played a major role in both centralized and shared cataloging. Beginning with the Library's printed card service which began in 1902 (and which, for many years, simply amounted to distributing duplicates of catalog cards prepared by its own staff for its own use), libraries around the country have made use of LC cataloging records or data in their own catalogs.

By the middle of the 1950s, even LC could not keep up with its current cataloging load, so it began welcoming cataloging records prepared by other major libraries. It used these records to supplement its own cataloging and also made them available to other libraries. Shared cataloging has been a major force in American cataloging ever since.

Besides shared bibliographic records, there is another kind of cataloging information that the library community benefits from sharing. This is name and subject authority data. As discussed in chapter 8, the Library of Congress has been making its subject authority list available since early in the twentieth century, through publishing *Library of Congress Subject Headings* (LCSH). In 1986, LCSH became available in machine-readable form, first on magnetic tape as the *Subject Authorities*, and later also on CD-ROM as *CDMARC Subjects*. In 1974, the Library of Congress began issuing its name authority records, first serially in book form,[1] then on microfiche, and finally on magnetic tape as the *Name Authorities* and on CD-ROM as *CDMARC Names*. Currently, the authorities databases are accessible from the library's website (http://authorities.loc.gov), and as part of Cataloger's Desktop and Classification Web, both of which are online tools developed and maintained by the Library of Congress.

At first, LC was almost the only agency involved in the large-scale collection and distribution of cataloging records. Now, spurred by the use of computer technology to facilitate library operations, there are many others, particularly the cooperatives called *bibliographic networks* or *bibliographic utilities*.

Bibliographic utilities are agencies with large cataloging databases that provide a wide range of bibliographic services to members or subscribers. Some are networks in which members contribute their original cataloging records to be shared with other members. There are also many commercial and government-supported processing centers that provide pre-cataloged books and other resources to libraries. Some of them create their own cataloging records; others adapt cataloging copy and either make it directly available to libraries or use it in their own products. Such processing centers offer a variety of services often tailored to individual libraries' needs. Many provide cataloging data to be integrated into on-line catalogs of member libraries, along with library materials ready to circulate.

MAJOR SOURCES OF CATALOGING COPY

Cataloging records, both bibliographic records and authority records, are available through subscriptions offered by the Library of Congress, and through bibliographic utilities. These records are also searchable for free on LC's websites: Library of Congress Online Catalog (http://catalog.loc.gov) for bibliographic records and *Library of Congress Authorities* (http://authorities.loc.gov) for authority records.

The Library of Congress

The Library of Congress has a long history of making cataloging data available (through several different vehicles) under the direction of the Cataloging Distribution Service (CDS, formerly the Card Distribution Service). In 1942, LC began publishing *The Library of Congress Catalog: A Cumulative Catalog of Books Represented by Library of Congress Printed Cards*, which made available, en masse, the author or main entry cataloging records of the vast holdings of the Library. In 1953, the title was changed to *National Union Catalog (NUC)*, and the scope was enlarged to include cataloging records of contributing North American libraries with holdings information for many items. In 1983, the Library of Congress discontinued the print version of *NUC* and began issuing it on microfiche.

Since March 1969, LC has been distributing cataloging data in machine-readable form, coded according to the MARC format, for most currently cataloged monographs. Magnetic tapes containing these records were distributed to subscribers weekly. Libraries that have the necessary computer facilities can load data to local catalog databases, or can use the tapes for various technical services functions.

Currently, the MARC Distribution Service (MDS), a part of CDS, offers a service in which MARC bibliographic and authority records in hundreds of languages (including non-Roman alphabet languages in their original scripts) are available through subscription. These records encompass a variety of resource types, including books, serials, electronic resources, maps, music, and visual materials. They can be transmitted via FTP (File Transfer Protocol), the protocol for exchanging files over the Internet.

Program for Cooperative Cataloging (PCC)

An important component of the cooperative cataloging activities worldwide is the Program for Cooperative Cataloging (PCC), which is "an international cooperative effort aimed at expanding access to library collections by providing useful, timely, and cost-effective cataloging that meets mutually accepted standards of libraries around the world."[2] PCC, an initiative of the Cooperative Cataloging Council (CCC), began work in 1992. Currently, PCC has four components:

NACO: the name authority cooperative
SACO: the subject authority cooperative
BIBCO: the monographic bibliographic record program
CONSER: the cooperative online serials program

Member libraries contribute to the various programs by creating authority and bibliographic records based on mutually agreed-upon standards and submitting them to the Library of Congress, which coordinates the activities of PCC. The Library of Congress also provides training and documentation for such activities. The resulting authority records are made available through the authority databases maintained by the Library of Congress and the bibliographic records are made available through the Library of Congress Online Catalog and OCLC's WorldCat.

Cataloging-in-Publication (CIP)

The Library of Congress established the Cataloging-in-Publication (CIP) program in 1971, with the objective of including cataloging data for a publication inside the publication itself. The program represents a cooperative effort between the Library of Congress and publishers, with the majority of American trade publishers participating. Selected federal government documents are also included. Publishers submit galleys of their books to the CIP Office at LC, where the material is processed through regular cataloging channels. LC cataloging staff members supply the data that require professional decisions: main entry, title proper, series statement, descriptive notes, subject headings, added entries, and Library of Congress and Dewey Decimal Classification numbers. For children's materials, a summary and alternative subject headings are also provided, as are National Library of Medicine subject headings and class numbers for medical books. The CIP information is then returned to the publisher for inclusion in the resource itself. For books, for example, the CIP information appears on the verso of the title page. Librarians or library assistants working with the item in hand can then prepare a complete cataloging record by filling in whatever else is needed, such as other title information, edition, publication information, physical description, and local call number.

Bibliographic Utilities

Over the last four decades, bibliographic utilities have been playing an increasingly larger role in distributing cataloging data. A bibliographic utility is an organization that offers bibliographic resources and services to subscribing libraries at much lower cost than to prepare the same records in house.

Most of the bibliographic utilities began as cooperative arrangements among small groups of participating libraries. Some of them have become enormous operations involving many libraries and have extended their services beyond the United States. Examples of bibliographic utilities include OCLC, begun as the Ohio College Library Center and later expanded to serve libraries in the United States and abroad, and RLIN (pronounced Arlin, the Research Libraries Information Network), begun in 1967 at Stanford University. WLN (the Western Library Network) began as the Washington Library Network serving libraries in the state of Washington and later expanded to serve many libraries outside the state.

OCLC (Online Computer Library Center)

Among the utilities, OCLC is the largest in scale and service. In 2007, its WorldCat (a union catalog of MARC records contributed by member libraries, including LC MARC records) totaled over 85 million records. It affords an apt example of what a bibliographic utility can do for member libraries.

OCLC was founded by Frederick G. Kilgour in 1967 as a consortium of forty-nine academic libraries in the state of Ohio. Its principal objectives were resource sharing and reduction of per-unit library costs.[3] It began operation in 1971 with its first subsystem, cataloging. Other subsystems, including serials control, online acquisitions, and online interlibrary loan requests, were implemented as time went on. Since 1973, access to its union catalog and services has been extended to libraries in states outside of Ohio and eventually abroad, an important step toward making OCLC the largest online bibliographic network in the world. To reflect its expanded scope, the name Ohio College Library Center was changed to OCLC Online Computer Library Center in 1977. OCLC Pacific was formed in 1976 to provide training and support to west coast OCLC members, and in 1999 OCLC Pacific merged with WLN. The result was the OCLC/WLN Pacific Northwest Service Center, now called OCLC Western.

OCLC's cataloging subsystem consists of an online union catalog set up as a shared cataloging operation. Early use of the network leaned heavily toward off-line catalog card production using MARC tapes from the Library of Congress. Now, libraries with proper equipment can download or import OCLC records directly to their own online catalog.

Since 1985, UK (United Kingdom) MARC records have also been incorporated into WorldCat. The LC Name Authority File was loaded as a separate file in 1984; and in 1987, the LC Subject Authority File was also added. These authority files are kept current as new and corrected data are received. With millions of bibliographic records and a large number of authority records available online, member libraries have been able to reduce cataloging costs considerably.

An important feature of WorldCat is that each bibliographic record has corresponding holdings records, giving each library's holdings information. As of 2007, WorldCat contains more than 85 million bibliographic records with over one billion holdings records in hundreds of languages for a wide range of library materials, including stone tablets to electronic books, wax recordings to MP3s, DVDs, and websites.

In 2005, OCLC launched its OCLC Open WorldCat program, making the records in WorldCat visible and freely accessible to Web users through popular Internet search sites such as Yahoo! and Google. In early 2006, OCLC incorporated the RLG (see below under Other Networks and Services) union catalog containing more than 48 million titles and more than 150 million holdings records.

Early OCLC cataloging systems allowed retrieval of records by only a limited number of search keys, none of which afforded subject access. Over the years, OCLC has implemented very sophisticated searching options as well as a number of progressively effective systems with enhanced features and capabilities for online cataloging operations. The current cataloging interface is called Connexion, which is based on an Oracle platform for its databases and the Web as its communications platform.

Other Networks and Services

There are a number of other networks and agencies that provide bibliographic services to libraries. Some networks are nationwide or regional. Some serve special types of libraries. A prominent example is RLG[4] which, like OCLC, was a not-for-profit organization. Its membership consisted of over 150 research libraries, archives, museums, and other cultural memory institutions. RLG was founded in 1974 by Columbia, Harvard, and Yale universities and the New York Public Library. One of its products was the RLG Union Catalog, a database containing bibliographic records covering a wide range of subjects and material types in almost 400 languages. Its major clientele consisted of academic and research libraries. Its RLIN21 Web interface offered sophisticated search and navigation capabilities supported by Web browsers. On July 1, 2006, RLG merged with OCLC, and RLG's programs continue to operate, as a new unit of OCLC.

In addition to networks such as OCLC, many commercial companies also offer bibliographic services, supplying completely processed library materials, both print and nonprint, with bibliographic records ready to be downloaded to local library systems. It is a fairly common practice among libraries, particularly small libraries, to outsource their cataloging operations to commercial companies. For example, in 2006 Amazon.com became a participant of the OCLC PromptCat program, whereby libraries receive complete MARC records from OCLC's WorldCat along with materials purchased from the vendor.[5]

ONLINE CATALOGING

Introduction

The focus of this section is the online cataloging environment, a situation in which, first, cataloging records are produced through the medium of large-scale computer-processing equipment and, second, local librarians work directly with such equipment.

In working with online catalogs, reference librarians as well as catalogers and collection development and acquisitions personnel need to know about how cataloging records are coded. For reference librarians, such knowledge is an important factor in effectiveness when using the catalog as a retrieval tool.

Even with the computer playing a significant role in the cataloging operations, the intellectual part of the cataloging process is still largely performed by human catalogers and is completed before the computer plays its part. This is true no matter how little fully original cataloging is done, because cataloging copy has to be screened and often altered before it can be used.

Online Cataloging Activities

The availability of facilities for the online processing of cataloging records has proven to be extremely helpful to libraries, not only in terms of catalog cost savings but also in terms of reducing the time between an order request and appearance of the purchased item on the shelves. The following discussion describes some of the processes involved in online cataloging.

Searching

For catalogers, the main purpose of searching is to ascertain whether there is a record in the database that can serve as cataloging copy. The most common search keys used in this regard are name, title, name-title, subject heading, LC control number, ISBN, ISSN, and a special control number in the database. These are elements that appear in cataloging records. The last, the special control number, is unique to a given record barring keying mistakes. Using the others will frequently call up more than one record, because the computer will respond with all the records containing the same search key. In such a case, the system displays brief descriptions, and the searcher then decides which particular record is to be displayed in full.

Once it is ascertained that a particular record is in the database, that record can then be used as needed. For cataloging, the next step is to compare the record with the item being cataloged. If their descriptions are a full match, the record then can be processed and downloaded for local use. However, if the record varies in certain details from what fits the item being cataloged, or if it differs from local cataloging norms, it can be modified to suit the item. The modifying process is called *editing*.

Editing

Editing can be performed online. One great advantage of online cataloging is its instant feedback. In editing, changes are made directly on the screen, and the modified or edited record will be shown instantly, allowing the cataloger to ensure that all necessary modifications have been made.

There are three basic editing operations, substituting, inserting, and deleting. When a data element found in cataloging copy is inappropriate, more suitable data may be substituted for it. An example is copying pertinent data, such as a valid name heading, from the authority file to the bibliographic record in hand. When additional information elements are required, they can be inserted; conversely, unwanted characters can be deleted.

Deriving Records

Frequently, there may be a record in the database for the same work but in a different format from the item being catalogued. For example, the searcher may locate a record created for a book in the database that matches the item being cataloged but that is in microform or electronic form. The source record can then be adapted by editing the details with regard to physical description and adding appropriate notes to fit the item in hand.

Inputting Cataloging Records

To store original cataloging data in machine-readable form in a database, records must be input in coded form. When there is no record in the database that can be used as a cataloging copy for the item in hand, the cataloger creates an original cataloging record, adding all additional data and tags called for in the MARC format. This newly created record is then input into the database. The inputting process is made relatively easy in online cataloging systems because a MARC worksheet or workform showing the most frequently used field tags needed in a typical record is displayed on the screen. Cataloging data are then entered in the appropriate fields.

Downloading and Transporting Records

After records have been created and verified, the next step is to transport them to the local system. For members of a cooperative such as OCLC, records can be efficiently exported to local systems via the Internet. Because the online systems in different libraries are likely to differ in system requirements and needed protocols, some adjustments may be needed before imported records can be used.

CONVERSION AND MAINTENANCE OF CATALOGING RECORDS

Before online catalogs came into being, the catalogs of most libraries were in card form, with some card sets produced in-house and some imported. With the advent of the online age, it was naturally considered desirable that the information on those cards be made machine-readable. Thus, countless library staff hours were spent on what is sometimes called *retrospective conversion*. The term *conversion* refers to the process of converting manually produced records to MARC records, a necessary step in a library's transition from the manual to the automated cataloging environment and in implementing an online catalog. Conversion involves coding data in cataloging records according to the MARC formats. It is a time-consuming task, in part because, during conversion, it is desirable to update old records, particularly their access points, to reflect current practice. As of this writing, most libraries have completed the conversion process; some may still have small portions of the catalog not completely converted. Fortunately, many bibliographic utilities and commercial companies offer retrospective conversion services. Use of such services is often the most cost-effective means for a library to effect its transition to an online catalog.

Maintenance refers to the process of correcting errors and keeping cataloging records compatible with current standards. Maintenance is an ongoing and highly labor-intensive process. For example, when a heading is revised, the authority record and all bibliographic records bearing the heading should be revised to conform to the current heading. Almost always, a changed heading requires changes in cross references as well. In parallel, when new headings are established, cross references are often required to link them to existing headings. In systems where authority files are integrated or linked with the bibliographic file, many heading changes can be accomplished automatically through making the change in the appropriate authority file. In systems with separate authority files, all changes must be made record by record. Record-by-record changes are sometimes necessary even with linked authority files. For instance, when the subject heading *Ophthalmoscope and ophthalmoscopy* is changed to two separate headings, it takes at least looking at the record and often at the item itself to know whether *Ophthalmoscopes* or *Ophthalmoscopy* (or both) should be assigned to each bibliographic record being affected by the change.

Maintenance is a never-ending process because a catalog is dynamic; it not only grows but changes as cataloging standards are refined and the technology of cataloging is improved. The most important objective in catalog maintenance is ensuring the quality of the catalog so that it can best serve the needs of its users. A secondary goal is to contain cataloging costs.

CONCLUSION

Library catalogs have come a long way from ancient inventory lists to the sophisticated online catalogs of today. Physical changes are the most obvious, from scroll and book catalogs to card catalogs, and from microform catalogs to online catalogs. Standards for preparing catalog entries have also changed, more through evolutionary processes than by large-scale, drastic leaps. While the ways people can approach a catalog or other information sources have changed dramatically, the primary function of a catalog or catalog-like instrument remains the same: to assist users in identifying, verifying, and retrieving useful information. To this end, the essence of a catalog record—the elements of bibliographic information that have proven useful over the years—has shown surprisingly little change in spite of how much technological advances have altered the way cataloging operations are performed and cataloging data are maintained. There is no question that the vast stores of recorded information now available virtually worldwide—in much more varied venues than traditional libraries—require a maximally effective system of resource description and retrieval mechanisms if they are to fulfill their information-bearing potential. What has worked fairly well for libraries may provide design clues for improved retrieval in a larger environment; it may even be that the library sector of the information world can be helpful in this regard. But for those engaged in the field of cataloging and classification, there remains a particular and very important question: How can we make the best use of our new technological powers to maintain the catalog in such a way that it can continue to serve the diverse needs of users through a wide range of systems presently operating, while at the same time remaining viable and adaptable to systems in the future, some of which have yet to be developed? Herein lies the challenge ahead.

NOTES

1. Library of Congress, *Library of Congress Name Headings with References* (Washington, D.C.: Library of Congress, 1974–1983).

2. "Program for Cooperative Cataloging," www.loc.gov/catdir/pcc/2001pcc.html (2 Mar. 2007).

3. Frederick G. Kilgour, "Ohio College Library Center," in *Encyclopedia of Library and Information Science* (New York: Marcel Dekker, 1977), v. 20, pp. 346–47.

4. OCLC/RLG, www.rlg.org/ (25 Feb. 2007).

5. *OCLC Abstracts* 9, no. 36 (Sept. 18, 2006), www5.oclc.org/downloads/design/abstracts/ (25 Feb. 2007).

APPENDIX A
MARC Bibliographic Records

INDEXING AND ABSTRACTING IN THEORY AND PRACTICE. 2003

000	00665cam 2200217 a 4500
001	2003501172
003	DLC
005	20031217092525.0
008	030321s2003 enka b 001 0 eng
010	$a2003501172
020	$a1856044823
040	$aDLC$cDLC$dDLC
050 00	$aZ695.9$b.L33 2003
100 1	$aLancaster, F. Wilfrid$q(Frederick Wilfrid),$d1933-
245 10	$aIndexing and abstracting in theory and practice / $cF.W. Lancaster.
250	$a3rd ed.
260	$aLondon :$bFacet Pub.,$c2003.
300	$axix, 451 p. :$bill. ;$c24 cm.
504	$aIncludes bibliographical references (p. 394-436) and index.
650 0	$aIndexing.
650 0	$aAbstracting.

ONLINE JOURNAL OF SPACE COMMUNICATION [ELECTRONIC JOURNAL]. 2002–

000	01507cas 2200385 a 4500
001	2002212979
003	DLC
005	20051015084425.0
006	m d
007	cr cnu
008	021009c20029999ohuqr1pss 0 a0eng
010	$a 2002212979
022 0	$a1542-0639
035	$a(OCoLC)ocm50756672

037    $bInstitute for Telecommunication Studies, 235 RTV
       Ohio University, Athens, Ohio 45701$cfree
040    $aDLC$cDLC$dOCoLC$dCU-S$dCSmarS
042    $ansdp$alc
050 00 $aTK5104
082 10 $a621$213
210 0 $aOnline j. space commun.
222 0 $aOnline journal of space communication
245 00 $aOnline journal of space communication$h[electronic
       resource].
260    $aAthens, OH :$bInstitute for Telecommunications
       Studies, Ohio University,$c2002-
310    $aFour times a year
362 0 $aIssue no. 1 (Apr. 2002)-
500    $aTitle from caption (viewed Oct. 7, 2002).
500    $aLatest issue consulted: Issue no. 2 (July 2002).
538    $aMode of access: World Wide Web.
550    $aA project of the Society of Satellite Professionals
       International, hosted by: the Institute for
       Telecommunications Studies, Ohio University.
650 0 $aArtificial satellites in telecommunication$vPeriodicals.
710 2 $aSociety of Satellite Professionals International.
710 2 $aOhio University.$bInstitute for Telecommunications
       Studies.
850    $aDLC
856 40 $uhttp://bibpurl.oclc.org/web/10568$uhttp://
       satjournal.tcom.ohiou.edu/

UNIVERSAL MAP (FIRM). *LEXINGTON, KENTUCKY, STREET MAP* [MAP]. 2006?

000   01386cem 2200337 a 4500
001   2006458616
003   DLC
005   20060905161002.0
007   aj canzn
008   060905s2006 miu a 1 eng
010    $a 2006458616
020    $a0762546727
034 1 aab31000
034 1 aab150000
040    $aDLC$cDLC
050 00 $aG3954.L4 2006$b.U51
052    $a3954$bL4

110 2 $aUniversal Map (Firm)
245 10 $aLexington, Kentucky, street map :$bincluding Berea, Burgin, Curdsville, Cynthiana, . . . & Winchester ; featuring airports, cemeteries, Fayette County vicinity map, . . . zip code boundaries /$cUniversalMAP.
246 3 $aUniversalMAP Lexington, Kentucky, street map
255      $aScale [ca. 1:31,000].
255      $aScale [ca. 1:150,000].
260      $aWilliamston, MI :$bUniversalMAP,$c[2006?]
300      $a2 maps :$bboth sides, col. ;$c60 x 57 cm. and 79 x 59 cm., folded to 24 x 11 cm.
500      $aTitle from panel.
500      $aAt head of title: UniversalMAP.
500      $aIncludes indexes, ancillary map of Central Lexington, and inset of "Major highway systems of Kentucky."
505 0 $aLexington, Kentucky [Lexington metropolitan area] — Lexington, Kentucky [Lexington region road map].
650 0 $aRoads$zKentucky$zLexington region$vMaps.
651 0 $aLexington (Ky.)$vMaps.
651 0 $aLexington Metropolitan Area (Ky.)$vMaps.

SORCE [ELECTRONIC RESOURCE]. 2003

000   01137cmm 2200325 a 4500
001   2005567624
         003DLC
005   20051028095702.0
007   co |||||||||||
008   030723s2003 mdu m eng d
010      $a 2005567624
040      $aIMF$cIMF$dDLC
042      $alccopycat
050 00 $aQC911
082 10 $a523.7$214
086 1 $aSFTW NAS 1.86:S 04/CD
245 00 $aSORCE$h[electronic resource] :$bsolar radiation and climate experiment.
246 3 $aSolar radiation and climate experiment
260      $a[Greenbelt, Md. :$bNASA,$c2003]
300      $a1 computer optical disc :$bsd., col. ;$c4 3/4 in.
538      $aSystem requirements: Any computer capable of running Adobe Acrobat Reader.
500      $aTitle from disc label.

500	$aAccompanying material may vary.
500	$a"NP-2003-1-525-GSFC."
610 20	$aGoddard Space Flight Center$vInteractive multimedia.
650 0	$aSolar radiation$xMeasurement$vInteractive multimedia.
650 0	$aArtificial satellites$zSun$vInteractive multimedia.
651 0	$aSun$vInteractive multimedia.
710 2	$aGoddard Space Flight Center.
753	$aIBM

DOWN [SOUND RECORDING]. 2005

000	00776cjm 22002173a 4500
001	2006587011
003	DLC
005	20060912092039.0
007	sd fsngnnmmned
008	060911s2005 xx ppn| | eng
010	$a 2006587011
024 1	$a642973514421
040	$aDLC$cDLC
050 00	$aSDB 48334
245 00	$aDown$h[sound recording].
260	$a[S.l.] :$bCentralized Music,$c[2005]
300	$a1 sound disc :$bdigital ;$c4 3/4 in.
511 0	$aPerformed by the group Drag of Gravity.
500	$aCompact disc.
505 0	$aThe threshold — The door — Freaks — Discontent — Miserable lies — First impressions — 120 — One more time — Anomaly — sympathy note — Anything but you — [symbol] — Thanks, for nothing — So help me.
500	$aBrief record.

AMERICAN VARIETY STAGE [ELECTRONIC RESOURCE]. 1996–

000	02127cmm 2200397 a 4500
001	96802670
003	DLC
005	20060123173713.0
008	961205m19969999dcu m eng
010	$a 96802670
040	$aDLC$cDLC$dDLC

043        $an-us—
050 00 $aPN1968.U5
082 10 $a793.8$212
245 00 $aAmerican variety stage$h[electronic resource]
           :$bvaudeville and popular entertainment, 1870-1920 /
           $cAmerican Memory, Library of Congress.
246 30 $aVaudeville and popular entertainment, 1870-1920
256        $aComputer data.
260        $a[Washington, D.C. :$bLibrary of Congress],$c1996-
538        $aSystem requirements: World Wide Web (WWW)
           browser software.
538        $aMode of access: Internet.
500        $aTitle from title screen dated Oct. 31, 1996.
500        $a"Groups of theater posters and sound recordings will
           be added to this anthology in the future."
520        $aMultimedia collection containing digitized versions of
           selected Library of Congress holdings. Represents
           diverse forms of popular entertainment, especially
           vaudeville, that thrived from 1870-1920. Includes 334
           English and Yiddish language playscripts, 146 theater
           playbills and programs, sixty-one motion pictures, and
           143 photographs and twenty-nine memorabilia items
           documenting the life and career of Harry Houdini.
505 1 $aHoudini — Theater playbills and programs — Sound
           recordings (coming soon) — Motion pictures — English
           playscripts — Yiddish playscripts
600 10 $aHoudini, Harry,$d1874-1926.
650 0 $aVaudeville$zUnited States$xHistory$y20th century.
650 0 $aVaudeville$zUnited States$xHistory$y19th century.
650 0 $aVaudeville$zUnited States$xFilm catalogs.
650 0 $aAmerican drama$y20th century.
650 0 $aAmerican drama$y19th century.
650 0 $aYiddish drama$z20th century.
650 0 $aYiddish drama$z19th century.
650 0 $aTheater programs$zUnited States.
650 0 $aPlaybills$zUnited States.
710 2 $aLibrary of Congress.$bNational Digital Library
           Program.
856 7 $uhttp://hdl.loc.gov/loc.gdc/collgdc.gc000048$2http

The following group of records represents various manifestations and
transformations of the same work, Jane Austen's *Pride and Prejudice*. The
records are from OCLC's WorldCat, reproduced with permission from
OCLC (Online Computer Library Center).

LCCN: 2005049349

Pride and prejudice / Jane Austen ; edited with an introduction and notes by Vivien Jones ; with the original Penguin classics introduction by Tony Tanner. 2005. (See figure A-1.)

Books	▼	Rec stat	p	Entered	20050713		Replaced	20060331082†20.7
Type	a	ELvl		Srce		Audn	Ctrl	Lang	eng
BLvl	m	Form		Conf	0	Biog	MRec	Ctry	nyu
		Cont	b	GPub		LitF	1	Indx	0
Desc	a	Ills		Fest	0	DtSt	r	Dates	2005 , 1813

010			2005049349
040			DLC ǂc DLC ǂd BAKER ǂd IBI
020			0143036238 (pbk.)
029	1		NLGGC ǂb 282914870
043			e-uk-en
050	0	0	PR4034 ǂb .P7 2005b
082	0	0	823/.7 ǂ2 22
090			ǂb
049			OCLC
100	1		Austen, Jane, ǂd 1775-1817.
245	1	0	Pride and prejudice / ǂc Jane Austen ; edited with an introduction and notes by Vivien Jones ; with the original Penguin classics introduction by Tony Tanner.
260			New York : ǂb Penguin Books, ǂc 2005, c1813.
300			392 p. ; ǂc 20 cm.
504			Includes bibliographical references.
650		0	Young women ǂv Fiction.
650		0	Social classes ǂv Fiction.
650		0	Courtship ǂv Fiction.
650		0	Sisters ǂv Fiction.
651		0	England ǂv Fiction.
655		7	Domestic fiction. ǂ2 lcsh
655		7	Love stories. ǂ2 gsafd
700	1		Jones, Vivien, ǂd 1952-
938			Baker & Taylor ǂb BKTY ǂc 10.00 ǂd 7.50 ǂi 0143036238 ǂn 0006448182 ǂs active

FIGURE A-1   MARC record from OCLC, LCCN 2005049349

LCCN: 2003102755

Pride and prejudice / Jane Austen ; with an introduction and notes by Carol Howard. 2003. (See figure A-2.)

Books	▼	Rec stat	c	Entered	20030220	Replaced	20041208095636.62
Type	a	ELvl		Srce		Audn		Ctrl		Lang	eng
BLvl	m	Form		Conf	0	Biog		MRec		Ctry	nyu
		Cont	b	GPub		LitF	1	Indx	0		
Desc	a	Ills		Fest	0	DtSt	r	Dates	2003	,	1813

010			2003102755
040			DLC ǂc DLC ǂd NZW
020			1593080204
043			e-uk-en
050	0	0	PR4034 ǂb .P7 2003c
082	0	0	823/.7 ǂ2 22
090			ǂb
049			OCLC
100	1		Austen, Jane, ǂd 1775-1817.
245	1	0	Pride and prejudice / ǂc Jane Austen ; with an introduction and notes by Carol Howard.
260			New York : ǂb Barnes & Noble Classics, ǂc c2003.
300			xxxvi, 376 p. ; ǂc 18 cm.
440		0	Barnes & Noble classics
504			Includes bibliographical references (p. [375]-376).
505	0		The world of Jane Austen and Pride and prejudice — Introduction — Pride and prejudice — Endnotes — Inspired by Pride and prejudice — Comments and questions — For further reading.
650		0	Social classes ǂv Fiction.
650		0	Young women ǂv Fiction.
650		0	Courtship ǂv Fiction.
650		0	Sisters ǂv Fiction.
651		0	England ǂv Fiction.
655		7	Domestic fiction. ǂ2 lcsh
655		7	Love stories. ǂ2 gsafd
856	4	2	ǂ3 Publisher description ǂu http://www.loc.gov/catdir/description/ste051/2003102755.html

FIGURE A-2   MARC record from OCLC, LCCN 2003102755

LCCN: 2001098528

Jane Austen's pride and prejudice / text by William Blanchard; illustrations by Richard Fortunato. 2002. (See figure A-3.)

Books			▼	Rec stat	c	Entered	20011115		Replaced	20040514265057.0	
Type	a	ELvl		Srce		Audn		Ctrl		Lang	eng
BLvl	m	Form		Cont	0	Biog		MRec		Ctry	nju
		Cont	b		GPub		LitF	0	Indx	0	
Desc	a	Ills	a		Fest	0	DtSt	s	Dates	2002	,

010			2001098528
040			DLC ǂc DLC
020			0878910425
050	0	0	PR4034.P72 ǂb B49 2002
082	0	0	823/.7 ǂ2 21
090			ǂb
049			OCLC
100	1		Blanchard, William.
245	1	0	Jane Austen's pride and prejudice / ǂc text by William Blanchard ; illustrations by Richard Fortunato.
246	1	8	Pride and prejudice
260			Piscataway, N.J. : ǂb Research & Education Association, ǂc c2002.
300			v, 86, [1] p. : ǂb ill. ; ǂc 21 cm.
440		0	MAXnotes
504			Includes bibliographical references (p. [87]).
600	1	0	Austen, Jane, ǂd 1775-1817. ǂt Pride and prejudice ǂx Examinations ǂv Study guides.

FIGURE A-3   MARC record from OCLC, LCCN 2001098528

LCCN: 2003096589

The annotated Pride and prejudice / Jane Austen ; annotated and edited, with an introduction, by David M. Shapard. 2004. (See figure A-4.)

Books		▼	Rec stat	c	Entered	20040315		Replaced	20050809011322.7
Type	a	ELvl		Srce		Audn		Ctrl		Lang	eng
BLvl	m	Form		Cont	0	Biog		MRec		Ctry	nyu
		Cont	b	GPub		LitF	1	Indx	1		
Desc	a	Ills	a b	Fest	0	DtSt	s	Dates	2004	,	

010			2003096589
040			DLC +c DLC +d QBX +d OCLCQ +d BAKER
020			0974505307 (alk. paper)
037			1229225 +b QBI
043			e-uk-en
060	0	0	PR4034 +b .P7 2004
082	0	0	823/.7 +2 22
090			+b
049			OCLC
100	1		Austen, Jane, +d 1775–1817.
240	1	0	Pride and prejudice
245	1	4	The annotated Pride and prejudice / +c Jane Austen ; annotated and edited, with an introduction, by David M. Shapard.
246	1	8	Annotated Pride & prejudice
260			Delmar, NY : +b Pheasant Books, +c c2004.
300			xxviii, 739 p. : +b ill., maps ; +c 24 cm.
504			Includes bibliographical references (p. 717–736) and index.
600	1	0	Austen, Jane, +d 1775–1817. +t Pride and prejudice.
650		0	Social classes +v Fiction.
650		0	Young women +v Fiction.
650		0	Courtship +v Fiction.
650		0	Sisters +v Fiction.
651		0	England +v Fiction.
655		7	Domestic fiction. +2 lcsh
655		7	Love stories. +2 gsafd
700	1		Shapard, David M.
938			Quality Books, Inc. +b QUAL +n qbi04500140
938			Baker & Taylor +b BKTY +c 29.95 +d 22.46 +i 0974505307 +n 0004354999 +s active +z B&T Title: The Annotated Pride & Prejudice

FIGURE A-4   MARC record from OCLC, LCCN 2003096589

#51541621

Pride and prejudice [text (large print)] / Jane Austen. 2000. (See figure A-5.)

Books		Rec stat	c	Entered	20030129		Replaced	20050101225657.20
Type	a	ELvl	I	Srce	d	Audn	Ctrl	Lang	eng
BLvl	m	Form	d	Conf	0	Biog	MRec	Ctry	cau
		Cont		GPub		LitF	f	Indx	0
Desc	a	Ills		Fest	0	DtSt	s	Dates	2000 ,

040			SJM ǂc SJM ǂd OCLCQ
020			0758319282
043			e-uk-en
090			PR4034 ǂb .P7 2000
090			ǂb
049			OCLC
100	1		Austen, Jane, ǂd 1775-1817.
245	1	0	Pride and prejudice ǂh [text (large print)] / ǂc Jane Austen.
250			[Large print ed.].
260			San Diego, Calif. : ǂb Huge Print Press, ǂc 2000.
300			272 p. ; ǂc 29 cm.
500			Date of publication from phone conversation with publisher, 7/02.
500			Printed in 16 point type.
651		0	England ǂv Fiction.
650		0	Social classes ǂv Fiction.
650		0	Young women ǂv Fiction.
650		0	Courtship ǂv Fiction.
650		0	Sisters ǂv Fiction.
650		0	Large type books.

FIGURE A-5   MARC record from OCLC, #51541621

#61287973

Orgueil et préjugés / Jane Austen. [2003]. (See figure A-6.)

| Books | | ▼ | Rec stat | c | Entered | 20050818 | | Replaced | 20050818162559.4 |

Type	a	ELvl	I	Srce	d	Audn		Ctrl		Lang	fre
BLvl	m	Form		Conf	0	Biog		MRec		Ctry	fr
		Cont		GPub		LitF	1	Indx	0		
Desc	a	Ills		Fest	0	DtSt	t	Dates	2003	,	1980

040			CGP ǂc CGP ǂd CGP
020			2264023821
041	1		fre ǂh eng
043			e-uk-en
090			ǂb
049			OCLC
100	1		Austen, Jane, ǂd 1775-1817.
240	1	0	Pride and prejudice. ǂl French
245	1	0	Orgueil et préjugés / ǂc Jane Austen ; traduit de l'anglais par V. Leconte et Ch. Pressoir ; préface de Virginia Woolf, traduite de l'anglais par Denise Getzler ; note biographique de Jacques Roubaud.
260			Paris : ǂb Christian Bourgois Éditeur, ǂc [2003], c1979.
300			379 p. ; ǂc 19 cm.
440		0	Éditions ; ǂv 10/18
650		0	Young women ǂz England ǂv Fiction.
650		0	Courtship ǂz England ǂv Fiction.

FIGURE A-6 MARC record from OCLC, #61287973

#63117271

Pride and prejudice [videorecording]. 2005. (See figure A-7.)

Visual Materials		▼	Rec stat	n	Entered	20060120		Replaced	20060120104733.5	
Type	g	ELvl	I	Srce	d	Audn	g	Ctrl		Lang	eng
BLvl	m	Form		GPub		Time	3 0 0	MRec		Ctry	enk
Desc	a	TMat	v	Tech	l	DtSt	s	Dates	2006	,	

040			MZF ǂc MZF
020			0767038266 : ǂc $49.99
020			0767038274 (v. 1)
020			0767038282 (v. 2)
028	4	2	AAE-70254–AAE-72066 ǂb A & E Home Video
090			PN1997 ǂb .P75 2005
090			ǂb
049			OCLC
245	0	0	Pride and prejudice ǂh [videorecording] / ǂc a co-production of BBC Television and BBC Worldwide Americas, Inc. in association with A & E Network.
250			Special ed. ; widescreen.
260			[London] : ǂb British Broadcasting Corporation ; ǂa New York : ǂb A & E Home Video ; ǂa New York : ǂb Distributed by New Video, ǂc c2005.
300			2 videodiscs (300 min.) : ǂb sd., col. ; ǂc 4 3/4 in.
500			Not rated.
500			Based on the novel by Jane Austen.
500			Originally produced for 1995 miniseries television broadcast.
500			Booklet (7 p.) includes list of chapters, and cast and crew reminiscences.
500			Dolby, digital, stereo.
546			Closed-captioned.
500			Bonus features exclusive to this edition listed on containers.
508			Producer, Sue Birtwistle ; director, Simon Langton ; dramatized by Andrew Davies ; photography, John Kenway ; film editor, Peter Coulson ; music, Carl Davis.
511	1		Colin Firth, Jennifer Ehle, Allison [i.e. Alison] Steadman, Benjamin Whitrow, Susannah Harker, Crispin Bonham-Carter, Anna Chancellor, Julia Sawalha, David Bamber, David Bark-Jones.
520			The story of lively and rebellious Elizabeth, one of five unmarried daughters living in the countryside of 19th century England, in a world where an advantageous marriage is a woman's sole occupation.
538			DVD.
650		0	Feature films.
650		0	DVD-Video discs.
600	1	0	Austen, Jane, ǂd 1775-1817 ǂv Film and video adaptations.
650		0	Young women ǂz England ǂv Drama.
650		0	Courtship ǂz England ǂv Drama.
650		0	Television adaptations.
650		0	Television mini-series.
651		0	England ǂx Social life and customs ǂy 19th century ǂv Drama.
650		0	Video recordings for the hearing impaired.
650		0	Love stories.
700	1		Firth, Colin, ǂd 1960-
700	1		Ehle, Jennifer, ǂd 1969-
700	1		Steadman, Alison, ǂd 1946-
700	1		Whitrow, Benjamin.
700	1		Harker, Susannah.
700	1		Bonham-Carter, Crispin.
700	1		Chancellor, Anna.
700	1		Sawalha, Julia, ǂd 1968-
700	1		Bamber, David.
700	1		Langton, Simon.
700	1		Austen, Jane, ǂd 1775-1817. ǂt Pride and prejudice.
710	2		Arts and Entertainment Network.
710	2		British Broadcasting Corporation.
710	2		A & E Home Video (Firm)
710	2		New Video Group.

FIGURE A-7   MARC record from OCLC, #63117271

#70803445

Pride and prejudice [sound recording]. 2003. (See figure A-8.)

Sound Recordings		Rec stat	n	Entered	20060802		Replaced	20060802094603.6
Type	i	ELvl	I	Srce	d	Audn		Ctrl		Lang	eng
BLvl	m	Form		Comp	nn	AccM		MRec		Ctry	vau
		Part		TrAr							
Desc	a	FMus	n	LTxt	f	DtSt	s	Dates	2002 ,	

007		s ‡b z ‡d u ‡e s ‡f n ‡g z ‡h n ‡i n ‡n d
040		OCD ‡c OCD
020		1598952625
024	3	9781598952629
090		‡b
049		OCLC
100	1	Austen, Jane, ‡d 1775-1817.
245	1 0	Pride and prejudice ‡h [sound recording] / ‡c Jane Austen.
250		Unabridged.
260		Falls Church, VA : ‡b Sound Room ; ‡a Cleveland : ‡b Findaway World, ‡c 2003.
300		1 sound media player (11 hrs.) : ‡b digital ; ‡c 8 x 5 cm. + ‡e earphones + AAA battery.
511	0	Read by Kate Redding.
520		The story of Mrs. Bennett's finding husbands for her five daughters.
538		Issued on Playaway, a dedicated audio media player.
650	0	Courtship ‡z Great Britain ‡v Fiction.
650	0	Family ‡v Fiction.
651	0	England ‡x Social life and customs ‡y 19th century ‡v Fiction.
655	0	Audiobooks.
700	1	Redding, Kate.

FIGURE A-8   MARC record from OCLC, #70803445

#50505644

First impressions [sound recording]. [2002]. (See figure A-9.)

Sound Recordings ▼	Rec stat	c	Entered	20020829		Replaced	20051120231548.2
Type	j	ELvl	l	Srce	d	Audn	Ctrl	Lang	eng
BLvl	m	Form		Comp	mc	AccM	MRec	Ctry	nyu
		Part		TrAr					
Desc	a	FMus	n	LTxt		DtSt	r	Dates	2002 , 1959

007		s ǂb d ǂd f ǂe u ǂf n ǂg g ǂh n ǂi n ǂm e ǂn u
040		JED ǂc JED ǂd ELW
024	1 0	021471903621
028	0 0	19036 ǂb DRG Theatre
028	0 0	A 59933 ǂb Sony
033	0 0	19590322
050	4	M1500.G65 ǂb F57 2002
082	4	782.13
090		ǂb
049		OCLC
100	1	Goldman, Robert.
245	1 0	First impressions ǂh [sound recording] : ǂb the new musical / ǂc music & lyrics by Robert Goldman, Glenn Paxton and George Weiss.
260		[New York] : ǂb DRG Theater : ǂb Manufactured by Sony, ǂc [2002]
300		1 sound disc (53 min.) : ǂb digital, stereo. ; ǂc 4 3/4 in.
306		005315
440	4	The Broadway collector series
500		DRG Theatre: 19036.
500		Sony: A 59933.
500		Compact disc.
500		Based on Jane Austen's Pride and prejudice and the play by Helen Jerome.
511	1	Polly Bergen, Farley Granger, Hermione Gingold; orchestra conducted by Frederick Dvonch.
508		Presented by George Gilbert and Edward Specter Productions, Inc.; produced for records by Goddard Lieberson.
518		Recorded Mar. 22, 1959.
500		Originally released as Columbia Masterworks OS 2014.
500		Program notes by George Dale laid in container.
505	0 0	ǂt Overture — ǂt Five daughters — ǂt I'm me — ǂt Have you heard the news? — ǂt Polka/The assembly dance/A perfect evening — ǂt As long as there's amother — ǂt Love will find out the way — ǂt A gentleman never falls wildly in love — ǂt Fragrant flower — ǂt I feel sorry for the girl — ǂt I suddenly find it agreeable — ǂt This really isn't me — ǂt Wasn't it a simply lovely wedding? — ǂt A house in town — ǂt The heart has won the game — ǂt Dance — ǂt Let's fetch the carriage — ǂt Finale.
650	0	Musicals.
700	1	Paxton, Glenn.
700	1	Weiss, George ǂq (George David)
700	1	Bergen, Polly, ǂd 1930-
700	1	Granger, Farley.
700	1	Gingold, Hermione, ǂd 1897-
700	1	Dvonch, Frederick.
700	1	Jerome, Helen, ǂd 1883-
700	1	Austen, Jane, ǂd 1775-1817. ǂt Pride and prejudice.

FIGURE A-9 MARC record from OCLC, #50505644

#60338843

Pride and prejudice [electronic resource]. 2004. (See figure A-10.)

Sound Recordings	▼	Rec stat	n	Entered	20050510		Replaced	20050630204911.3
Type	i	ELvl	I	Srce	d	Audn	g	Ctrl		Lang	eng
BLvl	m	Form	s	Comp	nn	AccM		MRec		Ctry	vau
		Part		TrAr							
Desc	a	FMus	n	LTxt	f	DtSt	s	Dates	2004	,	

007			s ‡b z ‡d z ‡e u ‡f n ‡g n ‡h n ‡i n ‡m u ‡n u
007			c ‡b r ‡d n ‡e n ‡f a
040			JZ6 ‡c JZ6
050	1	4	PR4034 ‡b .P7
082	0	4	823/.7 ‡2 22
090			‡b
049			OCLC
100	1		Austen, Jane, ‡d 1775-1817.
245	1	0	Pride and prejudice ‡h [electronic resource] / ‡c Jane Austen.
256			Computer data (digital audio).
260			Falls Church, Va. : ‡b Commuter's Library ; ‡a Wayne, N.J. : ‡b distributed by Audible, ‡c 2004.
306			091600
511	0		Narrated by Kate Reading.
500			Digital audio file that can be played back on a portable device or suitably equipped microcomputer.
500			Title supplied by cataloger from distributor web site.
500			Unabridged.
500			Duration: 9:16:00.
520			Intelligent Elizabeth Bennet must overcome her prejudice against the rich and overly proud Mr. Darcy before romance can blossom.
650		0	Social classes ‡v Fiction ‡v Sound recordings.
650		0	Young women ‡v Fiction ‡v Sound recordings.
650		0	Courtship ‡v Fiction ‡v Sound recordings.
650		0	Sisters ‡v Fiction ‡v Sound recordings.
651		0	England ‡x Social life and customs ‡y 19th century ‡v Fiction ‡v Sound recordings.
655		7	Domestic fiction. ‡2 lcsh
655		7	Love stories. ‡2 gsafd
700	1		Reading, Kate. ‡4 nrt
710	2		Commuter's Library (Firm) ‡4 pbl
710	2		Audible, Inc. ‡4 dst

FIGURE A-10   MARC record from OCLC, #60338843

APPENDIX B
MARC Authority Records

PERSONAL NAMES

William A. Katz, 1924–2004

000	00799cz 2200193n 4500
001	n 79092477
003	DLC
005	20060518052008.0
008	800507n| acannaabn |a aaa
010	$an 79092477 $zn 93025121 $zn 97014023
035	$a(OCoLC)oca00324772
040	$aDLC$beng$cDLC$dDLC$dUkOxU$dSdMadT
100 1	$aKatz, William A.,$d1924-2004
400 1	$aKatz, Bill,$d1924-2004
400 1	$aKatz, Willis Armstrong,$d1924-2004
400 1	$aKatz, William,$d1924-2004
670	$aLibrary Buildings Institute, Chicago, 1963.$bProblems in planning library facilities, 1964.
670	$aHis Your library, c1984:$bCIP t.p. (William Katz, SUNY at Albany)
670	$aIntegrating print and digital resources in library collections, 2006:$bprelims. (Dr. William (Bill) Katz; d. Sept. 12, 2004)

Jane Austen, 1775–1817

000	00524cz 2200169n 4500
001	n 79032879
003	DLC
005	20000413070350.0
008	790418n| acannaabn |a aaa
010	$an 79032879
035	$a(OCoLC)oca00266512
040	$aDLC$beng$cDLC$dDLC$dCtY-BR$dOCoLC
100 1	$aAusten, Jane,$d1775-1817

```
400 1    $aOstin, Dzhein,$d1775-1817
400 1    $aAo-ssu-ting,$d1775-1817
400 1    $aAo-ssu-ting, Chien,$d1775-1817
670      $aAo-ssu-ting yen chiu, 1985:$bt.p. (Ao-ssu-ting) p. 367
         (Chien Ao-ssu-ting)
```

Diana, Princess of Wales, 1961–1997

```
000      00794cz 2200205n 4500
001      n 81073496
003      DLC
005      20060206130114.0
008      810716n| acannaabn |a aaa
010      $an 81073496 $zn 82138607
040      $aDLC$cDLC$dDLC
100 0    $aDiana,$cPrincess of Wales,$d1961-1997
400 1    $aSpencer, Diana Frances,$cLady,$d1961-1997
400 0    $aDi,$cLady,$d1961-1997
670      $aDunlop, J. Charles and Diana, a royal romance, c1981
         (subj.)$bp. 6, etc. (Lady Diana Frances Spencer; b. July 1,
         1961)
670      $aLeete-Hodge, L. The Country Life book of the royal
         wedding, 1981:$btable of contents (Diana, Princess of
         Wales)
670      $aCarretier, M.-P. Lady Di chez elle, c1987.
670      $aThe Washington post, Aug. 31, 1997$b(Diana d. Aug.
         31, 1997 from a fatal car accident)
```

H. D. (Hilda Doolittle), 1886–1961

```
000      00830cz 2200217n 4500
001      n 78095822
003      DLC
005      20011122071903.0
008      790124n| acannaabn |a aaa
010      $an 78095822
035      $a(OCoLC)oca00230886
040      $aDLC$beng$cDLC$dDLC$dNBuU$dWaU$dOCoLC
053 0    $aPS3507.O726
100 0    $aH. D.$q(Hilda Doolittle),$d1886-1961
400 1    $aAldington, Hilda Doolittle,$d1886-1961
400 1    $aHelforth, John,$d1886-1961
400 1    $wnna$aDoolittle, Hilda,$d1886-1961
400 1    $aD., H.$q(Hilda Doolittle),$d1886-1961
400 0    $aHD$q(Hilda Doolittle),$d1886-1961
```

670 $aHer Sea garden, 1916.

670 $aContemp. auth., web-version, 10/21/96:$b(Born September 19, 1886, in Bethlehem, Pennsylvania, United States; died of a heart attack, September 27, 1961, in Zurich, Switzerland)

Eleanor Roosevelt, 1884–1962

000	00490cz 2200157n 4500
001	n 79144645
003	DLC
005	19850826130438.3
008	800310n| acannaab |a aaa
010	$an 79144645
040	$aDLC$cDLC$dDLC
100 10	$aRoosevelt, Eleanor,$d1884-1962.
400 10	$wnna$aRoosevelt, Eleanor Roosevelt,$d1884-1962
400 10	$aRoosevelt, Franklin D.,$cMrs.,$d1884-1962
400 10	$aRoosevelt, Anna Eleanor Roosevelt,$d1884-1962
670	$aHer When you grow up to vote, 1932.

Muhammad Ali, 1942–

000	00566cz 2200193n 4500
001	n 79054611
003	DLC
005	19840322000000.0
008	790622n| acannaab |a aaa
010	$an 79054611
040	$aDLC$cDLC
100 10	$aAli, Muhammad,$d1942-
400 10	$aClay, Cassius,$d1942-
400 00	$aCassius X,$d1942-
400 10	$aX, Cassius,$d1942-
400 10	$aAli, Muhammed,$d1942-
400 00	$aMuhammad Ali,$d1942-
670	$aHis I am the greatest! [Phonodisc] 1963.
670	$aKaletsky, R. Ali and me, c1982 (a.e.)$bp. 11 (Cassius Marcellus Clay)

PLACES

Kentucky

000	00663cz 2200205n 4500
001	n 79018583

```
003    DLC
005    20050727051945.0
008    790327n| acannaabn |a ana
010    $an 79018583 $zsh 85071957
035    $a(OCoLC)oca00252432
040    $aDLC$beng$cDLC$dDLC$dWaU$dViU
043    $an-us-ky
151    $aKentucky
451    $aKentuck
551    $aVirginia
667    $aAACR 1 form: Kentucky
670    $aThe buzzel about Kentuck, c1999.
675    $aBGN, Dec. 11, 1998;$aCol. Lipp. gaz., 1962 ; A
       hornbook of Virginia history, 1983: p. 121 (in 1789
       Virginia allowed Kentucky's nine counties to apply for
       statehood)
781 0  $zKentucky
```

Seattle, Washington

```
000    01442cz 2200229n 4500
001    n 79041965
003    DLC
005    20030619052713.0
008    790501n| acannaabn |a ana
010    $an 79041965
035    $a(OCoLC)oca00275410
040    $aDLC$beng$cDLC$dDLC$dWaU
043    $an-us-wa
151    $aSeattle (Wash.)
451    $wnnaa$aSeattle
451    $aCity of Seattle (Wash.)
551    $aSoutheast Seattle (Wash.)
670    $aU.S. Engineer Dept. Board of Engineers for Rivers and
       Harbors. Port and terminal facilities at the port of Seattle
       . . . 1941.
670    $aWashington place names origins, via WWW, March 2,
       1999$b(Seattle. The largest city in Washington is on Puget
       Sound in northwest King County. It extends 15 miles
       north-south, and about nine miles east-west, with the
       main business section centering around Elliott Bay. The
       city has diversified industries and businesses. It was
       named for Noah Sealth, chief of several Indian tribes
       when Seattle was established in 1851.)
```

670     $aInvolving all neighbors : building inclusive
communities in Seattle, c2000:$bcover (City of Seattle)
675     $aNUCMC data from Seattle Municipal Archives for
Southeast Seattle (Wash.). Town Council. Minutes, 1906
(Southeast Seattle was inc. on July 2, 1906, following a
merger with Hillman City and York, for the sole purpose
of being annexed to Seattle, Wash., on Jan. 7, 1907)
781 0 $zWashington (State)$zSeattle

Queens, New York, N.Y.

000   00529cz 2200181n 4500
001   n 81047346
003   DLC
005   20030619052755.0
008   810811n| acannaabn |a ana
010     $an 81047346
035     $a(OCoLC)oca00592901
040     $aDLC$beng$cDLC$dDLC$dWaU
043     $an-us-ny
151     $aQueens (New York, N.Y.)
410 1 $aNew York (N.Y.).$bQueens
451     $wnnaa$aQueens (Borough)
451     $aQueensborough, (N.Y.)
667     $aSUBJECT USAGE: This heading is not valid for use as
a geographic subdivision.

Georgetown, Washington, D.C.

000   01271cz 2200289n 4500
001   n 83166323
003   DLC
005   20030627052330.0
008   830811n| acannaabn |a ana
010     $an 83166323
035     $a(OCoLC)oca00988965
040     $aDLC$beng$cDLC$dDLC$dWaU
043     $an-us-dc
151     $aGeorgetown (Washington, D.C.)
410 1 $aWashington (D.C.).$bGeorgetown
451     $wnnaa$aGeorgetown, D.C.
451     $aGeorgetown (Md.)
451     $aGeorge Town (Washington, D.C.)
451     $aGeorge's Town (Washington, D.C.)
451     $aWest Washington (Washington, D.C.)

667    $aSUBJECT USAGE: This heading is not valid for use as a geographic subdivision.

667    $aUsed pre-AACR2 as subj. hdg. only

670    $aMitchell, M. Glimpses of Georgetown, past and present, 1983 (subj.)$bt.p. (Georgetown)

670    $aRand McNally comm. atlas, 1979, p. 273$b(District of Columbia listing: Georgetown, Sta. Washington P.O., part of Washington)

670    $aSoars, F. L. An 18th century map of George Town on Potomack, c1934.

670    $aRochambeau, J.-B.-D. de V. Camp a 1 mille 1/2 audela de George's Town, 1782.

670    $aMap of the city of Washington, District of Columbia, 1886?:$bmap recto (Georgetown; West Washington)

CORPORATE BODIES

United States Military Academy (a)

000   00724cz 2200193n 4500

001   n 79074300

003   DLC

005   20000119093739.0

008   790817n| acannaab |a ana

010    $an 79074300

040    $aDLC$cDLC$dDLC

110 2 $aUnited States Military Academy

410 2 $aU.S.M.A.

410 2 $aWest Point (Military academy)

410 2 $aUSMA

410 2 $aU.S. Military Academy, West Point

410 1 $wnna$aUnited States.$bMilitary Academy, West Point

510 1 $aUnited States.$bArmy.$bDept. of West Point

670    $aThomasville, Georgia, birth home of Lt. Henry Ossian Flipper, The Jack Hadley Black History Memorabilia, Inc. presents a buffalo soldier, 1998:$bt.p. (U.S. Military Academy, West Point)

United States Military Academy (b)

000   00496cz 2200145n 4500

001   n 82151415

003   DLC

005   19840322000000.0

```
008        830118n| acannaab |a ana
010        $an 82151415
040        $aDLC$cDLC
110 10     $aUnited States.$bArmy.$bDept. of West Point.
510 20     $aUnited States Military Academy
670        $aU.S. Military Academy, West Point. General orders.
           Feb. 8, 1881.
678        $aMilitary Academy and post of West Point were made a
           separate military department by 1877
```

Westminster Abbey

```
000        01251cz 2200265n 4500
001        n 80008753
003        DLC
005        19950701055411.5
008        800320n| acannaab| |a ana
010        $an 80008753
035        $a(OCoLC)oca00391308
040        $aDLC$cDLC$dDLC$dInU$dMnHi
110 20     $aWestminster Abbey
410 20     $aSt. Peter's (Westminster, London, England)
410 20     $aAbby Church of Westminster (London, England)
410 20     $aSaint Peter's (Westminster, London, England)
410 20     $aCollegiate Church of St. Peter (Westminster, London,
           England)
410 20     $aDean and Chapter of Westminster (London, England)
410 20     $aAbbey of St. Peter (Westminster, London, England)
410 20     $aAbbey Church of Westminster (London, England)
410 20     $aEcclesia Collegiata B. Petri Westmonasterii (London,
           England)
410 20     $aAbbey of Saint Peter (Westminster, London, England)
670        $aTanner, L. E. The history and treasures . . . 1953.
670        $aInU/Wing STC files$b(variants: St. Peter's; Abby
           Church of Westminster; Abbey of St. Peter; Abbey
           Church of Westminister; Ecclesia Collegiata B. Petri
           Westmonasterii)
670        $aAllegations for marriage licences issued by the Dean
           and Chapter of Westminster, 1558-1699, 1886.
```

SUBJECT HEADINGS

Computers

```
000        01143cz 2200325n 4500
001        sh 85029552
```

003	DLC
005	20020611123401.0
008	860211i| anannbabn |b ana
010	$ash 85029552
040	$aDLC$cDLC$dDLC
053 0	$aQA75.5$bQA76.95$cMathematics
053 0	$aTK7885$bTK7895$cElectrical engineering
150	$aComputers
360	$iheadings beginning with the word$aComputer
450	$aAutomatic computers
450	$aAutomatic data processors
450	$aComputer hardware
450	$aComputing machines (Computers)
450	$aElectronic brains
450	$wnne$aElectronic calculating-machines
450	$aElectronic computers
450	$aHardware, Computer
550	wgaComputer systems
550	wgaCybernetics
550	wgaMachine theory
550	$aCalculators
550	$aCyberspace
680	$iHere are entered works on modern electronic computers first developed after 1945. Works on present-day calculators, as well as on calculators and mechanical computers of pre-1945 vintage, are entered under$aCalculators.
681	$iNote under$aCalculators

Adolescent psychology

000	00376cz 2200157n 4500
001	sh 85000969
003	DLC
005	19871218164043.1
008	860211i| anannbab| |a ana
010	$ash 85000969
040	$aDLC$cDLC$dDLC
053	$aBF724
150 0	$aAdolescent psychology
450 0	$aAdolescence$xPsychology
450 0	$aTeenagers$xPsychology
550 0	wgaPsychology

UNIFORM TITLES

Jane Austen's *Pride and prejudice*

000	00564cz 2200157n 4500
001	n 2002041181
003	DLC
005	20040419141448.0
008	020814n| acannaabn |a aaa
010	$an 2002041181
040	$aDLC$beng$cDLC
100 1	$aAusten, Jane,$d1775-1817.$tPride and prejudice
400 1	$aAusten, Jane,$d1775-1817.$tJane Austen's Pride and prejudice
400 1	$aAusten, Jane,$d1775-1817.$tAnnotated Pride and prejudice
670	$aAusten, Jane. Jane Austen's Pride and prejudice, 2002.
670	$aAusten, Jane. The annotated Pride and prejudice, c2004.

APPENDIX C
Key to Exercises

CHAPTER 8

Exercise 8-1 (*Library of Congress Subject Headings,* 29th edition, 2006)

1. Journal of geographical information science
   Geographic information systems—Periodicals.
2. Geometric function theory in several complex variables
   Geometric function theory.
   Functions of several complex variables.
3. The communicative ethics controversy
   Communication—Moral and ethical aspects.
4. Dictionary of concepts in recreation and leisure studies
   Recreation—Dictionaries.
   Leisure—Dictionaries.
5. Geography in the curriculum
   Geography—Study and teaching.
6. Proceedings of a conference on condensed matter, particle physics and cosmology.
   Condensed matter—Congresses.
   Particles (Nuclear physics)—Congresses.
   Cosmology—Congresses.
7. A handbook for counseling the troubled and defiant child
   Problem children—Counseling of—Handbooks, manuals, etc.
   Child psychotherapy—Handbooks, manuals, etc.
8. Construction materials: types, uses, and applications
   Building materials.
9. Control theory of distributed parameter and applications: proceeding of a conference
   Control theory—Congresses.
   Distributed parameter systems—Congresses.
10. An introduction to urban geographic information systems
    Geography—Data processing.
    Cities and towns—Data processing.
11. Paleontology of vertebrates
    Vertebrates, Fossil.

12. The adolescent in the family
    Parent and teenager.
    Teenagers—Family relationships.
    Adolescent psychology.
13. The rhythm and intonation of spoken English
    English language—Rhythm.
    English language—Intonation.
    English language—Spoken English.
14. The biblical doctrine of salvation
    Salvation—Biblical teaching.
15. An English-Swedish, Swedish-English dictionary
    English language—Dictionaries—Swedish.
    Swedish language—Dictionaries—English.
16. A historical study of the doctrine of the Trinity
    Trinity—History of doctrines.
17. ABC: A child's first book
    Alphabet rhymes.
18. Twenty-three days with the Viet Cong: an American soldier's experience
    Vietnam War, 1961–1975—Personal narratives, American
19. The principal voyages and discoveries of the English nation to 1600
    Discoveries in geography—English.
    Voyages and travels.
20. Public attitudes toward life insurance
    Insurance, Life—Public opinion.

Exercise 8-2 (*Library of Congress Subject Headings*, 29th edition, 2006)

1A. Athens (Ga.)—Social conditions
    Athens (Greece)—Social conditions
    Brittany (France)—Social conditions
    Cambridge (England)—Social conditions
    Munich (Germany)—Social conditions
    New York (N.Y.)—Social conditions
    Ottawa (Ont.)—Social conditions
    Tennessee—Social conditions
    Rio de Janeiro (Brazil : State)—Social conditions
    Mississippi River Valley—Social conditions
B. Art—Georgia—Athens
    Art—Greece—Athens
    Art—France—Brittany
    Art—England—Cambridge

Art—Germany—Munich
Art—New York (State)—New York
Art—Ontario—Ottawa
Art—Tennessee
Art—Brazil—Rio de Janeiro (State)
Art—Mississippi River Valley

2A. Events leading to the American Civil War, 1837–1861
United States—History—1815–1861.
United States—History—Civil War, 1861–1865—Causes.

2B. A history of slavery and slave trades in Sub-Saharan Africa
Slavery—Africa, Sub-Saharan—History.
Slave-trade—Africa, Sub-Saharan—History.

2C. Profile of Ontario's provincial electoral districts based on statistics collected in the 1986 census
Ontario—Census, 1986.
Election districts—Ontario—Statistics.

2D. Popular culture in the United States during the Cold War
Popular culture—United States—History—20th century.
Cold War—Social aspects—United States.

2E. Lobbying for social changes in the United States
Lobbying—United States.
United States—Social policy.

2F. Christian life and the church in the Holy Roman Empire during the tenth century
Holy Roman Empire—Church history.
Christian life—History—Middle Ages, 600–1500.
Holy Roman Empire—Social conditions.

2G. Essays on the Hungarian Protestant Reformation in the 16th century
Reformation—Hungary.
Hungary—Church history—16th century.

2H. Violence in American families
Family violence—United States.

2I. Managing social services in the United States: designing, measuring, and financing
Social service—United States—Planning.
Social service—United States—Evaluation.
Social service—United States—Finance.

2J. U.S-Japan economic relations since World War II
United States—Foreign economic relations—Japan.
Japan—Foreign economic relations—United States.

2K. Social relations in Elizabethan London
London (England)—History—16th century.
London (England)—Social conditions.

2L. Public school choice in American education
Public schools—United States.
School choice—United States.
Education—United States—Parent participation.
Education and state—United States.

2M. The gypsies of Eastern Europe
Romanies—Europe, Eastern.
Europe, Eastern—Ethnic relations.

2N. The Taiwan uprising of February 28, 1947
Taiwan—History—February Twenty Eighth Incident, 1947.

2O. Working women look at their home lives
Home—United States.
Working mothers—United States—Attitudes.

2P. Norman illumination of manuscripts at Mont St. Michel, 966–1100
Illumination of books and manuscripts, Norman—France—Le Mont-Saint-Michel.

2Q. Life in a Japanese Zen Buddhist monastery
Monastic and religious life (Zen Buddhism)—Japan.

2R. The German community in Cincinnati
German Americans—Ohio—Cincinnati.

2S. A pictorial guide to San Francisco
San Francisco (Calif.)—Guidebooks.
San Francisco (Calif.)—Pictorial works.

2T. A catalog of Great Britain railway letter stamps
Railway letter stamps—Catalogs.
Postage stamps—Great Britain—Catalogs.

Exercise 8-3 (*Library of Congress Subject Headings*, 29th edition, 2006)

1. A history of modern German literature
German literature—19th century—History and criticism.
German literature—20th century—History and criticism.

2. Essays on American and British fiction
American fiction—History and criticism.
English fiction—History and criticism.

3. A study of the themes of order and restraint in the poetry of Philip Larkin, a British author
Larkin, Philip—Criticism and interpretation.
Self-control in literature.
Order in literature.

4. Women and literature in France
French literature—Women authors—History and criticism.
Women and literature—France.

5. Irony in Rabelais
   Rabelais, François, ca.1490–1553?—Criticism and interpretation.
   Irony in literature.
6. Memoirs of Richard Nixon
   Nixon, Richard M. (Richard Milhous), 1913–1994
   Presidents—United States—Biography.
   United States—Politics and government—1969–1974.
7. Columbus and the age of discovery
   Columbus, Christopher.
   Explorers—America—Biography.
   Explorers—Spain—Biography.
   America—Discovery and exploration—Spanish.
8. Bibliographies of studies in Victorian literature for the years
   1975–1984
   English literature—19th century—History and criticism—Bibliography.
9. A critical study of characterization in Jacobean tragedies
   English drama—17th century—History and criticism.
   English drama (Tragedy)—History and criticism.
   Characters and characteristics in literature.
10. A commentary on the epistles of Peter and Jude
    Bible. N.T. Peter—Commentaries.
    Bible. N.T. Jude—Commentaries.
11. A study of the theme of friendship in fifteenth-century Chinese
    literature
    Chinese literature—Ming dynasty, 1368–1644—History and criticism.
    Friendship in literature.
12. Mary Stuart in sixteenth and seventeenth century literature: a critical study
    Mary, Queen of Scots, 1542–1587—In literature.
    Literature, Modern—15th and 16th centuries—History and criticism.
    Literature, Modern—17th century—History and criticism.
13. A reader's guide to Walt Whitman
    Whitman, Walt, 1819–1892—Criticism and interpretation.
14. A journal of twentieth-century Spanish literature
    Spanish literature—20th century—Periodicals.

CHAPTER 10

Exercise 10-1 (*Sears List of Subject Headings*, 18th edition, 2004)

1. Reading habits of adolescents
   Teenagers—Books and reading.

2. Advertising and selling by mail
Advertising.
Mail-order business.
Direct selling.
3. Encyclopedia of science and technology
Science—Encyclopedias.
Technology—Encyclopedias.
4. *Library Journal*
Library science—Periodicals.
Libraries—Periodicals.
5. Handbook of chemistry and physics
Chemistry—Handbooks, manuals, etc.
Physics—Handbooks, manuals, etc.
6. History of the First World War
World War, 1914–1918.
7. *Journal of Plant Pathology*
Plant diseases—Periodicals.
8. A list of scientific journals
Science—Periodicals—Bibliography.
9. *Time* (magazine)
History—Periodicals.
10. A Russian-English dictionary of medical terms
Medicine—Dictionaries.
Russian language—Dictionaries—English.
11. A bibliography of library and information science
Library science—Bibliography.
Information science—Bibliography.
12. Opportunities in textile careers
Textile industry—Vocational guidance.
13. An amateur photographer's handbook
Photography—Handbooks, manuals, etc.
14. *Sears List of Subject Headings*
Subject headings.

Exercise 10-2 (*Sears List of Subject Headings,* 18th edition, 2004)

1. Museums in New York City
Museums—New York (N.Y.)
2. Popular songs in the U.S.A.
Popular music.
American songs.
3. Alternative work hours
Flexible hours of labor.

4. Canadian foreign policy, 1945–1954
   Canada—Foreign relations.
5. *The Eisenhower Years: A Historical Assessment*
   United States—History—1953–1961.
6. Party politics in Australia
   Political parties—Australia.
   Australia—Politics and government.
7. Directory of hospitals in Athens, Georgia
   Hospitals—Athens (Ga.)—Directories.
8. The reign of Elizabeth, 1558–1603
   Great Britain—History—1485–1603, Tudors.
9. A pictorial guide to San Francisco
   San Francisco (Calif.)—Guidebooks.
   San Francisco (Calif.)—Pictorial works.
10. *Famous American Military Leaders*
    United States—Armed forces—Biography.
11. *Norwegian Folk Tales: A Collection*
    Folklore—Norway.
12. *Getting to Know Iran and Iraq*
    Iran.
    Iraq.
13. *The Land and People of Switzerland*
    Switzerland—Civilization.
    Switzerland—Description and travel.

Exercise 10-3 (*Sears List of Subject Headings*, 18th edition, 2004)

1. Swedish word origins
   Swedish language—Etymology.
2. *Poems for Thanksgiving* (by various authors)
   Thanksgiving Day—Poetry—Collections.
   American poetry—Collections.
3. Russian grammar
   Russian language—Grammar.
4. *The Peace Corps in Action*
   Peace Corps (U.S.)
   American technical assistance.
5. *Chemicals of Life: Enzymes, Vitamins, Hormones*
   Enzymes.
   Vitamins.
   Hormones.
6. A history of the American Medical Association
   American Medical Association—History.

7. NATO and Europe
   North Atlantic Treaty Organization.
   Europe—History—1945–
8. The German community in Cincinnati
   German Americans—Cincinnati (Ohio).
9. *Wonders of the Himalayas*
   Himalaya Mountains.
10. A travel guide to Estonia, Latvia, and Lithuania
    Baltic States—Guidebooks.
11. *The Department of Defense: A History*
    United States. Dept. of Defense—History.
12. Sparrows of Asia
    Sparrows.
    Birds—Asia.

Exercise 10-4 (*Sears List of Subject Headings,* 18th edition, 2004)

1. Lives of famous French dramatists
   French dramatists—Biography.
2. *American Men and Women of Science*
   Scientists—Directories.
3. Short stories: a collection
   Short stories.
4. Stories of Maupassant
   Short stories, French.
5. Commentaries on the New Testament in the Bible
   Bible. N.T.—Commentaries.
6. Life of Pablo Picasso
   Picasso, Pablo, 1881–1963.
7. Modern American secret agents
   Spies—United States.
8. Famous New Yorkers
   New York (State)—Biography.
9. Life of Daniel Boone
   Boone, Daniel, 1734–1820.
10. *The Agony and the Ecstasy* (an American novel based on the life of Michelangelo)
    Michelangelo Buonarroti, 1475–1564—Fiction.
11. *Best Sports Stories*
    Short stories.
    Sports—Fiction—Collections.
12. *A Day in the Life of President Johnson* (Lyndon B.)
    Johnson, Lyndon B. (Lyndon Baines), 1908–1973.

13. *The Combat Nurses of World War II*
    Military nurses.
    World War, 1939–1945—Medical Care—Biography.
14. *Book of Poetry for Children*
    Children's poetry.
15. *A Man for All Seasons* (an English drama based on the life of Sir
    Thomas More)
    More, Sir Thomas, Saint, 1478–1535—Drama.
16. *A Study of Mark Twain's Novels*
    Twain, Mark, 1835–1910—Criticism.

CHAPTER 13

Exercise 13-1 (*Dewey Decimal Classification*, edition 22, 2003)

1. India under the British rule
   954.03
2. Discipline of students through punishments in the public schools
   371.54
3. Television commercials
   659.143
4. A thesaurus of water resources terms
   025.4933391
5. Planning public library buildings
   022.314
6. A bibliography on diagnostic x-ray techniques
   016.61607572
7. *American Libraries* (official journal of the American Library Association)
   020.5
8. Commentaries on the Gospel of John
   226.507
9. Colligative properties of electrolytic solutions
   541.3745
10. Unemployment in library services
    331.1378102
11. Embryology of vertebrates
    571.8616
12. Curriculum design in schools
    375.001
13. The Bolshevik Revolution and the Civil War in Russia
    947.0841

14. *Journal of Physical Oceanography*
    551.4605

Exercise 13-2 (Number 1)

The answers for exercise 13-2, number 1, are shown in Table C-1.

Exercise 13-2 (Number 2)

A. Financial management of special education in Ohio
   371.90681
B. Brooklyn Public Library
   027.474723
C. History of classical languages
   480.09
D. A dictionary of modern music and musicians
   780.922 (preferred) *or* 780.904
E. Popular music in the United States
   781.630973
F. European immigrants in the United States during the 1930s
   325.24097309043 [-09043 = 1930-1939]
G. The government of American cities
   320.85
H. Statistical methods used in social sciences
   300.015195 [519.5 = statistical math]
I. Foreign relations between Russia and Japan
   327.47052
J. The Nazi spy network in Switzerland during World War II
   940.5487494
K. Social conditions in Japan after World War II
   952.04
L. Masterpieces of painting in the Metropolitan Museum of Art: An
   exhibition catalog
   750.747471

TABLE C-1   DDC Exercise 13-B(1) Answers

	United States	Tennessee	Scotland	Egypt
Area table notation	−73	−768	−411	−62
History of	973	976.8	941.1	962
Tourist Guide to	917.304	917.6804	914.1104	916.204
Newspapers from	071.3	071.68	072.911	079.62
Folk songs from	782.4216200973	782.42162009768	782.42162009411	782.4216200962
Political condition in	320.973	320.9768	320.9411	320.962
Geology of	557.3	557.68	554.11	556.2

M. Life and health insurance laws (United States)
346.7308632

N. Illinois rules and regulations for fire prevention and safety, as amended 1968
344.7730537

O. Arizona library laws (a compilation)
344.79109202632

P. Tourist trade in Russia after World War II
338.47914709045

Exercise 13-3 (*Dewey Decimal Classification*, edition 22, 2003)

1. Swahili grammar
496.3925

2. A bibliography of anonymous works in German
014.31

3. A Chinese-English, English-Chinese dictionary
495.1321

4. Islamic painting
759.91767

5. Jewish population in the Netherlands
949.2004924 [-004924 = Jews (T5)]

6. *La Raza: the Mexican-Americans*
305.86872073

7. An exhibition of twentieth century American art from a Long Island collection
709.730747

8. Jewish families in New York City
305.892407471

9. A German version of the New Testament
225.531

10. World War II letters of Barbara Wooddall Taylor and Charles E. Taylor
940.5481730922

11. Italian-American women in Nassau County, New York, 1925-1981
974.7245004510082 [-747245 = Nassau County, NY; -004 = s.s; -51 = Italians (T5); -0082 = women (T1)]

12. Teaching English reading in the secondary school
428.40712 [-84 = reading; 0712 = 2nd. educ]

13. The Spanish-speaking people from Mexico in the United States
973.046872 [-004 = Racial groups (vol. 3, p.710), -04 under 973; -68 = Spanish American; -72 = Mexico]

14. Native Americans in the United States, 1820-1890
    973.0497 [-004 = Racial groups; -97 = Indians (T5)]

Exercise 13-4 (*Dewey Decimal Classification*, edition 22, 2003)

1. A collection of German literature for and by Jews
   830.808924
2. Characterization in Jacobean (English 1606–1625) tragedies: a critical study
   822.05120927
3. A collection of devotional poetry from colonial America
   811.1080382
4. A collection of seventeenth-century French drama
   842.408
5. A history of science fiction in the United States
   813.0876209
6. A study of the theme of friendship in fifteenth-century Chinese literature
   895.109353
7. Abraham Lincoln in American literature: a critical study
   810.9351
8. A study of the theme of alienation in twentieth-century American fiction
   813.509353 [alienation as a social theme]
   813.509382 [alienation as a religious theme]
   813.509384 [alienation as a philosophic concept]
9. The diaries of Mark Twain
   818.403
10. A history of Irish Gaelic poetry in the early period
    891.621109
11. A study of the theme of love in twentieth-century American poetry
    811.5093543
12. A study of the characters in seventeenth-century French drama
    842.40927
13. A study of Shakespeare's tragedies by Clifford Leech
    822.33
    D-Lxx [Lxx = Cutter number of author]
14. Collected poems of Byron
    821.7
15. The art of writing short stories
    808.31
16. An anthology of American short stories

813.0108
17. Literary history of the United States: twentieth century
    810.9005
18. A study of French Renaissance tragedy
    842.05120903 [-20512 = Tragedy (T3B)]
19. A study of feminine fiction in England, 1713-1799
    823.5099287 [-5 = Queen Anne, 1702-45; -099287 = woman (T3C)]
20. Study of literary criticism in Finnish universities
    801.9507114897
21. Essays on Russian and Polish literature
    891.709
22. Interpret the following Decimal classification numbers:
    338.4769009421 = The building industry in London, England
    338.926091724 = Information policy in developing countries
    551.2109989 = Volcanoes of the Antarctica
    782.4215520941 = Songs in British drama
    917.92003 = Utah place names

Exercise 13-5 (*Dewey Decimal Classification*, abridged edition 14, 2004)

1. Magnetism of the earth
   538
2. Guidance and counseling in schools
   371.4
3. Cataloging and classification of books in libraries
   025.3
4. *Séance: A Book of Spiritual Communications*
   133.9
5. A bibliography of bacteriology
   016.5793 *or* 579.3016
6. Landscaping for homes
   712
7. Acquisition of audiovisual materials in libraries
   025.2
8. The causes of the Civil War
   973.7
9. A bibliography of local transportation
   016.3884 *or* 388.4016
10. The kinesiology of weight lifting
    613.7
11. Designing dormitories
    727
12. *Kentuckiana: A Bibliography of Books about Kentucky*

016.9769 *or* 976.90016
13. A concordance to modern versions of the New Testament
    225.5
14. A critique of Marx's *Das Kapital*
    335.4
15. Smallpox vaccination
    614.5
16. Newspapers in Russia
    077
17. Position of women in the Old Testament
    221.8
18. Paintings from the United States
    759.13
19. An atlas of the moon
    912.99
20. Public library administration
    025.1
21. Greek mythology
    292.1
22. How to prepare for college entrance examinations
    378.1

Exercise 13-6 (*Dewey Decimal Classification*, abridged edition 14, 2004)

1. How to teach cooking
   641.507
2. A scientist's view with regard to life on Mars
   576.8
3. Labor union discrimination against black American textile workers
   331.6
4. Rocks from the moon
   552.0999
5. Flora and fauna of Alaska
   578.09798
6. Nursing education
   610.7307
7. A history of Kentucky during the Civil War
   976.9
8. Monetary policy of France
   332.4
9. History of political parties in Australia
   324.294009

10. An encyclopedia of engineering
    620.003
11. A travel guide to Florida
    917.5904
12. A bibliography of Ohio imprints
    015.771
13. A history of Christian churches in Iowa
    277.77
14. Journal of political science
    320.05
15. Farming in Iowa
    630.9777
16. A history of New Orleans
    976.3
17. Interior decoration in Sweden
    747.285
18. Social conditions in China
    306.0951
19. A history of Singapore
    959.57
20. A collection of fairy tales
    398.2
21. A gardener's handbook on diseases of flowers
    635.9
22. Political conditions in the United States
    320.973
23. Geology of Iran
    555.5
24. *American Restaurants Then and Now*
    647.9573 [647.95 = Eating and drinking places]
25. United States policy toward Latin America
    327.7308
26. Kentucky folklore
    398.09769
27. Macroeconomic policy in Britain, 1974-1987
    339.50941
28. *Early Education in the Public Schools in Massachusetts*
    372.2109744

Exercise 13-7 (*Dewey Decimal Classification*, abridged edition 14, 2004)

1. A history of American literature
   810.9

2. An encyclopedia of Norwegian literature
839.82
3. A biography of President Lyndon Baines Johnson
973.923092
4. A biography of Walter Cronkite, news broadcaster
070.1092
5. A teacher's handbook of Latin literature
870.7
6. A critical study of twentieth-century drama
809.2
7. An English-Japanese, Japanese-English dictionary
495.6
8. A critical study of Russian novels
891.73009
9. A history of Chinese poetry
895.1
10. The collected works of Henry Fielding
823
11. A handbook for sign language teachers
419.07
12. A critical study of the Afro-American as a character in American fiction
813.009
13. Remedial reading for French
448.4
14. A collection of Portuguese essays (by various authors)
869.4008
15. A study of political themes in twentieth-century British literature
820.9

Exercise 13-8 (*Cutter's Three-Figure Author Table*, 1969)

1. 973
   Ad17h Adams, Henry. *History of the United States of America.* 1962
2. 973
   Ad17f Adams, Henry. *The Formative Years: A History of the United States during the Administration of Jefferson and Madison.* 1948
3. 973
   Ad18m Adams, James Truslow. *The March of Democracy.* 1932–33
4. 973
   Ad19g Adams, Randolph G. *The Gateway to American History.* 1927

5. 973
   Ad19p   Adams, Randolph G. *Pilgrims, Indians and Patriots: The Pictorial History of America from the Colonial Age to the Revolution.* 1928
6. 973
   B193s   Baldwin, Leland Dewitt. *The Stream of American History.* 1965
7. 973
   B2275h   Bancroft, George. *History of the United States of America, from the Discovery of the Continent to 1789.* 1883–85
8. 973
   B367a   Beals, Carleton. *American Earth: the Biography of a Nation.* 1939
9. 973
   Sch38n   Schlesinger, Arthur Meier. *New Viewpoints in American History.* 1922
10. 973
    Sch38p   Schlesinger, Arthur Meier. *Political and Social History of the United States, 1829–1925.* 1925
11. 973
    Sch68h   Schouler, James. *History of the United States of America under the Constitution.* 1880–1913
12. 973
    Se48s   Sellers, Charles G. *A Synopsis of American History.* 1963
13. 973
    Sh16u   Shaler, Nathaniel S. *The United States of America.* 1894
14. 973
    Sh35m   Sheehan, Donald H. *The Making of American History.* 1950
15. 973
    Sh58c   Sherwood, James. *The Comic History of the United States.* 1870
16. 973
    Si97   *Six Presidents from the Empire State.* 1974
17. 973
    Sm54u   Smith, Dale O. *U.S. Military Doctrine: A Study and Appraisal.* 1955
18. 973
    Sm57u   Smith, Goldwin. *The United States: An Outline of Political History, 1492–1871.* 1893

Exercise 13-9 (*Cutter's Three-Figure Author Table,* 1969)

A. 92
   C475ar   Arthur, Sir G. *Concerning Winston Spencer Churchill* [1874–1965]

92
C475as   Ashley, M. P. *Churchill as Historian* [W. S. Churchill, 1874–1965]

92
H638b   Bullock, A. L. C. *Hitler: A Study in Tyranny*

92
C4745a   Churchill, Jennie Jerome, 1854–1921. *The Reminiscences of Lady Randolph Churchill*

92
C475c   Churchill, Randolph S., 1911–1968. *Winston S. Churchill* [1874–1965]

92
C475a   Churchill, Winston, Sir, 1874–1965. *A Roving Commission: My Early Life*

92
C4747c   Churchill, Winston, Sir, 1874–1965. *Lord Randolph Churchill* [1849–1895]

92
C4743f   Fishman, J. *My Darling Clementine* [wife of W. S. Churchill]

92
C475g   Gardner, B. *Churchill in Power* [W. S. Churchill, 1874–1965]

92
C475gr   Graebner, W. *My Dear Mr. Churchill* [W. S. Churchill, 1874–1965]

92
H638aZh   Hackett, Francis. *What Mein Kampf Means to America*

92
H638a   Hitler, Adolph. *Mein Kampf*

92
H638aE   Hitler, Adolph. *My Battle*

92
C4747j   James, R. R. *Lord Randolph Churchill* [1849–1895]

92
C4745k   Kraus, R. *Young Lady Randolph* [Churchill, 1854–1921]

92
C4745l   Leslie, Anita. *Jennie: The Life of Lady Randolph Churchill* [1854–1921]

92
C4745l1   Leslie, Anita. *Lady Randolph Churchill: The Story of Jennie Jerome* [1854–1921]

92
C4745m   Martin, R. G. *Jennie: The Life of Lady Randolph Churchill* [1854–1921]

92
H638s   Smith, B. F. *Adolph Hitler: His Family, Childhood and Youth*

B. 823.8
D555zb   Brook, G. L. *The Language of Dickens*
823.8
D555yc   Churchill, R. C. *A Bibliography of Dickensian Criticism*
823.8
D555tG   Dickens, Charles. *Eine Geschichte von zwei Städten* [a German translation of *A Tale of Two Cities*]
823.8
D555h   Dickens, Charles. *Hard Times*
823.8
D555tS   Dickens, Charles. *Historia de dos Ciudades* [a Spanish translation of *A Tale of Two Cities*]
823.8
D555tF   Dickens, Charles. *Paris et Londres en 1793* [a French translation of *A Tale of Two Cities*]
823.8
D555hF   Dickens, Charles. *Les temps difficiles* [a French translation of *Hard Times*]
823.8
D555hG   Dickens, Charles. *Schwere Zeiten* [a German translation of *Hard Times*]
823.8
D555t   Dickens, Charles. *A Tale of Two Cities.* 1934
823.8
D555t   Dickens, Charles. *A Tale of Two Cities.* 1970
823.8
D555tGd   Dickens, Charles. *Zwei Städte, Roman aus der französischen Revolution* [a German translation of *A Tale of Two Cities* by B. Dedek, 1924]
823.8
D555zz   *Dickens Studies Newsletter*
823.8
D555zzd   *The Dickensian: A Magazine for Dickens Lovers*
823.8
D555yh   Hayward, A. L. *The Dickens Encyclopedia*
823.8
D555tZ   *Twentieth Century Interpretations of A Tale of Two Cities: A Collection of Critical Essays*

CHAPTER 14

Exercise 14-1: Assign complete LC call numbers (i.e., class number + item number and date)

1. *Gardens for the new country place : contemporary country gardens and inspiring landscape elements* / by Paul Bennett ; [principal photography by Betsy Pinover Schiff]. 2003

SB457.53 .B46 2003

2. *Ramanujan's lost notebook* / George E. Andrews, Bruce C. Berndt. 2005- [Ramanujan was a mathematician from India]
   QA29.R3 A73 2005

3. *World guide to scientific associations and learned societies* / [editor, Helmut Opitz]. 8th ed. 2002
   Q10 .W67 2002

4. *The philosophy of science and technology studies* / Steve Fuller. 2006
   Q174.8 .F85 2006

5. *Sedimentary geology : sedimentary basins, depositional environments, petroleum formation* / Bernard Biju-Duval ; translated from the French by J. Edwin Swezey and Traduclair Translation Company. 2002
   QE571.B4813 2002

6. Conference on Recent Advances in Operator-Related Function Theory 2004 : Dublin, Ireland. *Recent advances in operator-related function theory.* 2006
   QA319.C66 2004

7. *Evolution of herbivory in terrestrial vertebrates : perspectives from the fossil record* / edited by Hans-Dieter Sues. 2000
   QE841 .E96 2000

8. *U.S. development aid—an historic first : achievements and failures in the twentieth century* / Samuel Hale Butterfield ; foreword by Maurice Williams. 2004
   HC60.B8758 2004

9. *Magnetic leadership : are you a good enough leader to be hired by the best employees?* / Victor Downing. 2005
   HD66 .D69 2005

10. *Back to the drawing board : designing corporate boards for a complex world* / Colin B. Carter and Jay W. Lorsch. 2004
    HD2745 .C366 2004

11. *Methods of discovery : heuristics for the social sciences* / Andrew Abbott. 2004
    H61.15 .A23 2004

12. *Boss talk : top CEOs share the ideas that drive the world's most successful companies* / the editors of the Wall Street Journal ; introduction by Tom Peters. 2002
    HD38.2 .B67 2002

13. *Pension plans : IRS programs for resolving deviations from tax-exemption requirements : report to the Chairman, Subcommittee on Oversight, Committee on Ways and Means, House of Representatives* / United States General Accounting Office. 2000 [main entry under: United States. General Accounting Office.]
    HJ4653.P5 U55 2000

14. *Women workers in brick factory : sordid saga from a district of West Bengal* / Amal Mandal. 2005
    HD6073.B82 M36 2005
15. *The economic dynamics of environmental law* / David M. Driesen. 2003
    HC110.E5 D74 2003

Exercise 14-2 (Library of Congress Classification)

1. *Monetary and financial management in Asia in the 21st century* / editor, Augustine H. H. Tan. 2002 [main entry under the title]
   HG1202 .M66 2002 [Table 8—551-555: Asia]
2. *Communism in history and theory. the European experience* / Donald F. Busky. 2002
   HX236.5 .B87 2002 [Table H9a]
3. *A tough act to follow? : the Telecommunications Act of 1996 and the separation of powers* / Harold W. Furchtgott-Roth. 2006
   HE7781 .F87 2006
4. *Ben Jonson in the Romantic Age* / Tom Lockwood. 2005
   PR2637.4.G7 L63 2005
5. *Staging anatomies : dissection and spectacle in early Stuart tragedy* / Hillary M. Nunn. 2005
   PR678.B63 N86 2005 [Table PR5]
6. *Love's sacrifice* / John Ford ; edited by A. T. Moore. 2002
   PR2524 .L58 2002 [Table P-PZ33]
7. *The Brontës* / Patricia Ingham. 2006
   PR4169 .I54 2006
8. *Medieval images, icons, and illustrated English literary texts : from Ruthwell Cross to the Ellesmere Chaucer* / Maidie Hilmo. 2004
   PR275.A77 H55 2004
9. *Kelly's people* / Walter Wager. 2002 [late 20th century American author]
   PS3573.A35 K45 2002 [Table P-PZ40]
10. *Miss Lulu Bett and stories* / Zona Gale [early twentieth century American author] ; edited by Barbara H. Solomon and Eileen Panetta. 2005
    PS3513.A34 A6 2005 [Table P-PZ40]
11. *All's well that ends well* / [William Shakespeare] ; edited by Russell Fraser ; with an introduction by Alexander Leggatt. 2003 [Table PR4: A2 = by editor]
    PR2801.A2 F7 2003
12. *Reinventing King Arthur : the Arthurian legends in Victorian culture* / Inga Bryden. 2005
    PR468.A78 B79 2005

13. *Jane Austen and religion : salvation and society in Georgian England* / Michael Giffin. 2002
PR4038.R4 G54 2002 [Table P-PZ33]

14. *Mark Twain himself : a pictorial biography* / produced by Milton Meltzer. 2002
PS1331 .A2 2002 [Table P-PZ31 modified: .A2 = Autobiography]

GLOSSARY

The following works were used in compiling this glossary:

The ALA Glossary of Library and Information Science. Heartsill Young, ed. Chicago: American Library Association, 1983.

Anglo-American Cataloguing Rules. 2nd ed., 2002 revision. Prepared under the direction of the Joint Steering Committee for Revision of AACR, a committee of the American Library Association, the Australian Committee on Cataloguing, the British Library, the Canadian Committee on Cataloguing, Chartered Institute of Library and Information Professionals, the Library of Congress. Chicago: American Library Association, 2002.

IFLA Study Group on the Functional Requirements for Bibliographic Records, *Functional Requirements for Bibliographic Records, Final Report* (München: K. G. Saur, 1998). UBCIM Publications, New Series; v. 19. Also available at www.ifla.org/VII/s13/frbr/frbr.htm (27 March 2007).

Lois Mai Chan, *Library of Congress Subject Headings: Principles and Application.* 4th ed. Westport, Conn.: Libraries Unlimited, 2005.

Melvil Dewey, *Dewey Decimal Classification and Relative Index*, Ed. 22, Joan S. Mitchell, Editor in Chief, Julianne Beall, Giles Martin, Winton E. Matthews, Jr., Gregory R. New, Assistant Editors. Dublin, Ohio: OCLC Online Computer Library Center, Inc., 2003.

Please consult these works for definitions of terms not included in this glossary.

access point. A name, term, code, etc. that can serve as a search key in information retrieval. *See also* heading.

access-point provision. Designating selected elements in the representation which the user can use as means to gain "entry" to the representation.

added entry. An additional access point by which a cataloging record can be retrieved. *See also* main entry.

administrative metadata. A type of metadata providing information regarding the management of an information resource or object, such as when and how it was created, file type and other technical information, as well as information regarding access.

alphabetical catalog. *See* dictionary catalog.

alphabetical specific catalog. A catalog containing subject entries based on the principle of specific and direct entry and arranged alphabetically. *See also* alphabetico-classed catalog; classed catalog; dictionary catalog.

alphabetico-classed catalog. A subject catalog in which entries are listed under broad subjects and subdivided hierarchically by topics. The entries on each level of the hierarchy are arranged alphabetically. *See also* alphabetical specific catalog; classed catalog; dictionary catalog.

analytical entry. A record for a part of a larger item for which a comprehensive record is also made.

analytico-synthetic classification. *See* faceted classification.

area. A section of the bibliographic description, comprising data elements of a particular category or set of categories. *See also* element.

array. A group of coordinate subjects on the same level of a hierarchical structure, e.g., oranges, lemons, limes, but not citrus fruit.

author number. *See* Cutter number.

author-title added entry. *See* name-title added entry.

author-title reference. *See* name-title reference.

authority control. The process of maintaining consistency in access points in a catalog.

authority file. A collection of authority records.

authority record. *See* name authority record; subject authority record.

bibliographic control. The operation or process by which recorded information is organized or arranged and thereby made readily retrievable. The term covers a range of bibliographic activities, including complete records of bibliographic items as published; standardization of bibliographic description; and provision of physical access through consortia, networks, or other cooperative endeavors.

bibliographic database. A collection of bibliographic records in machine-readable form.

bibliographic description. The description of a bibliographic item, consisting of information, including title and statement of responsibility, edition, publication and manufacturing, physical description, notes of useful information, and standard numbers, that together uniquely identifies the item. *See also* resource description.

bibliographic file. A collection of bibliographic records.

bibliographic record. A record containing details with regard to identification, physical and other characteristics, and subject access information of a bibliographic item. In a catalog, it is also called a catalog record.

bibliographic resource. An information item in tangible or intangible form that is used as the basis for bibliographic description.

bibliographic utility. A processing center or network providing services based on machine-readable cataloging data or metadata.

biographical heading. *See* class-of-persons heading.

book number. *See* item number.

Boolean operations. Logical or algebraic operations, formulated by George Boole, involving variables with two values, such as Value 1 *and* Value 2; Value 1 *or* Value 2; and Value 1 but *not* Value 2. Used in information retrieval to combine terms or sets, e.g., Children *and* Television; Children *or* Young adults; Children *not* Infants.

broad classification. (1) A classification scheme that does not provide for minute subdivision of topics. (2) Arrangement of works in conformity with the provisions of such a scheme. *See also* close classification.

call number. A composite symbol consisting of the class number, book or item number, and sometimes other data such as the date, volume number, and copy number, which provides identification of an individual item and its shelf location. *See also* Cutter number; item number; work mark.

catalog. (1) A list of materials prepared for a particular purpose, e.g., an exhibition catalog or a sales catalog. (2) In the narrower sense, a list of library resources contained in a collection, a library, or group of libraries, organized according to a definite scheme or plan.

catalog record. A basic unit in a catalog, containing cataloging data—bibliographic description, subject headings, and call number—of a particular item.

cataloging copy. A cataloging record prepared by an agency to be used by other agencies or libraries.

centralized cataloging. The preparation of cataloging records by one agency to be used by other agencies or libraries. *See also* shared cataloging.

chain. A series of subject terms each from a different level of a hierarchy, arranged either from general to specific or vice versa.

characteristic of division. *See* facet.

chief source of information. The part of a bibliographic item containing data as the preferred source based on which a bibliographic description is prepared.

chronological subdivision. A subdivision showing the period or span of time treated in a work or the period during which the work appeared. Also called period subdivision.

CIP (Cataloging-In-Publication). A system of providing cataloging information within or along with the material it represents.

citation order. The order by which the facets or elements of a compound or complex subject are arranged in a subject heading or class number. *See also* close classification.

class. (1) (*noun*) A group of objects exhibiting one or more common characteristics, usually identified by a specific notation in a classification scheme; (2) (*verb*) To assign a class number to an individual work. *See also* classify; classification (2).

class entry. A subject representation consisting of a string of hierarchically related terms beginning with the broadest term and leading to the subject in question, in the form of a chain. *See also* direct entry.

class number. Notation that designates the class to which a given item belongs.

class-of-persons heading. A subject heading used with biographies which consists of the name of a class of persons with appropriate subdivisions, e.g., Physicians—California—Biography; Poets, American—19th century—Biography. Also called biographical heading.

classed catalog. A subject catalog consisting of class entries arranged logically according to a systematic scheme of classification. Also called class catalog; classified subject catalog; systematic catalog. *See also* alphabetical specific catalog; alphabetico-classed catalog; dictionary catalog.

classification. A logical system for the arrangement of knowledge. *See also* class.

classification schedule. *See* schedule.

classificationist. A person who designs or develops a classification system or one who engages in the philosophy and theory of classification.

classifier. A person who applies a classification system to a body of knowledge or a collection of documents.

classify. (1) To arrange a collection of items according to a classification scheme; (2) To assign a class number to an individual item. *Also called* class.

close classification. (1) A classification providing for minute subdivision of topics; (2) Arrangement of works in conformity with the provisions of such a scheme. *See also* broad classification.

closed stacks. Parts or all of a collection not open for free access by users.

coextensive heading. A heading that represents precisely (not more generally or specifically than) the subject content of a work.

collective biography. A work consisting of two or more life histories. *See also* individual biography.

compiler. (1) One who produces a collection by selecting and putting together matter from the works of various persons or corporate bodies. (2) One who selects and puts together in one publication matter from the works of one person or corporate body.

completely revised schedule. Previously called a phoenix schedule, a term used in the Dewey Decimal Classification to refer to a completely new development of the schedule for a specific discipline. Except by chance, only the basic number for the discipline remains the same as in previous editions; all other numbers are freely reused.

compound surname. A surname consisting of two or more proper names, with or without a hyphen, or conjunction, and/or preposition.

content designation. A system of special codes (tags, indicators, and subfield codes) in a MARC 21 record used for the purpose of identifying a particular unit of information. *See also* tag; indicator; subfield code.

continuation. A supplement to, or a part issued in continuance of, a monograph, a serial, or a series.

controlled vocabulary. In subject analysis and retrieval, the use of an authorized subset of the language as indexing terms. *See also* free-text.

conventional name. A name, other than the real or official name, by which a corporate body, place, or thing is more familiarly known.

conventional title. *See* uniform title.

cooperative cataloging. *See* shared cataloging.

copy cataloging. The process of adapting an existing catalog record prepared by another library or agency. *See also* original cataloging.

core record. A level of catalog record that contains less-than-full bibliographic elements as defined by the Program for Cooperative Cataloging (PCC).

corporate body. An organization or group of persons that is identified by a particular name and that acts, or may act, as an entity. Examples include associations, institutions, business firms, nonprofit enterprises, governments, government agencies, religious bodies, local churches, and conferences.

cross classification. Placing works on the same subject in two different class numbers when a given work deals with two or more subdivisions of a subject, with each subdivision representing a different characteristic of division. Such a situation creates the possibility of inconsistent classification. Example: a work on weaving cotton cloth deals with two subdivisions of textile technology, cotton (material) and weaving (process), and may be classed with either. *See also* citation order.

cross-reference. *See* reference.

Cutter number. A system combining letters and numerals devised by Charles A. Cutter for the purpose of distinguishing works on the same subject (or sharing the same classification number) by different authors. Also called author number. *See also* call number; item number.

delimiter. A code (represented by the symbol $ or ≠) used to identify a subfield in a MARC 21 record.

description. *See* resource description.

descriptive cataloging. That part of cataloging consisting of the presentation of bibliographic description and the determination of access points through personal names, corporate names, and titles.

descriptive metadata. A type of metadata, consisting of data elements such as title, abstract, author, and keywords, describing an information resource or object.

dictionary catalog. A catalog in which all the entries (author, title, subject, series, etc.) and the cross-references are interfiled in one alphabetical sequence. The subject entries in a dictionary catalog are based on the principle of specific and direct entry. Also called an alphabetical catalog. *See also* alphabetical specific catalog; alphabetico-classed catalog; classed catalog.

direct entry. A subject representation containing the most specific word or phrase describing the subject. *See also* class entry.

direct subdivision. Geographic subdivision of subject headings by the name of a local place without interposition of the name of a larger geographic entity. *See also* geographic subdivision; indirect subdivision.

directory. In the MARC 21 record, a series of entries that contain the MARC tag, length, and starting location of each variable field within the record.

duplicate entry. Entry of the same subject heading in two different forms, e.g., United States—Foreign relations—France and France—Foreign relations—United States.

element. A unit of information with an area of bibliographic description. *See also* area.

encoding. The marking of the individual parts or elements of a record according to specific schemas to enable computer manipulation of the parts or elements for display and retrieval.

entry. (1) An access point; (2) A record of an information item in a catalog. *See also* heading.

entry word. The first word (other than an article) in a heading, which determines the location of the record in the catalog. *See also* heading.

enumerative classification. A classification scheme or subject headings system which lists subjects and their subdivisions and provides ready-made class marks or compound headings for them. *See also* faceted classification.

expression. The intellectual or artistic realization of a *work* in the form of alpha-numeric, musical, or choreographic notation, sound, image, object, movement, etc., or any combination of such forms (the second level of entities in FRBR).

facet. A component (based on a particular characteristic) of a complex subject, e.g., geographic facet, language facet, literary form facet.

facet analysis. The division of a subject into its component parts (facets). Each array of a facet consists of parts based on the same characteristic, e.g., English language, French language, German language, etc.

faceted classification. A classification scheme that identifies subjects by their component parts and requires fitting together the appropriate parts in order to provide a class mark for a work. For example, the Colon Classification is a faceted scheme, while the Dewey Decimal Classification is partially so. Also called analytico-synthetic classification. *See also* enumerative classification.

field. A unit of data in a MARC record, identified by a three-character numeric tag.

field terminator. A symbol used to signal the end of a field in a MARC record.

fixed field. A field with a fixed (i.e., predetermined) length in a MARC record. *See also* variable field.

fixed location. System of marking and arranging library materials by shelf and book marks so that their absolute position in room or tier and on the shelf is always the same.

form heading. A heading representing the literary genre, or physical, bibliographic, or artistic form of a work, e.g., Encyclopedias and dictionaries; Essays; Short stories; String quartets.

form subdivision. A division of a class number or subject heading which brings out the form of the work, e.g., -03 and -05 in Dewey Decimal Classification; —Dictionaries and —Periodicals in Library of Congress Subject Headings.

FRBR. *See* Functional Requirements for Bibliographic Records.

free-floating subdivision. A subdivision that may be used by a cataloger at the Library of Congress under any existing appropriate subject heading for the first time without establishing the usage editorially.

free-text. The use of natural language in information retrieval. *See also* controlled vocabulary.

Functional Requirements for Bibliographic Records (FRBR). A conceptual model that defines the bibliographic entities and the relationships among them. The three groups of entities are: (1) products of intellectual activities: work, expression, manifestation, and item; (2) persons and corporate bodies that are related to group 1 in terms of their role in the existence of the entities; and, (3) subjects of works, including concepts, objects, events, and places as well as the entities in groups 1 and 2.

general reference. A blanket reference to a group of headings rather than a particular heading. *See also* specific reference.

geographic qualifier. The name of a larger geographic entity added to a local place name, e.g., Cambridge (Mass.); Toledo (Spain).

geographic subdivision. A subdivision by the name of a place to which the subject represented by the main heading is limited. Also called local subdivision. *See also* direct subdivision; indirect subdivision.

half title. A title of a publication appearing on a leaf preceding the title page.

heading. A name, word, or phrase placed at the head of a catalog entry to provide an access point. *See also* access point; entry; entry word.

hierarchy. The arrangement of disciplines and subjects in an order ranging from the most general to the most specific.

holdings. Items belonging to a library's collection.

imprint. Details regarding the publication and distribution of a printed item.

indicator. One of two character positions at the beginning of each variable data field in a MARC 21 record, containing values that interpret or supplement the data found in the field.

indirect subdivision. Geographic subdivision of a subject heading with the interposition of a larger geographic entity between the main heading and the local subdivision. *See also* direct subdivision; geographic subdivision.

individual biography. A work devoted to the life of a single person. *See also* collective biography.

integrity of numbers. The policy of maintaining the stability of numbers in a classification scheme. Such a policy is opposed to revision, especially when the relocation of a subject is involved.

International Standard Bibliographic Description (ISBD). An internationally agreed-upon standard format for representing bibliographic information.

International Standard Book Number (ISBN). An internationally agreed-upon standard number that identifies a book uniquely.

International Standard Serial Number (ISSN). An internationally agreed-upon standard number that identifies a serial publication uniquely.

item. (1) A document or set of documents in any physical form, published, issued, or treated as an entity, and as such forming the basis for a single bibliographic description. (2) A single exemplar of a *manifestation*; it represents the lowest entity in bibliographic relationships in the FRBR (Functional Requirements for Bibliographic Records) model.

item number. That part of a call number which designates a specific individual work within its class. May consist of the author number and/or other elements such as a work mark, and an edition mark. An item number for a book is also called a book number. *See also* call number; Cutter number; work mark.

key heading. In Sears subject headings, a heading that serves as a model of subdivisions for headings in the same category.

keyword. A significant word in the title, subject heading strings, notes, abstract, other parts of a record, or the text, that can serve as an access point in retrieval.

leader. Data elements (numbers or coded values identified by relative character position) that provide information for the processing of the MARC record.

literary warrant. (1) The principle which allows a category to exist in a classification or thesaurus only if a work exists for that category. (2) The use of an actual collection or holdings of a library or actual published works as the basis for developing a classification scheme or thesaurus.

local subdivision. *See* geographic subdivision.

machine-readable cataloging. *See* MARC.

main entry. The primary access point. *See also* added entry.

main heading. In subject headings the first part of a heading excluding subdivisions.

manifestation. The physical embodiment of an *expression* of a *work*, representing the third level of FRBR entities.

MARC (Machine Readable Cataloging). A system in which cataloging records are prepared in a format which enables the computer to recognize the elements and manipulate them for various purposes.

MARC record. A catalog record in machine-readable form.

metadata. A collection of structured information that provides details regarding the attributes of information items or resources for the purposes of facilitating identification, discovery, as well as management of such resources.

mixed notation. A notational system using a combination of two or more kinds of symbols, e.g., letters and numerals.

mnemonics. Recurring concepts denoted by the same notational symbols in a classification scheme.

model heading. *See* pattern heading.

monograph. A bibliographic resource that is complete in one part or intended to be completed within a finite number of parts.

name authority file. A collection of name authority records.

name authority record. A record that shows a personal, corporate, or geographic heading in its established form, cites the authorities consulted in determining the choice of form of name, and indicates the references made to the heading. *See also* subject authority record.

name-title added entry. An added access point consisting of the name of a person or corporate body and the title of an item. Also called author-title added entry.

name-title reference. A cross reference containing the name of a person or a corporate body and the title of an item. Also called author-title reference.

network. (1) Two or more organizations engaged in a common pattern of information exchange through communications links, for some common objectives. (2) An interconnected or interrelated group of nodes.

notation. Numerals, letters, and/or other symbols used to represent the main and subordinate divisions of a classification scheme. *See also* mixed notation; pure notation.

notational synthesis. *See* number building.

number building. The process of making a class number more specific through addition of segments taken from auxiliary tables and/or other parts of the classification. *See also* synthesis.

online catalog. A catalog containing records encoded for access and display in an interactive mode.

open entry. An element within a cataloging record with a beginning but no ending date or number.

open stacks. A library or collection allowing users open access to the stacks.

organization. The method of arranging both surrogates and physical resources according to established orders: alphabetic (in most browsing lists or files), alpha-numeric (in Library or Congress classification order), or numeric (Dewey Decimal classification order).

original cataloging. The preparation of a cataloging record without the assistance of outside cataloging agencies. *See also* copy cataloging.

outsourcing. Having a specific task performed by an external agency or company.

pattern heading. A subject heading that serves as a model of subdivisions for headings in the same category. Subdivisions listed under a pattern heading may be used whenever appropriate under other headings in the same category. For example, Shakespeare, William, 1594–1616, serves as a pattern heading for literary authors; and Piano serves as a pattern heading for musical instruments. Also called model heading.

period subdivision. *See* chronological subdivision.

phoenix schedule. *See* completely revised schedule.

postcoordination. Combination of individual concepts into compound or complex subjects at the point of retrieval. *See also* precoordination.

precoordination. Combination of individual concepts into compound or complex subjects at the point of storage. *See also* postcoordination.

publication, distribution, etc., area. An area in bibliographic description giving details such as place, name, and date regarding the manufacturing and distribution of a bibliographic item. For a printed item, it is called Imprint.

pure notation. A notational system using one kind of symbol only, e.g., Arabic numerals or letters.

qualifer. A term (enclosed in parentheses) placed after a name heading or subject heading for the purpose of distinguishing between homographs or clarifying the meaning of the heading, e.g., Paris (France); Mercury (Planet); PL/I (Computer program language); Mont Blanc (Freighter); Naples (Italy : Province). *See also* geographic qualifier.

record. A unit in a file or database. *See also* bibliographic record; catalog record; name authority record; subject authority record.

record terminator. A symbol used to signal the end of a MARC 21 record.

refer-from reference. An indication of the terms of headings *from* which references are to be made to a given heading. It is the reverse of the indication of a *see* or *see also* reference and is represented by the symbols *UF* (used for) or *x* (*see* reference from); and *BT* (broader term) and *RT* (related term), or *xx* (*see also* reference from). In the MARC authority record, these terms are stored in fields 4XX and 5XX.

reference. A direction from one heading or access point to another. Also called cross-reference.

reference source. Any source, not limited to reference works, from which authoritative information may be obtained.

relative location. The arrangement of library materials according to their relations to each other and regardless of their locations on the shelves.

relocation. An adjustment in a classification system resulting in the shifting of a topic between successive editions from one number to another.

resource. An information item.

resource description. The process or the product of creating a surrogate (a bibliographic or metadata record) or a brief representation containing essential facts concerning an information item, based on established standards. *See also* bibliographic description.

schedule. The list containing the main part of a classification scheme, listing class numbers with captions and notes.

secondary entry. *See* added entry.

see also **reference.** A reference from a heading to a less comprehensive or otherwise related heading.

see **reference.** A reference from a term or name not used as a heading to one that is used.

segmentation mark. A slash (/) or prime mark (') used to indicate the end of an abridged number (as provided in the abridged edition of DDC) in a Dewey class number assigned from the full edition.

shared cataloging. The preparation by one of several participating agencies or libraries of a cataloging record which is made available to the other participating agencies or libraries. Also called cooperative cataloging. *See also* centralized cataloging.

shelflist. A file of cataloging records arranged by call number.

specific entry. Entry of a work under a heading that expresses its special subject or topic as distinguished from an entry for the class or broad subject which encompasses that special subject or topic.

specific reference. A reference from one heading to another. *See also* general reference.

standard subdivision. In Dewey Decimal Classification, a subdivision that represents a frequently recurring physical form (dictionaries, periodicals, etc.) or approach (history, research, etc.) applicable to any subject or discipline.

structural metadata. A type of metadata indicating how an item is structured, for example, how compound objects are put together or how pages are ordered to form chapters.

subdivision. The device of extending a subject heading by indicating one of its aspects—form, place, period, topic. *See also* form subdivision; geographic subdivision; chronological subdivision; topical subdivision.

subfield. A subunit within a field in a MARC 21 record.

subfield code. A two-character code identifying a subfield in the MARC 21 record, consisting of a delimiter (represented by $ or ‡) followed by a data element identifier (a lowercase alphabetic or numeric character).

subject. The overall content of a work, whether stated in the title or not; representing what the work is "about."

subject access point. An access point based on the subject of an item.

subject analysis. The process of identifying the intellectual content of a work. The results may be displayed in a catalog or bibliography by means of notational symbols as in a classification system, or by verbal terms such as subject headings or indexing terms.

subject analytical entry. A subject entry made for a part of a work.

subject authority file. A collection of subject authority records.

subject authority record. A record of a subject heading that shows its established form, cites the authorities consulted in determining the choice and form of the heading, and indicates the cross references made to and from the heading. *See also* name authority record.

subject catalog. A catalog consisting of subject entries only; the subject portion of a divided catalog.

subject cataloging. (1) The process of providing subject access points to bibliographic records. (2) The process of assigning subject headings.

subject heading. The term (a word or a group of words) denoting a subject under which all material on that subject is entered in a catalog.

subject-to-name reference. A reference from a subject heading to a name heading for the purpose of directing the user's attention from a particular field of interest to names of individuals or corporate bodies that are active or associated in some way with the field.

superimposition. The policy of adopting a new catalog code while leaving headings derived from an earlier code unrevised.

surrogate record. A collection of essential data (such as author, title, date, subject, location, etc.) regarding an information resource, assembled for the purpose of efficient access to and retrieval of the resource it represents.

syndetic device. The device used to connect related headings by means of cross-references.

synthesis. The process of composing a class number, subject heading, or indexing term by combining various elements in order to represent a compound or complex subject. *See also* number building.

table. A list in a classification scheme listing numbers to be combined with main numbers from the schedule. *See also* schedule.

tag. A three-character numeric code that identifies a field in a MARC 21 record.

thesaurus. A controlled vocabulary list of indexing terms (descriptors) consisting of a subset of a natural language and cross references from synonyms and related terms.

topical subdivision. A subdivision that represents an aspect of the main subject other than form, place, or period.

tracing. (1) The record of the headings under which an item is represented in a catalog. (2) The record of the references that have been made to a name or to the title of an item that is represented in a catalog.

uniform heading. The particular heading by which a subject or person that may be represented by different names or different forms of a name is to be listed in the catalog.

uniform title. A title of a work chosen from multiple titles by which the work has been known for the purpose of collocating and identifying works with different titles. Also called conventional title.

union catalog. A catalog representing the holdings of a group of libraries.

unique heading. A heading that represents only one person, corporate body, or subject.

universal bibliographic control. The ideal of achieving universal bibliographic information exchange and sharing through standard bibliographic description of all publications in the world, each created and distributed by a national agency in the country of origin.

variable field. A field with variable length in a MARC record. *See also* fixed field.

verso of the title page. The back side of the title page.

vocabulary control. The effort to standardize indexing terms by controlling synonyms and homographs and providing term relationships for the purpose of efficient and effective retrieval of information.

work. A distinct intellectual or artistic creation, representing the highest level in the FRBR conceptual model.

workform. A standardized framework or template for creating a catalog record by filling in data in appropriate places.

work mark. A part of call number based on the title of a work. *See also* item number; call number.

XML (eXtensible Markup Language). A markup language designed for Web documents to enable the inclusion of data about themselves *within* the document, i.e., allowing the documents to carry with them specifications that guide their processing independent of any specific software application.

BIBLIOGRAPHY

ALA Filing Rules. Chicago: American Library Association, 1980.

Anglo-American Cataloguing Rules. 2nd ed., 2002 revision. Prepared under the direction of the Joint Steering Committee for Revision of AACR, a committee of the American Library Association, the Australian Committee on Cataloguing, the British Library, the Canadian Committee on Cataloguing, Chartered Institute of Library and Information Professionals, the Library of Congress. Chicago: American Library Association, 2002.

Association for Library Collections & Technical Services, Cataloging and Classification Section, Subject Analysis Committee, Subcommittee on the Revision of the Guidelines on Subject Access to Individual Works of Fiction. *Guidelines on Subject Access to Individual Works of Fiction, Drama, Etc.,* 2nd ed. Chicago: American Library Association, 2000.

Attig, John. "The USMARC Formats—Underlying Principles." *Information Technology and Libraries* 1, no. 2 (June 1982): 169–74.

Auld, Larry. "Authority Control: An Eighty-Year Review." *Library Resources & Technical Services* 26 (October/December 1982): 319–30.

Austin, Derek, and Jeremy A. Digger. "PRECIS: The Preserved Context Index System." *Library Resources & Technical Services* 21 (Winter 1977): 13–30.

Avram, Henriette D. *MARC: Its History and Implications.* Washington, D.C.: Library of Congress, 1975.

Bates, Marcia J. "Rethinking Subject Cataloging in the Online Environment." *Library Resources & Technical Services* 33, no. 4 (1989): 400–412.

Berman, Sanford. *Prejudices and Antipathies: A Tract on the LC Subject Heads Concerning People.* Jefferson, N.C.: McFarland, 1993.

Berman, Sanford, ed. *Subject Cataloging: Critiques and Innovations.* New York: Haworth, 1985.

Bliss, Henry Evelyn. *Bliss Bibliographic Classification.* 2nd ed. Edited by J. Mills and Vanda Broughton, with the assistance of Valerie Lang. London; Boston: Butterworths, 1977–<1996>.

———. *A System of Bibliographic Classification.* 2nd ed. New York: H. W. Wilson Company, 1936.

———. *The Organization of Knowledge in Libraries.* 2nd ed. New York: The H. W. Wilson Company, 1939.

Borgman, Christine L. "From Acting Locally to Thinking Globally: A Brief

History of Library Automation." *Library Quarterly* 67, no. 3 (July 1997): 215–49.

Bourne, Charles P., and Trudi Bellardo Hahn. *A History of Online Information Services, 1963–1976.* Cambridge, Mass.: MIT Press, 2003.

British Museum. *The Catalogue of Printed Books in the British Museum.* London, 1841.

British Museum. Department of Printed Books. *Rules for Compiling the Catalogues of Printed Books, Maps and Music in the British Museum.* Rev. ed. London: British Museum; printed by order of the Trustees, 1936.

British Standards Institution. *Universal Decimal Classification.* Complete ed. London: BSI, 2005.

———. *Universal Decimal Classification.* 2nd ed. Abridged. London: BSI, 2003.

Brown, James Duff. *Subject Classification for the Arrangement of Libraries and the Organization of Information, with Tables, Indexes, etc., for the Subdivision of Subjects.* 3rd ed. Revised and enlarged by J. D. Stewart. London: Grafton & Co., 1939.

Byrne, Deborah J. *MARC Manual: Understanding and Using MARC Records.* 2nd ed. Englewood, Colo.: Libraries Unlimited, 1998.

Calhoun, Karen. "The Changing Nature of the Catalog and its Integration with Other Discovery Tools: Final Report, prepared for the Library of Congress, March 17, 2006." www.loc.gov/catdir/calhoun-report-final.pdf (28 Feb. 2007).

Caplan, Priscilla. *Metadata Fundamentals for All Librarians.* Chicago: American Library Association, 2003.

———. "International Metadata Initiatives: Lessons in Bibliographic Control." 61–79 in *Proceedings of the Bicentennial Conference on Bibliographic Control for the New Millennium: Confronting the Challenges of Networked Resources and the Web: Washington, D.C., November 15–17, 2000,* sponsored by the Library of Congress Cataloging Directorate; edited by Ann M. Sandberg-Fox. Washington, D.C.: Library of Congress, Cataloging Distribution Service, 2001. Also available at: www.loc.gov/catdir/bibcontrol/chan_paper.html (28 Feb. 2007).

Carlyle, Allyson. "Understanding FRBR as a Conceptual Model." *Library Resources & Technical Resources* 50, no. 4 (October 2006): 264–73.

Carpenter, Michael, and Elaine Svenonius. *Foundations of Cataloging: A Sourcebook.* Littleton, Colo.: Libraries Unlimited, 1985.

Cataloging & Classification Quarterly. 1, no. 1– (Fall 1980–).

Cataloging and the Organization of Information: Philosophies, Practices, and Challenges at the Onset of the 21st Century. Binghamton, N.Y.: Haworth Press, 2000. Also published as Volume 30, Numbers 1–3 of *Cataloging & Classification Quarterly.*

Cataloging Rules: Author and Title Entries. American ed. Chicago: American Library Association, 1980.

Cataloging Service. Bulletin 1–125 (June 1945–Spring 1978).

Cataloging Service Bulletin. No. 1- (Summer 1978-). Published quarterly.

Chan, Lois Mai. "Functions of a Subject Authority File." 9–30 in *Subject Authorities in the Online Environment: Papers from a Conference Program Held in San Francisco, June 29, 1987,* edited by Karen Markey Drabenstott. Chicago and London: American Library Association, 1991.

———. *A Guide to the Library of Congress Classification.* 5th ed. Englewood, Colo.: Libraries Unlimited, 1999.

———. "Library of Congress Classification as an Online Retrieval Tool: Potentials and Limitations." *Information Technology and Libraries* 5 (September 1986): 181–92.

———. *Library of Congress Subject Headings: Principles and Application.* 4th ed. Westport, Conn.: Libraries Unlimited, 2005.

———. "Still Robust at 100: A Century of LC Subject Headings." *The Library of Congress Information Bulletin* 57, no. 8 (August 1998): 200–201.

Chan, Lois Mai, Phyllis Richmond, and Elaine Svenonius. *Theory of Subject Analysis: A Sourcebook.* Littleton, Colo.: Libraries Unlimited, 1985.

Chan, Lois Mai, and Joan S. Mitchell. *Dewey Decimal Classification: Principles and Application.* 3rd ed. Dublin, Ohio: OCLC Online Computer Library Center, 2003.

Chan, Lois Mai, and Theodora Hodges, revised by Giles Martin. "Subject Cataloguing and Classification." 95–109 in *Technical Services Today and Tomorrow,* by Michael Gorman and Associates, 2nd ed., Englewood, Colo.: Libraries Unlimited, 1998.

Chan, Lois Mai, Eric Childress, Rebecca Dean, Edward T. O'Neill, and Diane Vizine-Goetz, "A Faceted Approach to Subject Data in the Dublin Core Metadata Record." *Journal of Internet Cataloging* 4, no. 1/2: (2001) 35–47.

Chu, Heting. *Information Representation and Retrieval in the Digital Age.* Medford, N.J.: Published for the American Society for Information Science and Technology by Information Today, 2003.

Coates, Eric. *Subject Catalogues: Headings and Structure.* London: Library Association, 1988.

Cochrane, Pauline A. "Universal Bibliographic Control: Its Role in the Availability of Information and Knowledge." *Library Resources & Technical Services* 34, no. 4 (October 1990): 423–31.

Comaromi, John P. *Book Numbers: A Historical Study and Practical Guide to Their Use.* Littleton, Colo.: Libraries Unlimited, 1981.

———. "Conception and Development of the Dewey Decimal Classification." *International Classification* 3 (1976): 11–15.

———. *The Eighteen Editions of the Dewey Decimal Classification.* Albany, N.Y.: Forest Press Division, Lake Placid Education Foundation, 1976.

The Concise AACR2. Prepared by Michael Gorman. 4th ed. Chicago: American Library Association; Ottawa: Canadian Library Association; London: Chartered Institute of Library and Information Professionals, 2004.

Cutter, Charles A. *C. A. Cutter's Three-Figure Author Table*. Swanson-Swift revision. Chicopee, Mass.: H. R. Huntting Company, 1969.

———. *C. A. Cutter's Two-Figure Author Table*. Swanson-Swift revision. Chicopee, Mass.: H. R. Huntting Company, 1969.

———. *Cutter-Sanborn Three-Figure Author Table*. Swanson-Swift revision. Chicopee, Mass.: H. R. Huntting Company, 1969.

———. *Expansive Classification: Part 1: The First Six Classifications*. Boston: C. A. Cutter, 1891–1893.

———. *Rules for a Dictionary Catalog*. 4th ed. rewritten. Washington, D.C.: Government Printing Office, 1904. Republished, London: The Library Association, 1953. First published under the title *Rules for a Printed Dictionary Catalogue* in 1876.

Dewey, Melvil. *Abridged Dewey Decimal Classification and Relative Index*. Ed. 14, edited by Joan S. Mitchell, Editor in Chief, Julianne Beall, Giles Martin, Winton E. Matthews, Jr., Gregory R. New, Assistant Editors. Dublin, Ohio: OCLC Online Computer Library Center, Inc., 2004.

———. *Dewey Decimal Classification and Relative Index*. Ed. 22, edited by Joan S. Mitchell, Editor in Chief, Julianne Beall, Giles Martin, Winton E. Matthews, Jr., Gregory R. New, Assistant Editors. Dublin, Ohio: OCLC Online Computer Library Center, Inc., 2003.

The Dublin Core Metadata Element Set, ANSI/NISO Z39.85-2001. Bethesda, Md.: NISO Press, 2001. Available: www.niso.org/standards/resources/Z39-85.pdf (28 Feb. 2007).

Dunkin, Paul S. *Cataloging U.S.A.* Chicago: American Library Association, 1969.

Ebenezer, Catherine. "Trends in Integrated Library Systems." *VINE* 32, no. 4 (2003): 19–45.

Evans, G. Edward, Sheila S. Intner, and Jean Weihs. *Introduction to Technical Services*. 7th ed. Greenwood Village, Colo.: Libraries Unlimited, 2002.

Foskett, A. C. *The Subject Approach to Information*. 5th ed. London: Library Association Publishing, 1996.

Fritz, Deborah A., *Cataloging with AACR2 and MARC21, for Books, Electronic Resources, Sound Recordings, Videorecordings, and Serials*. 2nd ed. Chicago: American Library Association, 2004.

Fritz, Deborah A. and Richard J. Fritz. *MARC21 for Everyone: A Practical Guide*. Chicago: American Library Association, 2003.

Furrie, Betty. *Understanding MARC Bibliographic: Machine-Readable Cataloging*. 7th ed. Washington, D.C.: Cataloging Distribution Service, Library of Congress, 2003. Also available: www.loc.gov/marc/umb (28 Feb. 2007).

Gorman, Michael. "Descriptive Cataloguing: Its Past, Present, and Future." 79–94 in *Technical Services Today and Tomorrow*, Michael Gorman et al., 2nd ed. Edited by Michael Gorman. Englewood, Colo.: Libraries Unlimited, 1998.

————. *The Concise AACR2.* 4th ed. Chicago: American Library Association, 2004.

Gorman, Michael, ed. *Technical Services Today and Tomorrow.* 2nd ed. Englewood, Colo.: Library Unlimited, 1998.

Hagler, Ronald. *The Bibliographic Record and Information Technology.* 3rd ed. Chicago: American Library Association, 1997.

Hahn, Trudi Bellardo. "Pioneers of the Online Age." 116–31 in *Historical Studies in Information Science,* edited by Trudi Bellardo Hahn and Michael Buckland. Medford, N.J.: Published for the American Society for Information Science by Information Today, 1998.

Hamdy, M. Nabil. *The Concept of Main Entry as Represented in the Anglo-American Cataloging Rules: A Critical Appraisal with Some Suggestions: Author Main Entry vs. Title Main Entry.* Littleton, Colo.: Libraries Unlimited, 1973.

Hanson, J. C. M. "The Library of Congress and Its New Catalogue: Some Unwritten History." In *Essays Offered to Herbert Putnam by His Colleagues and Friends on His Thirtieth Anniversary as Librarian of Congress: 5 April 1929.* New Haven: Yale University Press, 1929.

Harold, Elliotte Rusty, and W. Scott Means. *XML in a Nutshell,* 3rd ed. Sebastopol, Calif.: O'Reilly, 2004.

Haykin, David Judson. *Subject Headings: A Practical Guide.* Washington, D.C.: Government Printing Office, 1951.

Haynes, Elizabeth, and Joanna F. Fountain. *Unlocking the Mysteries of Cataloging: A Workbook of Examples.* Westport, Conn.: Libraries Unlimited, 2005.

Hildreth, Charles, ed. *The Online Catalogue: Developments and Directions.* London: Library Association, 1989.

Hillmann, Diane. "Using Dublin Core," 2005-11-07. http://dublincore.org/documents/2005/11/07/usageguide/ (28 Feb. 2007).

Hsieh-Yee, Ingrid. *Organizing Audiovisual and Electronic Resources for Access: A Cataloging Guide.* Englewood, Colo.: Libraries Unlimited, 1999.

Hunter, Eric J. *Classification Made Simple.* 2nd ed. Aldershot, Eng.; Burlington, Vt.: Ashgate, 2002.

IFLA Study Group on the Functional Requirements for Bibliographic Records. *Functional Requirements for Bibliographic Records, Final Report.* München: K. G. Saur, 1998. UBCIM Publications, New Series; v. 19. Also available at www.ifla.org/VII/s13/frbr/frbr.htm (28 Feb. 2007).

International Conference on Cataloguing Principles, Paris, 1961. *Report of International Conference on Cataloging Principles,* edited by A. H. Chaplin and Dorothy Anderson. London: Organizing Committee of the International Conference on Cataloguing Principles, 1963; Hamden, Conn.: Archon Books, 1969.

International Conference on Cataloguing Principles, Paris, 1961. *Statement of Principles: Adopted at the International Conference on Cataloguing Principles, Paris, October 1961.* Annotated ed., with commentary and examples by Eva Verona assisted by [others]. Definitive ed. London (c/o Dept. of Printed Books, British Museum, WC1B 3DG), International Federation of Library Associations (Committee on Cataloguing), 1971.

International Federation of Library Associations. Working Group on the General International Bibliographic Description. *ISBD(G): International Standard Bibliographic Description (General)*: Annotated Text. London: IFLA International Office for UBC, 1977.

International Standard Bibliographic Description. . . . München: K. G. Saur, 1971– . (Each standard covering a different type of material such as electronic resources, monographic publications, and printed music.)

Intner, Sheila S., and Jean Weihs. *Standard Cataloging for School and Public Libraries*. 3rd ed. Englewood, Colo.: Libraries Unlimited, 2001.

Intner, Sheila S., Susan S. Laziner, and Jean Weihs. *Metadata and Its Impact on Libraries*. Westport, Conn.: Libraries Unlimited, 2006.

Jewett, Charles C. "Smithsonian Catalogue System." 3–19 in *Smithsonian Report On the Construction of Catalogues of Libraries and of a General Catalogue and Their Publication by Means of Separate, Stereotyped Titles with Rules and Examples*. 2nd ed. Washington, D.C.: Smithsonian Institution, 1853; also in *Foundations of Cataloging: A Sourcebook*, edited by Michael Carpenter and Elaine Svenonius, 51–61. Littleton, Colo.: Libraries Unlimited, 1985.

Joint Steering Committee for Revision of Anglo-American Cataloguing Rules. *A Brief History of AACR.* www.collectionscanada.ca/jsc/history.html (28 Feb. 2007).

Jones, Wayne, Judith R. Ahronheim, and Josephine Crawford, ed. *Cataloging the Web: Metadata, AACR, and MARC 21*. Lanham, Md.: Scarecrow, 2002.

Kanellos, Michael. "The Hard Drive at 50: Half a Century of Hard Drives." *CNET News.com*, 11 September 2006. http://news.com.com/The+hard+drive+at+50/2009-1015_3-6112782.html (16 Oct. 2006).

Koch, Traugott. *Controlled Vocabularies, Thesauri and Classification Systems Available in the WWW. DC Subject*. 2003. www.lub.lu.se/metadata/subject-help.html (28 Feb. 2007).

Koch, Traugott, and Michael Day. *The Role of Classification Schemes in Internet Resource Description and Discovery*. Last updated: 28-Jan-1999. www.ukoln.ac.uk/metadata/desire/classification/ (1 March 2007).

LaMontagne, Leo E. *American Library Classification with Special Reference to the Library of Congress*. Hamden, Conn.: Shoe String Press, 1961.

Lancaster, F. W. *Indexing and Abstracting in Theory and Practice*. 3rd ed. London: Facet Pub., 2003.

———. *Vocabulary Control for Information Retrieval*. 2nd ed. Arlington, Va.: Information Resources Press, 1986.

Lancaster, F. Wilfrid, and Amy J. Warner. *Information Retrieval Today*. Arlington, Va.: Information Resources Press, 1993.

Langridge, D. W. *Subject Analysis: Principles and Procedures*. London: Bowker-Saur, 1989.

———. *Classification: Its Kinds, Elements, Systems and Applications*. London: Bowker-Saur, 1992.

Lehnus, Donald J. *Book Numbers: History, Principles, and Application*. Chicago: American Library Association, 1980.

Library of Congress, Cataloging Policy and Support Office. *Free-Floating Subdivisions: An Alphabetical Index*. Washington, D.C.: Library of Congress, Cataloging Distribution Service, 1989–.

———. *Subject Cataloging Manual: Subject Headings*. 5th ed. Washington, D.C.: Cataloging Distribution Service, Library of Congress, 1996.

———. *Subject Cataloging Manual: Classification*. 1st ed. Washington, D.C.: Cataloging Distribution Service, Library of Congress, 1992–.

———. *Subject Cataloging Manual: Shelflisting*. 2nd ed. Washington, D.C.: Cataloging Distribution Service, Library of Congress, 1995–.

———. *Subject Cataloging Manual: Subject Headings*. 5th ed. Washington, D.C.: Cataloging Distribution Service, Library of Congress, 1996–.

Library of Congress. MARC Development Office. *Information on the MARC System*. 4th ed. Washington, D.C.: Library of Congress, 1974.

Library of Congress. Processing Department. *Studies of Descriptive Cataloging: A Report to the Librarian of Congress by the Director of the Processing Department*. Washington, D.C.: Government Printing Office, 1946.

Library of Congress. Processing Services. *Library of Congress Filing Rules*. Prepared by John C. Rather and Susan C. Biebel. Washington, D.C.: Library of Congress, 1980.

Library of Congress. *Rules for Descriptive Cataloging in the Library of Congress*. Adopted by the American Library Association. Washington, D.C.: Library of Congress, 1949.

Library of Congress. Subject Cataloging Division. *LC Classification Outline*. www.loc.gov/catdir/cpso/lcco/ (1 March 2007).

———. *Library of Congress Subject Headings*. 8th ed.–. Washington, D.C.: Cataloging Distribution Service, Library of Congress, 1975–. Published annually, with weekly updates: *Weekly Lists*. www.loc.gov/aba/cataloging/subject/weeklylists (1 March 2007).

Library of Congress. *Subject Headings Used in the Dictionary Catalogs of the Library of Congress*. 1st ed.–7th ed. Washington, D.C.: Library of Congress, 1914–1966.

Library of Congress Authorities. http://authorities.loc.gov/ (1 March 2007).

Library of Congress Classification: A-Z. Washington, D.C.: Library of Congress. 1901–.

Library of Congress Online Catalog. http://catalog.loc.gov/ (1 March 2007).

Library of Congress Rule Interpretations. 2nd ed. Washington, D.C.: Cataloging Distribution Service, Library of Congress, 1989– (Kept up to date with quarterly updates and annual cumulations).

Library of Congress Subject Headings: Principles of Structure and Policies for

Application. Prepared by Lois Mai Chan for the Library of Congress. Washington, D.C.: Library of Congress, 1990.

Library Resources & Technical Services. Vol. 1, no. 1– (Winter 1957–). Published quarterly.

List of Subject Headings for Use in a Dictionary Catalog. Prepared by a Committee of the American Library Association. Boston: Published for the ALA Publishing Section by the Library Bureau, 1895.

Lubetzky, Seymour. *Cataloging Rules and Principles: A Critique of the A.L.A. Rules for Entry and a Proposed Design for Their Revision.* Prepared for the Board on Cataloging and Classification. Washington, D.C.: Library of Congress, Processing Department, 1953.

———. *Code of Cataloging Rules, Author and Title Entry: An Unfinished Draft for a New Edition of Cataloging Rules Prepared for the Catalog Code Revision Committee, with an Explanatory Commentary by Paul Dunkin.* Chicago: American Library Association, 1960.

———. *Principles of Cataloging: Final Report: Phase I: Descriptive Cataloging.* Los Angeles: Institute of Library Research, University of California, 1969.

———. "Principles of Descriptive Cataloging." 25–33 in *Studies of Descriptive Cataloging.* Washington, D.C.: Library of Congress, 1946; also in *Foundations of Cataloging: A Sourcebook,* edited by Michael Carpenter and Elaine Svenonius, 104–12. Littleton, Colo.: Libraries Unlimited, 1985.

———. *Writings on the Classical Art of Cataloging,* compiled and edited by Elaine Svenonius and Dorothy McGarry. Englewood, Colo.: Libraries Unlimited, 2001.

Luhn, Hans Peter. "Keyword in Context Index for Technical Literature (KWIC Index)." *American Documentation* 11 (1960): 288–95.

MacLennan, Alan. "Classification and the Internet." 59–68 in *The Future of Classification,* edited by Rita Marcella and Arthur Maltby. Brookfield, Vt.: Gower, 2000.

Maltby, Arthur. *Sayers' Manual of Classification for Librarians.* 5th ed. London: Deutsch, 1975.

Mann, Thomas. *Library Research Models: A Guide to Classification, Cataloging, and Computers.* New York: Oxford University Press, 1993.

MARC 21 Concise Formats, prepared by Network Development and MARC Standards Office, Library of Congress, 2000 ed.–. Washington, D.C.: Cataloging Distribution Service, Library of Congress, 2000–; updated annually. Also available at: www.loc.gov/marc/authority/ecad home.html (1 March 2007).

MARC 21 Format for Authority Data: Including Guidelines for Content Designation, prepared by Network Development and MARC Standards Office, Library of Congress, in cooperation with Standards and Support, National Library of Canada. Washington, D.C.: Library of Congress,

Cataloging Distribution Service; Ottawa: National Library of Canada, 1999–.

MARC 21 Format for Bibliographic Data: Including Guidelines for Content Designation, prepared by Network Development and MARC Standards Office, Library of Congress, in cooperation with Standards and Support, National Library of Canada. Washington, D.C.: Library of Congress, Cataloging Distribution Service, 1999–.

MARC 21 Format for Classification Data: Including Guidelines for Content Designation, prepared by Network Development and MARC Standards Office, Library of Congress in cooperation with Standards and Support, National Library of Canada. Washington, D.C.: Cataloging Distribution Service, Library of Congress, 2000–.

MARC 21 Format for Holdings Data: Including Guidelines for Content Designation, prepared by Network Development and MARC Standards Office, Library of Congress, in cooperation with Standards and Support, National Library of Canada. Washington, D.C.: Cataloging Distribution Service, Library of Congress, 2000–.

The MARC21 Formats: Background and Principles, prepared by MARBI in conjunction with Network Development and MARC Standards Office, Library of Congress. Revised November 1996. Washington, DC: Cataloging Distribution Service, Library of Congress, 1996. Also available at: www.loc.gov/marc/96principl.html/ (1 March 2007).

Marcella, Rita, and Arthur Maltby. *The Future of Classification*. Aldershot, Eng.; Brookfield, Vt.: Gower, 2000.

Markey, Karen. *Subject Searching in Library Catalogs Before and After the Introduction of Online Catalogs*. OCLC Library, Information and Computer Science Series, no. 4. Dublin, Ohio: OCLC, 1984.

Markuson, Barbara Evans. "Bibliographic Systems, 1945–1976." *Library Trends* 25 (July 1976): 311–27.

Maxwell, Robert L. *Maxwell's Guide to Authority Work*. Chicago: American Library Association, 2002.

———. *Maxwell's Handbook for AACR2: Explaining and Illustrating the Anglo-American Cataloguing Rules Through the 2003 Update*. 4th ed. Chicago: American Library Association, 2004.

McCallum, Sally H. "An Introduction to the Metadata Object Description Schema." *Library Hi Tech* 22, no. 1 (January 2004): 82–88.

———. "Library of Congress Metadata Landscape." *Zeitschrift für Bibliothekswesen und Bibliographie* 50, no. 4 (2003): 182–187.

McIlwaine, I. C. *The Universal Decimal Classification: A Guide to Its Use*. The Hague: UDC Consortium, 2000.

McKnight, Mark. *Music Classification Systems*. Lanham, Md.: Scarecrow Press, 2002.

Medical Subject Headings 1st ed.– Bethesda, Md.: U.S. Dept. of Health and Human Services, Public Health Service, National Institutes of Health, National Library of Medicine, 1960–2003 (last printed version). Online version: www.nlm.nih.gov/mesh/ (1 March 2007).

Medical Subject Headings. Annotated Alphabetic list. Bethesda, Md.: Medical Subject Headings Section, Library Operations, National Library of Medicine; [Springfield, Va.: National Technical Information Service, distributor, 19??–2003.]

Medical Subject Headings. MeSH Tree Structures. Bethesda, Md.: National Library of Medicine, 2004–. www.nlm.nih.gov/mesh/intro_trees 2007.html. (1 March 2007).

Medical Subject Headings. Tree Structures. Bethesda, Md.: Medical Subject Headings Section, Library Operations, National Library of Medicine, 1972–2003.

Miksa, Francis. *The Subject in the Dictionary Catalog from Cutter to the Present.* Chicago: American Library Association, 1983.

Miller, Rosalind E., and Jane C. Terwillegar. *Commonsense Cataloging: A Cataloger's Manual.* 4th ed. rev. New York: H. W. Wilson Co., 1990.

Mills, J. *A Modern Outline of Library Classification.* London: Chapman & Hall, 1960.

Millsap, Larry. "A History of the Online Catalog in North America." 79–91 in *Technical Services Management, 1965–1990: A Quarter Century of Change and a Look to the Future: Festschrift for Kathryn Luther Henderson,* edited by Linda C. Smith and Ruth C. Carter. New York: Haworth Press, 1996.

Milstead, Jessica, and Susan Feldman. "Metadata: Cataloging by Any Other Name . . ." and "Metadata Projects and Standards." *Online* (January 1999).

National Library of Medicine Classification: A Scheme for the Shelf Arrangement of Library Materials in the Field of Medicine and Its Related Sciences. 5th ed. rev. NIH Publication, no. 00-1535. Bethesda, Md.: National Library of Medicine, 1999 (last printed version); online version: www .nlm.nih.gov/class/. (1 March 2007).

NLM Classification. Bethesda, Md.: National Library of Medicine, 2002–. www.nlm.nih.gov/class/(1 March 2007).

OCLC. *Bibliographic Formats and Standards.* 3rd ed. Dublin, Ohio: OCLC, 2003. Also available at: www.oclc.org/bibformats (1 March 2007).

———. *OCLC Online Computer Library Center.* www.oclc.org/ (1 March 2007).

Olson, Hope A., and John J. Boll. *Subject Analysis in Online Catalogs.* 2nd ed. Englewood, Colo.: Libraries Unlimited, 2001.

O'Neill, Edward T., and Lois Mai Chan. "FAST (Faceted Application of Subject Terminology): A Simplified Vocabulary Based on The Library of Congress Subject Headings." *IFLA Journal* 29, no. 4 (December 2003): 336–42. Also available: www.ifla.org/IV/ifla69/papers/010e-ONeill_Mai-Chan.pdf (1 March 2007).

O'Neill, Edward T., Lois Mai Chan, Eric Childress, Rebecca Dean, Lynn El-Hoshy, and Diane Vizine-Goetz. "Form Subdivisions: Their Identification and Use in LCSH." *Library Resources & Technical Services* 45, no. 4 (2001): 187–97.

Osborn, Andrew D. "The Crisis in Cataloging." *Library Quarterly* 11 (October 1941): 393–411.

Palmer, Bernard I. *Itself an Education: Six Lectures on Classification.* 2nd ed. London: Library Association, 1971.

Panizzi, Anthony. "Mr. Panizzi to the Right Hon. the Earl of Ellesmere.— British Museum, January 29, 1848." 378–95 in Great Britain, Commissioners Appointed to Inquire into the Constitution and Government of the British Museum. *Appendix to the Report of the Commissioner Appointed to Inquire into the Constitution and Management of the British Museum.* London: Her Majesty's Stationery Office, 1850.

Panizzi, Anthony, et al. "Rules for the Compilation of the Catalogue." Vol. 1. Pp. v–ix in British Museum, *Catalogue of Printed Books in the British Museum.* London: British Museum; printed by order of the trustees, 1841.

Permuted Medical Subject Headings. Bethesda, Md.: National Library of Medicine; [Springfield, Va.]: U.S. Dept. of Commerce, National Technical Information Center [distributor], 1977–[2003?].

Perreault, Jean. "Authority Control, Old and New." *Libri* 32 (1982): 124–48.

Pettee, Julia. *Subject Headings: The History and Theory of the Alphabetical Subject Approach to Books.* New York: The H. W. Wilson Company, 1947.

Prevost, Marie Louise. "An Approach to Theory and Method in General Subject Headings." *Library Quarterly* 16 (April 1946): 140–51.

"Principles of the Sears List of Subject Headings." xv–xxix in *Sears List of Subject Headings*, 18th ed., Joseph Miller, Editor; Joan Goodsell, Associate Editor. New York: H. W. Wilson Company, 2004.

The Prussian Instructions: Rules for the Alphabetical Catalogs of the Prussian Libraries. Translated from the 2nd ed., authorized August 10, 1908, with an introduction and notes by Andrew D. Osborn. Ann Arbor, Mich.: University of Michigan Press, 1938.

Ranganathan, S. R. *Colon Classification.* 7th ed. Edited by M. A. Gopinath. Bangalore: Sarada Ranganathan Endowment for Library Science, 1987–.

———. *Elements of Library Classification.* 3rd ed. Bombay: Asia Pub. House, 1962.

———. *Prolegomena to Library Classification*, 3rd ed., assisted by M. A. Gopinath. London: Asia Publishing House, 1967.

RDA—Resource Description and Access. Joint Steering Committee for Revision of AACR, updated: 20 June 2006. www.collectionscanada.ca/jsc/rda.html (1 March 2007).

Rowley, Jennifer, and John Farrow. *Organizing Knowledge: An Introduction to Managing Access to Information.* 3rd ed. Burlington, Vt.: Ashgate, 2000.

Salton, Gerard. "Historical Notes: The Past Thirty Years in Information Retrieval." *Journal of the American Society for Information Science* 38, no. 5 (1987): 375–80.

Sayers, W. C. Berwick. *Sayers' Manual of Classification for Librarians.* 3rd ed., revised by Arthur Maltby. London: Andre Deutsch, 1955.

Scott, Edith. "The Evolution of Bibliographic Systems in the United States, 1876–1945." *Library Trends* 25 (July 1976): 293–310.

Sears List of Subject Headings. 18th ed., Joseph Miller, Editor; Joan Goodsell, Associate Editor. New York: H. W. Wilson Company, 2004.

Sears, Minnie Earl. *List of Subject Headings for Small Libraries, Compiled from Lists Used in Nine Representative Small Libraries.* New York: The H. W. Wilson Company; London: Grafton & Co., 1923.

Slavic, Aida. "UDC Translations: A 2004 Survey Report and Bibliography." *Extensions and Corrections to the UDC* 2 (2004): 58–80.

Smiraglia, Richard. *The Nature of "A Work": Implications for Knowledge Organization.* Lanham, Md.: Scarecrow Press, 2001.

"Sputnik and The Dawn of the Space Age." http://history.nasa.gov/sputnik/ (updated February 21, 2003; accessed 1 March 2007).

Strout, Ruth French. "The Development of the Catalog and Cataloging Codes." *Library Quarterly* 26 (October 1956): 254–75.

Studwell, William E. *Library of Congress Subject Headings: Philosophy, Practice, and Prospects.* New York: Haworth Press, 1990.

Super LCCS: Gale's Library of Congress Classification Schedules Combined with Additions and Changes Through . . . Detroit: Gale Research, Inc., c1994–.

Svenonius, Elaine, ed. *The Conceptual Foundations of Descriptive Cataloging.* San Diego, Calif.: Academic Press, 1989.

———. "Design of Controlled Vocabularies." Vol. 45, Supp. 10. Pp. 82–109 in Allen Kent, ed., *Encyclopedia of Library and Information Science.* New York: Marcel Dekker, 1990.

———. *The Intellectual Foundations of Information Organization.* Cambridge, Mass.: The MIT Press, 2000.

———. "LCSH: Semantics, Syntax and Specificity." *Cataloging and Classification Quarterly* 29, no. 1/2 (2000): 17–30.

Talmacs, Kerrie. "Authority Control." 129–39 in *Technical Services Today and Tomorrow.* 2nd ed. Englewood, Colo.: Libraries Unlimited, 1998.

Taube, Mortimer, and Associates. *Studies in Coordinate Indexing.* Washington, D.C.: Documentation, Inc., 1953.

Taylor, Arlene G. "Authority Control: Where It's Been and Where It's Going." In *Authority Control: Why It Matters.* Conference held at College of the Holy Cross, Worcester, Mass., sponsored by the NELINET Cataloging and Technical Services Advisory Committee, November 1, 1999. Available: www.nelinet.net/edserv/conf/cataloging/cts/1999/taylor.htm (1 March 2007).

———. "Cataloguing." 117–81 in *World Encyclopedia of Library and Information Services.* 3rd ed. Chicago: American Library Association, 1993.

————. *Introduction to Cataloging and Classification.* 10th ed. Westport, Conn.: Libraries Unlimited, 2006.

————. *The Organization of Information.* 2nd ed. Westport, Conn: Libraries Unlimited, 2004.

————. "Research and Theoretical Considerations in Authority Control." *Cataloging & Classification Quarterly* 9, no. 3 (1989): 29–57.

Taylor, Arlene G., and Barbara B. Tillett, eds. *Authority Control in Organizing and Accessing Information: Definition and International Experience.* New York: Haworth Information Press, 2004.

Taylor, Arlene G., with the assistance of Rosanna M. O'Neil. *Cataloging with Copy: A Decision-Maker's Handbook.* 2nd ed. Englewood, Colo.: Libraries Unlimited, 1988.

Tedd, Luch A. "OPACs through the Ages." *Library Review* (Glasgow, Scotland) 43, no. 4 (1994): 27–37.

Tillett, Barbara B., ed. *Authority Control in the Online Environment: Considerations and Practices.* New York: Haworth Press, 1989.

Tillett, Barbara B. "Authority Control: State of the Art and New Perspectives." *Cataloging & Classification Quarterly* 38, no. 3/4 (2004): 23–42.

————. "Considerations for Authority Control in the Online Environment." *Cataloging & Classification Quarterly* 9, no. 3 (1989): 1–13.

————. "FRBR (Functional Requirements for Bibliographic Records)." *Technicalities* 23, no. 5 (September/October 2003): 1, 11–13. Also available at: www.loc.gov/cds/FRBR.html (1 March 2007).

————. "A Taxonomy of Bibliographic Relationships." *Library Resources & Technical Services* 36 (April 1992): 162–88.

Understanding MARC Authority Records: Machine-Readable Cataloging. Prepared by Network Development and MARC Standards Office, Library of Congress. 2nd ed. Washington, D.C.: Cataloging Distribution Service, Library of Congress, 2004. Also available at: www.loc.gov/marc/uma/ (1 March 2007).

Vatican Library (Biblioteca Apostolica Vaticana). *Rules for the Catalog of Printed Books.* Translated from the 2nd Italian ed. by Thomas J. Shanahan, Victor A. Shaefer, Constantin T. Vesselowsky. Edited by Willis E. Wright. Chicago: American Library Association, 1948.

Williamson, Nancy J. "Classification in the Millennium." *Online & CDROM Review* 21, no. 5 (October 1997): 298–301.

Wilson, Patrick. *Two Kinds of Power: An Essay on Bibliographical Control.* Berkeley: University of California Press, 1978.

Young, Heartsill, ed. *ALA Glossary of Library and Information Science.* With the assistance of Terry Belange, et. al. Chicago: America Library Association, 1983.

INDEX

A and Z Cutter numbers, (LCC), 394
A and Z Cutter numbers, (DDC), 367–68, 370–71
AA (1908), 54–55
AACR (1967), 7, 15, 57–58
AACR2 (1978), 8, 58–59
AACR2R (1988, 1998, 2002), 64–114
AACR3. *See RDA: Resource Description and Access*
AC Subject headings, 255
access points (descriptive), 145–62; choice of, 146–59; form of, 164–89. *See also* main entries; main entry; added entries
access points (subject). *See* controlled vocabularies; subject authority control
accompanying material (bibliographical description), 102–3, 108
added entries, 161–62
additions to names: corporate, 177–78; geographic 174–75; government officials, 181–82; governments, 180–81; personal, 172–74
adjectival phrase headings (LCSH), 218
ALA (1941) draft code, 55–56
ALA (1949), 56–57
ALA list of subject headings, 198
Alexandrian library, 23
alternative headings for children's material, 255–56
ambiguous terms, qualifiers for, in LCSH, 220
American Library Association, 56, 57, 61, 288
American states and Canadian provinces table (LCC), 399
analysis, in description, 112–14
analytical added entries, 113, 162

Anglo-American Cataloging Rules. See AACR
anonymous works created before 1501, 183–84
anthologies and collections, LCSH headings for, 245
approximate-the-whole rule (DDC), 338, 356
areas, geographic: abridged DDC, 356–57; full DDC, 340–42; LCSH, 222–41; MeSH, 300–301
areas of description. *See* bibliographic description areas
associative references (LCSH), 239–40
author and authorship defined, 147–48
author notation in class numbers. *See* item numbers
author tables in Class P, 404–5
authority and bibliographic files, 26
authority control: maintenance and retrieval functions, 208; names and titles (*see* name authority control); principles, 164–65; subjects (*see* subject authority control)
authority file, 26, 27, 166, 167, 202, 206, 208, 214, 221–22, 265–66, 484–85, 487–89
authority records, 165–66; coded examples, 36, 507–15; contents, with example, 34–37, 165–67; cross references in, 185; revisions procedures, 166–67; *See also* name authority records; subject authority records
authority work, 27–28

Bacon, Francis, 320–21
Berners-Lee, Tim, 9
BIBCO (monographic bibliographic record program), 83, 483

ABOUT THE AUTHOR

Lois Mai Chan, professor at the School of Library and Information Science, University of Kentucky, Lexington, Kentucky, is the author of eight books and numerous articles and co-editor of two collections in the areas of knowledge organization and subject indexing. In 1989, Chan was awarded the Margaret Mann Citation for Outstanding Achievement in Cataloging and Classification given by the American Library Association. In 1992, she received the Distinguished Service Award from the Chinese-American Librarians Association. In 1999, Chan and Diane Vizine-Goetz were chosen for the Association for Library Collections & Technical Services' (ALCTS) Best of LRTS Award for the Best Article Published in 1998. In 2006, Chan received the Beta Phi Mu (International Honor Society for Library and Information Science) Award for distinguished service to education for librarianship. From 1986 to 1991, Chan served as the chair of the Decimal Classification Editorial Policy Committee. Currently, she is a member of the IFLA Standing Committee on Knowledge Management. Her research interests include knowledge organization, subject vocabulary, authority control, metadata, and organization and retrieval of Web resources.